ORTHO'S HOME IMPROVEMENT ENCYCLOPEDIA

Created and designed by the editorial staff of ORTHO Books.

Project Editor
Alan Ahlstrand

Writers
Robert J. Beckstrom
John Reed

Ortho Books

Publisher
Robert B. Loperena

Editorial Director
Christine Jordan

Production Director
Ernie S. Tasaki

Managing Editors
Robert J. Beckstrom
Michael D. Smith
Sally W. Smith

System Manager
Linda M. Bouchard

Editorial Assistants
Joni Christiansen
Sally J. French

Address all inquiries to
Ortho Books
Box 5006
San Ramon, CA 94583-0906

Copyright © 1985, 1994
Monsanto Company
All rights reserved under
international and Pan-American
copyright conventions.

4   5   6   7   8   9
        98   99

ISBN 0-89721-270-3

Library of Congress Catalog Card
Number 94-65698

Photographs
Ortho Photo Library

Book Designer
Karin Shakery

Illustrators
Edith Allgood
Ron Hildebrand
Ronda Hildebrand
Rik Olson
Mark Pechenik

Editorial Coordinator
Cass Dempsey

Page Composition
Laurie A. Steele

Copy Editor
Elizabeth von Radics

Production by
Indigo Design & Imaging

Indexer
Susan Coerr

Color Separations
Color Tech Corp.

Lithographed in the USA by
Banta Company

Contributors
B. Gay Ballard
Craig Bergquist
Lin Cotton
Tracy Craig
R.J. DeCristoforo
David Edwards
William Henkin
Ron Hildebrand
Margaret Lucke
A. Cort Sinnes
L. Ken Smith
Diane Snow
Jenepher Walker
T. Jeff Williams
William W. Wilson
Robert Yeager

Consultants
Blair Abee
Lyle Beckstrom
Mel Berry
Marc Buchanan
Curt Burbick
Claire Carter
Bob Clark
Dan Fuller
Michael Hamman
Tom Hearne
Tom Hise
Charley Huddleston
Glen Kitzenberger
Jon Larson
Bob Lombardi
Malcolm MacLeod
Chuck Rumwell
John Seltzer
Barbara Sutton
Lee Ward

THE SOLARIS GROUP
2527 Camino Ramon
San Ramon, CA 94583-0906

This edition of Ortho's classic *Home Improvement Encyclopedia* has been revised and updated to include changes in codes, materials, construction techniques, home design, and life-styles. There are plenty of thick, home-improvement books, but none is as comprehensive, beautiful, and easy to use.

For example, you don't have to wonder whether to search for windows in an outdoor or an indoor section; you will find them between Window Coverings and Wire. You don't have to cull through page after page to find out how to install a skylight. You will find what you need between Sinks and Solar Energy. You don't have to decide whether a trellis has been classified as an outdoor improvement or a shade structure to protect the furnishings inside. Just turn to Trellises. If you don't find what you are looking for, it is probably because it is listed under another name: Check the back cover for a complete list of topics. And that's all the direction you need.

As you will quickly discover, each topic is introduced by a general discussion and a list of Recommended Cross-References. Pay particular attention to the Recommended Cross-References, as they will provide you with additional germane information and ideas. Within each section, instructions are boxed together with the photographs and illustrations you need for reference; you won't have to hunt for illustration number MCMLXXXV on page III while lying on your back trying to locate the P-trap. Also eliminated is the need to keep flipping back and forth to an index while trying to remember if you should now check the fifth or the sixth page reference. However, for those times when you want to study a subject at your leisure, a complete index has been provided.

Ortho's Home Improvement Encyclopedia contains indoor and outdoor projects, easy repairs and more complex installations, material choices and planning aids, planter boxes that take an hour or more to build, and decks that require several weekends to erect. There are ideas to inspire the novice carpenter, hints to help the professional do-it-yourselfer, advice to encourage the all-thumbs homeowner, and information on kits for people who don't know—and don't want to know—the difference between a router and a sander.

We hope that just skimming these pages has made you realize that *Ortho's Home Improvement Encyclopedia* is as appropriate for the coffee table as it is for the workshop.

ATTICS

Many attics can be converted into additional living space if there is enough room and the project is structurally feasible. But even if the attic already has stairs and is presently used for storage, converting it to living space is a major project that must begin with proper planning. Read this section and the related cross-references, then consider which parts of the job you want to have done by professionals.

Give some thought to how the space will be used. As a playroom? An office?

A guest room? Don't limit your dreams. An attic does not have to look like the rest of the house. In fact, its unusual architectural lines create a unique appeal. It also has boundless finishing possibilities. For example, the space behind the low kneewalls can be used for built-in storage in order to maximize the potential floor space.

Consult an architect or builder to see if your project is feasible before developing your plans.

Generally, if the clearance from the bottom of the ridge board to the top of

the attic floor or ceiling joists below is at least 9 feet, there is enough space to build a minimum-sized room. Adding dormers is a major project in itself, but may change a marginal space into a more functional or charming room.

Recommended Cross-References
Doors, Dormers, Framing, Plumbing, Skylights, Stairs, Subfloors, Wallboard, Windows, Wiring.

Well-placed dormers and a skylight give this attic a well-lighted, cheery aspect; the efficient layout of the kitchen and storage areas adds to the feeling of spaciousness.

Space and Structural Requirements

Local codes will vary, but the following are typical requirements that affect attic conversions.

Ceiling Height and Room Size. Usually, 50 percent of the floor area used as habitable space must have a minimum ceiling height of 7½ feet. Habitable space does not include utility and storage areas, workshops, bathrooms, or hallways. A minimum ceiling height, usually 4 or 5 feet, may be required for any part of the room.

Except for kitchens, habitable living areas must be at least 7 feet wide and have an area of 70 square feet. Taking several key measurements will determine whether an attic will meet these space requirements. Begin by measuring how much floor area falls within the minimum ceiling height of 4 or 5 feet. Allow 6 inches or more for a new floor. Then calculate how much of this potential floor area will have a ceiling height of over 7½ feet, using 8 feet for your measurement (to allow for a new floor). If this floor area accounts for more than half of the minimum-room-size measurements, you can proceed. If not, you may be able to move the kneewalls in to reduce the floor area where ceiling height is less than 7½ feet, and still exceed the minimum room size. Otherwise, the attic will not meet minimum requirements for ceiling height.

Stair Dimensions. Codes specify stair dimensions, such as minimum width and allowable angle. The requirements differ for main stairs and service stairs. Usually, an attic space less than 400 square feet will not have main stair requirements. If there are no stairs, allow space for adding them. A stairway usually requires an opening about 3 feet wide and 10 to 12 feet long. Spiral stairs need an opening from 4 to 6 feet across.

Windows and Skylights. If the attic is designed for sleeping, the code requires at least one openable window that can be used as an emergency exit. The window must be of a minimum size and be within a certain distance from the floor.

Structure. Besides evaluating the potential space, also consider the structural requirements of an attic conversion. Is the foundation adequate for an additional floor? Have any walls on the first floor been removed or altered? Will the attic floor need new joists? Will walls or other structural bracing be needed in the attic to compensate for any collar ties that need to be removed? Is there space to run plumbing, electrical, or heating connections to the attic? If the attic space is crisscrossed by small framing members, the roof may be supported by trusses. These are carefully designed to work together; alterations may destroy their strength, leading to collapse of the roof. If you are in doubt, consult an architect or structural engineer.

An unused attic is transformed into a well-lighted reading room.

Structural Components

The floor joists may be the original ceiling joists of the rooms below (if they are the right size), or they may be new joists. They support a subfloor and finish floor for the living space, and perhaps a subfloor under the eaves for storage purposes.

The walls will vary in height, depending on the slope of the roof. Kneewalls (low walls that run the full length) are usually 4 or 5 feet high. They help support the rafters, and are necessary if any collar ties are removed to create more headroom. The end walls and partition walls that run across the attic do not bear any loads. They are the walls most suitable for windows or doors. The ceiling may be peaked or partially suspended on short, level rafters. The minimum height for the flat portion of the ceiling is 7½ feet.

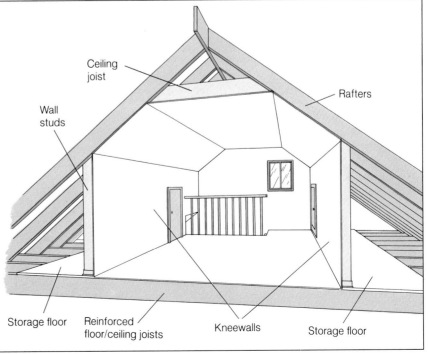

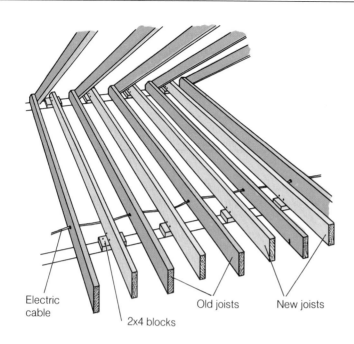

Electric cable

2x4 blocks

Old joists

New joists

Installing Floor Joists

Usually, the joists in an attic are intended only to support the ceiling below and not additional living space. They either need to be reinforced or have new floor joists installed between them. If the existing joists are 2 by 4s or 2 by 6s, install new floor joists. If they are 2 by 8s or larger, you can reinforce them.

Size. To determine the proper size of the floor joists, consult with your local building department or refer to joist span tables in the code. Be sure that your calculations of headroom and floor space account for the new joist size.

Reinforcing Joists. The simplest way to install a new support system is to nail reinforcing joists to the sides of existing ceiling joists. The new joists rest on the same wall plates as the old joists. The joist ends must be cut to fit into the slope of the roofline. Use a bevel gauge or cardboard template to determine the approximate angle; it does not have to be exact. Remove any insulation between the old joists in order to make room for the new joists.

When a joist is in place, toenail both ends into the cap plates below. If the angle of the roofline limits your nailing access, you should drill starter holes at the ends of the joist before nailing. Use a bit slightly smaller than the nail. When nailing sides of the new joists to old ones, stagger 16d nails every 12 inches.

If the ceiling below is lath and plaster, use a nail gun or pneumatic nailer to minimize damage to the plaster from vibrations. You can also use Phillips-head standard steel wood screws (not wallboard screws), installed with a high-powered variable-speed drill. Predrill the joists.

Obstructions such as wires running through the old joists may also prevent you from setting new joists directly on the cap plates. Try installing blocks on the cap plates, thereby elevating the new joists. These blocks can be made out of short lengths of 1 by 4 or 2 by 4.

New Joists. To provide better isolation from sound and reduce the potential of the ceiling below cracking, space the new joists evenly between the old. This creates a new floor system totally independent of the existing ceiling.

Raise the new joists with wood blocks nailed securely into the cap plates with 16d nails. Toenail the new joists into the blocks with three 16d nails at each connection. For long spans, lap two joists over the cap plate of the center bearing wall and nail them with 16d nails. Or butt the ends together, bracing on both sides with 2-foot lengths of ½-inch plywood.

If installing partition walls in the attic, double the joists under them. Separate the doubled joists by 3½ inches if you plan to run plumbing or wiring up into the partition wall.

Installing Utility Lines

Wiring, plumbing, and heating lines should be roughed in between the new joists and inspected before you install the new subfloor. The wiring may be extensions of existing circuits or come from a new circuit run from the main service panel, depending on the number of outlets needed and the capacity of your electrical system. If you are running plumbing into the attic, stub the pipes far enough above the floor to make it easy to connect to them when you rough pipes into the walls later.

Installing the Subfloor

Install subflooring over the area you plan to finish as living space, as well as under the eaves if you intend to use them for storage. Plywood is the easiest material to use. It should be tongue-and-groove and at least ⅝ inch thick. Use CDX plywood that is plugged and touch sanded (PTS) if the finish floor is to be resilient tile or sheet goods; otherwise, use plain CDX-grade plywood. Lay the plywood panels perpendicular to the joists, staggering the end joints by 4 feet. Leave ¹⁄₁₆- to ⅛-inch gaps between panels. To eliminate squeaks, attach the panels with construction adhesive as well as nails. Use 8d nails spaced every 6 inches around the perimeter and every 10 inches within the panel.

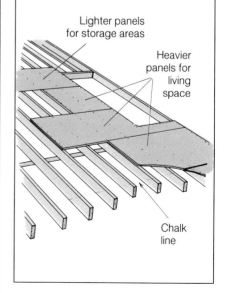

Lighter panels for storage areas

Heavier panels for living space

Chalk line

Constructing Kneewalls

If the code is not specific, make these any height (4 feet will allow you to use full panels of wallboard). If building a 5-foot wall, use 4 by 10 wallboard panels cut in half.

A 4-foot kneewall is especially easy to lay out with a 4-foot level. Mark the subfloor and rafter at each end of the kneewall and snap a chalk line between the marks. While the line is on the rafters, check for any that are out of line more than ¼ inch. Low rafters can be propped up or sistered (doubled); high ones can be shimmed down. The rafters must be even, both for the kneewall and for the ceiling wallboard.

Cut two plates the length of the wall and lay them doubled along the room side of the layout line for the bottom plate. Mark the center of a 96-inch stud and make a diagonal cut approximately equal to the roof slope. Stand one stud on the doubled plates and align the inside edge with the upper chalk mark. Mark the stud along the line of the rafter, cut it, and test it for fit at several other rafters. If it doesn't fit, adjust the rafters or the studs. The distance

from the floor to the rafter should be at least 4 feet 1 inch to allow for the ceiling wallboard and the finish floor. Any gap should be left at the bottom to be covered by baseboard.

Use the first stud as the template to mark the rest. Assemble the kneewalls on the floor with one plate at the bottom of the studs and the second plate at the top. The

studs don't need to align with the rafters, but keep them either 16 inches or 24 inches on center so the ends of the wallboard will rest on studs. Tilt the kneewalls into place. Check for plumb with a level, and shim as required. Nail the soleplate into the floor joists and the top plate into the rafters with 16d nails.

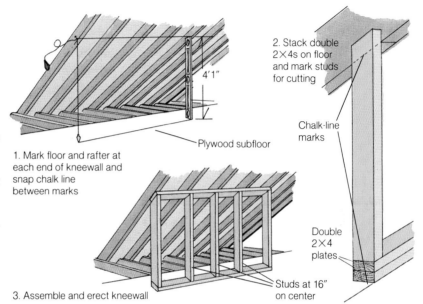

1. Mark floor and rafter at each end of kneewall and snap chalk line between marks

Plywood subfloor

2. Stack double 2×4s on floor and mark studs for cutting

Chalk-line marks

Double 2×4 plates

3. Assemble and erect kneewall

Studs at 16" on center

Installing Ceiling Joists

When building a peaked ceiling, the existing roof rafters are the only framing you need. Collar beams can be left exposed as long as they are 80 inches above the floor. If they are too low, raise or replace them one at a time; or remove them if you are certain that the kneewalls provide sufficient rafter support.

For a level ceiling, install ceiling joists that are high enough to give at least 7½ feet of headroom after the finish floor and ceiling are installed. Mark the bottom of the joist on the rafters by measuring up from the subfloor along a plumb line. Then add the finish floor and ceiling dimensions to the required minimum height of 7½ feet.

Use 2 by 4s or 2 by 6s for the joists, depending on the span. Cut both ends at the same angle as the slope of the roof to provide the maximum nailing surface, allowing at least ¼-inch clearance at each end. Lift each joist (crown side up if it is bowed) and tack one end to the rafter with a 16d nail. Check the level and nail the other end.

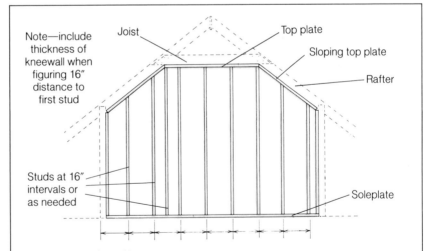

Note—include thickness of kneewall when figuring 16" distance to first stud

Joist

Top plate

Sloping top plate

Rafter

Studs at 16" intervals or as needed

Soleplate

Erecting End Walls

Cut a soleplate to fit between the two kneewalls and nail it in place. Simplify framing by placing it beneath one of the new ceiling joists.

Cut the horizontal top plate and nail it directly into a joist. If the wall falls between two joists, nail blocking between the joists and nail the top plate to the blocking. Another method is to install the blocking ¾ inch above the bottom of the joists and nail a 1 by 6 to the blocking before installing the top plate. Then

nail the top plate to the 1 by 6.

Install sloping top plates between the kneewalls and horizontal top plate. Nail them into rafters or to blocking installed between rafters.

Mark the stud locations along the soleplate. Measure for each stud along a plumb line, cut it, and then toenail it in place. Cut the tops of studs located under the sloping top plates at the same angle as the roof. Be sure to plumb each stud with a level before nailing.

BARBECUES

Barbecue units can be purchased at almost any department, hardware, or home center store. The variety of units offered ranges from inexpensive, simple hibachis to lavishly appointed outdoor stoves. Some are designed to place on top of a bench or table and some are freestanding, with or without wheels.

Because most built-in barbecues are customized to suit a particular setting, the design possibilities are endless. You can build a large outdoor fireplace, or include a small grill as part of a seating area. Materials, as long as they are fireproof, can be whatever you choose, but brick and stone are most commonly used.

The most basic barbecue design is a simple fire pit. You can cook on it and it radiates warmth in all directions. Check with your local fire department about open wood fires before you begin construction. You may need to install pipes for a natural gas or propane fire starter. These pipes can be disguised by covering them with non-explosive volcanic rocks for a warmer and more decorative effect.

Recommended Cross-References
Benches, Bricks, Patios.

A low wall defines a barbecue center large enough for entertaining a crowd. Curved bench seating surrounds the tiled firepit.

Fire Pits

Fire pits, like camp fires, have a universal appeal. The warmth of an open fire is a pleasant experience, and it can make a patio usable even when the weather is cool.

Raised Fire Pit. A two-brick-high wall is enough to contain the coals in this square fire pit. For a permanent installation, lay a gravel bed on top of either a drain or a 3-foot-deep dry well backfilled with crushed rock. Set the bricks into mortar with fireclay added. You can also merely dry lay the walls and remove the bricks when you have finished barbecuing.

If you wish to include a gas starter, install a valve outside the wall. Use drilled pipe shaped into a tee for the burner, setting it 6 inches below the top of the pit. Be sure to check local codes regarding requirements for the installation of gas lines.

The same design, or a round version, can be recessed into the ground so that the wall is flush with the surrounding patio.

Concrete Block Fire Pit. You can use slump concrete blocks set on end to give a fire pit a different look. However, if you do so, you must coat the inside of them with a mortar mixed with fireclay. Otherwise the blocks may not be able to withstand the heat of the fire.

Fire Pit Cover. In order to keep rain and animals out of the fire pit, it is a good idea to build a circular cover to place on top of the barbecue when it is not in use. Build this cover by nailing cut lengths of 2 by 4 to a piece of 1-inch exterior plywood.

Hibachi Table

A hibachi is one of the simplest and least expensive types of barbecues. The most common ones are made in a sturdy cast iron and are widely available in many sizes.

This table, featuring a fireproof box in the center, is a simple way to turn a portable hibachi into a built-in barbecue center. Even though the hibachi box is well fireproofed, never leave the unit unattended.

Because it is low, this table can be used as a bench when the hibachi is removed. The cutout can also double as a temporary planter—just pop in some colorful container plants.

Constructing a Hibachi Table. You can make the cutout either before or after assembling the top. Don't be too precise when cutting the hole—allowing air space is vital.

1. Cut all slab pieces to length. Mark the dowel locations on one piece, and, using this as a pattern, drill pilot holes in all pieces. Enlarge holes to size of dowel and insert dowels into one piece. Drive nails through the bottom edge. Keep adding pieces using ¼-inch plywood as a spacer. Nail each piece in place as you go.

2. Assemble the two leg sections so that the dowels fall directly above the centers of the 2 by 4s that make up the top slab. Drill four holes into the 2 by 4s for the leg dowels.

3. Build the box out of 1-by lumber that is pressure treated or of a naturally durable species. Measure the hibachi, including the protruding handles. Allow room for a ¼-inch-thick noncombustible lining and at least ½-inch of air space.

4. Set the top slab onto the legs and nail the hibachi box into the opening. Cut ¼-inch noncombustible sheets for lining the bottom and sides. Instead of conventional wood-working saws, cut with an abrasive disk in a power saw. Work slowly or score and break the sheets carefully. Wear a respirator and goggles. Attach each sheet with two or three screws.

5. Cover the top edges of the box with metal trim, as shown. Use right-angle roof flashing and cut it to length, or fashion your own pieces out of 20-gauge galvanized sheet metal. Nail on trim with 2d HDG box nails.

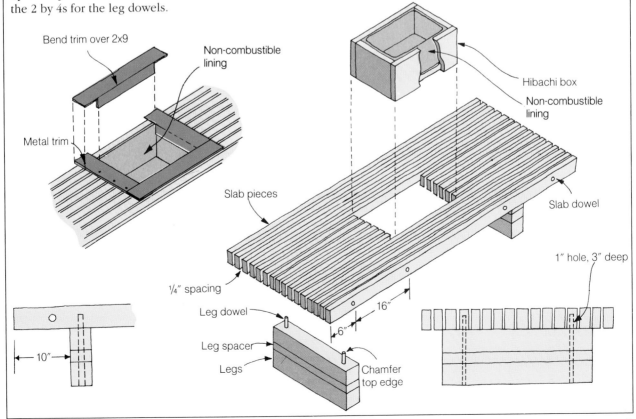

Bend trim over 2x9

Non-combustible lining

Metal trim

Hibachi box

Non-combustible lining

Slab pieces

Slab dowel

¼" spacing

Leg dowel

Leg spacer

Legs

Chamfer top edge

1" hole, 3" deep

16"

6"

10"

BASEMENTS

A full-sized basement under at least a portion of your house means the possibility of additional living space. If there is only a crawl space, it is usually more practical to build an addition aboveground than to excavate under the house. The obvious advantage in remodeling an existing basement is that it has outside walls, ceiling joists, and a rough floor. Access is rarely a problem, since most basements already have a stairway.

Code limitations for a basement conversion are similar to those for attics. Before you begin building, check your local codes regarding ceiling heights and stairways. The intended use of an area is often the key factor. If you do not plan to use the basement as habitable living space, the ceiling restrictions are usually less demanding.

In spite of the advantages of finishing a basement, many remodeling projects run into complications. Typically they have to do with excess moisture, rough walls and floors, and an assortment of exposed pipes and ducts. These problems must be overcome before you consider converting a basement into a usable living space.

Code Requirements

Building codes set standards for habitable basements to ensure that they are safe and comfortable. Local requirements vary; the most common are:
- Minimum ceiling height of 7 feet 6 inches
- Minimum height below ceiling projections (beams, pipes, ducts) of 7 feet
- A window area equal to 8 to 10 percent of the floor area
- Emergency egress
- A heat source that can maintain a temperature of 65° to 70° F.

Radon

Radon is a natural radioactive gas that is emitted from the soil in some areas. Because radon concentrates naturally in basements, you should test for it before you start. Radon problems are relatively easy to correct before a basement is finished, but more expensive and difficult afterward.

Recommended Cross-References
Ceilings, Drainage, Floors, Foundations, Framing, Insulation, Paneling, Pumps, Safety, Subfloors, Wallboard.

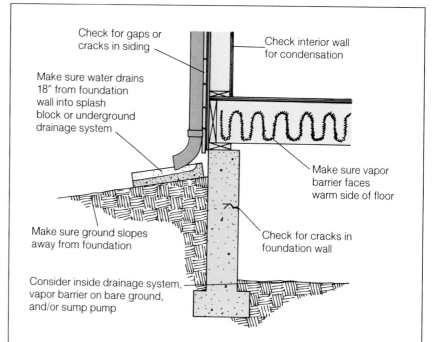

Check for gaps or cracks in siding

Check interior wall for condensation

Make sure water drains 18″ from foundation wall into splash block or underground drainage system

Make sure vapor barrier faces warm side of floor

Make sure ground slopes away from foundation

Check for cracks in foundation wall

Consider inside drainage system, vapor barrier on bare ground, and/or sump pump

Solving Moisture Problems
From the Outside. The best place to begin solving basement moisture problems is outside the house. Poor drainage around the foundation accounts for an overwhelming majority of leaky basements.

Start with an outside inspection. Check all gutters and downspouts for leaks and repair them. Provide splash blocks or leaders to carry the water away from the foundation, ideally 8 to 10 feet. Be sure the grading slopes away from the house, all around. The slope should be at least ½ inch per foot for the first 3 feet. If you find spots where water accumulates, install drain lines or surface trenches. Check the seal around the bottoms of doors and basement windows and recaulk if necessary.
From the Inside. Locate any cracks and open joints and fill them with an expansive mortar, such as epoxy cement. If they are leaking, use a special hydraulic cement. Check the joints between walls and floor. If moisture appears to be seeping through, widen the joint, fill it with epoxy cement, and seal with patching cement. Or install plastic baseboard channels. These collect the water and divert it to a floor drain.

Look for loose and crumbling joints between concrete blocks. Dig out ½ to ¾ inch of the old mortar, clean the joint thoroughly, dampen it, and repoint it with new mortar. Keep the mortar moist for four or five days to ensure proper curing.

After making these repairs, coat the walls and floor with a waterproof sealer. Use an alkyd-based concrete paint or a silicone or epoxy sealer. Most sealers can be brushed or rolled on like paint.

Seepage and Condensation
Dampness can also be caused by either seepage or condensation. To determine which one is causing the problem, cut a 12-inch square of heavy plastic and tape it to the floor or to any wall below grade level. Leave it in place for several days. If the area under the plastic becomes wet, the problem is seepage. If the surrounding wall becomes damp, the problem is condensation.
Seepage. First try sealing the walls and floor. If the problem persists, get professional advice. You may need to excavate, install drainage pipes, and waterproof the exterior walls. If seepage is the result of a high water table, install a sump pump and forget about finishing the basement.
Condensation. This is the result of too much humidity. Look for culprits such as an unvented clothes dryer or sweating pipes that need insulating. Try to improve ventilation either with more windows or a fan. If this does not help, install a dehumidifier. Wait several months and make sure the problem is solved before proceeding with your remodeling plans.

Floors

Preparing the Floor Surface. If the concrete floor in the basement is dry and reasonably smooth, you may be able to install a finish floor directly over it. Ceramic tiles, carpet, and some kinds of resilient tile or sheet goods are suitable for use below grade over concrete. First fill minor pits and low spots with patching cement and cover the entire floor with a waterproof sealer.

If the concrete floor in the basement is rough, uneven, sloped, or badly cracked, there are three ways to fix it: pour a leveling compound, replace the floor entirely, or install a wood subfloor.

Leveling compound is simply poured over the old concrete after preparing the surface according to the compound manufacturer's instructions. The compound forms a level surface that is smooth enough to use as a subfloor.

A more expensive and difficult alternative is to dig out the old concrete floor and pour a new one.

Installing a Wood Subfloor. In many cases, installing a subfloor over the concrete is called for when the existing floor is damp due to condensation and high humidity; when the concrete is rough, uneven, sloped, or badly cracked and you don't wish to use a leveling compound; or when you prefer the warmth and resiliency of a wood subfloor.

The two techniques for installing a wood subfloor over concrete are very similar—the choice is primarily a matter of preference.

Method 1. Sweep the concrete slab clean, seal it with asphalt primer, and spread a layer of asphalt mastic over the entire surface, 1/8 to 1/4 inch thick. Lay 15-pound felt building paper or sheets of 6-mil plastic polyethylene sheeting over the mastic, overlapping any edges by 6 inches. Walk over the surface to press the paper or plastic down into the asphalt. Snap chalk lines every 16 inches across the width of the floor.

Next, lay short lengths of pressure-treated 2 by 4s along the chalk lines to serve as sleepers. To allow for air circulation, leave a clearance of 1/2 to 3/4 inch between the ends of the sleepers and at the walls. Using a long straightedge, make sure the sleepers are level, and shim them as needed. Nail the sleepers to the slab with concrete nails long enough to prevent the sleepers from moving.

A powder-actuated gun works much better than a hammer for nailing into concrete. Hammering tends to shatter the concrete around the nails, reducing their holding power. Be sure to wear eye and ear protection when using a powder-actuated gun and follow all manufacturer's instructions.

Another way to fasten the sleepers is with hardened screws. Each box of these includes a masonry bit. To use

them, first drill a hole in the wood the same diameter as the screw shaft, so only the head of the screw will hold the wood. Drill a hole in the concrete with the masonry bit, then install the screws with a power screwdriver.

Nail either a 5/8- or 3/4-inch plywood subfloor over the sleepers, leaving 1/8- to 1/4-inch gaps between panels and a 1/2-inch gap at the walls. Provide ventilation under the floor to prevent musty odors or possible rot. Cut out 2- by 8-inch holes along the two walls that are perpendicular to the sleepers. Space them 6 feet apart and cover with floor-register grills after installing the finish floor.

Method 2. Sweep the floor clean, then brush or roll on a waterproofing sealer. When it dries, snap chalk lines 16 inches apart across the width of the floor. Along these marks, apply a mastic suitable for bonding wood to concrete. The easiest way is to buy mastic in a tube and use a caulking gun.

Lay random lengths of pressure-treated 1 by 4s over the mastic (1 by 2s or 1 by 3s can also be used). Leave a 1/4- to 1/2-inch gap between the ends and drive concrete nails into the floor every 24 inches. When the entire floor is covered, spread a layer of 6-mil polyethylene sheeting over the sleepers. Overlap the joints 6 inches. Then add a second layer of untreated 1 by 4s and nail to the sleepers below. Cover with a plywood subfloor, as described in method 1.

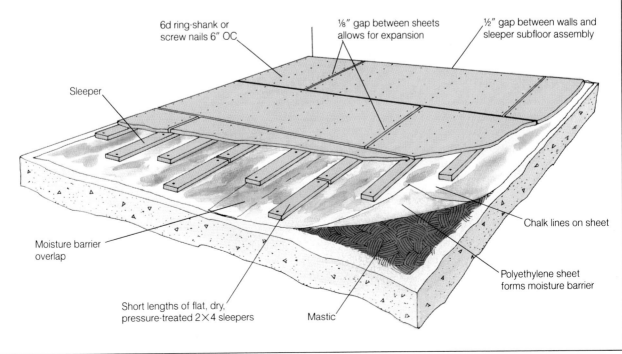

6d ring-shank or screw nails 6" OC

1/8" gap between sheets allows for expansion

1/2" gap between walls and sleeper subfloor assembly

Sleeper

Moisture barrier overlap

Short lengths of flat, dry, pressure-treated 2 × 4 sleepers

Mastic

Chalk lines on sheet

Polyethylene sheet forms moisture barrier

Walls

It is possible to leave the masonry or concrete walls of a basement exposed, or to cover them with suitable waterproof coatings that can be painted. Plaster mixes are also available that create a waterproof and very durable texture coating. In most instances, however, it is desirable to cover the basement walls with a finish material such as wallboard or paneling. This improves appearance and adds insulation. In mild climates the dead air space between the finish wall and the masonry wall is sufficient. In cold areas you should add batts or rigid panels for insulation. It is particularly important to insulate the section of wall above grade and the cavity along the rim joists above the mudsills.

Preparing the Walls. Before the walls can be finished, you must install a nailing surface over the masonry. This can be accomplished with furring strips—normally 1 by 2s laid flat against the wall—or a full-stud false wall built in front of the existing foundation wall. Generally, installing a false wall is easier than furring. It also simplifies the job of finishing the wall and gives better results. It requires more material and takes up more space. The choice depends on a number of factors. In general, furring strips can be used in the following cases:

1. If the walls are flat and plumb. Check the foundation with a plumb bob or long level held against a straightedge. If the walls are reasonably straight and plumb, fine. Minor problems can be corrected by putting shim stock behind the furring strips. Otherwise, it is more practical to frame a new false wall.

2. If ¾ inch of insulation is sufficient. Furring strips laid flat against the wall provide only a ¾-inch space for installing rigid insulation panels. Check the required R-value for your area. If you need more insulation and the floor area is too cramped to allow for a full-stud wall, it is possible to install insulation on the exterior of the foundation wall. If you are excavating a trench to solve moisture problems by waterproofing the wall anyway, this is an ideal time to install rigid panels and backfill against them. You should protect the portion that extends above grade.

3. If there have been no moisture problems. Attaching the strips to the wall with nails or screws could aggravate such problems.

After the walls are prepared, using either furring strips or a new stud wall, run wiring and plumbing behind them, insulate them, and cover them with wallboard or other finish material. As you cover the walls, keep in mind that all shutoff and drain valves, cleanout plugs, meters, and electrical junction boxes must remain accessible. Provide access panels by cutting an opening in the wallboard for each meter or valve. Cover each opening with ¼-inch plywood cut 2 inches larger than the opening. Hold the plywood in place over the opening and drill for expansion bolts at each corner; use wood screws if the corners are over studs. Secure the panel to the wall and paint it to match the walls.

Installing Furring Strips. If you are using insulation batts or no insulation at all, first cover the walls with a plastic moisture barrier, such as 4-mil polyethylene sheeting. Make sure the joints are overlapped and tight. Cut the sheets an extra inch or two long. Trim them later. Staple the top to the edge of the mudsill.

Snap vertical chalk lines 48 inches on center. Along each line attach 1 by 2 furring strips with 1½-inch concrete nails every 16 inches. Or use lead or fiber expansion shields and wood screws instead. Space them 36 inches apart. Snap horizontal chalk lines 16 inches apart and install short pieces of furring along them. To allow for air circulation, leave a ¼-inch gap between each end and the vertical furring strips. Be sure to fur completely around any window openings. If you are using insulating batts, install the vapor barrier toward the inside of the room. If the batts are unfaced, add a vapor barrier of plastic sheeting after the insulation is in place.

If you are using rigid insulation panels, install the furring first. The space between the furring can be modified to fit the panel dimensions, but keep in mind that you also need uniformly spaced nailers for the finish material. Glue the insulation panels directly to the foundation wall according to the manufacturer's instructions, then install a plastic vapor barrier over the strips and panels. Because this furring is in direct contact with masonry, it should be pressure treated or naturally durable.

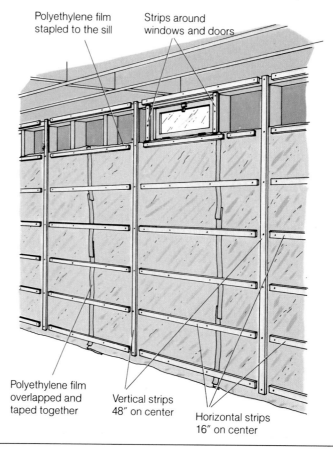

Polyethylene film stapled to the sill

Strips around windows and doors

Polyethylene film overlapped and taped together

Vertical strips 48" on center

Horizontal strips 16" on center

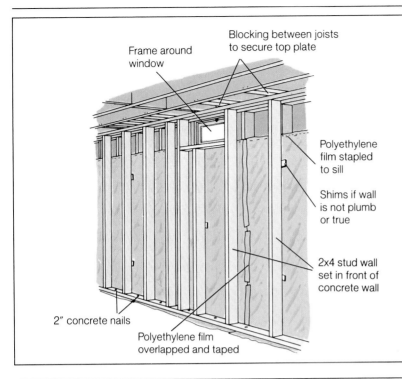

Frame around window

Blocking between joists to secure top plate

Polyethylene film stapled to sill

Shims if wall is not plumb or true

2x4 stud wall set in front of concrete wall

2" concrete nails

Polyethylene film overlapped and taped

Building a False Wall

If furring strips are not appropriate, building a false wall in front of the foundation wall is the solution. The wall can be framed using standard stud-wall techniques, with the following differences:

● Cover the foundation wall with a plastic moisture barrier stapled to the mudsill. Cut the sheets long enough to lap under the soleplate of the new wall.

● If the foundation is out of plumb or not flat, use shim stock or 1 by 2 blocks behind the wall.

● If there are pipes that run along the foundation wall, attach 1 by 2 or 2 by 4 blocks to clear them.

● If the floor is concrete, attach the solid plate with 2-inch concrete nails, 16 inches on center. If a new subfloor has been installed, 10d common nails are sufficient.

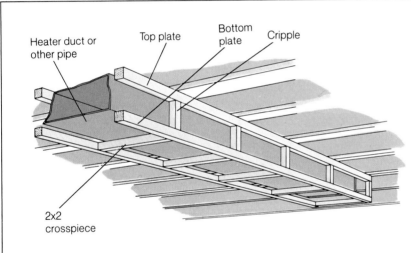

Heater duct or other pipe

Top plate

Bottom plate

Cripple

2x2 crosspiece

Framing Around Duct Work

You can box in exposed plumbing and duct work, so long as there is 80 inches of headroom beneath the finished box.

Construct two sides of the framework and attach them to the ceiling by hand-nailing (difficult) or with a nail gun (easier). You can also attach the framework with 3-inch wallboard screws. Predrill the screw holes through the framework but not into the ceiling. Once the framework is attached, nail crosspieces between the bottom plates and cover the framework with wallboard or paneling.

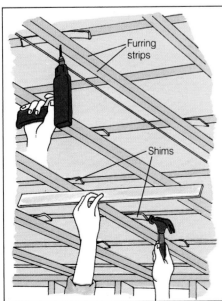

Furring strips

Shims

Furring Ceilings

Even if the ceiling is level, you may wish to fur it down to avoid rerouting wires and pipes that are attached to the bottoms of the ceiling joists. A ceiling furred with resilient channel will provide sound insulation. Furring is necessary in order to install a wallboard ceiling.

First, sight along the bottom of the floor joists. Correct sagging joists by jacking them up and reinforcing them with sister joists glued and nailed to the original joist. The sister joists don't have to be as deep as the original.

Use furring strips deep enough to extend below any pipes or wires that are attached to the joists.

Establish a baseline at each end of the ceiling. Use a water level or measure down from the lowest point of the joists (usually the middle). Measure down 2 inches from this mark and extend the line across the wall. Stretch a level string tightly from wall to wall, at right angles to the joists. Install strings in the same way for every third furring piece (every 4 feet). When you install the furring, keep it a consistent distance above the string line.

Attach the furring with nails or screws. Screws allow for easy shimming; simply loosen them at the appropriate points, insert shims between the furring and joists, and tighten the screws.

BATHROOM LAYOUT

A successful bathroom design is one that reflects the life-style of its users. Adults with identical schedules need a bathroom laid out differently than one used by children or occasional guests or one that includes a laundry.

Take a look at present patterns of bathroom use in your household. Are people always waiting for someone to get out of the bathroom? Is there enough room for two people? How often is the tub used? Can guests get to the bathroom without going through someone's bedroom?

Recommended Cross-References

Bathtubs, Faucets & Valves, Floors, Lighting: Indoor, Plumbing, Shelves, Showers, Storage: Indoor, Toilets, Vanities, Washbasins, Washers & Dryers.

These six plans show different layouts for one proposed project. The original layout includes a hallway and linen closet on the right, with an entrance from the hall. The bathtub is along the top wall, the toilet and basin along the lower wall. Main walls and the basic position of the toilet stay the same, but these plans show how closets, shelves, and fixtures can all be changed.

Enlarging the Space

A bathroom should be about 8 by 10 feet, although 7 by 8 feet can be quite adequate. Even if you cannot move major walls, there are still ways to add precious inches.

One way is to annex an adjacent closet. Even though you will probably need the equivalent space for storage, you can make the bathroom feel larger by converting the closet space into a cabinet with some open shelves and a counter.

Another space-saver is to change a hinged door into a pocket door. Even though it is not as quiet to use, and it requires making a large hole in the wall to install the new door, it may be worth the effort if you are remodeling completely. Before making the hole, check to see if you will have to move any plumbing.

You can also bump out the exterior wall to make a window seat or a shelving unit, or you can install a greenhouse window. These additions create space without the need for a new foundation or for making major structural changes.

It is possible to expand a room visually by eliminating partition walls. For instance, if the bathtub does not take up an entire wall and needs to be enclosed at one end, build a low shelf or a divider just high enough for a shower enclosure, rather than a full-height wall.

Natural light makes a bathroom appear larger. If there already is a window above the tub or shower, use a transparent or translucent shower curtain or shower door to let in the light. Install a large mirror on one wall to reflect light, or flood the room with sunshine by installing a skylight in an appropriate position.

Many people have realized that there is nothing wrong with having a vanity, or even a bathtub, in the bedroom. This does require moving and adding plumbing and vents, but it frees up space in the bathroom for the remaining fixtures.

Finally, consider incorporating outdoor space into a ground-level bathroom design. Fence in a private garden and connect it to the bathroom with a sliding glass door.

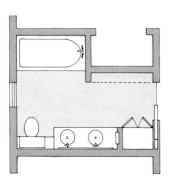

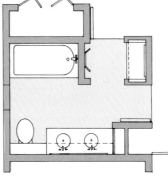

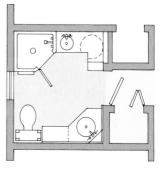

Plan 1
Problem. To provide two basins, an enlarged floor area, and ample storage within the bathroom itself.
Solution. The hinged door is replaced by a pocket door. The hallway linen closet is replaced with a new storage unit within the bathroom. The original closet wall is moved to allow for a vanity with two basins. The medicine cabinet is recessed into the wall. A narrow shelf unit on the back of the bedroom closet creates floor-to-ceiling storage. The original tub is still suitable and therefore remains.

Plan 2
Problem. Because both parents and children have to share this bathroom, there is a need for separate entrances and separate mirrors.
Solution. The original bedroom closet is converted into a dressing room with access to the bathroom. The bathroom includes a full-length, three-sided mirror and a dressing table. A new, enlarged bedroom closet replaces the old one. Door to the linen closet is moved around to the hallway side. Bathroom door now opens directly from the main hall. Shelf unit over the vanity provides towel storage in the bathroom while the shelf unit over the toilet provides storage for odds and ends.

Plan 3
Problem. Provide two separate washing areas and plenty of floor space to clear up a traffic jam at the washbasin in the morning.
Solution. Existing linen closet is retained. Bathroom door swings out to create more space. A bifold door makes access to the linen closet easy. The bedroom closet is reduced to gain space. Bathtub is replaced with a shower. A custom-built vanity includes a basin, a lazy susan under the counter, and drawers underneath. A vanity in the opposite corner is set at the same angle as the shower front; it has corner shelves above. Mirrors are hung above vanities. Shelf unit is hung over the toilet.

Code Requirements

Local plumbing codes vary but the following minimum clearances are fairly typical:

Washbasins. There should be at least 21 inches in front of a washbasin, preferably 24 inches. If the washbasin is beside a bathtub, allow at least 6 inches between the two fixtures.

Toilets. Allow for at least 24 inches in front and 15 inches from the centerline of the toilet to a tub or a wall on the side. There should be at least 4 inches between a toilet tank and a washbasin.

Showers. These must be at least 32 inches square and there must be at least 28 inches of clear space in front to allow for the door swing.

Tubs. The size of the tub determines the space needed. Allow space to get in and out easily.

Keep in mind that code requirements are usually the minimum measurements allowable. For comfort and for ease of cleaning, it is always advisable to provide extra clearance whenever you can.

Basic Fixtures

To begin your actual layout, determine the exact size and shape of the available space. Locate doors and windows, then major fixtures, such as the toilet, bathtub, shower, bidet, and basin, and plan the other accessories around them.

Use a priority list to help you decide which fixtures to include. For instance, if limited space or a tight budget make it necessary to choose, would you rather have two basins and a shower or one basin and a tub? Two basins side by side or in separate compartments? A large storage cabinet or a separate shower and tub? A brand new tub or the old tub and a skylight?

A good planning aid is to make a floor plan of the empty space to scale. Include doors and door swings, windows, radiators, and any obstructions. Then make a cutout of every possible fixture, drawn to the same scale. This way you can move the cutouts around on the floor plan to see how different arrangements will work.

Possible Pitfalls

When juggling so many variables, it is easy to make a simple error or a wrong assumption that may defeat the entire scheme. These reminders will help you to avoid mistakes:

● Plumbing is not a sacred cow. Although it is more economical and convenient to cluster fixtures on the same wall or back to back, do not feel wedded to a particular layout because of the plumbing hookups. It is better to move a few pipes than to settle for a compromise solution.

● When making drawings, include door swings and wall thicknesses.

● It should not be necessary to shut the door in order to use the basin.

● If a washbasin and a toilet are at right angles to each other, be sure there is enough clearance.

● Try to avoid windows in tub and shower enclosures. They are difficult to seal properly.

● Avoid placing the toilet so that it is directly opposite the basin. Stagger the two fixtures if they can't be on separate walls.

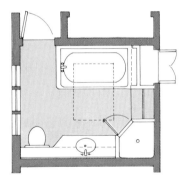

Plan 4

Problem. Create a private and luxurious bathroom. Make access only from the master bedroom.

Solution. Bedroom closet is removed to make room for a sunken bathtub. A new closet replaces the old one and a built-in dresser unit is added. New pocket door is added. Original toilet is left in place, with storage above. A low divider between toilet and vanity creates some privacy. New vanity has two basins. The original linen closet is retained.

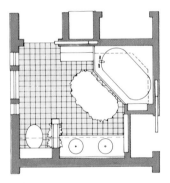

Plan 5

Problem. The children have grown up and the bathroom needs to be converted into a spacious, relaxing room off the main bedroom.

Solution. Original bedroom closet is replaced with a whirlpool tub and a utility closet that opens into the hall. A built-in, cushioned bench is added, with a storage unit above for towels and linen. Old linen closet is replaced with a shower. Spacious vanity has one basin. Skylight is new. Vanity counter extends over a new low-line toilet. An open wall allows for a large window unit or patio doors. New entrance to the bedroom has a hinged door. New closet replaces the old one.

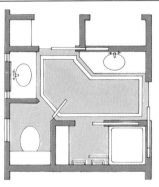

Plan 6

Problem. Bathroom is shared by the whole family and needs to be divided into private compartments.

Solution. A new shower compartment is created by removing the old linen closet and vanity. The compartment includes towel bars, a bench with storage beneath, and a pocket door. The toilet is enclosed in its own compartment containing a storage cabinet. New window provides light. New vanity and basin have narrow windows on either side. Original bedroom closet is replaced by a second vanity. New closet replaces the old one. New pocket door provides an entrance from the bedroom. Drawer unit added in the entryway.

BATHTUBS

Replacing a bathtub or installing a new one is a major project that usually involves some framing, rough plumbing, tiling, putting in plumbing fixtures and flooring, and installing accessories. Although bathtubs vary in size, shape, and basic materials, the techniques of installation are similar for all models. Most manufacturers include instructions with the tub.

Old bathtubs were made of porcelainized cast iron, which is still a popular choice. Later they were made of enameled steel, which was much cheaper and easier to handle, but not as durable. Now tubs are available in acrylic and fiberglass-reinforced plastics. Not only are the new plastics warmer and more comfortable to the touch, but they are also inexpensive, lightweight, and easier to fabricate into intricate shapes. Some tubs can be ordered already equipped with pumps and jets for massage, ready to

install. Although the plastic tubs are not as durable as those of cast iron or steel, they hold up well under careful use. They are particularly vulnerable to scratches and dulling.

Choosing a Bathtub
In addition to style preferences and cost, consider available space when selecting a new bathtub. If you are replacing an older tub, choose a new one that has the same dimensions and the same drain outlet (left or right side). Most old and new tubs are 30 inches wide by 60 inches long, so matching the size should not be difficult. You can always choose a different height, depending on the depth of water you prefer. If you are installing a new tub altogether, there is a wide choice of sizes to fit whatever space is available, from large double tubs to square tubs that tuck into a corner.

If you are buying a larger-than-standard size, be sure you can get the new tub into the bathroom. To solve this problem, some tub-and-shower units come in separate sections.

Also consider the weight of the tub, especially if you must cut any joists for plumbing. If you intend to replace a lightweight tub with one of cast iron, remember that a cast-iron tub full of water can weigh up to 1,500 pounds—not the perfect choice for a second-floor bathroom. A final consideration is durability. Some tub damage is difficult if not impossible to repair. An inexpensive tub that is prone to chips, dents, scratches, or cracks may turn out to be an expensive investment in the long run if it has to be replaced.

Recommended Cross-References
Bathroom Layout, Faucets & Valves, Plumbing, Tile, Wallboard.

Removing an Old Tub
Removing a built-in bathtub requires a considerable amount of work. You will also have to demolish some finished wall surfaces.

First disconnect all the pipes. If the tub is freestanding, just carry it away. If it is built-in, strip away the tile or other wall material for a few inches around its rim to reveal the studs and framing. Then, prying the tub up from the floor slightly, slide it away from the wall and carry it out. If it is cast iron and you are unable to lug it away intact, smash it into pieces with a sledgehammer. Wear eye and ear protection, gloves, and heavy clothing. If a steel or fiberglass tub won't fit through the doorway, consider whether removing the door and jamb trim will create enough room. If not, cut the tub up with a reciprocating saw and a blade appropriate for the tub material.

Refinishing
A possible alternative to replacing an old tub is to have it professionally refinished. There is a wide range of finishes available; some dealers offer custom colors. Metal trim can also be replated.

New finishes are quite durable if you use nonabrasive cleaners. The longest-lasting jobs require professional installation.

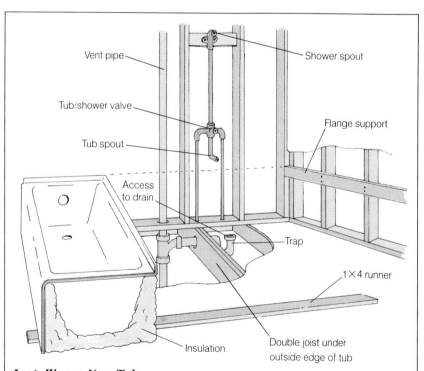

Labels: Vent pipe · Tub/shower valve · Tub spout · Access to drain · Insulation · Shower spout · Flange support · Trap · 1×4 runner · Double joist under outside edge of tub

Installing a New Tub
1. Positioning a New Tub. Fit the new tub exactly against the studs. If the space is too long, frame in a short wall to use as a shelf.

Rough-in the drain and faucet plumbing. Most new tubs have only two holes: the drain and the overflow. Some luxury tubs have one or two faucet mounts on the rim of the tub. The water supply pipes must be installed and connected before putting the tub in place.

A typical assembly is ½-inch cold-

water and ½-inch hot-water supply pipes connecting to a mixer valve (faucet). A short ½-inch pipe runs down from the valve and terminates in an elbow with a short stub, to which the spout is connected later. Another ½-inch pipe runs from the valve and connects to an elbow with a short stub, to which the showerhead is connected later. When buying a mixer valve, specify whether the connection will be soldered copper (CU) or threaded fittings (IP).

2. Installing an Access Panel. Most local codes require that bathtub plumbing be accessible. When the tub is on the ground floor, this access can be from the basement or crawl space below. Just cut a hole in the floor, approximately 8 by 12 inches, under the head of the tub. If your bathroom is on a slab or an upper floor, build an access door or removable panel in the room or hall that shares the head wall of the tub.

If the tub is steel or plastic, you will have to nail either 2 by 4 or 1 by 6 cleats to the studs to rest the flange on. Be sure these boards are at exactly the right height and are level. The instruction sheet with the tub will provide the proper dimensions. Cast-iron tubs don't need these cleats.

Before setting the tub in place, make sure there is plenty of room to work on the drain from below the floor or through the access door. Even on an upstairs floor it is a good idea to remove some of the subfloor adjacent to the access opening.

It is customary to wait until the tub is in place before finishing the bathroom floor, but if you are installing vinyl sheet flooring you may want to wait until it has been laid before positioning the tub. If the tub is installed first, the flooring has to be butted up to the tub. Unless this joint is caulked and sealed very thoroughly, moisture will lift the flooring and may cause structural damage in time. Installing the tub after the flooring prevents this problem.

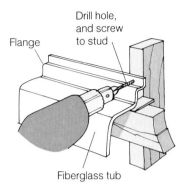

Drill hole, and screw to stud
Flange
Fiberglass tub

3. Positioning the Tub. First, stuff insulating material into hollow cavities around the tub. (This will help to keep the bath water warm.) Then slide the tub in place against the studs. Rest the flange on the cleats and screw it to the studs.

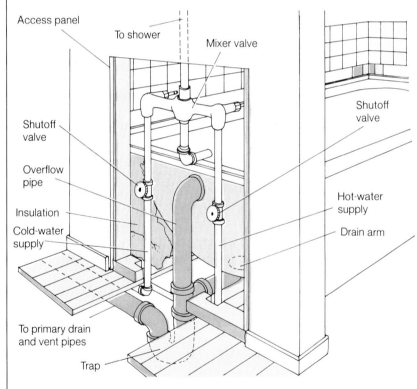

Access panel
To shower
Mixer valve
Shutoff valve
Shutoff valve
Overflow pipe
Hot-water supply
Insulation
Drain arm
Cold-water supply
To primary drain and vent pipes
Trap

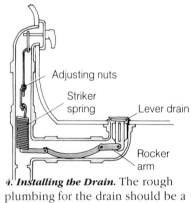

Adjusting nuts
Striker spring
Lever drain
Rocker arm

4. Installing the Drain. The rough plumbing for the drain should be a 1½-inch-diameter trap below floor level, with the inlet centered directly beneath the drain. It should have a slip nut or other means to connect to the waste-and-overflow pipe coming from the tub.

The tub itself does not come with any pipes, so you have to get a tub drain assembly, which consists of the drain arm, overflow pipe, and connecting tee. Assemble this unit according to the manufacturer's directions and place it in position. You will need a helper to hold it. Then, working from inside the tub, put lots of plumber's putty around the drain hole and screw in the strainer fitting. Tighten it by inserting the plastic-coated handles of a pair of pliers or a special wrench for this purpose. Do not overtighten; just make it snug. Install the overflow cover with the screws that came with it. Then, working under the tub, connect the overflow assembly to the trap by tightening the compression nut with a spud wrench or spanner. Test the drain with a few buckets of water. Then install the stopper mechanism.

5. Finishing the Enclosure. Finish the walls around the tub with moisture-resistant wallboard or other backing and whatever final finish material you choose. Replace the stub-outs for the spout and showerhead with proper nipples of the right length. Then screw on the fixtures.

6. Caulking. After the tile or other wall material and doors or curtain rod are installed, the final step in installing a tub is to caulk all the joints. To make a neat joint between

tub and tile, put tape along the edge of the tub. Then apply caulk, finger it smooth, and pull up the tape to reveal a straight, clean line.

A bath platform for a drop-in bathtub is an alternative to a sunken tub. Specific plumbing requirements may include access to whirlpool equipment, holes for a deck-mounted faucet, and a vacuum breaker for a spout located below the rim of the tub.

Building a Tub Enclosure

1. Framing the Tub. Make a frame of 2 by 4s with supporting studs placed every 16 inches. Build one frame for each exposed side of the tub. The frames should be below the rim just enough to fit the combined thickness of the plywood and tile. When you cut the studs, remember to subtract an additional 3 inches for the top and sole plates. Construct the frames and attach them to the walls and floor with nails and construction adhesive. Use toggle or Molly bolts if there are no studs to nail into.

2. Building the Surround. To extend the storage ledge on any exposed side of tub, merely build an extra frame identical to the first one. Set it parallel to the first frame as far away as the desired width of the ledge. For ledges wider than 16 inches, add a third frame halfway between the inside and outside frames, or provide blocking between the two frames to support the top piece of plywood, no more than 16 inches on center.

3. Covering the Framework. Cover the tops and sides of the frames with ½-inch CDX plywood or moisture-resistant wallboard. Caulk all joints between tub and covering, and seal the plywood or wallboard with a moisture-resistant primer. Then cover the backing with tile, wood, or other finish material. To prevent water damage, seal the finish material and caulk joints well.

4. Caulking Around the Tub. After the tile or other wall material and doors or curtain rod are installed, caulk all the joints. To make a neat joint, put tape along the edge of the tub. Cut the tip of the nozzle about ³⁄₁₆ inch. Hold the caulking gun at a 45-degree angle as you push it forward. When you have finished applying the caulk, smooth it with a soapy finger. Let the caulk set, then pull up the tape to reveal a clean, straight line.

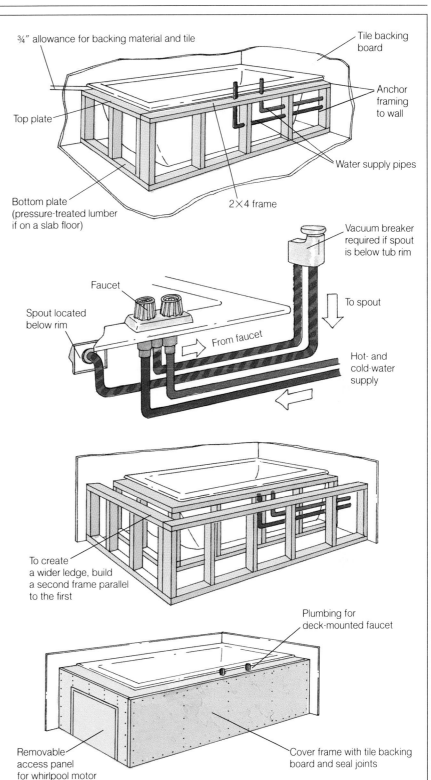

¾″ allowance for backing material and tile

Tile backing board

Top plate

Anchor framing to wall

Water supply pipes

Bottom plate (pressure-treated lumber if on a slab floor)

2×4 frame

Vacuum breaker required if spout is below tub rim

Faucet

Spout located below rim

From faucet

To spout

Hot- and cold-water supply

To create a wider ledge, build a second frame parallel to the first

Plumbing for deck-mounted faucet

Removable access panel for whirlpool motor

Cover frame with tile backing board and seal joints

BENCHES

Benches help to make outdoor spaces more relaxing and inviting. They eliminate the need for space-consuming furniture and they define spaces or separate activity areas. They belong on decks, on patios, in arbors, under trees, at the edge of lawns, or just about any place in the garden that suggests a quiet retreat.

Benches are commonly 15 or 16 inches high and 16 to 20 inches wide. Simple designs are a good way to practice your carpentry skills and get useful, attractive results. If you are adding a built-in bench to a deck, use the same detail for the top surface and attach legs permanently to the deck joists or fascia board. You can also use the railing posts as supports for a bench, bolting horizontal cleats to them and nailing the bench top to the cleats. Or, if your local building code allows, you can edge a deck with a bench instead of a railing.

To reduce splintering of the bench surface, use clear, straight-grained, small-dimension lumber. The smaller boards also keep the top from collecting water, and it will dry out more quickly.

A bench can be finished the same way as a deck or other outdoor structure, with paint, stain, or a clear sealer. Avoid preservatives that have been restricted for consumer use, since prolonged skin contact may be a health hazard. Use a sealer instead. It is a good idea to sand the bench surface well before finishing it. This helps reduce splinters.

Recommended Cross-References
Decks, Garden Walls, Joinery, Paths, Patios, Planters, Railings, Wood.

Benches should be designed to suit the location in which they are placed and either follow existing contours or, by their shape, define an area. Use materials that either match the surface on which the bench stands or ones that will blend in and be unobtrusive in a natural setting.

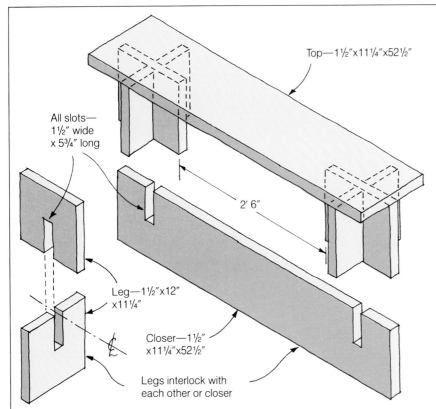

Top—1½"x11¼"x52½"

All slots—
1½" wide
x 5¾" long

2' 6"

Leg—1½"x12"
x11¼"

Closer—1½"
x11¼"x52½"

Legs interlock with
each other or closer

Plank Bench

These unique benches can be used individually or as modules that can be grouped for various uses. They can even be stacked to serve as a temporary counter or bar. You have a choice of two styles of legs. In one

style the legs are two separate pedestals, each supporting one end of the bench. In the other, a continuous 2 by 12 forms the support for the top.

Work with a good grade of kiln-dried lumber to minimize warping. You must cut the slots carefully, so

make a cardboard pattern to mark the cutting lines on each piece. Size the slots so that the pieces slide together snugly but do not bind. Binding will eventually cause splits or cracks. Use screws or 16d nails to secure the tops to the legs.

Deck-Top Bench

Cut pieces of 2 by 4 to length. Mark the dowel locations on one piece and drill a small pilot hole at each center point. Using this as a pattern, drill holes into each of the other pieces. Enlarge the holes to 1¼ inches, to fit the dowels.

Insert the dowels into one piece and drive nails through the bottom edge to hold it in place. Keep adding pieces, nailing in similar fashion, using a scrap of ½-inch plywood as a spacer. Trim dowels flush with the face of the final piece.

Assemble legs and rails with 2 carriage bolts through each leg then place the slab upside-down and position the leg assemblies. Center the position for each lag screw over a slab piece. Drill ⁵⁄₁₆-inch holes through the rails and ³⁄₁₆-inch holes partway into the slab pieces. Install the lag screws, and the bench is ready to turn over and use.

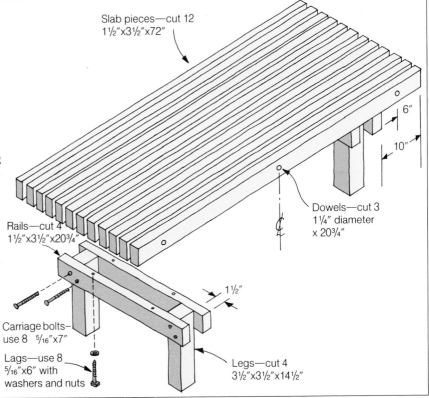

Slab pieces—cut 12
1½"x3½"x72"

6"

10"

Dowels—cut 3
1¼" diameter
x 20¾"

Rails—cut 4
1½"x3½"x20¾"

1½"

Carriage bolts—
use 8 ⁵⁄₁₆"x7"

Lags—use 8
⁵⁄₁₆"x6" with
washers and nuts

Legs—cut 4
3½"x3½"x14½"

BOARD SIDING

Board siding has long been a favorite material for covering the exterior of a home because it has a rich and handsome finish and is relatively easy to install. The price of board siding varies with the type and grade of lumber. If you are installing an interlocking pattern, buy a dry rather than a wet grade of lumber. Green lumber is adequate for shiplap or board-and-batten siding. Durable wood species, such as redwood and cedar, are superior for damp climates or for areas of the house that are constantly subjected to moisture. Pine and Douglas fir siding, which are much less expensive, are suitable for exposures that get enough sun to dry out easily.

Store siding so that it is protected from the weather. Sort out the most attractive pieces for highly visible locations.

Recommended Cross-References
Caulking, Doors, Flashing, Framing, Insulation, Paint, Shingle Siding, Siding, Windows, Wood.

Scaffolding

If you are working alone or more than 8 feet above the ground, scaffolding will increase safety and speed the work. It is usually more practical to have a scaffolding company deliver, erect, and pick up the scaffolding rather than rent it from a full-service rental outlet. The scaffolding company may also charge less for a full month (their usual minimum) than a rental outlet charges for a few days.

Covering New Walls

Sheath the walls with ³/₈-inch exterior-grade plywood. Wrap 15-pound asphalt, red resin, or other building paper around the house, stapling it to the plywood and wrapping at least 6 inches around corners. Start at the bottom, lapping each successive course at least 4 inches over the one below it. Make end laps 6 inches.

When the paper is up, snap vertical chalk lines on the paper over the center of each stud. If the roof is closed in, mark the stud locations on the underside of the roof sheathing before applying the paper.

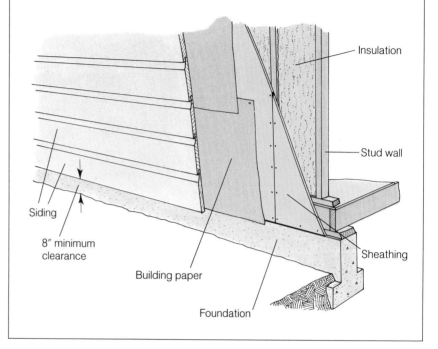

- Insulation
- Stud wall
- Sheathing
- Siding
- 8″ minimum clearance
- Building paper
- Foundation

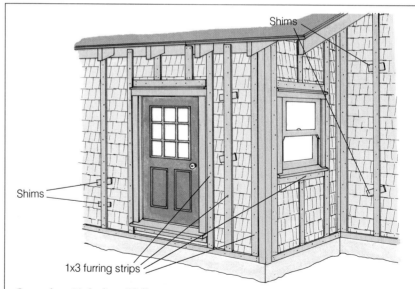

- Shims
- Shims
- 1x3 furring strips

Covering Existing Siding

For ventilation in an uninsulated home with no vapor barrier, drill ¹/₂-inch holes through the old siding and sheathing at the top and bottom of each stud cavity. Nail on 1-inch-thick sheets of rigid insulation; leave a ¹/₈-inch gap at corners and the top edge for moisture to escape. It is important to locate all the studs. You may be able to spot them if the nails are exposed. Otherwise, pry off the top piece of siding and snap vertical chalk lines over the studs.

If you are applying siding over an irregular surface, such as shingles, install 1 by 3 furring strips first. Sight down the wall, and shim behind any spots that bow inward. Butt furring strips up against the existing corner and window trim, or remove the trim and install jamb extenders.

Types of Horizontal Siding

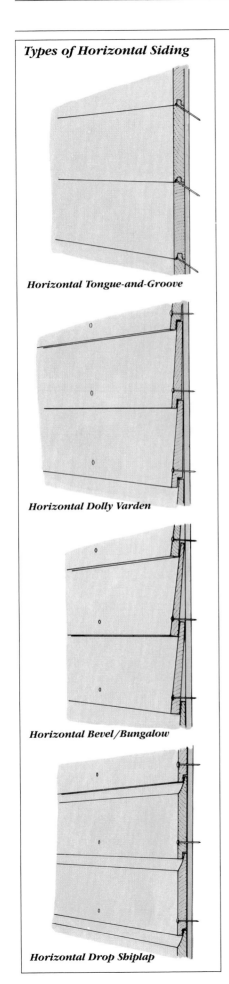

Horizontal Tongue-and-Groove

Horizontal Dolly Varden

Horizontal Bevel/Bungalow

Horizontal Drop Shiplap

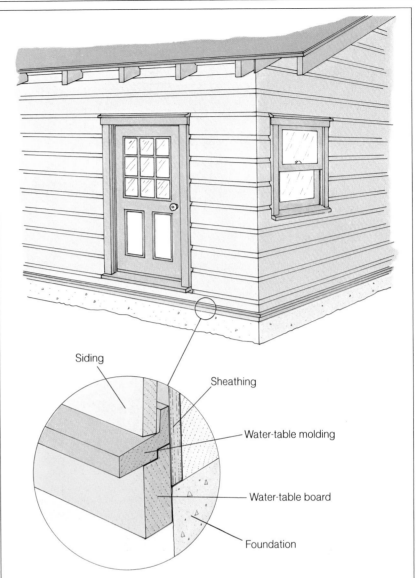

Siding

Sheathing

Water-table molding

Water-table board

Foundation

Planning the Installation

Try to plan a horizontal installation so that all joints will meet at the corners and be aligned, if possible, with the tops of the doors and windows. The classic way to begin putting on the siding is to nail on a water-table board and water-table molding, although many contemporary builders forego doing it.

Story Pole

Making a story pole is an easy way to figure out where each board should lie. To make one, mark a 1 by 4, starting with marks for the bottom course, and showing locations of window sills and drip caps above the windows. Measure between these marks, and divide by the board width. Make any necessary adjustments, then mark the story pole for each course of boards. When you move around the house, use the story pole to keep the boards aligned.

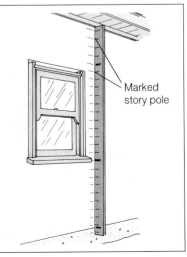

Marked story pole

Installing Horizontal Boards

Put the story pole in place at each corner, and transfer the marks to the corner boards. Periodically check your work against these marks, as well as with a level.

To determine placement of the first board, snap a level string line around the house to represent the starting line. Snap it against the foundation or along the base of the existing siding. If one wall is lower than this line, use the story pole to measure the starting place for the boards on that wall.

For clapboard or hardboard siding, nail a starter board around the bottom of the house to set the first piece of siding at an angle.

Once the preparations are complete, align the first board and face-nail it into each stud, using 8d HDG siding nails or casing nails. Align, then blind-nail subsequent boards. If you are using redwood or cedar that is not going to be either painted or sealed, use aluminum instead of galvanized nails.

Don't position end joints between studs. Cut both pieces at a 45-degree bevel, rather than 90 degrees, so that they overlap slightly. Predrill the ends of boards before nailing them.

Tongue-and-Groove Boards. If you are blind-nailing tongue-and-groove boards, set small-headed nails so that the head will not interfere with the placement of the next board. If you tap a board down to fit, use a beater block to protect it.

Gable Ends. Set the angle of the rafter or roof sheathing on a bevel gauge and transfer the angle to the ends of siding boards for the gable.

Corner Treatments. Horizontal siding requires special corner treatment to cover the exposed board ends.

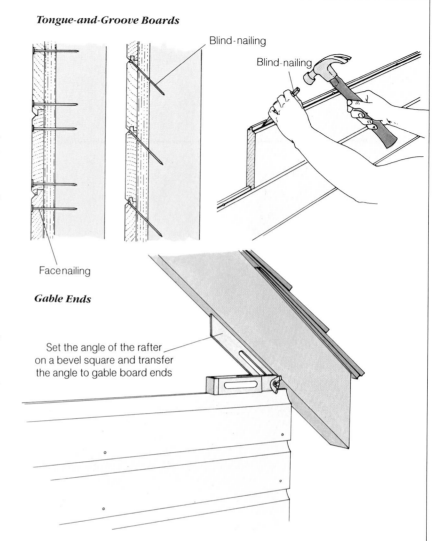

Tongue-and-Groove Boards

Facenailing

Blind-nailing

Blind-nailing

Gable Ends

Set the angle of the rafter on a bevel square and transfer the angle to gable board ends

For outside corners, use a vertical 1 by 4 and 1 by 3 overlapping each other for a tight seal. Cut the siding so that the ends butt smoothly and tightly against this trim. Then caulk the joints after all boards are in place.

Another method is to use metal corner pieces. Nail siding in place so that the ends just meet at the corners. Slip on the metal corner pieces and nail with small brads.

Nail a 1 by 1 or 1 by 2 into the corner. Then butt the ends of the siding boards against it. Caulk the edges after the siding is in place.

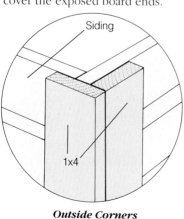

Siding

1x4

Outside Corners

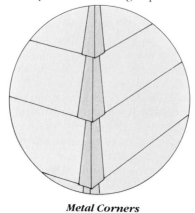

Metal Corners

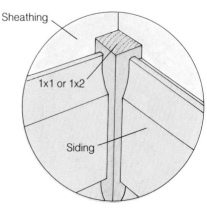

Sheathing

1x1 or 1x2

Siding

Inside Corners

Installing Vertical Boards

Redwood and cedar are commonly used for vertical siding and, very often, are left to weather naturally. Pine or Douglas fir can also be used if the boards are painted or stained.

The boards are usually ³/₄ inch thick and range in widths from 3¹/₂ inches to 11¹/₄ inches. Some styles, such as channel siding, have rabbeted edges for a weathertight fit. Shiplap and tongue-and-groove boards are also commonly used. Standard-dimension lumber can be used, either surfaced or rough, as long as the joints are covered by battens. The battens are generally 1 by 2, 1 by 3, or 1 by 4. Choose a size in proportion with the siding boards.

Preparing the Walls. To apply vertical board siding over exposed studs, place blocks between the studs at 24-inch intervals to provide a nailing surface. To keep the blocks straight, snap a chalk line across the edges of the studs. The blocks also help prevent the studs from warping. Next, cover the framing with 15-pound felt, starting from the bottom. Lap the top edges from 2 to 4 inches and the ends 6 inches. Felt is not needed when putting new siding over existing siding. Install flashing over any doors and windows that do not have integral drip caps.

For existing walls that are straight and smooth, drill a 1-inch hole in the top and bottom of each stud cavity and nail 1-inch rigid insulation panels to the siding. Leave a ¹/₈-inch gap between panels at the top for ventilation. If the existing walls are irregular, nail horizontal furring strips every 24 inches.

Installing the Siding. Start at one corner and use a level to make sure the first board is plumb. Keep the board vertical even if the building is out of plumb; trim will cover the discrepancy. Start tongue-and-groove siding with the groove edge at the corner. Install the rest of the boards the same way as horizontal siding. You can run boards all the way up to the roof, or finish the gable with boards running in a different direction.

Lapping End Joints. All end joints should be cut with a 45-degree bevel so that the top pieces lap over the bottom pieces to prevent leaks. Make sure you caulk each joint before nailing the top board in place.

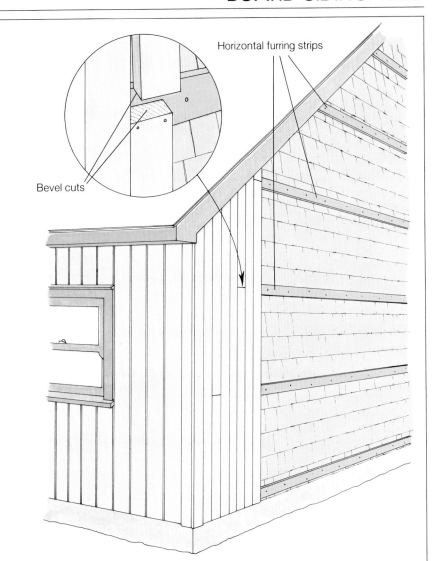

Horizontal furring strips

Bevel cuts

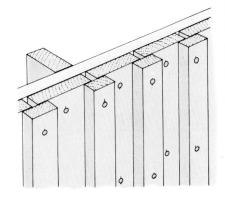

Board-and-Batten Siding. Nail each board with one centered nail to each furring strip. Allow a ¹/₄-inch expansion gap between boards. After nailing, let boards season a few weeks before nailing on the battens. An alternative pattern, called batten-and-board, is to nail the boards to the battens. Leave a gap between boards.

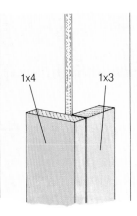

1x4   1x3

Corner Trim. Trim corners with 1 by 4s or a combination of 1 by 4s and 1 by 3s. For maximum durability, coat each piece with primer, let it dry, and then apply a bead of caulk on the back before installing it.

Covering Gable Ends

Gable ends can be done in several different ways. If the main siding is vertical, you can bring it all the way up to the roof sheathing. This works best with narrow patterns. Another option is to use horizontal siding or even shingles on the gable section for more contrast, especially if the vertical siding consists of boards wider than 6 inches.

Finish the underside of the rake eaves the same way as the cornice eaves. If you do not cover them with a soffit, nail trim along the top edge of the siding where it meets the roof sheathing for a more finished look.

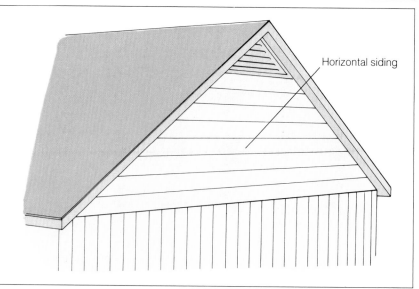

Horizontal siding

Finishing the Eaves

You can leave the eaves completely open or you can finish with a frieze board trimmed with molding. For a boxed look, build either a sloped or a level soffit. To build a level soffit, cut the bottom of the rafters square. For ventilation, drill 2-inch holes and insert vent plugs.

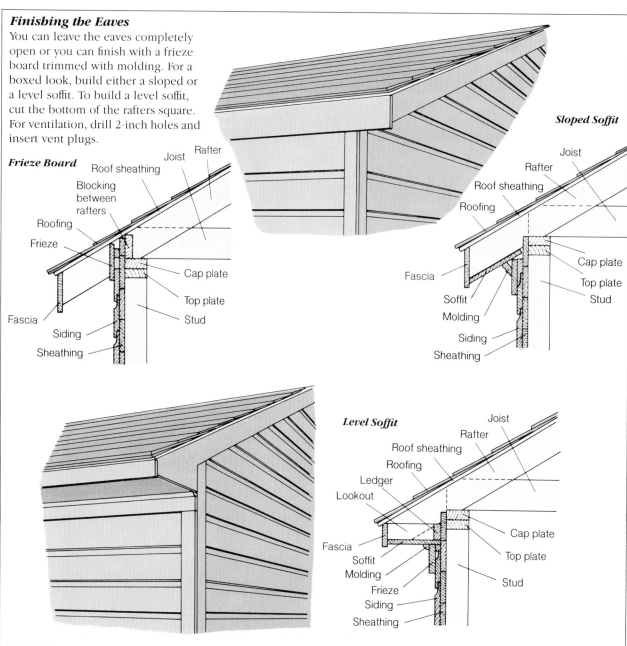

Frieze Board
Joist
Rafter
Roof sheathing
Blocking between rafters
Roofing
Frieze
Cap plate
Top plate
Fascia
Stud
Siding
Sheathing

Sloped Soffit
Joist
Rafter
Roof sheathing
Roofing
Cap plate
Top plate
Fascia
Stud
Soffit
Molding
Siding
Sheathing

Level Soffit
Joist
Rafter
Roof sheathing
Roofing
Ledger
Lookout
Cap plate
Top plate
Fascia
Stud
Soffit
Molding
Frieze
Siding
Sheathing

Repairing Board Siding

Most repairs of board siding involve removing a section of damaged board and replacing it with a new piece to match. If you have trouble finding a board to match, remove one from an inconspicuous part of your house, such as the garage or the bottom board behind some shrubbery, and replace it with the closest match you can find. For extensive repairs, you may find a lumberyard that will mill custom boards. Just take in a sample, and they can either order cutting blades or make their own. However, this will be costly.

If you are patching a large section or splicing a new wall into an existing wall, do not make all the cuts over the same stud. Instead, cut alternating boards over the same stud, using a different stud for the rest. This will make a less conspicuous splice between the new and old siding. Caulk the ends of boards.

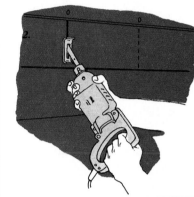

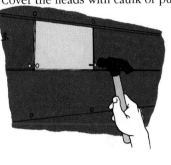

Repairing Lapped Siding

1. Cut nails on either side of the damaged section by sliding a hacksaw blade between the boards.
2. Holding out the damaged board with wedges, saw vertical cuts on each side of the damaged area directly over the studs with a backsaw or circular saw.

Complete cuts with a keyhole saw, reciprocating saw, or circular saw.
3. Remove the damaged piece and cut a new piece to replace it. Predrill holes at the ends, caulk both ends, and nail with 6d or 8d HDG nails. Cover the heads with caulk or putty.

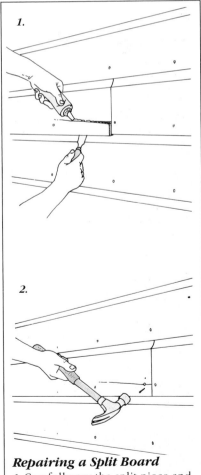

1.

2.

Repairing a Split Board
1. Carefully pry the split piece and apply an epoxy resin cement.
2. Predrill. Nail at an angle.

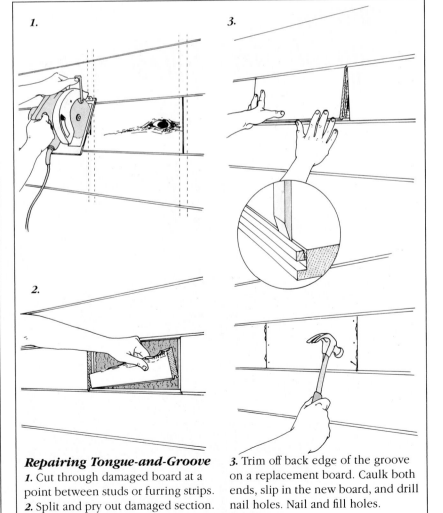

1.

2.

3.

Repairing Tongue-and-Groove
1. Cut through damaged board at a point between studs or furring strips.
2. Split and pry out damaged section.

3. Trim off back edge of the groove on a replacement board. Caulk both ends, slip in the new board, and drill nail holes. Nail and fill holes.

BRACING

Two of the most powerful natural events, earthquakes and hurricanes, can destroy a house in seconds. However, some reasonably simple, inexpensive reinforcement techniques can help your home survive.

Recommended Cross-References
Emergencies, Foundations, Framing, Windows.

Hurricanes

Hurricanes cause damage from wind, wind-driven objects, waves, and flooding. Generally, the closer a building is to an affected coastline, the more susceptible it is to hurricane damage.

Hurricanes can pulverize building with waves or blow them off their foundations. In addition, roofs can be lifted off and falling trees can inflict structural damage.

Building code specifications for hurricane reinforcement vary widely from area to area. In general, the object of reinforcement is to tie a building securely to the foundation and to attach the parts of the building securely together. Some roof configurations are safer than others; hip roofs deflect pressure from wind, whereas gable ends face it directly. Steeply pitched roofs reduce the low-pressure effect on the side of the building away from the wind, whereas low-pitch roofs increase it. This low pressure can lift the roof completely off a building.

A dangerous but easily prevented effect of hurricanes is flying glass from windows. Storm windows and shutters of steel, vinyl, and wood are available to protect the glass.

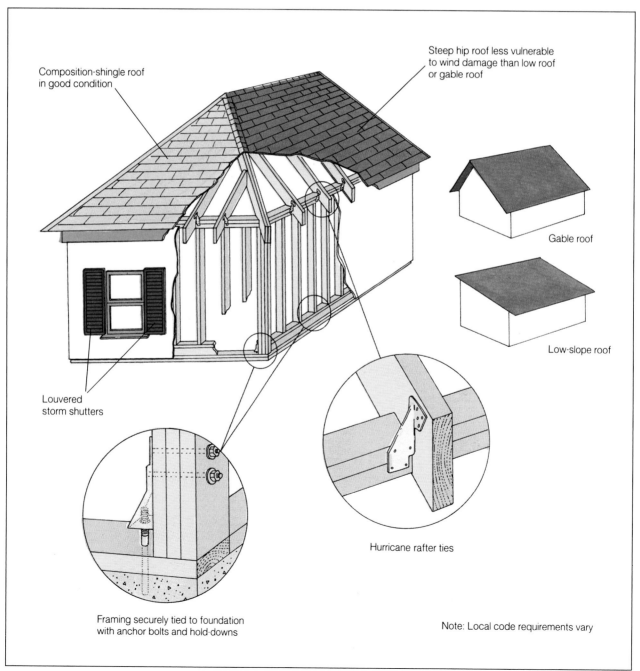

Composition-shingle roof in good condition

Steep hip roof less vulnerable to wind damage than low roof or gable roof

Gable roof

Low-slope roof

Louvered storm shutters

Hurricane rafter ties

Framing securely tied to foundation with anchor bolts and hold-downs

Note: Local code requirements vary

Earthquakes

Major earthquakes are not just a West Coast phenomenon. Scientists believe three of the biggest earthquakes in North America occurred in southern Missouri during 1811 and 1812. If these quakes happened today, more than a million structures—most built with no consideration of earthquake resistance—would be affected. Large, damaging earthquakes also occurred in South Carolina and New England during the past 240 years.

How Buildings Fail. Earthquakes produce strong side-to-side shaking motions that can break connections between parts of the building. In the worst cases, the motion slides the building off its foundation.

Unreinforced masonry structures are usually the most vulnerable to earthquakes. The shaking causes the mortar joints to crack and the walls to start moving independently, pounding themselves to bits. Then the joints between the floors, walls, and roof separate, allowing the floors to fall and the walls to collapse.

Wood-frame houses generally resist earthquake damage. Modern wood-frame structures, which use plywood or other panel sheathing, are even stronger. Three conditions make a wood-frame house vulnerable to earthquakes: If the house is weakly attached to the foundation (or not attached at all) it may slide off. This will cause severe damage or complete destruction. Second, kneewalls, short stud walls sometimes used between the foundation and the floor, may collapse unless they are braced. Finally, serious rot or insect damage can weaken structural connections so much that they fail in an earthquake.

Types of Reinforcement. Masonry structures are reinforced during construction with rebar embedded in the material. Reinforcing an existing brick building is a job for professionals.

Wood-frame structures are reinforced with anchor bolts, shear walls, hold-downs, and metal ties at framing connections.

A brief inspection of the crawl space beneath the house will tell you whether some of the most essential reinforcement has been done. There should be anchor bolts holding the mudsill to the foundation. If the house has kneewalls (also called cripple walls) they should be reinforced with plywood shear walls.

The absence of either anchor bolts or shear walls places a house at much greater risk of destruction during a quake.

If there are no anchor bolts, installing them is the first priority.

The next step is to reinforce kneewalls with shear walls.

The third step, installing hold-downs and metal framing connectors, is more complicated. Consult the local building code for specific requirements. The advice of an architect or structural engineer is recommended.

In addition to major structural reinforcement, some very simple steps can reduce earthquake losses. One is to attach the water heater and tall pieces of furniture, such as bookcases, to the wall studs with lag screws and plumber's tape. If the water heater falls during an earthquake, it can cause a gas leak and fire. The water heater is also a source of drinking water if the quake is severe enough to disrupt the normal water supply. Another step is to place heavy items, such as large cans of food, on lower shelves. Valuable breakable items such as glassware should be placed in cabinets with doors so they won't be tossed onto the floor.

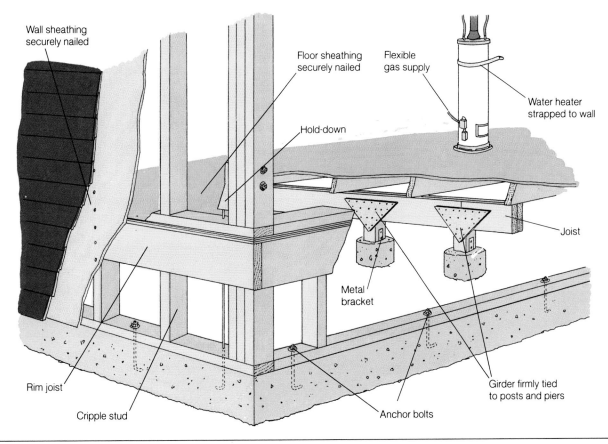

Wall sheathing securely nailed

Floor sheathing securely nailed

Flexible gas supply

Water heater strapped to wall

Hold-down

Joist

Metal bracket

Rim joist

Cripple stud

Anchor bolts

Girder firmly tied to posts and piers

BRICK

Few building materials are as simple and basic, and at the same time as elegant and versatile, as brick. Brick is equally at home in traditonal, contemporary, rustic, formal, or stately settings. It is ideal for walls, steps, paving, small structures, or decorative veneers. For these reasons, as well as the fact that it is easy to work with, brick has long been a favorite material for home-improvement projects.

Brick is particularly suitable for the garden. It blends well with greenery, and it can be laid in a variety of patterns. As a paving surface, it is nonskid and nonglare, and as a wall material it combines strength with design flexibility.

Most of these projects can be done by a novice bricklayer. Some just need bricks laid in a simple pattern on a sand base; others require careful layout and extensive preparation.

Recommended Cross-References
Barbecues, Chimneys & Stovepipes, Concrete, Fireplaces, Garden Walls, Paths, Patios, Steps.

Simple techniques can create dramatic results; the jack-on-jack border pattern of this basket-weave brick walkway (below) defines the edges and provides a pleasing contrast. In a more complicated project (above), contrast is gained by using bands of ceramic tile between the brick steps.

Shopping for Brick

Bricks are made from clay that is shaped, dried, and fired in a kiln. They come in a bewildering variety of sizes, shapes, colors, and textures. However, because of shipping costs, the selection at your local supplier is usually limited to those kinds that are manufactured in your vicinity.

Types of Brick. The main categories are common brick, face brick, and specialty brick.

Common brick, also called building brick, can be found virtually everywhere in existing buildings, but face brick is now the all-purpose type. Common brick has a rough texture and is the least expensive brick to buy new. Most common brick is wire cut and has straight, rough sides. Sand-molded brick has a smoother texture and has slightly tapered sides for easy release from the molds. Another style of common brick—clinker brick—is hard baked and often shows patches of black oven burns.

Common brick is rated for durability. There are three grades: SW (severe weathering), MW (moderate weathering), and NW (non-weathering). Use SW brick outdoors where frost occurs. MW brick is suitable for mild climates; and NW brick should be used indoors except for floors.

Face brick, or facing brick, is intended for use when a finished appearance is desired. It is harder than common brick, and at least one surface is smooth, textured, or even glazed. Size is also more uniform than that of common brick. Generally, dealers offer face brick, whereas common brick is often sold as seconds.

Some bricks are made specifically for certain situations. Firebrick is used for barbecues, fireplaces, and other high-temperature locations. The mortar must also have fireclay mixed into it. Another specialty brick is split brick or half brick. It is used for veneers or for paving where normal brick would be too thick; it is installed just like tile.

Used brick includes all categories of brick. Often the corners are rounded and there is a white mortar residue; these imperfections add to the charm. The quality and weathering durability of used brick are often uncertain, however. If the brick will be subjected to freezing temperatures, manufactured used brick is a better choice than genuine used brick.

Estimating the Amount. When ordering brick, you need to know the size of the job and the size of each brick. Brick is sized in two ways: the actual size and the nominal size. The actual size refers to the literal dimensions, whereas the nominal size includes mortar joints. To complicate matters, sizes aren't always uniform. Dimensions for common bricks may vary as much as $1/2$ inch. Generally, the actual size of a common brick is 8 inches long by $3^1/_4$ inches wide by $2^1/_4$ inches thick.

Once you know the brick size, you can determine how many are needed for each square foot of surface you are covering. As a rule of thumb, estimate 5 bricks per square foot of paving to lay a patio or walkway. To build a wall, calculate length and height to find out the square footage of one side. After choosing a brick pattern and deciding how thick you want the wall to be, estimate how many bricks are required for each square foot of wall surface. Multiply that figure by the total square footage.

Choosing a Pattern

One way to decide on a pattern is to lay out bricks in different ways to see what looks best. If you are not sure which pattern to use, stick with a basic one and avoid mixing patterns.

Half-Basket Weave

Jack-on-Jack

Running Bond

Herringbone

Ladder Weave

Basket Weave

Laying Bricks in Mortar

Installing the Base. Excavate, level, and compact the soil to allow for the concrete base. If drainage or freezing is a problem, excavate deeper and install 4 inches of gravel or sand. Build forms for a 4-inch concrete base, allowing for a ¼ inch-per-foot slope for drainage.

Pour a 4-inch concrete slab, reinforcing it with wire mesh if the soil is unstable. Screed the concrete so that it is even with the top of the forms. It should have a slight slope for drainage. Finish the slab with a wood float making sure that you get a rough enough surface that will allow for good mortar adhesion.

Allow the slab to cure for one or two days before laying the brick.

Mixing the Mortar. The ratio of mortar ingredients varies for different brick installations. For most garden projects, a satisfactory mix would be 1 part cement, 1 part hydrated lime, and 6 parts sand. Add only enough water for a buttery, firm consistency.

Applying the Grout. For a large job, let the bricks set overnight before grouting so that you can stand on them without disturbing the pattern or the level. If you are only paving a small area and you can reach all the bricks from the edge, you don't have to wait. Mix grout in the same way as mortar. Color is often added to the grout to make the joints blend in with the bricks. Colored grout mixes are expensive, but convenient for small jobs where the extra cost is minimal. For larger projects, it is much more economical to add a dry coloring agent to regular grout.

Either squeeze grout into the joints with a grout bag (like a bag for icing a cake) or sling the grout into the joints with a small brick trowel. If you must work on newly laid bricks, kneel on small sheets of plywood. Your weight will be distributed evenly over several bricks, reducing the risk of disturbing them.

Smoothing and Cleaning the Joints. Use a joint tool to smooth the grout into an even concave shape. Wipe fresh grout off the bricks with a wet sponge. If it dries on the bricks, wait for the mortar to cure. Then add 1 part muriatic acid to 10 parts water, wash the bricks, and rinse after one hour. When working with muriatic acid, be sure to wear rubber gloves and protect your eyes.

1. Do a dry layout on the concrete base to determine the pattern.

2. If using brick as an edging, butter the ends and lay the entire frame.

3. Butter the end and side of each brick and fill in the area between the edgings.

4. Scrape off the excess mortar, then, using an appropriate tool, press and smooth the grout.

Choosing a Base

Mortar Base. This is actually a concrete slab, either an existing patio or a rough slab poured in place for the brickwork. The bricks are embedded in a layer of mortar placed on top of the concrete. Additional mortar is used to grout joints between the bricks, and is sometimes colored for different effects.

Sand Base. A sand base is simpler to install than a mortar one, although the bricks may settle and buckle. Make the base at least 1 inch deep. In cold climates, it must be at least 4 inches deep and extend 4 inches beyond the edge of the bricks, to minimize the heaving caused by the expansion of frozen soil. In a sand installation, butt the bricks tightly together or leave a slight gap and fill it with sand. Hold the edges of the paving in place with a border of boards, concrete, or mortared brick.

Sand and Mortar. With this method, you lay bricks over a sand base and then mortar the joints. You can mix up the mortar and fill the joints or sweep dry mortar into the joints and spray them with water or let rainfall do the job for you. The success of this method depends completely on the stability of the base.

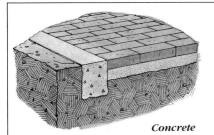

Concrete

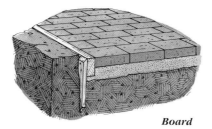

Board

Bricks Laid Flat

Installing Edging

The edging or border for a brick patio keeps the brick from shifting. This is especially important in a brick-on-sand installation where rain will cause the sand to seep out unless there is a solid frame that will prevent this from happening. The materials that are most commonly used for an edging or border are rot-resistant wood (redwood, cedar, pressure-treated lumber, or railroad ties), brick, or concrete.

Concrete. Use concrete for permanence. Make it decorative by adding a coloring agent or aggregate.

Brick. Place a row of brick, either flat or on end, around the perimeter of the patio. Set them in concrete, making sure that they will be flush with the surface of the patio.

Boards. Use redwood, cedar, or pressure-treated wood that will resist rot. Dig a ditch approximately 5 inches deep and place the boards on edge. Support them with 1-foot long, 1 by 2 stakes. Drive in these stakes every 4 feet and nail them to the outside of the boards so that the tops of the stakes are about an inch below the top of the edging board.

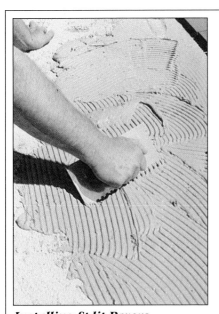

Installing Split Pavers

1. When the depth of brick is a problem, thin bricks can be set in ½ inch of mortar like common bricks. However, if a low height is critical, use a special epoxy mortar, spreading a thin layer directly on the concrete with a notched trowel.

2. Set bricks into the mortar or epoxy adhesive and tap them into place. The mortar should not fill the joint spaces or become stuck to the tops of the bricks. Wipe any mortar off immediately with a wet sponge.

3. Rather than using a brick chisel and hammer, it is better to cut thin pavers with a masonry cut-off blade in an ordinary power saw. This method is easier and will result in a smooth, clean cut.

Laying Bricks on a Sand Base

Bricks laid on sand will settle and buckle to some extent, but this can be minimized by setting a good base and securing the edges with a permanent border. A 2 by 4 edging of treated or decay-resistant wood such as redwood or railroad ties is adequate, but a more permanent and attractive edging is a border of bricks mortared to a concrete footing. If you want to emphasize the border, the bricks can be set on edge or on end. The concrete base should be at least 4 inches thick. In areas with severe winters, the base should be at least 8 inches thick with ½-inch reinforcing bars set into it. Opposing edges should be different heights so that the pavement will slope ¼ inch per foot and drain properly. Prepare the bed by excavating the soil deeply enough for adding the sand, then level and compact it. To control weeds, spray the excavated area thoroughly with a weed killer and lay down 6-mil plastic sheeting.

1. Spread a layer of damp, coarse sand over the subgrade. Level it by dragging a screed board across the bed. Both ends of a screed board are notched to the depth of one brick, so when an end is placed on the border, the bottom of the board will level the sand to the depth of one brick.

2. Starting at the first section, set the bricks in place. Keep the joints tight, no more than ⅛ inch wide unless you plan to grout them with mortar. After placing several bricks, level and set them by laying a short 2 by 4 across them and tapping the board. If a brick is too low, lift it out and place more sand under it.

3. Repeat steps 1 and 2 for the next and all remaining sections.

4. After all the bricks are in place, spread a layer of fine sand over the whole area and sweep it. Sweep, adding sand as necessary until the joints are filled. Wet the bricks with a fine spray. When they are dry, add more sand to the joints. Repeat the process until all the joints are full.

1.

2.

3.

4.

Laying Bricks With Dry Mortar

This method of laying brick is a middle ground between the permanence of a wet mortar installation and the ease of a brick-in-sand one. The brick can be laid on a sand bed or into wet concrete but rather than buttering the bricks, you merely sweep in the grout and water it.

Set bricks in the desired pattern, spacing them ⅜ inch apart. Mix 1 part masonry cement to 3 parts dry sand and sweep the mixture over the bricks until all the joints are filled. In order to avoid staining the brick, carefully sweep each brick as clean as possible before continuing with the next step. Set up a hose long enough to reach the bricked area and turn the nozzle on fine mist. Carefully spray the entire area making sure that the water penetrates into all the joints. Wait approximately 15 minutes to allow the grout lines to settle and spray the entire area again to make sure that the mortar is thoroughly saturated.

By the time the brick dries, the mortar will probably have settled again. Sweep in some more dry mortar, filling all the joints, and repeat the fine watering process.

Loose Bricks

Individual bricks can be removed from walls or paving and replaced quite easily. If many bricks are loose or cracked, structural problems may need to be dealt with first. Chip away the mortar of a loose brick, then split it with a hammer and chisel and pry it out. Clean the hole, wet it, then smooth in a layer of mortar (1 part cement, 1 part hydrated lime, 3 parts sand) on the bottom. At this point either apply mortar to the sides and top of the new brick and set it in place or set the brick in place and then pack mortar in as needed; use the method most convenient to the site. Finish the joints to match the rest of the wall or paving.

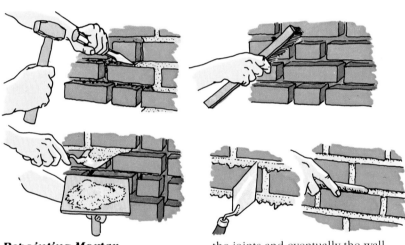

Repointing Mortar

One of the most common problems with bricks is the crumbling away of old mortar. As this happens, water works itself deeper and deeper into the joints and eventually the wall decays. This kind of damage can be minimized if, when the brick mason finishes each course of bricks, he or she shapes the joints. This method is called pointing; some of the more common styles are shown here.

If you find that mortar is crumbling away from a joint, repoint promptly. Using a masonry cutting disk on a power drill will quickly clean out much of the joint. Finish the job with a small cold chisel (a cape chisel is ideal), then scrub clean with a wire brush. The opening should be at least $\frac{1}{2}$ inch deep.

Wet the area to be repointed so as not to dry out the mortar. Fill the joint with mortar by holding the trowel just below the joint and forcing mortar into it. Do this with an appropriate tool or a stick.

Repoint the joint to match existing work. Pointing tools are handy for this and are inexpensive enough for one-time use. Use a trowel to repoint raked, weathered, or struck joints.

Pointing Styles

Flush, weathered, and struck joints can be pointed with a trowel. Other joints need a pointing tool.

Efflorescence

This whitish deposit that discolors bricks is caused by salts in the brick leaching out to the surface. Efflorescence is a fairly common problem that frequently occurs just after brick work is completed, when water from the mortar and other brick-laying procedures has dissolved the salts. It is also not unusual for this condition to occur in older walls, particularly the basement walls, when moisture creeps through mortar and bricks.

To remove efflorescence, scrub the wall with water. If that fails, mix 1 part muriatic acid with 9 parts of water and scrub the wall, rinsing it with clean water. If a stronger solution is needed, try a dilution of 1 to 4. Always add acid to water and not water to acid. Wear rubber gloves and protective goggles. If the efflorescence recurs, you must solve the moisture problem that causes it.

It is hard to improve on built-in cabinets as a storage system. Cabinets are a major design feature (and expense) of any kitchen remodel. Whether you are planning to build your own cabinets, to buy and install ready-made units, or to have the work completely done by professionals, there are many decisions to make before investing in cabinets. Besides cost, the main factors to consider when planning and selecting cabinets are appearance, efficiency, capacity, and quality.

Recommended Cross-References
Countertops, Dishwashers, Hinges, Pulls & Knobs, Hoods & Vents, Joinery, Kitchen Layout, Ranges, Ovens & Cooktops, Shelves, Storage: Indoor, Vanities.

Efficiency and Capacity
The primary function of a cabinet is to provide concealed storage space. In spite of the fact that all cabinets perform this function in basically the same way, some installations work better than others. This is because the storage space is located where it is needed and because it has features that make it easy to use.

The core of cabinet planning is a good working layout of the kitchen—one that includes enough activity space, that allows a smooth flow of traffic, that organizes the work spaces into an efficient triangle totaling 23 feet or less, that accommodates appliances well, and that provides adequate lighting. If the total space is not planned well, the cabinets will not work well either. Beautiful, new cabinets will not overcome an inefficient kitchen by themselves.

Conversely, an efficient kitchen layout will not automatically meet all storage needs. The size, placement, and style of the cabinets should be refined keeping all the following principles in mind:
- The minimum total frontage of all base cabinets, not counting sink cabinets or corner spaces, should be 13 feet for small kitchens and 16 feet for medium and large kitchens.
- The minimum frontage of wall cabinets should be 12 feet for small kitchens and 16 feet for medium and large kitchens.
- Cabinets should be arranged so that every item has room to be stored in the area where it has primary use.
- Base cabinets with large drawers or pull-out shelves are more efficient than fixed-shelf cabinets.
- Corner cabinets with lazy-susan arrangements are more efficient than those with fixed shelves. The type with doors attached to a revolving tray tend to pinch fingers. It is better for corner cabinets to have diagonal doors or right-angle doors.
- Wall cabinets with adjustable shelves reduce wasted space.
- The top shelf inside a wall cabinet should be no higher than 6 feet for maximum accessibility.
- Sink bases are available with a tilt-down front panel. The recess behind conceals a small tray for storing sponges and scrubbers.
- It is customary for wall cabinets above a sink or stove to be no lower than 5 feet from the floor and within 72 inches of the sink. This includes the hood for cabinets over a stove.
- The cabinet over a refrigerator should be 24 inches instead of 12 inches deep, if it is not connected to other 12-inch wall cabinets. This depth makes it more accessible, and provides a perfect storage space for large, awkward items that are seldom used. Placing a cabinet here also has the advantage of dissuading members of the family from using the top of the refrigerator as a general dumping ground.
- If the minimum frontage for base and wall cabinets cannot be met, or if additional window space is a higher priority than convenient wall cabinets, try locating a tall storage unit along a short wall. These units are 7 feet tall, 12 to 24 inches deep, and 18 to 36 inches wide. Some include small shelves in the doors or pull-out shelves and bins.
- Because the area around the sink is the most used, it therefore needs the most storage space.
- For base cabinets with fixed shelves and two doors, the most efficient style is one that has overlapping doors thereby eliminating the need for a center stile.
- While wall cabinets can be designed to extend to the ceiling, the extra space is not easily accessible. It is usually better to install standard-height cabinets and fill the space with a soffit or use it for displaying seldom-used items.

Appearance
Clever and efficient storage is not the only function of cabinets. They are a strong design element that must be chosen carefully, both for overall appearance and for small design details.

The style options are considerable, given the range of colors and materials. However, cabinet design falls into only two categories: the contemporary European look and the traditional look. Traditional cabinets have exposed face frames, while European cabinets have full-overlay doors and drawers that cover the entire front of the cabinet.

Both styles of cabinet come in a variety of face designs and materials, including solid wood, veneers, and laminates. The type you choose depends on which color, texture, and line you feel are most appropriate for your kitchen. Do not limit your choice because of existing appliances, floorcoverings, wallcoverings, or current fads. Accessories can change, but you will probably be living with the cabinets for a long time.

Cabinet details are important. Hinges and pulls can be either smart design accents or eyesores that call attention to themselves. If the overall look of the kitchen is streamlined and austere, exposed hinges will look out of place. If the kitchen is warm and somewhat busy looking, the hinges can add visual interest. Door handles and drawer pulls should harmonize with other elements in the kitchen, not introduce a new color or shape.

Strong horizontal lines of these light oak cabinets give the effect of lengthening a small kitchen. Mug recess allows extra headroom above the sink. Below the sink, what appears to be a drawer is actually a drop-down flap that hides soap, sponges, and scourers.

Quality

Cabinets come in three ranges of quality—low, medium, and high—with prices to match.

Cabinets are expensive and usually last for years, so take your time when making a selection. Talk to dealers, cabinetmakers, installers, and friends who have installed cabinets.

● Particleboard was once a sign of low quality, but no longer. Even the highest-quality cabinets may use particleboard. Particleboard itself varies in quality; generally, the thicker, denser, and heavier the materials, the more durable the construction. The weight can be a disadvantage during shipping and installation; plywood offers the same strength with less weight.

● Solid wood refers to plywood, natural wood boards, and particleboard covered with veneer. Typically, particleboard in medium- to high-quality cabinets is covered with wood veneer on the outside and a vinyl or melamine coating on the inside. Vinyl is usually used as an outside coating only on low-quality cabinets.

● Manufacturers of high-quality cabinets spend significant amounts of time checking cabinet doors and panels for consistency of stain color and grain appearance. The rejects are sometimes sold and may appear on low-quality cabinets.

● In general, the finish is thicker on high-quality cabinets. A low-quality finish may have visible sanding marks, feel rough, or simply not look deep or rich. Low-quality finishes are also likely to wear more quickly.

● High-quality cabinets usually offer more styles and options. Operation of doors and drawers is smoother. Joints are tight, fasteners don't poke through the box, and there is no glue visible at joints.

● To test the fit of drawers, pull them out a few inches and try to move them from side to side. Some movement is likely, but high-quality drawers will move less. Side-to-side movement is especially significant on large drawers.

● To test drawer slides, pull the drawer out all the way and push downward on it. The drawer slide shouldn't bow or deform. Two side slides are generally better than a single center slide.

● Hinges and catches should feel secure. The best type of hinges are self-closing, and a sturdy door catch releases the door smoothly and easily when you pull on it.

Types

The three main types of cabinets are stock, modular, and custom. Stock cabinets are mass-produced and commonly kept in stock by dealers. They are usually of low to medium quality.

Modular cabinets are more commonly found in kitchen showrooms. After you select and order the cabinets, they are assembled from modular components at a factory and shipped to you.

Custom cabinets are made to your specifications by a local cabinetmaker who will design the units to fit your particular space. This may be less expensive than buying from a kitchen showroom or specialty store, even though the service and quality are comparable. If you select custom cabinets, ask the cabinetmaker for references and apply the same standards of quality that you would to ready-made units. Bear in mind that unusual designs may be expensive.

It helps to know some basic terminology when planning and ordering cabinets. These terms may vary, but the following are the most common.

Base Cabinet: The lower cabinet on which the countertop rests.

Wall Cabinet: The upper cabinet that is hung on a wall.

Utility Cabinet: A tall storage unit that may have shelves, or an open cabinet that functions as a broom closet.

Sink Front: A cabinet face without a deck or box. It is installed in front of a sink and attached to the base cabinets on either side. You have to build your own deck.

Specialty Cabinets: These include corner cabinets (either "blind" or "lazy susan" units), island and peninsula cabinets, and built-in oven cabinets.

Box: The main body of the cabinet is called a box. It is also referred to as a case or carcass. The box is made from plywood or particleboard, with wood braces on the top and back to give more backing for attaching cabinets to walls and countertops.

Face Frame: The entire front framework of a cabinet, consisting of horizontal rails and vertical stiles or mullions. It is usually made from the same material as the doors and drawer fronts. Not all cabinet styles have face frames.

Deck: The permanent bottom shelf of a cabinet.

Base or Base Frame: The pedestal that elevates a base cabinet off the floor, usually 4 to 4⅝ inches (higher for European cabinets).

Toe Kick: A recessed space under base cabinets that allows you to stand close to the cabinet without your foot bumping into it. It is usually 3 inches deep.

End Panels: Decorative pieces of plywood or similar material that cover exposed cabinet sides.

Fillers: Narrow pieces of face-frame material intended to fill the empty spaces created when a row of cabinets does not quite fit wall to wall. Fillers can be ripped to the exact width of the space.

Dimensions

Except for unique situations that require a custom design, cabinet dimensions are standardized throughout the industry. Base cabinets are always 24 inches deep (the countertop is usually 25½ inches), and 34½ inches high, so that by adding a 1½-inch-thick countertop the total will be the normal 36 inches above the floor. Wall cabinets are 12 inches deep and from 12 to 48 inches wide. Most are 30 inches high; when they are installed 18 inches above the countertop, the tops are 7 feet above the floor. Wall cabinets are also available in 12-, 15-, 18-, and 24-inch heights for installations over sinks, ranges, refrigerators, and windows. Allow at least 30 inches of clearance above a cooktop, even when a range hood is under the cabinet. A bar counter is generally 42 inches high. Built-in desks or tables are usually 29 to 30 inches high.

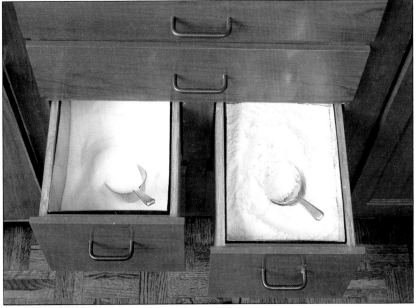

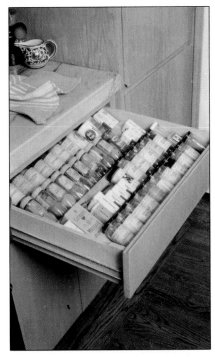

When choosing cabinets, look for ones that offer special features. Efficient storage makes it easy to keep drawers and shelves organized. Pull-out shelves beneath a cooktop *(top left)* keep pots and pans handy. Preparation center *(top right)* houses mechanism for blending and processing. Vertical dividers *(center left)* separate baking trays. Lined drawers *(center right)* contain flour and sugar. Spice drawer *(far left)* eliminates losing small bottles at the back of a shelf. Deep drawers *(left)* are often more useful than cabinets.

Preparation

Whether you have constructed your own kitchen cabinets or purchased ready-made units, installing them is a meticulous and demanding task. It's easy to underestimate the time required to do it right. For a kitchen of average size, figure on putting in about a week of work.

In a successful cabinet installation, the units are level, plumb, and square; all joints are tight and flush; and the doors and drawers are aligned. Carefully study the following techniques and the manufacturer's instructions before you start to work. Note especially the differences between frame and frameless cabinet installations. There is no margin for error with frameless cabinets; if they are not perfectly square and straight, the doors and drawers will not fit properly.

All the walls and ceilings should be smooth, and the soffits, if any, should be finished, unless you are adding them later. Painting should be completed, wallcoverings may be up, and wiring for undercounter lighting should be installed. If the finish floor is down, protect it with plywood or cardboard while the cabinets are being installed. Remove artwork and other valuable objects from the walls.

Inspect all the cabinets for defects and verify the sizes. Make sure that the doors fit, that none of the boxes is warped, and that all the drawers slide perfectly. Remove all the doors; mark on each door which cabinet it belongs with.

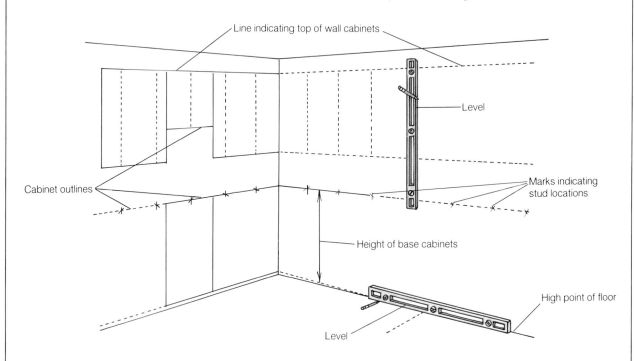

Line indicating top of wall cabinets

Level

Cabinet outlines

Marks indicating stud locations

Height of base cabinets

High point of floor

Level

Marking the Layout

Start the layout for the cabinets by locating the highest point of the floor in the area where the base units will be installed. Use a long level or a straightedge with a level on it. If the highest point is not against the wall, use a level and a pencil to transfer the height of that point to the wall. Having marked the wall at the appropriate height, measure up from the mark and make a second mark at the height of the base cabinets (usually 34½ inches). Add an allowance for the thickness of the finish floor if it is not yet down. Using the straightedge and a level, draw a line on the wall to represent the tops of all the base cabinets. (The line will be covered by the counter or the backsplash. Make heavy marks on the wall only where they will be covered; elsewhere use a faint pencil line.)

Draw another level line for the tops of the wall cabinets. Most wall cabinets are 30 inches tall and 18 inches above the countertop. For most installations, then, this line will be 84 inches above the highest point of the floor (36 + 18 + 30).

If the wall cabinets extend up to a soffit or to the ceiling, check them for level. Find the lowest point of the ceiling or soffit in the area over the cabinets and draw a level line on the wall at that height for the cabinet tops. You can now see how much of a gap there will be between the ceiling or soffit and the cabinets. After the cabinets are installed, cover this gap with a strip of molding.

If the installation includes a full-height cabinet, measure it now to make sure that it will fit beneath the ceiling or soffit. You may have to trim the top or the base, according to the manufacturer's instructions.

Using the lines on the wall for horizontal guides and a level for plumb, lay out the cabinet dimensions on the wall. Make sure that they line up properly with each other and with the various corners, windows, sinks, appliances, and so forth. Make any necessary adjustments.

Next mark the location of each stud just above the line for the base cabinets. To find a stud, tap lightly on the wall and listen for a solid sound. Probe the area with a hammer and nail until you locate both edges of the stud. Mark the exact center of the stud on the wall. Using a level, draw a vertical line through this mark. Repeat for each stud behind the upper cabinets. If there is blocking between the studs, mark a horizontal line at the center of the blocking where the cabinets will be hung.

CABINETS

Installing Wall Cabinets

Start a run of wall cabinets with a full-height unit or a corner unit if you have one. Otherwise start at whichever end will not require a filler piece. The first cabinet must be perfectly level, plumb, and square or the entire run will be out of alignment.

Measure where the studs line up behind the first cabinet and transfer these measurements to the inside of the cabinet at the top and bottom hanger rails. Countersink and drill screw holes through the back of the cabinet at these marks.

If the cabinets are frameless, they may require a metal support rail, provided by the manufacturer. Install this rail next. Cut the rail to length and screw it securely to each stud at the height recommended by the manufacturer.

To begin, lift the first cabinet into place and slide a brace up under it. You will need a helper to stabilize the cabinet while you do this. Attach the cabinet to the studs with 3-inch screws, tightening only one of the top screws and leaving the others slightly loose. Place a shim behind the cabinet next to a screw, at any point where the wall bows inward. Use a level to check that the cabinet is plumb and horizontal in all directions.

Now transfer the stud dimensions to the inside of the second cabinet and countersink and drill the screw holes. Drill two more screw holes through the vertical stile on the side that will be attached to the first cabinet. Drill where the hinges will cover up the screw heads.

Lift the second cabinet into place and support it, but do not screw it into the back wall. Instead, clamp the two cabinets together so that the joint between them is tight and flush. Use wood shims to protect the cabinet finish from the clamps. Choose a drill bit slightly smaller than the shank of a 1½-inch screw and center it in the first side hole of the second cabinet. Drill about two thirds of the way into the adjoining stile of the first cabinet.

Do the same for the second side hole. Now lubricate two 1½-inch screws with bar soap and drive them firmly into the holes that you have just drilled. If the cabinets are tall or if the face frames do not align perfectly, predrill more holes and add more screws. Then attach the cabinet to the back wall in the same way as you did the first cabinet.

Repeat this process for all the wall cabinets in the same run. If a vent hood will be mounted to a wall cabinet, cut holes in the cabinet for the duct before you install the cabinet.

For frameless cabinets the side holes are already partially drilled, about 3 inches back and 2 to 3 inches up from the bottom or down from the top. Simply complete the drilling. Special fasteners go into these holes; they screw into each other, leaving a smooth head on each side that is covered with a plastic cap.

If the final cabinet will end next to a sidewall, there may be a gap that needs a filler piece. These come in 3-inch and 6-inch widths and must be cut to fit snugly. Before you install that cabinet, attach the filler piece to the stile in the same way as you would attach two cabinets together. Then take a series of measurements between the wall and the last cabinet installed. Transfer these measurements to the face of the final cabinet, marking them on the filler piece. Now connect the marks with a line. Cut along the line with a fine-toothed keyhole saw, angling the back of the cut toward the cabinet. The cut will follow any deviations in the wall so that the filler piece will fit perfectly. Filler pieces for corners are installed in the same way, but they need not be scribed and cut. When the full run of wall cabinets is in place, check for level, plumb, and square (measure diagonals). Use shims to make any necessary adjustments.

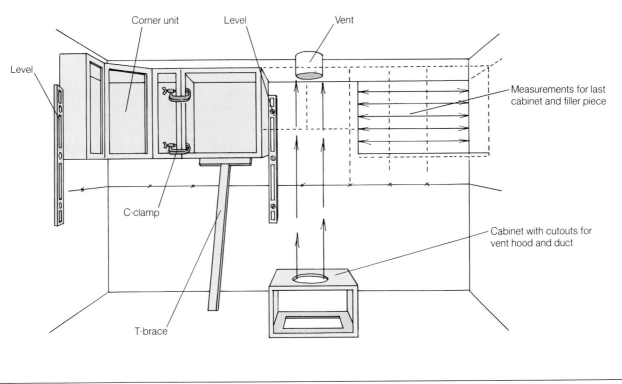

Corner unit

Level

Vent

Level

Measurements for last cabinet and filler piece

C-clamp

Cabinet with cutouts for vent hood and duct

T-brace

Installing Base Cabinets

It is usually easier to install the wall cabinets before the base cabinets. However, if the backsplash will be full-height laminate that extends up to the wall cabinets, the base cabinets and the countertop must be installed first. It is also better to install the base cabinets first if there is a full-height cabinet in the middle of a run.

Frame and frameless base units are installed in the same way as wall cabinets, except that with the frameless style there is no margin for error. Start with a corner unit, unless a cabinet in the middle of a run must be perfectly aligned with some other feature, such as a window or the sink plumbing. Set the cabinet in place and shim under the base until the top is even with the layout line. Countersink and

drill through the top rail at each stud and attach the rail to the stud with 3-inch screws. If the wall is not straight, place shims behind the cabinet, using a level to check the top, sides, and front. Hold the level against the frame, not against a door or drawer.

Set the second unit in place and attach it to the first unit. Screw it to the back wall.

Complete the run of base cabinets. Some of them, such as lazy susan corner units and sink fronts, have no box to attach to the wall. They are held in place only at the face frames. (With frameless styles the sink fronts have sides that extend back just far enough to attach them to the adjacent cabinets.) Because these units have no backs, you will have to provide support for the countertop

along the backside. Screw cleats of 1-by lumber to the wall just below the layout line.

You will also need to fabricate a floor for some sink fronts. Cut it out of a piece of ½-inch to ¾-inch plywood and support it on cleats screwed to the wall and to the adjacent cabinets. Seal it or paint it before you install it.

If there will be an appliance in the middle of a run—a dishwasher, trash compactor, or slide-in range—you must allow for it when you install the base cabinets. Check the appliance specifications to determine the exact width of the space. To keep the cabinets on both sides aligned, bridge the gap with a long straightedge at the front and back. Install fill pieces at the end of the run and at the corners, just as you did for the wall cabinets.

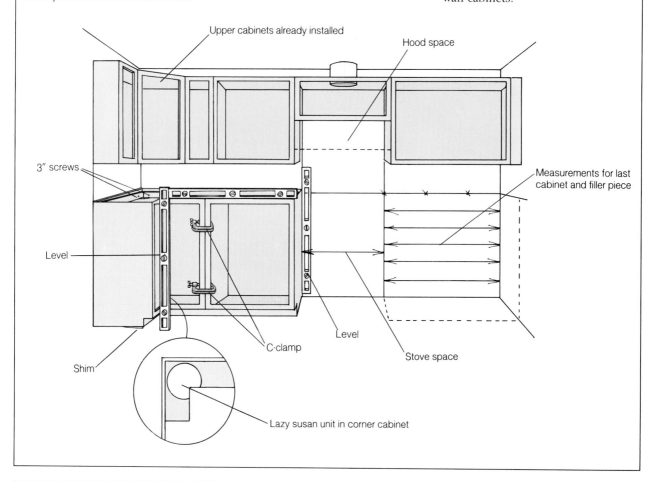

Upper cabinets already installed

Hood space

Measurements for last cabinet and filler piece

3" screws

Level

Shim

C-clamp

Level

Stove space

Lazy susan unit in corner cabinet

Tool Checklist

The tools you will need for installing cabinets are a ⅜-inch or ¼-inch electric drill, preferably variable speed; a countersink bit; an assortment of screwdrivers; a tape measure; a hammer; 2-foot and 4-foot levels; a 6-foot straightedge or a long level; adjustable clamps or C-clamps; a stepladder; shims; a flat pry bar; masking tape; and a bar of soap. An extra electric drill with a Phillips-screwdriver bit is handy to have. You will also need a supply of 1½-inch, 2½-inch, and 3-inch quick-drive wood screws; 3d, 4d, and 6d finishing nails; 1-inch brads; and whatever particular connecting screws are provided with frameless cabinets.

Finishing Touches

Finish panels, doors, trim, and handles are the most noticeable features of a cabinet installation. Take care to attach them correctly. Try to set aside one day just to do this part of the job; don't try to do it at the end of a long day's work.

In some lines of manufactured cabinets, finish panels must be installed on all the exposed faces of every unit. These panels come either precut or as a full sheet of plywood paneling from which you cut out each piece to fit. If the panels have grain patterns, match each one carefully with the patterns on the adjacent cabinets.

Measure and cut each panel to size. Spread contact cement on the back of each panel and on the side of the cabinet where the panel will be positioned. Let it set for the amount of time specified in the instructions. Press the panel in place, clamp it, and leave it overnight to dry. If necessary, use 3d nails to help hold it in place. The nail heads can be countersunk and the holes filled with putty after the cement dries.

When you put the doors back on the cabinets, some of them may not line up perfectly. Most hinges have a mechanism for making slight adjustments to correct this problem.

Before you install trim pieces, be sure that the cabinets are aligned and securely fastened. Cut the trim to length with a miter box, and stain or paint the trim, including the cut ends, before you attach it. Predrill the trim and fasten it with 3d, 4d, or 6d finishing nails. Sink the heads with a nail set and fill the holes.

For frameless units attach the trim pieces from inside the cabinet, using screws. Predrill holes through the cabinet large enough to take the screws; use a smaller bit to drill pilot holes in the trim itself. Most manufacturers provide plastic caps to cover the screw heads.

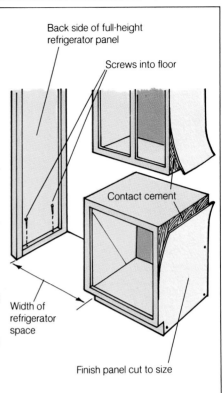

Back side of full-height refrigerator panel

Screws into floor

Contact cement

Width of refrigerator space

Finish panel cut to size

Cabinet Doors and Hinges

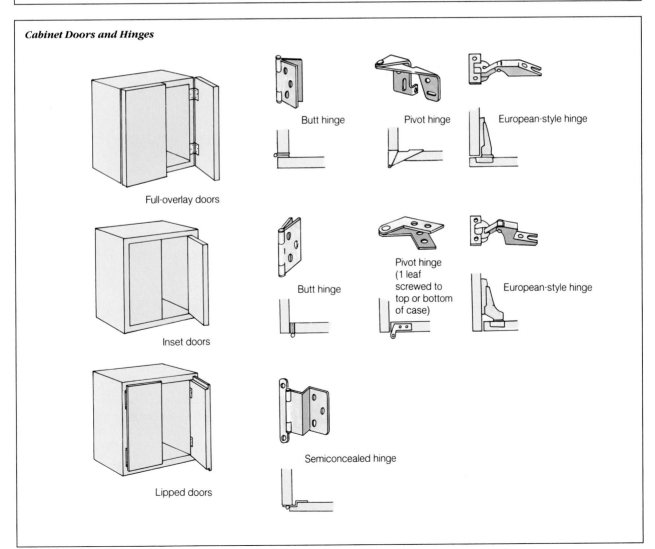

Full-overlay doors

Butt hinge

Pivot hinge

European-style hinge

Inset doors

Butt hinge

Pivot hinge (1 leaf screwed to top or bottom of case)

European-style hinge

Lipped doors

Semiconcealed hinge

Vanities and wall-mounted storage units are popular bathroom cabinets. They create valuable space, conceal plumbing hookups, and become an attractive design element.

Bathroom cabinets are available in almost as wide a range of styles and materials as kitchen cabinets. Vanities are usually open in the back to accommodate plumbing, so the bathroom wall behind the cabinet should be finished well enough for exposure under the sink.

Vanities are shorter than kitchen base cabinets, usually 29 to 30 inches high. This is a satisfactory height for most people, but it can be surprisingly irritating for people who are taller than average. The following installation steps include ways to raise the height of a vanity when you install it.

Recommended Cross-References
Bathroom Layout, Countertops, Hinges, Pulls & Knobs, Joinery, Shelves, Storage: Indoor, Vanities.

This bathroom appears spacious because of the light color scheme and good storage. Double vanity rests on a long cabinet, and open shelves top additional cabinets.

Vanity Styles

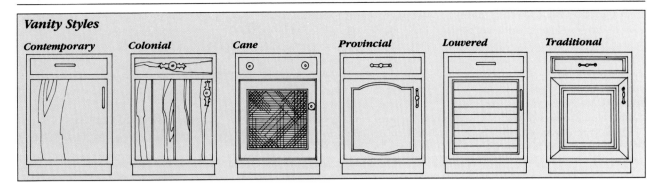

Contemporary   Colonial   Cane   Provincial   Louvered   Traditional

Installing a Bathroom Cabinet

1. Leveling the Cabinet. Be sure the floor is level. If it is not, add shims beneath the cabinet so that water does not pool at one end of the countertop or run off onto the floor. If you add shims, check the countertop with a level.

2. Raising the Height. There are several different ways that you can increase the height of a vanity:

● Buy a kitchen base cabinet instead of a bathroom vanity, which is 34½ inches high without the countertop, and 24 inches deep.

● Build a plywood base out of 2 by 4s and set the vanity on it. Laying the 2 by 4s flat adds 1½ inches; setting them on edge gains 3½ inches.

● Raise the toe kick by turning the cabinet upside down and screwing wood cleats to the bottom.

● Elevate the countertop by screwing wood cleats to the top of the vanity before installing the countertop. Finish the faces of the cleats to match the rest of the vanity.

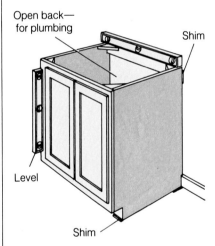

Open back—for plumbing
Shim
Level
Shim

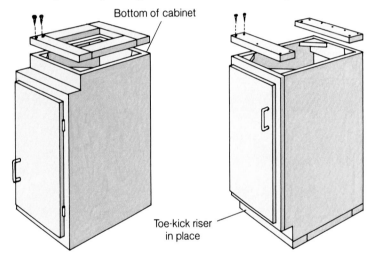

Bottom of cabinet
Toe-kick riser in place

3. Attaching the Vanity. Measure the cabinet and, using a level, draw a line on the wall at that height. If the vanity is in a corner, mark both walls. Drill pilot holes into the hanging cleat on the cabinet in spots where the holes line up on the studs, and drive a 2½-inch screw into every stud. Be sure the weight rests on the floor. Shim behind the screws if the front of the cabinet lifts off the floor.

4. Attaching More Than One Unit. If you are combining two or more units, clamp them together with C-clamps. Drill pilot holes into the side of the stile on one cabinet and screw into the adjacent cabinet, making sure cabinets are level and face frames are flush. Tightening screws will often pull a unit out of line. If this happens, add or remove shims.

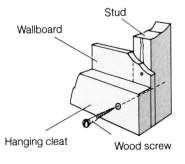

Stud
Wallboard
Hanging cleat
Wood screw

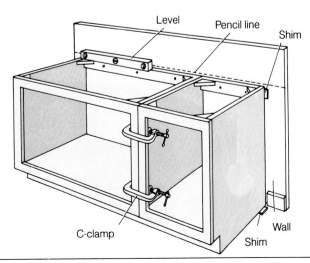

Level   Pencil line   Shim
C-clamp
Shim
Wall

CARPET

With the wide range of colors, fibers, and textures to choose from, carpet is one of the most luxurious choices of flooring. The softness and resilience of carpet invite you to sit down or stretch out on it, and the broad expanse of color provides an excellent background for any decor.

Three steps are involved in having a new carpet: selecting the carpet, preparing the floor, and installing the carpet. Most homeowners leave the floor preparation and carpet installation to professionals, but there is no reason why a reasonably handy person could not take care of the initial preparation for laying any type of carpet and the installation of cushion-backed carpeting.

Selecting a Carpet

The color, appearance, and texture of a carpet are probably your most immediate concerns, but other factors should be considered as well. The chart below compares different carpet materials and will help you choose the best type for your needs. The highest-quality carpet is not necessarily the best choice, since you may not want to live with the same carpet forever.

Preparing the Floor

Except for cushion-backed carpet or very thin goods, carpet conceals defects and irregularities beneath it quite well. The thicker the carpet or pad, the more successful the effect will be. Carpet installations usually require a little floor preparation: The subfloor surface must be dry, free of debris, and as smooth as possible.

To replace an existing carpet, remove all metal edgings. Then pry one corner of the carpet loose from the tackless strip and pull up the entire piece. Reuse the pad and tackless strip if they are in good condition.

To lay carpet over a wood floor or resilient flooring, sweep it clean and nail down any loose boards or tiles. Patch cracks or holes larger than ¼ inch with a quick-drying filler or nail down a particle-board underlayment.

When installing carpet on top of concrete, make sure the floor is dry and that there are no moisture problems. Floors with radiant-heat pipes deserve special consideration if you are installing conventional (not cushion-backed) carpet. Because the tackless strip has to be nailed into the concrete, you risk puncturing the pipes. To locate the pipes, moisten the concrete around the perimeter of the room wherever you intend to install pieces of tackless strip. Then turn up the heat. Mark the areas that dry first; these are spots to avoid when nailing.

Cushion-Backed Carpet

This type of carpet must be glued to a very smooth surface. If the subfloor or finished floor surface is rough, install ¼- to ½-inch underlayment-grade plywood over it. Fill joints and surface depressions with a filler compound.

To remove cushion-backed carpet, cut it into 12-inch-wide bands. Work each band free with a wide putty knife or other scraping tool. Scrape off any remaining chunks of foam backing or adhesive. Then sand off the residue with a floor sander or install a plywood underlayment.

To lay conventional carpet over cushion-backed carpet, just remove a band around the edge of the room that is wide enough for the new tackless strips. The remaining cushion-backed carpet now serves as a pad.

Recommended Cross-References
Floors, Subfloors.

Carpet Materials

	Wool	Nylon	Polyester	Acrylic	Polypropylene Olefin
Resiliency	Excellent. Feels springy underfoot.	Very good. Resists crushing.	Fair. May crush.	Good. Almost as resilient as wool.	Differs depending on type of pile and carpet construction.
Resistance to Soil	Very good. When soiled may be difficult to clean.	Very good. More easily cleaned than wool.	Fair. Cleans well.	Good. Must be treated after deep cleaning.	Very good—doesn't hold soil.
Abrasion	Very good.	Very good.	Excellent.	Low.	Very good.
Static	Tends to hold static unless treated.	Metal threads almost always included to resist static.	Not prone to static.	Will not hold static.	Will not hold static.
Fading	Direct sunlight will damage fiber over time.	May be damaged by prolonged exposure to sunlight.	Damaged by heat and sunlight.	Good. High color life.	Usually treated to resist fading.
Mildew and Pests	Usually treated by the manufacturer to prevent damage.	Fiber naturally resists damage from mildew and pests.	Treated to resist mildew. Not likely to attract pests.	Fiber naturally resists damage from mildew and pests.	Fiber naturally resists damage from mildew and pests.
Relative Cost	High.	Medium to high.	Low to medium.	Low to medium.	Low.

Wall-to-wall, plush carpet cushions this floor with elegance, warmth, and comfort. The uninterrupted flow up the stairs emphasizes the expansive quality of the architecture.

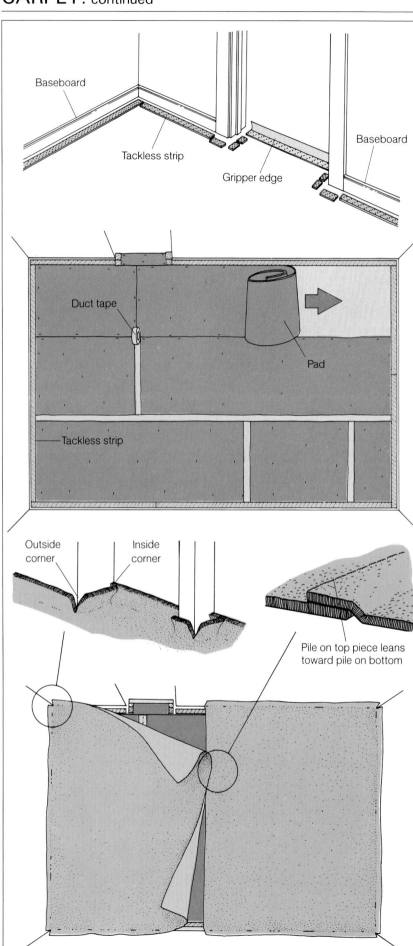

Baseboard

Tackless strip

Gripper edge

Baseboard

Duct tape

Pad

Tackless strip

Outside corner

Inside corner

Pile on top piece leans toward pile on bottom

Carpet Installation

1. Installing Tackless Strip. Cut pieces of tackless strip to length with a saw or shears. Starting in a corner, nail the strip around the perimeter of the room. Each piece should have at least two nails. The pins should point toward the wall. Leave a gap between the strip and the wall that equals two thirds of the thickness of the carpet.

Use masonry nails to nail tackless strip to concrete floors. Where sections do not hold well, add a second row of strip in front of the first. If there is resilient tile glued to the concrete, you should remove it where you are nailing the strip.

2. Installing the Pad. Cut a piece of the pad long enough to cover one end of the room. Place the long edge and one of the ends up against the tackless strip. Lap the other end over the strip. Staple the pad every 6 to 12 inches all the way around the edge. Continue cutting and stapling the pad until the entire floor is covered. Butt the edges; don't overlap them. To trim any excess pad overlapping the tackless strip, run a utility knife along the strip. Allow a slight space between the pad and the strip to keep the pad from riding up on the pins when the carpet is installed. Cover seams with duct tape.

3. Rough-Fitting Carpet Pieces. Making sure the cutting surface is clean, cut each piece of carpet off the roll. Make rough cuts 4 to 6 inches longer than finished dimensions to allow for trimming later on. Plan all cuts so that the pile will lean in the same direction on all pieces.

To make a cut, snap a chalk line along the back of the carpet and cut from that side with a sharp utility knife. Only carpet with loop pile in straight rows should be cut from the face side.

Unroll the pieces so that the pile faces in the proper direction. The excess along each side should curl up the walls slightly. At corners and obstructions, make vertical slits through the excess portion to allow the carpet to lie flat. Slits should reach almost to the floor. Overlap pieces that will be seamed together by an inch or so.

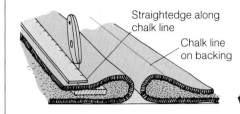

Straightedge along chalk line
Chalk line on backing

Edge of top piece guides knife

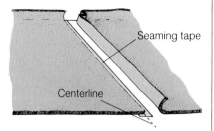

Seaming tape
Centerline

4. Cutting the Seam Edges. A good seam requires that the edges of both pieces are perfectly straight. Cut new edges on both pieces with a chalk line, straightedge, and sharp knife. Make sure an edge is square before cutting it, by folding the carpet back and measuring from the crease to the chalk line at both ends.

5. Cutting Seam Edges of Loop Pile. Dress the edges of loop pile by cutting from the face with a row cutter. Use the top piece to guide the cutting of the bottom piece.

6. Positioning the Seaming Tape. Cut a length of hot-melt seaming tape to the exact length of the seam. Center it under the seam, adhesive side up. Square the two pieces of carpet so that they butt against each other.

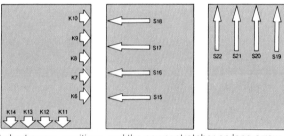

Use the knee kicker at short-arrow positions and the power stretcher on long-arrow points, following the numerical order indicated

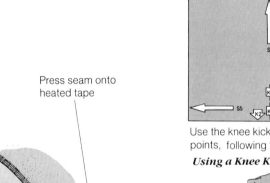

Press seam onto heated tape

Using a Knee Kicker

Knob adjusts bite   Knee pad

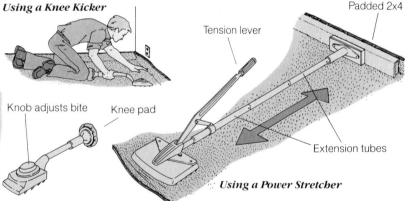

Tension lever
Padded 2x4
Extension tubes

Using a Power Stretcher

7. Melting the Adhesive. Heat the tape with a seaming iron by gliding the iron slowly from one end of the seam to the other. As the iron passes over the melted adhesive, quickly pinch the carpet pieces together over it. Place heavy objects on each section of bonded seam as you push the iron forward.

8. Stretching Carpet Into Place. Start at one corner and dig the head of the knee kicker into the carpet about an inch from the wall. Lean on the handle and swiftly kick the cushion with your knee. As you proceed, kick by kick, hold the secured carpet onto the strip so that it won't unhook.

See the diagram for kicking and stretching patterns. For short distances, such as across hallways or small bedrooms, it is possible to use just a knee kicker. In larger rooms, use a power stretcher with extension tubes that make it possible to stretch carpet across a room of any size.

Set the head of the power stretcher 6 inches from the wall and adjust the

extension tubes so that the foot rests against the opposite wall. Press down on the lever to stretch the carpet toward the wall in front. The lever should lock with a gentle and easy push. With the handle locked and the carpet stretched, fasten the section of carpet held by the head onto the tackless strip. Release the head, move the power stretcher 18 inches, and repeat the operation.

Move the foot of the stretcher along the opposite wall as you proceed. Protect baseboards or a weak wall with a piece of padded 2 by 4 placed between the wall and the foot. The 2 by 4 should be long enough to span 3 or 4 studs.

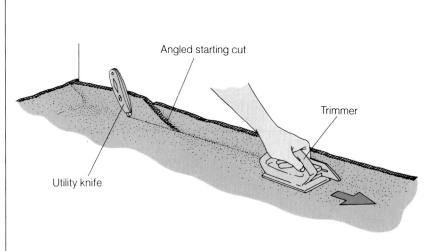

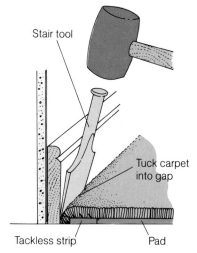

9. Trimming Carpet to Fit. Trim the excess carpet around the edges with a wall trimmer. Adjust the trimmer to the thickness of the carpet. Starting at the lapped end, slice downward at an angle until the trimmer is flat

against the floor. Then hold the trimmer against both the wall and the floor, and plow along the edge of the carpet. When you approach the end, carefully trim the last few inches with a utility knife.

10. Tucking in the Edges. Tuck the trimmed carpet edge into the gap between the tackless strip and the baseboard. Push a broad screwdriver or stair tool into the narrow section of carpet that crosses the gap, rather than down onto the edge of the carpet itself. Otherwise, the carpet will bulge and lift off the strip pins.

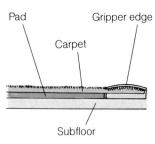

Gripper Edge

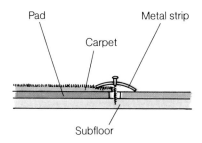

Metal Strip

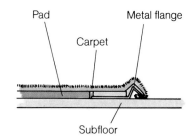

Binding Strip

11. Finishing Door Openings. At doorways, trim the edge of the carpet so that it centers under the closed door. Finish this edge with a metal strip suitable for the type of subflooring.

If the subfloor is concrete, nail a special gripper edge across the doorway before the carpet is installed. The teeth bite into the carpet, and

the curved metal flange is hammered down over the edge to bind the carpet and hold it in place.

If the subfloor is a nailable surface, the easiest way to finish it is to nail a metal strip over the joint between the carpet and the adjacent floor covering. Before installing the strip, tack the carpet to the floor.

Or, you can finish the edge of a carpet with a binding strip that is concealed by the carpet. It gives the finished carpet a folded edge.

When using a metal strip that will show, be sure to protect it when hammering it into position by placing a piece of scrap wood between the strip and the hammer.

Cushion-Backed Carpet

Cushion-backed carpet has its own bonded foam backing. It requires no stretching since it simply affixes to the existing floor with the appropriate adhesive. The existing floor needs to be prepared carefully because defects will show through the finished carpet.

Open knotholes or gouges in the subfloor should be filled and sanded. Since board subfloors or tongue-and-groove floors will show through the carpet, cover them with a ¼-inch underlayment.

Concrete subfloors must be completely free of moisture, since the foam backing acts like a sponge. If moisture is minimal, try applying a coat of sealer to the subfloor. If the moisture persists, do not lay the carpet. Using cushion-backed carpet over plywood floors on sleepers or nailing it directly to concrete is not recommended; use conventional carpet instead. You can lay cushion-backed carpet directly on a tile floor, as long as it is flat, dry, and you fill all grout lines with a latex-type underlayment.

Before you begin to work with the carpet, install a toothless binder bar with a flange that clamps down over the carpet at any door openings. If there are no seams, just rough cut the piece of carpet, place it in position, and proceed with step 5. Always cut cushion-backed carpet on the face side.

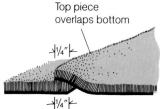

Edge aligned with chalk line

Chalk line

1. Positioning the First Piece. Rough-cut the first piece of carpet and position it, allowing a 3-inch excess at the wall. Snap a chalk line on the floor where the seam will fall. Align one edge carefully to this chalk line.

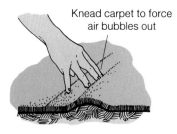

Top piece overlaps bottom

¼″

¼″

2. Overlapping the Seam. Place the second piece of carpet so the edge overlaps the bottom piece by ¼ inch.

Adhesive

First piece—flush to chalk line

Adhesive band

Seaming fluid along edge of primary backing

3. Adhering the Seam Edges. Fold both edges of the carpet back about 2 or 3 feet and trowel a thin, even coat of adhesive onto the exposed floor. Unroll the bottom piece into place, carefully keeping the edge aligned to the chalk line. Knead the carpet to force air bubbles out.

Apply seaming fluid to the adhered piece of carpet along the edge of the primary backing material. Cut the nozzle of the dispenser at an angle so that when you run the tip along the floor, the bead of seaming fluid flows onto the carpet backing, not onto the foam or pile.

Knead carpet to force air bubbles out

4. Joining the Seam. Glue the seam together by joining the second piece of carpet to the first. Be sure that any pattern lines up. Since you allowed a ¼-inch overlap, the edges should press tightly against each other. Work any bulge away from the seam. Let the seam adhesive dry thoroughly.

Glue the rest of the carpet by folding the wall edges back toward the center to expose the floor. Trowel adhesive onto the floor, then roll the carpet toward the wall so that it covers the area spread with glue. Work out any wrinkles, creases, or bumps as you go. Repeat for the other half of the carpet.

5. Fitting, Trimming, and Tucking Edges. Trim and finish the edges. Use a stair tool to seat and crease the edge of the carpet against the wall. Trim the carpet with a knife, leaving an excess margin equal to the thickness of the carpet. Tuck this margin down at the wall.

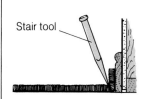

Stair tool

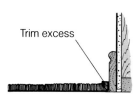

Trim excess

Tuck margin at wall

CARPORTS

A carport is a covered parking space, usually attached to the house, that is not completely enclosed by walls. There are two improvement projects that involve carports. One is to convert an existing carport into storage space or living space by enclosing it.

The other is to build a new carport. Sometimes a new carport is needed to replace an old one. But it can also be a roundabout way of adding new living space to some homes without building a room addition. If you are wondering how to add an extra room in a home that has an attached garage, you might consider building a carport and converting the garage into an extra room.

Recommended Cross-References
Concrete, Doors, Flashing, Footings, Foundations, Framing, Garages, Gutters & Downspouts, Roofs, Siding, Storage: Outdoor, Windows.

Planning
Consult with your local building department about necessary permits and code restrictions. Local codes may specify minimum dimensions for parking spaces, minimum driveway area, or maximum driveway slope. In addition to setback limits and specifications concerning the maximum percentage of the lot that can be covered by site improvements, these restrictions will affect the size and location of your carport.

Planning will be much easier if you already have a driveway beside your house with a setback that allows room for a new structure. If your driveway is on the property line or within the setback, you will probably have to build a fire wall. Check with your building department before making any plans; you may not be allowed to build at all.

Building a Carport
The actual plan for a carport is quite simple. It should be at least 12 feet wide and 20 feet long for one car, or 20 by 20 feet for two cars. The roof should have a minimum slope of 1 in 12, but a slope of 3 in 12 or steeper is better in snow areas. The roof usually slopes away from the house, so the house must be tall enough for the low side of the carport roof to be at least 8 feet high. Otherwise, the roof will have to cantilever over the top of the house to attain the proper slope.

Floor and Footings. Although a gravel floor may be adequate in some cases, the best design incorporates a concrete slab at least 4 inches thick. Most codes require that a new slab extend into the ground even farther, usually to a minimum depth of 12 inches or to the frost line. To build a new slab, excavate to the depth of the concrete plus 4 inches to accommodate a sand base. Excavate around the perimeter for a footing 12 inches wide. Build forms around the outside of the footing, so their tops are at the desired final elevation. Place a 3-inch layer of sand on the bottom of the slab area—not in the footing trench. Cover the sand with a layer of 6-mil polyethylene sheeting to provide a vapor barrier, and cover the sheeting with the rest of the sand. Put steel reinforcing bars in the footing and steel mesh in the slab. When you pour the concrete, place a metal anchor at each post location while the concrete is fresh. The slab should slope away from the house.

If the existing driveway does not have a sufficient footing to support the posts or a wall, build individual footings for all the posts. Break holes in the driveway at each post location, and excavate to the depth of the footings. Fill the holes with concrete and place post anchors in them.

Posts. Locate posts 6 to 8 feet on center, depending on the size of your beam. A 4 by 4 post is adequate for most carports, but 4 by 6 stock and steel columns are also common. When the concrete is cured, install the posts. Attach each one to the post base with 1/2-inch-diameter carriage bolts. Brace each post in two directions with diagonal braces after plumbing it with a level. Do not cut them to length until all are erected.

When all the posts are up, measure and mark both corner posts at the

height at which the beam will rest. Stretch a chalk line between these marks and snap it against the posts. Repeat the procedure on the other posts. Mark cut lines, saw off the tops of the posts, then attach the beam on top with a metal beam connector. An alternative method is to measure longer posts and bolt a 2-by stringer to each side. The inside stringer should be slightly higher than the outside stringer, so that the sloped rafters will rest on both.

Rafters. Rafters, supported by the beam and a ledger bolted to the house wall, will span the width of the carport. To install the ledger, mark a level line along the wall of the house at a height that yields the required slope. Two-by rafter stock makes a fine ledger. Cut to length and mark the rafter spacing. Nail joist hangers where the rafters will attach. Determine the location of the studs and secure the ledger to them with lag bolts.

If the span is long, consider using 4-by lumber. Once you have selected stock, your next task is to cut a pattern rafter. Using a carpenter's square, mark the plumb cut at the house end. After making the plumb cut, calculate the dimension of the bird's mouth by using rafter framing techniques. Finish cutting the pattern rafter, then test it to see if it fits. Make any necessary adjustments, and cut out the rest of the rafters. You may have to notch the bottom of each plumb cut slightly so that it will fit into the joist hanger. Nail the rafters into the joist hangers and toenail them into the beam. Install blocking over the beam and at the midpoint. If the rafters overhang the beam, attach a fascia board.

Roof. Roofing plywood should be at least 1/2 inch thick. Nail plywood over the rafters, laying sheets perpendicular to the rafters and staggering the end joints at least 4 feet. Install flashing around the edges and along the house wall. Install roofing trim to match the house, and install a gutter and a downspout on the outside edge of the roof.

Walls. If you do not need walls, finish the underside of the roof and paint the carport. If you want walls along the back or side, install framing between the posts and cover it with exterior plywood or sheathing and siding material to match the house.

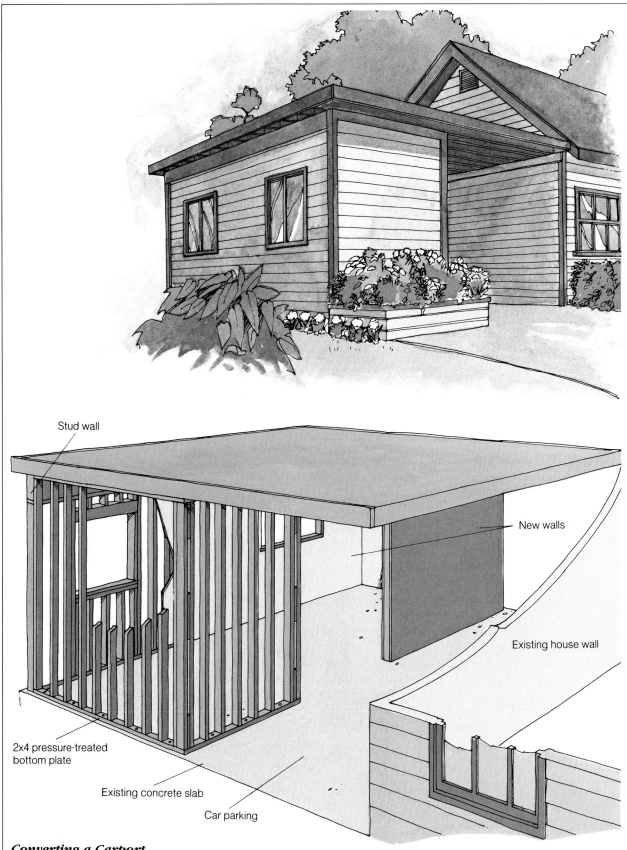

Stud wall

New walls

Existing house wall

2x4 pressure-treated
bottom plate

Existing concrete slab

Car parking

Converting a Carport

If a carport is not being used, or if an alternative area for parking is available, it may be desirable to use the space for covered storage. You will want to add walls to enclose all or part of the space. First ensure that the roof and floor are sound. After making necessary repairs, lay out the wall locations on the floor, lining them up with the edge of the floor or convenient roof framing members. It may be easier to build a wall directly beneath a roof beam or in line with existing posts than to line it up with the edge of the floor.

CAULKING & ADHESIVES

The purpose of caulking, like weather stripping, is to make your house more draft resistant and to help reduce the infiltration of air, dirt, noise, moisture, and insects.

Leaks occur where different structural components of the house join together, such as joints between the siding and the foundation, or where cracks have opened up from the natural settling and shifting of the house over time. Although these fissures may be minor at the outset, they can lead to serious problems, causing heat loss in the winter and increased cooling costs during hot weather.

Caulk, properly applied, is the best way to seal these cracks and leaks. It is one of the least expensive ways to preserve your house and save energy. In combination with weather stripping, caulking may save enough energy to pay for all the materials you use within one year.

Where to Caulk
You should caulk all cracks and joints around the exterior first. The most likely spots are where two building sections meet each other, such as joints between the chimney and house, between siding and door or window frames, between the roof and walls, between a porch and the house, or between steps and the house. Cracks are also likely wherever the shell of the building is pierced by a pipe, wire, roof vents, faucets, plumbing cleanouts, foundation vents, and air conditioners.

Other spots to seal are joints between dissimilar building materials, such as concrete and wood or metal and brick. These joints are particularly vulnerable to infiltration because materials expand and contract at different rates and under different weather conditions. Therefore, they require caulk that stays flexible and adheres well.

Indoors, caulk may be used effectively wherever cracks occur between walls and ceilings, between floors and walls, and around windows and doors. You should caulk wherever pipes and wires penetrate into the living area of the house, such as under sinks. Finally, seal all joints around bathtubs and sinks to prevent moisture getting behind the walls and damaging structural members.

When to Caulk
The best time to caulk is on exactly those days when you would rather be doing something else: the warm days of late April, May, early June, September, and early October. Why? These days are warm enough for the caulk to flow and set up easily, but not uncomfortably hot. If you caulk during the colder months, wrap a heating pad around the caulking gun. Check the manufacturer's directions for minimum temperature requirements. Always caulk when the weather and the surfaces are dry.

What Caulk to Use
The chart below compares the durability and performance of various types of caulk. Always buy the best grade of caulk. The most important considerations are whether you intend to paint the caulk and whether you are caulking fixed joints (where identical materials meet) or joints that expand and contract.

Tube caulks (for caulking guns) work best for most cracks. For larger openings, spray in canned fiberglass or foam insulation before caulking.

Safety Precautions
Work carefully on a ladder. Place it so that the feet are one quarter of the ladder's height away from the house. Avoid placing a metal ladder near electrical wires.

Do not use caulk near an open flame, and do not smoke while caulking. Most caulking compounds are flammable and give off noxious odors when in proximity to high heat.

Recommended Cross-References
Insulation, Paint, Siding, Weather Stripping.

Comparison of Caulking Materials

Caulking Material	Life	Application	Remarks
Oil base	1–2 years	All household surfaces.	Least expensive, least durable of all caulks. Oil tends to seep out and may stain unprimed surfaces, while drying out caulk itself, leading to shrinking, cracking, and the need for replacement.
Latex base	3–10 years	Indoors; outside only if painted, and not where seal moves or is subject to moisture. Only for narrow joints (less than ¼").	Because it is water soluble, should not be used where it will become damp. Insufficiently flexible to withstand frequent expansion and contraction, and should not be used on moveable joints. May disintegrate on concrete or cement.
Acrylic latex	10 years	All applications, indoors and out. For joints up to ½" × ½".	Durable, fast-curing (about 1 hour), does not stain. Should not be painted.
Butyl rubber	3–10 years	Outdoors, especially on metal and stone; effective where water may collect such as eaves and downspouts, since it is water-resistant. Only for narrow or moderately narrow joints (less than ½").	Needs no paint. May take more than a week to cure. Will shrink over time.
Elastomeric *(synthetic base: silicone, polysulfide, or polyurethane)*	20 years +	All applications, but does not adhere to paint. Polysulfide doesn't adhere to porous materials. Some polyurethanes work well in damp conditions.	Highly flexible, long-lasting caulk. May be used on large joints. Some require surface priming before application. Some cannot be painted.
Polyurethane or Urea Formaldehyde Foam	Varies with exposure	Not a true caulking material but excellent for filling large cracks.	Available in aerosol cans. Expands tremendously. Must not be exposed to direct sunlight. Excellent as a filler before caulking.

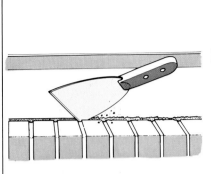

How To Caulk

Preparation. Thoroughly clean the crack or joint to be caulked. Use a putty knife to scrape away loose paint, old caulk, and other debris, and remove them with a brush. Use a cleaning solvent on grease spots or on any metal surface. Check the caulk instructions to see if priming is necessary. Allow the crack to dry thoroughly before applying caulk.

Filling Cracks. Cracks over 1/2 inch wide should be filled before caulking. Use strips of fiberglass or foam insulation from an aerosol can. Using

a screwdriver or putty knife, pack the material tightly into the crack so that the caulk will have a firm base.

Applying Caulk. After all joints are clean and dry and large cracks are

packed with filler, apply caulk. Run a continuous bead of caulk along the entire length of the crack. In order to widen the bead, cut off as much of the nozzle tip as necessary.

Using a Caulking Gun

1. Pull the plunger all the way back and insert the cartridge, seating the bottom end first. Squeeze the trigger a few times until the plunger makes contact with the tube.

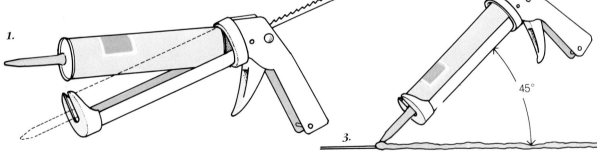

1.

3.

45°

2.

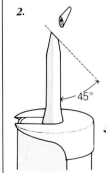

2. Cut off the tip of the nozzle at an angle; the closer to the top, the finer the bead. Start with a fine bead and enlarge it if necessary. Puncture the seal inside the nozzle with a long nail or stiff wire.

45°

4.

3. Force caulk into the crack by pushing the gun forward at an angle and squeezing the trigger. The caulk should be as deep as the width of the crack and should adhere firmly to both sides. Stop pulling the trigger and release the plunger just before you reach the end of the crack.

4. Moisten your finger with soapy water (for latex) or mineral oil to smooth the caulk and clean off adjacent surfaces.

5. Release the plunger and insert a nail into the nozzle. Wipe off any excess caulk and cover the nozzle with foil or plastic.

5.

Adhesives

An adhesive is any substance that holds things together by bonding. There are no universal adhesives. Some have very limited uses; others are more versatile.

Polyvinyl Acetate. This is the generic term for the water-based white or yellow glue widely used in households and for general construction. Yellow glues have greater holding power than white glues. However, both types tend to soften at temperatures above 110° F and allow creep (movement in a glued joint), so they are not considered structural adhesives. Polyvinyl acetate glues are inexpensive and widely available. They are suitable for interior use only.

Resorcinol and Urea-formaldehyde. These are strong, waterproof glues that must be mixed with water for each use. The mixed glue must be used quickly, usually within a few hours. Ambient temperature must be at least 70° F. The joints must be clamped. The harder the material being joined, the tighter it must be clamped.

These types of glue work best with very fine glue lines; they are not suitable as fillers. They don't work with wet or oily wood.

Urea-formaldehyde and resorcinol glues are toxic and release fumes. Avoid contact with skin and eyes. Ventilate the work area.

Epoxy. These glues consist of a resin and a hardener, supplied in separate containers and mixed just before use. They generate heat and can bond with almost any material, even underwater. In some cases, they are stronger than the materials they bond together. They resist heat, corrosion, water, shrinkage, and creep. However, epoxy bonds in wood deteriorate when exposed to water, even though the adhesive itself isn't damaged.

Cyanocrylate. Also known as super glues, these are expensive, but they bond most plastics, wood, ceramic, and metals. They are poor fillers, but set very rapidly without clamping. They are cleaned up with acetone or fingernail-polish remover. The fumes are irritating and the glue will bond skin quickly.

Contact Cement. This glue provides instant bonding and resistance to water and heat. It is widely used for veneers and laminate countertops. Contact cement is supplied in solvent-based and water-based varieties, but most water-based contact cements are not as strong and don't adhere as quickly as solvent-based formulations.

The cement is applied to two surfaces and allowed to dry, then the surfaces are pressed together. Running a roller over the materials helps them bond. The joined materials can be worked immediately, but there is no margin for error in aligning them.

Construction Adhesives. These are used to bond panels, tiles, wallboard, and flooring material. When used on walls and subfloors, they reduce the number of fasteners needed, increase strength, and reduce sound transmission.

Other Adhesives. There are many adhesives besides the widely used ones. Polyurethane foams are usually used to insulate and caulk, but they stick to almost anything and are effective fillers. Hot-melt glues are easy to use, set up in a few seconds, and provide adequate light-duty or temporary bonding. Other adhesives include solvent-adhesives for plastic pipe, asphaltic cements such as roof tar, and cementitious adhesives such as mortar and thinset. Casein and hide glues are used in woodworking. Starches are used for wallcoverings. Anaerobic adhesives are used in low-oxygen locations, such as on bolt threads. Adhesive tapes are used for carpet, heating, electrical wiring, and insulation.

Double-Cylinder Epoxy Gun

Types of Adhesives

Type	Description	Uses
Hide glue	Granules must be dissolved in warm water and glue kept warm while using. Gluepots and brushes are available for this purpose.	Gluing joints and veneers
Powdered casein	Mix 15 minutes before using. Glue is somewhat water-resistant.	Gluing oily woods such as teak and yew
Polyvinyl acetate	This water-based white or yellow glue is inexpensive. It sets quickly, dries clear, but is not waterproof. Clamp work while glue sets.	Multipurpose; for interior use only
Contact cement	Contact cement is water-resistant. Solvent-based contact cement is flammable and noxious.	Bonding veneers and laminates
Mastic cement	This puttylike adhesive is available in cans or cartridges. Some, but not all, mastics are waterproof.	Adhering materials to vertical and horizontal surfaces
Resorcinol	A catalyst (two-component) glue for use in high-moisture situations.	Kitchen and bathroom cabinet construction, outdoor projects
Epoxy	A catalyst glue suitable for joining wood to other materials.	Adhering wood to glass or metal
Aliphatic resin glue	Slower setting and more heat resistant than polyvinyl.	General-purpose glue

Tips for Gluing Wood

● Softer woods tend to absorb some adhesive and thus hold better. Hardwoods are more impermeable. Moisture prevents an adequate bond, so avoid gluing wood when it is green.

● Pressure is necessary for all wood gluing. It forces the glue to spread uniformly, pushes out air bubbles, and presses the two surfaces tightly against each other. To determine how much pressure is needed, use this rule of thumb: When you are working with a thin adhesive, such as polyvinyl acetate, use only moderate pressure; with thicker glues, such as plastic resins, use heavy pressure.

● The best way to apply even pressure over the entire joint is with clamps. The type and number to use depends largely on the project, but most joints require at least two. Always put a piece of scrap wood on both ends of the clamp to distribute pressure more evenly and to prevent marring the workpiece. When you glue long pieces together, such as for a tabletop, use at least three bar or pipe clamps. The two clamps near the ends should be across the top, while the middle clamp is underneath. This helps prevent buckling.

● The setting time for adhesives depends on the type you use and the surrounding air temperature. Follow the manufacturer's instructions carefully.

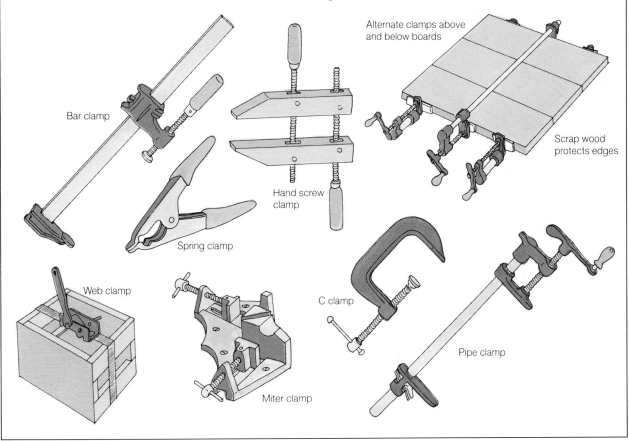

Bar clamp

Spring clamp

Hand screw clamp

Web clamp

Miter clamp

C clamp

Pipe clamp

Alternate clamps above and below boards

Scrap wood protects edges

CEILINGS

For many builders, finishing a room automatically means an 8-foot-high ceiling of painted plaster or wallboard. This option is common because it is inexpensive and flexible. However, the trend in contemporary design is to "break out of the box." This may involve elevating the ceiling, vaulting it, or adding relief with interesting materials and trim details. Today, ceiling materials include wood paneling, individual siding boards, tongue-and-groove roof decking, exposed beams, suspended lighting grids, suspended panels, spray-on textures, fiberglass insulating panels, and, of course, wallboard.

Ceilings have a strong impact on the ambience of a room. A low ceiling makes a cozy and intimate area or an oppressive one; a high ceiling creates an atmosphere that can either inspire or overwhelm. When you settle on a ceiling height, be sure that it is appropriate for the scale of the room, the type and amount of furnishings, and the mood desired.

Color and pattern can play optical games. In general, a dark-colored or heavily patterned ceiling will look much lower than the same ceiling painted in a light color.

Energy Efficiency
Some existing ceilings, such as exposed beam, are poor insulators. Unless you are prepared to tear off the roof and insulate from above, you may want to redesign the ceiling in order to add insulation. Generally, high ceilings make a room more difficult to heat, although a ceiling fan will help to circulate warm air.

Lighting
Think about the lighting when you plan your ceiling. Recessed fixtures usually require at least an 8-inch space. When using suspended or flush-mounted light fixtures of a particular style, the ceiling should complement them.

Recommended Cross-References
Attics, Framing, Insulation, Lighting: Indoor, Moldings, Paint, Paneling, Roofs, Wallboard, Walls.

The recessed skylight in this ceiling (above) bathes the breakfast area in natural light while strategically placed recessed fixtures illuminate work areas. Exposed-beam ceiling (below) is lightened by painting it white.

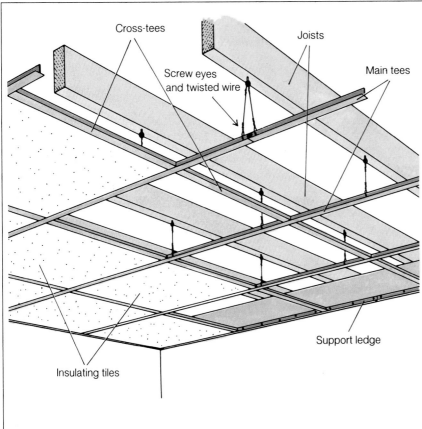

Cross-tees

Joists

Screw eyes
and twisted wire

Main tees

Support ledge

Insulating tiles

Suspended Ceiling

Although it provides less headroom, a suspended ceiling muffles sound and conceals duct work or uneven joists. The panels themselves are usually insulating tiles, but can also be light fixtures or smooth acrylic panels. This type of ceiling is easy and fast to install, and can be attached either before or after finishing the walls.

Start by attaching the outer support ledge (wall angles) all around the room. Use a level to position each piece, rather than measuring from the floor or ceiling. Hang the main tee supports perpendicular to the joists, spacing them according to the size of the panels you are using. Suspend the main tees from wires every 4 feet. Attach the wires to the joists, letting them hang 2 inches lower than the tees. Where tees join end to end, hang a wire on each side of the splice. When all the wires are hung, feed them through the holes in the tees and twist them, making sure all the tees are level. Fill in the secondary cross-tees and lay in each panel. If necessary, cut them to fit.

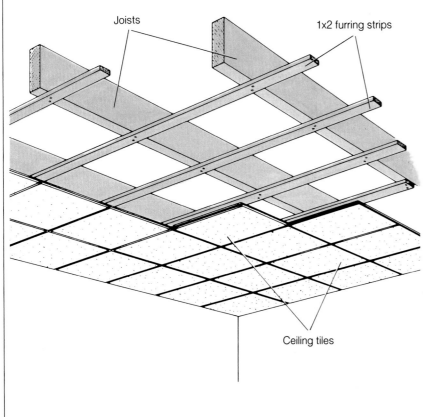

Joists

1x2 furring strips

Ceiling tiles

Tiled Ceiling

Ceiling tiles are made from either organic fibers, which are usually $\frac{1}{2}$ inch thick, or mineral fibers, which won't burn and are usually $\frac{3}{4}$ inch thick. Both come in squares or rectangles, 12 by 12 and 12 by 24 being the most popular.

Tiles can be applied over any flat surface or, if the code allows, nailed directly onto 1 by 2 or 1 by 3 furring strips, leveled if necessary. To avoid too many cut tiles around the edges, start by marking the exact center of the room. Measure from this point out to the wall to determine how many rows of tiles will fit on each side. If there is a half row or less at the outer edge, adjust the center point. Attach the tiles with a staple gun, or mastic. With mastic, start by installing four tiles in the center and working outward. If you staple, start at one edge and work across so the stapling flange is always exposed.

CHIMNEYS & STOVEPIPES

As wood becomes increasingly popular for heating homes, more attention must be paid to chimneys and stovepipes. Although faulty stoves are responsible for their share of tragic accidents, most fires occur as a result of badly installed or maintained chimneys and stovepipes.

If you are installing a new fireplace or wood-burning stove, you must install the chimney or stovepipe according to local code requirements, even if you are using an existing chimney. Always have a fire or building official inspect a new chimney or stovepipe, or a new stove that has been attached to an old chimney or stovepipe. Careful use and maintenance are also essential. Even a proper installation is no guarantee that a chimney or stovepipe won't fail, possibly causing a disastrous fire. Maintain constant vigilance.

The main problem with modern, efficient wood-burning stoves and fireplaces is creosote buildup. If the creosote ignites, it can become a roaring inferno, hot enough to destroy some types of chimneys or stovepipes. Even if there is no fire, creosote is caustic enough to cause real damage. Always use materials that have been tested and approved for your area, and install them according to local codes. High-quality materials cost more, but they are definitely worth it.

Recommended Cross-References
Bricks, Fireplaces, Flashing, Heating, Roofs, Wood-Burning Stoves.

New Chimneys and Stovepipes

For your own safety, check through the following list of musts before installing a chimney or stovepipe.

- The diameter of the chimney or cross-sectional area of the fireplace throat should be sufficiently wide relative to the size of the fireplace. In most areas, codes demand that masonry chimneys have a minimum cross-sectional area of 50 square inches. Flue pipes for wood-burning stoves vary according to the size of the stove. A pipe that is 8 inches in diameter is equivalent to 50 square inches.
- There must be a minimum clearance between the chimney and all combustible materials. Building codes typically require a minimum of 1 inch. Because this clearance creates a gap around the chimney where it penetrates a ceiling or roof, the gap is usually filled with a non-combustible material such as plaster or fiberglass insulation. Flashing covers the gap on the roof.
- The walls of a masonry chimney must be at least 4 inches thick if they are made of brick and about 12 inches thick if they consist of hollow concrete block.
- Chimneys must be lined from top to bottom with a flue of $5/8$-inch fireclay tile, 2-inch fire brick, or other code-approved material. All joints must be grouted. Metal chimneys must have at least double-wall construction and any other specifications required by code.
- Chimneys should only support their own weight, unless they are structurally reinforced as load-bearing members.
- The height of a chimney depends on local codes. A typical requirement in many codes is for the chimney to terminate at least 2 feet above the highest point of the building within 10 feet of the chimney.
- Even if it is not required by your local codes, putting a cleanout in a metal stovepipe makes it much easier to maintain.

Existing Chimneys and Stovepipes

When cleaning or working on an existing chimney, note the following precautions.

- Install a rain cap to prevent moisture from deteriorating the inside of the chimney, especially where acid rain is prevalent.
- Be sure all bricks and mortar joints are sound. Remove loose mortar from joints and repoint them. Replace loose bricks.
- Install a spark arrester to prevent external fires.
- Do not hook up a new wood stove to an existing chimney without consulting local codes for requirements such as a metal transition piece or an insulated flue lining. An older chimney may not be enough protection for the intense heat of a wood stove without adding a new lining. If a new lining is necessary, retrofit systems are available consisting of a flexible stainless steel flue pipe that is inserted down the chimney and surrounded by noncombustible insulating material.
- Do not vent two appliances into the same chimney.
- Take precautions against creosote buildup. Wood stoves and newer, more efficient fireplaces have a negative side effect of causing creosote to form in the chimney. When exhaust gases cool rapidly, the heavier particles condense into a tarlike substance that coats the flue. Creosote buildup is extremely dangerous because it can lead to chimney fires.

Precautions include eliminating the creosote and preventing it altogether. Clean your chimney at least once a year to get rid of creosote accumulation that is thicker than $1/4$ inch. If you do the work yourself, use brushes that match the size and shape of the flue. To keep creosote from forming, install a stove with a catalytic combuster or consider installing one in an existing stove. You can also reduce creosote buildup by insulating the chimney—the walls do not cool down enough to cause the creosote to condense. To insulate an existing masonry chimney, insert a stainless steel flue liner down the chimney and pour a special insulating material around it.

- Burn a hot fire in your wood stove for about 30 minutes every day to burn off excess creosote in the chimney.
- Do not burn unseasoned wood. Doing so causes creosote to form.

Installing a Rain Cap

The mixture of rain, soot, and fireplace gases can produce an acid that deteriorates the chimney surface. To prevent deterioration and to minimize downdrafts, install a rain cap. Chip away enough concrete from each corner of the chimney top to accommodate a brick. Mortar a stack of bricks on each corner to a height of at least 12 inches. Attach concrete or flagstone cap over the four stacks.

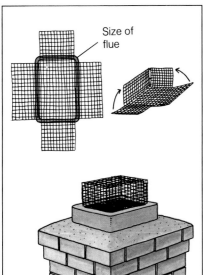

Size of flue

Installing a Spark Arrester

To protect your roof and neighboring houses, you should have a wire spark arrester. Make one from heavy galvanized mesh with a 1-inch grid. Cut the mesh into a rectangle that will wedge into the flue opening. Or cut the mesh large enough to fit over the opening. Then wire it to the flue.

Cleaning a Chimney

Clean your chimney at the start of each heating season and two or three times during the season, depending on use. Although chimney sweeps have specialized equipment, you can do the job yourself with brushes that you rent, buy, or improvise.

Start by removing the fireplace grate and opening the damper. Block off the fireplace opening with a large piece of cardboard or plywood. Stuff rags around the barrier.

Do the actual cleaning from the roof. Dress in old clothes and wear a dust mask. Tie a weight and cleaning brush onto a rope and lower them into the chimney. Work the brush up and down vigorously along the entire length of the chimney. If you do not have a brush, place some rocks and crushed newspaper in a burlap sack that you lower down the chimney.

After retrieving the rope and brush or sack, remove the barrier from the fireplace opening and shovel up the soot. Use a brush or broom to knock soot down from the damper and shelf. After you have swept the fireplace, give it a final cleaning with an old vacuum.

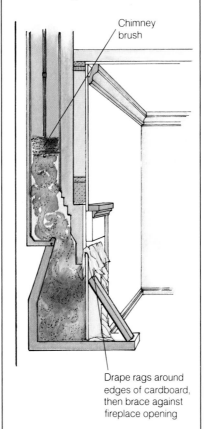

Chimney brush

Drape rags around edges of cardboard, then brace against fireplace opening

Relining a Chimney

Unlined chimneys, or those with cracked tile liners, can allow the heat from a chimney fire to start a house fire. Chimneys with these conditions can be relined rather than replaced.

There are two relining methods. With both methods, the old liner is removed.

With one method, a vinyl or rubber hose is inserted into the chimney and inflated. Lightweight concrete is poured around the hose, which is then deflated and removed after the concrete sets.

With the second method, a stainless steel liner is inserted into the chimney. The liner is surrounded with lightweight concrete and either connected directly to a wood stove or used as a fireplace chimney.

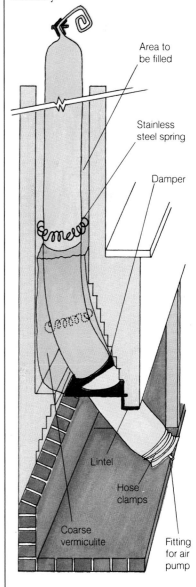

Area to be filled

Stainless steel spring

Damper

Lintel

Hose clamps

Coarse vermiculite

Fitting for air pump

CLOSETS

For most people, additional closet space is very near the top of a home improvement wish list. Somehow, there is never enough room for everything and you can never find what you're looking for. Two storage problem solvers are organizing an existing closet and building a new one.

Organizing a Closet

You can double the storage capacity of an ordinary closet by installing an efficient system of poles, shelves, drawers, hooks, and pullouts. Ready-made components are available from closet specialty shops, or you can build your own modular units. Instead of a single horizontal shelf at the top of the closet, install vertical shelving units from floor to ceiling. For most efficiency, make the shelves adjustable.

Pull-Out Storage

Pull-out storage consists of drawers, baskets, and bins. All can be incorporated into a closet. Drawers can replace a bureau, and vinyl-coated baskets and plastic bins provide color, a view of the contents, and ventilation.

Poles

Shirts, pants, and dresses can be reorganized dramatically merely by installing several short poles at different levels. This allows you to devote a small section to longer garments and double up in the rest of the closet. For instance, shirts and blouses can hang on a high pole, while skirts and jackets can be hung on a lower one directly below it.

Doors

You can increase storage space by utilizing the back of the closet door. It's easy to install hooks, racks, shelves, bins, or grid systems on any door except bifold or bypass ones.

Recommended Cross-References

Doors, Framing, Moldings, Shelves, Storage: Indoor, Wallboard.

Slats nailed to the wall (left) provide a rack for sports equipment. Brightly colored washtubs (above) corral toys. The drawer unit, topped with a cushion, can be used as a bench. Bifold louver doors (opposite) conceal drawers, shelves, and hanging storage.

Building a New Closet

1. Planning the Closet. Personal closets should allow each person 8 to 10 square feet of storage space and be wide enough so that each person in the family has 4 to 5 linear feet (8 to 10 square feet) of closet space. They should be from 24 to 30 inches deep. Linen closets should be at least 20 inches deep. If possible, doors should open full width.

Unless you particularly need a nook above the closet, build the walls all the way to the ceiling. This creates a more permanent look and increases storage capacity.

2. Framing the Walls. Try to plan a layout so that the closet walls can be tied into existing wall studs. If this is not possible, add a new stud or horizontal blocking.

Assemble the front wall on the floor, positioned so that it can be lifted into place. Build the wall ½ inch shorter than the floor-to-ceiling height, so it clears the ceiling when you raise it. If there will be a return wall, construct a corner post out of two studs and blocking, as shown.

Check local code requirements for the header size; typical sizes are 4 by 4 for openings up to 4 feet, 4 by 6 for those 4 to 6 feet wide, and 4 by 8 for those 6 to 8 feet wide. Do not cut out the section of soleplate within the doorway until the wall is in place; instead, cut halfway through the underside of the soleplate before lifting the wall.

3. Finishing the Walls. Lift the front wall into place. Check it for plumb and nail the soleplate into the floor with 16d nails, except in the door opening. Slide shims between the top plate and ceiling at all the joist locations. Nail through the shims into the top plate. Nail end studs into the studs of the existing wall.

Build and erect any side walls in the same way. Nail the front end stud into the corner of the front wall and the back end stud into a stud in the existing wall.

Remove the soleplate in the door opening by completing the saw cuts. Install wiring for an overhead light fixture. After attaching wallboard or other finish material, you are ready to install the doors.

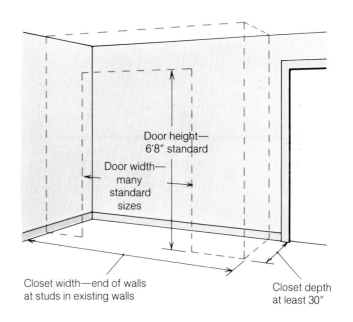

Door height— 6'8" standard

Door width— many standard sizes

Closet width—end of walls at studs in existing walls

Closet depth at least 30"

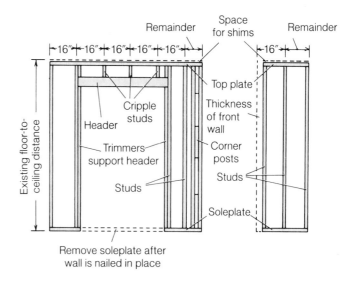

Remainder

Space for shims

Remainder

Cripple studs

Header

Top plate

Thickness of front wall

Trimmers support header

Corner posts

Existing floor-to-ceiling distance

Studs

Studs

Soleplate

Remove soleplate after wall is nailed in place

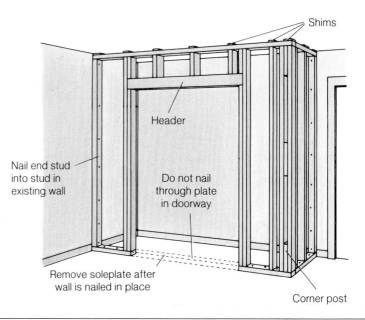

Shims

Header

Nail end stud into stud in existing wall

Do not nail through plate in doorway

Remove soleplate after wall is nailed in place

Corner post

Closet Organizers. These systems can make use of wasted space in a closet. Ready-to-assemble systems come in a variety of styles. Most include shelves, closet poles, and drawers or baskets. They are usually made of wire or particleboard. Some modular closet organizers can be custom-made to fit the size and shape of your closet.

Wire organizers are relatively easy to cut into needed lengths. Some come with mounting hardware that can be attached directly to the closet wall, eliminating the need to locate the studs.

Organizers come with complete installation instructions. An average system can usually be installed in half a day or less.

Designing the System. Before you select an organizing system, make a list of what will be kept in the closet. Place the items in categories according to size, shape, and whether they will be on hangers, on hooks, on racks, or laid flat. Consider also how often you will use each item; those that rarely see the light of day can be placed at the sides, on a high shelf, or in the corners, whereas those you use often should be easily accessible. If seldom-used items are stored out of sight (in a drawer or cupboard), it's not a bad idea to label the drawer front or cupboard door so you don't forget what's inside.

Place the highest closet shelf approximately 7 feet from the floor. This will leave 12 inches of storage space on the shelf. Be sure that any light fixture is positioned so that nothing piled on the shelf can touch the bulb. Allow for the fact that stored items may project several inches beyond the shelf.

Baskets or drawers work best in the center third of the closet. This allows them to be used without interfering with the doors or side compartments.

Average items of clothing on hangers require 1 inch of horizontal space. Bulky winter clothing requires 2 to 3 inches. Shirts and blouses need approximately 40 to 42 inches of vertical space; suits need 42 inches; and unfolded slacks need 50 inches. If your closet organizer doesn't include a rack or bag for shoes, allow 10 inches of vertical floor or shelf space for men's shoes, and 9 inches for women's.

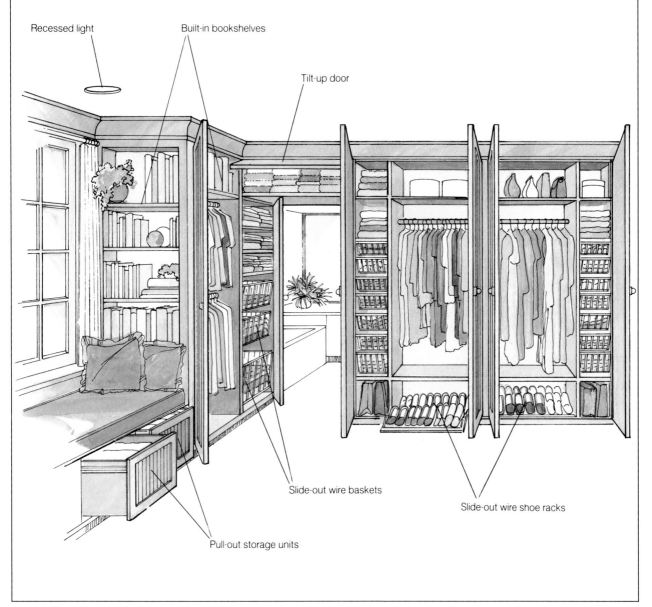

Recessed light

Built-in bookshelves

Tilt-up door

Slide-out wire baskets

Slide-out wire shoe racks

Pull-out storage units

CONCRETE

Concrete is an indispensable building material that fills a variety of structural and decorative needs. Working with concrete may seem intimidating, but it is actually fairly easy, although the work must be done properly to ensure strong, durable, and attractive results. By understanding what concrete is made of and how it attains strength you can undertake most projects with confidence. The following principles should guide you in working with concrete, whether your project is a weekend one or a major structural improvement.

It is necessary to plan any concrete project ahead of time. Estimate materials so you have enough concrete to complete the job at one time, but not so much extra that disposing of it becomes a problem. All the preparations should be complete before you begin the actual mixing and placing of concrete. This way you can finish the pour in one operation. Thorough planning also eliminates errors; once the concrete is in place, you are pretty much stuck with the results. Caution: Handling wet concrete may irritate skin. Read all product labels carefully.

Recommended Cross-References
Basements, Drainage, Floors, Footings, Foundations, Garden Walls, Paths, Patios, Ponds, Pools, Steps.

A walk with curved edges and an exposed aggregate finish shows how concrete can be an effective element in landscaping.

Proportioning Concrete
Concrete has three basic ingredients: cement, aggregate, and water. The proper ratio produces a mix with the greatest strength and the most workable consistency.

Cement is the magic ingredient—the glue that holds the mix together and gives it strength. It is a manufactured chemical product that is often called "portland cement," named after Portland stone, a building material popular in nineteenth century England, when cement was invented. Cement is a fine, dry powder that, when mixed with water, solidifies and attains incredible strength.

Aggregate, a combination of sand and gravel, is the bulk of the mix. It must be clean so that the cement can adhere, and must include enough small material to fill the spaces between the larger rocks.

The size of aggregate refers to the largest rocks in the mix. The size that is needed varies with the type of job. Typical aggregate sizes for residential use are ³/₈ inch and ³/₄ inch. Use ³/₈-inch aggregate for tight spaces, such as when you are filling the cells of concrete blocks or pumping concrete through a 3-inch-diameter hose. A ³/₄-inch aggregate mix is common for foundations, footings, and slabs. Aggregate size should not exceed one third the thickness of a slab or one fifth the narrowest dimension between wall forms.

Water is the third essential ingredient of concrete. It combines with the cement to form a chemical reaction, called hydration, that results in a hard, solid material. Successful hydration depends on getting the proper water/cement ratio. For most residential installations, this ratio is approximately 1 to 2, by weight. A common mistake is to use too much water, which weakens the concrete.

Some concrete mixes include other ingredients, called admixtures. The most common is air entrainment, used for outdoor concrete in climates where freezing and thawing or de-icing salts would otherwise cause surface deterioration. The air-entrainment agent makes the cement paste froth during mixing, creating microscopic air bubbles in the hardened concrete. Other admixtures improve the consistency of the concrete under unusual conditions, such as extremely hot weather or when it is necessary to delay finishing time.

The proportions of various ingredients in a mix determine the strength and consistency of concrete. Know that proportions change according to the size of aggregate.

Proportions for 1 Cubic Yard of Concrete (in Pounds)

Type of Project	Aggregate Size	Cement	Sand	Gravel	Total Aggregate	Water	Air-Entrainment
Foundations	⅜	565	1630	1190	2820	285	-
and Footings	¾	520	1310	1730	3040	260	-
	1	490	1260	1870	3130	245	-
Slabs, Patios,	⅜	580	1570	1190	2760	290	7 %
and Foundations	¾	580	1250	1730	2980	290	6 %
in Cold Climates	1	535	1170	1870	3040	270	6 %

Note: 1 sack of cement equals 94 pounds. Water weighs 8 pounds per gallon.

Mixing Your Own Concrete

If you need only a small quantity of concrete—1 yard or less—mix it by hand or in a small cement mixer. To make a 1-cubic-foot batch, divide each of the proportions in the chart by 27 (there are 27 cubic feet in 1 cubic yard). For instance, the first row of ingredients would become: 22 pounds of cement, 105 pounds of aggregate, and 11 pounds of water. You can easily repeat this recipe for each succeeding batch by weighing the first batch of ingredients in buckets on a bathroom scale. Use a separate container for each ingredient, marking on the side of the container how high it needs to be filled to reach the desired weight. Fill the buckets to the same marks for the remaining batches.

Mix the dry ingredients together first, then add the water. For best results the machine should mix the entire batch for at least two or three minutes. When you are through with the mixer, clean it out by throwing one or two shovelfuls of gravel and some water in it. Let them scour the inside of the mixer for a while, and then dump them.

Ordering Ready-Mix Concrete

If you need more than 1 yard, or you want air entrainment in the mix, have the concrete delivered by a ready-mix company. The following are things to specify when ordering:

Cement Content. Use the proportions chart to calculate the number of sacks of cement you will need in each cubic yard.

Aggregate Size. For most jobs ¾-inch aggregate is suitable, but if you are having the concrete pumped by a small cement truck that only has a 3-inch hose, you will need to specify ⅜-inch aggregate.

Water/Cement Ratio. Specify .5 or .55.

Slump. This term is used to describe the consistency of fresh concrete. It refers to the number of inches a 12-inch-high tower of concrete slumps when it is fresh. A 1-inch slump is a very stiff mix, a 10-inch slump very soupy. For residential projects 4 inches is average.

Air Entrainment. Consult the proportions chart for the percentage of air entrainment to be added for concrete poured in cold climates.

Strength. You may be asked to specify the strength or load-bearing capacity of your concrete. Most residential needs vary from a minimum strength of 2,000 pounds per square inch (psi) to over 4,000 psi. Be aware that the proper handling and curing of the concrete, not just the correct proportions, are needed to attain the specified strength.

In addition to the per-yard delivery charge, be aware of other fees you may have to pay. A short-load charge is an additional fee for small orders (generally less than 4 yards). A stand-by charge is also customary. This is for any additional time the truck must remain at your site after the allotted per-yard time limit expires (usually about 5 minutes per yard). The amount can skyrocket if you are not prepared when the truck arrives.

If the truck cannot get close to your forms (for instance, a patio in a backyard), arrange for a pump truck to arrive shortly before the concrete. Rent one from the ready-mix companies or an independent pumping company. Even if you think the concrete truck might reach your forms by backing into the driveway, it is better to have the concrete pumped than to take a chance on having to pay for a broken sidewalk.

Estimating Concrete

Whether you order ready-mix or the materials to mix your own, estimate the volume of concrete you need in cubic yards. The easiest way to determine cubic yards is to calculate the job in cubic feet and then divide the total by 27, which is the number of cubic feet per cubic yard.

If the project is a patio or other slab, first determine the thickness in fractions of a foot. For instance, a 4-inch-thick slab is ⅓ foot thick. Then multiply this figure by the total surface area of the slab. The surface area for rectangles is length times width and for circles it is pi (3.14) times the radius squared. If the shape is too complicated for a simple formula, divide it up into smaller shapes and calculate each one separately. Then find the total and multiply it by the thickness of the slab. Just be sure all your measurements are in feet, or fractions of a foot, and not inches.

If the project is a wall or long footing, multiply the length (in feet) by the area of the cross section. For instance, the cross section of a footing for a garden wall might be 12 inches wide and 6 inches high. Thus, the area of the cross section would be 1 foot times ½ foot, which equals ½ foot. Multiply this figure by the length of the footing to yield the cubic feet of concrete that will be needed for the job.

Example: If the footing is 30 feet long, the calculation would be: ½ × 30 = 15 cubic feet.

Once you have figured the volume needed as precisely as possible, add another 5 percent for waste. Then convert the number of cubic feet into cubic yards by dividing by 27. Round off to the nearest tenth of a yard, for example, 2.4 cubic yards.

CONCRETE: continued

Demolition

Concrete must often be removed from construction sites in order to remodel. Dismantling large concrete walls such as basement or retaining walls should be left to professionals. Smaller jobs, such as breaking up patios and porch footings, can be done by homeowners.

The best tool is a jackhammer. Rent the largest you can handle. Wear gloves and use eye and ear protection. Wear boots (preferably steel-toed). If the concrete contains wire mesh, cut it with bolt cutters as it's exposed.

Start 4 to 6 inches from the edge of a slab. Angle the jackhammer bit toward the outer edge. This will break off pieces that are small enough to be picked up. Concrete can't be compressed, so in order to break it, pieces must be separated. For this reason, starting from the center of the slab will only pulverize the concrete and make a hole rather than break up the slab.

When the hammer starts to open a crack, let the tip penetrate an inch or two, then lean the hammer at a 45-degree angle and stop hammering (continuing will drive the hammer into the soil under the slab). This will open a wide crack, so the broken piece will not obstruct removal of the next piece. Continue until the entire slab is broken up.

A sledgehammer requires either finesse or brute strength. As with the jackhammer, start near the edge. Excavate dirt to provide room for the concrete to split. If possible, undermine the edge of the slab so the piece being struck is not supported from below. Another method is to dig a small hole under the edge of the slab, then insert a pry bar or timber and pry the slab upward. Strike the raised slab with hard blows in the center between the points of support.

Preparing the Site

All concrete work involves some excavation and grading. Walls and continuous footings need a trench. Flatwork, such as a patio or slab, requires removing enough soil for the gravel base, plus whatever concrete will be below grade. Where the ground is very firm and the climate is mild, a sand or gravel base may not be required. Always remove all vegetation and debris.

Dig carefully when you excavate. Concrete must be placed on undisturbed soil. If you dig too deeply, you cannot throw dirt back into the hole; you must use more concrete. The base of the excavation should be flat and level, especially on a sloping site. The sides should be as straight as possible, and the corners between sides and bottom should be square rather than rounded.

Forms and Reinforcement

Flatwork and most footings are shallow enough to be formed with simple boards held in place by stakes. Concrete structures taller than 12 inches require a more sophisticated form system: either lumber held in place with metal ties or plywood with extensive 2 by 4 bracing. Any wall higher than 3 feet should be designed and built by professionals.

Building codes insist on steel reinforcement in certain concrete structures—either round bars or welded wire mesh. If there is a lot of steel to cut and bend, rent special tools. Codes also specify concrete cover, which is the minimum thickness of concrete that must surround the steel—usually 3 inches if the footing is below ground and 1½ inches if above ground.

Placing Concrete

Wet the forms and the bottom of the excavation first. Pour concrete immediately after mixing it. Avoid dragging it or spreading it around; otherwise the heavier aggregates will sink to the bottom.

When the concrete is in place, use a rod, stick, or square-edged shovel to consolidate it. Rent a concrete vibrating machine for large jobs. Only agitate the concrete enough to settle it into place. Bang the outside of the forms with a hammer to release air pockets.

After the concrete settles, level the top by dragging a screed (a piece of 2 by 4) across the top of the forms. Use a sawing motion to push excess concrete along in front of the screed and fill in low spots behind it. Screeding does not smooth the surface; it only levels it.

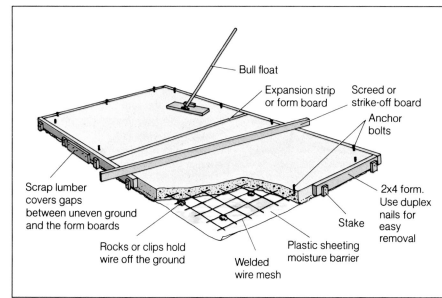

Bull float

Expansion strip or form board

Screed or strike-off board

Anchor bolts

Scrap lumber covers gaps between uneven ground and the form boards

2x4 form. Use duplex nails for easy removal

Stake

Rocks or clips hold wire off the ground

Plastic sheeting moisture barrier

Welded wire mesh

Typical Flatwork Forms

Most residential slabs are 4 inches thick, so use 2 by 4s staked every 4 feet. Adjust forms for a ¼ inch per foot drainage slope. On a large slab, place expansion material or decorative boards every 10 feet. Expansion strips allow the slab to expand and contract without cracking.

Patios and walks do not usually require reinforcing steel, but driveways, basement floors, and other structural slabs do. Use welded wire mesh, which comes in 6-foot-wide rolls. Cut the wire with bolt cutters, and use special holding devices to place it in the middle of the slab. If ground moisture is a problem, install 6-mil plastic sheeting.

Finishing the Surface

Immediately after screeding, do a preliminary smoothing with a tool called a float. Some floats are made of wood, and others are made of aluminum or magnesium for air-entrained concrete. A bull float has a long handle for reaching the center of large slabs. Run the float back and forth over the concrete, with the leading edge raised slightly, thus pushing the aggregate down and flattening the surface. Floating does not produce a perfectly smooth surface, but it does level it enough for finishing later. Clean up the perimeter edges by running a trowel between the forms and the fresh concrete.

After floating, wait for the surface bleed water to evaporate before doing the final finish operations. This may take from a few minutes to several hours, depending on the weather, but usually there is enough time to clean the tools and take a break. Begin finishing the concrete when troweling activity does not cause immediate puddling. Footings and simple walls do not require careful finishing.

Various finish surfaces, each producing a different texture and appearance, are possible for slabs and prominent walls. For a casual, rustic effect, leave the floated surface as it is. Refine the look with an edger and groover. Run the edger back and forth against the side forms, and run the groover against a temporary straightedge (a straight piece of 2 by 4) held up off the concrete surface.

A surface scratched with a broom is skid resistant and shows fine lines all running in the same direction. This texture is simple to produce. Merely drag a damp, stiff-bristled broom lightly over a floated surface.

The smoothest surface is produced by steel troweling. An initial troweling can be done shortly after floating, but for smoother surfaces you must trowel again after the concrete stiffens and barely responds to light troweling activity. When working in the center of a slab, be careful not to ruin your smooth surface. Use ply-wood knee boards to distribute your weight evenly over the entire area.

Exposed aggregate is another finish. It is produced by "seeding" decorative stones into the surface after screeding. Wet the stones before spreading them over the slab. Then embed them below the surface with a float, level the surface, and wait for the concrete to set. When set, use a broom and a fine water spray from a hose to flush away the surface concrete and expose the top portion of the seeded stones.

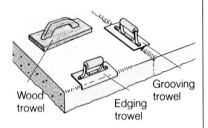

Wood trowel   Edging trowel   Grooving trowel

Curing Concrete

One remarkable property of concrete is that it gains strength over time. Whereas day-old concrete has a compressive strength of only a few hundred psi, the strength increases to 1,500 psi after 3 days, 2,000 psi after 7 days, and as much as 4,000 psi or more after 28 days. However, if the water evaporates too soon, the chemical reaction is arrested, and the concrete never reaches full strength. Freezing also disrupts the hydration process and will ruin the concrete.

To ensure that the concrete attains full strength, prevent water from evaporating after the initial bleed water has disappeared. This is called curing. For walls and footings, leave the forms on for at least seven days. If stripped sooner, the fresh concrete should be sprayed with a special curing compound. Cure slabs by wetting the surface constantly, covering the surface with plastic sheeting, or spraying on a curing compound to seal in the moisture. Keep the slab moist for at least a week, ideally 28 days. Do not use a spray-on curing compound if you plan to paint the slab or install flooring with adhesives.

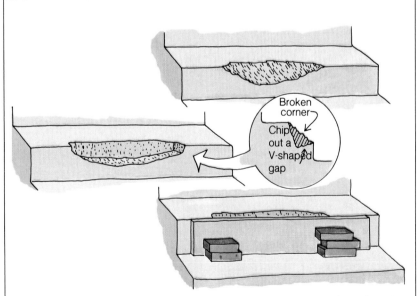

Broken corner
Chip out a V-shaped gap

Repairing Concrete

The most common repairs are patching holes and filling cracks. For patches, enlarge the hole so that all parts of it are at least 1 inch deep. Clean out the hole. If possible, etch the old concrete with diluted muriatic acid. Rinse thoroughly and apply a liquid bonding agent before filling the hole with new concrete. For cracks, enlarge to a V-shaped gap and fill with special expansive mortar. Use hydraulic cement if there are signs of water seepage.

COOLING

The goal of home cooling is comfort. Emphasizing this self-evident notion is necessary because it is too easy to associate cooling with some kind of mechanical system, something you buy and install in your home.

A better way to think of cooling is as a list of strategies for reducing heat. Many of them are simple and inexpensive projects that you can do to your home. The idea behind all of them is that our bodies become overheated in three different ways.

First, we experience discomfort when the air temperature around us is too high. Most cooling systems concentrate on reducing this temperature, although it may not actually be necessary because we may feel overheated for one of the other reasons.

We may feel uncomfortable because the air around us is too still for our bodies' cooling system to function, even at temperatures within our comfort range. Conversely, a slight breeze may make us feel comfortable, even if the surrounding air temperature is higher than we normally like.

The third source of discomfort is hot objects radiating heat directly at us. Some heat sources, like the sun or a stove, are concentrated, but our bodies respond to all the surfaces around us. When the walls, ceiling, floor, and furnishings of a room have absorbed heat and are radiating it back toward us, instead of perceiving it as coming from these sources, we naturally blame the hot weather—even if the air temperature is comfortable.

The strategies for cooling your home that follow are designed to minimize one or more of these sources of discomfort.

Recommended Cross-References
Fans, Heating, Insulation, Ventilation, Windows.

Sunshine in the winter and shade in the summer—let nature do your cooling for you. This house, nestled in an oak and maple forest, is comfortable all year round.

Reducing Heat Gain

The sun is the main source of direct radiant heat, as well as the indirect cause of high air temperatures.

Shading the Windows. Anytime sunlight comes directly through a window, it has a double heating effect: It heats any surface it touches and it warms the air. If you shade the window from the inside with curtains or drapes, they stop the direct radiant heat but still allow the air trapped behind them to heat up.

Better shading comes from awnings, overhangs, vines, or trees. Awnings and overhangs attached to the house should be louvered or have other venting means to eliminate the hot air that they trap against the house. You must also plan them with the daily and seasonal changes of the sun in mind. When the sun is high in the sky, little overhang is needed to shade a window. When the sun is lower, such as in the morning and evening and all day during the winter, it shines beneath the overhang. Make the width of the overhang from $1/4$ to $1/2$ of the height of the window, depending on latitude, and position it about 8 inches above the window for each foot of overhang width.

East windows and west windows are difficult to shade with horizontal overhangs because the sun is so low in the morning and afternoon. Vertical baffles work better. An even better shading device is foliage—either trees, shrubs, or vines. If the winter sunshine is going to be beneficial rather than problematical, use deciduous species of trees and shrubs.

Another way to shade windows is with the use of screening materials. Some shades are made of film and attach to the inside of the window. Some are made of clothlike woven material that you can hang on the outside of doors or windows that you want to open. These shading devices are designed for maximum visibility and minimum heat gain.

Shading Pavements. Even if the sun does not hit your house directly, it may be heating up dark driveways or patios, or it may be reflecting heat from pavements. Use trees, high fences, and overhangs for shading.

Reflecting the Heat. Increase the reflectivity of your roof with light-colored roofing materials. Install large sheets of aluminum building foil under the roof to reflect heat away from the attic. Staple it directly to the rafters. Use low-E window glass to reduce the transmission of heat from the outside.

Insulating Ceilings and Roofs. Insulation is more cost-effective in cold climates than in hot ones because the temperature difference between indoors and outdoors is greater. Most areas of the country need insulation for the cold weather and benefit from it during the summer as well. In hot climates it may not be worth installing insulation unless you rely heavily on air-conditioning and need to increase its efficiency.

Eliminating Heat Sources. Appliances create heat and humidity. If possible, locate washers, clothes dryers, and water heaters in the garage or other areas outside of the house. Otherwise, be sure that the dryer is vented to the outside and that the bathroom and kitchen have exhaust vents.

Increasing Air Movement

Air circulation is not only important for body comfort, but it also draws absorbed heat away from objects and surfaces that might otherwise radiate it to the occupants of the house.

Creating Cross-Ventilation. If you live where there are natural breezes, you can use them for most of your cooling needs. Open a door or window on opposite walls in every room. To give cross-breezes a boost as they go through the house, open low windows where breezes enter and high windows where they leave.

Another way to enhance air circulation is with an open floor plan. You can't very well rearrange the walls of an existing home, but for new designs, keep interior walls and partitions to a minimum to maximize cooling benefits.

If the windows are not in line with the prevailing breeze, place fencing or other solid diverters outside the windows to direct the breeze into the house.

Installing a Ceiling Fan. Large paddle fans are popular in contemporary homes. When operated at low speed, they are efficient and ensure a constant movement of air, around 200 cubic feet per minute.

Installing a High Vent. A venting skylight, an openable window near the ceiling, or a special cupola installed on the roof and connected to the living space with a shaft, all effectively exhaust hot household air if the outdoor temperature is cooler than the one indoors. For these vents to work best, open low windows or vents around the house to draw in cooler air to replace the escaping hot air. If you have a fan, place it at one of the high vents or windows to speed the escape of hot air.

Installing an Attic Fan. Small fans in the gable or roof that exhaust hot air from the attic do not actually increase air movement in the rest of the house, but they make it easier to cool the house, and they increase the efficiency of fans or other mechanical devices.

Installing a Whole-House Fan. Large attic fans keep air moving through the house and out through a central hole in the ceiling. Their main purpose is to cool the various surfaces and objects in the house, but they can also improve the efficiency of central air conditioning, especially at night when the outside air drawn into the house has cooled down.

Building a Solar Greenhouse. Ironically, the sun—the source of uncomfortable outdoor temperatures—is also a free energy source for cooling the house. A sun space with openable vents near the top and vents strategically placed to draw hot air out of the house can act as a powerful fan whenever the sun shines.

Cooling the Indoor Air

The final strategy for cooling a home is to reduce the air temperature with an air conditioner. The two options are central air-conditioning for the entire house or a room air conditioner. A central system is often incorporated with a heating system, and is best left to professionals. If you have a room air conditioner, maintaining it periodically will improve its performance and longevity. Even a layer of dirt only thousandths of an inch thick will reduce efficiency by 10 to 15 percent.

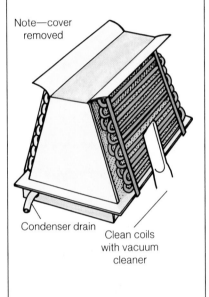

Note—cover removed

Condenser drain

Clean coils with vacuum cleaner

Maintaining a Room Air Conditioner or Heat Pump

At the beginning of the cooling season and then as often as every few weeks, change or clean the filter on a room air conditioner or heat pump.

Unplug the unit, then remove the front panel and filter. Wash the filter in mild detergent, then rinse, dry, and replace it. Be careful not to tear it. Clean condenser coil fins with a vacuum cleaner or brush. Straighten bent fins with a fin comb.

Do not touch the capacitor; electricity is stored here. You can get a shock even if the unit is unplugged.

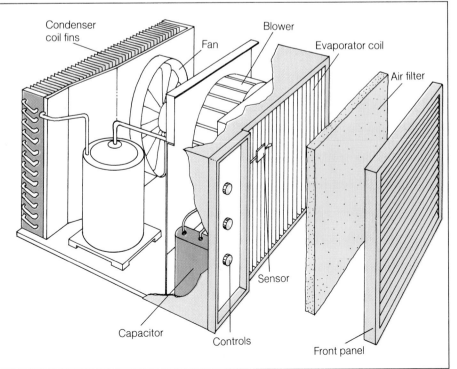

Condenser coil fins

Fan

Blower

Evaporator coil

Air filter

Sensor

Capacitor

Controls

Front panel

Using granite tile is a relatively inexpensive way to construct a natural stone countertop.

Over the years, the role of the counter-top has expanded from a tiny drain-board tucked around the kitchen sink to an expansive work surface found in dining rooms, bathrooms, offices, dens, and laundry rooms, as well as in the kitchen. What was once a strict-ly utilitarian surface has become a major design element used to provide everything from a bold accent to a subdued background that highlights other features in the room.

You will certainly be planning new countertops if you are replacing cabinetry, but even if you aren't, you might consider replacing existing countertops in your home. Doing so is an excellent project for adding in-stant sparkle to a room at a relatively low cost.

Whether you buy a ready-made countertop and install it yourself, or-der one custom-made to specific di-mensions, or build one from scratch, several details need to be planned. One concerns the edges. Some materi-als are thick enough to have attrac-tive edges. The edges of thinner mate-rials need to be covered, either with the same or a contrasting material. There are also a few options for the backsplash: It can be low or extend up the wall, be of the same or a different material, and be joined to the coun-tertop with a sloping curve or at an abrupt angle. The most fundamental detail of all is to measure carefully before ordering a top. Be sure to lo-cate cutouts for any sinks or cooktops and allow for any obstructions or in-sets. Measure where the backsplash needs to be lower for windowsills. Line up the countertop with the edges of wall cabinets. Plan finished edges around peninsulas and islands.

Recommended Cross-References
Bathroom Layout, Cabinets, Kitch-en Layout, Sinks & Garbage Dispos-ers, Tile, Vanities, Washbasins.

Ceramic tile can be given a distinctive look when coupled with ornate edge tiles.

Countertop Materials

The material used for a countertop has to be practical in addition to harmonizing with the other materi-als in a room.

Laminate. Plastic laminate is easy to maintain and comes in many colors and patterns but is subject to scorch and cut marks.

Prelaminated countertops, with or without edging and backsplashes, are available in ready-made sections that you cut to length. They come with mitered ends for L-shaped cor-ners—just join them together with appropriate drawbolts.

The widest selection of sizes and colors is available when you have the countertop custom-made.

Marble. Marble is often used as an inset in a kitchen countertop be-cause the cool, smooth surface is ideal for working with pastry and candy. Marble is very heavy, it scratches easily, and can crack, but it doesn't burn.

Search antique stores or wreck-ing yards for old pieces of marble or buy a new piece from a marble supplier.

Solid-Surface. This material is durable and resistant to moisture, stains, cracks, and heat. It is sold under such names as Corian®, Sur-rell®, Avonite®, and cast polymer.

Solid-surface material is available in several preformed shapes and sizes. It comes in thicknesses of ¼, ½, and ¾ inch. The material can be glued to a supporting surface, although this is not required with thicker layers.

Surfaces are plain, veined, or speckled. Since the color perme-ates the materials, worn counter-tops can be sanded and polished. Solid-surface material costs ap-proximately 3 to 4 times as much as plastic laminate. It can also be worked like wood with carbide-tipped power tools. This raises irritat-ing dust, however, so be sure to wear a mask if you do the work yourself.

Tile. Ceramic tiles come in a large variety of shapes, sizes, colors, and patterns. Bullnose and cove pieces are available to finish edges. Glazed tiles are impervious to water, grease, and stains; unglazed tiles are porous and permeable and, for this reason, are not recommended for kitchen countertops.

Tiling a countertop is not difficult. It is more tedious than complicated.

Woodblock. Genuine woodblock or butcher block is made of thick, lami-nated pieces of hardwood that are either oiled or untreated. It is gener-ally used on only a portion of a countertop or as a separate chopping block. The porous surface is easily marred and stained, although burn and scratch marks can be eliminated with periodic sanding.

Woodblock countertops come in standard lengths that can be cut to fit. After cutting, all you need to do is screw on a backsplash (if required), set the countertop in place, and screw it to the cabinets from under-neath. Use a scroll saw or a drum sander to round the corners of an island or peninsula. When wood-block is near a sink, seal the top, bottom, and all exposed sides.

Wood Edging. Wood edging is popular with plastic laminate and synthetic-marble countertops because of the warm look it gives. Wood and most countertop materials expand at dif-ferent rates, which can allow mois-ture into a poorly made joint. For this reason, wood edging should be in-stalled by a professional.

Plastic Laminate

The most commonly used kitchen countertop is plastic laminate bonded to particleboard or plywood. This usually has a lipped or rolled front edge and coved corners between the top surface and the backsplash. Making this kind of countertop is best left to a professional, who will take accurate measurements and deliver a finished unit that you can screw or nail to your base cabinets. If you make your own plastic laminate countertop, don't attempt to roll edges or cove corners.

Measurements. Stock countertops are available in 2-foot increments. If you want a custom size, you will need to provide measurements. Check with the dealer first to find out exactly which dimensions are needed. For an extra charge, some dealers will send out an estimator, who will take measurements and plan for details such as backsplashes, windowsills, and out-of-square corners.

Sketch the countertop. Double-check every measurement, and note the dimensions clearly on the drawing. Make all measurements in inches (not feet and inches) to avoid confusion. Be sure to note the depth of the base cabinets; some older ones are shallower than modern countertops and sinks. For countertops that will fit between two walls, measure the width at the back as well as at the front. If the walls are not perfectly parallel, one of the

measurements will be longer; use the longer measurement. Mark the centerline of the sink cutout. Include a template of the sink cutout if you have one.

Exposed edges, including those that butt refrigerators or ranges, should have finished ends. These are usually supplied by the countertop dealer, as are backsplashes.

Once the sketch is made, label it clearly, put your name on it, and make a photocopy to keep. It will come in handy if you need to have a mistake corrected.

Custom-made countertops take about two weeks.

Removing the Old Countertop. Laminate countertops are secured to the base cabinets with screws and occasionally with glue. If necessary, remove drawers and cabinet doors to provide access to the screws. Remove the screws (a cordless screwdriver will save time). Disconnect the sink plumbing. Lift out the countertop. If it is too heavy to lift, you can cut it into pieces, but be careful not to cut into the cabinets below.

Preparation. After the old counter is removed, check the base cabinets for level. If the cabinets are uneven, raise any low points on the countertop mounting surface with shims. Don't try to reposition the cabinets.

Installation. Cut sections to length and lay one section in place. If it fits between two walls and is mitered, nip off the overhanging rear corner,

then glue it back on later. It will almost certainly break off if you don't. Fit the counter section against the wall, then scribe it with a pencil or a compass set to the width of the widest gap between the countertop and wall.

Cut off the excess countertop. Work from the top to avoid chipping. Use a file, belt sander, jigsaw, or circular saw. Tape the bottom of either type of saw to prevent scratches. Be sure the saw blade is sharp.

Laminate countertops with rolled backsplashes come with a back overhang of approximately ¼ inch. This makes scribing quite easy. After the ends are scribed, push the counter back and scribe the back edge. Cut off the excess as before. In this situation, a file or sander is best; a saw may remove too much material.

Make the sink cutout before you join any miters because you may have to turn the countertop over to finish the cutout.

Test-fit all of the pieces before you attach the countertop. Make sure the fronts fit flush at the seam. Miter joints are usually secured with wood glue and specially designed clamps; test the fit of these as well.

Pull the countertop away from the wall if necessary to connect the joints. Push it back into position, make sure the screws won't penetrate the countertop surface, and then secure it to the base cabinets.

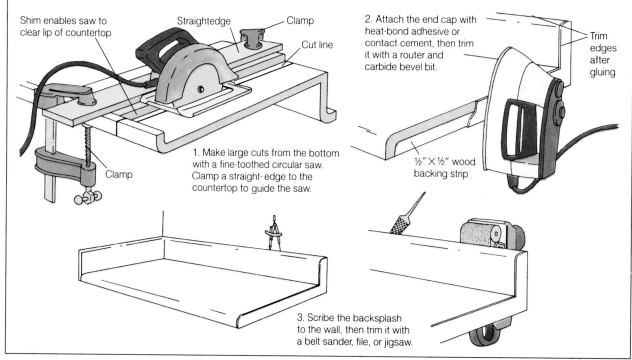

Shim enables saw to clear lip of countertop

Straightedge

Clamp

Cut line

Clamp

1. Make large cuts from the bottom with a fine-toothed circular saw. Clamp a straight-edge to the countertop to guide the saw.

2. Attach the end cap with heat-bond adhesive or contact cement, then trim it with a router and carbide bevel bit.

Trim edges after gluing

½" × ½" wood backing strip

3. Scribe the backsplash to the wall, then trim it with a belt sander, file, or jigsaw.

4. Turn the top over and attach the trim pieces by gluing them to the underside of the edge, using a recommended glue. Clamp, and let the joints dry overnight. Scrape off any residue or wipe it off with a drop of acetone on a rag. Apply silicone or other mastic to the top edges of the cabinet or shims. Place the countertop in position, press down firmly, and let the glue dry. Finally, attach the backsplash to the counter, fitting it snugly against the wall, with the recommended adhesive. Seal all joints and seams with silicone, wiping away the excess and smoothing the seams with a wet rag wrapped around your finger.

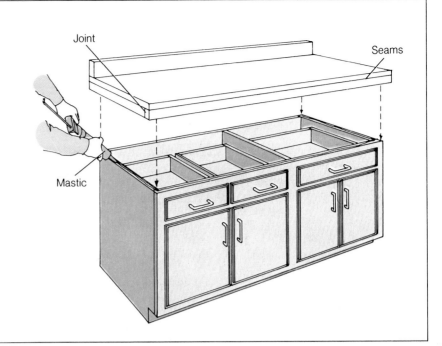

Installing a Marble Insert

1. Measure the area for the top and backsplash. If it will be lower than adjacent counter surfaces, measure for side pieces, too. Take these measurements to a marble dealer and have the pieces cut and edged.

Position the counter, back, and side pieces to make sure they are even with other counter surfaces and backsplashes. If not, raise the marble or the adjacent countertop with shims glued and nailed to the top edges of the cabinet.

2. Gluing the slab in place may be unnecessary because marble is extremely heavy. However, to prevent any shifting, apply glue to the cabinet edges before setting the slab in place. Use a recommended adhesive to attach the sides and backsplash.

Run a bead of silicone sealant around the edges, seams, and sides of adjacent counter surfaces. Smooth it with a dampened rag wrapped around your finger, and let it cure before using the countertop.

Measuring for a Countertop

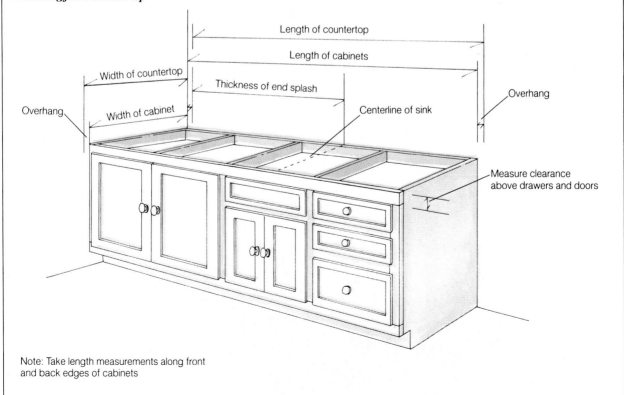

Note: Take length measurements along front and back edges of cabinets

DECKS

Planning Considerations

For dramatic beauty and additional living space at a reasonable cost, few home improvement projects can rival a new deck. A successful deck should harmonize with the house and yard and be in scale—neither overwhelming nor dwarfed by its setting. Angles should be in the same family (i.e., 30, 60, and 90 degrees, or 45 and 90). Consider how the deck looks from below as well as above, and choose details and a color that is in keeping with the character of the house.

The starting point of a successful deck project is careful planning, whether you are using a kit, a plan from a book, or a custom design. Do you want a quiet retreat? A platform for sunbathing or displaying plants? A children's play area? The more you clarify how the deck will be used, the better you can estimate the appropriate size and location. Are you building a deck to get you into the sun or out of it? Will a breeze be a welcome relief or an unwanted intruder? Study the patterns of sun, shade, and winds in your yard as you plan your deck. Observe how these patterns change according to the season.

Your deck should be accessible from living spaces and the kitchen and located where it capitalizes on dramatic vistas or intimate views. The doorway should be at least 36 inches wide, easy to open with one hand, and ideally made of glass (tempered or safety) to reinforce the continuity of space.

A deck that does not offer seclusion and feel secure is not comfortable. To prevent raised decks from putting people "on stage," locate the deck where the house, fences, or plantings shelter it, or add screens, extend fence heights, or even lower parts of the deck to gain privacy. Add benches or perimeter plants around low decks to give a sense of enclosure.

Size and location may be restricted by local zoning laws, as well as obstructions such as buried gas lines or water pipes. Building codes will certainly affect structural design.

Recommended Cross-References
Benches, Concrete, Planters, Railings, Steps, Wood, Zoning, Codes & Permits.

The size, shape, and design of a deck are controlled by those same elements of your backyard. As these decks illustrate, the scope is limited only by your imagination.

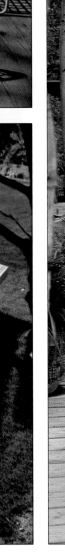

Types of Decks

Ground-Level Deck. A low platform is quick and easy to build and generally does not require a building permit if it is not attached to the house. Check your local codes for requirements concerning attached decks.

The simplest design is to lay decking boards over sleepers, usually 2 by 4s or 4 by 4s laid directly on the ground. They should be pressure-treated lumber or an all-heart grade of a naturally durable species. For greater protection, it is a good idea to lay them on a 3-inch bed of gravel instead of on the ground, or use 4 by 6 beams set on masonry footings.

The distance between the sleepers should be no greater than the maximum span that is allowed for the decking boards you use. Leave a 1/8- to 1/4-inch gap between the decking boards, and a 1-inch space between the deck and the house.

Low, Attached Platform. Another simple and very common type of deck is a floor-level platform for homes built over a low crawl space or basement. The main supports are a ledger bolted to the side of the house and a beam set on permanent footings. The size of the beam depends on its distance from the ledger and the spans between its footings; correct size can be determined from a table of minimum beam sizes.

The ledger and beam provide support for joists, which are spaced according to the maximum span allowed for the decking boards. If the joists are spaced 32 inches or less apart, use 2-inch lumber set on edge. If they are spaced further apart, use 4 by 4s or 4 by 6s. Whether the joists should be 2 by 6 or 2 by 8 depends on the length of the span and how closely they are spaced together. Consult a joist span table to determine appropriate size.

If the deck is higher than 10 or 12 inches from the ground, you should provide steps, a wood platform, or concrete landing for easier access.

Hillside Deck. A deck is an excellent way to make a sloping corner of the yard more usable. You can extend an existing patio with such a deck, build it completely freestanding, or even attach it to the house. It is supported on posts that are firmly anchored to footings set into the slope. The basic joist and beam structure is the same

as for the low platform. Beam and joist sizes depend on the span.

The depth and size of the footings depend on local codes. Slopes usually require a deeper footing than level grades; sometimes the piers must be connected with concrete grade beams. Get professional advice if your slope drops more than 3 feet per 10 feet of horizontal distance.

The length of the 4 by 4 posts varies with the site. If the posts are taller than 5 feet, cross-brace with 2 by 4s; use 2 by 6s if the posts are longer than 8 feet.

Railings are needed on decks over a certain height—usually 30 inches. Attach railing posts to the joists or to a fascia board nailed around the edge of the deck, or extend the support posts.

Split-Level Raised Deck. A multilevel deck provides visual interest. Decks can be built at any height. Because a one-step change in level can be hazardous, try to separate the levels with more than one step or at least change the deck board pattern to make the step easier to see.

The ledger, beams, joists, and decking are the same as for the low, attached platform.

The fascia board around the outside of the deck can be installed so that the top edge is covered by decking or is flush with the surface.

Elements of Deck Framing

The basic deck structure shown here can be used for almost any deck design, and consists of a framework of beams and joists which in turn supports the main decking boards. The joists are attached to the house with a ledger board bolted to the house. The ledger supports either a cleat on which all the joists rest or onto which you can fasten individual joist hangers for each joist. The joists are also supported by beams that rest on posts. The beams are 4 by 4s or they can be built up from three or more thicknesses of 2 by 4s. Sometimes, 2 by 12 stringers are bolted to each side of the posts in place of the thicker beams that rest on top of the posts. This design allows the posts to extend up through the deck to become supports for the railing.

The 4 by 4 posts are spaced according to the size and spacing of the beams. Each post has a concrete footing. In many areas, the posts can be buried directly in the ground instead of resting on separate footings, as long as they are pressure-treated lumber suitable for ground contact and they are backfilled with gravel.

Joists with spans longer than 10 feet must have blocking or bridging between them. Blocking should consist of solid pieces of joist material or 1 by 4 cross-braces. It is usually installed at the midpoint of the joist spans or over beams.

The decking boards are the most prominent part of the deck. The most common size is 2 by 6, which can span from 2 to 4 feet, depending on species and grade. Other popular sizes are 2 by 4 and 2 by 3, but 1 by 6 is also a good board for decking as long as the joists are spaced no more than 16 inches apart.

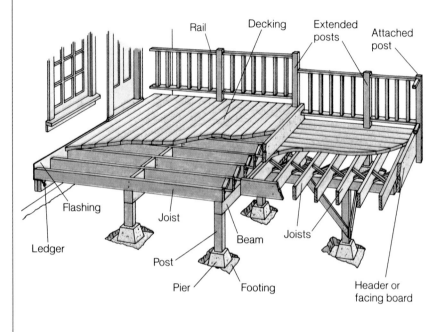

Rail — Decking — Extended posts — Attached post — Flashing — Joist — Beam — Joists — Ledger — Post — Header or facing board — Pier — Footing

Typical Deck Details

Stairs can be added to a deck by doubling the end joist or providing a separate double header below it. Attach the stair stringers to the double header with joist hangers.

This low deck is more permanent than a platform on sleepers. The joists are suspended between the beams instead of set on top of them to keep the height down.

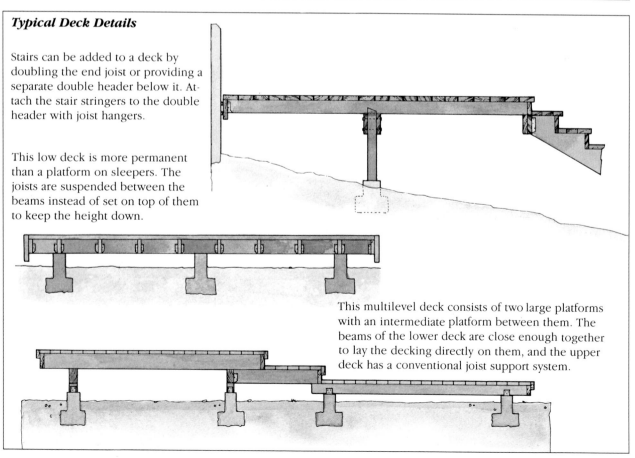

This multilevel deck consists of two large platforms with an intermediate platform between them. The beams of the lower deck are close enough together to lay the decking directly on them, and the upper deck has a conventional joist support system.

Laying Out Footings

Check with your local code for footing depths and dimensions. In some regions pressure-treated posts can be buried directly in the ground. To locate the footings, lay out string lines between the ledger and the batter boards. They should represent the outside corners of the posts. Use a 3-4-5 triangle to square the strings. Then excavate the holes and build concrete footings.

To resist frost heaving, footings must be placed below the frost line and made wider at the bottom than at the top.

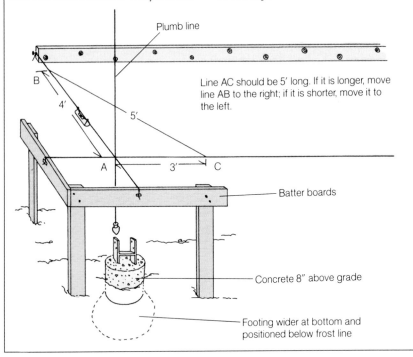

Plumb line

Line AC should be 5' long. If it is longer, move line AB to the right; if it is shorter, move it to the left.

B

4'

5'

A   3'   C

Batter boards

Concrete 8" above grade

Footing wider at bottom and positioned below frost line

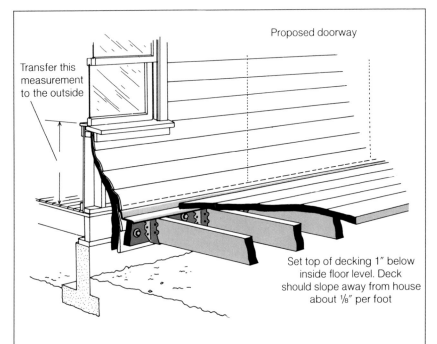

Transfer this measurement to the outside

Proposed doorway

Set top of decking 1" below inside floor level. Deck should slope away from house about 1/8" per foot

Attaching a Ledger Board

Cut the ledger to length. Determine height—usually so that the surface of the deck will be 1 inch below the doorway—and mark a level line on the wall for the top of the ledger.

To protect the ledger from decay, prime the back or use pressure-treated lumber. Either cover the ledger with flashing after it is installed or use extra washers to create a 3/4-inch air space behind it.

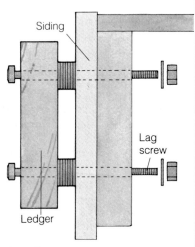

Siding

Lag screw

Ledger

Attachments

Attaching to Wood. Attach a ledger to a wood-framed house with 3/8- or 1/2-inch lag screws or machine bolts 16 to 24 inches apart. Drill pilot holes for bolts and squeeze caulk into the holes.

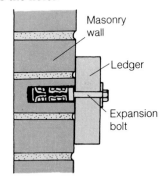

Masonry wall

Ledger

Expansion bolt

Attaching to Masonry. Use expansion bolts when attaching a ledger to a masonry wall. For additional support, place 2 by 6 supports against the house under the ledger every 4 feet.

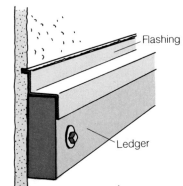

Flashing

Ledger

Attaching to Stucco. Use lag screws and the same method described for fastening on a wood-frame house.

Install flashing by making a 3/8-inch-deep groove in the stucco, bending the top of the flashing to fit in the groove, and sealing with butyl rubber.

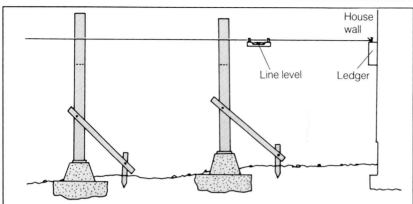

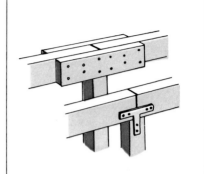

Erecting Posts

Cut each post longer than needed and attach it to its pier, toenailing it if the pier is a precast block, or bolting it if the pier has a metal bracket. Use the layout strings to align the posts accurately. Plumb each post with a level, then temporarily brace it in both directions with bits of scrap lumber and stakes.

If the posts are not going to extend to the deck railing, mark them for cutting by measuring down from the level string line a distance equal to the depth of both the joist and the beam. Scribe cutting lines and saw off the tops of the posts.

Installing Beams

Paint primer or sealer on the tops of the posts and lay the beams over them. Use metal connectors to attach the beams to the posts. Any splices between beams must be centered over the posts and must have a metal connector or cleats on both sides.

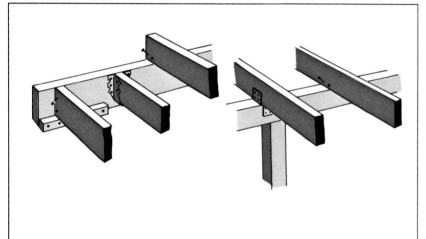

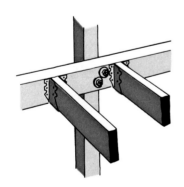

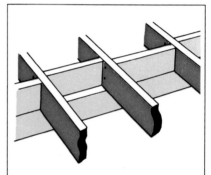

Installing Blocking

Install blocking between joists placed over any beams and at the center of any joist spans that are longer than 10 feet.

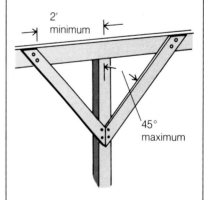

Attaching Joists

To keep the joists evenly spaced, mark a layout pattern on the ledger and beams, indicating at each mark on which side the joist goes. Be sure to start all layouts from the same end of the deck. Attach the joists using the methods shown above. After all the joists are installed, trim them to the same length and nail a rim joist across the ends. Install blocking between the joists, staggering the pieces so that they are easier to nail.

Bracing Tall Posts

If the posts are taller than 5 feet, brace them diagonally with 2 by 4 knee braces, as shown, or with full diagonal braces between the footings and the beams.

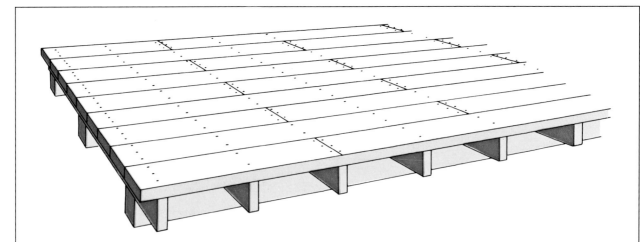

Laying Out the Deck Boards

Most deck boards have variations in color or frequency of knots. Therefore, before you start nailing, lay them in place on the joists in order to check their appearance. While doing this layout, plan the joint pattern and lay the boards accordingly. Stagger the joints and be careful not to place them or unattractive boards along the outer edges of the deck or in front of doorways or stairs. Place boards so that the grain pattern at the end of the board shows the bark side facing up.

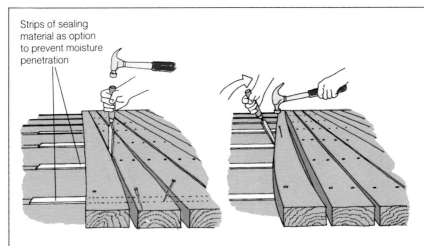

Strips of sealing material as option to prevent moisture penetration

Installing Deck Boards

Decking can be glued with certain outdoor adhesives, nailed, or secured with a combination of nails and deck clips. Adhesives and nails with deck clips give a clean, nail-free appearance; nails alone work better if some of the boards are crooked. Nails should be corrosion-resistant, such as aluminum or high-quality HDG. Use 12d or 16d common nails for 2-inch lumber, 10d for 1-inch. Drive nails at a slight angle toward each other, approximately $\frac{1}{2}$ to $\frac{3}{4}$ inch from the edge of the board. Drill holes at the ends of boards to prevent splitting. To keep the nailing lines straight, stretch a string along each row. Leave a $\frac{3}{16}$-inch gap between boards. Use a chisel hammered into the joists as a pry to force crooked boards into alignment.

To install deck clips, toenail both sides of the first board to the joists. Nail the clips to the edge of the next board, one alongside each joist. Slip the clips under the first board, then toenail the exposed edge of the second board to the joists. Install the remaining boards in the same way.

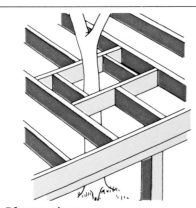

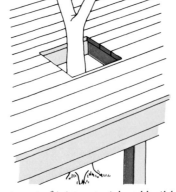

Obstructions

Extra supports are needed when building a deck around a tree trunk or other obstruction. Cut the supports out of joist material and build a frame, as shown. Attach this frame to the 2 full-length joists as well as to the interrupted one.

Trimming Deck Boards

Snap a chalk line across the ends of the deck boards and use this as your cutting line. Trim boards with a power saw or handsaw. Leave the edges exposed or cover them with a fascia board.

Decking Patterns

The simplest and most straightforward decking pattern is to lay all the boards perpendicular to the joists, but there are many ways to vary this layout. In some cases you can vary the decking pattern without altering the structure, such as laying boards diagonally across the joists or in a herringbone pattern. However, be sure the decking boards are strong enough for the increased distance they have to span. If you want to change the direction of the boards completely, or if you wish to lay out an elaborate design, you will have to alter the framing.

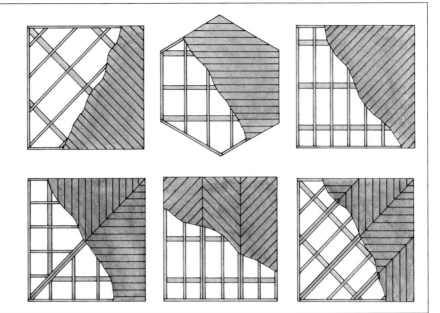

Decking on Edge

Decking that is laid on edge creates a very refined and highly textured look, although it requires substantially more lumber than decking laid flat. The compensation is that the decking can span greater distances than normal, up to 8 feet for high-strength grades of 2 by 4. Decking laid on edge also has no visible nailheads, but does require spacers to stabilize the boards and prevent them from warping.

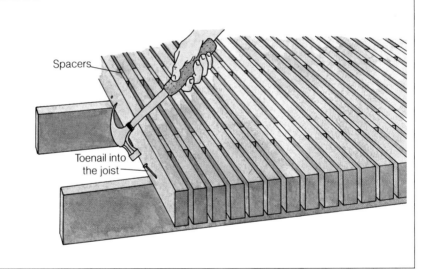

Parquet Deck

A deck consisting of individual modules laid in criss-cross fashion will create a parquet design. Typical modules are 3 feet square and made of 2 by 4s, although other configurations are possible. This type of decking can be laid over the same structure used for conventional decking, set directly onto a patio, a rooftop, or even laid on the ground if you use lumber suitable for ground contact and allow for drainage.

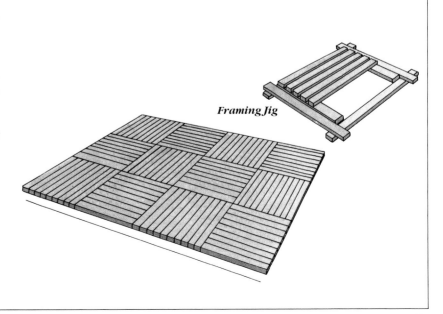

Framing Jig

Finishing the Deck

Complete any railings, stairs, benches, or other amenities you wish to install on the deck. Then apply whatever finish you have selected, letting the wood season for a few weeks first. If you desire a weathered gray look, do nothing to the deck, simply let it age naturally. The wood should either be pressure treated or it should be an all-heart grade of a durable species.

Bleaching Oil. You can accelerate the weathering process by applying a bleaching oil. Wait at least 60 days if the wood is pressure-treated, then apply the bleach with a brush or roller, wait the specified period of time, and hose off the deck.

Clear Sealer. Applying a clear sealer prolongs the look of new wood. It slows down the weathering process, although it does not retard it altogether. Use a sealer that penetrates the wood, rather than forming a hard shell on the surface.

Stain. Another way to retain the color of the new wood is to stain the deck with a color that matches it. A wide range of stains is also available for giving the wood a completely different color. There are two types of stain: semitransparent (light-bodied) and solid (full-bodied). The semitransparent stains have less pigment and reveal the grain of the wood better; they are preferred for the deck surface itself because the wear will not be as noticeable. Solid stains are more durable, hide defects better, and have to be renewed less frequently. Use an oil-based instead of a water-based stain. Before staining wait at least 60 days for the deck to season. Most stains are applied by brushing or rolling, one coat for solid and two for semitransparent.

Paint. Another finish option is painting the deck, either all of it or certain parts such as railings and understructure. The wood should be thoroughly seasoned, although you can prime it at the time of construction and then wait 60 days. For best results, apply a water-repellant sealer before priming. The primer should be zinc free, preferably oil based, and chemically compatible with the top coats. Use acrylic latex or a high-gloss alkyd paint specified for decks and porches for the two topcoats.

Sizing Lumber for a Deck

The charts on these two pages will enable you to size posts, beams, joists, and decking boards for your deck. They will also tell you the maximum distances you can span with a board of a particular size. The figures take the varying strengths of different species and grades of lumber into account. You may find that the span you have in mind is too great for a particular grade of lumber, but can be accomplished by a stronger species or grade of the same size.

These charts assume a "live" load on the deck of 40 pounds per square foot. This includes all furniture, people, planters, or anything other than the deck itself. For an even more substantial deck, or if you anticipate concentrated loads, like a large pile of firewood or heavy snow, use lumber one or two sizes larger than the size indicated in the chart.

Span refers to the maximum distance a member can bridge between two supports. Spacing refers to the distance between identical members, such as joists or beams (a ledger attached to the house would be considered a beam). Notice that the maximum spans for the same board vary according to how close it is to like members (its spacing).

Minimum Post Sizes (wood beam supports)

Species Group	Post Size (inches)	Load Area: Beam Spacing x Post Spacing (square feet)									
		36	48	60	72	84	96	108	120	132	144
1	4x4	Up to 12'————————→Up to 10' Up to 8'									
	4x6				Up to 12'————————→Up to 10'						
	6x6									Up to 12'	
2	4x4	Up to 12'	Up to 10'————————→Up to 8'————————→								
	4x6			Up to 12'————————→Up to 10'————————→							
	6x6					Up to 12'————————→					
3	4x4	Up to 12'	Up to 10'—→Up to 8'————————→Up to 6'————————→								
	4x6		Up to 12'—→Up to 10'————→Up to 8'————————→								
	6x6			Up to 12'————————————————→							

Based on 40 psf deck live load plus 10 psf dead load. Grade is Standard and better for 4 by 4 inch posts and No. 1 and better for larger sizes.
Group 1—Douglas fir, larch, and southern pine; Group 2—Hem fir and Douglas fir south; Group 3—Western pines and cedars, redwood, and spruces.
Example: If the beam supports are spaced 8 feet 6 inches, on center, and the posts are 11 feet 6 inches, then the load area is 98. Use next larger area: 108.

Maximum Allowable Spans for Spaced Deck Boards

Species Group	Maximum Allowable Span (inches)					
	Laid Flat				Laid on Edge	
	1x6	2x3	2x4	2x6	2x3	2x4
1	24	28	32	48	84	96
2	16	24	28	42	72	84
3	16	24	24	36	60	72

These spans are based on the assumption that more than one floor board carries normal loads. If concentrated loads are a rule, spans should be reduced accordingly.
Group1—Douglas fir, larch, and southern pine; Group 2—Hem fir and Douglas fir south; Group3—Western pines and cedars, redwood, and spruces.
Based on Construction grade or better (Select Structural Appearance, No. 1 or No. 2).

Beam Spans (Post Spacing)

Species Group	Beam Size (inches)	4	5	6	7	8	9	10	11	12
						Beam Spacing (feet) (distance between posts)				
1	4x6	Up to 6'								
	3x8	Up to 8'		Up to 7'	Up to 6'					
	4x8	Up to 10'	Up to 9'	Up to 8'	Up to 7'		Up to 6'			
	3x10	Up to 11'	Up to 10'	Up to 9'	Up to 8'		Up to 7'		Up to 6'	
	4x10	Up to 12'	Up to 11'	Up to 10'	Up to 9'		Up to 8'		Up to 7'	
	3x12		Up to 12'	Up to 11'	Up to 10'	Up to 9'		Up to 8'		
	4x12			Up to 12'		Up to 11'	Up to 10'		Up to 9'	
	6x10			Up to 12'	Up to 11'	Up to 10'		Up to 9'		
2	4x6	Up to 6'								
	3x8	Up to 7'		Up to 6'						
	4x8	Up to 9'	Up to 8'	Up to 7'		Up to 6'				
	3x10	Up to 10'	Up to 9'	Up to 8'	Up to 7'		Up to 6'			
	4x10	Up to 11'	Up to 10'	Up to 9'	Up to 8'		Up to 7'			Up to 6'
	3x12	Up to 12'	Up to 11'	Up to 10'	Up to 9'	Up to 8'		Up to 7'		
	4x12		Up to 12'	Up to 11'	Up to 10'		Up to 9'		Up to 8'	
	6x10			Up to 12'	Up to 11'	Up to 10'		Up to 9'		
3	4x6	Up to 6'								
	3x8	Up to 7'	Up to 6'							
	4x8	Up to 8'	Up to 7'	Up to 6'						
	3x10	Up to 9'	Up to 8'	Up to 7'	Up to 6'					
	4x10	Up to 10'	Up to 9'	Up to 8'		Up to 7'		Up to 6'		
	3x12	Up to 11'	Up to 10'	Up to 9'	Up to 8'	Up to 7'			Up to 6'	
	4x12	Up to 12'	Up to 11'	Up to 10'	Up to 9'		Up to 8'		Up to 7'	
	6x10		Up to 12'	Up to 11'	Up to 10'	Up to 9'		Up to 8'		

Beams are on edge. Spans are center-to-center distances between posts or supports. (Based on 40 psf deck live load plus 10 psf dead load. Grade is No. 2 or better; No. 2, medium-grain southern pine.) Group 1—Douglas fir, larch, and southern pine; Group 2—Hem fir and Douglas fir south; Group 3—Western pines and cedars, redwood, and spruces.
Example: If the beams are 9' 8" apart and the species is Group 2, use the 10-foot column; 3x10 up to 6' spans, 4x10 up to 7', etc.

Joist Spans (Beam Spacing)

Species Group	Joist Size (inches)	Joist Spacing (inches)		
		16	24	32
1	2x6	9' 11"	7' 11"	6' 2"
	2x8	12'	10' 6"	8' 1"
	2x10	15' 3"	13' 4"	10' 4"
2	2x6	8' 7"	7' 0"	5' 8"
	2x8	11' 4"	9' 3"	7' 6"
	2x10	14' 6"	11' 10"	9' 6"
3	2x6	7' 9"	6' 2"	5' 0"
	2x8	10' 2"	8' 1"	6' 8"
	2x10	13' 0"	10' 4"	8' 6"

Joists are on edge. Spans are center-to-center distances between beams or supports.
Based on 40 psf deck live loads plus 10 psf dead load. Grade is No. 2 or better; No. 2 medium-grain southern pine. Group 1—Douglas fir, larch, and southern pine; Group 2—Hem fir and Douglas fir south; Group 3—Western pines and cedars, redwood, and spruces.

DISHWASHERS

It's hard to imagine a remodeled kitchen that doesn't include this friendly little box that hums while it does your dishes. Even if you don't have room under the counter now, you can get a portable unit that can be adapted for installation under the counter when you remodel.

A built-in dishwasher is easy to plan for; except for an occasional 18-inch version, virtually all models are 24 inches wide. Your main decisions involve design, performance, and available features, such as preheating units and energy-saving cycles. Color is not usually a problem. Since most models come with front panels in several different colors and textures, just slip the one of your choice to the front.

Recommended Cross-References
Electrical System, Kitchen Layout, Plumbing, Sinks & Garbage Disposers.

Locating a Dishwasher

Try to locate the dishwasher as close to the sink as possible. Allow at least 24 inches of free clearance in front of the dishwasher for door swing. This is especially critical when it is directly opposite an oven with a swing-down door. If you cannot set the dishwasher next to the sink, try to keep them in the same plane so that the door swing will not interfere with the use of the sink. If dishwasher and sink have to be at right angles, locate the dishwasher at least 15 to 20 inches from the corner so that you do not have to back away from the sink to open the dishwasher door.

If you locate a dishwasher at the end of a run of cabinets, there are two ways to cover the exposed side. One is a plywood end panel that you can order with your cabinets. The other is a side panel that attaches to the dishwasher, available from most manufacturers. When installing the dishwasher in a corner, do not set it so close to the flanking cabinets that the door will hit drawers or cabinet doors that are left ajar. Allow at least 2 inches of clearance.

Installing a Dishwasher

1. Preparing the Opening. It is usually best to install new flooring first so that the dishwasher can be removed for repairs or be replaced without tearing up the floor. The flooring material should cover the space under the dishwasher so its edge won't form a dam and trap any water that leaks. Vinyl floors are especially suitable because they are water-resistant and can be tightly sealed. Before installing a dishwasher, check the manufacturer's specifications for all clearances and rough-in dimensions. The specifications will also indicate where pipes and wires can run without interfering with the mechanisms. Most cabinet openings should be 24⅛ to 24½ inches wide. If the installation is next to a sink, you can tap into the plumbing. Most dishwashers require water that is somewhere between 120° and 140° F, unless they have a preheating feature.

2. Roughing-In the Drain Hose. A ⅝-inch diameter (inside) drain hose comes with the dishwasher. It is usually 6 or 7 feet long. If it is not long enough, buy more hose and join it by slipping a short piece of copper tubing inside both hose ends and clamping the ends of the hoses tightly around the tubing.

Most codes require that the drain hose have an air gap to prevent overflow from a clogged sink drain from siphoning back into the dishwasher. This device is mounted in a hole in the sink deck or countertop. The drain hose is connected to the air-

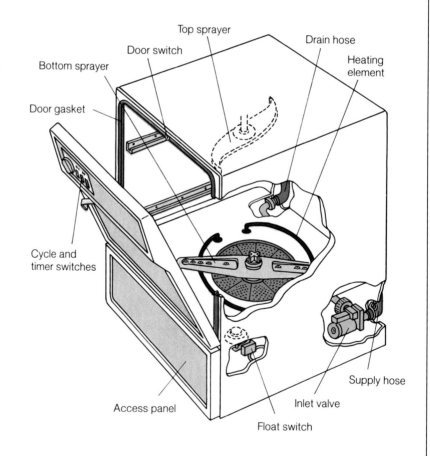

gap inlet under the counter, and another short hose connects the outlet to the disposer or sink drain. Water can flow only one way through the air gap. If you are not required to install an air gap, you should still loop the drain hose up to the bottom of the countertop and attach it there with a clamp. Then run the hose into the disposer or sink drain.

3. *Roughing In the Hot-Water Supply.*
The dishwasher should have its own valve. Install a tee in the hot-water supply pipe running to the sink faucet or run a new hot-water line under the floor and stub up into the dishwasher space. Check specifications for the size of tubing needed to connect the valve to the dishwasher (usually ⅜ inch), and be sure the valve has an outlet for a compression fitting the size of the tubing.

4. *Roughing In the Electrical Wiring.*
Dishwashers are usually required to be on a separate circuit protected by one 20-amp breaker, but in some cases you may be able to wire the dishwasher into the same circuit as the disposer. Check your local code. If the dishwasher requires its own junction box or outlet, check the manufacturer's specifications for locating it. Some units have a standard household cord for plugging into a wall receptacle, often located in the dishwasher space or under the sink. Others have a short cable for wiring directly to the junction box. Still others include their own junction box for mounting on the floor.

5. *Installing the Dishwasher.* Slide the dishwasher into place and secure it to the floor with lag bolts or heavy screws. Make connections, usually underneath the unit, according to the manufacturer's instructions. Turn on the circuit breaker and the water supply valves and run the machine through a test cycle. If everything checks out, secure it to the countertop and install the base panel.

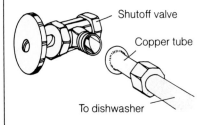

Shutoff valve
Copper tube
To dishwasher

Repairing a Dishwasher

The basic maintenance task for a dishwasher is cleaning the water jets on the sprayer. Unscrew the nut that holds the spray arm, lift it out, and use a piece of wire to pick out any food particles wedged in the holes.

Caution. Before undertaking any of the repairs outlined below, unplug the machine or deaden the circuit.

Dishwasher Won't Run. The door must be tightly closed to activate the switch. Wait a few moments; the machine may just be between cycles. If not, open the door and make sure nothing is jammed against the spray arm. Check the fuse or circuit breaker. Push the red reset button, if there is one, close the door tightly, and try again. If the dishwasher still doesn't work, call in a professional.

Dishwasher Overfills. Most dishwashers are prevented from overfilling by a float in the tub. It rises and falls, controlling the amount of water being let it. If the tub is overfilling, jiggle the float to make sure the arm is free. If this doesn't work, shut off the power to the dishwasher, disconnect the leads to the float switch, unscrew it, and replace it.

Dishwasher Won't Drain. Some dishwashers are drained by the motor reversing and pumping out the waste water. Other models have drains. First, check to see if yours has a drain and if it is clogged. If not, call for professional help.

Dishwasher Leaks. Check that the door gasket is in place. If cracked or broken, replace it. Tighten the clamps on the water supply hose.

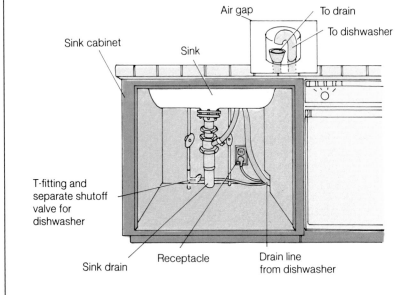

Air gap
To drain
To dishwasher
Sink cabinet
Sink
T-fitting and separate shutoff valve for dishwasher
Sink drain
Receptacle
Drain line from dishwasher

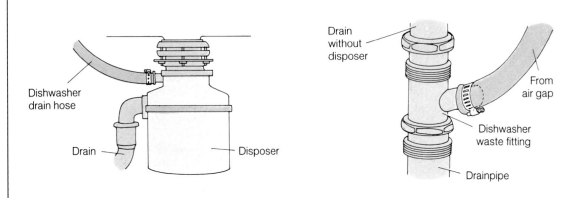

Dishwasher drain hose
Drain
Disposer
Drain without disposer
From air gap
Dishwasher waste fitting
Drainpipe

DOORBELLS

Although they have many sounds, shapes, and designs, all doorbells operate in basically the same way. The bell, chimes, buzzer, or recorded sound track use low-voltage current, which is provided by a transformer that steps 120-volt house current down to the lower voltage (20 volts or less).

Low-voltage wires, usually 18 or 20 gauge, connect the transformer to the doorbell and push button. A circuit is created by connecting one wire between the transformer and the button, another between the button and the doorbell, and a third between the doorbell and the transformer. Pushing the button completes this circuit and makes the bell ring.

Additional bells or push buttons can be wired into the circuit as shown in the diagrams below.

Recommended Cross-References
Electrical System, Wiring.

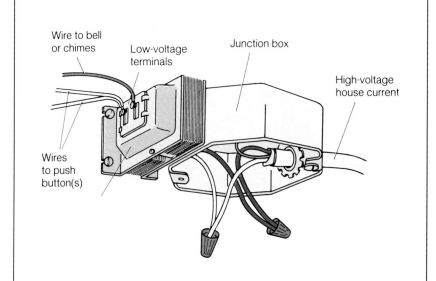

The Transformer

The transformer changes 120-volt house current into low-voltage current for the doorbell. It is wired into one of the house circuits at a junction box in the attic, basement, or a closet. Be sure to turn off the circuit before working on the transformer.

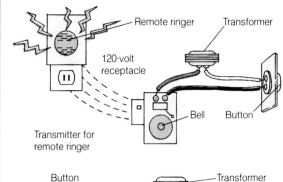

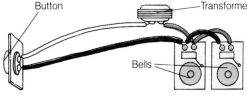

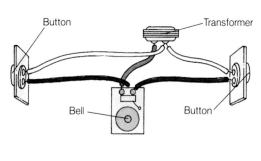

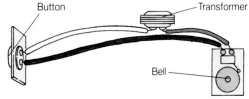

Circuits

One Button. The circuit between the bell and transformer is interrupted by the button.

Two Buttons. Connect the bell to the transformer with one wire and run a separate switch loop for each button.

Two Bells. Wire the circuit as if there were only one bell. Then connect the second bell to the first one.

Remote Ringer. This device, which plugs into a standard wall outlet, sounds when the doorbell rings. It can be located as far as 50 feet from the doorbell.

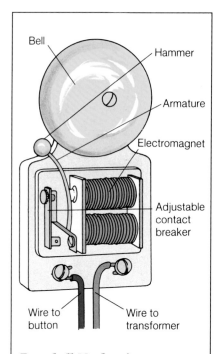

Doorbell Mechanism

Doorbells, chimes, and buzzers all have an electromagnet that is activated when the circuit is completed to the transformer. Pushing the door button is the usual way to complete the circuit. Then the electromagnet pulls the armature, causing the hammer to strike the bell. This also causes the contact breaker to open up, momentarily turning off the magnet and letting the armature spring back to remake the circuit. The whole process is repeated several times a second.

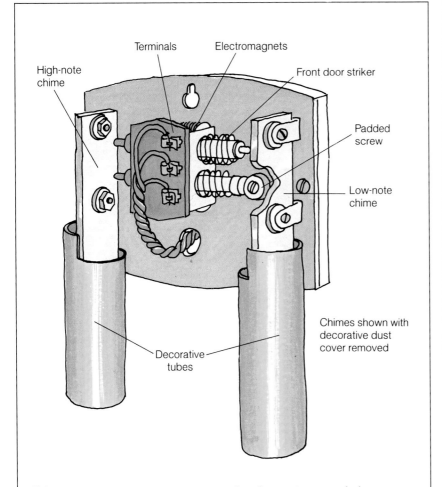

High-note chime

Terminals

Electromagnets

Front door striker

Padded screw

Low-note chime

Decorative tubes

Chimes shown with decorative dust cover removed

Chimes

When the front-door button is pressed, current energizes the top electromagnet, pulling the top striker to hit the high-note chime. Releasing the button breaks the circuit, and the spring pulls the striker back to the low-note chime. When the back-door button is pressed, the sequence is the same, except that the back-door striker is not allowed to ring the low-note chime when it springs back. A padded screw is in the way on some units; on others the end of the striker is padded so that it hits the bar but makes no noise.

Installing a New Doorbell

If you are upgrading an existing doorbell with new chimes or another mechanism, simply remove the old bell and connect the wires to the terminals of the new unit. Be very careful to connect the wires to the proper terminals if you have both a front-door and back-door button or a second bell, because if the connections are reversed you will hear the wrong bell each time. Test this by pushing the door button before mounting the bell unit to the wall. Then remove the old button and attach the new button to the same wires. If you are installing a new system where none exists, you will have to wire a transformer to one of the house circuits, as well as run 18- or 20-gauge wires behind walls or under floors to connect the transformer to the button and bell unit. Plan your installation for the most convenient wiring, locating the transformer where an accessible junction box already exists and locating the bell where wires can easily be fished through the walls. Be sure to turn off the circuit breaker or house current when you hook up the transformer at the junction box. Most transformers have a threaded sleeve around the high-voltage wires that you insert into a knockout hole in the junction box. The sleeve includes a nut that is used to secure the sleeve to the box.

Repairing a Doorbell

The following steps will help you fix a doorbell that doesn't ring or rings very faintly.

First, be sure that none of the fuses or circuit breakers are off. The problem may simply be no power. Then check the push-button unit. Problems often occur here because it is exposed to the elements and to dirt. Unscrew the unit from the wall and check the wire connections. If they have worked loose, tighten them and test the button again.

If the bell still doesn't ring, unscrew the two wires from the button and touch them to each other, holding them by the insulation. If the bell rings, it probably means that the button is defective. Straighten, clean, and sand the contacts and try it again. If it doesn't work, replace it with a new one.

When holding the button wires together produces only a faint ring or no ring at all, the problem could be in the bell itself. First, clean off any dirt, paint, or grease that may have accumulated on the striker, the bell, or any of the contacts. This is usually the cause of a faint sound.

If you are still having problems, check all the wires where they connect to the bell terminals to see if any have broken or become loose. Also check the wires where they connect to the transformer, and check any exposed sections of wire that you can get at. Wrap any frayed areas with electrician's tape and repair any breaks by stripping the ends and connecting them with wire nuts.

If these checks do not uncover the problem, the bell or transformer needs replacing. Unless you have electrical testing equipment, the only way to tell which one to replace is by trial and error. If you need a new bell anyway, buy one and install it. If it doesn't work, the transformer also needs replacing. If you already have an expensive bell or chime unit, try your luck with a new transformer; they are much less expensive.

DOORS

Whether you are upgrading an existing door, creating a new doorway, or installing a door in a new building, the techniques for installation are basically the same for all of these projects. The first thing to understand is the different types of doors.

Exterior Doors

Front doors are commonly 1¾ inches thick and at least 80 inches high, like all doors, and 36 inches wide. Back doors are sometimes as narrow as 32 inches. Exterior doors should be solid panel or solid core: The space between the front and back surfaces of the door is filled with wood, foam, or particleboard. A solid-core door not only offers more security, but is also less subject to the warping brought on by humidity and different temperatures inside and outside. Exterior doors are usually hung on three 4-inch butts (hinges), unless they are sliding doors. The jambs are commonly 5⅛ inches wide, but vary with the thickness of the exterior wall.

The front door is the first impression of your home. It is the main entrance, and it enhances the character and tone you have created.

Although a wide variety is available, most doors are either flush or paneled. Paneled doors have a framework of vertical stiles and horizontal rails, glued together with dowels, which frame individual wood panels, panes of glass, or a combination of both. Flush doors are made by covering a solid core of lumber or compressed wood fibers with thin sheets of plywood or veneer. The surface is either smooth or decorated with wood moldings. A variation of the flush door is a steel door filled with foam insulation. This type of door offers both security and energy efficiency; it is finished to resemble painted wood doors and is usually sold in a prehung package.

Interior Doors

Interior doors are usually 1⅜ inches thick and 80 inches high. They are generally hung with two 3½-inch butts. Since interior walls are thinner than exterior ones, doorjambs are only 4⅝ inches wide.

Interior doors are paneled or flush. The flush doors have a core that is either hollow or honeycombed cardboard rather than solid wood. If you are replacing an old paneled door, try to match it unless you are changing the architectural character of the rooms as well.

Other styles of interior doors include sliding closet doors, bifold doors, and pocket doors.

Recommended Cross-References
Garages, Hinges, Pulls & Knobs, Locks, Security, Thresholds, Weather Stripping, Windows.

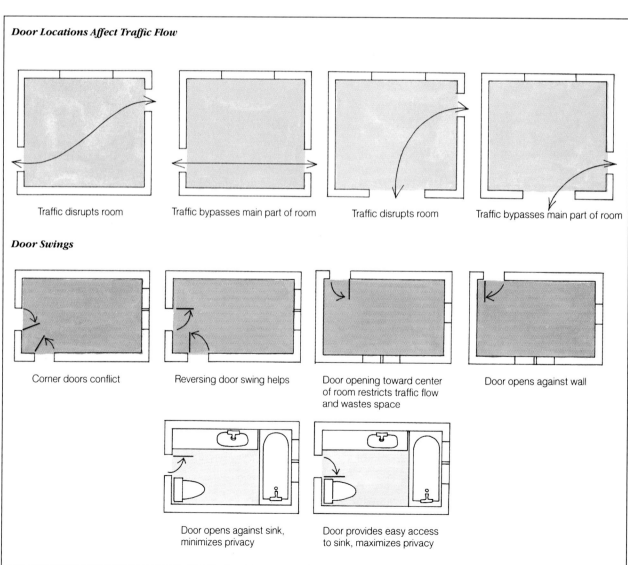

Door Locations Affect Traffic Flow

Traffic disrupts room

Traffic bypasses main part of room

Traffic disrupts room

Traffic bypasses main part of room

Door Swings

Corner doors conflict

Reversing door swing helps

Door opening toward center of room restricts traffic flow and wastes space

Door opens against wall

Door opens against sink, minimizes privacy

Door provides easy access to sink, maximizes privacy

Entry door with transparent panels

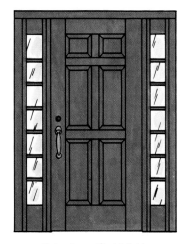

Entry door with sidelights

Dutch door

Double sliding French doors with transom

Double entry doors with transom and sidelights

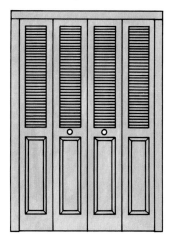

Bifold doors

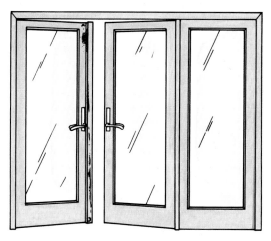

Three-piece patio door with double door and fixed panel

Choosing a Prehung Door

Both exterior and interior doors come in prehung packages. Such a unit includes the side and head jambs, the stops, and the door already mounted on hinges. Although the unit is more expensive than the components would be if purchased separately, it saves hours of painstaking work. You can also order the door with holes already drilled for the lockset. Installing a door used to require the services of a skilled carpenter, but the prehung door has changed that.

Now you just put it into place and nail. Well, almost. Both interior and exterior prehung doors are installed in the same manner. However, a sill must be installed with exterior doors. Techniques for installing a sill are covered in the section that follows on how to hang a door.

The prehung door is factory-assembled with the door hinged and mounted on the side jamb. Before ordering a door, you must determine which way it will open. A right-handed door swings to the right when opened from inside the room into which the door opens; a left-handed door opens to the left.

Prehung doors come in three basic styles. In one, the door is mounted inside the fully assembled jambs. In another, it is mounted to the hinge jamb only and you must nail together the head jamb and other side jamb. In the third style, called a split jamb, tongue-and-groove jambs are fitted together from opposite sides of the opening, and the door is already hung from the hinge jamb. Aside from these differences, prehung doors are installed in the same way.

Preparing the Opening

Frame a rough opening with a king stud and trimmer stud on each side and a header across the top that is sufficiently heavy to carry the load above it. This rough opening should be ½ inch to 1 inch wider than the prehung unit and 1 inch higher. Install the wall-coverings on both sides of the framing and trim flush with the opening. The combined thickness of the stud and both wallcoverings will determine the width of the jamb stock; this is usually 4⅝ inches for interior jambs and 5⅛ inches for exterior ones.

Strips of flashing paper or 15-pound felt building paper should be tacked around the rough opening before the door is hung. First, install a strip across the bottom of the door opening. You can use staples or roofing nails. This bottom strip should overlap the building paper below it. Then install strips on the sides, overlapping the bottom strip. The strips on the side of the opening should run up under the building paper above the opening. Place a strip of flashing paper on the top of the opening. It should overlap the side strips and nailing fin.

If the opening is for an exterior door in a brick wall, lay out the dimensions carefully, so that as much of the cutting as possible will follow the mortar joints. Break a hole through the center of the opening with a hammer and chisel or a hammer drill, and remove bricks individually with a hammer and pry bar or masonry chisel. Remove whole bricks around the edges of the opening, leaving a sawtooth pattern, then fill in alternating courses with half bricks to trim out the opening. If the opening is wider than 4 feet or the wall bears heavy loads, shore up the wall with bracing before cutting a hole in it. To complete the preparation for the door, head off the top of the opening with a lintel of concrete or angle iron.

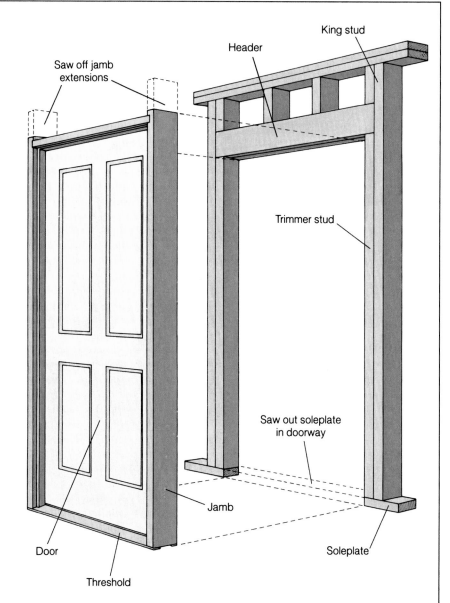

Saw off jamb extensions

King stud

Header

Saw out soleplate in doorway

Trimmer stud

Jamb

Soleplate

Door

Threshold

Installing the Door

Prehung packages come in different stages of assembly. Although some are fully assembled, with the jambs, hinges, and door in place, most packages are not. All, however, contain all the materials. The jambs are already cut to length; all you have to do is nail the side jambs to the head jamb with 10d finishing nails. If the package you buy already has the hinges attached to the jamb and door, pull the pins and detach the door while you nail the jambs together. Leave the door off until you place the jambset in the door opening. If necessary, trim off excess jamb extensions above the head jamb so they fit in the rough opening, leaving 1/2 inch to 1 inch.

If the prehung package is fully assembled, do not remove any temporary straps or braces that are attached to the unit until the door is in place. With many exterior doors the hinges are attached with long, heavy screws. If they penetrate through the side jamb far enough to interfere with clearances between the jamb and studs, saw off the excess.

Set the door in the rough opening, centering it between the jambs. Use pairs of tapered shims to fill the gap between the jambs and studs, at the locations shown in the illustration. Adjust the thickness of the shims by sliding them toward or away from each other.

The first place to nail the jambs to the studs is through the shims behind the top hinge. Drive a 12d finishing nail at this point to hold the unit in place. Then use a long level to check the hinge jamb for plumb, adjusting shims in or out until the jamb is straight and plumb along its entire length. When it is, nail a 12d finishing nail through the center of the jamb at each shim location.

Next, level the head jamb by adjusting the shims above it and nailing it into the header. Then measure the width of the jambs at the top of the door, making sure the door can shut between them. Adjust the shims behind the side jamb opposite the top hinge and nail. Then use the same measurement at the middle and bottom of the door opening to adjust the remaining shims, and nail the jamb to the stud. As you continue nailing, check from time to time to make sure the door shuts freely.

To complete the installation, snap off the free ends of the shims by scoring them with a utility knife and tapping them with a hammer. Then install the lockset and striker plate. Finally, install casings or other trim to match existing doors and windows. If the door is an exterior door, fill the gaps between jambs and framing with insulation before installing the trim.

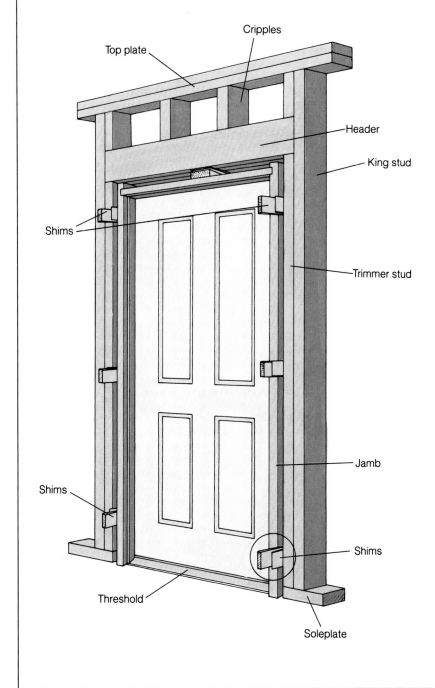

Cripples

Top plate

Header

King stud

Shims

Trimmer stud

Jamb

Shims

Shims

Threshold

Soleplate

Framing Your Own Door

If you are replacing an existing door or jambs, or if you are installing a new door that was not purchased prehung, plan to install the door in stages rather than as one unit. You will need the door, side and head jambs, hinges, doorstops, a lockset, and trim. For an exterior door, you will also need sill and threshold material. The techniques described here are for exterior doors, but are the same for interior doors, except that you do not need to install a sill.

1. Constructing the Jambs. Buy a set of jambs or rip finished lumber to the same width as the wall thickness. If you make your own jamb stock, also rout a ½-inch-deep rabbet at the top of each side jamb into which the head jamb will fit. Assemble all three pieces of the jamb with glue and three 8d nails in each side.

2. Installing a Sill. Sill stock is made of hardwood, has a bevel that slopes downward away from the door to shed water, and should have a drip groove on the underside, close to the outside edge.

In new construction the floor joists must be trimmed to accept the sill so that the back edge of the sill is flush with the finish floor. A threshold will cover the joint between the sill and the floor. If you are installing a new door in an existing house, cut away enough of the flooring to expose the joists. Make the cut directly under the inside edge of where the closed door will fall.

3. Adding a Sill Support. If the joists run parallel to the sill, you must add a support member for the edge of the subflooring that was cut away, as well as for the back of the sill. Do this by nailing two blocks, of the same dimensions as the joists, between the joists on either side of the door opening. Cut two support joists to length and nail them through the blocks, as illustrated. One supports the flooring and the other catches the inner edge of the sill. Use a saw and chisel to notch the tops of the

joists at the edge of the house. Make the notches 2 inches deep, then fit the sill into this trimmed area, making sure that it is level. Shim as necessary. Predrill the nail holes, then nail the sill in place. Fill the joint below the sill with caulk and cover it with a strip of trim material.

4. Installing the Jambs. Prepare the rough opening the same as for a prehung door. Set the jambs into the opening, and place pairs of shims behind all hinge locations. Plumb the hinge jamb with a long level and nail it with 12d finishing nails at each set of shims. Level and nail the head jamb, checking with a carpenter's square to make sure it is square to the hinge jamb. Then measure the distance between the side jambs so that the door will shut freely, and nail the latch jamb, after shimming it in three or four places.

5. Trimming the Shims. After checking for plumb and square and nailing the frame in position, cut off the shims flush with the edges of the jambs.

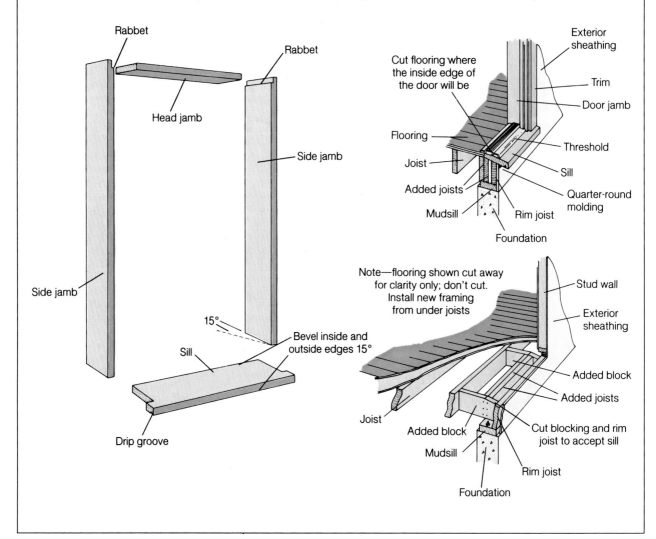

Rabbet

Rabbet

Head jamb

Side jamb

Side jamb

Sill

15°

Bevel inside and outside edges 15°

Drip groove

Cut flooring where the inside edge of the door will be

Flooring

Joist

Added joists

Mudsill

Exterior sheathing

Trim

Door jamb

Threshold

Sill

Quarter-round molding

Rim joist

Foundation

Note—flooring shown cut away for clarity only; don't cut. Install new framing from under joists

Stud wall

Exterior sheathing

Added block

Added joists

Cut blocking and rim joist to accept sill

Joist

Added block

Mudsill

Rim joist

Foundation

6. Install Hardware and Finishing Touches. Install the hinges on the door first. Be sure that the door is approximately ¼ inch narrower than the jamb opening. If you need to trim it, plane or saw the hinge side. The latch side should be beveled.

To be able to mark where the hinges are to go on the door and the jamb, set the door in place and temporarily shim it to make a ⅛-inch clearance on both sides. Then mark the hinge positions on the jamb and the stile edge of the door. Usually the top of the top hinge is 7 inches from the top of the door and the bottom of the bottom hinge is 11 inches from the bottom of the door. (Center the middle hinge between them for exterior doors.)

Take the door down, and trace each hinge outline on the edge of the door with a sharp pencil or knife, allowing each hinge leaf to extend ¼

inch beyond the edge of the door so that the knuckle will clear the casing. Make the knuckle inside, not outside, the house. Using a sharp chisel or a router, cut mortises to the thickness of the hinges. Then screw the hinges to the door, predrilling for each screw. Be sure to drill straight holes; if you drive the screw in at an angle it will pull the hinge out of alignment.

Cut mortises in the jamb the same way as for the door, tracing the outline of each hinge on the jamb and then chiseling out the mortise. A trick to hanging a door is to mark and attach the top hinge first. Screw the top hinge to the jamb, then mark the other hinges and cut them.

When the door is up, check that it closes without binding anywhere. It should have about ⅛-inch clearance on each side. Make adjustments by placing a thin cardboard shim be-

hind a hinge or by deepening the mortise. Cut the bottom of the door to allow clearance for any carpeting, the threshold, or weather stripping.

Use stop material 1⅛ or 1⅜ inches wide. Hold the door closed in its proper position, and have a helper trace the outside edge of the door along the jambs with a sharp pencil. Then measure and cut the stops to length, and nail them with their outside edges on the pencil line. For greater security, install jamb stock made for exterior doors; the stops are milled as an integral part of the jamb and cannot be pried off.

Install the threshold, lockset, weather stripping, and trim, using techniques described in other sections of this book. You can either paint the door or finish it with a stain or clear finish. Applying a double coat of oil-based sanding sealer will ensure a handsome appearance.

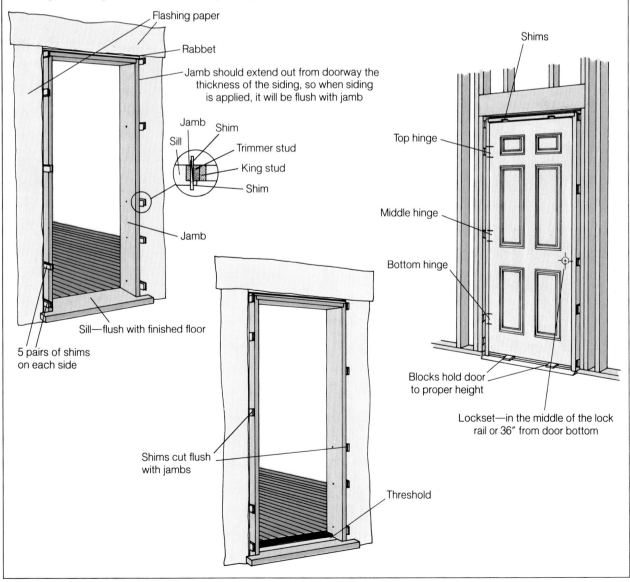

Sliding Glass Doors

To instantly transform a house, nothing succeeds quite like a sliding glass door. Standard sizes are 80 inches high and 5 feet, 6 feet, or 8 feet wide. Most local codes require that the glass be tempered or laminated safety plate. If you live in a cold climate, buy dual-glazed doors to conserve energy.

Sliding doors usually have wood or aluminum frames. If you choose aluminum, look for doors with an insulated thermal break that prevents the aluminum from conducting cold into the house. For security, choose a door with a good lock. Most sliding doors come with a screw in the top jamb that prevents it from being pried out of the lower track.

Preparing the Opening. Frame the opening with king studs, trimmer studs, and a header sized to carry the load above the opening. The rough opening should be ½ inch larger than the door unit on both sides and the top. Be sure that the header is level and the studs plumb. Use shims to correct minor variations. Make sure the subfloor is sound; install a filler board if the subfloor needs to be brought up to the proper height. Unless it is provided with the sliding-door unit, install drip flashing or a drip cap across the top of the opening, tucking it under the siding.

Installing the Doors

1. Attaching the Framing. Fasten the jambs and threshold with screws into a single frame before installing them. Before putting the frame in place, lay two thick beads of caulk along the floor near the edge of the opening to provide a weathertight seal. Also caulk around the outside of the opening if the unit has flanges or integral casings.

From the outside, have someone help you place the frame in the opening and align it so that there is an equal gap on both sides. Step on the sill to distribute the caulk.

Level the sill, shimming if necessary, and fasten it to the floor with screws. Do not drive them all the way in until the rest of the frame is set properly. Use a level and a long straightedge to plumb the side jambs. Even if the jambs are straight, use five pairs of shims on each side to keep them solidly in place. Do the same to level and straighten the head jamb. After checking the corners with a carpenter's square and measuring the opening at several places to make sure the doors will fit, attach the jambs to the sides of the opening. Styles differ: from metal flanges on the exterior side of the jambs for nailing to the siding, to wood casings, to predrilled holes in the jambs for screws. If the sill overhangs the opening, nail a strip of wood along the bottom for extra support.

2. Positioning the Doors. Put the stationary door in place in one of the channels, depending on where you want the door that slides. You may have to use a hacksaw to complete a cut started along the top of a metal door before it will fit. Push the door snugly against the side jamb, tapping it with a board, if necessary. Secure it to the frame with brackets or screws.

Place the sliding door into the frame. On wooden doors, first put the security screws into the head jamb, then remove the head stop. Position the bottom of the door first, with the rollers resting on a rail in the sill, then press the top firmly against the weather stripping. Screw the head stop back in place.

On metal doors, first remove the security screw. Slip the top of the door into the head jamb channel, then lift the door and set the rollers on the rail. Open door, and install security screw in the head jamb.

Slide the door back and forth to check the movement. If it does not glide or close smoothly, adjust the rollers at the bottom corners.

3. Finishing Touches. Patch the wall and add trim on the outside and inside, as needed. Be sure to install drip flashing along the top edge if it is not provided with the unit.

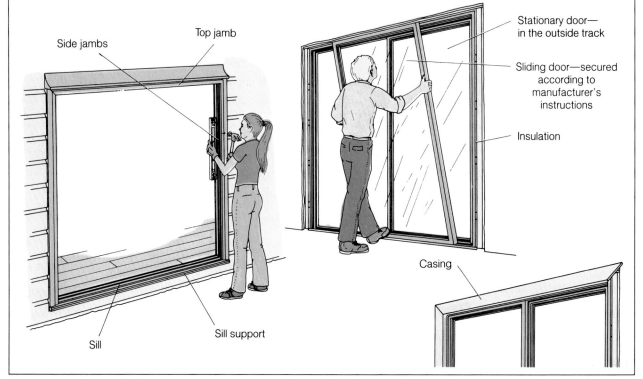

Side jambs

Top jamb

Sill

Sill support

Stationary door— in the outside track

Sliding door—secured according to manufacturer's instructions

Insulation

Casing

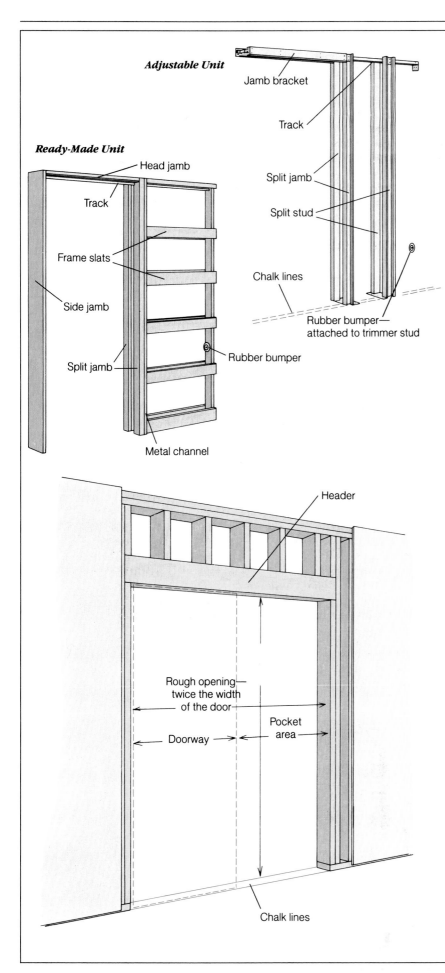

Adjustable Unit

Jamb bracket

Track

Split jamb

Split stud

Chalk lines

Rubber bumper—
attached to trimmer stud

Ready-Made Unit

Head jamb

Track

Frame slats

Side jamb

Split jamb

Rubber bumper

Metal channel

Header

Rough opening—
twice the width
of the door

Pocket
area

Doorway

Chalk lines

Pocket Doors

Preparing the Opening. Frame a rough opening that is ¹/₂ inch to 1 inch wider and taller than the complete pocket frame. If you are cutting into an existing wall, lay out the opening so that the latch jamb of the door starts at the edge of an existing stud. Then lay out the rough opening dimensions and cut back to the stud closest to the end of the pocket frame. Install new trimmer studs and a header across the entire opening.

Installing a Ready-Made Unit. Set the pocket frame into the side of the opening where the door will be recessed, making sure it is plumb and level. Nail it to the framing.

Install the side jamb and head jamb making sure they are plumb and level before nailing. Then screw the overhead track to the center of the head jamb. After mounting the wheels on the top of the door, lift it in place so that the wheels hook onto the track. Adjust the wheels until the door hangs straight. Finish the walls and trim the opening.

Installing an Adjustable Unit. Kits are available that include everything but the door. First place the overhead track in the opening so that both ends butt against the trimmer studs. After checking that it is centered and level, nail it to the studs.

Snap chalk lines on the floor between the outside edges of the trimmer studs. Then place the split jamb at the edge of the door opening and screw the top of the jamb to the track. Screw the bottom flange to the floor, using the chalk lines and a level to check plumb. Repeat this step with the second split stud.

Mount the wheels to the door and hang it on the track, adjusting the wheel mechanisms to make the door the proper height. Install door guides at the base of the split jamb, adjusting them to allow ¹/₈-inch clearance from the door. Then install the bumper where the midpoint of the door will hit it. Adjust the bumper with shims or washers so that the door will extend ³/₈ inch beyond the split jamb when it is recessed.

Cover the exposed trimmer stud with jamb stock and the framing with wallboard. Use 1¹/₈-inch doorstop material to conceal the track and split jambs. Leave a ¹/₈-inch clearance on both sides, then trim the opening with casing material.

Sliding Closet Doors

Sliding doors are commonly used for closets because they are inexpensive and easy to install. Virtually any type of door slides: flush, paneled, or louvered. Some doors are mirrored, which can enhance the bedroom decor. Because they are heavy, mirrored doors are installed in metal frames like sliding glass doors.

The basic hardware for sliding closet doors consists of an overhead track, a pair of wheels that attach to the top of each door, and door guides that are fastened to the floor. Hardware of good quality will also include a floor track with rollers built into it to guide the doors smoothly and keep them from rattling. You can buy this hardware separately and use inexpensive hollow-core doors, or buy the doors and hardware in a kit.

The doors should be 1½ inches shorter than the opening to allow 1¼ inches for the track and ¼-inch clearance above the floor or carpet. Each door should be ½ inch wider than half of the width of the opening, so that they overlap by 1 inch when closed. If you cannot find doors of the proper width, either make them narrower by trimming the edges with a power saw or add trim to the inside of the doorway.

1. Installing the Track. Frame the door opening with side and head jambs. Most overhead track is adjustable. If it is not, cut it to length with a hacksaw. Then place the track against the overhead jamb. Mark the jamb where the predrilled screw holes are located, remove the track, and drill pilot holes for the screws. Then install the track with the open channels facing the closet. You can conceal the track with an extra-wide top casing or a separate strip of wood nailed to the jamb.

2. Hanging the Doors. Mount a pair of wheels on the top edge of the doors, about 2 inches in from each end of the door. With the overhead track installed and the wheels mounted, hang the inside door on the inside channel first, then hang the outside door. Push the doors back against the side jambs, and check how straight they hang by comparing them to the jambs. If a door hangs unevenly, loosen the adjusting screws on the wheel mounts and raise or lower one corner of the door until it is hanging straight. If the hardware includes a bottom track, remove the doors and set the guide track on the floor between the door jambs. Replace the doors, center the track under them, and raise or lower the doors by turning the adjusting screw until they

ride on the rollers. Remove the doors, screw the track to the floor, and replace the doors.

3. Attach Floor Guides. If hardware does not include a track with rollers for the door bottoms, you can help keep the doors from swinging and banging into each other by using a metal or plastic floor guide. Screw the guide to the floor between the doors in the center of the opening where they meet. If the guide is adjustable, move the side pieces until there is a ⅛-inch clearance from the doors. If the guide is too low, place a shim under it to raise it.

Finish the installation by trimming around the doors. Install casings around the opening and a strip of molding across the head jamb to hide the overhead track.

4. Adjusting the Nut. Some wheel mechanisms have an adjusting nut that is loosened and tightened with a small wrench that comes with the hardware. The turning motion will move the door up and down or it will loosen the door so that you can move it. Hold the door steady while you tighten the nut.

5. Adjusting the Dial. Some doors have a dial mechanism that raises or lowers the door. Loosen the set screw, turn the dial to adjust the door, then retighten the set screw.

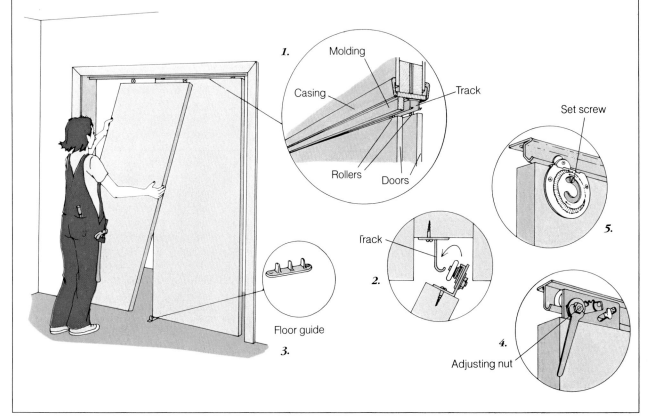

1. Molding
Casing
Track
Rollers
Doors
Set screw
5.
Track
2.
Floor guide
3.
Adjusting nut
4.

Bifold Doors

Bifold doors come to the rescue in places where a conventional door would be in the way. When open, they fit neatly against the door jambs; when closed, they provide a warm and interesting break in a wall. Bifold doors are available louvered, paneled, or flush.

Bifold doors are easily installed in an existing door frame. They come in different widths for pairing together. Use two pairs for wider openings. If the doors do not fit the opening exactly, you can narrow all the doors an equal amount by trimming them at the sides or building up the sides of the opening to create a narrower space.

Hardware includes an overhead track, a bottom pivot for each pair of doors, a slide guide, and an adjustable bolt that goes in the bottom corner of each pivot door. The hardware is available separately or as part of a complete package that usually includes four doors.

1. Installing Track. Cut the overhead track to fit inside the opening. Insert the rubber or spring-cushioned bumper into the track, locating it where the slide guides attached to the top of the doors will hit it. Slip the pivot guides into each end of the track and screw the track into the center of the head jamb.

2. Installing Brackets. Position the bottom brackets on the floor by dropping a plumb bob from each pivot guide in the top track. Screw the bottom brackets to the side jambs, leaving all adjusting screws loose for later adjustment. If you plan to install carpet later, allow for the carpet by placing plywood shims under floor brackets before attaching.

3. Installing Doors. Measure the opening carefully and trim the doors equally to allow a total clearance of 1/4 to 1/2 inch, depending on the number of hinges and doors. Install the hinges that join each pair of doors. Then install the top and bottom pivots and the slide guide necessary for each pair.

Set each pair of doors in place. Set the bottom pivot into the bottom bracket first. Tilt the door toward the center of the opening and slide the top pivot guide to the center of the track so that you can insert the top pivot of the door into it. Then tilt the door back to a vertical position, inserting the slide guide into the track as you push on the door.

4. Adjusting the Guides. When the door is back to the jamb and in a plumb position, tighten the top and bottom adjusting screws. Open the door to test it for clearance. If it binds on the top track or is too low, adjust the height by turning the adjusting nut located on the bottom pivot of the door. Repeat the same process for the second pair of doors.

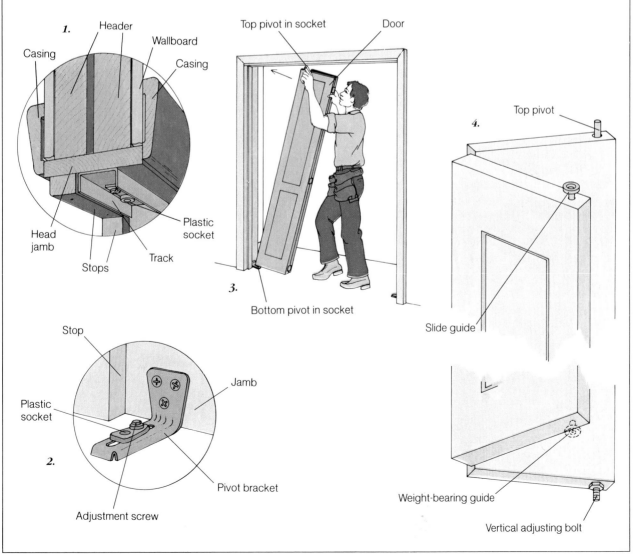

1. Header · Casing · Wallboard · Casing · Head jamb · Stops · Track · Plastic socket

Top pivot in socket · Door · **3.** · Bottom pivot in socket

2. Stop · Plastic socket · Adjustment screw · Jamb · Pivot bracket

4. Top pivot · Slide guide · Weight-bearing guide · Vertical adjusting bolt

Installing a New Threshold

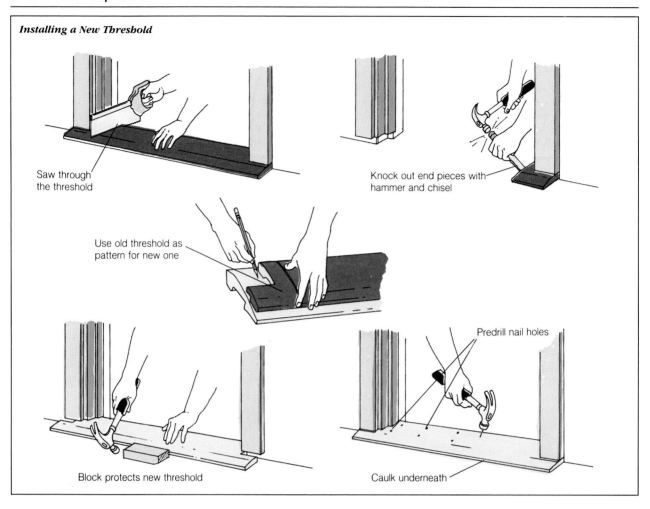

Saw through the threshold

Knock out end pieces with hammer and chisel

Use old threshold as pattern for new one

Block protects new threshold

Predrill nail holes

Caulk underneath

Trimming a Door

Mark the door while it is still hung. Then take it down and place it on sawhorses. Use a pencil and a straightedge to mark a cutting line and then clamp on a straightedge. To prevent the door from splintering, scribe the cutting line with a sharp knife. On the latch edge of the door, bevel-cut at 5 degrees.

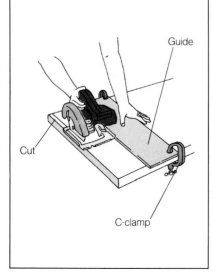

Guide

Cut

C-clamp

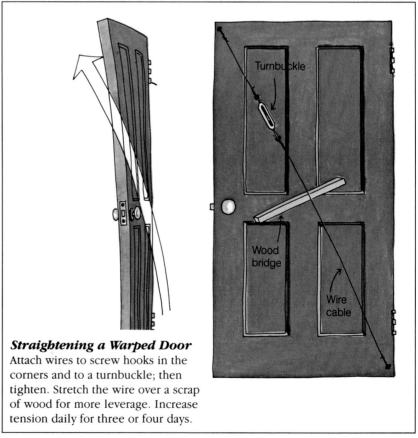

Turnbuckle

Wood bridge

Wire cable

Straightening a Warped Door

Attach wires to screw hooks in the corners and to a turnbuckle; then tighten. Stretch the wire over a scrap of wood for more leverage. Increase tension daily for three or four days.

Shimming Hinges

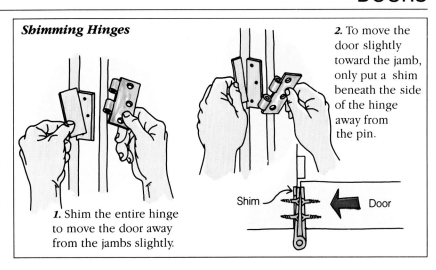

1. Shim the entire hinge to move the door away from the jambs slightly.

2. To move the door slightly toward the jamb, only put a shim beneath the side of the hinge away from the pin.

Shim   Door

Setting Hinges

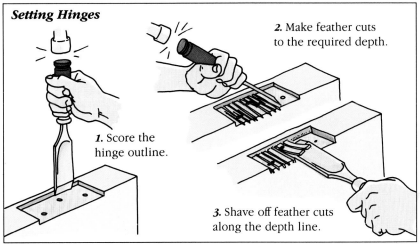

1. Score the hinge outline.

2. Make feather cuts to the required depth.

3. Shave off feather cuts along the depth line.

Realigning Hinge Knuckles

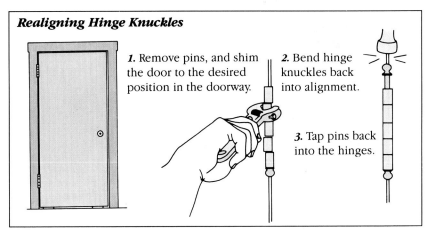

1. Remove pins, and shim the door to the desired position in the doorway.

2. Bend hinge knuckles back into alignment.

3. Tap pins back into the hinges.

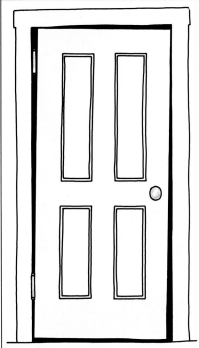

Binding Doors

1. Slide paper between the door and jamb—it will bind where the door is sticking. If a door sticks at the top of the latch side, tighten the top hinge screws, chisel the top hinge mortise more deeply, or shim the bottom hinge.

2. To correct sticking at the bottom of the latch side, tighten screws, deepen the mortise of the bottom hinge, or shim the top hinge. If the door binds on the hinge side, shim one or both hinges, as needed. If these methods fail, plane off part of the door and repaint.

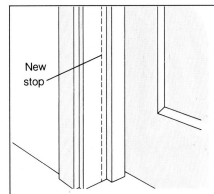

New stop

Moving a Doorstop

When a door is slightly out of line and you don't want to straighten it, you may be able to move the door-stops to conform to the door. Pry the stop from the jamb taking care not to damage it. Close the door, then place the stop against the jamb and flush with the door. Nail the stop in this new position.

DORMERS

Adding a dormer alters the exterior of a house dramatically. Ideally, an addition should be built with materials that match the existing ones and harmonize with the architecture.

A new dormer can transform a small, dark attic into a bright and spacious living area. Adding one or more windows improves light and ventilation, and can increase the usable floor space by as much as 30 to 40 percent. If you compare the cost of building a dormer to adding on a complete room, a new dormer is an appealing project indeed.

Adding a dormer demands careful planning and skillful carpentry. If you have relatively little building experience, you would be wise to seek professional assistance for at least part of the job. You may want to work alongside the contractor, learning as you go. Or have the contractor handle the more difficult aspects, such as cutting into the roof and framing the shell. Then finish the job yourself, employing many of the techniques described in other sections of this book.

It is a good idea to ask the advice of a designer or architect. At the outset, you need to know if the project is structurally feasible. If the attic is undeveloped, you must verify whether the foundation, first-floor walls, and floor joists can carry a new floor load. You should also know whether the dormer walls will be sufficient reinforcement when you cut a hole in the roof. Usually they will be.

You must plan the size and shape of the dormer carefully to maximize the available living space. The optimum size reflects a delicate balance between your needs and the structural and aesthetic possibilities of the space. Another reason for obtaining design help is that the dormer will dramatically alter the exterior appearance of the house. Good design is essential. The dormer should match the style of the existing architecture. Generally, the same type of windows, siding, and roofing should be used, and any details such as overhangs and fascia should be repeated. Most important, the dormer should blend smoothly with the rest of the house, complementing the overall design. In fact, it should not even look like an addition.

Planning the Dormer

The first step in planning the new dormer is to determine the size and slope of the existing roof so that you can draw an accurate end view of it. (See the next page.)

Once you have an accurate drawing of the roof, experiment with different dormer dimensions to see how they will fit into the roof. Several factors come into play at this point. One is where you want the top of the dormer roof to connect to the house roof. The best-looking connection is usually just below the ridge, but if you need more headroom or if the house ridge is so high that the resulting dormer roof will look like a ski jump, relocate the connection for better appearance.

The slope of the dormer roof influences overall design. The general appearance of the roof must be kept in mind, as well as code requirements for different roofing materials. For example, if you plan to roof the dormer with wooden shingles to match the existing roof, the slope must be at least 4 in 12. If you want less of a slope, then you will have to choose a different roofing material. The minimum slope for composition shingles is 3 in 12; roll roofing can be as low as 1 in 12. If the dormer is high enough so that you cannot see the dormer roof, it may not matter what roofing material you use, but it is best to match the roofing with what is on the rest of the house.

A third consideration that will affect the size and shape of the dormer is the minimum ceiling height. Most codes require that at least one half of the ceiling in a room be 80 inches or higher, and that the ceiling over the other half have a minimum height of usually 48 or 60 inches. Since the dormer will be part of a larger room, you have to calculate how high the dormer ceiling must be to satisfy the minimum height requirement for the total square footage of the room.

Recommended Cross-References
Attics, Flashing, Framing, Insulation, Roofs, Siding, Subfloors, Wallboard, Windows.

Dormer Shapes
There are two basic shapes for a dormer. Although the shed shape is easier to build, your choice should depend on how well the dormer blends in with the other architectural details on your home.

Gable Dormer. While a gable dormer has charm and appeal, reflecting the basic lines of the house, it cannot be very large. It adds light but little floor space, and often requires one or two more dormers to balance the exterior proportions of the house.

Shed Dormer. A shed dormer adds more living space than a gable dormer, and can even extend across the entire length of the roof. The front can be built directly over an exterior wall, but in most cases it looks better when it is set further back.

Gable Dormer

Shed Dormer

Calculating the Slope of a Roof

Roof slope is measured as the number of inches of vertical rise per 12 inches of horizontal run, and is always expressed as x in 12, where "x" is the vertical rise.

One method of calculating slope is to measure the total span of the house and divide it by 2 to find the run. Then measure the rise of the roof ridge above the walls. Once you know both figures, multiply the rise by 12 and divide that figure by the run. The result is the number of inches of rise in 12 inches of run.

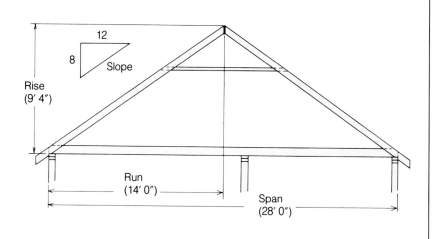

Measuring the Slope of a Roof

An easy way to measure roof slope is to hold a carpenter's level against the bottom of a rafter, as shown. Mark the level where it is exactly 12 inches from the end you hold against the rafter. Then, holding the level in place, measure the vertical distance between that mark and the bottom of the rafter. That figure is the number of inches of rise in 12 inches of run.

This method of calculation may not be as accurate as the first since the rafter may be sagging, but it is adequate enough for planning. An alternative is to take the level and tape measure up on the roof itself. Hold the level horizontally, letting the bottom corner touch the roof, and measure down from the 12-inch mark to the surface of the roof.

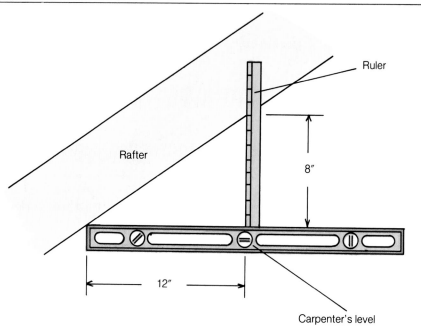

Drawing the Plan

Start by drawing an accurate end view of the existing roof, showing the rafters and attic joists. Also determine the minimum slope of the dormer roof and the minimum ceiling height of the new space, as described on the previous page. These dimensions, as well as aesthetic considerations, such as the best place to connect the dormer to the roof ridge and the best location for the front wall, will help you experiment with different dormer configurations to arrive at the best plan.

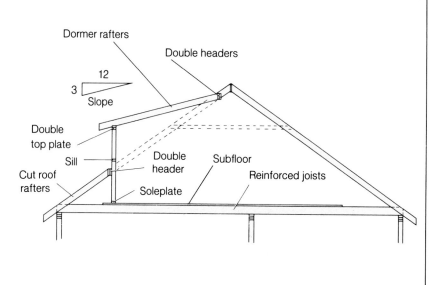

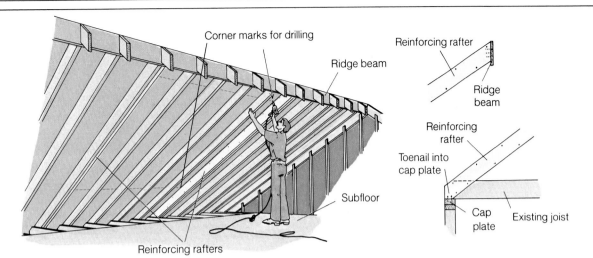

Corner marks for drilling

Ridge beam

Reinforcing rafter

Ridge beam

Reinforcing rafter

Toenail into cap plate

Cap plate

Existing joist

Subfloor

Reinforcing rafters

Installing a Dormer

1. Laying Out the Opening. Before you start work on the opening, make sure the attic floor is adequately supported for the new space and covered with subflooring. Lay out dormer dimensions on the floor. Then hold a plumb bob over each corner and mark where the line hits the roof. These marks are the corners of the roof opening.

Double the rafters on either side of the proposed opening. Use a bev-el gauge to cut the angled ends and nail with 10d nails, 12 inches on center. Cutting will be done in the roof surface. Therefore, transfer the corner marks by drilling holes or driving nails up through the roof.

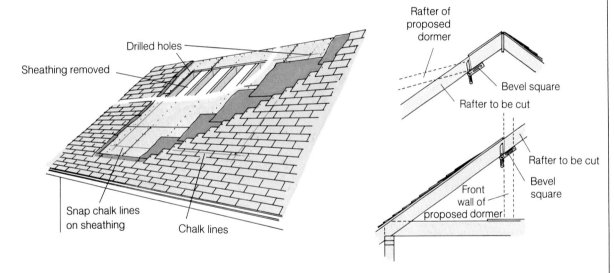

Drilled holes

Sheathing removed

Snap chalk lines on sheathing

Chalk lines

Rafter of proposed dormer

Bevel square

Rafter to be cut

Rafter to be cut

Bevel square

Front wall of proposed dormer

2. Cutting the Roof Opening. Snap chalk lines between the four corners. Strip off the roofing, going beyond the lines 10 or 12 inches. Resnap the chalk lines onto the sheathing. Cut through the sheathing along the chalk lines and remove it. Mark the rafters for cutting, as shown, but do not cut yet.

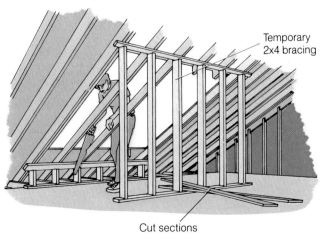

Temporary 2x4 bracing

Cut sections

3. Cutting the Rafters. Brace the rafters before cutting them. Nail 2 by 4s to the bottom of the rafters, just above and below the opening. Nail 2 by 4 soleplates to the subfloor and wedge studs between the two plates under every rafter. Have a helper hold each rafter as you cut it, setting it down gently so as not to jar the ceiling.

4. Installing Headers. To install double headers across the cut ends of the rafters, nail 3-inch joist hangers to the double rafters at each corner of the opening. Then cut a header from rafter stock, set it into the joist hangers, and nail it into all the rafter ends. Cut another piece, slide it into the same joist hangers, and nail it. Repeat for the top header.

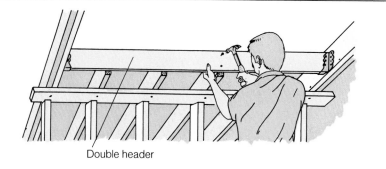

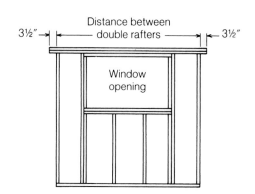

Double header

5. Framing the Front Wall. Remove the temporary bracing. Frame the front wall on the floor of the attic. The length of the wall is the distance between the double rafters, but make the double top plate long enough to extend beyond the end studs 3½ inches on each side. Use standard framing techniques for the studs and window opening.

Distance between double rafters

3½″   3½″

Window opening

6. Erecting the Front Wall. Stand the wall up and set it in place. Nail a diagonal brace to it, plumb the wall, and secure the brace to a block nailed into the floor. Nail the sole-plate into the floor, at the joists. Then nail the studs, toenailing them into the header and facenailing the end studs into the double rafters.

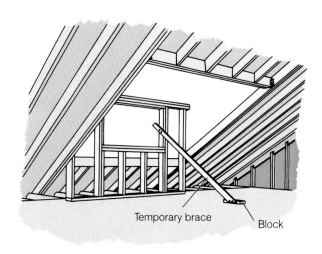

Temporary brace

Block

7. Installing Corner Posts. Build corner posts for the wall with two 2 by 4s and scraps of ³⁄₈-inch plywood. Measure them to fit between the top plate of the new wall and the exposed roof sheathing, cutting the bottoms at the same angle as the roofline. Set each one of the posts in place, checking for plumb, and toenailing them into the rafters, wall studs, and top plate.

Corner posts

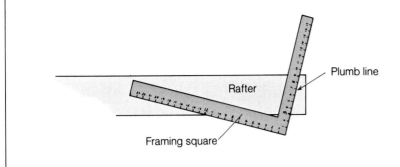

8. Marking for Rafter Cuts. Cut rafters from lumber sized to span the opening, usually 2 by 6 or 2 by 8. Mark the plumb cut for the top of the rafter with a framing square held against it, as shown. The measurement along the bottom of the square is 12 inches; along the vertical arm it is the same as the roof slope of the dormer (shown in the plan). Scribe a mark onto the rafter along the vertical arm of the square. Cut along that line.

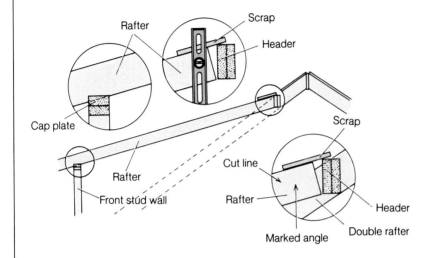

9. Alternative Marking Method. If you do not know the slope of the dormer, you can mark for the plumb cut by holding the rafter stock so that the bottom edge aligns with the inner edge of the cap plate, as shown. At the upper end, hold a piece of scrap wood along the top of the rafter so that it rests on the header. Position a straightedge against the rafter next to the header. Mark the plumb cut, cut the rafter, and check it for fit.

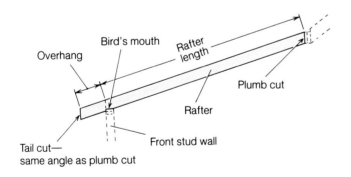

10. Cutting the Bird's Mouth. Position the rafter so that the plumb cut rests flush against the header and the lower edge intersects the inside edge of the cap plate of the wall. Trace a mark on the rafter against the top and outside edge of the cap plate. Cut out this notch, called the bird's mouth, and test the rafter for it. Make any adjustments and use this rafter for a pattern to cut the other rafters, except for the outside two.

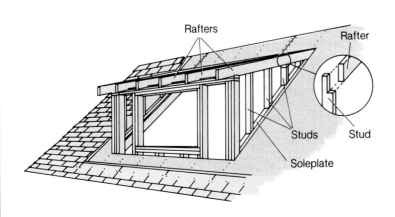

11. Installing the Rafters. Lay out the rafter locations along the cap plate and header, 16 or 24 inches on center, depending on the span. Secure the top ends to the header with joist hangers. Secure the bottom ends by toenailing into the cap plate. The tops of the end rafters should be angled to fit against the roofline. Close in the dormer by framing the end walls and installing sheathing, roofing, siding, and windows.

DRAINAGE

Improving the drainage outside your home will yield long-lasting benefits. Failure to correct inadequate drainage could lead to disastrous consequences ranging from drowned plants to structural damage.

Water is the major cause of structural problems in a home, such as decay, fungus, wood-destroying insects, and settling or upheaval of the foundation.

Provide drainage with surface ditches or underground pipes. Most underground drainage systems consist of continuous lengths of corrugated, flexible polyethylene pipe or 10- and 20-foot sections of rigid polyethylene pipe joined by fittings. Clay tiles and bituminized fiber pipe are less common. Perforated pipe collects subsurface water in the uphill portions of the system. Solid pipes connect to the perforated pipes and carry water to the discharge point.

Recommended Cross-References
Basements, Foundations, Gutters & Downspouts.

Use a corrugated drain line to lower a high water table, carry water away from low spots, or collect runoff from a slope.

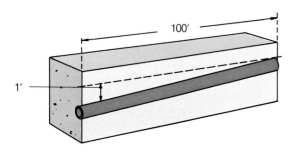

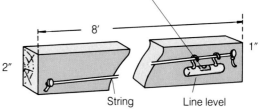

Note: When the bubble in the line level is centered, the board is at a pitch of 1' in 100'

8'

2"

1"

String   Line level

Yard Drainage

If natural surface drainage is inadequate or if the water table is very high, drain low spots with a system of buried pipes. To determine if the water table is high, dig a hole 12 to 18 inches deep. If it fills with water, the table is too high.

If the source of the water is a slope, place an underground interceptor line across the base of the slope to collect the water. Divert the water around and away from the house. If the water is concentrated in one spot, such as a low area in the yard or a window well next to your

basement, install a small catch basin at that point and run a drain line.

To plan a drain line, first determine where you want to discharge the water. A street gutter, a drainage ditch, and a swale are potential discharge sites. Do not discharge water onto your neighbor's property. If you cannot divert it from your property, dig a dry well to percolate water beneath the clay or hardpan that prevents natural seepage.

Lay the drain lines back from the outfall. If you have only one low spot, one line will do. Always install a cleanout in the high end of the

system. Cleanouts work best with smooth-walled pipe; ribbed pipe may be damaged by cleaning tools. Dig the trenches so the pipe will slope toward the outfall at a rate of 1 foot per 100 feet. Make a portable gauging device to help you measure the slope. Set an 8-foot 2 by 4 on edge. Tack a piece of string so one end is 1 inch below the top of the board and the other end is 2 inches below the top. Hang a line level on the string. When one end of the board is raised so the string is level, the board is at the proper slope for the drain line.

Foundation Drainage

Always install drain lines when you build a new foundation. If an existing foundation has moisture problems, try to resolve them by improving surface drainage. A little detective work may save you some labor. If all the moisture concentrates along an upslope wall, a diversion line farther up the yard may eliminate the need to excavate against the foundation. Measure the effectiveness of the new line by taping squares of plastic on the wall in several places. If moisture accumulates behind most of them, it will be necessary to dig around the foundation and apply waterproofing as well as installing the drainage system.

Excavate to the base of the footing, but not below it. Slope the trench 1 to 2 inches per 100 inches. End the line in a catch basin or drainage ditch downslope from the house.

Place 2 inches of sand or 1 inch of drain rock in the bottom of the trench before you lay the pipe. Use 4-inch pipe that connects with fittings or 4-inch continuous flexible tubing. Use perforated pipe where you want to collect water and solid pipe to carry water away. Wrap the perforated pipe with filter material to prevent it from being clogged with mud.

Next, waterproof the walls. The old standbys of parging cement and asphalt are still around, but newer coatings are a better choice. These include plastic backed with clay as well as other membranes. If you must excavate near the foundation for a drain line, these membranes are much better than simply coating a masonry wall. Protect it from gravel and other backfill with a 1/2-inch layer of rigid insulating foam.

Cover the pipe with 2 to 3 inches of drain rock. Place burlap or roofing felt over the rock to keep the topsoil from clogging it, then fill the trench with topsoil. Grade the area to slope away from the foundation.

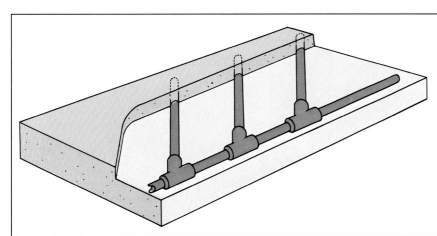

Herringbone Drainage Pattern

If you need to drain a large area in your yard, place perforated 4-inch pipes in a herringbone pattern. Space the branch lines 10 to 20 feet apart, sloping them toward the main trunk at a rate of 1 foot per 100 feet. Single or double Y-shaped connectors for either rigid or corrugated pipe are readily available from plumbing-supply stores. Construct the outfall section using unperforated pipe.

Cross Section of a Drain Line

A typical trench is 12 inches wide and as deep as needed. The pipe is surrounded by 1-inch drain rock, pea gravel, or a coarse sand and gravel mix. The type of fill depends on the size of holes in the pipe. Place the pipe so the holes are close to the bottom but not on it.

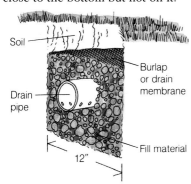

Soil

Drain pipe

Burlap or drain membrane

Fill material

12″

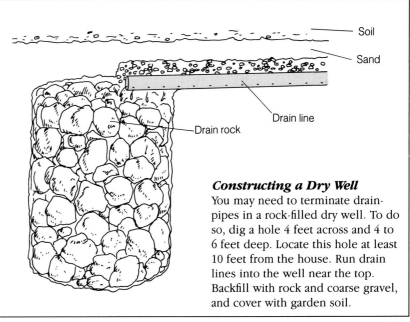

Soil

Sand

Drain line

Drain rock

Constructing a Dry Well

You may need to terminate drainpipes in a rock-filled dry well. To do so, dig a hole 4 feet across and 4 to 6 feet deep. Locate this hole at least 10 feet from the house. Run drain lines into the well near the top. Backfill with rock and coarse gravel, and cover with garden soil.

DRAWERS

A drawer is just a box made of five basic pieces: a front, a back, two sides, and a base. Construction can be simple, with butt joints and a laminated face or, if you want to practice your carpentry skills, the sides can be rabbeted to accept the back and front and dadoed to accept the base.

To achieve a tight fit, the following three points should be kept in mind when you construct a drawer:

● *Measure and cut all of the pieces* precisely; because the drawer fits into a restricted opening, there is little, if any, room for error.

● *Build a strong drawer.* Although some experts suggest leaving the bottom unglued to allow for expansion, it is best to glue all of the joints, including where the bottom meets the sides. Secure all joints with nails or clamps to ensure a strong bond.

● *Make sure the drawer slides easily;* it should not wobble or bind. If you use drawer slides or roller guides, align them very carefully. A grooved drawer that slides on wood rails will slide much more smoothly if the rails are coated with candle wax, soap, or some other lubricant.

Recommended Cross-References
Cabinets, Caulking & Adhesives, Hinges, Pulls & Knobs, Joinery.

Sequence of Construction

Choose a drawer design that you can build with confidence. The plans on this page show two basic designs that are easy to build and, because of the overlapping face piece, do not require a perfect fit to look well finished.

1. Determine the size of the drawer by measuring the opening carefully. As a rule of thumb, drawers should not be wider than 30 inches or deeper than 12 inches. If the opening is larger, divide it in half for two drawers.

2. Allow for any additional space needed for the sliding mechanism. Some are located on the top or bottom of the drawer and do not take up drawer space. Others, usually mounted on the sides of the drawer, require that the drawer be narrower so that they have room to clear the sides of the opening.

3. Measure and cut the sides to equal length and the front and back to equal length. The front and back normally fit between the sides to prevent heavy sliding objects from knocking them out.

4. Make a face for the drawer that is large enough to cover all the gaps around the drawer opening. It can be simple paint-grade plywood or a sanded and finished piece of dimension lumber. Glue it to the drawer front and screw it from the back with four short screws. This method is called paste-a-face.

5. Attach drawer guide hardware.

Joint Construction

A butt joint is the easier joint to make, but a rabbet joint will result in a much stronger drawer.

Butt Joint: 1. Cut the side, front, and back pieces out of 1-by lumber or ½-inch plywood.

2. Glue and screw the front and back between the sides, working on a flat surface to keep all edges even.

3. Cut the base out of ⅛-inch hardboard. Glue and nail it to the frame.

4. Cut the face from a piece of ½-inch plywood or other material 1 inch larger than the drawer front all around. Glue and screw in place.

5. Attach the drawer pull and all the drawer glide hardware.

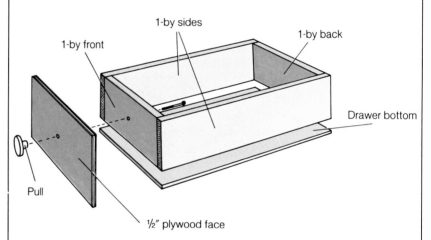

Pull
1-by front
1-by sides
1-by back
Drawer bottom
½" plywood face

Rabbet Joint: 1. Cut sides to length. Rabbet the ends, removing two thirds of the stock. Cut the front and back pieces. Try a dry-run assembly and make any necessary adjustments.

2. Cut grooves ½ inch up from the bottom on all four pieces. Make them wide enough to accept the base plus about one third of the thickness of the wood.

3. Cut the base, allowing for the depth of the grooves. Check for fit.

4. Put glue on all the joints and grooves. Assemble the pieces and secure them with finishing nails.

5. Attach drawer face, a pull, and all of the glide hardware.

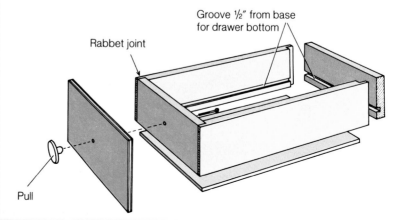

Rabbet joint
Groove ½" from base for drawer bottom
Pull

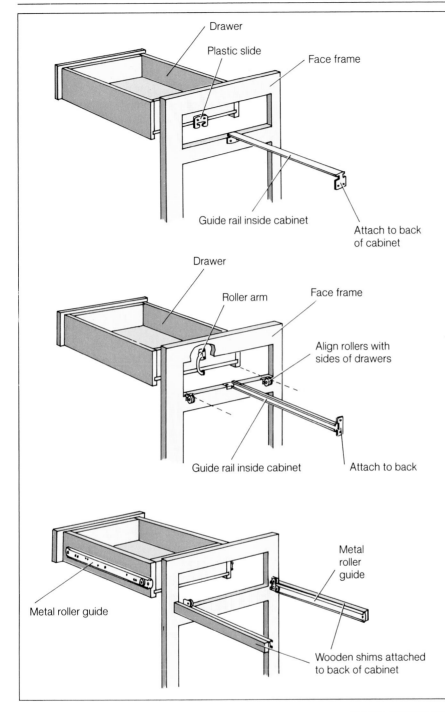

Drawer

Plastic slide

Face frame

Guide rail inside cabinet

Attach to back
of cabinet

Drawer

Roller arm

Face frame

Align rollers with
sides of drawers

Guide rail inside cabinet

Attach to back

Metal
roller
guide

Metal roller guide

Wooden shims attached
to back of cabinet

Guides

Center Slide Guide. This is the simplest type of guide. The drawer slides on the face frame, but is guided by a plastic slide that fits over a metal rail. To install, center the plastic slide on the back of the drawer and attach it with screws. Cut the guide rail to length and install it in the cabinet, making sure it is centered and level. Screw the brackets into the face frame and into the back of the cabinet.

Center Guide and Rollers. This drawer glides more smoothly because there are three rollers. The sides of the drawer glide on two of them, and the centered guiding mechanism attached to the back of the drawer is on a third roller.

Install the roller arm to the back of the drawer with screws. Attach the two side rollers to the face frame so that the tops barely protrude. Attach the guide to the front and back of the cabinet, measuring carefully to center and level it.

Side Roller Guides. With this smooth and stable mechanism, guides are attached to both the drawer sides and the sides of the cabinet opening. The drawer guides slide into the cabinet guides and glide on rollers.

Attach 1 by 2 wooden shims inside the cabinet so that the tops are the specified distance above the bottom rail of the face frame and the inside faces are flush with the sides of the opening. Attach the metal roller guides, then set the drawer into the opening and mark where the bottom of its guides line up with the cabinet's. Remove the drawer and attach the guides to the sides.

Rails and Grooves

This drawer has grooved sides that slide over rails attached to the inside of a cabinet. This method requires extreme precision in drawer construction. The drawer fronts must fit flush, rather than overlapping an opening, so all gaps between them must be narrow enough to look clean but wide enough to allow drawers to slide past each other. The cabinet sides must also be strong enough to keep the rails stable and

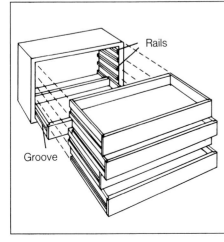

Rails

Groove

the drawers from wobbling.

The front pieces are the actual faces, and must be sized so the gap around them is no thicker than a matchbook cover. When the side pieces are cut and rabbeted, cut a groove along the outside of each piece. Center the groove. Then assemble the drawers.

Cut and tack the rails inside the cabinet. Test each drawer and make adjustments to the rails. Then glue and nail or screw them in place.

ELECTRICAL SYSTEM

Before you do any wiring you should have a basic understanding of the electrical system in your home. The following pages show how electricity enters your home, how it is distributed to the lights, switches, outlets, and appliances, and how safety backup systems, such as circuit breakers and ground wires, work.

Electricity deserves respect. You should take safety precautions whenever you work around it, obtain proper permits, and pay strict attention to all code requirements. This does not mean that it is an unpredictable force that must remain shrouded in mystery and ignorance. It is actually one of the simplest, most logical systems in your entire house, and can be very enjoyable to work on.

A basic understanding of your electrical system starts with the simplified notion that electricity must travel in circles. It starts somewhere, does some work somewhere else, and needs to return "home." The entire path is called a circuit.

Next you need to learn three basic terms: volts, amps, and watts.

Volts is a measurement of electrical pressure. In house wiring it is at a constant of 120 or 240 volts. Amps (amperes) is a measurement of the electricity flowing past a given point. For practical purposes, think of it as the number of electrons commuting to work. When the work demand is heavy, it is rush hour (high amperage); when there is no demand, traffic is slow (low amperage). Sometimes the highway gets overcrowded (overheating of a wire). This can cause serious problems unless a gatekeeper stops the flow of traffic (fuse blows).

In house wiring, the amperage rating usually refers to the amount of electricity a wire can handle before the protective system (fuse or circuit breaker) rescues it. For instance, if the whole house is rated at 125 amps, the main wires entering the meter are large enough for that much amperage. If the total demand in the house is higher, the wires overheat unless they are protected by a main breaker. If a circuit is rated at 20 amps, the wires can handle that much amper-age before the breaker automatically isolates the wire from the source of electricity.

Watts is a measurement of the actual power being used. It is what your meter measures and what you get billed for. Watts is the measurement commonly used for telling how much electricity an appliance or fixture will use when it is on.

One way to become familiar with these terms is to use them in a basic electrical formula, the only one you will need to know. It is easy to memorize, easy to use, and comes in handy lots of times: $Volts \times Amps = Watts$ ($V \times A = W$) or $Watts / Volts = Amps$ ($W / V = A$). With this formula, you can figure out how many amps a 240-volt clothes dryer will need if it is rated at 7,200 watts ($7,200 / 240 =$ ———). The answer is 30, which tells you how many amps the wire to the dryer will need to carry.

Recommended Cross-References
Doorbells, Lighting: Indoor & Outdoor, Receptacles, Switches, Wire, Wiring.

How You Get Electricity
Electricity enters the home through wires hung from a power pole or buried underground. Most homes are served by three wires: two "hot" wires of 120 volts each and one "neutral" wire that provides a return path to complete the electrical circuit. Such a system has 120 volts for normal household needs and the capability of 240 volts for heavy-duty appliances. Older homes that have two wires (one hot and one neutral) have only a 120-volt capability.

At the head of the electrical system is the meter. It is connected to the hot wires and measures incoming electricity. Next is the main disconnect, which allows you to turn off the entire electrical system. It might be a pull-down lever, a pull-out fuse block, or a large circuit breaker; it is located in a separate box by the meter or in the service panel. Local codes specify the location so that emergency crews can find it quickly.

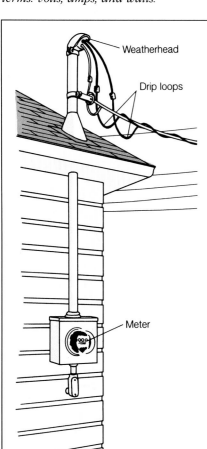

Weatherhead

Drip loops

Meter

Meter/Main Box

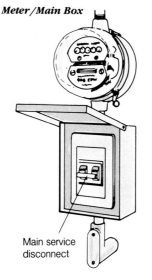

Main service disconnect

Service Panel

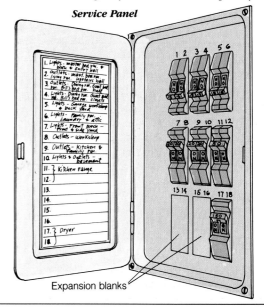

Expansion blanks

Inside the Service Panel

After the main disconnect, the electricity is distributed throughout the house by several circuits. The point of distribution is the service panel. In older homes it is a fuse box; in modern electrical systems it is a circuit-breaker panel. Subpanels may also be in the house for particular appliances or because of a room addition, but each one is connected to its own circuit breaker in the main service panel.

The illustration shows the inside of a typical combination service panel. For clarity, only one of the circuit breakers is shown in addition to the main disconnect. If the main disconnect is not in the panel, three large wires will still come from the meter and disconnect. In either case the two hot wires, at 120 volts each, are connected to two fingerlike bars in the middle of the panel. These are insulated from each other and from the rest of the panel by a heavy plastic shield. These fingers are called power buses and are controlled by the main disconnect switch.

The neutral wire (usually white) bypasses the main disconnect and attaches to a neutral bus bar. Because it provides an unbroken path for the safe return of electricity to the main power system, a neutral wire should never have a switch or any other device on it. The neutral bus is insulated from the box, and grounds in all boxes except the type that includes the main disconnect. In this box, the ground wires and neutral conductors (officially the grounded conductors) are joined or bonded together, and can even share the same bus bar.

In an old subpanel without a ground bar, check to see if the neutrals are insulated from the box. If there is no electrical continuity, you may add a ground bus bar if there is room. Run a ground wire from the bus bar to an approved ground. Check local code requirements. The job of the ground bus is to connect the system ground to ground wires from all the circuits.

Each circuit that is up to current code has its own hot wire and neutral wire and is grounded. The hot wire, which provides electricity to appliances or fixtures along the circuit, is connected to its own circuit breaker. The breaker, which is snapped onto a flange on the plastic shield, has contacts that grip one of the power buses. When the breaker is switched to the *on* position, power flows from the bus into the hot wire of the circuit. It completes its path by returning along the neutral wire to the neutral bus bar. The backup grounding wire or conduit is connected to the ground bus.

All the circuit breakers are arrayed along both sides of the plastic shield, drawing 120 volts from one power bus or the other. Any individual circuit can be deadened by tripping the circuit breaker. Circuits that require 240 volts have two hot wires connected to a double breaker. It has contacts that grip both power buses, so that each of its wires carries 120 volts. (No single wire carries 240 volts.) The size of the panel determines the number of circuit breakers in the system. When installing a panel, it is wise to have three or four blank spaces so that you can add extra breakers in the future.

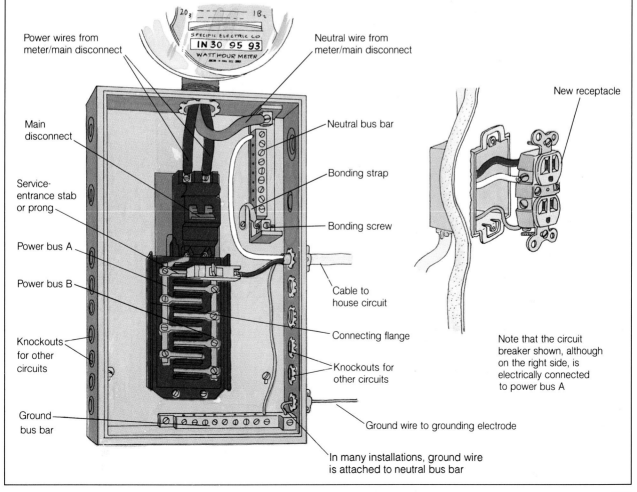

Power wires from meter/main disconnect

Neutral wire from meter/main disconnect

Main disconnect

Neutral bus bar

Bonding strap

Service-entrance stab or prong

Bonding screw

Power bus A

Power bus B

Cable to house circuit

Knockouts for other circuits

Connecting flange

Knockouts for other circuits

Ground bus bar

Ground wire to grounding electrode

New receptacle

Note that the circuit breaker shown, although on the right side, is electrically connected to power bus A

In many installations, ground wire is attached to neutral bus bar

Planning Circuits

Although it is possible to have all the lights and appliances in the house on one circuit, it is highly impractical. First, the system would have to have very large wires to handle the electrical demand. Second, if a fuse blew or a breaker tripped, everything in the house would shut down. In all new homes the electrical load is divided into several circuits.

The number of circuits depends on the size of the house and the number of major appliances. The National Electrical Code (NEC)® helps you find an answer by specifying the three types of circuits required: individual appliance, small appliance, and general-purpose.

Individual-Appliance Circuits. Any 240-volt appliances require their own circuits, as well as any 120-volt appliances and motors that are permanently installed. Each appliance must be served by its own circuit, and no other outlets, fixtures, or appliances can be wired onto that circuit. Each 120-volt circuit must be wired with No. 12 wire and protected by a 20-amp circuit breaker. The 240-volt circuits must have wire and breakers sized for the wattage of the particular appliance. The chart below gives the typical voltage, wire, and breaker size of appliances that require their own circuits.

Small-Appliance Circuits. Certain rooms of the house are required to have 20-amp circuits that are separate from the general-lighting circuits or individual-appliance circuits. Originally, the kitchen was the only room designated in this way, but with increasing use of high-wattage appliances throughout the house, the Code continually changes to include more rooms. The list now includes two such circuits for a kitchen, and one each for a dining room, a laundry room, a family room, and a breakfast nook. In some areas, all of the outlets in a house must be on 20-amp circuits that are separate from the lighting circuits.

General-Purpose Circuits. According to the Code, there must be one general-purpose circuit, sometimes called a lighting circuit, for every 600 square feet of floor space in the house, or 3 watts of power for every square foot. The Code also specifies a minimum of three such circuits, no matter how small the house.

It is common practice, however, to provide one circuit for every 500 square feet, even if it means a higher cost initially. This saves expensive upgrading later on and reduces any chance of overloading circuits. And if you are even remotely considering expanding living space into the garage or attic, you should include these areas in your electrical planning as well.

The Code allows these circuits to be wired with No. 14 wire and 15-amp breakers, but if they include receptacles as well as lights, you might want to use No. 12 wire with 20-amp breakers for higher capacity. Using the $V \times A = W$ formula, you can calculate the difference:
120 volts $\times$ 15 amps = 1,800 watts
120 volts $\times$ 20 amps = 2,400 watts
If you use No. 12 wire, it is possible to accommodate an additional 600 watts per circuit.

Calculating Amperage Needs

If you are sizing a service panel, the number of circuits will only tell you how large a panel to buy for it to have enough blanks for all the breakers. You will also need to know how large the main breaker–entrance conductors should be. The Code has a formula for calculating amperage.

1. List the wattage of each circuit, allowing for the following adjustments:
2. Add the total.
Total watts = 40,800
3. Subtract the first 10,000 watts.
40,800 − 10,000 = 30,800
4. Find 40 percent of the remainder.
30,800 $\times$ .40 = 12,320
5. Add back the first 10,000 watts.
12,320 + 10,000 = 22,320
6. To find amps, divide the total by 240 volts. 22,320 / 240 = 93 amps

In this example, then, the entrance wires and main breaker should be large enough for at least 100 amps. Just to be safe, it would be better to use 125 amps.

If you have an electrical heating or cooling system, add the higher wattage of the two to the total of step 5 above.

Appliances Requiring Individual Circuits

Appliance (Amps)	Typical Voltage	Wire Size (Copper-AWG)	Breaker Size
Kitchen range	240	6	50
Built-in oven	240	8	40
Cooktop	240	8	40
Water heater	240	10	30
Clothes dryer	240	8	40
Central electric heat	240	6	50
Air-conditioning	240	8	40
Food freezer	120	12	20
Dishwasher	120	12	20
Garbage disposer	120	12	20
Trash compactor	120	12	20
Fixed bathroom heater	120/240	12	20
Furnace motor	120	12	20
Well pump	120	12	20
Any permanent appliance rated at more than 1,000 watts	120	12	20

Calculating Size of Electrical Service

Circuit	Adjustment	Example (Watts)	
General purpose	3 watts per square foot	1,500 sq ft house =	4,500
Small appliance	1,500 watts each circuit	2 K, 1 DR, 1 Laundry =	6,000
Kitchen range	Check name plate		12,000
Clothes dryer	Check name plate		5,000
Dishwasher	Check name plate		1,500
Garbage disposer	Check name plate		800
Water heater	Check name plate		5,000
Central heating	65% of total rating	Rating = 9,230 $\times$ .65 =	6,000
Central air conditioner	Don't add if heating is electric; otherwise, 100%		

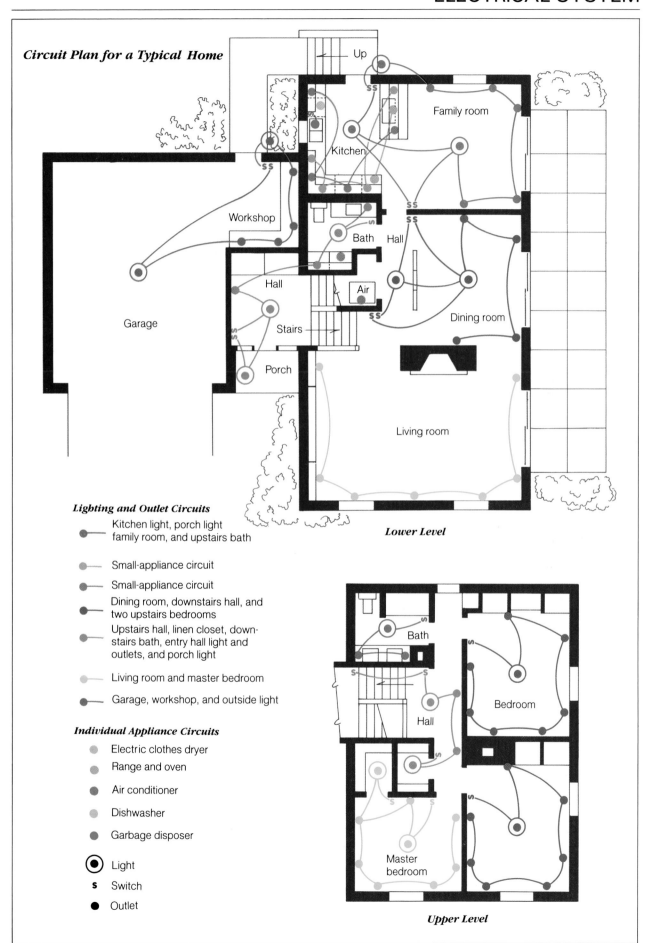

Circuit Plan for a Typical Home

Up

Family room

Kitchen

Workshop

Bath   Hall

Hall

Air

Garage

Stairs

Dining room

Porch

Living room

Lower Level

Lighting and Outlet Circuits

Kitchen light, porch light family room, and upstairs bath

Small-appliance circuit

Small-appliance circuit

Dining room, downstairs hall, and two upstairs bedrooms

Upstairs hall, linen closet, downstairs bath, entry hall light and outlets, and porch light

Living room and master bedroom

Garage, workshop, and outside light

Individual Appliance Circuits

Electric clothes dryer

Range and oven

Air conditioner

Dishwasher

Garbage disposer

⊙ Light

s Switch

● Outlet

Bath

Hall

Bedroom

Master bedroom

Upper Level

The Grounding System

Electricity follows the path of least resistance, usually the hot and neutral wires. When a neutral wire is broken or cannot provide an easy path for electricity to return "home" on, or when a hot wire comes loose, the electrical charge in the hot wire seeks an alternative path to complete its circuit. Because the earth itself will complete the circuit, the charge will jump through anything that touches the ground. This is dangerous. The hot wire may cause persistent sparking, or it may be dangerously idle, waiting for a path to discharge.

The job of the grounding system is to provide that easy path, diverting the charge to the ground so quickly that the sudden surge in the wires causes the circuit breaker to overload and trip. Ground wires accompany all hot and neutral wires and must be connected to every receptacle, switch, fixture, and appliance.

These wires converge at the ground bus bar, which is connected to the ground by a No. 6 or larger wire. The critical link in the entire system is the connection of this wire to the ground itself. A cold-water pipe used to be sufficient, but plastic plumbing materials now make it necessary to augment this connection with at least one of the connections shown here. These are all called grounding electrodes. Many local codes require that the ground wire continue uninterrupted to a second ground, such as additional rod or water pipe.

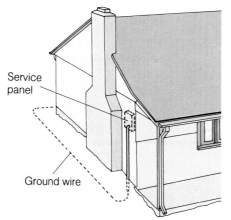

Buried. Connect the ground wire coming from the service panel to No. 2 or larger copper wire buried 2½ feet deep for 20 or more feet alongside the house.

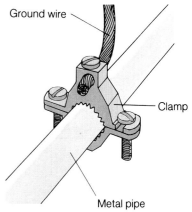

Attached to Pipe. Slip large ground wires into a clamp connected to a metal cold-water pipe. A bonding jumper may be required at the water meter.

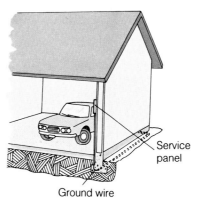

Attached to Rebar. Connect the ground wire from the service panel to 20 feet or more of ½-inch steel rebar or No. 4 or larger solid copper wire enclosed in concrete, usually the foundation of the house.

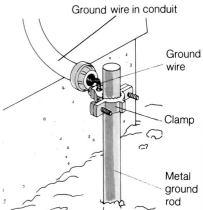

Ground Rod. Connect the ground wire to an approved copper or copper-clad ground rod driven to a depth required by local code.

Electrical Surges

Surges (sudden increases in power) can destroy the microprocessors used in microwave ovens, refrigerators, ranges, VCRs, personal computers, and televisions. Surges are produced by changes in power transmission through the lines, electric motors switching on in the house, and lightning strikes on telephone or power lines. Surges happen so quickly they may not be noticed, but even small ones have a cumulative effect.

Protection from small surges can be accomplished with multiple-outlet strips ("power strips") that plug into wall outlets. These work by dumping the excess current, sometimes into the ground conductor. They wear out and need to be replaced occasionally. The best ones come with a test button to tell you whether they are still working.

There are also surge protectors that can handle the large loads caused by lightning strikes. These are slower to respond but have high capacity. Check with your local electric utility before installing this type of protector. If lightning storms are common in your area, you may want to install a high-capacity surge protector in addition to the plug-in types that handle small surges.

Surge protectors should be listed by Underwriters' Laboratories (UL).

Using a Voltage Tester

This handy device lights up whenever household current passes through it. Use it to test whether wires or devices are hot and to see if outlets are properly grounded. To test for current, hold one of the prongs against a known ground and touch the other prong to all wires and connections. If the tester lights up, the wire is hot. Try all possible combinations with both prongs.

To check for proper grounding, hold one prong in the short (hot) slot of a receptacle and touch the other prong to the grounding hole and then the faceplate screw. It should light up both times.

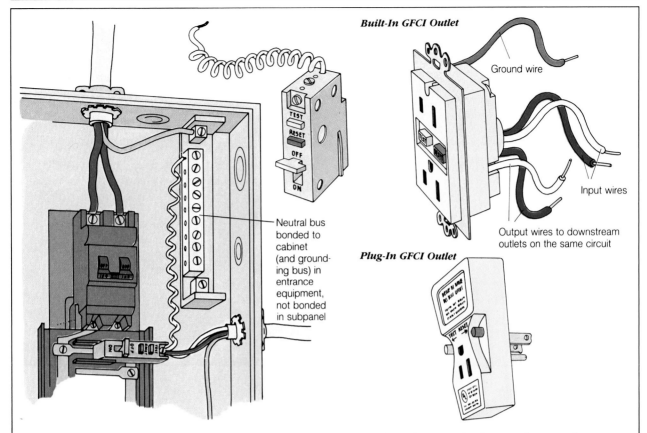

Built-In GFCI Outlet

Ground wire

Input wires

Output wires to downstream outlets on the same circuit

Neutral bus bonded to cabinet (and grounding bus) in entrance equipment, not bonded in subpanel

Plug-In GFCI Outlet

Ground Fault Circuit Interrupters

The Code now requires that all receptacles located in the bathroom, outdoors, by the kitchen sink, and in the garage be protected by a GFCI device. Also check your local code; it is possible that there are additional locations requiring this device.

A GFCI constantly monitors the circuit for any voltage leaks that might cause shock, and shuts off the outlet or circuit that it is protecting. You can reset it by pushing a button on the device. There are three ways that you can protect outlets: with a portable device that plugs into an ordinary receptacle, with a built-in outlet, and with a circuit breaker that protects the entire circuit.

Safety and Common Sense

The grounding system should never be considered a blanket insurance policy against electrical hazards, particularly when you are doing electrical wiring. The best backup system is caution and common sense. These safety rules are the most vital aspect of any electrical work.

The Circuit. Always deaden the circuit you are working on. Trip the breaker or remove the fuse. Then padlock the box shut or post a sign on it to warn others that you are working on that circuit.

The Wires. Before touching any wires, make sure they are dead by checking with a voltage tester.

Tools. When working with electricity, use plastic- or rubber-handled tools.

Damp Floors. Never stand on a wet or damp floor while working with electricity. Instead, stand on a rubber mat or dry boards.

Touching Pipes. Never touch any plumbing or gas pipes when working with electricity.

Ladders. Avoid using aluminum ladders near overhead entrance wires.

Rubber Gloves. Wear rubber gloves when working in the service box. A slip of a bare finger could put you in contact with a hot wire.

Service Panel. Make sure the service panel is securely screwed to the wall. It could slip unexpectedly and catch you unaware.

Fuses. Never use a fuse with an amperage rating higher than that specified for the circuit.

Plugs. Always pull the plug, not the cord, out of an electrical socket. Teach children to do the same.

Extension Cords. Avoid running extension cords across doorways or other traffic corridors or under rugs.

Grounded Fixtures. Never touch faucets or other grounded fixtures while holding an electric razor, hair dryer, or other appliance.

GFCI Outlets. When using power tools outdoors or on concrete floors in contact with the earth, always make sure the electrical outlet is GFCI protected.

Voltage Tester. After completing any electrical work, turn on the power and use a voltage tester to check your work. Buy two or three of them and keep them handy.

FANS

Whole-House Attic Fan
Two people can install a whole-house attic fan fairly easily. The fan will increase the comfort level throughout your house, satisfy all your cooling needs on many days, and give your air conditioner a boost when the days are especially hot. Unlike a ceiling fan, which only circulates air within the house, a whole-house fan requires that the attic and house be open to each other in order to ventilate.

Recommended Cross-References
Cooling, Insulation, Ventilation, Wiring.

Attic Fan
Unlike a whole-house fan, an attic fan ventilates only the attic. It is not intended as a substitute for vents, but it does enhance their ability to release pent-up heat from the attic.

Bathroom Fans
An exhaust fan is desirable in any bathroom, and it is required in bathrooms that have no windows that can be opened. All bathroom fans should be ducted to the outside through a roof or nearby wall. If possible, listen to a fan of the model you select before buying; some are objectionably noisy.

Air Circulation
Moving air replaces stale air and odors in a home. Air movement is important for body comfort in hot weather, and moving air cools surfaces and furnishings, reducing the amount of radiant heat in a room. Fresh moving air also inhibits the growth of mildew and other fungi that can damage a house. The air within a home should be exchanged completely at least once each hour, although two or three complete exchanges are preferable. Bathroom fans should exchange the air in a bathroom completely every 5 minutes.

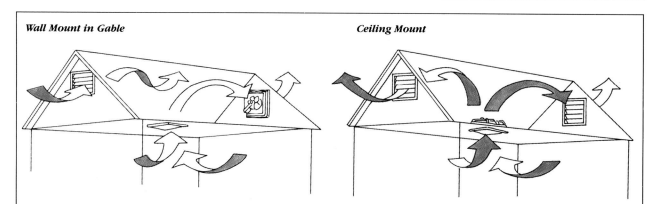

Wall Mount in Gable

Ceiling Mount

Whole-House Fan Locations
To use any of these installations, you must have two air passages—one from the living space to the fan and another from the fan to the outside. Fans are usually 24 inches, 30 inches, or 36 inches in diameter and, when in position, should have at least 2 to 3 inches of clearance above them. Be sure to follow the manufacturer's instructions.

A fan draws air from all parts of the house. Some doors or windows must be open before you turn on your fan, or pilot lights may go out and the air flow may draw soot from your chimney. If the fan is in a spot where children or animals could reach it, be sure to put a barrier or safety cage around the fan.

Before you begin work, be sure you have complete instructions from the manufacturer. In most cases you will need to run a separate electrical circuit for the fan; check with your local building department. Each fan style requires its own method of installation. The steps shown on the opposite page are common for most installations, however.

Installing a Bathroom Fan
Set the housing in place between two ceiling joists. Install a termination cap in the wall or in the roof by cutting a hole approximately 4½ inches in diameter through the sheathing and attaching the cap from the outside. Run 4-inch flexible duct from the fan housing to the termination cap, using a tightening band or sheet-metal screws to secure it at each end.

Run a two-wire No. 12 feeder cable from the fan to the circuit-breaker panel. Then run cable from the fan to a switch box on the wall. Use one 2-wire, one 3-wire, or two 2-wire cables (all with ground

wires), depending on how many switches are needed to control the fan motor, the radiant-heat lamp, the light, and so on. Because all of the wires in this switch loop will be hot, mark any white wires with black electrical tape.

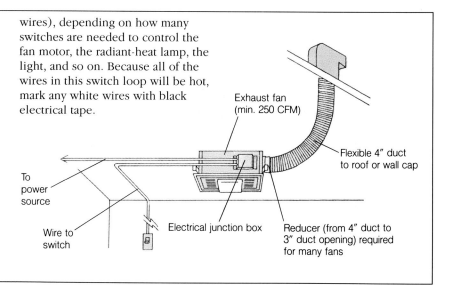

Exhaust fan (min. 250 CFM)

Flexible 4" duct to roof or wall cap

To power source

Wire to switch

Electrical junction box

Reducer (from 4" duct to 3" duct opening) required for many fans

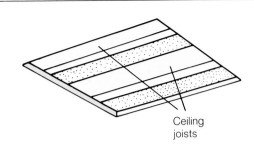

Ceiling
joists

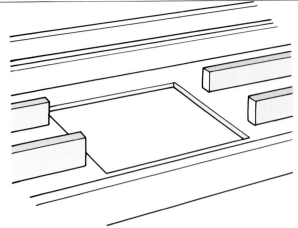

Installing a Whole-House Fan

1. Cut an opening in the ceiling the same size as the fan shutter. If the attic is insulated, use plastic sheeting or pieces of plywood to make baffles to hold insulation back. If the insulation is loose fill, check with the fan manufacturer about the advisability of installing the fan.

2. Cut sections out of the ceiling joists where the fan fit. Cut joists so there will be 1½ inches of clearance around the opening.

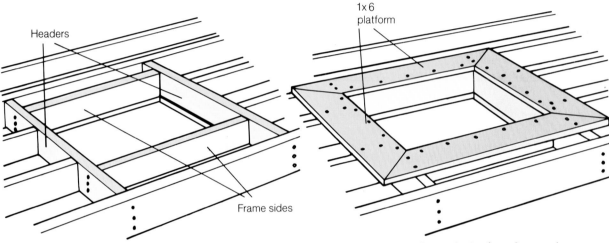

Headers

Frame sides

1x6
platform

3. Support the cut joists with headers between the full-length joists. Double up any headers that span more than 4 feet. Frame the other two sides of the opening by installing blocking between the headers.

4. Build a platform of 1 by 6s to fit over the framing. Miter the corners so that the available framing will support the platform.

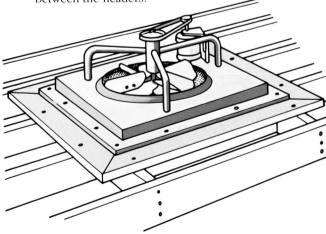

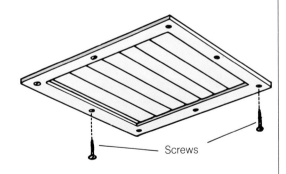

Screws

5. Set the fan in place, toenailing through the frame to secure it. Then run wiring for the fan. If you use nonmetallic cable, run the cable through holes drilled in the centers of the joists or staple cable beside the joists. If you run cable over the tops of the joists, nail 1 by 4s next to the cable to form a shield.

6. Install the shutter from below, driving wood screws through the ceiling into the frame.

FASTENING HARDWARE

In any project, the right connectors save effort and ensure a lasting job. Fasteners are perhaps the most essential components of a project, but they are often last-minute additions to the materials list or may not even appear on it. The selection here shows the major types of fasteners you will find at a hardware store and will help you choose the right ones. The selection is by no means complete, but you can augment it with common sense and attention to these guidelines:

● Use your tape measure to determine sizes if you aren't familiar with the antique classification systems that some fasteners use: Sort nails by pennyweight, or d, and screws by gauge, or number (No.).

● In many cases a substitute fastener will do, although one is usually more appropriate than all the others. The best fastener is the strongest, the most attractive, and the easiest to install.

● If you intend to do many projects, buy more fasteners than you need for one project. You will build up an inventory that could save you many trips to the store. When you buy in bulk you may also save money.

● Any nails, bolts, or screws that you use outdoors should be of high-quality, corrosion-resistant materials.

● Adhesives are an excellent type of fastener. Many adhesives are stronger and more convenient than the metal fasteners they replace. Adhesives have become indispensable. You will use adhesives to attach paneling, wallboard, subflooring, decking, furring strips, molding, countertops, and rigid insulation.

Recommended Cross-References
Most entries.

Bolts

Bolts require nuts (usually with washers) to complete a connection. They are specified by diameter, length, and the number of threads per inch. Carriage bolts have a round head for a more attractive appearance. The heads of machine bolts fit into a wrench, so they are easier to tighten.

Lag Screws

Usually larger than conventional screws, lag screws are driven by a wrench. They do not require nuts, but usually have washers.

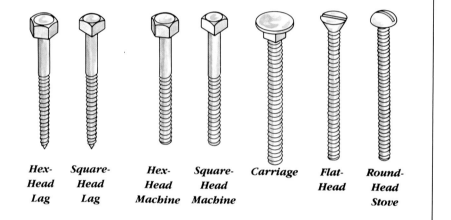

Hex-Head Lag   **Square-Head Lag**   **Hex-Head Machine**   **Square-Head Machine**   **Carriage**   **Flat-Head**   **Round-Head Stove**

Specialized Fasteners

Fasteners exist for particular situations, such as fastening to concrete or wallboard.

Expansion Shields. The most common method of attaching to concrete uses an expansion shield and a lag screw. Drill a hole into the concrete with a rotary hammer. Place the shield in the hole, insert the lag screw through the bracket or furring strip into the shield, and then tighten the screw.

Anchor Bolts. These are used with concrete or masonry. Drill a hole into the surface the same diameter as the anchor and at least ½ inch longer than the distance the anchor will penetrate. Clean dust from the hole. Drive in the anchor with a nut and washer on it. Tighten the nut to expand the base. The anchor should tighten without rotating to develop its rated withdrawal resistance.

Toggle Bolts. Also known as butterfly bolts, these use a folding nut that can be pushed through a small hole, then unfolded to grip the backside of the surface being fastened to. The bolt should be inserted through the piece being fastened before the nut is inserted into the hole.

Hollow Wall Anchors. Drill a hole the same diameter as the anchor. Insert the anchor with the screw and tighten the screw to expand the anchor and lock it in place. Remove the screw, insert it through the piece being attached, and reinstall the screw in the anchor.

Plastic Anchors. Drill a hole and insert the anchor. Install the screw with the piece being attached. Tightening the screw expands and secures the anchor.

Screw Anchors. These are used with wallboard only. Screw the anchor into the wall, then install the screw.

Drive Anchors. These are also used with wallboard only. Drive the anchor as you would a nail. Its legs will expand and secure it when a screw is driven into it.

Hot-Melt Anchors. These are used to fasten lightweight objects only. They are quick and easy to use and do not leave holes in walls.

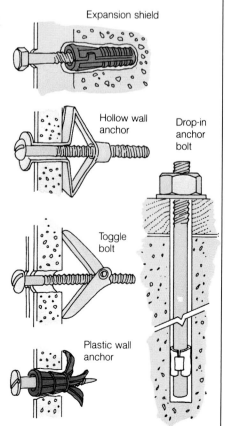

Expansion shield

Hollow wall anchor

Drop-in anchor bolt

Toggle bolt

Plastic wall anchor

Nails

Each type of nail comes in various lengths, designated by the term *penny* (d). It is not known whether this term derives from the cost (pence), or the weight (pennyweight). Most types are bright (uncoated steel that rusts easily); better ones are coated with zinc to prevent corrosion; and the best are hot dipped rather than electroplated. Some nails also come in copper, aluminum, or stainless steel, and some have a vinyl cement coating making them easier to drive.

Nails come by the pound or in 50-pound cases. If planning a large project, buy 16d nails by the case—you will find many uses for this basic framing nail. (For outdoor projects, buy hot-dipped galvanized ones.)

The nails shown are suitable for the following purposes:
Casing. Trim where the head does not countersink.
Finishing. Trim, cabinetry.
Box. Sheathing, siding, exterior trim.
Masonry. Concrete, stucco, brick.
Wallboard. Wallboard.
Roofing. Composition roofing and building paper.
Aluminum Roofing. Aluminum roofing, skylights, and flashing.

Brads. Molding, paneling, parquet.
Common. Framing, construction.
In addition to the nails shown, you can also get the following:
Cut. Flooring and concrete block.
Concrete. Furring, sleepers.
Corrugated Fastener. Picture frames.
Duplex. Temporary bracing, scaffolds, and foundation forms.
Flat-Head Wire Brad. Thin veneers.
Ring-Shank. Plywood subflooring and floor repairs.
Spiral-Shank. Floors, some framing.

Note—nailing instructions often include the term ''o.c.'' meaning on center

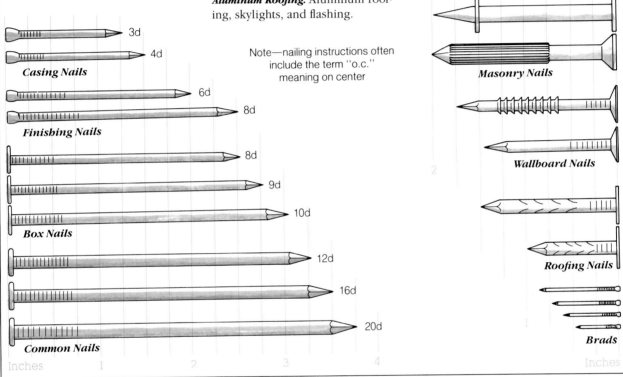

3d
4d
Casing Nails

6d
8d
Finishing Nails

8d
9d
10d
Box Nails

12d
16d
20d
Common Nails

Inches   1   2   3   4   Inches

Masonry Nails

Wallboard Nails

Roofing Nails

Brads

Screws

Oval-head
Round-head
Slotted
Flat-head
Bugle-head
Wallboard screw
Robertson square drive
One-way
Phillips-head

The three basic types of screws are wood screws, sheet-metal screws, and drive screws, but different sizes, gauges, heads, points, and materials create dozens of variations. You should keep an assortment on hand.

Among wood screws, slotted-head screws are the most common, but Phillips-head screws are easier to drive and do not damage as readily. Robertson, or square-drive, screws offer the surest grip for driving.

Some sheet-metal screws have hex heads for driving with a nut driver. Self-drilling screws have a special groove point that enables them to cut their way through sheet metal without requiring a pilot hole.

Drive screws, also called wallboard screws or bugle-heads, were developed for use with power screwdrivers and have taken the place of nails for many carpentry and woodworking applications. The screw shank is threaded and tapered all the way to the head and has a very sharp point for easy starting. The head flares into a bugle shape for countersinking. A small-sized variation is the trim head, which is small enough to be hidden in the wood when countersunk. Drive screws are available for driving into wood or sheet metal, have Phillips or Robertson heads, and come in many different sizes, coatings, and strengths.

FAUCETS & VALVES

Installing or repairing a faucet is an easy project that gives instant results. You know if everything is working as soon as you turn on the water—sometimes sooner. The following pages present techniques for installing, replacing, and repairing most types of faucets and valves.

Some faucets (such as hose bibbs, laundry faucets, and most tub or shower valves), attach directly to the water pipes of the house. To install or repair them, you have to shut off the main valve. Other faucets (such as kitchen sinks, washbasins, and some tub or shower valves) have intermediate stops close to the fixture for turning off the water. If you install new plumbing, you will have to attach stops before you hook up the faucets.

Types of Faucets

All faucets—tub faucets, sink faucets, hose faucets, and so on—fall into two categories distinguished by how they work. One type is the compression faucet, which has a revolving handle that opens and closes a stem against an opening inside called a valve seat. The stem has a washer on it that fits tightly against the valve seat when the faucet is closed. When the washer wears from age and use, it does not fit tightly and the faucet leaks. Use a compression faucet for hose bibbs, washing machine hookups, and any dual-handle sink fixtures.

The second type of faucet is a mixing faucet. This is sometimes called a washerless faucet. Instead of screwtype handles, the mixing faucet has a single lever or knob that adjusts both temperature and flow of the water. Although several different designs are available, all mixing faucets close off the hot- and cold-water ports with a sliding mechanism rather than a stem and washer that screw down against a seat. Because the sliding mechanism is simple and not subject to the grinding action found in a compression fixture, a mixing faucet lasts longer without repair. Most contemporary homes use mixing faucets for sinks, bathtubs, showers, and washbasins.

Recommended Cross-References
Bathtubs, Pipe, Plumbing, Showers, Sinks & Garbage Disposers, Washbasins.

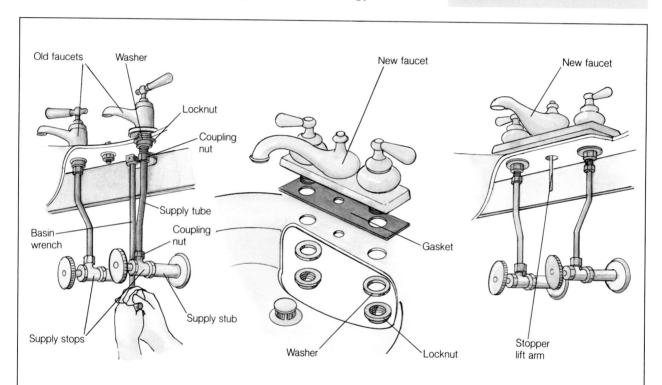

Installing Sink Faucets

Sink faucets have fittings on the bottom that extend down through the sink deck. Be sure the spacing of the fittings matches the spacing of the holes in the sink. Holes in most sink decks are either 4 inches apart or 8 inches apart.

1. Removing Old Faucets. Turn off the supply stops. Then, using a basin wrench, disconnect the old faucets. Most sinks have 3/8-inch supply tubes with 1/2-inch nuts.

2. Attaching the Faucet. If you are putting in a new sink, it is easier to install the faucet before placing the

sink. If the sink is already in place, however, use a basin wrench, a tool that enables you to reach up into the narrow space behind the sink to tighten or loosen the locknuts and compression nuts.

To install a faucet, slide the sealing gasket over the fittings and insert them down through the holes in the sink. Some faucets come equipped with long supply tubes instead of threaded fittings; guide the tubes through the center hole. To make the seal more watertight, apply a bead of tub caulk around the bottom edge of the faucet before positioning it.

Secure the faucet to the sink deck by screwing the locknuts to the fittings from below. Some models have separate mounting bolts that are not part of the plumbing fittings.

3. Installing the Supply Tubes. Attach the supply tubes to the fittings with coupling nuts. Connect the faucet fittings to the supply tubes from the hot- and cold-water stops, using the compression nuts that are supplied with the faucet. Bend the tubes gently so that they are in alignment with the fittings. Tighten the nuts until they are secure.

Supply Stops

The most difficult aspect of working with supply stops is deciding which kind to buy. Three variable features distinguish them. The first is the direction of flow. On some stops the inlet and outlet are in a straight line. On angle stops, the inlet and outlet are at a right angle. Angle stops are the most common for sinks.

The second variable is the type of inlet. The size must match the size of the pipe, which is usually ½ inch. Some inlets are threaded to screw onto iron pipe (IP) or a male adapter. Others have a compression fitting that you attach to copper pipe.

The third variable is the type of outlet, which must match the size of the supply tube. Most supply tubes are ⅜ inch. Outlets have either slip-joint or compression fittings, depending on the type of supply tube. These are not interchangeable.

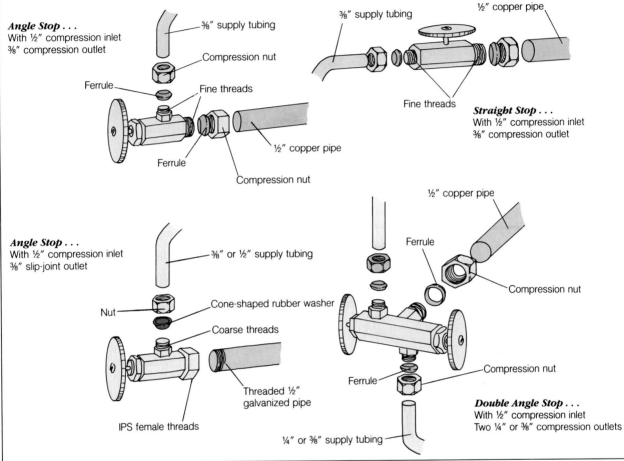

Angle Stop . . .
With ½" compression inlet
⅜" compression outlet

⅜" supply tubing
Compression nut
Ferrule
Fine threads
Ferrule
½" copper pipe
Compression nut

⅜" supply tubing
Fine threads
½" copper pipe

Straight Stop . . .
With ½" compression inlet
⅜" compression outlet

Angle Stop . . .
With ½" compression inlet
⅜" slip-joint outlet

⅜" or ½" supply tubing
Nut
Cone-shaped rubber washer
Coarse threads
Threaded ½"
galvanized pipe
IPS female threads

½" copper pipe
Ferrule
Compression nut
Ferrule
Compression nut
¼" or ⅜" supply tubing

Double Angle Stop . . .
With ½" compression inlet
Two ¼" or ⅜" compression outlets

Installing a Hose Bibb

If you run a new pipe to the bibb, terminate it with a threaded nipple or male adapter. If the bibb has male threads, attach a coupling to the pipe. Apply joint compound and screw on the bibb. Many localities require hose bibbs to be of the siphon-breaker type. This prevents contaminants from being sucked into the water system if pressure drops. Freeze-proof hose bibbs are recommended for cold climates.

Installing a Supply Stop on Copper Pipe

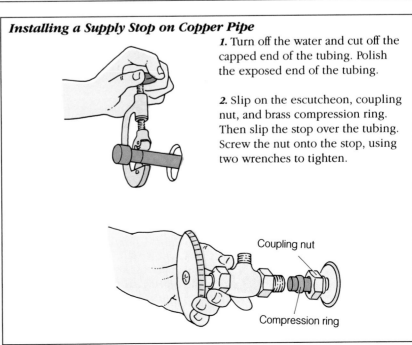

1. Turn off the water and cut off the capped end of the tubing. Polish the exposed end of the tubing.

2. Slip on the escutcheon, coupling nut, and brass compression ring. Then slip the stop over the tubing. Screw the nut onto the stop, using two wrenches to tighten.

Coupling nut
Compression ring

FAUCETS & VALVES: continued

Installing Tub/Shower Faucets

Tub and shower faucets (called valves by plumbers because pipe attaches to both inlet and outlet) are installed at the same time as the rough plumbing. The faucets come in several styles. Your selection will depend on whether you want to control the spout and shower functions with one, two, or three handles. The plumbing for all three arrangements is basically the same. The installation consists of connections to the hot and cold supply pipes and outlet connections for the tub spout, showerhead, or both.

When you buy the valve, specify whether the fittings should be IP (for threaded iron pipe) or CU (for copper tubing). Run pipes for the showerhead and spout as part of the rough plumbing. Then attach short nipples to the elbows. When the bathroom walls are finished, replace the nipples with the spout and showerhead and install the handles.

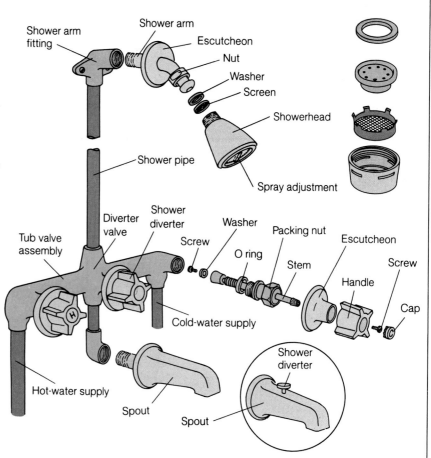

Types of Valves

Valves are a real necessity in several places in the home. A main valve allows you to turn off all the water entering your home. A valve in the inlet pipe of a water heater allows you to isolate the water heater from the rest of the plumbing system.

Some valves serve special functions. The bleeder valve, also called a stop-and-waste or drainable valve, has an outlet on the side. This allows you to backdrain the system when it is blocked. It also enables you to drain all water from the system—a necessity in cold-weather regions where pipes can freeze in winter.

A check valve is a one-way valve that prevents water from flowing back through it. In a domestic water system, use a check valve between the well and pump to keep water from draining back into the well.

A TPRV (temperature-pressure relief valve) is required on all water heaters to release built-up pressure. A PRV (pressure relief valve) is required on solar collectors, located at the topmost point of the system.

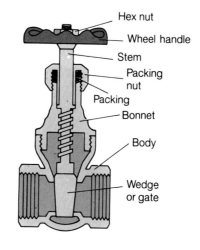

Gate Valve. Turning the handle of this valve causes a gate in the supply pipe to open or close. The gate valve does not have a baffle that distinguishes the inlet from the outlet. Because the water travels straight through, use gate valves where pressure is low; use a gate valve as a main valve or to connect a water heater.

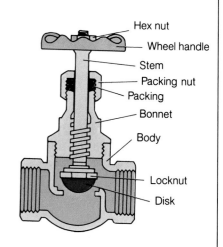

Globe Valve. A globe valve works like a compression faucet, with a hard washer that seats into an opening inside the valve. It regulates the rate of flow by adjusting the opening, and closes more tightly than a gate valve. The inlet and outlet sides are different; an arrow on the outside of the valve indicates the direction of flow.

Repairing a Faucet

You can improve the flow of water by cleaning the aerator—a simple maintenance chore. Just disassemble the aerator and clean out the holes with a pin or by blowing through them. Remember the sequence of parts so that you can put them back together correctly.

If a faucet leaks around the handle or does not shut off completely, the repair is a bit more involved. For compression faucets, which have handles that turn, remove the stem and replace the washer. On a combination faucet with two handles and one spout, you can determine which side needs repair by turning off the stops below the sink one at a time.

If you have a washerless faucet, the model of the fixture will determine the repair. Some have replaceable cartridges. Repair others with new seals and gaskets. Always bring old parts to the store when you look for new parts.

Compression Faucet

Turn off the water at the stop and remove the faucet handle and packing nut. If the handle is stubborn, pry gently on both sides with two screwdrivers, being careful not to damage the sink. Remove the stem. The bottom of the stem should contain the old washer held by a brass screw. Replace the washer with one of the same size. If the screw is missing or damaged, replace it with a brass screw. Because washers come in so many shapes and sizes, it is advisable to bring the valve to the store so you can try the new washer.

Check the seat for damage. It must be smooth. You can dress the seat with an inexpensive refacing tool. Or, if the fixture has an allen wrench fitting, you can remove and replace it.

If the faucet leaks around the handle or if the packing washer looks worn, replace the washer as well. If you are not able to find a replacement, a few coils of packing string around the worn washer will do.

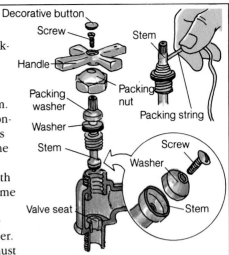

Seat Dressing

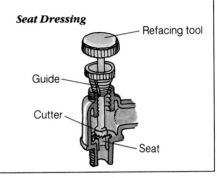

Washerless Faucets

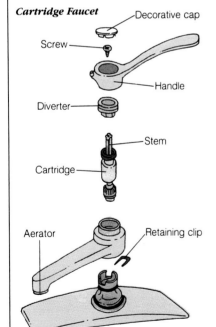

Cartridge Faucet. Cartridge faucets are of two types. Repair both kinds by replacing the cartridge.

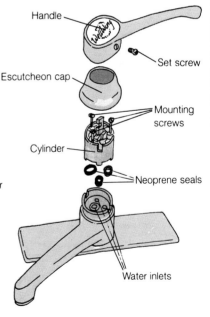

Ball Faucet. Worn gaskets cause most leaks in this type of faucet. The culprit is usually the large O-ring around the base or one of the small grommets inside. Use needle nose pliers to remove the smaller rings—be sure to keep track of the spring and seat.

Disk Faucet. A disk faucet has two plastic or ceramic disks, an upper one that can be rotated and a lower one that is part of the faucet body. Disk faucets depend on replaceable rubber seals, usually set into the fixed disk, to ensure a positive seal.

Compared with many home-improvement projects, a fence is not difficult to build. Once you master a few basic steps, the work is repetitive and proceeds at a comfortable pace.

What makes a good fence? It must be well built, easy to maintain, and long lasting. But it also has to be attractive and look like it belongs.

Reasons for Building a Fence

Most fences are intended to protect property, secure pets or children, and provide privacy. But it is important to clarify how a fence will accomplish these things. In some cases a low, open fence makes the home more secure than a tall fence, because neighbors can spot intruders. A fence around a swimming pool, on the other hand, generally has to be 4 to 6 feet tall in order to provide privacy and keep out small children.

Another reason for a fence is wind protection. A high, solid fence at the property line will not screen the wind from a patio 20 feet away, because the wind just swirls over the top and continues unabated. An open fence is actually better. It at least tames the wind, if not blocks it. The best solution is a tall fence directly adjacent to the area needing shelter. Screening out objectionable views is a good argu-

ment for a fence. You may find that the screen does not have to be full height to do so. Or a fence with staggered heights may be apropos because it blocks out some views but preserves desirable ones.

A fence can also provide shade, reflect light into dark rooms of the house, block unwanted noise, or even become a temporary barrier for heavy construction in the backyard. Each of these needs affects the shape, color, size, and construction of a fence.

Maintaining a Fence

Besides function, consider the maintenance. It is a mistake to base a fence design solely on cost. Nothing can make a property look more run-down than a sagging, warped fence. It pays to think in terms of longevity, even though the initial cost is greater.

Considering the Neighbors

Your new fence will affect your neighbors, just as their fences and yards affect how you design your fence. Before you start to build, talk with your neighbors. Sometimes this can lead to splitting costs. In order to maintaining good relations with neighbors, advise them that you plan to build and try to design a fence that will blend with their yard as well as yours.

Checking Height Requirements

Verify property lines and check deed restrictions and building codes for height and other requirements. Normally, fences on the front property line are limited to 42 inches high; side and back fences, up to 6 feet. A higher fence is allowed if it is set in from the property line and the height is within a 45-degree angle that begins at a point 6 feet above the property line.

Aesthetic Considerations

A fence should harmonize with its surroundings. It should be level if the ground is fairly level, and it should either step down or follow the contour of a steep slope. The size should be in proportion to the site, neither dominating nor being dwarfed by its setting. The materials should be in keeping with your home, whether it is rustic or formal, lively or subdued.

Recommended Cross-References
Concrete, Gates, Fastening Hardware, Garden Walls, Joinery, Siding, Wood.

This elegant fence (opposite) creates privacy and protection without being overwhelming. It consists of the basic fence components of posts, rails, and infill.

Building on a Slope

There are two ways to design a fence for sloping terrain. One is to make the fence parallel with the ground, framing each bay so it mirrors the slope. All posts and infill materials are the same length. This approach suits almost any terrain, whether it is steep, gentle, or irregular. Post-and-rail, narrow boards, pickets, stakes, and slats work best.

The second method is to step the fence down the slope. This method works best for gentle, even slopes. Posts are all the same length, but each bay is built so the top and bottom are level rather than parallel to the slope. Any kind of fencing material works, including infill materials that are set between the framing rather than nailed to it.

Both styles are attractive. The contour design looks more natural and flowing, the stepped design more architectural and crisp. A good way to judge which style will work is to draw the slope to scale on paper and sketch each type of fence on it.

A Low Picket Fence

This classic design fits almost any setting, either formal or informal. It also controls pets and children without obstructing views.

Set posts 6 to 8 feet apart. Cut them about 6 inches shorter than the fence height. Nail the top rail to the tops of the posts, the bottom rail between the posts, about 6 inches above the ground. The rails should be level. Pickets can sometimes be ordered from a lumberyard. If you cut your own, make simple pointed stakes with a circular saw or fancy shapes with a jigsaw. Stretch and level a string line across the bottom of the posts for aligning the pickets.

Stacked Rails

The rails can be 4 by 4s, 6 by 6s, or any other large-scale timbers. They are stacked on top of each other and either spiked together or threaded onto vertical pipes or rebar. The rows are staggered for stability.

Because it has no posts for stability, this fence works best with dimensioned timbers. For even more stability, pour a concrete foundation to set the bottom rails on. Attach the rails to each other by threading them over pipes set into the concrete or by nailing each rail into the one below it with 12-inch spikes. The length of the rails can vary. The ones shown here are 10 feet long.

Post-and-Rail

This traditional fence has several design variations and can be built from split or dimensioned lumber. One style has double posts with the rails wired between them, such as shown here. Others use mortise-and-tenon joints, which saves on the amount of lumber needed and allows the fence to move without breaking apart, but is quite difficult to build.

Dig holes for the double posts, and stretch a level string line for aligning the tops. Set the posts in place, secure them either with concrete or tightly-packed gravel, and cut the tops to length. Stack rails between the posts, as shown, setting the bottom rails on stones or nailing them to the posts so they are level. When all rails are in place, wire the tops of the posts tightly together with galvanized or copper wire.

Grapestake

The grapestake fence is usually made of split redwood and can be high or low. The grapestakes can extend above the framing for a ragged effect or be topped off by a cap rail for a more finished appearance.

Use 4 by 4 posts on 6-foot centers. Cut posts 3 or 4 inches shorter than the fence, and cap with a 2 by 4 rail. For a bottom rail, nail 2 by 4s between the posts, 6 to 18 inches above the ground. The top and bottom rails should be level, unless the fence follows a sloping contour. Nail grapestakes to the rails, at the top and the bottom.

Wire

A chain link fence is strong and provides good security, but it needs to be camouflaged with vines or other plantings. It is even stronger when threaded with lath pieces.

Another type of wire fence is made with welded wire fabric. This has rectangular openings available in various sizes, such as 2 by 4, 1 by 2, or larger.

Both chain link and welded wire mesh are available with vinyl coatings, either black or white, or in colors like brown or green. The brighter colors call attention to the fence, whereas the darker colors are more subdued.

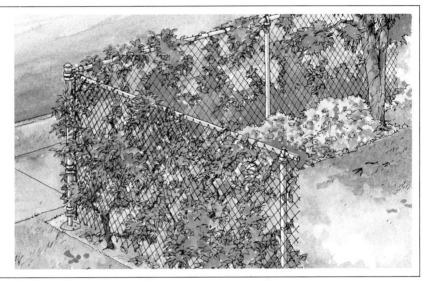

Translucent Panels

Plastic and fiberglass panels can be used for fences where retaining the view or natural light are critical. They are available either translucent or opaque. You can use these materials for the entire fence, or for a screen at the top. Remember that these materials are synthetic and should be used in natural settings with discretion. Some materials will discolor and scratch over time, but others are quite durable.

Posts should be set closer than in most other fences because the panels require a very rigid frame. Set them no more than 4 feet apart. Install the bottom and top rails, and any middle rails, so they are perfectly level as well as square to the posts. Use 2 by 2 nailers to hold the panels in place, and allow at least a 1/4-inch expansion gap all around.

Vertical Boards

Vertical boards offer design flexibility. They can be arranged in various patterns, either butted tightly together, spaced like slats, set in a slanted angle like louvers, or nailed on both sides of the framing in staggered fashion. Any size of dimension lumber can be used, although the larger sizes are stronger, more economical, and easier to install.

The most common construction is to use 4 by 4 posts and set them 8 feet apart. A top rail is set on top of the post, and a bottom rail installed between them. The fencing boards are then nailed to one side of the framing or the other. In some cases, they are nailed on both sides, or even installed between the rails.

Board-and-Batten

Vertical boards with battens nailed over the joints create a solid screen that is an effective sound barrier. A board-and-batten fence is also a good wind block. When the battens are the same size as the boards, the design is called board-on-board.

Use rough sawn boards. These are less expensive and cracks or defects are less obvious. The framework is the same as a vertical board fence, and the boards are mounted on it with gaps between them that will be covered up by the battens. The battens should overlap the board on each side by at least 1/2 inch.

Siding Material

Building a fence in the same material used to clad your house provides an integrated look.

If siding, such as shingles, is applied to both sides of the fence, the fence framing is the same as a stud wall. Set the posts 6 to 8 feet apart, with top and bottom rails between them. Place intermediate vertical 2 by 4s between the rails every 2 feet. Then cover the two sides of the fence with 1/2-inch CDX pressure-treated plywood. Attach a sheet metal cap to prevent moisture from seeping inside. Or, wrap 30-pound felt paper over the top of the framing before installing the shingles. Nail the shingles to the plywood the same way as house shingles, omitting the building paper.

Lattice

Lattice allows breezes into the garden while preserving some of the view. It works well for tall fences because it is light to support and does not look overpowering.

The framework for a lattice fence is held up by posts set in the ground every 6 to 8 feet, depending on the size of lath sections. Nail rails between the posts, top and bottom. An option is to install a kickboard beneath the bottom rail. Then nail a frame of 1 by 2 stops around the inside of each bay created by the posts and rails. Attach the lattice to these stops, and cover the edges with another set of stops. Lattice is available in prefabricated panels; for a more substantial fence it can be built at the site with 1 by 2 lath.

Woven Boards

This fence, also called basket weave, admits some breeze, but is tight enough for privacy.

Set posts 8 feet on center, with 8-foot horizontal bender boards. Sandwich the ends between 1 by 1s and a center 1 by 2 nailed to the posts. Place vertical 1 by 3s at regular intervals, and interweave the bender boards around them. Nail the bender boards at the ends and to the spacers. A 2 by 4 cap rail and vertical bender board nailed onto the posts give the fence a finished look. Stain or natural weathering are the most successful finishes.

Clapboard

Horizontal siding material makes an effective, durable, but fairly expensive fence as both sides are usually covered. One of the least expensive siding materials is clapboard or simply lap siding. You should match the existing siding of the house.

Set posts at 8-foot intervals. The top and bottom rails are 2 by 4s, with intermediate vertical studs placed every 2 feet between them. Use pressure-treated framing materials because they will be covered and there will be no air circulation. Cover the framing with the clapboard siding, starting from the bottom and working up. Finish off the fence with a 1 by 8 or 2 by 8 cap to give it a trim appearance and to reduce moisture infiltration. Paint to match the house.

FENCES: continued

Fence Tops

The top of your fence is a prominent design element that can be dressed up in a number of ways. Some utilize the same materials as the fence and others add a new design element. The more intricate designs work better on simple board fences rather than a fence that is already elaborate.

Rail. This simple top features a 2 by 6 cap rail nailed on the tops of the posts. The posts are longer than normal fence posts, usually 15 to 18 inches. The posts should be no more than 6 feet apart to prevent sagging of the cap rail. The top rail of the fence itself must be installed between the posts the same way as a bottom rail, but all other construction is the same.

Divided Rail. This variation of the previous design is especially suitable where posts are already too far apart for a 2 by 6 cap rail to span without sagging. Simply insert intermediate 2 by 4 blocking every 2 to 3 feet. Cut all the blocks to the same length, rather than measure for each individual block. This style of top emphasizes the framed sections.

Lattice. The lattice infill of this top creates a contrast to the solid board fencing below it. Lattice is an excellent material because it looks light and provides some visibility. The posts for this design are extended above the fence height as with other tops, and then bridged with a cap rail. The lattice is held in place with 1 by 1 or 1 by 2 stops.

Arbor. An arbored fence top provides a pleasing accent to a fence. If it is on a fence that straddles a property line, be sure you have your neighbor's agreement and cooperation. The short horizontal cleats are usually 2 by 6s, but can be 2 by 4s or even 2 by 6s cut into a decorative shape. Nail them to the posts with at least three nails each, or bolt with two bolts. The vertical slats are 2 by 2s.

Gabled Roof. This is made out of shingles nailed to plywood. (Make sure that the exposed face is finished.) If you prefer, make the sheathing out of spaced 1 by 4 boards. The structure is supported by 2 by 6 rafters sloped at a 45-degree angle. You can make decorative cuts on the ends of the rafters, or leave them plain.

Installing the Posts

Do a layout using string lines and batterboards. The line should represent one side of the posts, rather than the center, so it can remain while posts are erected. To locate each posthole, divide the distance between corner posts into equal spaces that do not exceed 8 feet. Dig the holes with an auger or clamshell digger—shovels make the holes too large. Depths vary with height and frost conditions, but minimums are 24 inches for 6-foot fences and 18 inches for 4-foot fences.

Use pressure-treated lumber or an all-heart grade of a durable species for posts. Usually, 4 by 4s are large enough, but unsupported corners and posts for heavy gates should be 6 by 6s, set 3 feet deep.

Fill the bottom of each hole with 4 inches of rock or gravel. Set corner posts first, aligning them to the string line and bracing them diagonally in both directions after plumbing them with a level. Stretch an upper string line between the tops.

Align the rest of the posts to these two string lines, bracing each one in two directions. Backfill the holes with concrete or well-tamped gravel, mounding them at the top for water runoff. In heavy frost areas, pour a foot of concrete into the bottom of each hole, add a layer of gravel, and fill the top 6 inches with concrete. Then slide a tapered shingle between each side of the post and the concrete to create an expansion gap. After the concrete sets, remove the shingles and fill the gaps with tar.

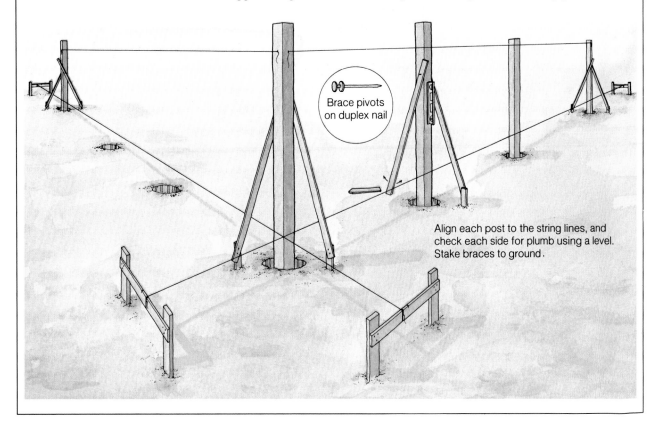

Brace pivots on duplex nail

Align each post to the string lines, and check each side for plumb using a level. Stake braces to ground.

Installing the Rails

Wait at least 24 hours for the concrete to set. Then, mark the posts and cut off the tops. The height depends on the design. You can:
- Cut so that the top rails are flush with the tops of the boards.
- Cut so that the posts are 6 to 12 inches shorter than the finished height of the fence and the boards extend above the top rails.
- Cut so that the tops are higher than the boards and either bevel the post tops or attach cap rails. Attach the top rails first. Usually they are set on top of the posts and facenailed with two 16d nails at each post. Use 2 by 4s long enough to span two or three bays, and locate all of the joints over the posts.

Cut the bottom rails to fit between the posts. There are several ways to attach them. The strongest is with metal fence clips that are nailed to the posts. These can be angles that go below the rails, or have pockets that the rails slip into. Or, you can toenail the ends of the rails into the posts, using 8d nails and predrilling the holes to prevent splitting. Use dado or mortise-and-tenon joints for a more crafted look. However, the joints can trap moisture and must be well treated to prevent decay.

Installing the Infill

Nail the fence boards to the frame or recess them by nailing them to 2 by 2 stops attached to the posts and rails. Use a level to check vertical boards for plumb. If they extend above the top rail, level the tops by stretching and leveling a string near the ground and setting the bottom of each board just above it.

If the joints are wide, use a scrap of wood for uniform spacing. Make it long enough to cover both rails. Tack a small block near the top of the piece of wood and it will hang from the top rail by itself, leaving both hands free for nailing. Use top-quality galvanized nails and drill pilot holes into narrow boards.

FIREPLACES

Over the years, the words hearth and home have become synonymous with warmth and comfort; the fireplace has become the symbol.

With the increased use of wood as a residential heating fuel, current interest in the heating efficiency of a fireplace has become as important as traditional romantic appeal. New developments have made it possible to install a traditional-looking fireplace without having to go to the expense of building a brick chimney.

Recommended Cross-References

Brick, Chimneys & Stovepipes, Heating, Wood-Burning Stoves.

Types of Fireplaces

Homes built 50 to 100 years ago were often designed to take advantage of a centrally located fireplace with a solid brick, heat-retentive chimney reaching up several stories through the center of the house.

Masonry. Recently, fireplaces have become merely decorative, often built on the outside wall. Many have a clay flue inside a brick chimney, surrounded by 6 to 12 inches of dead space. In almost every case, these fireplaces actually make for a net heat loss.

Freestanding. A freestanding fire-place is a variation of the masonry fireplace. It is basically a hood made out of sheet metal and hung over some sort of grate, with a pipe or chimney to duct the smoke away. The metal hood heats evenly, radiating the heat in all directions. As with any old-style fireplace, the heat-loss factor due to the chimney effect is greater than the heat gain.

Zero-Clearance. A prefabricated metal fireplace, called a zero-clearance fireplace, can be built into a wall or an existing fireplace. These are inexpensive and easy to install but are only about 10 percent efficient.

Improving Efficiency

Reducing the chimney effect does not increase the actual warmth from the fire. If your home has more than one fireplace, a simple way to improve heat output is to use only the fireplace that is located near the center of the house and block off any that are located on exterior walls.

You can also increase heat output by circulating room air so that it gets heated by the fire and distributed back into the room, rather than forced up the chimney.

Dampers. The first improvement you should make to a fireplace is to install a damper so that you can close off the chimney when the fireplace is not being used.

Glass Doors. Installing glass doors across the fireplace opening will prevent room air from escaping. The fire still draws air through vents below the doors, but only enough to burn the fuel.

While glass doors certainly improve the overall efficiency of a fireplace and still enable you to see the fire, they do have one drawback: They reduce direct radiant heat.

Outside Air. Another improvement, which is even more effective when it is combined with the glass doors, is to duct air into the fireplace from the outside. Then the fireplace does not use room air for combustion at all. If you have glass doors, the vents can be sealed completely.

Warm-Air Ducts. If you are building a new fireplace, install ducts around it so that cool air is drawn in, circulated around the firebox, and expelled back into the room. (The ducts are completely self-contained; the air never mixes with the chimney smoke.) If you want to have the warmed air blown out at floor level so that it will heat the room even better, install a fan in the duct system that will reverse the natural convective currents.

Heat Exchangers. If you have an existing fireplace and are not able to build a duct system around it, install a small-scale duct system in the fire box, called a heat exchanger. This consists of hollow tubes bent into a shape that fits around the fire. Cool air from the floor is sucked into the bottom of each tube, heated by the fire, and expelled out the top tubes into the room. The metal tubing must be able to withstand the intense heat of the flames, and the system works best if the intake air is from an outside source rather than from the room. It takes some fiddling and fine-tuning to position the exchanger so that the tubes release the maximum amount of hot air without accumulating soot. The best heat-exchanger units come equipped with glass doors.

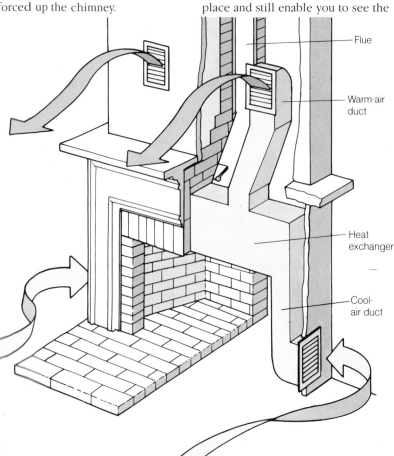

- Flue
- Warm-air duct
- Heat exchanger
- Cool-air duct

Heat Loss

Not only do many fireplaces heat poorly, but they are insidious robbers of the heated air that is already in the home. Unless the damper is closed, heated room air will escape through the chimney. This loss of heat can account for as much as 20 percent of the air that is heated by a furnace every hour.

When the fireplace is in use, an even greater heat loss is caused by the "chimney effect." The room actually gets colder instead of warmer because the fire consumes oxygen from the room, which must be replaced by air from other sources. If the house is poorly insulated, this air comes in through various cracks, chinks, and holes in the walls, doors, windows, and floors. If the room is well insulated, the source of new air to supply combustion for the fireplace is from other rooms in the house, making the furnace work harder to warm those rooms again. For this reason, new fireplaces, whether metal or masonry, require an outside source of combustion air and glass doors to seal off the fireplace from the warm house air. With these changes, a fireplace can be nearly as efficient as a wood-burning stove, particularly if fan-driven heat exchangers are used.

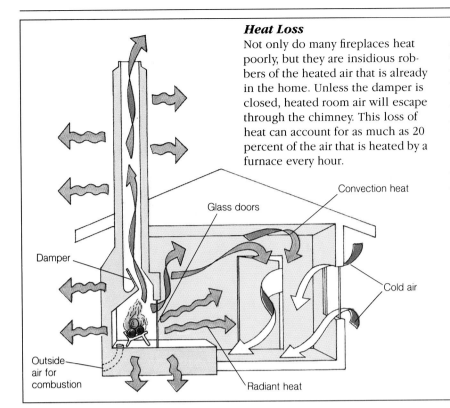

Convection heat
Glass doors
Damper
Cold air
Outside air for combustion
Radiant heat

Zero-Clearance Fireplaces

A zero-clearance fireplace can be installed on an interior wall with the chimney running straight up through the attic, or on an exterior wall with the chimney running up the outside of the house and boxed in with siding materials to match the house. Manufacturers provide complete installation instructions. Observe local codes.

Start by setting the unit directly on the subfloor in front of the wall. Cut a hole in the wall or ceiling for the chimney pipe to pass through, insert a metal collar in the hole, and run the pipe from the fireplace outlet through the collar. Build a frame of 2 by 4s around the fireplace, cover it with wallboard, and finish it. For exterior installations, build a frame of 2 by 4s to box in the chimney. Add sections to the pipe where it comes through the wall until the chimney reaches the required height. Strap the sections to the frame. Cover the frame with siding, cap it with a flashing collar, and install a spark arrester. If you are running the chimney pipe straight up through the roof, build a box on top of the roof as you would for an exterior wall. Cover all roof connections with metal flashing.

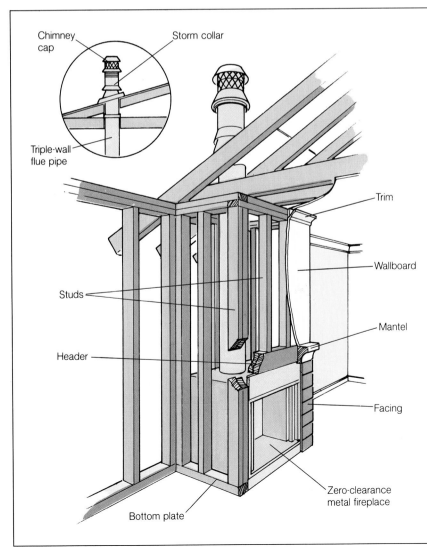

Chimney cap
Storm collar
Triple-wall flue pipe
Trim
Wallboard
Studs
Mantel
Header
Facing
Zero-clearance metal fireplace
Bottom plate

FLASHING

Flashing is any sheet material used to cover joints on the outside of a house so that rain or other moisture will not penetrate. It augments roofing and siding materials, covering such joints as holes around vent pipes, cracks where roofs intersect with vertical walls, horizontal gaps between plywood siding panels, or joints around skylights and chimneys.

Flashing is more permanent than ordinary caulking, and should outlast roofing and siding materials that are replaced every 10 to 25 years. The best flashing materials are copper, lead, stainless steel, and alloys such as terne metal, but aluminum and galvanized steel are much less expensive and hold up fairly well if they are installed properly. Preformed shapes, such as roof vents, step flashing, and angled lengths, will satisfy most of your flashing needs. If a ready-made shape is not available, you can order a custom shape from a sheet-metal shop or fabricate your own from roll material.

Recommended Cross-References
Bricks, Caulking, Doors, Roofs, Siding, Skylights, Windows.

Flashing for Doors/Windows
Doors and windows have cracks where water can penetrate behind the siding, causing invisible damage. Most prehung units include an integral flashing system that prevents this problem. However, windows and doors that were installed before these systems were available, and many custom installations today, must have external flashing to cover the joint above the trim. Cut and nail a length of Z-flashing so that the top edge tucks under the siding and the bottom edge laps over the window trim.

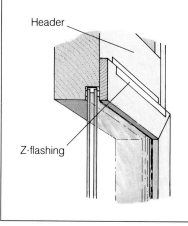

Header

Z-flashing

Flashing for Plywood Siding
Horizontal seams between plywood panels are vulnerable to moisture penetration because they interrupt the natural downward course of the water. Water tends to soak into the seam and even wick upward behind it. To prevent this problem, always install Z-flashing along horizontal joints in the manner shown. Flashing is available in different sizes to match the thickness of the plywood, such as $3/8$, $1/2$, or $5/8$ inch. Always leave a $1/4$-inch gap between the bottom of an upper panel and the flashing.

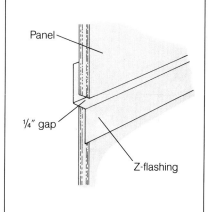

Panel

$1/4''$ gap

Z-flashing

Sheet Metal or Lead

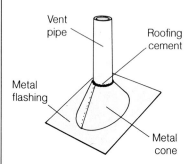

Vent pipe

Roofing cement

Metal flashing

Metal cone

Two-Piece Plastic

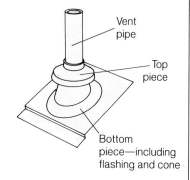

Vent pipe

Top piece

Bottom piece—including flashing and cone

Rubber Sleeve

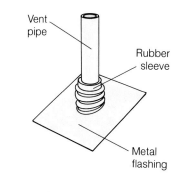

Vent pipe

Rubber sleeve

Metal flashing

Vent Flashing
Vent flashing is required wherever a plumbing vent, flue pipe, or other conduit penetrates a roof. Install the flashing as if it were a shingle, with the top tucked under the shingles above it and the bottom lapped over the shingles below it. The three styles illustrated work well for composition- or wood-shingle roofs. For roll roofing, you must embed the flashing in roofing cement and nail it all around. Use special lead flashing on tile roofs. Buy flashing collars that match the diameter of the pipe. If the bright metal is objectionable, paint the flashing before installing it.

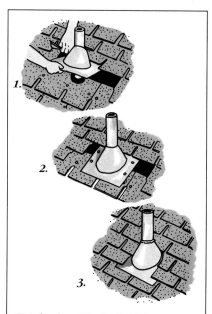

Replacing Vent Flashing
1. Remove old flashing and one or two shingles above it. Slide new flashing under one row of shingles.
2. Nail flashing in place, positioning all nails where they will be covered by shingles.
3. Replace shingles and seal or caulk the joint between flashing and vent.

Flashing in Valleys

You must install flashing along the entire length of a valley before roofing over it. Most codes specify a double layer of roll roofing or a continuous length of metal flashing.

Metal W-flashing is recommended for wood shingle roofs. The pre-formed rib down the center of W-flashing prevents water on one side of the roof valley from crossing over and running under the shingles on the other side. For wood shingles and composition shingles that are not woven across the valley, snap chalk lines on the flashing so that the distance between the shingles widens $1/8$ inch per foot, top to bottom.

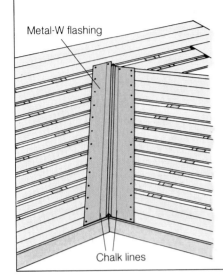

Metal-W flashing

Chalk lines

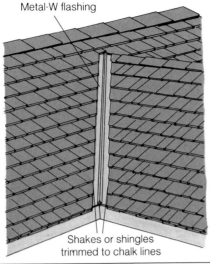

Metal-W flashing

Shakes or shingles trimmed to chalk lines

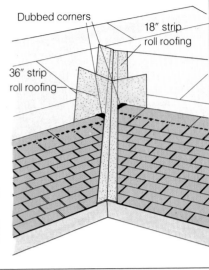

Dubbed corners

18″ strip roll roofing

36″ strip roll roofing

Where Roofs Intersect Walls

There are many situations in which a roof intersects a wall, such as two-story homes with roofing over part of the first story or homes with a lean-to attached to one side. If the joint is horizontal (not sloped), use a continuous piece of metal, at least 10 inches wide and bent at an angle that corresponds to the roof slope. The top edge should tuck up under the siding and the bottom edge should lap over the roofing. You may have to tack the bottom flap down with a few roofing nails so that it lies flat.

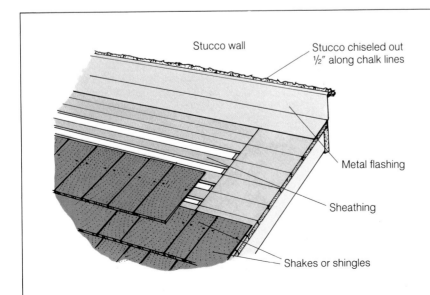

Metal flashing—bent lengthwise

Flashing With Stucco

If the existing siding is stucco, it is too complicated to try to tuck the top edge of continuous flashing under it. That would involve removing a band of stucco, installing the flashing against the exposed sheathing, and restuccoing over it. An easier method is to chisel or saw a groove into the stucco, bend the flashing so it will fit into it, and fill the groove with caulk or new stucco. Use a power saw with a masonry blade to cut the groove. Set the blade at a slight angle so that the kerf slopes downward away from the house. When shingling, make sure you tuck the shingles under the flashing.

Stucco wall

Stucco chiseled out $1/2$″ along chalk lines

Metal flashing

Sheathing

Shakes or shingles

FLASHING: continued

Step Flashing

Where a sloping roof intersects a vertical wall, including the sides of skylight curbs and chimneys, the only flashing that works is step flashing. Never use a continuous piece of angle flashing along such joints; if water gets underneath the shingles it will never get back out again. With step flashing, any water that gets into the joint and finds its way under a shingle will quickly be diverted to the surface of the next shingle down and flow harmlessly down the roof.

Step flashing comes in several different sizes, and you can even fabricate your own, but the most common is made in 10-inch squares bent in half at a right angle. As you start each new course of shingles, install a piece of step flashing. Place it over the shingle below and then cover it with the first shingle of its own course. The vertical flap laps on the outside of the step flashing from the previous course. Install or replace the siding when the roof is finished.

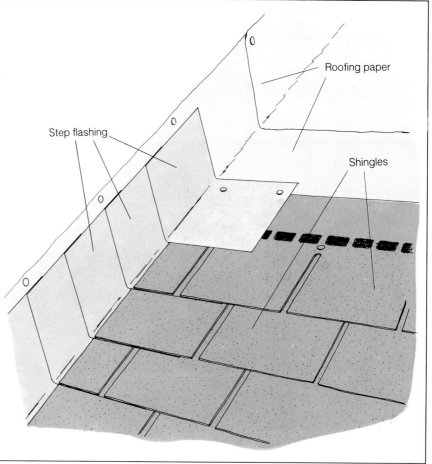

Roofing paper

Step flashing

Shingles

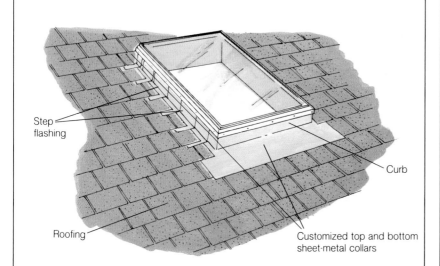

Step flashing

Roofing

Curb

Customized top and bottom sheet-metal collars

Flashing for a Skylight

Use step flashing on the sides and have special collars custom-made at a sheet-metal shop for the top and bottom. Give the supplier both the height and the outside dimensions of the skylight curb. Do not worry about angles, because all the flashing is bent at a 90-degree angle.

After the curb is in place, install roofing up to the bottom edge and cover the roofing with the bottom sheet-metal collar. Continue roofing up both sides of the skylight, using step flashing against the curb. Before installing the next course of shingles across the top of the skylight, nail the top collar in place. Then roof over the flashing.

Eave and Rake Flashing

Eave flashing is a metal drip edge that prevents rainwater from soaking back up under the edges of the roofing material. In cold climates, wider eave flashing protects against moisture damage from ice dams. Rake flashing is a similar material that runs along the edges of a gable end to prevent rain and snow from being blown under the roofing paper underlayment.

Drip edges at eaves are nailed to the roof decking beneath the underlayment. Those at rakes are nailed on top of the underlayment and some roofing materials, such as composition shingles.

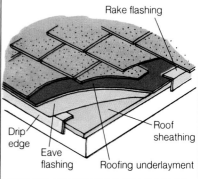

Rake flashing

Drip edge

Eave flashing

Roof sheathing

Roofing underlayment

138

Installing Chimney Flashing

Leaks around the chimney are a major source of damage to the roof structure, often undetected until expensive repairs must be made. They can be prevented with proper flashing, which must take into account the likelihood that snow and water will build up behind the chimney, as well as the fact that the chimney and house usually settle at different rates, creating an unstable joint.

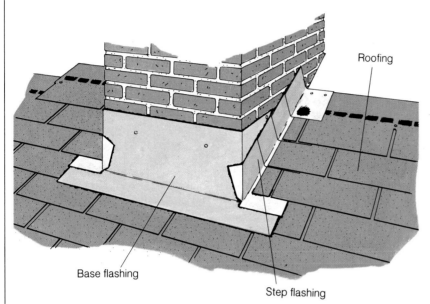

Roofing

Base flashing

Step flashing

Applying Base Flashing. Using sheet aluminum, fashion a piece of base flashing large enough to lap around the sides by about 10 inches. Coat the bottom of the bricks and the roof shingles just below the chimney with asphalt sealant. Put the base flashing in place, pressing it into the sealant. Drive nails into the mortar to hold it in place. Install step flashing up both sides, embedding each piece into the sealant.

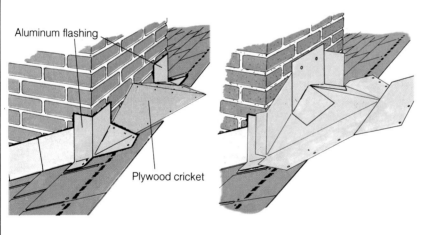

Aluminum flashing

Plywood cricket

Building a Cricket. In heavy snow areas, or if the chimney is wider than 2 feet, build a cricket on the upslope side. Cut two pieces of ½-inch exterior plywood and nail them to the roof. Cover them with a large sheet of aluminum flashing bent to the shape of the cricket and extending approximately 6 inches up the chimney. Cut slits at each end of the main crease so that the flashing lies flat. Cover these slits with smaller pieces of flashing. Drive all nails into the chimney mortar or into the up side of the the flashing. Do not nail into the cricket.

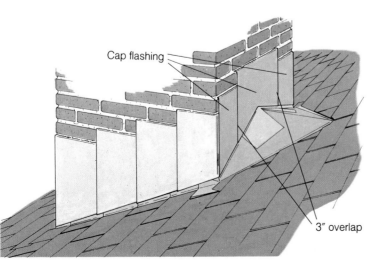

Cap flashing

3″ overlap

Applying Cap Flashing. Install cap flashing to drape down over all the step and base flashing. Embed each piece in a mortar joint, bent so it covers the flashing below it. Start at the bottom, installing the first piece in a mortar joint 2 bricks above the top of the base flashing. Chisel mortar out from between the bricks to a depth of 1½ inches. Cut and bend a piece of flashing so it will extend down to within 1 inch of the roof. Fit it into the groove and seal it in place by packing fresh mortar into the joint. Repeat the process up both sides of the chimney, wrapping the last pieces around the corner. Do the same across the top. Always overlap the previous piece by 3 inches.

FLOORS

The part of the floor we are most familiar with is the finish floor, which is essentially a membrane over the real floor—the structural floor that holds everything up and keeps out moisture and drafts. The floor system *is actually a series of layers. Not all floors have all the layers, but it is important to understand how they relate to each other. This knowledge is necessary whether you are repairing a damaged floor, installing new floor* *coverings, or building a new floor.*

Recommended Cross-References
Attics, Basements, Carpet, Concrete, Framing, Resilient Flooring, Subfloors, Tile, Wood Floors.

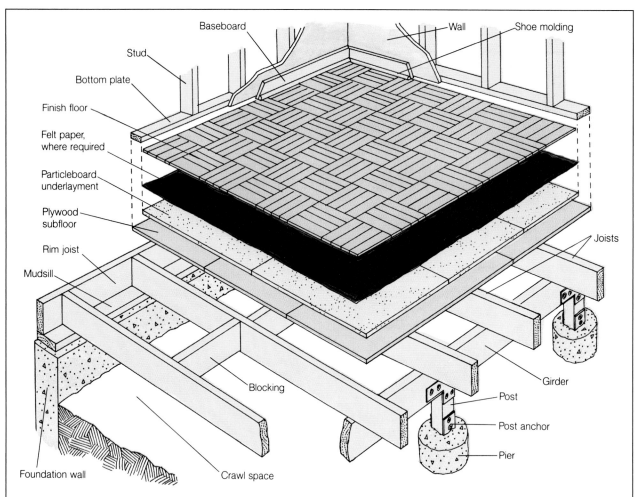

Anatomy of a Wood-Frame Floor

Most floors have a wood-frame construction that spans a crawl space, a basement, or downstairs rooms. The main framing members, which are called joists, are held up by primary structural components such as foundation mudsills, girders, and bearing walls. The size and spacing of the joists depend on the distance they have to span.

The subfloor is the main platform; it can be made of plywood, dimensional lumber, or tongue-and-groove boards. Some subfloors also double as the finish floor, such as ¾-inch tongue-and-groove wood, but most subfloors are covered by finish-floor material. A thin underlayment of smooth plywood or particleboard is installed over the subfloor if the finish flooring requires it.

Underlayment

Finish floors need a stable, smooth surface beneath them. Although some types of hardwood flooring can be attached to subfloors or even directly to the joists, others require underlayment. Underlayment is also necessary for sheet vinyl, vinyl tiles, ceramic tiles, and some carpets.

Tile backing board is the best underlayment for ceramic tile. The backing board and subfloor must have a combined thickness of 1⅛ inches. Particleboard or plywood are used under other types of floors.

Installing Underlayment. Remove the baseboard and cut back any casing with a backsaw.

Lay out the underlayment with the joints staggered. If the subfloor is plywood, place the underlayment at right angles to the plywood sheets. Avoid using small pieces of underlayment beneath a vinyl floor.

Cut the underlayment so the bor-der is ⅜ inch from the walls. Mark cutouts for pipes or door openings with a compass and cut them with a jigsaw.

Attach the underlayment with construction adhesive and 8d ring-shank or concrete-coated nails. Nail into the floor joists. At the edges and at any seams that do not fall on a joist, use 1¼-inch ring-shank nails or wallboard screws.

If the finish floor is vinyl, fill all seams and nail holes.

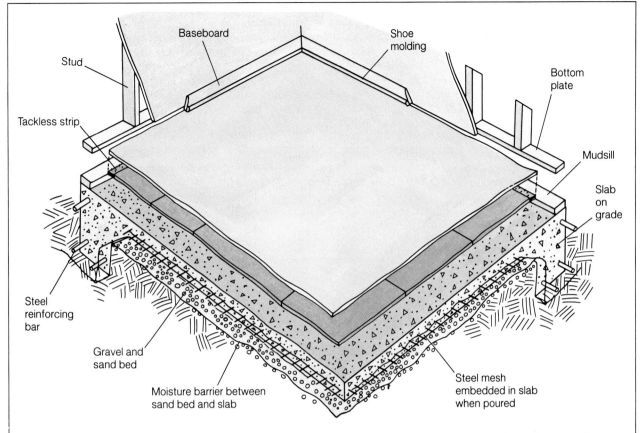

Baseboard

Shoe molding

Stud

Bottom plate

Tackless strip

Mudsill

Slab on grade

Steel reinforcing bar

Gravel and sand bed

Moisture barrier between sand bed and slab

Steel mesh embedded in slab when poured

Anatomy of a Concrete Slab

Some floors are concrete slabs. They are hard and unyielding, but can be covered with carpeting or with a wood subfloor. They make an excellent surface for thin or brittle floor coverings, such as tile and resilient flooring, which are glued directly onto the concrete. Concrete is not a waterproof material; it can wick moisture up from the ground. To prevent this, a properly constructed slab will have a moisture barrier under it or be adequately sealed before flooring is installed.

Choosing a Floor Covering

Because the floor is such an important part of the way a room looks, you will want to select new flooring carefully. Your tastes may change, so the simpler the floor treatment, the more flexibility you will have in the design and use of the room over time. It is much easier and less expensive to change the color of your walls or to introduce new furnishings than it is to install a new floor.

As a general guide, good design is simple design—although simplicity is not always easy to achieve. It requires a high level of restraint, thoughtfulness in planning, and care in execution. If you do opt for a dramatic and exciting floor, then be bold. Let it be the keynote for the rest of the decor. More often, however, floors play a background role, pulling the other elements of the room together.

The most common types of floor covering are wood strip, wood block, resilient tile, resilient sheet, ceramic tile, and carpet. Wood is a traditional favorite that can add quality, permanence, and livability to any room. The grain gives a floor texture. Wood-strip floors, especially wide planking, create a strong linear pattern. Wood-block and parquet floors have a dynamic pattern.

Resilient Tile and Sheet Flooring. This type of covering comes in a wide range of colors and patterns, making it appropriate for any room. Resilient flooring is durable, comfortable, and easy to maintain. Sheet materials come in room-size widths that create broad expanses of color and pattern.

Ceramic Tile. Tile and other masonry materials, such as brick and stone, create a feeling of permanence and substance. The effect can be either rustic or formal. Because of the grout lines, they create a strong pattern. Choose a color and width for the grout lines to accentuate or subdue this pattern.

Carpet. Wall-to-wall carpeting or area rugs offer the advantages of softness, warmth, comfort, and a wide choice of colors. Carpet is suitable for open expanses or intimate spaces, and can be used in any room. It needs to be maintained, and is not as permanent as other floor materials.

FOOTINGS

Many outdoor structures, including decks, gazebos, and arbors, require an independent foundation for each bearing post. These small concrete structures are usually referred to as footings, although technically they are piers set on footings.

Footing dimensions are determined by local codes. Because they support wood posts or beams, footings typically extend a minimum of 8 inches above grade. This portion, called a pier, is usually 8 inches or more across, and assumes various shapes—either round cylinders or blocks with straight or beveled sides.

The pier extends into the ground far enough to rest on the footing itself. The footing is usually 18 inches square by 6 inches thick (sometimes 12), and buried at a depth prescribed by code, which can be anywhere from a minimum of 12 inches to 6 feet or more, depending on the depth of the frost line. Footings on steep slopes usually have a depth requirement greater than the code minimum.

It is possible to buy precast piers and embed them in footings of fresh concrete, but a more acceptable practice is to build a simple form for the pier and pour it along with the footing, making a unified concrete structure. This allows for the use of metal post anchors for the connection between pier and post, and also makes it easier to level the tops of piers if they all have to be the same height.

For a simple structure that will not be bearing loads, you can eliminate the pier section and set the post just slightly above the grade if the post is pressure treated or is a naturally durable species of lumber.

Recommended Cross-References
Arbors, Concrete, Decks, Fences, Foundations, Gazebos.

Simple Footings

Some garden projects, such as fences or arbors, do not require footings capable of bearing floor loads. They only need a concrete base to keep posts out of the ground that otherwise would be buried. This way the posts will not be vulnerable to decay, and they can easily be replaced or repaired if necessary.

You make this type of footing by excavating a hole in the ground and filling it with concrete. This type of footing does not even need a pier to raise the post above grade if the post is of pressure-treated lumber suitable for ground contact or a naturally durable species of lumber.

Excavating. Excavate holes at least 12 inches wide and 6 inches deep (deeper where codes or frost conditions demand). Fill them with concrete. Position a metal post anchor in the wet concrete.

Positioning the Anchor. Tamp the metal anchor into the fresh concrete when it has set enough to hold its shape, but is still soft.

Leveling the Footings. Position and level each footing, sloping the fresh concrete away from the metal anchor so that water will drain away from the post.

Cylinder Piers

A deep footing hole will require pouring a tremendous amount of concrete. The most efficient way to deal with this problem is to extend the pier all the way to the footing, using a fiber forming tube. The round shape uses the least amount of concrete to attain the required cross-sectional dimension. Fiber tubes are readily available from concrete suppliers. If the pier is not deep, an alternative to buying ready-made tubes is to make your own out of roll roofing material.

Leveling Forms

In some cases you may need to level several piers, for instance if you are building a low deck that has beams resting directly on the piers rather than on posts. The simplest way to do this is to build forms for the piers so that the top edges are all level. This way you can pour the concrete and level it off at the top of the forms. You don't have to adjust the level of the wet concrete.

Sometimes, the forms are too far apart to use a level. If this is the case, there are several ways to adjust forms. One is to find a straight board that is long enough to reach all the forms from a central location. Set it on edge, place a carpenter's level on top, and make any adjustments. You can also use a line level. This is a small cartridge-shaped device that hangs on a string and indicates how level the string is when it is pulled taut. It is easy to use and quite accurate up to distances of 15 to 20 feet if you pull the string very taut and place the line level dead center. Another simple device is a water level. This is a long piece of plastic tubing with colored water in it. When the two ends are held up, no matter how far apart they are, the height of the water in one end will always be the same height as the water in the other end, as long as neither end is capped and the tubing is not partially in the shade and partially in direct sunlight (the part in the sun will receive more heat, and expand more than the shaded end, giving a false reading). A final method for leveling is to borrow or rent a builder's level, which is like a transit. However, the other methods are much simpler and adequate for footings.

Site-Formed Piers

1. Locating and Building Forms. Lay out the footing locations using string lines and batter boards. The lines should represent the outside edges of the posts. You will need them later in order to place the metal anchors accurately and erect the posts.

To mark a footing location, drop a plumb bob down from the intersection of two string lines. Using the plumb bob as the starting corner, trace the outline of a post on the ground. Then, using the post outline as the center, draw the outline of a footing around it.

2. Excavating Holes. Dig footing holes carefully. A posthole digger will keep the sides vertical and the hole from enlarging as you go deeper. Level the bottom of the hole and square the corners, using a square rather than a pointed shovel. Only dig to the required depth; there is no point in wasting concrete and you cannot throw dirt back in the hole—footings must rest on undisturbed soil.

3. Building Forms for the Piers. If the footings are shallow and do not require using a long forming tube, build simple pier forms out of scrap lumber. A square shape is fine, with two of the sides long enough to straddle the footing hole and the other two, 8 inches long, nailed between them. Nail the forms securely so that they will withstand the pressure of the wet concrete, and brace them or put heavy weights on them to keep them from floating upward.

To customize the piers with a graceful design, nail cambered (beveled) strips of wood inside the four corners of the form or along the top edge, or both. After the concrete is set and the forms are removed, the footing will have beveled edges wherever you put these strips.

4. Mixing and Pouring the Concrete. Use a concrete mix that is 1 part portland cement, 2 parts sand, and 3 parts gravel. Keep it stiff for maximum strength. If you have to make several footings, you will probably need a yard or more of concrete. In that case, it is best to order ready-mixed concrete.

For deep footings, wire pieces of $1/2$-inch reinforcing rod (rebar) into the forms so that they extend down into the footing cavities. Fill holes and forms with concrete. Use a stick or piece of rebar to consolidate the concrete and remove air pockets. Also hammer the sides of the form to release air pockets.

5. Setting the Anchors. Use a concrete trowel or a scrap of wood to smooth the concrete on the top of each form. Embed each anchor in the wet concrete, aligning it with the string lines and using a level to make sure it is plumb. Rock the anchor slightly to seat it firmly.

6. Curing the Concrete. Leave the forms on the pier for at least 3 days. For the best cure, moisten the concrete 2 or 3 times a day, or cover it with plastic to retard evaporation.

7. Stripping the Forms. Dismantle and remove all the forms. The piers are now ready to receive the posts or beams.

FOUNDATIONS

Most homeowners do not undertake extensive foundation projects themselves, but many are able to correct minor defects or build the foundation for a room addition. Even if you are not planning a project that involves any foundation work, you should have a basic knowledge of what your foundation does and how to recognize serious problems.

It is important to keep in mind the main functions of a foundation when you are inspecting it, analyzing problems, or planning extensive new work. These functions are important in determining the design details and the materials that will be needed.

• It carries the weight of the house to solid ground. Solid ground means undisturbed soil that is at least 12 inches below grade, and much deeper for special conditions, such as soils that are subject to much freezing or expansion or soils on steep grades. Spread footings distribute the weight, and in some cases deep piers carry the weight as far as bedrock or more stable soil.

• The foundation keeps the wood structure of the house above the ground. Foundation materials, such as concrete, masonry, and pressure-treated lumber, must hold any other wood at least 8 inches above grade to prevent decay and insect damage.

• It provides a level and stable base for the house. The foundation compensates for an uneven building site and should be constructed to counteract any tendencies of the ground to settle or heave.

• The foundation provides an anchor from wind and seismic forces, which can move a house and damage it. A house needs more than its own weight to hold it in place. The mass of the foundation and the fact that it is buried in the ground are what hold a house in place under stress—as long as the house is secured to the foundation and is tied together well itself.

• It keeps moisture out of the crawl space or basement. The foundation itself does not actually do this; lack of moisture depends on waterproofing materials and an effective drainage system. The foundation does give some protection and it provides a stable structure on which to install waterproofing materials.

Recommended Cross-References
Basements, Bracing, Concrete, Drainage, Floors, Footings, Gutters & Downspouts, Insulation, Ventilation.

Preventing Damage
Major foundation and structural damage are symptoms caused by other problems. In some cases the problem is one of poor foundation design or a failure of the soil bed. Most often, however, the symptoms are the result of simple conditions that any homeowner can correct. The following steps will help prevent damage from occurring or cure problems that are still minor.

• Grade the soil around the foundation so that it slopes away from the house $\frac{1}{2}$ inch per foot for at least 30 inches.

• Fix gutters and downspouts so that water is carried away from the foundation, ideally 10 feet or more.

• Dig trenches or install diversion drains upslope from the house.

• Install waterproofing material and a drain system around a badly leaking foundation.

• Patch visible holes or cracks.

• Inspect periodically for mud tubes, sawdust, or other evidence of termites or powderpost beetles.

• Install anchor bolts to connect the mudsill to the foundation.

• Remove all dirt that is within 8 inches of any wood.

Types of Foundations
This home rests on three types of foundations:

Perimeter. A perimeter foundation creates a crawl space under the house. Most perimeter foundations are made of poured concrete or concrete block, although it is not at all unusual to find brick foundations in older buildings. Separate piers support girders and other concentrated loads within the perimeter.

Slab. A slab built on grade functions as both the foundation and floor system. It is an economical type of foundation but can only be built in areas where soil conditions will permit such construction. The slab must have deep footings under all the perimeter and bearing walls, and should always be at least 8 inches above grade.

Basement. A basement foundation has higher walls than a perimeter foundation. It is built on a footing and has separate footings for supporting columns. The basement floor usually consists of a concrete slab poured after the footings and walls are completed.

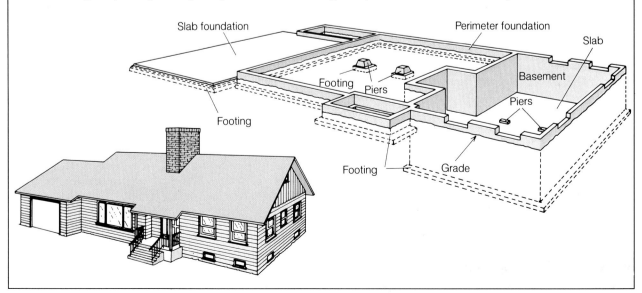

Laying Out Foundations

A foundation must have the right dimensions and be perfectly square. The layout technique described establishes string lines for the outside edges of a foundation and batter boards for the corners. This way, it is easy to adjust the string lines.

Start at the corner where the ground is highest (point A) or at the edge of the house if you are laying out a room addition. Build batter boards 3 feet behind that point. Then measure the approximate distance to point B and build another set of batter boards 3 feet behind it. Level them with the first set by using a line level, transit, or hydrolevel. Stretch a string line between the two sets that crosses over points A and B.

Build another set of batter boards 3 feet behind the approximate position of point C, and stretch a string line back to the batter board behind point B. Use a 3-4-5 right triangle (with longer multiples, use 6-8-10) to square the two string lines.

Then build batter boards at point D and stretch the last two string lines. All the batter boards should be level with each other. The string lines will be used as a reference for leveling the forms later on. Adjust the string lines back and forth on the batter boards until the four intersections are exactly as far apart as the foundation dimensions. The two diagonal measurements will be equal if the corners are square.

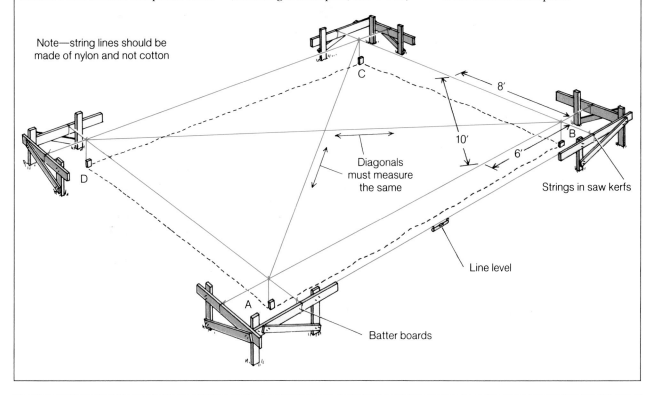

Note—string lines should be made of nylon and not cotton

C

8′

10′

6′

B

Diagonals must measure the same

Strings in saw kerfs

Line level

D

A

Batter boards

Extending Perimeter Foundations

If you are building a room addition, it must usually have the same type of foundation as the rest of the house. Excavate trenches for a perimeter foundation to the same depth as the house, or deeper if required by code. Drill ⅝-inch holes into the existing foundation, 7 inches deep, with a rotary hammer. Cement anchor bolts or lengths of rebar into them with epoxy mortar. Build forms to the height of the existing wall, and low forms for the footing if the trench is too wide. Place rebar for the new foundation. Clean the old wall and coat it with a latex-modified bonding agent before pouring new concrete.

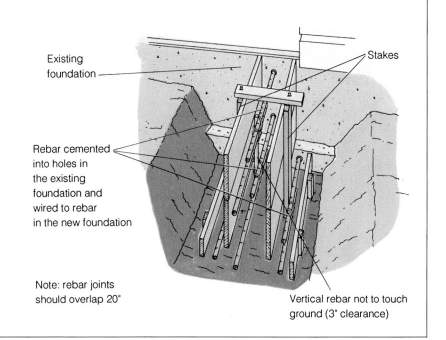

Existing foundation

Stakes

Rebar cemented into holes in the existing foundation and wired to rebar in the new foundation

Note: rebar joints should overlap 20″

Vertical rebar not to touch ground (3″ clearance)

Perimeter Foundation

This type of foundation consists of a wall that rests on a footing and runs continuously around the perimeter of the house. The wall and footing are reinforced with horizontal rebars and poured as one unit. Local codes vary, but most require the wall to be 6 inches thick for a one-story house and 8 inches thick for two stories. The wall must extend at least 8 inches above grade. The footing must be 12 inches wide for one story and 15 inches for two. It must at least have the same thickness as the wall. The footing must usually have a minimum depth of 12 inches, although certain frost conditions will require much deeper footings.

The floor system rests on the mudsill or a short cripple wall built on the mudsill. The floor must have minimum clearances of 12 inches beneath girders and 18 inches beneath joists. Girder ends that do not rest on the mudsill or cripple wall are supported by a short extension or by pockets formed into the foundation wall. The bottoms of any posts holding up the girder must be at least 8 inches above grade.

Inspecting a Perimeter Foundation.

Before you begin any major structural projects in your home, be sure the perimeter foundation meets the standards described above. Inspect it for problems as well, and seek professional consultation before you proceed with the project. Bring a flashlight and chipping hammer with you on your tour of the foundation.

Old foundations may have weak concrete from poor mixing or inferior materials. The rebar may even be exposed in some places. Masonry foundations are also suspect. Look for crumbling mortar and excessive moisture. Hit the wall with your hammer a few times; the hammer should bounce.

Before the inverted-T foundation was devised, most perimeter foundations were "battered" (or beveled) on the inside. Some had no footings at all. These foundations tend to lean and eventually roll over. This problem can be detected from the outside of the house because the top part of the foundation bulges outward slightly and the walls tend to be crooked.

Hairline cracks are natural and acceptable, but any crack wider than $1/16$ inch deserves observation. Make two or three continuous marks across the crack with a crayon and watch for movement over a few months' time. Extensive cracking indicates the absence of rebar or the settlement and upheaval of the soil bed, both serious problems.

With some foundation walls, the siding or even the mudsill may be so close to grade that dirt rests against it. Look for similar conditions around interior posts.

Building a Perimeter Foundation.
Most perimeter foundations are constructed from poured concrete in one continuous pour, referred to as a monolithic pour, but these foundations can also be built with concrete block

that is laid on a concrete footing.

To build forms for a poured concrete foundation, lay out string lines to represent the outside edge of the wall (not the footing). Mark lines on the ground for excavating the footing trenches, using a plumb bob to transfer the string line positions onto the ground. Take into account that the footing is wider than the wall.

Excavate to the code-required depth for the footing. If the soil is firm you can use it for the footing forms. The bottom of the trench should be level, the sides straight, and the corners square.

The forms for the wall can be constructed out of plywood with 2 by 4 braces, but it is simpler to use 2-by lumber. (It can be reused for floor joists.) Nail these boards to stakes driven into the bottom of the trench, positioning them so the distance between the inside faces of the lumber will be exactly the required width of the wall. Space the stakes every 3 or 4 feet.

To keep the heavy concrete from forcing the form boards apart, insert special metal ties between them. These ties will become encased in the concrete, but the wedges or other devices at each end make it possible to free the boards from the concrete when it hardens.

Set all the rebar in place before the pour and tie it securely with wire. Pour the concrete, insert anchor bolts for the mudsill, and let the concrete cure for at least 5 days before removing the forms.

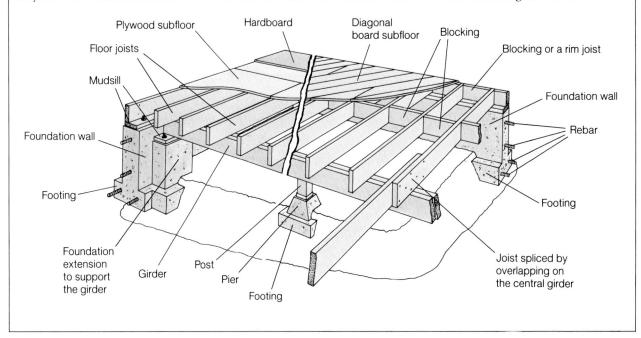

Plywood subfloor • Hardboard • Diagonal board subfloor • Blocking • Blocking or a rim joist • Floor joists • Foundation wall • Mudsill • Rebar • Foundation wall • Footing • Footing • Foundation extension to support the girder • Girder • Post • Pier • Footing • Joist spliced by overlapping on the central girder

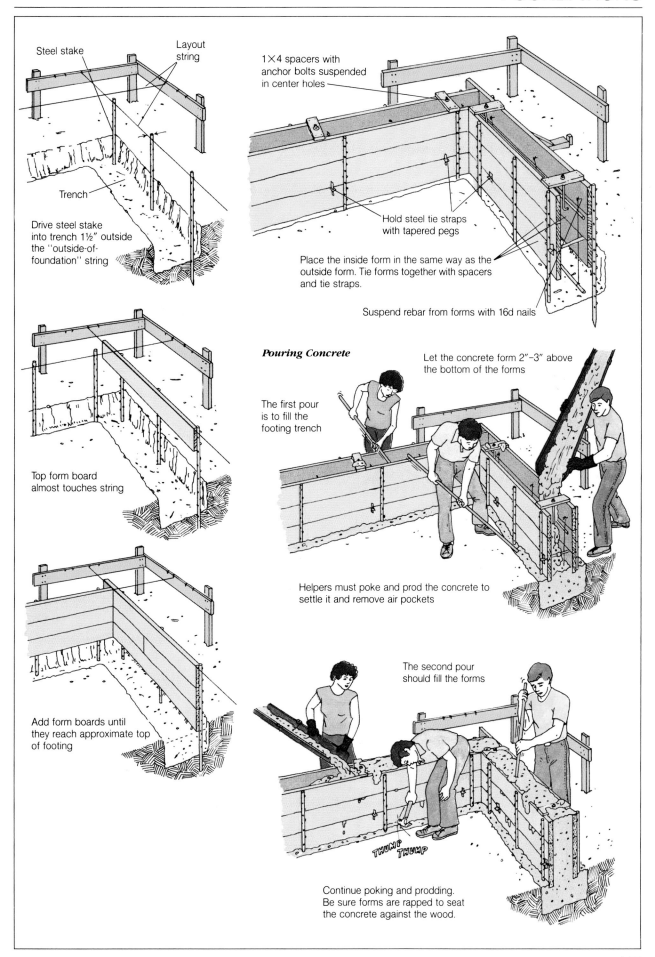

Steel stake

Layout string

Trench

Drive steel stake into trench 1½" outside the "outside-of-foundation" string

Top form board almost touches string

Add form boards until they reach approximate top of footing

1×4 spacers with anchor bolts suspended in center holes

Hold steel tie straps with tapered pegs

Place the inside form in the same way as the outside form. Tie forms together with spacers and tie straps.

Suspend rebar from forms with 16d nails

Pouring Concrete

Let the concrete form 2"–3" above the bottom of the forms

The first pour is to fill the footing trench

Helpers must poke and prod the concrete to settle it and remove air pockets

The second pour should fill the forms

THUMP THUMP

Continue poking and prodding. Be sure forms are rapped to seat the concrete against the wood.

Concrete-Block Foundation

Foundation walls are often built of concrete block instead of poured concrete—especially walls over 3 feet, which may otherwise require specific forming techniques and even an engineered design.

1. The Block Wall. A block wall still requires a continuous concrete footing. Check your local code for the required thickness and depth.

Some codes require that the wall have reinforcing steel in it, both vertical and horizontal, and that the wall be filled with concrete. A course of blocks that has horizontal rebar in it is called a bond beam; it uses blocks with holes at each end for the steel to pass through.

2. Excavating for the Footing. A simple way to build a footing is to excavate a trench to the required dimensions and fill it with concrete. Where deeper excavations are required, just fill the bottom of the trench to the thickness of the footing.

A footing for concrete blocks must be perfectly level because the mortar under the first course cannot be thicker than 1/2 inch at any point. To guide the concrete finishing, set grade stakes every 4 feet and level them. The bottom of the trench should be level as well. If the site is sloped, build the footing in steps. The height of each step must be equal to the height of one or more blocks, so that courses will line up.

3. Pouring the Concrete. Place horizontal rebars in the trench. Use dobies (small concrete blocks with wires attached) or rocks to hold them 3 inches above the ground and 3 inches in from the sides. Cut short sections of rebar for any vertical pieces. Bend the section ends into an L shape and set them aside for inserting in the concrete later.

Fill the trench with concrete, screeding it to the top of the stakes. Use a wood or magnesium float to make the surface slightly rough. After the concrete has set a bit, place the vertical rebars in it. They should line up with the cells of the blocks and be no farther apart than the maximum required by your local code. Bend them at the bottom, and insert them so that they clear the ground by 3 inches.

4. Building Footing Forms. For a large job or unstable soils, build forms to reduce concrete waste and to ensure a more accurate footing. Dig the trench at least 12 inches wider than the footing.

Once the trench is dug, start the forms at one of the outside corners. Use 2 by 8 lumber for an 8-inch footing, keeping the lumber about 1/2 inch off the ground if it is only 7 1/2 inches wide. Position the outside forms first, staking them every 18 inches. Then build the inside forms, tying them to the outside forms with 1 by 2s every 2 feet. Place horizontal rebar inside the forms and fill them with concrete, using the same method as for the trench. Screed the concrete flush with the top of the forms and place the vertical rebars. You can begin laying the concrete blocks the next day, but do not remove the forms until the concrete cures.

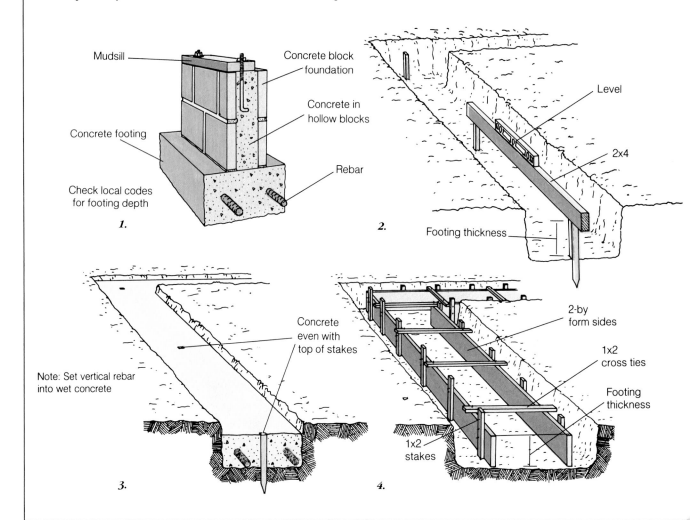

Mudsill
Concrete block foundation
Concrete footing
Concrete in hollow blocks
Check local codes for footing depth
Rebar

1.

Level
2x4
Footing thickness

2.

Concrete even with top of stakes
Note: Set vertical rebar into wet concrete

3.

2-by form sides
1x2 cross ties
Footing thickness
1x2 stakes

4.

When the footings are complete, you can begin the wall. Concrete blocks are normally 6, 8, or 10 inches wide, 8 inches high, and 16 inches long, although other sizes may be available. The sizes referred to are always nominal sizes. The blocks themselves actually measure about 3/8 inch less to allow for the mortar at each joint. An 8-inch block is standard for a foundation wall. Half-blocks, which are 8 inches square, are also common and are used for corners and to terminate walls at doorways or other openings.

A good mortar mix is 1 part masonry cement and 3 parts sand. It dries out quickly, so mix it in batches no larger than half a wheelbarrowful.

5. Laying Out the Blocks. The first step is to lay out a dry run, putting 3/8-inch spacers between the blocks to make sure they fit. Then take the blocks off the footing and locate the two outside corners of the first course, known as a lead in block work. Spread a layer of mortar at one end and place the corner block into it, pressing it down to within 3/8 inch of the footing. Lay a block at the other corner in the same way, and stretch a line between them to guide the rest of the first lead.

Be sure to set the blocks right side up. You can tell the top of a block because the web is wider than it is on the bottom of the block, providing a broader surface to lay mortar on for the next course.

6. Setting the Blocks. Lay mortar on the footing and butter one end of each block as you set it in place. You can speed up the laying process by buttering several blocks at one time, standing them on their ends near where you are working and spreading mortar on all their ends at once. As you lay each block, keep the buttered end raised slightly and then lower it and fit it snugly against the preceding block in one smooth motion. Use your trowel handle to tap the block level, and scrape away any excess mortar with the blade. Constantly check your work with a level to make sure each lead is level, and hold the level vertically against the side of the wall as you build upward to be sure it is plumb. Butter both ends of the last block.

7. Setting the Anchors. Fill the cells with concrete after the finished wall has dried overnight. Even if the codes do not require concrete in every space, you will need to fill holes every 4 to 6 feet for setting anchor bolts. The anchor bolts should be 1/2 inch thick and at least 10 inches long. Embed them 7 inches into the concrete while it is still fresh. Make sure an anchor bolt is within 12 inches of the end of each piece of mudsill.

Wait to install the mudsill until the concrete cures and the anchor bolts are firm. In some areas a metal termite shield must also be installed under the mudsill. If the wall encloses a basement or other heated space, you should also place a thin layer of fiberglass insulation between the wall and the mudsill. In areas where codes do not require concrete to reinforce the wall, the blocks are filled with insulating material, such as vermiculite, before the mudsill is installed.

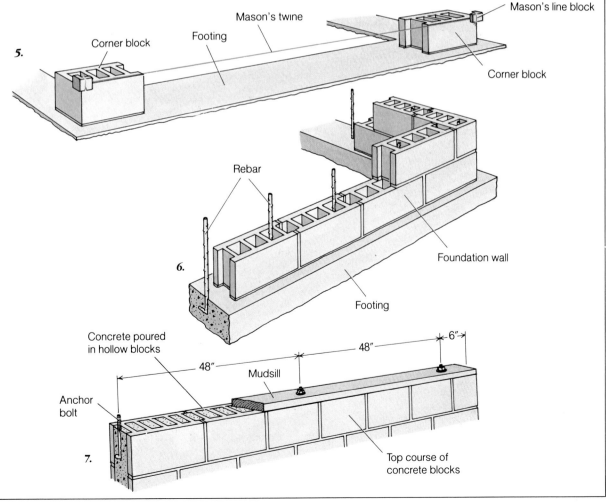

5. Corner block · Footing · Mason's twine · Mason's line block · Corner block

6. Rebar · Foundation wall · Footing

7. Concrete poured in hollow blocks · Anchor bolt · 48″ · Mudsill · 48″ · 6″ · Top course of concrete blocks

FRAMING

Any project that involves adding space, altering existing space, or putting a hole in a wall, floor, or roof will probably require some framing. Framing is a satisfying and dramatic stage of any project. It is fairly easy to do, although certain structural and code considerations must be satisfied. Never undertake a project involving structural changes or additions until you have a proper permit and understand the function of each framing member involved. Otherwise, you

may weaken the house without knowing it. You must also arrange for an inspection before covering up any of the new framing.

In new construction, such as a room addition, framing is basically a textbook operation. In remodeling an existing structure, however, you must be prepared to improvise and make adjustments for unique situations. You may find unorthodox framing conditions inside a wall, under a floor, or in an attic, and you will have

to work around them. Your goal should always be to make the house stronger when you finish than it was when you began. The framing practices described in this section are required by most building codes.

Recommended Cross-References
Attics, Basements, Bracing, Carports, Dormers, Fastening Hardware, Floors, Foundations, Garages, Joinery, Roofs, Sheds, Skylights, Stairs, Subfloors, Walls, Wood.

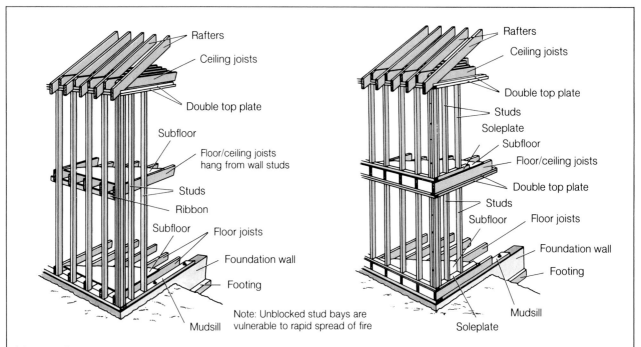

Types of Framing
Some homes are framed with heavy timbers, but most wood-frame houses use 2-by lumber. Old houses may have a balloon framing system, in which long studs extend from the foundation to the roof. But by far the most common system is platform framing. This system, which was introduced at the beginning of this century, uses short wall studs that extend between floors.

Framing Floors
Joists are the basic framing members for floors. Joists for the first floor bear on the foundation mudsills or short cripple walls, with large girders or beams supporting them at midpoint. Joists for upper floors rest on bearing walls. Joists are doubled wherever they carry a concentrated load, such as a bearing wall or bathtub. The joists are set on edge. Rim joists (also called band joists) at their ends prevent them from turning over. They are strengthened by a putting line of blocking or cross-bridging over girders and every 8 feet along open spans. Sometimes blocking is used instead of, or in addition to, rim joists.
Sizing Girders. These members must

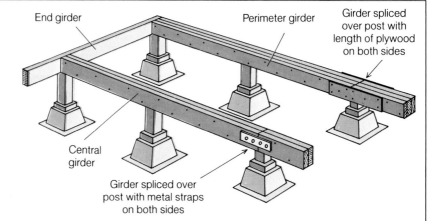

be sized according to the load they carry. Codes have formulas for sizes. A girder can be solid lumber or several 2-inch-wide boards nailed together—a built-up girder. Steel girders, such as I beams, will span long distances. In all cases the posts are spaced according to the girder span and they are always supported on foundation footings.

Installing Joists

Codes specify size and spacing for joists. You can increase the span if you space the joists 12 inches instead of 16 inches on center.

Select the straightest joists for the outside edges. Measure both diagonals, check for square, make any adjustments, then toenail joists to the mudsill or cripple wall. Lay out joist spacings on the rim joists and across the top of the girders, starting from the same end. Facenail each joist to the rim joist and toenail it to the bearing surface. Any joist must have at least 1½ inches of bearing surface. Install joists with the crown, or curved edge, up.

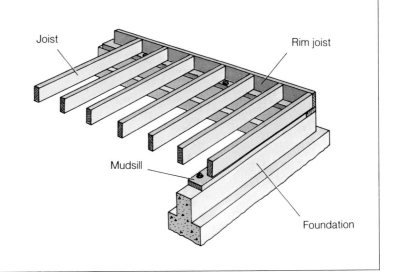

Splicing Joists

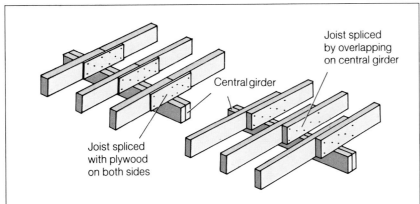

Long spans require two joists, which must be joined at a girder. Connect them with plywood or metal braces on each side or lap them, extending past the girder an inch or two. If they overlap, they will not be continuous throughout the floor system, which must be taken into account if you install a plywood subfloor. An alternative attaching method is to use joist hangers.

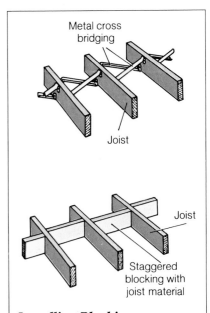

Installing Blocking

Cut solid blocking out of joist material, measuring for each piece at the rim joists rather than where you will be installing it. Stagger the blocks so that you will be able to facenail them at each end.

An alternative is to use metal cross-bridging. Attach the top, but wait until the subfloor is installed before nailing the bottom of the metal cross-bridging in place.

Extending an Existing Floor

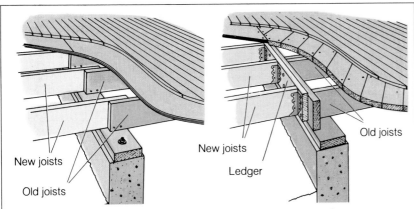

If the floor of a room addition will be at the same level as the existing floor and if you can install the new joists so that they run in the same direction as the old ones, use the same size lumber and rest the joists on the mudsill or wall plate that supports the existing floor. Remove the rim joist, lap the new joists against the old, and install blocking.

If the new subfloor or joists are a different dimension from the existing floor, attach a ledger and install the new joists with joist hangers taking the difference into account.

Framing Walls

Stud walls consist of a soleplate nailed to the subfloor, vertical studs, and a double top plate, with extra studs and blocking added where walls intersect. Openings are framed with headers and extra studs. The terminology for the parts discussed may vary in different parts of the country and carpenters and contractors may have their own vernacular but they all serve the same function.

Studs. Studs are normally spaced every 16 inches or 24 inches, on center. If the wall bears a floor, the studs must be spaced no more than every 16 inches, on center. Studs are usually 2 by 4s, but must be 2 by 6 if the wall bears more than two floors. In cold climates, 2 by 6s are often used for exterior walls because they can hold more insulation.

The standard height of most ceilings is 8 feet, so the studs are typically 92¼ inches tall. Higher ceilings require longer studs. If you are ordering studs for a large project, figure one stud for every lineal foot of wall. The extras will get used up fast for blocking and cripple studs. A good practice is to use standard framing lumber for most of the wall, but to use kiln-dried studs to frame doors and large windows to ensure that they will be absolutely straight.

Plates. The soleplate and top plates are the same size lumber as the studs, usually 2 by 4s. Use long lumber for plates, splicing lengths together for long walls. Although the soleplate does not extend across doorways, if you are framing a wall on the floor and lifting it into position, it is easier to use a continuous soleplate and then cut out the doorway section after the wall is in place. If you are building walls on a concrete slab, use pressure-treated lumber or a durable species of wood for the soleplates.

Bearing walls require a double top plate, consisting of a top plate and a cap plate nailed onto it. A single top plate is allowed on partition walls. However, if you are framing many walls at one time, you can avoid confusion and having to cut studs to different lengths if you frame all the walls with double top plates.

When framing a wall, first attach only the top plate. Install the cap plates after all the walls are up. This makes it possible to overlap the top plate and cap plate at the corners, making a stronger connection. Any splice in a top plate must be centered over a stud, and splices in cap plates must be at least 4 feet from splices in top plates.

Openings. Frame openings with a header across the top. The header should be the same width as the studs, either solid 4-by lumber or two pieces of 2-by material sandwiched together with ⅜-inch plywood spacers between them. The depth of the header depends on its span and the loads concentrated above it. For instance, you can use a 4 by 6 header to span 6 feet if the wall has no floors above it, but this same header can span only 4 feet if it is carrying another floor as well as the roof load.

Each end of the header bears on a shorter stud called a trimmer stud or jack stud, which must extend all the way to the soleplate. Trimmer studs are flanked by full-length studs, sometimes called king studs. Regardless of where an opening occurs, the 16-inch layout of joists continues from one end of the wall to the other. Cripple studs, used to fill in spaces above headers and below sills, should follow this layout.

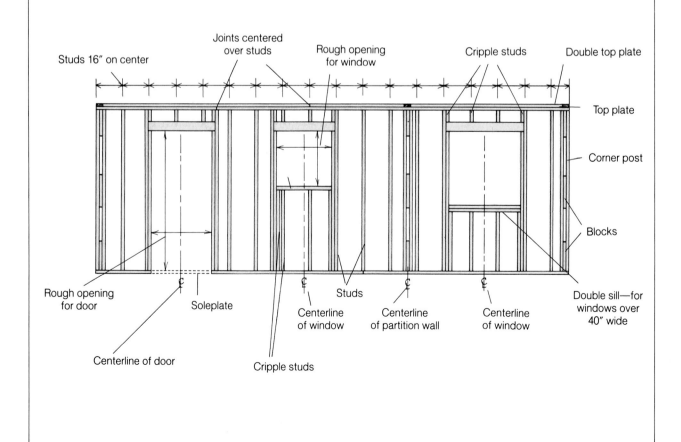

Studs 16" on center

Joints centered over studs

Rough opening for window

Cripple studs

Double top plate

Top plate

Corner post

Blocks

Rough opening for door

Soleplate

Studs

Centerline of window

Centerline of partition wall

Centerline of window

Double sill—for windows over 40" wide

Centerline of door

Cripple studs

Laying Out a Wall. Construct the longest walls first. Begin by marking stud locations on the soleplate and top plate. To ensure that the layout starts from the same end, mark both plates at the same time. Because the first measurement starts at the corner of the wall rather than the center of a stud, it should be 15¼ inches; the rest are 16 inches apart. One trick for making this measurement less confusing is to tack a scrap of ¾-inch-thick wood onto the end of the plates and hook the tape measure over it. This makes the first 16-inch mark automatically 15¼ inches from the end of the plates.

Building a Wall. Construct new walls by framing them on the floor and raising them into place. Build the corner posts first, using two studs and short blocking. Frame each opening with a header, trimmer studs, king studs, and sill, if needed. Lay these assemblies in place, along with all the field joists, between the soleplate and top plate, aligning them with the layout marks. Then facenail each plate into all the studs with two 16d common nails at each end. Finally, cut and install the cripple studs, toenailing each one into the header with four 8d nails.

Raising the Walls. Before lifting a wall, snap a chalk line onto the floor for aligning the soleplate. Then lift the wall into place. Nail the soleplate into the floor at every joist (every 16 inches). Using a plumb bob, plumb stick, or long level, align the wall so that it is plumb in both directions. Brace it temporarily with 2 by 4s.

Leave the temporary bracing in place until you are ready to install permanent bracing. Most codes allow three types: metal straps, 1-by boards that are notched into the exterior face of the wall frame, and solid sheathing panels. Plywood sheathing is the best type, because it can withstand tremendous wind or earthquake forces if it is nailed properly with as few seams as possible.

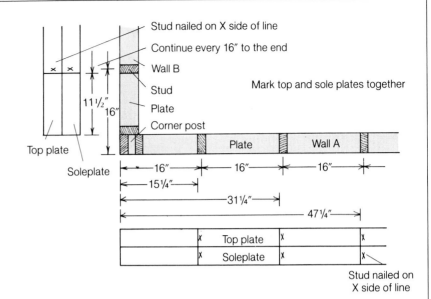

Stud nailed on X side of line
Continue every 16" to the end
Wall B
Stud
Plate
Corner post

Mark top and sole plates together

Top plate
Soleplate

11½"
16"

Plate   Wall A

16"   16"   16"
15¼"
31¼"
47¼"

	Top plate		
X		X	X
X	Soleplate	X	X

Stud nailed on X side of line

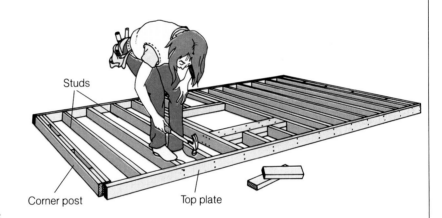

Studs
Corner post
Top plate

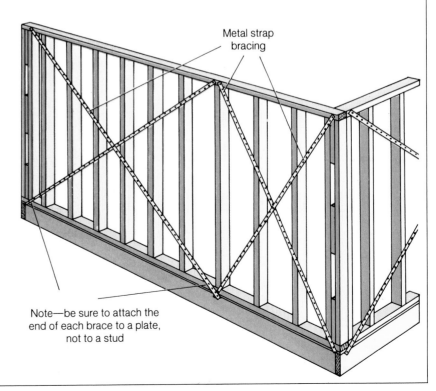

Metal strap bracing

Note—be sure to attach the end of each brace to a plate, not to a stud

153

Framing Roofs

Most roofs are framed with ceiling joists, rafters, and a ridge board. Sometimes collar ties connect pairs of rafters near the midpoint, lower if they take the place of the ceiling joists. The ceiling joists and collar ties prevent the rafters from spreading the walls apart; they should not be removed. The ridge board does not support the rafters. It provides a surface for the ends of the rafters to bear against.

Roofs with sloped or cathedral ceilings have a different roof system. The ridge end of each rafter is supported by a beam, at least 3 inches wide, that has a post or bearing wall holding up each end. The rafters on either side of the ridge beam do not function as pairs, but are independent of each other.

The peaked gable wall at the end of a roof is framed like a standard stud wall, then short studs are cut to fit between the cap plates and the rafters. The eave that projects beyond the gable wall terminates in a pair of barge rafters, also called verge or rake rafters. They are held in place by outriggers or lookouts, which are cantilevered 2 by 4s that are laid flat and placed into notches in the gable rafters.

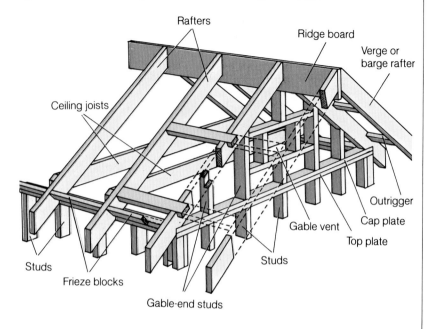

Laying Out Rafters

First you need to know the run and the slope. The run is half the span of the building. The slope is the number of inches of rise for every foot of run; it is expressed as "something in 12." For example, if a building is 24 feet wide (a 12-foot run) and the slope is 6 in 12, the rafters should be 2 by 8, 24 inches on center.

Mark the plumb cut by setting the square on one end of the board. As this is a 6-in-12 roof, the tongue (the narrow part) intersects the edge of the board at the 6-inch mark and the blade (the wide part) at the 12-inch mark. Hold the square this way to make all the marks.

Determine the rafter length with the formula $a^2 + b^2 = c^2$ (a and b are the rise and run). Or, look at the tables stamped on the blade of the rafter square. The 13.42 under the 6-inch mark means that for every inch of run, you need 13.42 inches of length. If the run is 12 feet, the rafter length for a 6-in-12 roof is 161 inches, or 13 feet, 5 inches.

Measure down from the plumb cut a distance equal to the rafter length and mark the top edge of the board. Holding the tongue of the square against this mark, set the square so that it is 6 in 12 and scribe a line.

Slide the square, in its 6-in-12 position, back toward the original plumb cut until it creates a line for the seat of the bird's mouth that is exactly the width of the cap plate (3½ inches for a 2 by 4 plate). Mark the position.

Mark the tail cut by sliding the square beyond the bird's mouth the distance of the overhang.

Move the mark for the plumb cut toward the bird's mouth. The distance should be exactly one half the thickness of the ridge board (3/8 inch for a 3/4-inch-thick board).

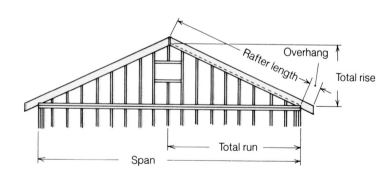

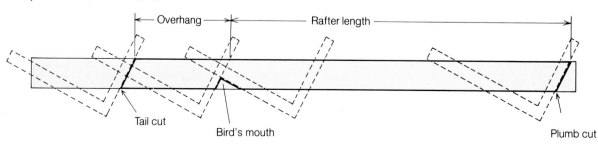

Installing the Rafters

Mark the locations of the ceiling joists and rafters at the tops of the walls. Make the outside of the first rafter flush with the gable wall. Set the first ceiling joist in from the wall to make room for the gable studs and to provide a nailer for the ceiling.

Size the ceiling joists according to the span, spacing, and species of lumber you are using. Toenail the ceiling joists to the wall plates. This framework gives you a platform to work on while you erect the rafters. In areas where wind or earthquakes are a hazard, you must use metal framing clips to connect the joists and rafters to the plates.

Lay out the first rafter, then cut it and use it for a pattern to lay out the second rafter. Test the two rafters with a dry run, using a scrap of ridge board, to see if the cuts fit snugly. After making adjustments as needed, use these rafters as patterns for laying out and cutting the rest.

Choose stock for the ridge board that is one size deeper than the rafter stock (1 by 10 for 2 by 8 rafters, for example). Lay out the rafter locations along both sides of the ridge board, allowing 18 inches for the gable overhang.

Have at least two helpers when you install the rafters. Hold the first two rafters in place, with the ridgeboard sandwiched between them, and nail each end into the wall plate. Then nail the top ends into the ridge board, facenailing one side and toenailing the other. Alternate this nailing sequence at the ridge as you work your way along the rafters.

Be sure the ridge board is level and centered over the house. If you have to splice it for a long roof, the splice must fall where a pair of rafters meet, not in the space between rafters.

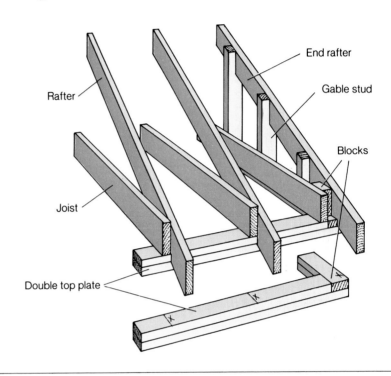

Rafter

End rafter

Gable stud

Blocks

Joist

Double top plate

Extending a Roof

The techniques for tying the new roof framing to the old vary with the design. If the addition is at the gable end, the new rafters can be framed parallel to the old. Simply double the existing rake rafter and use it for starting the new rafter layout.

If the ridge of the new roof runs perpendicular to the ridge of the existing roof, the connection is a bit more complicated. The easiest technique is to strip away roofing material from the old roof so that the sheathing is exposed. Then cut a pair of rafters for the new roof and hold them in place with the ridge board in between. Level the ridge board and establish the point where it will intersect the roof sheathing. Nail 2 by 4 plates between this point and the walls of the addition.

Cut an angle on the end of the ridgeboard so that the ridgeboard will lie on the apex of the two plates. Nail that end in place and hold the other end with temporary bracing so that it is level. Cut and install all the full-length rafters. Then cut jack rafters to fit between the 2 by 4 plates and the ridge, installing them as shown. Finally, install the lookouts and barge rafters.

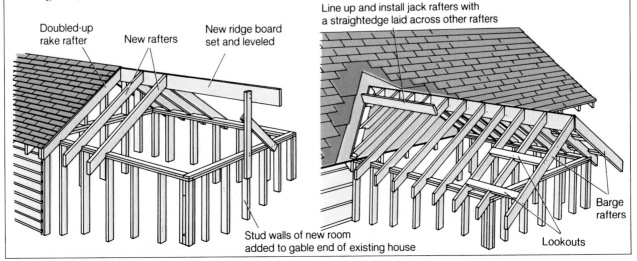

Doubled-up rake rafter

New rafters

New ridge board set and leveled

Line up and install jack rafters with a straightedge laid across other rafters

Stud walls of new room added to gable end of existing house

Barge rafters

Lookouts

FRAMING: continued

Reference Tables
Codes specify the minimum spans for various horizontal framing members and the number and placement of nails for framing connections.

These tables are typical of most model codes, but check with your local building officials to make sure the figures are in compliance with the tables they use.

Nailing Schedule

Connection	Number and Size of Common Nail	How Nailed
Joist to sill or girder	3 8d	Toenail
Built-up girders and beams of 3 members	20d 32″ o.c. at top and bottom staggered	Facenail
Bridging to joist, each end	2 8d	Toenail
Ledger strip (ribbon) @ ea. joist	3 16d	Facenail
1 by 6 subfloor, to each joist	2 8d	Facenail
Wider than 1 by 6 subfloor	3 8d	Facenail
2″ subfloor to joist or girder	2 16d	Facenail
Soleplate to joist or blocking	16d @ 16″ o.c.	Facenail
Soleplate to stud	2 16d	End nail
	4 8d	Toenail
Top plate to stud	2 16d	End nail
Doubled studs	16d @ 16″ o.c.	Facenail
Built-up corner studs	16d @ 24″ o.c.	Facenail
Doubled top plates	16d @ 16″ o.c.	Facenail
Top plates, laps, and intersections	2 16d	Facenail
Continuous header, 2 pieces	16d @ 16″ o.c. along each edge	Facenail
Continuous header to stud	4 8d	Toenail
Ceiling joists to plate	3 8d	Toenail
Ceiling joists, laps over partitions	3 16d	Facenail
Ceiling joists to parallel rafters	3 16d	Facenail
Rafter to plate	3 8d	Toenail
1″ brace to each stud and plate	2 8d	Facenail
1 by 8 sheathing or less, each bearing	2 8d	Facenail
Wider than 1 by 8 sheathing, each bearing	3 8d	Facenail

Header Sizes
Most codes do not have tables for sizing headers over doors and windows, but only have formulas for calculating beam sizes. However, the following sizes are generally accepted rules of thumb for headers in various situations.

Location	Size of Header (4x or built-up 2x)	Maximum Span
Single Story or Top Story	4x4	4 feet
	4x6	6 feet
	4x8	8 feet
	4x10	10 feet
	4x12	12 feet
Lower Floor, With Floor Above	4x4	3 feet
	4x6	4 feet
	4x8	7 feet
	4x10	8 feet
	4x12	9 feet

Note: Increase sizes where accumulated loads concentrate on a header.

Using Span Tables
The tables on the next page look complicated because they must account for the different strengths of various grades and species of lumber. The numbers across the top of each chart represent the range of strengths found in commercially available lumber. Some typical lumber grades and their strengths are listed at the bottom of this column to make it easier for you to use the charts. More complete tables are printed in code books and carpentry manuals.

There are separate tables for floor joists, ceiling joists, and rafters. To use a table, determine the span from your working plans, decide whether to space the members on 16-inch or 24-inch centers, then compare the various span limits for different sizes of lumber within the same column. Choose a vertical column that corresponds to the strength of lumber you plan to use. If you are not sure, pick 1.0 or 1.1. If your span is too long for the size of lumber you need to use, move up to a stronger grade of lumber until you find one that works.

Typical Lumber Strengths

Balsam Fir	No. 1:	E=1.2 F_b=1150–1440
	No. 2:	E=1.1 F_b=950–1190
California Redwood	No. 1:	E=1.1 F_b=1350–1690
	No. 2:	E=1.0 F_b=1100–1370
Douglas Fir (Larch)	No. 1:	E=1.8 F_b=1750–2190
	No. 2:	E=1.7 F_b=1450–1810
Douglas Fir (South)	No. 2:	E=1.3 F_b=1350–1690
Northern Pine	No. 1:	E=1.4 F_b=1400–1750
	No. 2:	E=1.3 F_b=1100–1380
Lodgepole Pine	No. 1:	E=1.5 F_b=1300–1620
	No. 2:	E=1.3 F_b=1050–1310
Southern Pine	No. 2:	E=1.6 F_b=1400–1750

Note: The symbol E stands for Modulus of Elasticity, a measurement of tensile strength; F_b stands for Fiber Stress in Bending.

Floor Joists

Allowable spans for 40 pounds per square foot live load. Listed in feet and inches. The figures labeled o.c. mean inches on center.

Joist Size	Joist Spacing	Modules of Elasticity, *E*, in 1,000,000 psi													
		0.8	0.9	1.0	1.1	1.2	1.3	1.4	1.5	1.6	1.7	1.8	1.9	2.0	2.2
2x6	16 o.c.	7-9	8-0	8-4	8-4	8-10	9-1	9-4	9-6	9-9	9-11	10-2	10-4	10-6	10-10
	24 o.c.	6-9	7-0	7-3	7-6	7-9	7-11	8-2	8-4	8-6	8-8	8-10	9-0	9-2	9-6
2x8	16 o.c.	10-2	10-7	11-0	11-4	11-8	12-0	12-3	12-7	12-10	13-1	13-4	13-7	13-10	14-3
	24-0	8-11	9-3	9-7	9-11	10-2	10-6	10-9	11-0	11-3	11-5	11-8	11-11	12-1	12-6
2x10	16 o.c.	13-0	13-6	14-0	14-6	14-11	15-3	15-8	16-0	16-5	16-9	17-0	17-4	17-8	18-3
	24 o.c.	11-4	11-10	12-3	12-8	13-0	13-4	13-8	14-0	14-4	14-7	14-11	15-2	15-5	15-11
2x12	16 o.c.	15-10	16-5	17-0	17-7	18-1	18-7	19-1	19-6	19-11	20-4	20-9	21-1	21-6	22-2
	24 o.c.	13-10	14-4	14-11	15-4	15-10	16-3	16-8	17-0	17-5	17-9	18-1	18-5	18-9	19-4

Ceiling Joists

Allowable spans for 10 pounds per square foot live load (wallboard ceiling). Listed in feet and inches.

2x4	16 o.c.	8-11	9-4	9-8	9-11	10-3	10-6	10-9	11-0	11-3	11-6	11-9	11-11	12-2	12-6
	24 o.c.	7-10	8-1	8-5	8-8	8-11	9-2	9-5	9-8	9-10	10-0	10-3	10-5	10-7	10-11
2x6	16 o.c.	14-1	14-7	15-2	15-7	16-1	16-6	16-11	17-4	17-8	18-1	18-5	18-9	19-1	19-8
	24 o.c.	12-3	12-9	13-3	13-8	14-1	14-5	14-9	15-2	15-6	15-9	16-1	16-4	16-8	17-2
2x8	16 o.c.	18-6	19-3	19-11	20-7	21-2	21-9	2-4	22-10	23-4	23-10	24-3	24-8	25-2	25-11
	24 o.c.	16-2	16-10	17-5	18-0	18-6	19-0	19-6	19-11	20-5	20-10	21-2	21-7	21-11	22-8
2x10	16 o.c.	23-8	24-7	25-5	26-3	27-1	27-9	28-6	29-2	29-9	30-5	31-0	31-6	32-6	33-1
	24 o.c.	20-8	21-6	22-3	22-11	23-8	24-3	24-10	25-5	26-0	26-6	27-1	27-6	28-0	28-11

Low Sloped Rafters

Allowable spans for roofs 3 in 12 or less (or any high slope rafter); 30 pounds per square foot live load (supporting drywall ceiling and heavy roof cover). Listed in feet and inches.

Rafter Size	Rafter Spacing	Allowable Extreme Fiber Stress in Bending Fb psi													
		500	600	700	800	900	1000	1100	1200	1300	1400	1500	1600	1700	1800	1900
2x6	16-0	6-6	7-1	7-8	8-2	8-8	9-2	9-7	10-0	10-5	10-10	11-3	11-7	11-11	12-4	12-8
	24 o.c.	5-4	5-10	6-3	6-8	7-1	7-6	7-10	8-2	8-6	8-10	9-2	9-6	9-9	10-0	10-4
2x8	16 o.c.	8-7	9-4	10-1	10-10	11-6	12-1	12-8	13-3	13-9	14-4	14-10	15-3	15-9	16-3	16-8
	24 o.c.	7-0	7-8	8-3	8-10	9-4	9-10	10-4	10-10	11-3	11-8	12-1	12-6	12-10	13-3	13-7
2x10	16 o.c.	10-11	11-11	12-11	13-9	14-8	15-5	16-2	16-11	17-7	18-3	18-11	19-6	20-1	20-8	21-3
	24 o.c.	8-11	9-9	10-6	11-3	11-11	12-7	13-2	13-9	14-4	14-11	15-5	15-11	16-5	16-11	17-4
2x12	16-0	13-3	14-6	15-8	16-9	17-9	18-9	19-8	20-6	21-5	22-2	23-0	23-9	24-5	25-2	25-10
	24 o.c.	10-10	11-10	12-10	13-8	14-6	15-4	16-1	16-9	17-5	18-1	18-9	19-4	20-0	20-6	21-1

High Slope Rafters

Allowable spans only for slope greater than 3 in 12; 30 pounds per square foot live loads (supporting drywall ceiling and heavy roof covering) Listed in feet and inches.

2x4	16 o.c.	4-1	4-6	4-11	5-3	5-6	5-10	6-1	6-5	6-8	6-11	7-2	7-5	7-7	7-10	8-0
	24 o.c.	3-4	3-8	4-0	4-3	4-6	4-9	5-0	5-3	5-5	5-8	5-10	6-0	6-3	6-5	6-7
2x6	16 o.c.	6-6	7-1	7-8	8-2	8-8	9-2	9-7	10-0	10-5	10-10	11-3	11-7	11-11	12-4	12-8
	24 o.c.	5-4	5-10	6-3	6-8	7-1	7-6	7-10	8-2	8-6	8-10	9-2	9-6	9-9	10-0	10-4
2x8	16 o.c.	8-7	9-4	10-1	10-10	11-6	12-1	12-8	13-3	13-9	14-4	14-10	15-3	15-9	16-3	16-8
	24 o.c.	7-0	7-8	8-3	8-10	9-4	9-10	10-4	10-10	11-3	11-8	12-1	12-6	12-10	13-3	13-7
2x10	16 o.c.	10-11	11-11	12-11	13-9	14-8	15-5	16-2	16-11	17-7	18-3	18-11	19-6	20-1	20-8	21-3
	24 o.c.	8-11	9-9	10-6	11-3	11-11	12-7	13-2	13-9	14-4	13-11	15-5	15-11	16-5	16-11	17-4

FURNACES

Forced-air heating systems depend on a furnace to heat the air, using oil, gas, coal, or wood for fuel. A boiler is the heating plant of steam and hot water systems, which have basically the same heating principles as forced-air systems. Because of high heating costs and the relative inefficiency of older (five years or more) furnaces, you are probably interested in the many ways homeowners can increase the efficiency of their heating plants.

Before turning your attention to the furnace itself, be sure the heating system is not wasting whatever heat the furnace produces. The house should be insulated, caulked, and weather stripped. Be sure to insulate all the heating ducts or hot-water pipes and seal any leaks. You should also balance the distribution of heat by adjusting the register dampers or hot-water valves until each room is receiving just the amount of heat it needs. Finally, correct any faults in the thermostat and consider replacing it with a new electronic type that monitors furnace operation far more efficiently than old automatic controls.

A furnace is rated by something called combustion efficiency—the percentage of heat actually produced compared with the heat potential in the fuel. The efficiency of most gas- and oil-fired furnaces installed twenty or so years ago is between 50 and 65 percent. Until a short time ago new furnaces had ratings of 75 percent, but the current generation of furnaces claims efficiency ratings of 95 percent or more. If you need to replace a unit, you may find that the higher cost of these new furnaces is more than offset by the long-range savings in fuel, depending on climate and individual circumstances. In the meantime, there are ways to improve the efficiency of an existing furnace without replacing it.

Recommended Cross-References
Gas, Heating, Insulation.

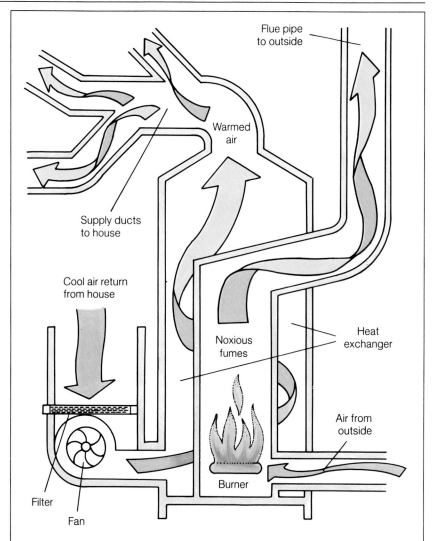

Servicing a Furnace

No furnace will keep functioning efficiently without regular maintenance. Ideally, you should have a furnace inspected and serviced annually by a qualified professional before the heating season begins. If you do your own maintenance, have it inspected professionally every three to five years.

The first maintenance chore is to clean or replace the furnace filter once a month. You should also start every heating season with a thorough cleaning, repeating this step as often as necessary. Before cleaning it, be sure the furnace is switched off and cool. On a forced-air type, open the fan compartment and vacuum away all lint, dust, and debris. Then clean out the fire box or burner compartment. Use the vacuum brush attachment to remove soot and other debris from the walls of the chamber. Some walls are made of fragile fibrous materials, so vacuum carefully. If possible, remove the flue connec-

tion and vacuum it and the flue.

If you have a forced-air system, service the blower. Check the fan belt for tension; it should "give" about ½ inch. Moving the motor bracket adjusts the fan best. You can also change the controls on the blower so it cycles the air at lower temperatures, allowing the blower to work even when the burner is not.

If the furnace is oil fired, oil the bearings in the pump motor. Locate the fuel filter in the main oil line and change it once a year.

Every two to five years the burners should be checked for proper adjustment, so that they mix the right amount of fuel and air for efficient combustion. For oil furnaces, this requires testing the smoke emissions. Black smudges around the inspection door to the burner compartment are a telltale sign that an adjustment is needed. Even though gas burners can be adjusted by watching the flame, this should be done by a professional.

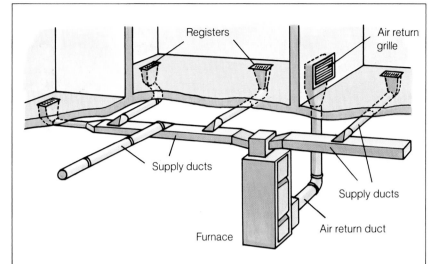

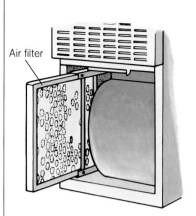

How Heat Is Distributed

A forced-air system blows heated air from the furnace to the living area through a system of supply ducts to room registers. The openings of these registers can usually be regu- lated by means of small levers that increase or decrease the amount of heat flowing into a room while the furnace is on. A separate set of ducts returns the air from the living space to the furnace.

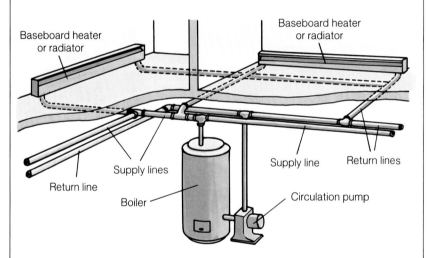

Pipe systems use steam or hot water to circulate heat from a boiler (which is heated by a furnace) to radiators or baseboard heaters in the living area. Like forced-air systems, most hot-water pipe systems return water to be reheated through a sec- ond set of pipes. For the most part, steam that condenses to water in the radiator returns to the boiler through the same pipe in which it first went to the radiator.

Fuel-Saving Devices

There are three devices you can have installed that will have a dramatic impact on fuel savings, especially for oil-fired units. One is a flame reten- tion burner for oil furnaces. Another is a conversion unit that changes an oil-fired furnace to gas fired. The third is an electronic spark igniter to replace pilot lights on gas furnaces.

Replacing Furnace Filters

Changing a furnace air filter is a job that is easy and inexpensive to do yourself. The purpose of a filter on a forced-air furnace is to keep dust, soot, and other airborne grime out of the air that blows into your living area. Because air has more trouble passing through a dirt-laden filter, your furnace has to work harder when the filter gets dirty. Change the filter at least a couple of times during the primary heating season, and as often as every month if you live in a dusty area or if your fur- nace has to work long hours. If your central air-conditioning unit also circulates through your fur- nace filter, you may have to replace the filter during the cooling season as well. The expense of a new filter—a dollar or two, depending on the size—will quickly be rec- ompensed by lower energy bills. And it will save strain on your fur- nace in the long run, too.

It isn't hard to change a furnace air filter. If, after reading the fol- lowing instructions, you still have questions about how to do it, ask your furnace service person to demonstrate the process during the next routine visit, so that you can do the task with confidence.

First, turn off the thermostat. Then locate the metal panel that covers the filter on the furnace, near the blower. Remove the panel and slide the filter out. Slide the new filter in according to the air- flow directions marked on it.

GARAGES

A garage is probably not high on your list of improvement projects, unless you want to upgrade the door or convert the garage into new living space. Garages contain safety hazards and potential structural problems that you should investigate, however. Even if you do not plan any garage projects, make sure the following items have been taken care of:

• Eliminate fire hazards. Move combustible materials, such as paint thinner and gasoline, away from appliances and exposed wood walls. Incidentally, most states prohibit the storage of more than 1 gallon of gasoline. Make sure that the access to attic space has a door that closes. The door to the house should have a solid core and should be at least one step above the garage floor. Make sure that any gas-burning appliances are at least 18 inches off the floor.

• Minimize structural damage from moisture by making sure the floor slopes toward a drain and that the garage has adequate ventilation.

• Make sure all outlets are protected by ground fault circuit interrupters.

• Correct a garage door that falls rapidly—it is a danger. Make sure the springs on a garage door have safety bars that prevent them from flying if they break.

Recommended Cross-References
Carports, Doors, Floors, Foundations, Framing, Insulation, Siding, Subfloors, Windows.

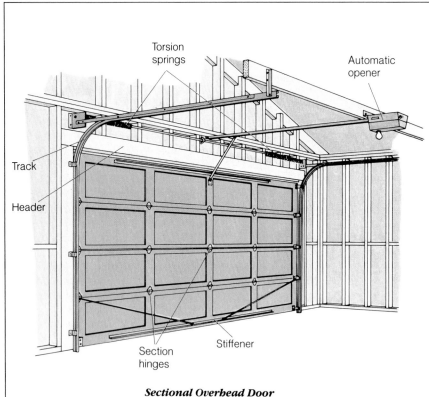

Sectional Overhead Door

Labels: Torsion springs, Automatic opener, Track, Header, Section hinges, Stiffener

Installing a Door or Opener

Hire a professional to install a sectional overhead door or purchase one in kit form to install yourself. Standard sizes are 8, 9, and 10 feet wide for single doors and 16 or 18 feet for double doors. Heights vary from 78 inches to 84 inches.

Automatic doors are available as overhead sectional models or overhead swing types. The track must be installed within ¼ inch of the center of the door. Most types are chain driven, but a screw drive is available on more expensive models. Features to consider include a timed light that turns off automatically, a key switch to install outside, and, if you have a low ceiling, minimum overhead clearance. All openers should reverse automatically if the door hits an obstruction. If an existing opener doesn't have this feature, replace it. Test the automatic reverse monthly and have it adjusted or repaired if necessary.

Converting a Garage

Where codes allow, a garage provides a means to gain new living space. In most cases the space is dry, well ventilated, and completely weatherized. The floor is solid and the walls are usually ready to finish with wallboard or paneling. If codes require enclosed off-street parking, you may be able to add a carport to the side of the garage or house to replace the lost garage.

Each project has unique conditions that may require different procedures, but a typical garage conversion involves the following steps:

1. Removing the Garage Door. Doors vary, but most are heavy and dangerous to remove. Get professional help unless you are familiar with the mechanism. If the door is spring balanced, prop it open with several 2 by 4s. Find the bolts or hooks that release the tension on the springs, and disconnect them carefully. Then remove the props, close the door slowly, and disassemble all the hardware and tracks. Remove the door from the frame and also any exterior trim around the opening.

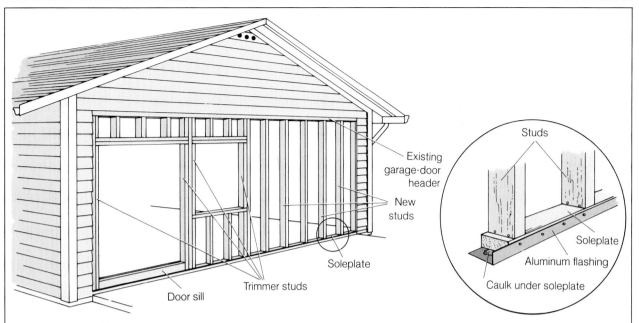

Existing garage-door header

New studs

Trimmer studs

Soleplate

Door sill

Studs

Soleplate

Aluminum flashing

Caulk under soleplate

2. Framing a New Wall. Follow standard framing techniques, except you do not need a double top plate because of the support provided by the header over the door. Either frame the wall with only one top plate and lift it into place, or forego a top plate and toenail all the studs into the header. The soleplate should be pressure-treated lumber or a durable wood species. Either connect the soleplate to the slab with concrete nails, or drill holes 24 to 30 inches apart for lag shields. Set the soleplate on a bead of caulk, then bolt the plate to the shields. As an added precaution, install a termite barrier made of bent metal flashing.

3. Installing Windows and Doors. If the garage will be a bedroom, many building codes require that it have an openable window. If you frame a door or window in the new wall, the header can be two 2 by 4s because the garage-door header actually bears the weight of anything above. Install the window and door after the sheathing is in place.

4. Installing Sheathing and Siding. Sheathing for the new wall should be the same thickness as the existing sheathing. Fasten the new panels horizontally with 8d nails spaced 6 inches apart at the edges and 12 inches inside the field. Leave expansion gaps of $1/8$ inch at the edges and $1/16$ inch at the ends.

If the new wall is an end wall, the simplest course is usually to remove the remaining panels and install new siding on the entire wall. If the new wall forms part of the long side of

the room, patch new panels into the siding that once surrounded the garage door. To conceal the joints in horizontal boards, cut 2 to 3 feet of board from every other row of siding. When you install the new siding, the joints will be staggered and therefore less noticeable.

5. Building the Subfloor. In some cases, you can install finish flooring directly over the concrete slab or install a wood subfloor as you would in a basement. In most cases, however, the floor of a garage requires insulation because it is at grade level. You may also want to raise the floor to the same level as that in the rest of the house. If so, build a subfloor leaving room for insulation. Allow at least $7 1/2$ feet of headroom between the finish floor and ceiling.

Depending on the size of the garage, one or two joist lengths will span the width. Lay the lengths on shims, sleepers, or girders. If necessary, place short posts under the girders, use deeper joists, or both. Toenail the ends of the joists to the existing wall framing. If wallboard covers the framing, remove the wallboard along the bottom for access. Install a polyethylene vapor barrier over the garage floor before you install the floor framing. If the joist spans are longer than 8 feet, install blocking between the joists at midspan. Use $5/8$-inch tongue-and-groove plywood for the subfloor.

6. Finishing the Walls. In some garages the studs are exposed. If so, all you have to do is run wiring and utility lines along them, install insu-

lation and a vapor barrier, and cover with wallboard.

If the walls are already covered with wallboard, probe behind to see if the walls are insulated. If not, either have a contractor blow in loose-fill insulation or strip off the wallboard and install insulation and new wallboard yourself. If you use loose fill, create a vapor barrier by painting the wallboard. Use two coats of oil-based enamel or one coat of sealer and one of alkyd.

7. Installing the Ceiling. If rafters and collar beams frame the roof, they may be the right height from which to hang a finish ceiling. Collar beams should fall at least every 16 inches, on center. If your collar beams don't measure up, add new beams as necessary. If the roof is framed with rafters and ceiling joists or with trusses (trussed roofs usually appear cluttered with bracing and metal connectors), hang the finish ceiling from the bottoms of the joists. Again, install additional supports if the joists fall more than 16 inches apart, on center. The new joists will be long and tend to sag. Support them at midspan with strongbacks that attach to original joists. After installing the new ceiling material add insulation between the joists. Don't forget to include a scuttle for access to the attic space you have created.

8. Finishing the Interior. Tape all the joints and texture the wall and ceiling surfaces. Install trim and other finish details, then paint the room. Install carpet, resilient flooring, or a wood floor over the subfloor.

Garden walls serve many functions. They can create privacy, screen out wind and noise, define an activity area, retain sloping ground, or accent a garden design. Low walls can double as a seating platform, and taller walls provide a handsome background for specimen garden plants. Walls impart a feeling of permanence and quality. Most walls—especially those lower than 3 feet—are within the homeowner's ability to build—as long as there is some help handling the materials. Your main considerations in planning a wall are height, material, and structural design.

Recommended Cross-References

Barbecues, Brick, Concrete, Drainage, Fences, Footings, Foundations, Gates, Lighting: Outdoor, Patios, Planters, Security, Steps, Stucco.

A simple retaining wall of stacked stones blends well with these plants and defines the flower bed (opposite, top). A low garden wall gives a more permanent look to a portable spa (opposite, bottom).

A stone wall and bench help to create a separate sitting area in this patio (above, right). The wall gives the space a sense of protection and intimacy, but its low height and use of natural stone preserve the outdoor feel of the space and keep it from feeling restrictive.

This brick wall (bottom, right), which suggests privacy, tradition, and formality, is softened by the cascading greenery and slatted, curving gate.

Height

The height of a wall is a critical factor in many respects. Codes and zoning ordinances set limits for wall and fence heights, usually 6 feet for side yards and backyards and 42 inches at the sidewalk line. You will probably need a building permit if you build above a certain height, typically 3 feet or more. Ordinances often require that masonry retaining walls taller than 3 feet be designed by an engineer, and some areas even require that an engineer design all freestanding walls.

Wall height is also important for aesthetic reasons. Low walls fit the scale of virtually any yard, but a tall wall can have a confining effect if it encloses a small space. On small lots it may be better to build a low masonry wall topped with a wood fence or a trellis and vines. A wall with openings or gridwork also lessens the feeling of confinement and takes advantage of views.

A tall, solid wall does increase security and blocks noise. To block wind, however, the wall must be right next to the area you want to shelter, or you are better off using a wall or fence with open spacing to subdue the wind by filtering rather than deflection.

There are countless places in the garden where a low wall would be appropriate: surrounding a raised planter, terracing a sloped yard, edging a driveway or walk, bordering a patio, defining a barbecue area, or serving as a fence along a sidewalk or property line.

Materials

Several materials work well for garden walls and create interesting effects. The same material can be used for formal or informal walls, rustic or refined, tall or short. Choose a material that matches an architectural feature of the house or garden or that blends with the character of the area. If you combine materials in the same wall, do not use more than two, and use one of them sparingly. If access to the site is difficult, build with small units that are easy to carry. Use smaller units or irregular or rounded stones for curving walls.

Brick. A traditional favorite, brick is an excellent material for garden walls because it is durable, blends well with outdoor settings, and is easy to handle. It is ideal for tall walls because each unit is easy to lift, although brick does require a great amount of mortar and joint dressing. It is also expensive and brick construction is time-consuming.

Stone. Stone is very attractive and makes an appropriate material for garden walls, especially if you have the good fortune to possess natural stones on your building site. Building stone walls that last for centuries is an art, but with a few simple techniques and great patience you can produce a garden wall that will give you pride and satisfaction for many years.

Wood. Wood is not as permanent as masonry, but is much easier to handle. A wood wall in an area with proper drainage will last for years if it is pressure treated or if the lumber is of a durable species. Used railroad ties are a good choice for retaining walls, although pressure-treated timbers are a more uniform size and can be stained more easily. The simplest wall is of 2-by planking held in place by posts.

Concrete. Although concrete block is usually easier to work with, a poured concrete wall may be more appropriate where strength or a smooth surface is desired. Short walls are built in the same manner as a simple foundation wall. They require carefully built forms, but you can recoup form-building time when you pour because the wall and footing can be poured together. Any wall over 3 feet tall requires special forming and steel reinforcement. Consider having a contractor build any major concrete retaining wall, then covering it yourself with a stone or brick veneer.

Concrete Block. Concrete block is inexpensive, easy to work with, and produces a strong wall quickly. The favorite block for garden walls is slump block, which has irregular faces that provide interesting relief. Other decorative types are also available, or build a wall of structural block and cover it with a veneer of brick, facing stones, stucco, or another more attractive material.

Adobe. A variation on bricks and blocks, adobe is a common wall material in the Southwest. It is not as durable as other materials and is losing favor to slump blocks. Adobe is either covered with stucco for weather protection, or stabilized with asphalt emulsion, then sealed with a clear sealer. Most blocks are 4 inches thick, 16 inches long, and from 4 to 12 inches wide.

Wall Footings

Except for those made of loose-laid stone or wood, all garden walls should be supported by a continuous concrete footing. The width and thickness of the footing depend on the size of the wall, and the depth depends on local soil conditions. Most footings are twice the width of the wall, but the footing of a retaining wall is usually two thirds the height of the wall. The footing should be at least 8 inches thick for low walls; construct 12-inch footings for walls over 2 feet tall. Depth also depends on the local frost line. The minimum depth for a footing is 12 inches below grade. If a footing is deeper, some of the wall will be below grade.

A footing should have a 6-inch layer of gravel beneath it. This controls the heaving that occurs in locations where there is unstable soil or deep frost. Be sure to dig the trench deep enough; in areas that get a lot of frost, the top of the gravel should be above the frost line. Also be sure that the footing does not encroach on your neighbor's property.

Footing should contain at least one horizontal rebar—two or three would be better. Also place vertical rebar every 24 inches in the footing to protrude up into a brick or concrete block wall. Stone is usually too irregular to accommodate it, although you may be able to lay stone around a few bars.

It is important to provide drainage behind a retaining wall. If the soil behind the wall becomes saturated, it could force the wall to crack or lean. Weep holes at the bottom of a wall can provide drainage. If the diameter of the holes is 1 inch or larger, space the holes 2 feet apart. Smaller holes require closer spacing. Weep holes tend to clog with debris unless you place fiberglass mesh behind them. In some cases the water that seeps through will be a nuisance. If so, instead of weep holes, bury drainpipe behind the wall to divert water around it.

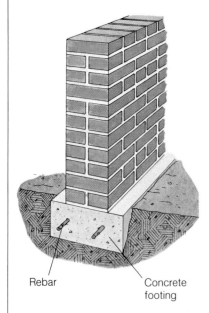

Rebar   Concrete
footing

Brick Walls

To provide stability most brick walls are of two rows of bricks (a single row is called a wythe). The space between wythes is the thickness of a mortar joint, which makes it possible to span both wythes with a single brick (a brick placed this way is called a header). For a strong wall, place headers at regular intervals, and also install vertical rebar in the space between wythes. Also, thickening a wall into a column, called a pilaster, every 12 feet will make for a much stronger wall. Wythes may contain bricks set on edge, but this type of wall is much weaker.

Footings. Build a reinforced concrete footing twice the width of the wall (16 inches) and at least 8 inches

thick. The top of the footing should be level. If you step it down for a sloped site, the height of each step should be a multiple of the thickness of one brick, plus mortar. If you are bringing a lawn up to the edge of the wall, the footing on the lawn side should be high enough to form a level mowing strip flush with the surface of the lawn. If you prefer a brick strip, bring the footing within one brick of grade level.

Mortar. A typical mortar mixture is 3½ parts sand, 1 part portland cement, ½ to 1¼ parts hydrated lime, and enough water to make the mortar stick to a vertical surface without running. You will have to experiment with the water and lime to allow for weather conditions, moisture in the sand, and moisture in the bricks. Mix up the mortar in small batches, preparing no more than what you will use in one hour.

First Course. Dampen the pile of bricks before you start. Spread enough mortar on the footing for three bricks. The mortar bed should be almost as wide as a brick, about 1 inch thick, with a depressed hollow running down the center, which masons call a furrow. Place the first brick at the corner, parallel to the footing. "Butter" one end of the next brick with mortar and nudge that end against the first brick. Do the same with the third brick. Tap the bricks down into the mortar bed with the butt of your trowel, and use a level to make sure they are all the same height. Do the same thing at the far end of the wall, or at an intermediate

point if the wall is long. When you lay the corner brick at that end, place it so the distance between both corner bricks is divisible by an even number of bricks. After you lay the three bricks at the far end, stretch a mason's line between the corner bricks, secure it ¼ inch out from the wall, and align it with the top edge of the bricks.

Complete the first course along both sides of the wall, using the string line as a guide. When you insert the last brick in each wythe, called a closure brick, mortar the ends of the bricks already laid as well as both ends of the closure brick. Then check along both rows of bricks with a level, tapping any stray bricks into alignment, and scrape off excess mortar from the joints. Each joint should be ⅜ to ½ inch wide.

Leads. After the first course is complete, start the second course at both ends. To create the offset spacing for the running bond pattern, set the first brick of the second course across the wall rather than along it. Instead of completing the second course, lay only a few bricks, then start the third course. Continue building courses at each end—staggering the joints of the corner bricks—until you have a stack four to five courses high. These stacks are called leads. Stretch a line between the two leads for the second course, fill it in, and repeat until the wall is filled between both leads. Complete the wall in this fashion.

Ties. Brick ties are strips of corrugated metal placed in the mortar between courses to bond both sides of the wall together. Use them on every fourth or fifth course. Space ties 2 to 3 feet apart and staggered in relation to the ties in previous courses.

Joints. As the mortar sets up, usually after three or four courses, go back and strike the joints. Joints can be of several styles, but the easiest joint that provides sufficient strength and weather protection is a concave joint. Shape a concave joint with a tool called a sled runner or a piece of ½-inch copper pipe. Compressing the mortar makes the joint strong. When you finish the wall, sweep away all excess mortar and make sure each joint is smooth and compact.

Concrete Block Walls

Concrete block is widely available in several sizes, colors, and styles. The common size for garden walls is 8 by 8 by 16 inches, although blocks that are 6 inches high are also popular. Besides the standard block, you may need special shapes. Half blocks begin alternate courses when you want to stagger joints. Corner blocks have finished faces on three sides. Bond blocks accommodate horizontal rebar and caps finish the top.

The style and color of concrete blocks vary even more than the size. Some are textured or sculpted on one side to resemble natural stone. Others have molded patterns and designs. A popular shape for garden projects is the slump block, which has irregular curved sides. Even if you use ordinary straight-sided blocks you can avoid a monotonous wall by covering the blocks with stucco or painting them.

Retaining Walls. Retaining walls require vertical and horizontal rebar as well as grout inside the cells, but a freestanding wall—especially a low one—may not require either.

Footings. For most walls the footing should be 16 inches wide and 12 inches thick. Lay out the blocks before building to determine the exact length. As in building a brick wall, adjust any steps in the footing to the height of the blocks. Incorporate a mowing strip if the wall abuts a lawn, and center vertical rebar inside the block cells.

Mortar. For most projects, a good mixture is 1 part cement, ½ part hydrated lime, and 4 ½ parts sand. Mortar should not run but should not resist when you push the block into place. Mix in color additives if you wish to match colored block.

First Course. Lay blocks after the footing cures. Do not wet the blocks; do a dry run to see where the two corner blocks will fall. All joints should be ⅜ to ½ inch wide. With the dry blocks in place, mark the joint locations on the footing and stretch a string line along the top edge of the course. Remove the blocks and mix mortar stiff enough to withstand the weight of the wall. Lay a 1-inch mortar bed for the first three blocks, furrowing it in the middle.

After the corner block is in place,

lay the next two blocks, mortaring one end of each block before placing it. Blocks are manufactured so the web is wider on one side than the other. With the wide web up, they hold mortar better.

Continue, three blocks at a time, until you reach the end of the first course. If you are creating weep holes for a retaining wall, use special blocks with holes or leave mortar out of some of the joints. Lay the concrete closure block by buttering both ends. Use a level to check alignment.

Remaining Courses. Use a half block to start the next course, unless your wall has a corner. If your wall has a corner, alternate the direction in which full blocks lie in each course. Place mortar on the webs of the first course and "butter" the end of each block that you place in the second course. Repeat this process to complete the wall.

If you build a tall wall, be sure to wire new rebar to the vertical pieces embedded in the footing as you work your way up. Lay a bond beam for horizontal rebar every fifth course, or according to code. After the joints are struck, fill the cells that have vertical rebar with grout. If you are pouring a cap across the top of a wall without grout, use building paper to keep the concrete from falling into the empty cells. If you build a retaining wall, however, grout the entire wall. If you intend to veneer the wall with stones or brick, insert metal ties in the mortar every 2 feet in alternating courses.

Rebar

Concrete footing

Joints. As you work, keep scraping the excess mortar from the joints and reusing it by mixing it with mortar on your board. Strike the joints before they are too hard to show a thumb print. Use a tool called a sled runner or a bent piece of ¾-inch copper pipe to make concave joints. Compress the mortar in the joints and trim off the mortar that is forced out by striking it off with the edge of a trowel. For an extra clean joint, go over it again with the runner, after the mortar has partially dried.

When the mortar is dry, go over all the joints with a wire brush to remove mortar fragments or dirt.

Loose-Laid Stone Walls

Stone laid without mortar is excellent for low freestanding and retaining walls. It demands exacting skill, but you can build a serviceable wall with patience and a few simple techniques. Dry stone walls are somewhat forgiving in that the wall can shift slightly without cracking or breaking, and parts that do come loose can be replaced without much trouble. Loose-laid stone walls cannot be expected to hold back an unstable hill, however, and are unsafe if they are higher than 3 feet.

Flat or stratified stones are the easiest to work with because they can be laid in courses and even trimmed. Round and irregular stones can be used for mortarless construction, although constructing a wall out of them requires a lot of skill and patience. One of the easiest and least expensive materials to use is broken concrete, because it has a uniform thickness, a smooth face on one side, and breaks fairly easily. Soften the jagged look with plants in nooks and crannies of the finished wall.

Preparation. Dig a trench 12 inches deep or to frost line, and backfill it with a 6-inch layer of sand or gravel. If the soil is unstable pour a shallow concrete footing. The width of a retaining wall should equal one half the height. The base and height of a freestanding wall should be equal.

Sort through the stones and set aside the flattest and broadest for the final top course. Also look for stones wide or long enough to stretch across the width of the wall near the bottom. These bondstones, or headers, stabilize the wall. Organize the stones in piles placed at regular intervals along the site so they will be handy when you need them.

Retaining Walls. To build a retaining wall against a slope with underground seepage, install a drainpipe behind the base before you begin or after laying the first course.

Begin the first course by setting bondstones at each end and at 4-foot intervals. Finish the base course with the largest stones you have left. Always place stones with the flat side down, and fill in spaces with smaller stones. Then spread a layer of sandy soil over the top of the course to serve as a kind of mortar. If you lay drainpipe, be sure it is in place. Cover the pipe with burlap or newspapers to keep soil from clogging it. Backfill the course with gravel or with the native soil if it is sandy.

Continue laying courses in the same manner. Tilt the wall toward the slope at least 1 inch per 24 inches of rise. This tilt is called a batter, and you can keep it uniform by building a simple V-shaped gauge out of two 1 by 3s or similar stock. The two legs should be as long as the wall is high, and separated by 1 or 2 inches at a point 24 inches from the apex. As you hold it against the wall, plumb the outside leg. The batter of the wall should conform to the angle of the inside leg.

With each course, move more dirt down from the hill to spread over the stones and to backfill behind the wall. By the time you reach the top, there will be a plateau ranging from a few feet to several yards wide. If you plant ivy or other vines, the roots will further bind the wall in place.

Freestanding Wall. A freestanding wall is similar to a retaining wall, except that the base is wider and you build up the ends before filling in the courses. Also, tilt all stones downward toward the middle, and batter both sides of the wall. Instead of filling cavities with sandy soil, use small stones and rubble. Cap the wall with large, flat stones.

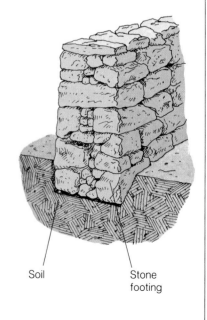

Soil   Stone
              footing

Mortared Stone Walls

A stone wall with mortar looks refined and permanent, and the sides can be vertical instead of battered. Building a mortared wall requires the same care as a loose-laid wall, however, and should not depend on the mortar to act as a glue. Stones are still held in place by their own weight; the mortar only acts as a filler. Mortared walls also require a substantial concrete footing to keep them from settling and cracking, and a drain system for retaining walls. Get professional help for any wall more than 3 feet high.

Almost any type of stone can be used. If your property is plagued by rocks, or if a ready source of fieldstone or river rock is close at hand, you should certainly use them. Otherwise you will have to buy stone. The least expensive are round, undressed stones, known as rubble. They are difficult to work with, but are certainly worth the time and effort if the price is right.

Stone with straight sides that can be laid in courses is the easiest to work with and the most expensive to buy. Volcanic rock, often used for interior stonework, is lightweight and easy to cut with a chisel or saw, but it is also expensive. Stratified stone, known as ashlar, is also easy to handle and can be laid in regular courses. Dressed stone, which has nearly square sides, can be cut to your specifications. To save money, buy semidressed stone, which is chiseled into fairly regular shapes.

Lay out the stones ahead of time so you can reach them conveniently as you work, before the mortar has time to set up. Spread large stones at regular intervals and have plenty of small filler stones on hand.

Footings. The footing should be 12 inches thick and wide enough to extend 6 inches beyond the wall on both sides. The footing should be below frost line and have a 6-inch layer of gravel beneath it to prevent heaving. Place at least two horizontal rebars and a few short vertical rebars in the footing if the voids between the stones will accommodate them.

Mortar. The mortar in a stone wall should be richer than the mortar in a brick wall and should not contain lime, which might stain the stones. Mix 3 parts sand to 1 part portland cement, with ½ part fireclay added for better consistency. The mortar should be dry enough so that it balls up in your hand but not so dry that it crumbles. To estimate how much you'll need, build a small section; the amount varies enormously. Wear gloves; handling mortar and rough stones is very hard on your hands.

First Course. The stones must be clean for the mortar to stick. Spread a 1-inch layer of mortar over the footing at one end and lay a bondstone. Then spread more mortar, lay large stones along the outside edges of the wall, and fill in the center with small stones, rubble, and mortar. Complete the course in this manner, laying a bondstone every 5 or 6 feet.

Remaining Courses. Do a dry layout, making sure the stones are staggered, then lay mortar over the first course and set the stones. If too much mortar oozes out, hold the stone in place with wood shims. When the mortar sets, pull out the shims and fill the voids. Check the sides often with a level to see if they are plumb. Batter the walls 1 inch per 2 feet unless the stones are stable enough to keep the wall vertical.

Joints. Strike the joints as you would strike joints in a brick or block wall, although you do not have to be as precise with stone. Deep joints leave prominent shadows, and shallow joints create a network of mortar lines. Remove any excess mortar from the face of the stone as quickly as possible, and wash the wall with clear water after all the joints have dried. Soapy water should remove stains; only use muriatic acid diluted 1 to 10 with water as a last resort.

Veneers. If you want to make an existing concrete block wall appear more rustic, or if you want to save on the amount of stone you need to purchase, you can use stones as a veneer. To resemble a solid stone wall, a faced wall should have some relief. Mortar the stones to the wall as well as to each other, and be sure there are metal wall ties protruding from the concrete block joints that can be embedded in the mortar of the stone wall. An alternative is to wrap the block wall with stucco mesh, apply a scratch coat of stucco, then embed flat, porous stones in the next coat.

Slip Forms. Another way to build a stone wall is to use forms as you would if you poured a concrete wall. Fill a form with stones and concrete. Work slowly so you can arrange stones against the forms, filling the holes with small stones to avoid having wide bands of concrete showing. By filling the inside cavity with concrete and horizontal rebar, you can build a very strong wall with a smooth stone face.

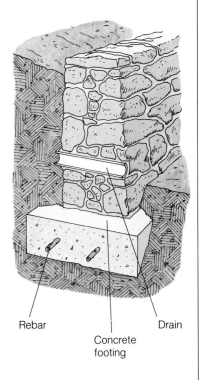

Rebar   Drain

Concrete footing

Horizontal Wood Plank Walls

Wood can be used very effectively in retaining walls. The simplest type is a plank wall of horizontal 2 by 12s held in place with unsurfaced 4 by 4 posts. Use heart grades of cedar, cypress, redwood, or black locust, or lumber that has been pressure treated for ground contact.

Setting the Posts. Sink the posts at least 30 inches into the ground. Place gravel in the bottom of the hole, then backfill around the posts with concrete. Lean the posts into the hill slightly. Set the planks inside of the posts, level them, and nail them with 16d HDG common nails. End joints should be behind posts. Leave a ³/₁₆-inch gap between planks for seepage, and install a drainpipe covered with drain rock behind the wall before backfilling with soil.

Deadmen. A deadman, or buried timber, attaches to the wall at one end and anchors at the other end with a pipe. Install a deadman with a minimum length of 3 feet at each post to strengthen a plank wall substantially. Use decay-resistant lumber no smaller than a 4 by 4 for each deadman. Bolt one end to the post and aim the other end uphill. Drill a hole in the uphill end and drive a 3-foot length of ³/₄-inch pipe through it to anchor it. Cover all the deadmen as you backfill behind the wall.

Capping. Cap the wall with a 2 by 8 to serve as a bench. If the wall is too tall, use the deadmen as bench supports by extending them through the wall at least 16 inches about 16 inches off the ground. Make sure the deadmen are level, then nail planks across them to serve as a bench.

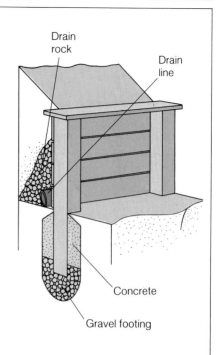

Drain rock
Drain line
Concrete
Gravel footing

Vertical Wood Timber Walls

Use railroad ties, treated posts, telephone poles, or special garden posts to build a stockade wall. They can be round or square, as long as they butt together tightly enough to hold back the soil. It's extremely hard work cutting railroad ties with a hand saw; use a chainsaw, a large circular saw, or have the posts cut to length by your supplier.

To build the wall, excavate a trench deep enough to bury the posts. The trench for a retaining wall should be one half to two thirds the length of the posts. The trench for a freestanding wall should be one third the length of the posts. Set the posts so they lean slightly into the hillside and backfill the trench with concrete or firmly packed soil. Pin the posts together by nailing a long 2 by 6 along the back of the wall near the top. Install a drainpipe covered with drain rock behind the wall, and, if the posts are an irregular shape, attach a strip of aluminum flashing to prevent the soil from leaking.

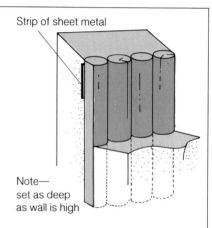

Strip of sheet metal

Note—
set as deep
as wall is high

Horizontal Timber Wall

Timbers are easy to build with and they blend well into any garden setting. You can use irregular and rugged timbers for a rustic look or milled timbers for a more formal setting. They can be stained to match the color of the house or other garden features, and their appearance improves with age as they weather and take on a more permanent look.

Properly treated timbers can last up to 35 years or more and they will survive the shifting and settling of unstable soils better than masonry walls. Timber walls are also easier to repair or replace than masonry ones.

Used railroad ties make a rugged and durable retaining wall because they are heavy and are treated for prolonged ground contact. They are generally 8 feet long, 8 inches wide, and 6 to 8 inches high. Select ties that are dry, since wet creosote is harmful to plants and people.

If you prefer a look that is not as rugged as railroad ties, buy pressure-treated timbers. They are longer and the preservative injected into them is usually more benign than creosote. The color—either beige or green—blends into gardens well. When working with either ties or pressure-treated lumber, wear gloves and avoid inhaling sawdust. Do not burn the scraps of wood; get rid of them

in an approved dumping area.

Excavation. Dig a trench across the bottom of the slope deep enough to embed the first timber. In a climate with severe winters, dig 6 inches deeper and lay a bed of gravel. In addition, excavate into the hill behind the site to accommodate a deadman every 8 feet or so. The trench should be perpendicular to the wall and deep enough to allow the deadmen to intersect the wall at the third or fourth course of timbers.

First Course. Lay the first course of timbers in the trench, using a string line to keep the row straight. Tamp the timbers into the soil or gravel and level them. To increase strength drill 3/4-inch diameter holes at the ends of each timber and drive 30-inch lengths of 1/2-inch pipe through them into the ground. An alternative is to wait until the third or fourth course, then drive pipes all the way through and into the ground. Use a heavy-duty 1/2-inch drill with a long ship's auger for the bit. Make sure you have something to brace yourself against as you hold the drill. Lay drainpipe behind the timbers and cover it with crushed rock.

Remaining Courses. Lay the second course of timbers over the first, lapping them wherever the wall has corners. Offset any end joints by at least 2 feet. Add the third course,

then drill through the three courses every 4 to 6 feet and drive 1/2-inch pipes through the holes into the ground. Short lengths of number 5 rebar can substitute for pipes.

As you lay the fourth course, set deadmen so one end rests on the wall, the other in the trench. Drill a hole through both ends, penetrating at least two timbers at the wall end, and drive pipes through them. A short length of timber lying across and beneath the deadman and pinned to the uphill end with the pipe will increase stability.

The rest of the timbers in the fourth course should butt up to the deadmen. Install the next two courses in the same way. If the wall is higher than five courses, install deadmen at least every third course.

If you need to cut timbers or ties, use a chain saw or an 18-inch-diameter circular saw. Watch out for gravel or nails that might be embedded in the wood, and wear goggles. Coat the cut ends with a preservative.

Backfill the wall with gravel as you build it, then bring soil from the slope down in behind the gravel. If you use pressure-treated timbers, you can stain them after letting them season for at least two months. A very dark color can seem oppressive; beige, light green, or gray are more suitable colors for most gardens.

GATES

The design of a gate should be appealing—welcoming visitors to your home. But since a gate is opened and closed so often, the two most important attributes are that it work properly and that it be wide enough.

Make a gate opening as wide as possible; 4 feet is comfortable, although 6 to 8 feet looks better for formal entryways. Some gates, such as for driveways, can be as wide as 20 feet. If the opening is 4 feet or less, a single gate is adequate. If it is between 4 and 8 feet, there should be a pair of gates. Double gates are no more inconvenient than single gates, since one side can be kept shut most of the time. Whether there is one gate or two, wide openings require special bracing, sometimes even a wheel, under the swing edge of the gate.

A gate should always swing inward toward private space, not outward toward public space. The hinges can be placed on either side of a single gate. If the gate will swing into a sloping hillside, mount the hinges on the downhill post. If the gate is made to swing against a wall or section of fence, mount the hinges on that side. If a pathway approaches the gate from an angle, hinge the gate so that it opens toward the path, rather than blocking it off. If none of these factors is an issue, hinge the gate on the right side as it opens toward you.

Three simple techniques will keep most gates from sagging or leaning:
● Brace the hinge post so that it won't lean toward the gate by building a diagonal wooden brace into the adjacent section of fencing or by attaching a cable between the top of the post and the bottom of the next fence post over. Provide a turnbuckle for tightening the cable. For tall or heavy gates, use 6 by 6 posts instead of 4 by 4 ones, setting them deep into the ground. Whenever possible, hang gates from house walls rather than from free-standing posts.
● Build diagonal bracing into the gate itself. This can be a 2 by 4 brace that runs from the bottom hinge to the top of the latch side or a cable that stretches from the top hinge to the bottom of the latch side.
● Attach heavy-duty hinges securely with lag bolts or long screws.

Recommended Cross-References
Fences, Garden Walls, Wood.

Materials and Design

A gate in the middle of a fence looks integrated when it is made from the same materials as the fence. However, a gate design does not have to duplicate that of the fence unless you want the gate to blend in. A gate is constructed differently enough for it to stand out at least a little from the rest of the fence.

If the gate is in a solid fence and privacy is not critical, a special touch is to space the gate materials so that they form an open grillwork instead of a solid facade. The gate design will contrast with the fence, and the gate will be inviting by revealing a glimpse of the yard and house beyond. Another way to vary the gate is to make it slightly taller than the fence by extending the infill up or by shaping it into a decorative pattern. If the fence is painted, particularly when it is solid, painting the gate a different color provides an interesting focal point. Using hardware, trim, or decorative objects gives a gate a distinctive character, although imagination must be tempered by sensitivity to the overall setting.

While gates for an opening in a masonry wall cannot possibly be the same material, the design should be complementary. Because walls are substantial, the gate should also have a feeling of strength. Wood gates should be solid and made of large-dimensioned lumber.

Hardware

Choose the latch and hinges before you build the gate, so that you can construct the gate for proper mounting of the hardware.

Latches. Latches come in many different types and styles. A dead bolt is the most secure type; it requires a key to open the gate from the outside. A thumb catch is a good type of latch for entry gates because it has a friendly, inviting handle that can be operated with one hand. Another type of latch has the same closing mechanism as a thumb catch, but opens from the outside with a small wire or string instead of a prominent handle. A cane bolt holds one side of a double gate constantly steady. It slips into a hole in the pavement and can be lifted out to open both gates. A latch that is mounted on top of the gate and a slide bolt are two other kinds, not to mention homemade varieties, such as a simple loop that collars both the latch post and gate to hold the gate shut.

Hinges. Gate hinges are as varied as gate latches. Short gates, less than 4 feet tall, can hang on two hinges, but taller gates need three. Plain butt hinges work for light gates, and can be mounted so that only the knuckles show. Heavier gates need longer hinges, such as straps or tees. Some hinges have a bolt instead of a leaf for mounting to the gate post or masonry column.

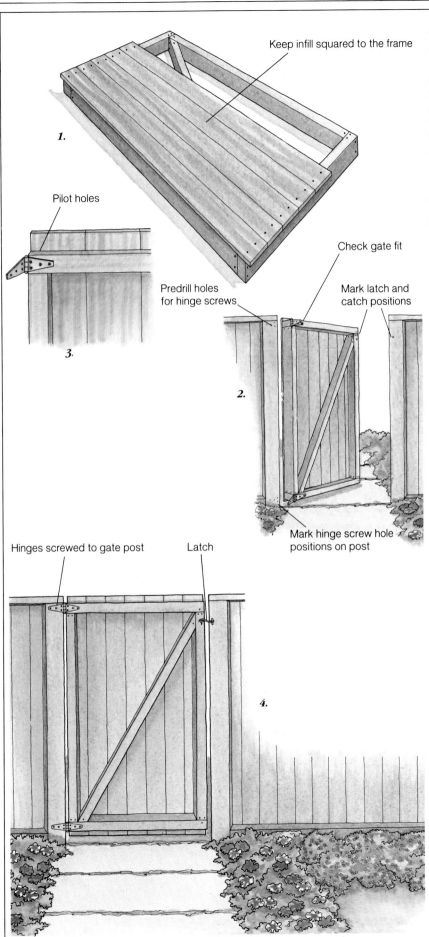

Keep infill squared to the frame

1.

Pilot holes

3.

Predrill holes
for hinge screws

2.

Check gate fit

Mark latch and
catch positions

Mark hinge screw hole
positions on post

Hinges screwed to gate post

Latch

4.

Wood Gate Construction

This type of gate depends on strong vertical members to hold it together. If the infill material is small-dimensioned lumber or if it is to be spaced for a lighter effect, modify the frame so that 2 by 4s are on each side as well as across the top and bottom. The gate still needs a diagonal brace, either a solid 2 by 4 or a thin cable running in the opposite direction with a turnbuckle to adjust tension.

1. Measure the opening. If it is out of plumb, try to straighten the posts. If you cannot, make adjustments in the gate itself. Allow 1/2 inch for hinge clearance, and another 1/2 inch on the latch side for swing clearance.

Select straight, dry lumber. Cut and lay out three 2 by 4s in a "Z" pattern, so that the bottom corner of the diagonal brace will be on the hinge side of the gate. Nail the infill to this frame, using more nails than you would for fencing. For a stronger gate, assemble the frame with lapped or rabbeted joints and nail it together before attaching the infill.

2. Place the gate in the opening and check it for fit, setting it on blocks if necessary. Take it down and make any adjustments to the gate.

3. Attach heavy-duty hinges to the gate, screwing or bolting them to the horizontal frame pieces. The knuckles should be centered about 1/4 inch outside of the gate, and should be in perfect vertical alignment with each other. To conceal the hinges entirely, use the butt style and screw the leaves into the end instead of the face of each horizontal framing member. This is not as strong as face-mounting because you are screwing the hinge into end grain.

4. Set the gate in the opening so that the hinges are positioned against the post. Use blocks to temporarily steady the gate, making sure it has equal clearance all around. Mount the hinges to the post with heavy screws or lag bolts, testing it for swing after one or two screws are in each hinge. If it swings properly, install the rest of the screws.

Install the latch. To save wear and tear on the latch, nail a wood stop to the post or onto the edge of the gate itself. Use material that matches the gate. It is also a good idea to mount a gate spring or improvise a weight-and-chain device so that the gate will swing shut automatically.

The warm, natural look of its materials, as well as its simple, open design, help this gazebo to blend attractively into the hillside behind it.

A gazebo is an outdoor structure that emphasizes fun more than function. Nobody really needs one, but they're nice to have. Other structures do a better job of providing shade, because they can be larger; or of staging outdoor entertaining, because they can hold more people; or of offering shelter, because they can be more weatherproof. But gazebos have an irresistible charm that combines nostalgia for the Victorian past with the feeling of intimacy and the quality of extravagance.

Gazebos come in many shapes and sizes, but the traditional style has an octagon shape, a wood floor, low railings, and gobs of gingerbread. Building such a structure is a major project; variations on this theme are much easier to build. One way to simplify the project is to build a

square gazebo, thus eliminating most of the time-consuming angles of a hexagon or octagon. Another way to make construction easier is to use lath or slats for the roof instead of shingle roofing, although this limits its use to fair weather.

The frills and ornamentation that are the hallmark of gazebos do not have to be sacrificed for ease of construction. You can use lattice, moldings, or prefabricated gingerbread pieces to dress up the simplest structure. Lighting for nighttime use is one of the easiest and most dramatic ways to glamorize a gazebo at minimal cost.

The easiest gazebos to build are from kits, which are available from home centers or through mail-order houses that advertise in garden magazines. Some kits are very elaborate

and require extensive cutting, although all the materials and a complete set of plans are included. Others have prefabricated pieces that can be assembled with little more than a screwdriver, hammer, and wrench. Another alternative is to buy a comprehensive set of plans or a book with complete plans and build the gazebo yourself.

Be sure to check with your local building department before starting any construction. You may need a permit, and there may be restrictions about where you can locate an outdoor structure.

Recommended Cross-References
Benches, Decks, Footings, Framing, Lattice, Lighting: Outdoor, Roofs, Trellises.

Gazebo Construction

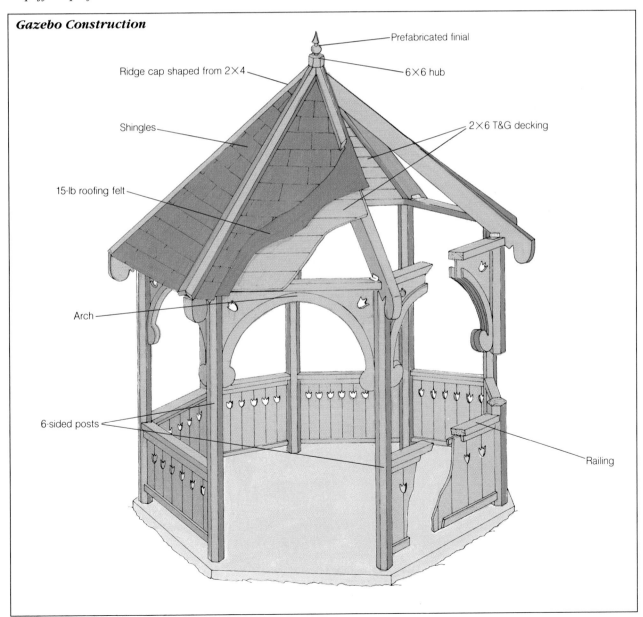

Prefabricated finial

Ridge cap shaped from 2×4

6×6 hub

Shingles

2×6 T&G decking

15-lb roofing felt

Arch

6-sided posts

Railing

GLASS

Into every life some broken glass must fall. Who knows when you will have to replace a broken window or perhaps frame a picture? If you order new windows, you will need to specify glass and you should be aware of the many types available.

Recommended Cross-References
Cooling, Greenhouses, Insulation, Solar Energy, Windows.

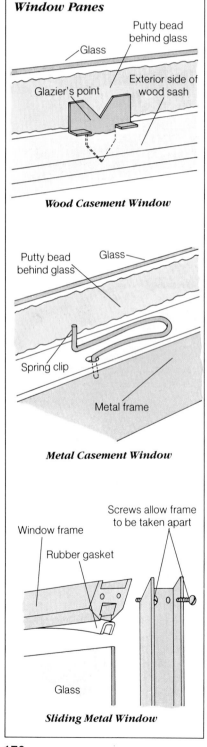

Window Panes

Putty bead behind glass
Glass
Glazier's point
Exterior side of wood sash

Wood Casement Window

Putty bead behind glass
Glass
Spring clip
Metal frame

Metal Casement Window

Screws allow frame to be taken apart
Window frame
Rubber gasket
Glass

Sliding Metal Window

Types of Glass

Window Glass. Sheet glass was used for windows in nearly all old houses. It was manufactured in one of four thicknesses: single-strength ($\frac{3}{32}$ inch); double-strength ($\frac{1}{8}$ inch); and heavy ($\frac{3}{16}$ or $\frac{9}{32}$ inch).

Plate glass was used for large windows, shelves, and tabletops. It is at least ¼ inch thick. It was rolled flat while hot and plastic, then ground smooth and polished. Although glass is no longer manufactured by this method, the term is used generally to describe thick glass.

Float glass has replaced both sheet and plate glass. It is made by pouring molten glass over a bed of molten metal. The glass floats on top of the metal and cools gradually. The resulting surfaces are smooth, parallel, and virtually free of distortion.

Safety Glass. Most codes require the use of specialty glass in skylights, overhead windows, large glass doors, shower doors, and windows within 18 inches of the floor. Codes usually specify one of three types of glass: tempered glass, laminated safety plate, or wire glass. Tempered glass is the most common. When it breaks, it disintegrates into small beads instead of large shards. Most manufacturers offer tempered glass as an option when you order prefabricated windows. The windows in a car are made of laminated safety glass. A thin adhesive film between two layers of glass keeps glass fragments from flying when the windows break. Wire glass is not often used in homes, but is an approved safety glass in many locations. It is a type of laminated glass with thin wire mesh between the layers.

Obscure Glass. Install obscure, or frosted, glass in bathrooms, entrance-hall windows, basement windows, and in other settings that demand privacy or diffused sunlight. Obscure glass is available in the same thicknesses as window glass.

Insulating Glass. Glass is a poor insulator. The insulation provided by insulating glass is due to an air space between two separate panes, not to an innate quality of the glass. The most effective insulating windows have a space from $\frac{3}{16}$ to $\frac{5}{8}$ inch wide and are sealed all around the edges. Units made of insulating glass are also called double-glazed or double-

pane windows because each unit uses two sheets of glass. Triple-glazed windows are also available, but the benefits they provide may not justify the cost. In some insulating windows, the manufacturer has replaced all the air in the space with a gas, usually carbon dioxide, argon, or krypton. These units can provide up to 20 percent more insulation than units of regular insulating glass.

These windows are often expensive and difficult to replace when broken. It may be impossible to replace just the glass; instead, the entire sash (panes of glass and immediate frame) must be replaced.

Low-Emissivity Glass. This type of glass, abbreviated low-E glass, has a clear, thin coating that admits full sunlight but holds back some of the heat that tries to escape. Low-E glass is particularly effective in double-glazed units where the coating is on the inside face of the exterior pane or is suspended between the panes. Such units earn insulating values as high as R-5, a marked improvement over most double-glazed windows.

Reflective Glass. Reflective glass has a metallic coating that reduces the penetration of sunlight. Reflective windows usually appear silver or gray and are like one-way mirrors. Use reflective glass in rooms that are subject to overheating.

Tinted Glass. Tinted, or heat-absorbing glass, reduces sunlight and glare. The tinting material is not a coating but a metallic oxide that is mixed into the ingredients. Iron oxide produces a bluish-green tint. Nickel oxide, cobalt oxide, or selenium produce a bronze or gray tint. The intensity of the color depends on the thickness of the glass. The view through tinted glass is brighter than the view through reflective glass and the ability of tinted glass to reduce heat gain is commensurately less.

Low-Iron Glass. Glass without iron oxide admits as much as 20 percent more light than ordinary window glass. The edges of low-iron glass do not have the familiar greenish tint of ordinary glass. The clarity of low-iron glass makes it a good choice for a picture frame. Also use it where you desire solar heat gain, such as in windows that face south or in solar collector panels.

Alternative Glazings

Acrylic. Acrylic is a kind of plastic that outperforms glass in some situations. It is lighter and stronger than glass, and when acrylic is new it is almost as transparent. Acrylic is prone to scratches, however, and will not stay clear more than a few years. Acrylic also expands and contracts a great deal. It insulates almost as poorly as glass, although double-glazed panels are more effective. Use acrylic in a domed skylight, a sunroom, or a greenhouse.

Polycarbonate. Polycarbonate plastic is much stronger than acrylic. It is useful where security is a concern. Polycarbonate is vulnerable to the ultraviolet rays in sunlight and is not quite as transparent as acrylic. It also expands and contracts a great deal.

Fiberglass. Polyester panels with fiberglass reinforcing fibers are available in flat or corrugated sheets. They are easy to handle, fairly stable in terms of thermal expansion, and are able to withstand ultraviolet rays. Although they appear cloudy, fiber-

glass panels allow as much solar heat gain as low-iron glass.

Films. Films may improve the insulating, shading, or reflecting performance of your windows. Some films are clear and emulate low-E glass. Some are tinted bronze, gray, or gold. Other films are silver and reflective. Some films help glass retain interior heat while allowing maximum solar gain. Others block direct sunlight. Be selective in applying films. A film is formulated to serve a specific purpose—don't expect it to do more than one job. Insulating films are most effective when applied on windows that face north. If you want to reduce heat gain, apply the appropriate film on windows that face east or west. Apply film to windows that face south only if heat gain is a problem all year. Whatever film you select, follow the manufacturer's instructions carefully, especially if you apply the film to double-glazed windows. Some window manufacturers void their warranty if films are applied improperly.

Cutting Glass

You can take measurements to a supplier and have glass cut, but it is not difficult to cut it yourself.

To cut glass, all you need is a steel framing square and a glass cutter. Practice the technique on a scrap before cutting a large piece of glass. Mark the point where the cut begins by lightly nicking the glass with the cutter. Wipe the line to be cut with kerosene or turpentine, which helps reduce the chances of chipping the glass. Then slide a steel framing square along the line to guide your

cutter. Make the cut in a smooth, single sweep. Just score the glass; pressing too hard will chip it. Don't try to go over the line a second time—you'll just get a sloppy break. Instead, turn the glass over and score it on the other side.

Move the glass to the edge of the work table, or place a dowel under the score and bend it downward. Do this right away while the score is still fresh, because—believe it or not—the glass will start to heal if you wait. If all goes well, the glass will snap cleanly along the scored line.

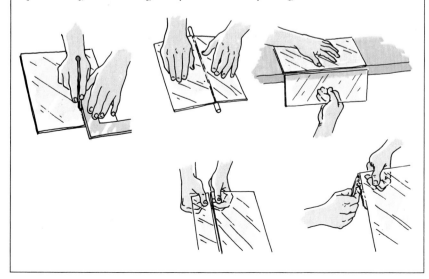

Replacing Broken Glass

1. Remove glass shards.

2. Chip out old putty and points.

3. Coat bare wood with sealer.

4. Apply cushion layer of putty.

5. Put in glass with glazier's point.

6. Press putty onto edge of glass.

7. Smooth putty with a putty knife.

8. Paint, after a week or so, when the putty is dry to the touch.

GREENHOUSES

A greenhouse, once a luxury afforded only by the wealthy, is a structure almost anyone can build from scratch or from a kit. Different designs fit different spaces: a tiny backyard, a rooftop, a balcony, or even a window.

Although a greenhouse is traditionally found in the garden, you can attach one to your home and even use it to help heat and expand the living space of the house.

The benefits are evident whenever you set foot in a greenhouse; it is like entering another world. It may be snowing outside, but inside you are among exotic arrays of tropical flowers or standing beside a flourishing garden of ripening vegetables.

Recommended Cross-References
Drainage, Foundations, Framing, Glass, Plumbing, Solariums, Windows, Wiring.

The simple construction of this greenhouse makes it a practical project for homeowners; and the uncluttered, efficient interior layout is a boon to gardeners.

Planning

Start by listing the purposes the greenhouse will serve. Some greenhouses display plants, others are a site for propagating and growing plants, and others serve to extend the growing season for only one or two months. Functions will help you choose location, size, and construction materials.

Size. A greenhouse should be at least 6 feet wide. The layout should allow you to walk through easily and provide room for benches on both sides.

Style. Greenhouses come in all shapes and styles. The type you choose depends on how permanent you want the structure to be, where you want to locate it, whether you live in a snowy climate, and the dictates of your taste.

The simplest greenhouse is probably an A-frame structure with two sloping sides joined at the top. An A-frame is relatively easy to construct and it sheds snow well, but provides limited headroom and is hard to ventilate. Add headroom to an A-frame by bending the sides so they converge more gradually at the top.

Attached or Freestanding. A greenhouse that attaches to a wall of the house is generally cheaper and easier to build than a detached greenhouse. Utilities are readily available and access is convenient. An attached greenhouse will help to heat the home, but you must shut it off at night to prevent excessive heat loss.

Kits. Consider time, cost, and complexity of design in deciding how much of the work to do yourself. Kits for simple rectangular greenhouses can take as long as a week to build and equip properly—you have to prepare the site, build the floor, and install plumbing and wiring. If you are comfortable with basic framing and paving techniques, you are probably better off building a simple greenhouse structure from scratch.

Energy Efficiency. Greenhouses need a secondary heat source to warm them during seasons when the sun does not shine directly on them. Some use gas or electric heaters. Solar greenhouses include heat-absorbing materials, such as masonry or water barrels, a calculated ratio of glass area to potential heat gain, and window insulation that retains heat during cold periods. If you consider a solar greenhouse, include these features in the design. An attached solar greenhouse or solarium is not difficult to construct. The benefit is an abundance of free heat that you can even use to heat your home.

Costs. As you plan your greenhouse, consider the cost of heating and cooling. Also consider the possible reassessment of your property, as well as the tax credits you could claim if the greenhouse qualifies as an energy-saving improvement.

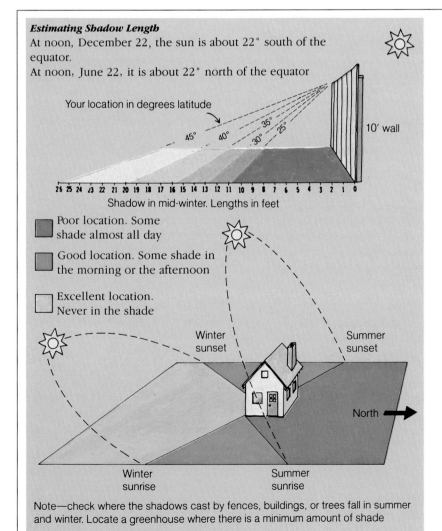

Estimating Shadow Length

At noon, December 22, the sun is about 22° south of the equator.
At noon, June 22, it is about 22° north of the equator

Your location in degrees latitude

45° 40° 35° 30° 25°

10' wall

26 25 24 23 22 21 20 19 18 17 16 15 14 13 12 11 10 9 8 7 6 5 4 3 2 1 0
Shadow in mid-winter. Lengths in feet

- Poor location. Some shade almost all day
- Good location. Some shade in the morning or the afternoon
- Excellent location. Never in the shade

Winter sunset   Summer sunset

Winter sunrise   Summer sunrise

North

Note—check where the shadows cast by fences, buildings, or trees fall in summer and winter. Locate a greenhouse where there is a minimum amount of shade

Choosing a Site

The primary consideration is sunshine. Choose a site where the sun will not be blocked by houses, walls, or trees. Keep in mind that in winter the sun is considerably lower than it is in summer. The sun should shine directly on the greenhouse for at least four hours on December 21 if you plan to use it in winter.

A simple formula helps to determine the effect of obstacles. If an obstacle lies directly south of your proposed greenhouse, the distance between them should equal 2½ times the height of the obstacle. For instance, if a wall is 10 feet tall, the greenhouse should be 25 feet away from it. If the obstacle is a deciduous tree, however, you may want to place the greenhouse closer to it to receive summer shade. Remember that in the summer the hottest sun will come from directly overhead and slightly to the north of due west in the late afternoon.

Also consider drainage and soil. Try to avoid building in depressions that will catch rain and snow or in boggy areas where soil is constantly wet and unstable. If the ground slopes behind the greenhouse, it may be necessary to put in drainpipes or gravel ditches to divert runoff. The site should also be close to water and electrical hookups.

Controlling the Environment

Owning a greenhouse is more like having a pet than having a garden. Because of extremes in temperature and humidity, the plants cannot survive long without attention. You will minister to your plants by weatherizing, heating, cooling, and humidifying the greenhouse. To minimize the time you need to spend tending the greenhouse, automate as many of the systems as possible.

Tightening the Joints. Ensure that the greenhouse is as airtight as possible by weather stripping the door and vents and sealing all the joints between roof and walls with caulk that stays flexible. Check that all the glazing is snug to the frame. Before you install the heating system, search for cracks and line them with plastic sheeting or sealant. In climates that suffer severe cold, line all the walls and roof with a layer of clear plastic sheeting at least 4 mils thick. Staple it to a framework mounted between 1 to 6 inches inside the glazing.

Heating. The basic considerations in heating a greenhouse are providing and distributing warmth and doing so at a reasonable cost. Most heating systems are gas or electric, but you should use as many solar heating techniques as possible in order to keep utility costs down. Wood and coal can also be used for heating greenhouses. Always favor a system that will operate automatically.

To determine your heating needs, figure the total surface area (SA) of the ceiling and walls; do not include the floor area. Calculate the degree rise (DR), which is the difference between the coldest outdoor temperature in the past several years and the temperature you want to maintain in the greenhouse. A typical greenhouse temperature is 55° F. Now consider the insulating factor (IF). Assign a value of 1.5 to glass glazing, 1.2 to fiberglass glazing, and 0.8 to a double layer of glass and plastic. Multiply SA times DR times IF to yield the heat loss per hour in BTUs. The output of the heater should be equal to the heat loss. To convert BTUs to kilowatts to apply the figure to an electric heater, divide the number of BTUs by 3,413.

Large heaters are expensive to buy and operate. Operating a large heater may be expensive enough to warrant the purchase of a small heater for auxiliary day-to-day use. A battery-powered, temperature-sensitive alarm can alert you to conditions that require the use of the large unit. Reduce operating costs by installing solar collectors, in the form of thermal mass. Place dark-colored 55-gallon drums along the back wall. Pour water to within 3 inches of the top of the drums. A concrete slab, water bottles, rocks, and concrete blocks also store solar heat. If practical, construct a solid, rather than a glazed, north wall. Insulate it and incorporate thermal mass into it.

The air in the greenhouse must circulate or all the heat will collect under the ceiling. A heater with a combination fan and thermostat is a favorite with greenhouse owners because it distributes warm air evenly throughout the greenhouse. A small fan near the ceiling is also effective.

Cooling. In much of the country, cooling the greenhouse in the summer is a greater problem than heating it in winter. In many areas, simple shades, fans, and an open roof vent are sufficient; where summer temperatures are constantly above 80 degrees, you need to install more elaborate cooling systems.

If you require cooling appliances, install an automatic system with thermostats. Buy a two-speed fan and use the lower speed during spring and fall. The thermostats should be designed for greenhouse use so humidity will not damage them. In addition, conditions may warrant thermal pistons that open and close vents, screens to block sunlight, and, in extremely hot regions, an evaporative cooler.

Humidity Control. If the humidity is too low, plants suffer. If humidity is too high, they are susceptible to leaf mold and stem rot. Correct low humidity by misting or watering the floor two or three times a day. Only extremely dry areas or severe winters necessitate a humidifier. Too much humidity is more common than too little. Your plants suffer from too much humidity if the leaves do not dry out during the night. Correct the problem by installing a fan that will improve air circulation. If humidity causes excess condensation on the windows, it may be necessary to install sheets of plastic film on the inside of the windows or insulate the windows on the outside at night.

Outfitting the Greenhouse

With the basic shell and the floor in place, you are ready to install benches and other permanent structures. Place benches in long rows with an aisle down the center. Or place short benches at right angles to the center aisle. Devote no more than one quarter of total floor space to aisles.

Ideal benches are attractive as well as functional. Make simple platforms by nailing crosspieces to the wall studs. Support the free ends with short legs, then lay long planks over them. The benches should be easy to reach, a width of 32 to 36 inches is typical. Place shelves above the benches on the back wall and below the benches on both sides according to your need for display and storage space.

Designate a shady area as a potting center. Build a rim around the bench to keep soil from spilling over. Other amenities include a sink, tool racks, shelves, and locked storage cabinets.

Your final chore before placing plants in the greenhouse is to sanitize it. The quickest and easiest way to sanitize is to wash everything down with a fresh solution of 1 part liquid household chlorine bleach to 10 parts water. Apply the solution with a sprayer. Scrub all surfaces, including crevices, crannies, benches, walls, and floors.

The greenhouse is now ready for plants although you still need to fine-tune the environment.

Warming Cables

A warming cable encourages propagation by maintaining a constant soil temperature. Arrange the cable to distribute heat evenly throughout the flat. The cable should never cross itself.

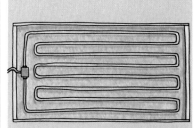

Note—warming cables should be arranged in a manner as shown here. Spaces should be equal widths and the cable must never cross over itself

Cold Frames

A greenhouse doesn't have to be an 8 feet by 12 feet structure. You can get a lot of pleasure out of a mini version—a cold frame. The traditional cold frame has a clear top that is angled to directly face the low winter sun. It is often made with scrap lumber found around the house and either a glass or plastic top. A fence or wall on the north side provides wind protection. White or silver paint on the inside helps reflect more light to the plants. If you want to adapt an old window, notch the horizontal mullions or dividers to make sure that water can escape.

Place a thermometer inside the frame and shield it from the direct rays of the sun. When the temperature is high, open the top to permit air circulation. Close it again when the temperatures start to drop. This will conserve the radiation that has been absorbed by the soil.

In actual practice, the frames are usually opened in the morning and then closed as soon as the direct rays of the sun have passed over.

Window Greenhouse

Install a prefabricated greenhouse as a window in an existing or new opening. A window greenhouse provides an attractive addition that can be enjoyed by both the indoor grower and people passing by.

The window greenhouse is a big step up from a windowsill garden. The greenhouse is more than just a bay window with room for plants; it closes on the inside so the plants are not subject to the drying effects of the house. They are in their own environment. The small size of a window greenhouse can create a problem, however. As soon as sunlight hits the window, the greenhouse warms rapidly. At night, it cools quickly. Vents that connect to the outside and vents from the room enable you to stabilize the greenhouse environment.

The location of a window greenhouse depends on the effect you want to achieve and the plants you want to grow. To get maximum sunlight, especially during the winter months, choose a window that faces south. A window that faces east gets morning and midday sun. A western window gets sun only in late afternoon, and a northern window gets little sun unless you live in the south. If you put a unit where the plants you want to grow will not get enough sunlight, install fluorescent lighting to supplement natural light.

Step-by-Step Installation. 1. Measure the existing window and order a greenhouse of similar size. Remove the existing window.
2. Make a frame with 1 by 6 stock.
3. Weather strip the framing.
4. Lift the greenhouse into place.
5. Screw it firmly to the framing.
6. Install the shelves and your plants.
7. Add a shade where necessary.

GUTTERS & DOWNSPOUTS

Gutters collect runoff and channel it into downspouts that direct water away from the house and foundation. Without them, water drips onto people's heads and onto border gardens, causing bad tempers and soil erosion. Worse, when the soil is saturated, water may seep into crawl space or through basement walls.

Selecting Component Parts

Gutters and downspouts are most commonly of galvanized metal, aluminum, or vinyl. You can buy painted or unpainted galvanized and aluminum gutters; the choice allows you to paint them to match your house. Vinyl gutters come in a wide array of colors. Many suppliers also carry copper and wood gutters, but they are a lot more expensive.

Gutters and downspouts are normally sold in 10-foot lengths, which are the easiest to handle. (You can usually order longer lengths.) Standard gutter widths are 4 inches, 5 inches, or 6 inches.

As a general rule, you should use 4-inch-wide gutters when the roof area is up to 750 square feet, 5-inch gutters with roofs up to 1,500 square feet, and 6-inch gutters with roofs that are more than 1,500 square feet.

Recommended Cross-References
Drainage, Roofs.

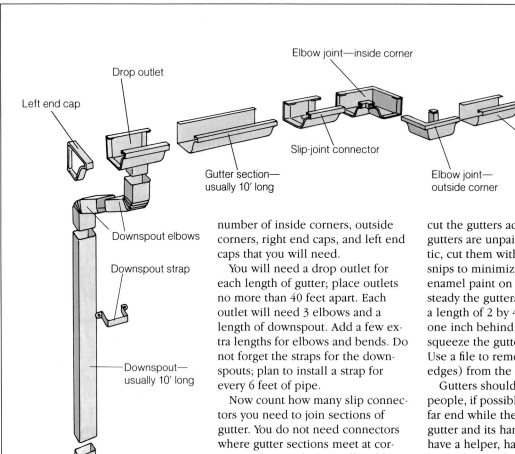

Left end cap

Drop outlet

Elbow joint—inside corner

Right end cap

Slip-joint connector

Gutter section—
usually 10' long

Elbow joint—
outside corner

Gutter section

Downspout elbows

Downspout strap

Downspout—
usually 10' long

Downspout
elbow

Splash block

Installation

Before you start, make sure that you have all the necessary parts.

Estimating Your Needs. First, measure the length of all the eaves to calculate the number of 10-foot gutter sections. Plan to install one bracket every 3 to 4 feet. Then count the number of inside corners, outside corners, right end caps, and left end caps that you will need.

You will need a drop outlet for each length of gutter; place outlets no more than 40 feet apart. Each outlet will need 3 elbows and a length of downspout. Add a few extra lengths for elbows and bends. Do not forget the straps for the downspouts; plan to install a strap for every 6 feet of pipe.

Now count how many slip connectors you need to join sections of gutter. You do not need connectors where gutter sections meet at corners or drop outlets. Finally, add up the number of splash blocks or leaders you will need under all the downspouts to divert water away from the house.

Installing the Gutters. Gutters should slope about 1 inch for every 20 feet. If you have a run of 40 feet or more, slope the gutters from the middle of the run and put a downspout at each end. To lay out the gutter slope, tack a nail to the fascia board at the high end of the slope. Measure the run, dropping 1 inch every 20 feet. Tack a nail at the final position and snap a chalk line between the two nails. Use the line as a guide.

Lay out all the components on the ground. Measure the gutter runs and note the downspout locations. Then cut the gutters accordingly. If the gutters are unpainted metal or plastic, cut them with a hacksaw. Use tin snips to minimize the shattering of enamel paint on painted gutters. To steady the gutters while sawing, slip a length of 2 by 4 in the gutter about one inch behind the cut. Then squeeze the gutter against the block. Use a file to remove burrs (ragged edges) from the cut edge.

Gutters should be installed by two people, if possible. One supports the far end while the other installs the gutter and its hangers. If you do not have a helper, hang the far end in a loop of string from the guide nail; then work toward it. When all the pieces are secure, go back and caulk each joint to prevent leaks.

Installing the Downspouts. Connect the downspout elbows to the drainpipe on the drop outlet by drilling holes on opposite sides and inserting sheet-metal screws. Connect the elbows to the downspouts in the same manner. Bend the straps to fit the downspout, then screw straps to the siding. Fit the elbow on the end of the downspout and place a splash block under it. If you wish to carry the water farther from the house, attach a length of downspout to the elbow. You can bury the extension and run it to a dry well or to an outlet further down the hill.

Gutters

Gutters are normally metal (sometimes corrugated for additional strength) or plastic. Wooden gutters are available, although they may be hard to find. The most common shapes are forged (ogee), half-round, and square.

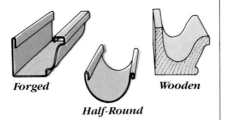

Forged

Half-Round

Wooden

Downspout Guards

To prevent a downspout from filling with leaves and other debris, install a downspout guard. A downspout guard is a perforated cover that you can insert in or over the drain hole. Or you can fashion your own from a piece of perforated metal. Clean guards out periodically to prevent the gutters from backfilling.

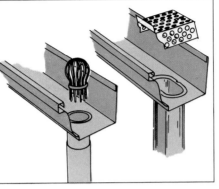

Gutter Covers

Vinyl-coated screens cover the gutter and keep out leaves and other debris. Install a cover by sliding it under the first course of shingles until it is flush with the front edge of the gutter.

Gutter Hangers

Gutters hang from eaves in a number of ways. You can use straps (these must be installed before the roofing is applied), brackets, or drive a long spike across the gutter through a spacer tube (ferrule).

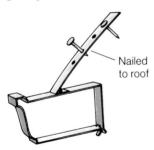

Nailed to roof

Straps. Nail strap to roof beneath shingles. Insert gutter from below and hook the hanger to itself under the gutter at the fascia.

Nailed to fascia

Clips. Nail hanger to the fascia. Insert gutter from above and snap the clip across the top.

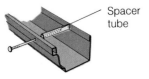

Spacer tube

Spikes. Drive spike through gutter and spacer tube into fascia.

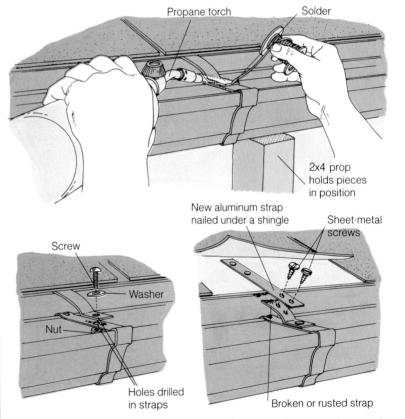

Propane torch

Solder

2x4 prop holds pieces in position

New aluminum strap nailed under a shingle

Sheet-metal screws

Screw

Washer

Nut

Holes drilled in straps

Broken or rusted strap

Repairing Gutter Supports

Many gutters droop and fail simply because the supports need repair. The most common problem is the separation of the bracket from its supporting strap. There are three different methods of connecting them:

1. Soldering. Support the gutter with a long 2 by 4. Clean bracket and strap with solvent so they are free of grease and dirt. Then coat the two surfaces with flux, heat them with a torch, and touch the solder to the joint when it is hot enough.

2. Bolts. Drill a hole through both pieces and connect them with a stove bolt.

3. Sheet-Metal Screws. If you need to attach a new aluminum strap, drill small pilot holes in the old bracket. Install the new strap with sheet-metal screws.

HEATING

Installing a complete heating system is a major project and not something a homeowner is likely to do. However, you should be able to maintain and even "tune up" your existing heating system. Also, being aware of new heating systems and equipment that provide energy-efficient alternatives to the outmoded equipment of yesterday will make you better able to upgrade your present system or plan a completely new heating system if you are remodeling or adding a room.

Heating systems vary widely in the type of energy they use and the means of distributing it. Some homes rely on space heaters, such as wall furnaces, wood stoves, or portable heaters, but most homes have a central heating system. The five most common types are warm air, hot water, hybrid, electric radiant, and heat pumps. In addition, solar energy is used to heat homes with hot-water systems, solariums, and direct solar radiation.

Recommended Cross-References
Cooling, Furnaces, Insulation, Solar Energy, Solariums, Wood-Burning Stoves.

Warm-Air Heating

A central furnace heats air that is circulated throughout the house by a system of metal ducts. Warm-air furnaces usually burn fuel (oil, wood, gas, or coal) to produce heat, but some use electrical resistance coils. This heated air is replaced by cooler air that returns to the furnace through a cold-air return located near the floor of the living space. All combustion fumes are vented through a flue or chimney that is separate from the duct system of the furnace.

Warm-air furnaces can be used to humidify the air. In areas of severe cold, it is difficult to keep air humidity high enough for comfort. A humidity level below 30 percent is uncomfortable. It irritates throat and nose membranes and can narrow the temperature range in which we feel comfortable, since dry air causes the body to lose

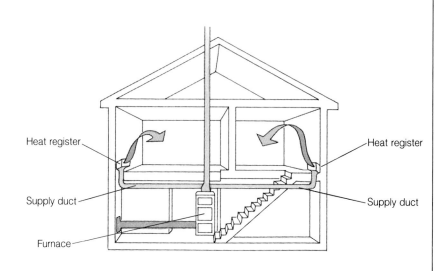

Heat register
Supply duct
Furnace
Heat register
Supply duct

water faster, thus losing heat. Warm-air systems can be equipped with humidistats that switch on at a predetermined humidity level.

There are four ways to increase the efficiency of a warm-air system. One is to improve air circulation and reduce drafts. Another is to replace the furnace with a more efficient model. A third is to tune up the system. A fourth is to install a programmable thermostat.

Improving Circulation

Warm-air heating can create drafts and stratified temperature layers that cause discomfort, even though the system supplies adequate heat.

Warm air rises and cool air drops. Air next to outside walls, especially next to doors and windows, loses heat much more rapidly than air next to an inside wall. The resulting air currents rise on the warm side of the room and drop on the cool side. If the heat registers are on interior walls, or even worse, in the ceiling or high on the walls, the natural current will be boosted, resulting in drafts and stratified layers of air at different temperatures. Your head may feel hot while your feet feel cold.

Proper mixing occurs when heat is applied to the coldest points, such as under large windows. This mixes cool and warm air directly and heats the room evenly.

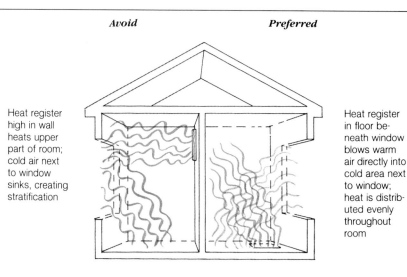

Avoid — Heat register high in wall heats upper part of room; cold air next to window sinks, creating stratification

Preferred — Heat register in floor beneath window blows warm air directly into cold area next to window; heat is distributed evenly throughout room

Poor air circulation can be improved by adding heat registers to cold locations. Reducing localized heat loss by installing storm windows, heavy drapes, and weatherstripping will also help. Keep doors near stairways closed. Make sure carpet is not blocking heat registers.

Drafts can be reduced by insulating the house. The less time the furnace needs to be on, the fewer drafts it will create.

Replacing the Furnace

This is usually a job for professionals, but knowing how to calculate the efficiency of a furnace can help you pick the right one.

As the efficiency ratings of furnaces rise, so do the prices. However, a more efficient furnace will pay for its extra cost with fuel savings. These can be calculated if you know the average fuel cost per year, the efficiency rating, and the price of the furnace. For example:

Calculating Cost Savings

	Efficiency	Installed Cost	Annual Fuel Cost	Payback (in years)
Furnace A	60%	$1,300	$700	—
Furnace B	80%	$1,800	$525	2.86*
Furnace C	95%	$2,800	$442	5.81*

*Additional cost of furnace divided by annual fuel savings.

Tuning Up the System

First, make sure the thermostat is accurate and the anticipator control adjusted so that it will shut off the furnace before it overheats. Then adjust the dampers on all the registers so that each room receives only the heat it needs. This will take several days of trial and error. Finally, clean the furnace periodically. Change filters, make sure the fan belts are properly adjusted, and check the flame controls.

Make sure the furnace receives enough combustion air from outside. Carefully seal all joints in the duct system with aluminum tape and wrap the ducts with insulation (call a professional if the ducts already have asbestos insulation).

Programmable Thermostats

These adjust the temperature setting just as people do manually, but with greater efficiency. They can be set to turn on the furnace before you get up or return from work. In addition, they can be set for different schedules on different days; the most elaborate models, coupled with duct controls, can sense the heat in various rooms and keep them at different temperatures.

When you shop for a programmable thermostat, make sure the thermostat is compatible with your heating system (and cooling system, if you have one). Most will work with forced-air, hot-water, radiant-heat, and steam systems.

Go through the programming steps before you buy. Some models take as long as half an hour to set; others may require you to wait until the time of day coincides with that on the thermostat clock before starting the program.

Program schedules vary. Some include the same schedule for every day; others offer two schedules, one for weekdays and the other for weekends. Some have three schedules, one for weekdays, one for Saturdays, and another for Sundays. Still others can be set for a different program each day.

The number of cycles per day also varies. Two cycles per day are generally enough; however, if a large number of people enter and leave the house, or if you need heat for only brief periods in the morning and evening, four cycles per day will provide additional savings.

Programmable thermostats should always have a manual override, so you can turn on the heat when you want to without reprogramming the thermostat. A vacation override is also a useful feature; it allows the temperature to be reset for a prolonged, indefinite period without reprogramming the thermostat.

A toll-free number for technical assistance is another plus, especially for models with a complicated programming process.

Most simple programmable thermostats can be installed in about an hour with a screwdriver, a drill, and a knife or wire-stripping tool. The thermostat wiring carries low-voltage current, which is quite safe.

Turn off the power to the furnace or air conditioner at the breaker panel and disconnect the appliance if possible. Some furnaces have separate switches or fuses or cords that can be disconnected.

Read the manufacturer's instructions and follow them if they differ from this sequence.

Remove the old thermostat. Label the wires. Wrap the wires around a pencil or similar object to keep them from falling into the wall.

Clean the ends of the wires with steel wool. There should be about ½ inch of exposed conductor at the end of each wire.

Position the base of the thermostat so the wires can come through. Level the plate and lightly outline it on the wall with a pencil. Mark the locations of the mounting screws.

Remove the plate and drill screw holes. Mount the plate and pull the wires through.

Connect the wires to the correct terminals, then attach the thermostat cover and controls.

Program the thermostat according to the manufacturer's instructions.

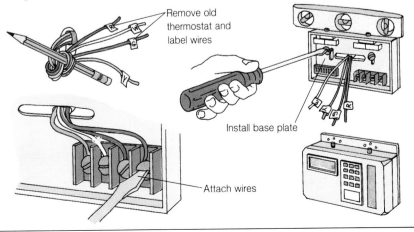

Remove old thermostat and label wires

Install base plate

Attach wires

HEATING

Heat Pump

This is a combination heating and cooling system that works like a central air conditioner, with a reverse cycle for heating. An electric pump circulates refrigerant through a compressor, condenser, evaporator, and tubing. As the refrigerant circulates, it changes from liquid to gas and back again. When it changes into gas it absorbs heat, and when it changes into liquid it releases heat. Depending on which direction it is flowing, the heat pump absorbs the heat from the inside of the house and releases it on the outside, or absorbs it from the outside and releases it on the inside. This works well for cooling in the summer and heating in mild winters, but in cold weather it does not find enough heat outside the house to absorb. Therefore, the system must be linked to an auxiliary heat source for cold-weather operation. One source is electric heat, which tends to be very expensive. Hot water and natural water from a deep well are much more efficient and economical options.

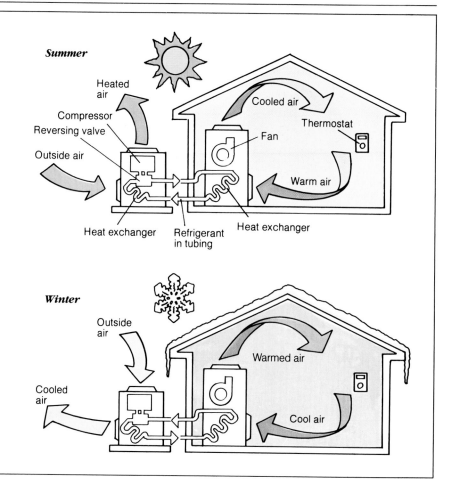

Hybrid Systems

Hybrid heating systems combine the components of several types of heating systems to take advantage of the best characteristics of each. Some systems combine two heat sources, such as a furnace and a heat pump, to optimize efficiency. Others combine a heat source traditionally used with one type of heating system with the distribution system normally used with another.

Hybrid Heat Pumps. Heat pumps are more efficient than fossil fuels so long as the outdoor temperature is moderate. When temperatures drop, fossil-fuel furnaces are more cost-effective to operate, and they produce warmer air. In a conventional heat-pump system, electric resistance heat is used when heating demands exceed the heating capabilities of the heat pump. Hybrid heat-pump systems use fossil fuels to provide supplemental heat, usually a warm-air system.

Hydronic Warm Air. This system has a boiler that heats water, but instead of the hot water being circulated throughout the house, it is

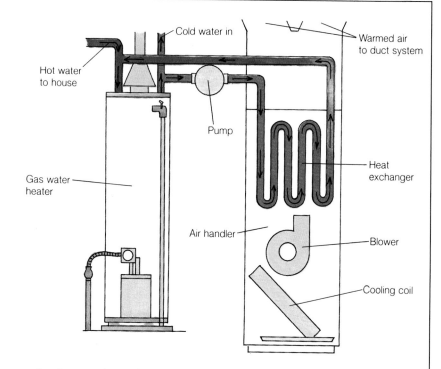

used to heat air that is then circulated through a traditional system of warm-air ducts. The boiler may be a traditional water heater, of larger capacity than normal, or a specialized boiler for hot-water systems. The water is piped through coils in a heat exchanger, which blows air over the coils and distributes it throughout the house.

Electric Radiant Heating

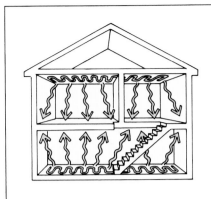

Homes equipped with electric radiant heating have no furnace, ducts, flue, or chimney. The source of heat is electricity flowing through resistance wiring, which can be installed in the ceiling between two layers of wallboard or beneath the plaster.

With radiant heating the actual air temperature of a room does not have to be as high as with forced-air heating. The surfaces radiate heat.

In mild climates the wiring is often located in the floor, embedded in a concrete slab. If the wiring is not in the floor or ceiling, baseboard panels are mounted along the floor. Some electric baseboards use only resistance wiring to heat the room. Other types heat water that is permanently sealed in tubing within the heater, which continues to heat the room for a while after the electricity is turned off. While electric resistance heating is quiet and comfortable, it is very expensive to operate.

Hot-Water Heating

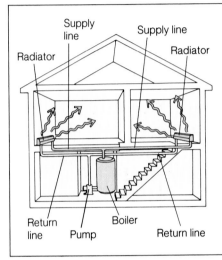

Supply line

Supply line

Radiator

Radiator

Return line

Pump

Boiler

Return line

In a hot-water system, also called a hydronic system, the furnace is a boiler fueled by oil, gas, electricity, or coal. The boiler heats water to about 200° F. A pump circulates the hot water throughout the house in ½-inch copper or galvanized piping. The heat is transferred from the pipes to the room by baseboard radiators, most often located on the outside walls.

Older systems heat the water above 212° F to make steam, which is carried upward to cast-iron radiators, condenses, and falls back down through the piping to the boiler. This system works by gravity.

With this type of system the temperature of each room can be controlled with separate thermostats.

Hydronic systems can be used as alternative heat sources. For instance, water can be circulated through solar panels, or through a heat exchanger connected to solar panels, to boost the temperature of the water before it enters the boiler.

Hot water also works as a source for radiant heating systems, with pipes embedded in a concrete slab or even run beneath a wood floor.

Wall Heaters

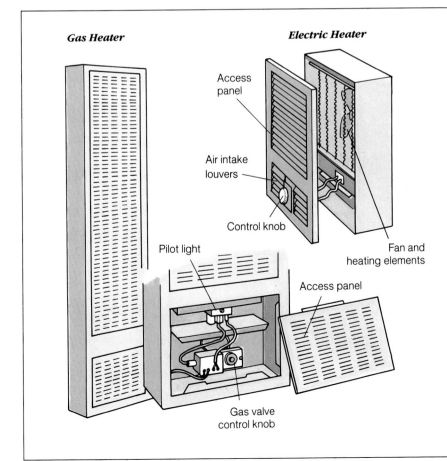

Gas Heater

Electric Heater

Access panel

Air intake louvers

Control knob

Pilot light

Fan and heating elements

Access panel

Gas valve control knob

A small heater, using either gas or electricity, can be mounted on a wall to heat an individual room. Some types include an air conditioner, and one type uses heat from a gas water heater instead of having its own burner. If the heating requirements of a home are low or if a new room addition needs heat, a wall heater may be sufficient.

Gas heaters have a burner that warms air, which then rises out into the room by convection. A flue carries the burned gases to the outside. Gas heaters cannot be installed in a bedroom unless they have a sealed air intake from the outside. Otherwise, they may deplete the oxygen supply in the room. Unvented heaters should always be turned off before bedtime and should be used with care in all rooms.

Electric heaters have resistance coils that warm the air as it moves across them. Some have fans to help circulate the air into the room. Most wall-mounted heaters can operate on 120 volts or 240 volts, and must have their own circuit.

HINGES, PULLS & KNOBS

Hinges, pulls, and knobs are basic hardware items that are chosen for their decorative value as much as for their practical function. The array of options is enormous, but the choices narrow considerably depending on the kind of doors to which they will attach and the overall design scheme.

Mounting hinges, pulls, and knobs is usually one of the last steps in a home-improvement project. Although this is a pleasurable task that is easy to do, it should not be done with the notion that the project is almost finished. Haste leads to waste and to mistakes that you will be reminded of every day—when a door sticks, pulls are not aligned, or a door swings the wrong way. This is a job for putterers, as well as for those with a feel for balance and design.

Most hardware requires only basic hand tools for installation, although a router, table saw, or drill may be needed to attach certain recessed hinges. A gimlet is handy for starting screws; it resembles a screwdriver but has a threaded point at the end for making pilot holes without a drill. Always mount hinges on the door first.

Recommended Cross-References
Cabinets, Doors, Drawers, Gates, Vanities.

Cabinet Doors and Hinges

Lap Doors. Attach lap doors, or full overlay doors, directly to the cabinet sides with butt, pivot, or "European" hinges. Butt hinges can be seen from the side and require room for the doors to clear. Pivot hinges do not need side clearance, but show slightly at the top and bottom of the cabinet face. More expensive European hinges do not show at all.

Flush Doors. Butt hinges for flush doors are mortised into the sides of the cabinet to reduce the size of the gap. Pivot hinges are mortised into the top and bottom of each door. Decorative face hinges can be mounted to show either one or both leaves. The Soss hinge, named for its inventor, is completely concealed.

Lip Doors. Lip doors use hinges that show one narrow leaf. They do not have to be mortised into the doors or frame. The bent leaf, also called an offset, comes in sizes that fit rabbets of different thicknesses, so be sure you have the right size. Like other types of hinges, one variation includes a leaf spring for self-closing.

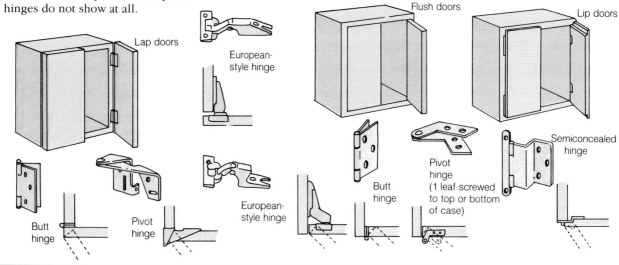

Pulls, Knobs, and Decorative Hardware

Because fads change, the safest designs to choose are simple or classical shapes. If a sleek and uncluttered look is desired, you can even avoid hardware altogether, relying on finger grooves under the cabinet doors and drawers, and touch latches on full-sized doors.

If you are changing the pulls or knobs on existing cabinets, check to see whether the existing hardware is mounted with one or two screws.

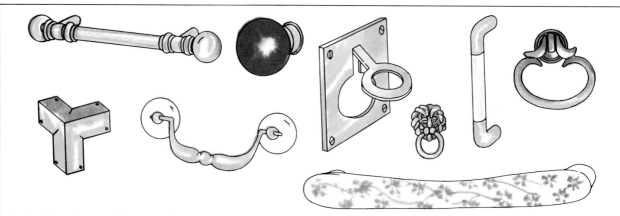

You are better off replacing it with the same kind so that you can use the same holes. For a similar reason, choose pulls for new cabinets carefully; remember that the holes you drill for mounting now will affect any future hardware changes.

Sticking Doors

Doors that stick or bind are a nuisance; luckily they are often easy to repair without removing the door and trimming it. During seasons of high humidity the door or door frame may swell, so do not make irreversible adjustments if the door also shrinks during dry seasons.

Slide paper between the door and the jamb; it will bind where the door is sticking. If a door sticks at the top of the latch side, fix it by tightening the top hinge screws, chiseling the top hinge mortise deeper, or shimming the bottom hinge.

Move the door to the right or left simply by inserting a shim behind the hinge thick enough to swing the pin one way or the other. Use a full shim behind the hinge to move the door away from the hinge jamb. Use a half shim to pivot the hinge pin so that the door moves toward the hinge jamb. If there is not enough room for the shim, mortise the hinge.

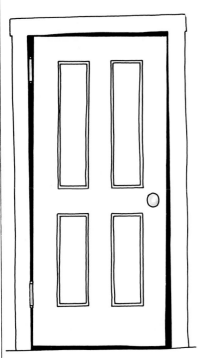

Slide paper between
the door and the jamb

Shimming a Hinge

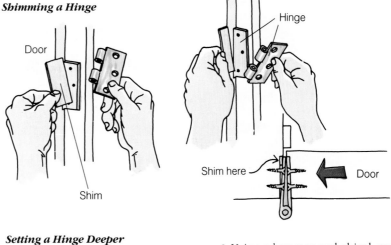

Door

Shim

Hinge

Shim here

Door

Setting a Hinge Deeper

1. Score the hinge outline.

2. Using a hammer and chisel, make feather cuts to the new hinge depth.

3. Shave off the feather cuts along the depth line.

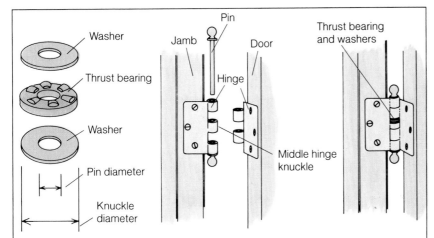

Washer

Thrust bearing

Washer

Pin diameter

Knuckle diameter

Pin

Jamb

Hinge

Door

Thrust bearing and washers

Middle hinge knuckle

Hinges for Heavy Doors

To keep a heavy door from wearing down the hinge knuckles and in order to make it swing more easily, buy hinges with thrust bearings or install your own. You can find them at a bearing supplier or full-service hardware dealer. To make room for the bearing and washers, file off the middle hinge knuckle.

Tightening Loose Doorknobs

Loosen the setscrew behind the knob. Holding the other knob stationary, turn the loose knob clockwise to fit it tightly against the rose. Tighten the setscrew against a flat side of the spindle.

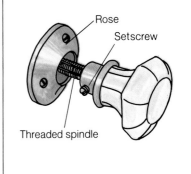

Rose

Setscrew

Threaded spindle

Many cabinet manufacturers offer enclosures specifically designed to conceal range hoods.

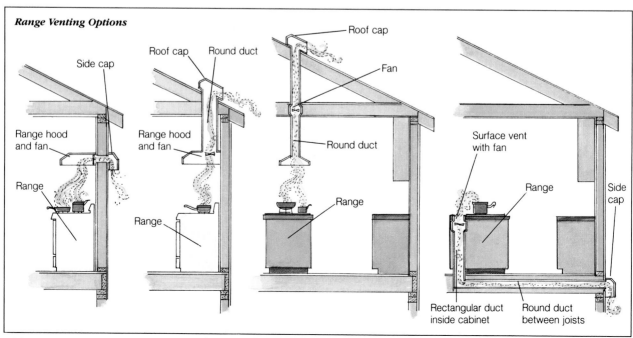

Range Venting Options

Side cap

Range hood and fan

Range

Roof cap

Round duct

Range hood and fan

Range

Roof cap

Fan

Round duct

Range

Surface vent with fan

Range

Side cap

Rectangular duct inside cabinet

Round duct between joists

Ranges and cooktops require some means of removing smoke, grease, heat, and moisture from the kitchen. The most common is an overhead hood, either hung from the wall, usually beneath a cabinet, or hung from the ceiling. Hoods come in various widths and heights, and should be at least as wide as the range or cooktop. Down-draft venting, which is built into some models of cooktops and ranges, is the other type of venting device. Most hoods and vents are ducted, venting all smoke, grease, heat, and moisture to the outside, either through the roof or wall. Ductless hoods and vents filter out the smoke and grease, but recirculate the heat and moisture into the kitchen.

The Home Ventilating Institute rates the power of a fan or blower (the quieter squirrel-cage type) in cubic feet per minute (CFM). Better hoods have a minimum capacity of 300 CFM. It also rates loudness in somes; less than 8 somes is desirable.

Openings in the top of a vent are either round or rectangular. Some have two knockouts to enable you to run the duct into either the right or left side of the cabinet above.

Recommended Cross-References
Cabinets, Flashing, Ranges, Ovens & Cooktops, Wiring.

Down-Venting Cooktops
On some cooktops, the vent is built right into the unit itself, and does not require separate installation. The vent should be ducted to the outside, either through the cabinets to an exterior wall or down through the crawl space under the floor. The duct should terminate outside the wall in a wall cap.

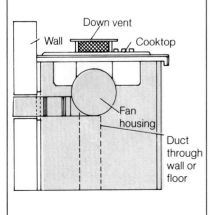

Range Hoods
Most range hoods are 6 inches high, although some are as high as 30 inches. They are 18 to 24 inches deep, sloping upward to the standard cabinet depth of 12 inches. They come in widths to match ranges and cooktops, 30, 36, or 48 inches. For energy conservation, many include a damper that prevents room heat from escaping when the unit is off.

Installing Under a Cabinet. If you are mounting a ducted hood under a cabinet, cut holes in the cabinet for the hood outlet and duct before installing the cabinet. Mark holes for cutting by setting the cabinet upside down on the floor and laying the hood upside down on top of it. Trace the hood outlet onto the cabinet, cut it out, and cut another hole for the duct. If the cabinet is already hung, measure for the holes as carefully as you can before cutting them out.

Wiring. Run nonmetallic cable behind the wall and bring it out through a small hole in a place where the electrical junction box of the hood will cover it. Strip away 6 to 8 inches of sheathing from the end of the cable and attach a cable clamp at that point, just outside the wall.

Venting. Run a 7-inch duct pipe into the cabinet from the attic or an exterior wall behind the cabinet. The pipe should vent all the way to the outside, terminating in a roof cap or wall cap. Secure each joint with sheet-metal screws and tape it with approved duct tape. Connect a transition fitting to the round duct for the rectangular opening in the hood, as well as any elbows needed for changing the direction of the duct in the cabinet. If an elbow won't fit, make a cardboard template showing cutouts and have a sheet-metal shop make up a metal box.

Attaching the Hood. Lift or prop the hood into place and mark where the screw holes line up against the bottom of the cabinet. Take the hood down and, on these marks, drill pilot holes for the screws. Lift the hood back up, feed the wires into the junction box, and screw it to the bottom of the cabinet.

Using wire nuts, connect the wires inside the junction box. Screw the ground wire to the grounding screw in the hood. Then connect the hood collar to the duct transition piece with sheet-metal screws and wrap the joint with duct tape.

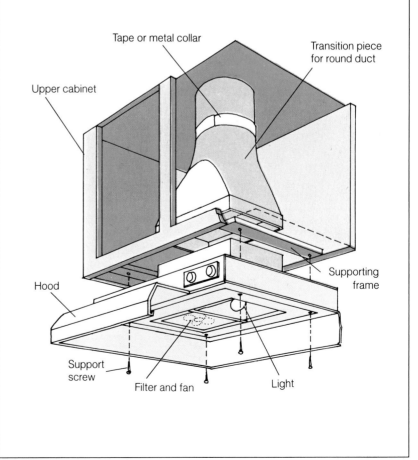

HOT TUBS & SPAS

Adding a hot tub or spa to your outdoor living area is an improvement that will afford much pleasure. A hot tub is less expensive than a swimming pool, uses less water, and is easier to install and maintain. Either is conducive to relaxation and socializing. A hot tub or spa fits into a small space, making it an ideal choice for an out-of-the-way place. Many homeowners install their hot tubs or spas themselves. Whether purchased as a self-contained unit or as separate components, the equipment includes a tub, pump, filter, heater, thermostat, piping, and insulated cover. Optional features include water jets and built-in lighting.

Even if you buy a complete unit, you will need to do more than just hook it up. A spa without a deck around it, steps leading up to it, and a privacy fence around it will look as ungainly as an unframed above-ground swimming pool. The whole point of having a spa is to be able to luxuriate in the soothing water. Therefore, you must build an appropriate setting.

Recommended Cross-References
Decks, Electrical System, Fences, Lighting: Indoor & Outdoor, Plumbing, Pools, Steps.

Thoughtful design of the surroundings can give an inexpensive manufactured spa the look of a custom installation.

Location

There are many factors to consider when you choose a location for your tub or spa. One is privacy. Take advantage of plants, fences, walls, or existing screens, or build a fence or even an enclosed structure similar to a Japanese bathhouse. Another factor is convenience. Make sure the tub is close to a dressing area.

Take advantage of attractive vistas, and consider using the tub or spa as a focal point in a garden or patio. Install lighting in and around the tub so you can use it at night.

Climate is a major factor; consider sunlight, shade, wind, and snow. Generally, an outdoor spa should take advantage of late afternoon sunshine (unless you are in a hot climate) and be sheltered from prevailing breezes. In cold climates, the installation should have valves for draining the equipment and tub separately, so you can keep the equipment from freezing without having to drain the tub. Also avoid placing a tub or spa beneath eaves where snow will slide into it.

Any indoor installation requires an adequate foundation for the tub and proper ventilation to reduce condensation.

Tub or Spa?

Basically, hot tubs are wooden barrels and spas are shells manufactured of plastic materials. This distinction is complicated by the fact that some hot tubs have acrylic liners and some spas are freestanding units with wood skirting or are made from concrete. However, tubs and spas have other basic differences—in maintenance, durability, appearance, and operation—all of which are fundamental considerations.

Beveled wood staves held in place by iron compression hoops form the sides of a hot tub. A dado groove near the bottom of the staves holds the wood floor in place. Most tubs are made of redwood—usually vertical-grain, all-heart grades. Some are made from less expensive grades that include sapwood, cedar, oak, or teak. Depending on the species and grade of wood, a tub will last from 10 to 15 years. Make sure the wood is kiln dried so that it swells evenly when the tub is filled with water. The constant swelling of the staves renders the tub watertight.

A tub can be any size or shape, but round tubs 5 or 6 feet in diameter and $2\frac{1}{2}$, 4, or 5 feet tall are most common. Some tubs are less than 4 feet in diameter and others are as wide as 12 feet. A standard 5-by-4-foot tub holds 500 gallons of water and weighs 5,000 pounds when full of water and bathers.

Install a hot tub at ground level or on a reinforced deck. A tub requires a substantial foundation—either a steel-reinforced concrete slab at grade level or a system of footings and piers for elevated tubs. The floor, not the sides, carries the weight of the tub.

Tubs have a rustic and natural appearance; they blend well with decks, gardens, greenhouses, or patios. Hot tubs are harder to clean and maintain than spas because of the texture of the wood and the angles and corners inherent in their design. On the other hand, tubs are easier to transport and relocate and generally cost less.

Early spas were made of fiberglass covered with gelcoat. More modern materials include formed acrylic reinforced with fiberglass and formed Centrex® thermoplastic, which needs no reinforcement. The outside of the spa varies. Some are designed to be installed in the ground or in a specially designed box that is filled with sand. Others are freestanding with wood skirting.

Spas present more design options than hot tubs, ranging from straight-sided squares and octagons to circular, free-form shapes. Spas are available in a wide range of colors, and their sleek texture helps make them a distinctive design element in any indoor or outdoor setting. Typical sizes are 5 to 6 feet across and 4 feet deep, although spas are usually narrower across the bottom because of their contoured seats.

The support equipment and installation are similar for hot tubs and spas. Both are available as complete, freestanding packages, or as separate components that require assembly. The simplest installation is at grade level on an existing slab, and the most involved are in-ground spas or elevated hot tubs. Most building codes require a building permit for either installation.

Installation

Installation techniques vary for different models of hot tubs and spas, but they all include the same basic features. The tub or spa must be well supported. Tubs require a solid concrete slab, usually 6 inches thick, if they are installed on the ground. The slab needs to be only slightly larger than the tub. A freestanding spa should have the same type of slab, but if it is a sunken spa, excavate a hole, then backfill it with sand. If you install the tub or spa on a deck, add extra beams below the deck and at least four independent posts and footings to support them. They should be cross-braced as well.

The tub or spa should also be convenient to pipe hookups. At the bottom is a drain that is the primary outlet for a pipe that goes to the pump. Most pumps are centrifugal, and must be large enough for the size of tub and number of inlet jets (usually $\frac{3}{4}$ horsepower [hp] for 1 or 2 jets, 1 hp for 3 jets, $1\frac{1}{2}$ hp for 4 jets, and 2 hp for 6 jets). The pipe is plastic, usually PVC or CPVC, and $1\frac{1}{2}$ inches or 2 inches in diameter.

The pump keeps the water moving through the pipe, which goes to the filter. Filters vary in their effectiveness. Cartridge filters have membranes of paper or fabric and are the least expensive. Replace a cartridge filter every year or two. Sand filters work better, and the best filters use diatomaceous earth (DE).

The water must be heated as well as filtered. In some systems the heater is in the same circuit as the pump, usually between the filter and tub. In other systems, water goes directly from the filter to the tub, and the heater is on a separate loop of pipes. Water circulates through the heater by convection, sometimes boosted by a small pump. With either system, the heater is powered by gas, electricity, or solar energy. Models vary widely in their output of BTUs and the speed with which they are able to heat all the water in the tub.

Water jets require their own circulation system. The system includes a blower that introduces air into the pipes to create greater water pressure.

The pipes that connect the various units have valves for draining or isolating different parts of the system as well as jets where the pipes connect to the tank. The system is usually closed; it is not included in the supply system of the house. In some cases, where codes allow, the filtering system may connect to house plumbing with a certain type of valve that prevents backflow.

Wiring for a hot tub or spa must be in strict accordance with local codes. Electric heaters and most pumps are on their own circuits, usually 240-volt. Lights and auxiliary water-jet systems use 120 volts. GFCI (ground fault circuit interrupters) must protect all wiring, and switches must be specific outdoor types that are out of reach of anyone in the tub.

INSULATION

In a narrow sense, insulation is material added to slow down the transfer of heat. In a broad sense, it is the entire process of making a home more comfortable and energy efficient, and includes caulking, weather stripping, and window insulation.

In a new building or addition insulation is automatically installed. But to make an existing house warmer in winter and cooler in summer, you should evaluate how well your house conserves energy. Otherwise, you may launch into a complicated insulation project when less expensive or more effective projects should be done first.

How does a house lose precious heat in the winter and admit unwanted heat in the summer? Mainly through holes, most of which escape notice because they are so obvious. An ordinary single-glazed window, for instance, may allow as much as 20 times more heat to escape than the wall that surrounds it, even though the wall is far larger than the window. An uninsulated roof or ceiling may take a third of all the heat your house consumes. Poorly sealed cracks around the foundation, sill, chimney, or siding can account for 10 percent of your heating, and a ¼-inch gap under a door is equivalent to a 3-inch-square hole in your wall. If your house has many such cracks and gaps, they can add up to a hole the size of a picture window.

Where should you begin? The best strategy is to start with projects that offer the highest long-range payback for the money and effort expended. The following list ranks heat robbers from the highest to the lowest. Some items, such as insulating walls, may be more effective than their position on the list indicates. It is the expense of doing the improvement that makes it relatively inefficient.

- *Weather stripping around doors and windows*
- *Caulking cracks*
- *Insulating windows and doors*
- *Insulating attics*
- *Insulating heating ducts*
- *Insulating floors or basement*
- *Insulating walls*

Recommended Cross-References
Caulking, Cooling, Furnaces, Heating, Solar Energy, Ventilation, Water Heaters, Weather Stripping, Windows.

Where to Insulate
After taking care of all the weather stripping and caulking, you can turn your attention to insulation. The basic principle of insulating a house is to surround the conditioned living space (occupied areas that are either heated or air-conditioned) with insulating material.

The illustration at right shows typical surfaces that need insulation. Generally, it is best to start at the top and work down until the entire living space is wrapped in a blanket, although there may be good reasons for changing this order. Some surfaces may be difficult to get to and others may be insulated enough already. The type of construction is also a factor. A single-story home built on a cement slab can lose tremendous amounts of heat through the exposed perimeter if it is not insulated properly.

Remember, you do not have to insulate everything at once. You can do small amounts at a time. There is also the law of diminishing returns: The more your home is already insulated, the less the monetary return on new insulation.

1. Attic and Roof. If the attic is not a living space, insulate your ceiling. This is an easy project that involves rolling out blanket insulation or blowing in loose fill.

If the attic is a living area, insulate the ceiling and walls, as well as any attic floor under the eaves. Some of these spaces are readily accessible, but others may be covered with interior finish walls or ceiling material. Your choices then are to blow in loose fill from the outside or strip off the finish wall or ceiling material and install blanket insulation.

Ceilings that are also roofs commonly lose heat, especially the type with exposed beams and attractive roof boards. One solution is to apply panels of rigid insulation to the inside of the roof boards. Most types of insulation must then be covered with wallboard because they are flammable. If the ceiling is too attractive to cover, install insulation on top of the roof. This involves ripping off the roofing material, installing a vapor barrier and rigid panels over the roof sheathing, nailing ½-inch plywood over the insulation, and reroofing.

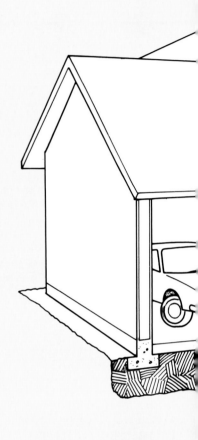

2. Exterior Walls and Windows. Insulating exterior walls is easy during new construction or remodeling, but is a major project in an existing house. Usually, loose insulation is blown into the stud cavities through holes that are drilled in the exterior wall and then plugged. Or rigid insulation is attached to the outside of the house and new siding is installed.

Realize that it does not do much good to insulate walls unless you do something about the windows first, even after they are caulked and weather stripped. Glass is a poor insulator—about R-1, compared with about R-4 for a wall that is not insulated and R-11 for a wall that is.

There are two options for insulat-

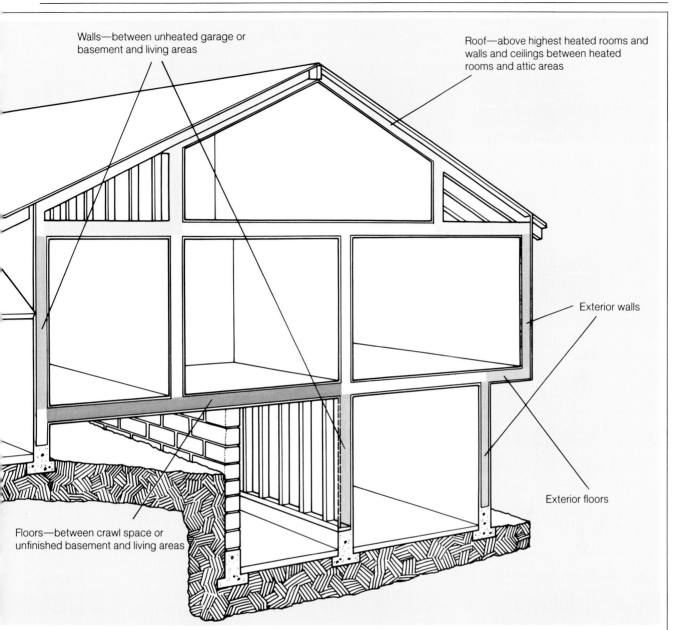

Walls—between unheated garage or basement and living areas

Roof—above highest heated rooms and walls and ceilings between heated rooms and attic areas

Exterior walls

Exterior floors

Floors—between crawl space or unfinished basement and living areas

ing windows. One is to add another layer of glazing, either by replacing the windows with double-glazed units or by installing storm windows (or sheets of plastic) over them. The other option is to cover the windows each night with movable insulation, such as multilayered Mylar shades.

3. Walls Between Living Space and Unheated Space. These walls are often easier to insulate than exterior walls because one side is not finished. Just install blanket insulation between the exposed studs, with the vapor barrier toward the living space. If both sides of the wall are covered, blow in loose insulation or strip off the finish on one side and install blanket insulation.

4. Exterior Floors. If a floor is cantilevered out beyond the downstairs wall, blow in insulation from the wall side of each joist cavity. Or strip off the soffit boards, install blanket insulation between the joists, and replace the boards.

5. Floors Over Unheated Areas. Floors over unheated crawl spaces and basements are fairly easy to insulate, although not very pleasant to do if the space is cramped. Install blanket insulation between the exposed joists, with the vapor barrier facing up. Hold the blankets in place with wire clips, chicken wire, or netting improvised from fishing line or tie wire. It is also important to solve any moisture problems under the house.

6. Foundations and Basement Walls. Basements and heated crawl spaces can be insulated from the outside or from the inside. If the inside walls are already finished, or if excavating around the foundation is easy to do, the best method is to install rigid panels around the outside of the foundation. These panels must cover the part of the basement wall that extends above the ground, in addition to whatever can be exposed by excavating. This is also the method that should be used for insulating around concrete slabs.

If the basement walls have not been finished yet, they can be insulated from the inside with blanket insulation or rigid panels.

Amount of Insulation Needed

The purpose of insulation is to hold in the heat during the winter and keep it out during the summer. Some materials do this better than others, so a scale has been developed for comparing different insulating materials. The measurement, called R-value, is a relative rating that indicates how well a material resists heat transfer. The higher the resistance, the higher the R-value.

The map below shows how much R-value the insulation should have for the attic, floors, and walls of homes in various regions of the country. The map is only intended to illustrate general differences among regions; it does not account for the significant variations that can occur within a region. To find out the recommended R-value for your area, consult with your local building department. Many states and counties have adopted rigorous energy-saving standards for new construction and remodeling. Sometimes compliance with the code is mandatory; in other cases the standards are intended only as guidelines.

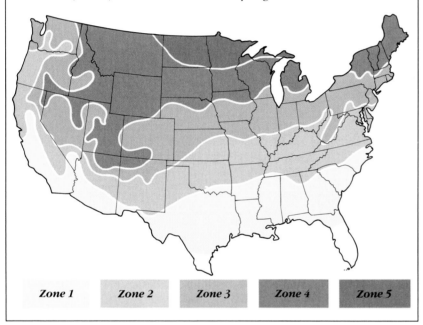

Zone 1   Zone 2   Zone 3   Zone 4   Zone 5

Recommended R-Values

Heating Zone	Attic Floors	Floors Over Unheated Crawl Space or Basement	Exterior Walls
1	R-30	R-11	R-12
2	R-30	R-13	R-19
3	R-38	R-19	R-19
4	R-49	R-22	R-19
5	R-49	R-22	R-22

Inch Equivalents of Various Insulations for Different R-Values

Insulation	R-11	R-19	R-22	R-30	R-38
Fiberglass batts/blankets	3.5″	6.0″	6.5″	10.0″	12.5″
Rock wool batts/blankets	3.0″	5.5″	6.0″	9.0″	10.5″
Fiberglass loose fill	5.0″	8.5″	10.0″	13.5″	17.5″
Rock wool loose fill	4.0″	6.5″	7.5″	10.5″	13.5″
Cellulose loose fill	3.0″	5.0″	6.0″	8.0″	10.5″
Molded polystyrene board	3.0″	5.0″	6.0″	8.0″	10.5″
Extruded polystyrene board	2.5″	4.0″	4.5″	6.0″	7.5″

Types of Insulation

Which type of insulating material is best for your project? All things being equal, you want to use whatever has the highest R-value. However, since all things are never equal, there are other factors you should consider:

Convenience. When doing the work yourself, choose the material that is easiest to install. That usually means fiberglass blankets or batts, since they are readily available and do not require specialized tools to install. Rock wool blankets have a slightly higher R-value, but are not as easy to find. Although you need to rent equipment for blowing in loose fill, the convenience makes it worthwhile especially if the alternative is crawling around in a low attic for one or two days.

Suitability. Consider the nature of the space to be insulated. If it is open framing, use blankets or batts. If the framing members are not spaced regularly for a ceiling or unfinished floor, pour loose fill between them. If it is a cavity enclosed by finished walls and ceilings, you will have to use blown fill. On the outside surface of a wall or roof, use rigid panels.

Dimension. Rigid panels give the most R-value per inch, making them ideal for tight spaces or where additional wall thickness must be kept to a minimum. If you have 2 by 4 stud walls and want to insulate to R-19, you need more than batts, blankets, or blown fill between the studs. Use rigid panels or fill the stud cavities with low-R material and add thin rigid panels under the wallboard or siding.

Flammability. When installing rigid panels between the exposed rafters of a sloped ceiling, you must either cover the panels with wallboard or use fiberglass panels. Any type of cellulose insulation must be treated with a fire retardant.

Moisture Resistance. Some types of loose insulation, such as cellulose, compact together and become useless when wet. This is no problem if walls are properly sealed and protected with a vapor barrier, but may be a factor in regions that get periodic flooding or high humidity. The most durable insulating material is extruded polystyrene, which can even be submerged.

Types of Insulation

Form	R-Value per inch	Materials	Principal Use	Installation Method	Comments
Blankets or Batts	3.7 3.3	Rock wool Fiberglass	Walls, floors, ceilings, attics, roofs	Fitted between wood-frame studs, joists, and beams	Most common form do-it-yourselfers use; suited for standard stud and joist spacing without obstructions; batts easier to handle
Loose or Blown Fill	2.9 2.2 3.3 2.4 2.7	Rock wool Fiberglass Cellulose fiber Vermiculite Perlite	Floors, walls, hard-to-reach places, finished areas	Poured between joists or blown into place with specialized equipment	Easy to use in irregularly shaped areas; blown fill, the only option for finished areas, should be installed by a professional
Rigid Panels	4.0 5.0 6.3 4.4	Molded polystyrene Extruded polystyrene Isocyanurate board Fiberglass board	Unfinished walls, basement masonry, walls, exterior surfaces	Cut to fit and secured in place; must be covered with finishing material for fire safety	High insulating value for relatively little thickness; plastic boards are highly flammable

Vapor Barriers

Insulation is so beneficial that it is hard to realize that it also causes a major problem in cold-weather climates. It does such a good job of keeping heat out of the attic and wall cavities that any water vapor carried by warm, moist air passing through the insulation into these areas immediately condenses into moisture upon hitting the colder air. The moisture gets trapped and almost inevitably causes wood decay and structural damage to foundations, roof, and walls.

One way to control this problem is to keep moisture from escaping into the insulation. This is done by installing a vapor barrier between all insulation and living spaces.

The other control is to ventilate the space above attic and roof insulation. Do not insulate a ceiling unless the attic has 1 square foot of vent for every 300 square feet of ceiling area. If you are insulating between roof rafters with blankets or loose fill, leave at least 1 inch of air space above the insulation and ventilate it at the soffit and ridge.

Installing a Vapor Barrier

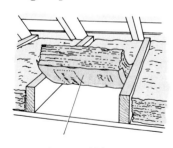

Vapor barrier toward living area

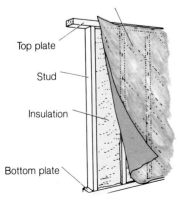

Top plate

Stud

Insulation

Bottom plate

Venting Attic Space

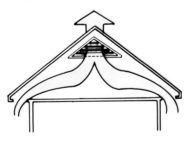

Backdrafting

Backdrafting occurs when a house is so tightly sealed that exhaust fans, such as the range hood or bathroom fan, can't draw enough outside air to equalize the pressure in the house. As a result, air is sucked down flues, such as those for gas water heaters and furnaces, drawing carbon monoxide into the house.

To check for backdrafting, close off all sources of outside air, such as doors and windows. Turn on all of the exhaust fans in the house and cause a combustion appliance to come on (for example, run hot water until the water heater starts up). Light a match, put it out so it smokes, and hold the smoking match next to the appliance flue. The smoke should quickly travel up the flue. If it doesn't, backdrafting is probably taking place. This condition is dangerous; consult your local utility or a heating professional for advice on correcting it.

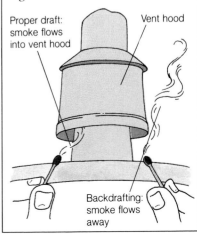

Proper draft: smoke flows into vent hood

Vent hood

Backdrafting: smoke flows away

Insulating With Loose Fill

1. Install a vapor barrier and baffle all fixtures, vents, and other openings.

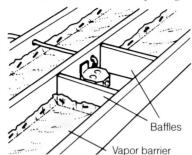

Baffles

Vapor barrier

2. Pour the insulation between the joists, making sure it gets into the corners and around bracings.

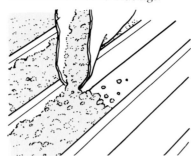

3. Spread and fluff the fill with a rake. Level it off with a notched board.

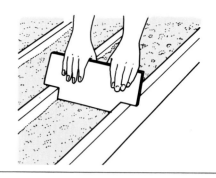

Insulating With Batts

1. Beginning at the eaves at one side of the attic, place the batts between the joists with the vapor barrier facing toward the space you want to insulate. Work toward the center, pressing the insulation into place.

2. Make a nonflammable buffer between insulation and chimney by wrapping the chimney with a metal barrier, from the base to 2 inches above the joists. Surround it with noncombustible material.

3. Place insulation under the wiring. Keep aluminum vapor barriers away from the wiring to prevent causing a short circuit. Separate the layers of insulation to surround cross-braces.

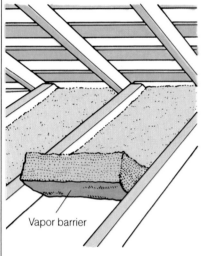

Vapor barrier

Metal barrier

Noncombustible material

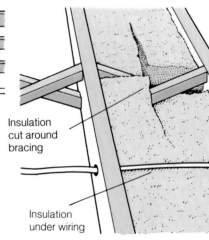

Insulation cut around bracing

Insulation under wiring

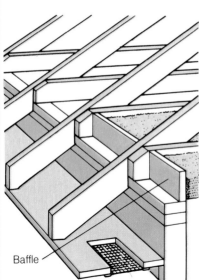

Baffle

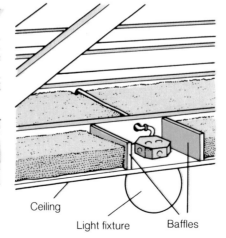

Ceiling

Light fixture

Baffles

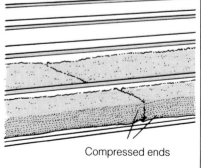

Compressed ends

4. Do not block vents or ducts. Place a baffle between the vent or duct and the insulation.

5. Keep insulation at least 3 inches away from lighting fixtures or heating vents. If you insulate a 100-watt fixture, heat can build up to the point of starting wood to smolder.

6. When you near the center of the attic, start over again from the eaves on the other side. Compress the ends together where they meet in the center of the room.

Cutting Blankets or Batts

If you have to cut a batt or blanket, place it on a wide piece of plywood or other hard surface. Using one of the temporary flooring boards to compress the insulation at the cutting line and also as a straightedge for cutting, cut the insulation with a utility knife. If the utility knife is not long enough, any strong, long, sharp serrated kitchen knife will do.

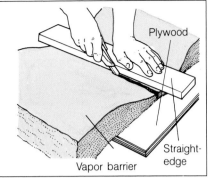

Plywood

Straight-edge

Vapor barrier

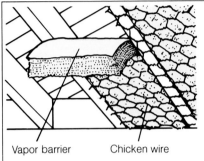

Vapor barrier   Chicken wire

Nails and wire netting

Insulating Under Floors

When you are installing insulation under a floor to protect the living space above, make sure the vapor barrier faces up, toward the space you want to insulate. Hold the insulation in place with chicken wire or a homemade system of wire netting nailed to the joists.

Insulating an Unfinished Wall

When adding insulation to an unfinished wall, you may have to build a series of 2 by 3 studs before adding batts or rigid panel insulation. If the insulation has no vapor barrier, cover the insulated wall with heavy-duty foil or 2-mil polyethylene sheeting, stapling the vapor barrier into the studs. Repair any gashes with waterproof insulating tape. If the insulation is flammable, make sure to use a fire-retardant wallboard when finishing off the wall.

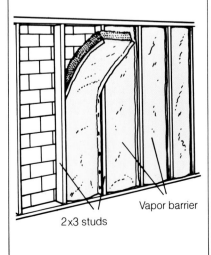

Vapor barrier

2x3 studs

Adding to Insulation

When adding to preexisting insulation, it is important to keep moisture from accumulating within and between the separate layers. If possible, add batts or blankets without a vapor barrier. If the new insulation does have a vapor barrier, slash liberally to the foil. Then set the insulation in place perpendicular to the old insulation, with the slashed foil facing it.

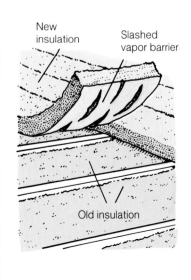

New insulation

Slashed vapor barrier

Old insulation

Insulating the Outside of a Basement or Foundation

A basement or crawl space that is heated needs to be insulated. If the inside walls are already finished or if it is easy to excavate around the foundation, the best method is to install rigid insulation panels around the outside edge of the foundation. This is a particularly good project to do if there is a moisture problem in the basement and you need to install a drainage system or waterproof the outside of the walls.

Use rigid panels at least 1 inch thick. They should have a high resistance to moisture and have interlocking joints to minimize heat leaks. It is critical that they cover the part of the foundation that extends above the ground, because this area is the most vulnerable to heat loss. The exposed section of insulation must be covered with flashing, stucco, or other building material to prevent deterioration from sunlight as well as any physical damage.

How far to extend the insulation down the wall depends on your willingness to dig. Happily, you do not have to dig all the way to the footings to get good results; even 12 or 18 inches below grade helps. The main thing is to cover the foundation wall above grade. This is particularly important for the perimeter of slab foundations.

It is also possible to insulate basement walls from the inside. All moisture problems must be solved first. Then furr out the walls with 2 by 4 studs and install blanket insulation between them, or attach rigid insulation panels directly to the concrete or masonry walls with adhesive. Use the rigid panels if the floor space is too limited for full stud walls. However, the insulation must be covered with 1/2-inch wallboard. Whichever method you use, be sure to insulate the rim joist cavity above the mudsill belonging to the foundation wall.

Insulating Windows

One way to insulate windows is to double the glass. The resulting R-value is actually higher than the sum of the two panes of glass because the air that gets trapped between them acts as an insulator. However, for optimum insulation the air space should be no wider than ¾ inch and should either be sealed or have condensation vents.

There are two ways to double the glass. One is to replace the old windows with new double-glazed windows. While this method is expensive, it is much less tedious than putting up storm windows every winter. The windows are also more efficient and less likely to have condensation problems. A compromise solution is to install storm windows permanently on existing windows. They are less expensive than replacing the entire unit, and make a tight seal around the edges. They can be removed periodically for cleaning. A very temporary solution for insulating a single-glazed window is to install plastic sheeting over it.

Although adding another pane of glass to windows cuts heat loss by more than half, the R-value is still no higher than 3 or 3.5, compared with at least R-11 for the rest of an insulated wall. Besides their insulating ability, double-glazed windows have an additional benefit: They are warm to the touch. This quality does not influence the air temperature of the room or directly contribute to lower heating bills, but it has a significant effect on body comfort. Our bodies radiate heat toward cold surfaces, even when they are several feet away. The fewer such surfaces in a room, the more comfortable we feel.

Aside from double-glass panes, the most effective way to insulate windows is to cover them with an insulating device on cold nights. This is called movable insulation and can consist of shutters, shades, or even drapes. The most effective type seals tightly around the windows so that no air currents get behind them and draw warm air out of the room. You can make your own device from quilted fabrics or rigid insulating panels covered with hardboard, or you can buy ready-made products.

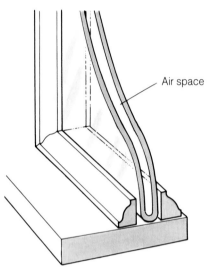

Sealed Double-Glazed Window

Air space

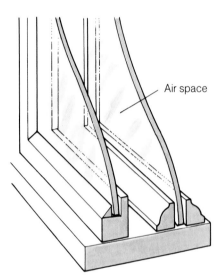

Storm Window

Air space

Interior Window Insulation

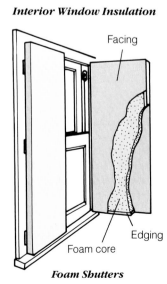

Facing

Edging

Foam core

Foam Shutters

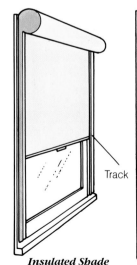

Track

Insulated Shade

Curtain Wall

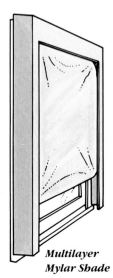

Multilayer Mylar Shade

Insulating a Water Heater

Insulating blankets are readily available for water heaters, but you can also make your own. All you need is duct tape and a roll of R-11 fiberglass. Cut 3 or 4 sections that equal the height of the heater and tape them together. Trim one edge so that the blanket fits around the tank, and cut out openings for the controls and the drain faucet. Don't cover the burner access or the flue collar of a gas heater.

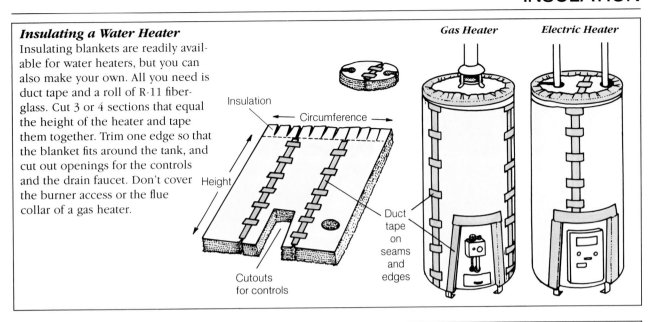

Gas Heater   *Electric Heater*

Insulation

Circumference

Height

Duct tape on seams and edges

Cutouts for controls

Duct Insulation

1. Run air through the ducts to check for leaks. Seal leaks with duct tape.
2. Without crushing the insulation, wrap the blankets around the ducts. Keep vapor barrier on the outside if the ducts are for air conditioning.
3. Where the blankets meet, and at the wrapping junctures, seal the insulation tightly with duct tape. Do not block any air intakes, and keep the tape and insulation out of contact with light fixtures, chimneys, and flue pipes.
4. Cut the insulation that reaches beyond the duct so that there are 2 parallel cuts that extend the height of the duct. Fold the flap of insulation you have just created over the end of the duct and tape it closed. Fold the 2 remaining ends of insulation over the first, and tape them.

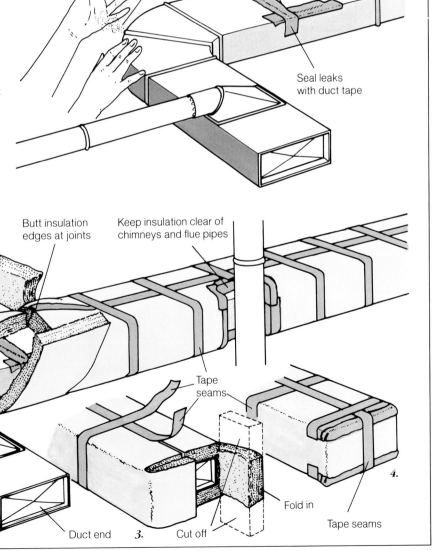

1.

Feel for escaping air

Seal leaks with duct tape

Butt insulation edges at joints

Keep insulation clear of chimneys and flue pipes

Vapor barrier

2.

Tape seams

Duct end

3.   Cut off

Fold in

4.

Tape seams

JOINERY

Many ingenious methods of joining two pieces of wood together have been devised over the centuries. Making a fine wood joint requires care and patience, but the results are strong and beautiful.

Although joints can be made with hand tools (a backsaw, sharp chisel, drill, and hammer), power tools simplify the process and ensure straight, accurate cuts. Three basic power tools that enable you to make almost any kind of joint are a table saw, a router, and a power miter saw. If you plan to do extensive woodworking, consider buying specialized, single-purpose tools to simplify the making of complicated joints. Such tools include a doweling jig, a dovetail template, and a biscuit joiner, which cuts matching grooves in pieces of wood so thin, biscuit-shaped splines can be inserted into them.

Each of the following joints can be made without a shopful of equipment. Most are simple and can be done fairly quickly. The keys to a successful joint are cutting the pieces accurately and fastening them securely. Always use sharp tools. Cut the pieces so that each joint closes with gentle hand pressure. If they fit loosely, the glue alone won't hold them. The closer the fit, the stronger the joint will be.

Most joints can be fastened with adhesives and screws or nails. Although many kinds of glue are on the market, woodworker's glue is adequate for most interior purposes. Clamp glued joints as soon as possible, and let them set overnight. Conceal nail heads by countersinking them. Fill the resulting holes with a stainable wood filler or, if the boards are already stained, putty from a putty stick that matches the stain color. Screw heads can be concealed by countersinking them and plugging the holes. Prefabricated plugs are available for this, or you can saw dowels into short sections or cut plugs from scrap wood with a plug cutter. Some joints require specialized fasteners, such as drawbolts or threaded plugs.

Understanding how joints are made will help you repair furniture, as most repairs involve failed joints.

Recommended Cross-References
Cabinets, Caulking & Adhesives, Fastening Hardware, Shelves, Storage: Indoor, Tools, Wood.

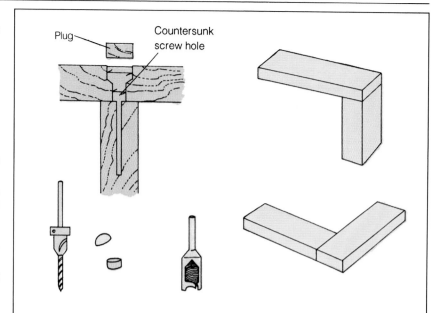

Butt Joint
Although a butt joint is simple to make, it has relatively little strength. Cut the butt end perfectly square so that it fits smoothly and tightly against the other board. Clamp the boards together securely before drilling a countersunk screw hole. Make sure the hole through the first piece is large enough that the threads don't bite. If the threads do bite in the first piece the screw passes through, the screw will not pull the joint together tightly. The hole can be drilled in one pass with a countersink drill; if you don't have one, drill each part of the hole separately with standard drills in different sizes. For a nice finish, plug the holes with matching or contrasting wood. You can make plugs with a plug cutter or buy them ready-made.

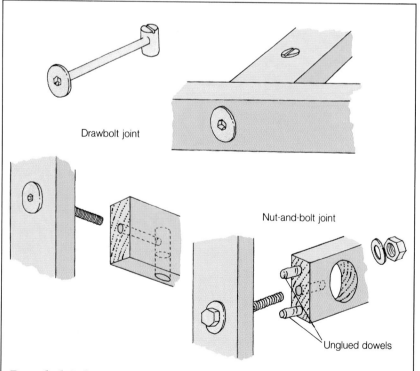

Drawbolt Joint
These very strong joints are easy to assemble, forgiving of minor imperfections, and easy to disassemble and reassemble once made. They can be fashioned with a standard bolt, nut, and washers, or you can buy specialty parts for high-quality work.

Lap Joints

Full-Lap Joint. First mark the position of the lapping board on the sides and top of the cross-board with a scribe or sharp pencil. Finish the line with a try square.

Cut the notch with a sharp backsaw. Fit the lapping board in the notch and fasten with glue and either screws or nails.

Half-Lap Joint. Because the lapping board is also notched, the cross-board requires a shallower notch. Lay the lapping board over the cross-board and mark them. Use a try square to draw the final marks. Measure the thickness of the lapping board, marking the center point on both edges. Mark the same dimension on the edges of the cross-board. Scribe the cutting marks with the square and cut out the notches. Fasten the joint with glue and nails or screws.

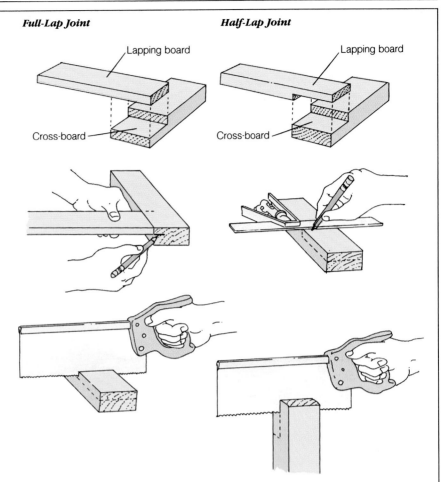

Full-Lap Joint

Lapping board

Cross-board

Half-Lap Joint

Lapping board

Cross-board

Blind-Dowel Joint

Use at least two dowels in any joint. Clamp together the two pieces of wood to be joined. Check that all edges are flush, then on both pieces mark the dowel locations across the joint. Use a doweling jig to hold the drill bit in precise alignment. If you don't have one, measure precisely with a try square where the holes are to be drilled on each edge. You can ensure greater accuracy by drilling holes in one piece, inserting dowel centers in them, and then tapping the two pieces of wood together.

Drill the dowel holes 1/16 inch deeper than the dowels.

Drive the dowels into one piece and tap the other piece onto them. If the dowels fit, gently pry the joint apart and then glue it back together. Apply glue to the holes and mating surfaces, not the dowels. If the dowels do not fit, fill the holes with new dowels, cut them flush, and start over again. It is possible that you will have to redrill only one side.

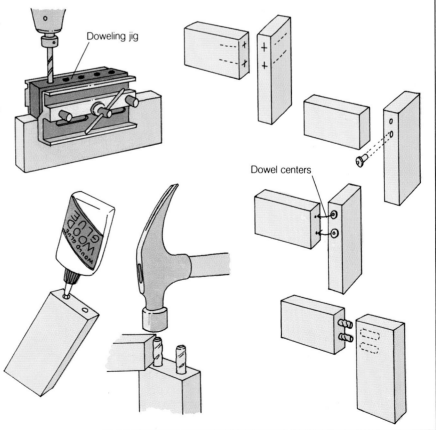

Doweling jig

Dowel centers

Dado Joints

Plain Dado. Dado joints are excellent for bookshelves and similar cabinetwork. They help to stabilize the case and they make interesting edges when several dado joints show. A dado goes across the grain; a dado groove goes with the grain. Dadoes are best done with a router or a power saw with dado blades, but you can also use a handsaw and chisel. The depth of cuts is usually one-third of the thickness of the board.

Rabbet Joint. A rabbet joint is a modified dado. Instead of a notch in the side of a board, a rabbet joint has a notch at the end. Use the same techniques as for a dado joint.

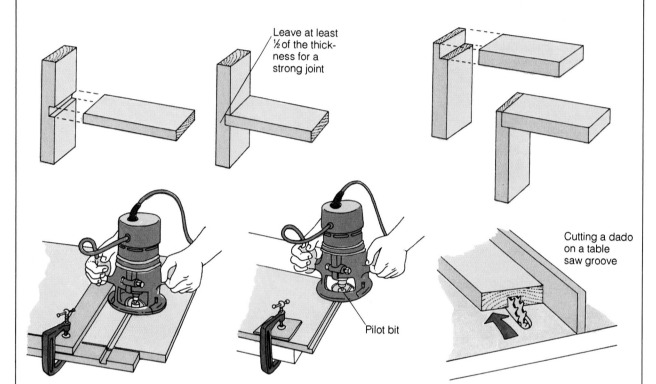

Plain Dado

Leave at least ½ of the thickness for a strong joint

Rabbet Joint

Cutting a dado with a router

Pilot bit

Cutting a rabbet with a router

Cutting a dado on a table saw groove

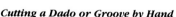

Cutting a Dado or Groove by Hand

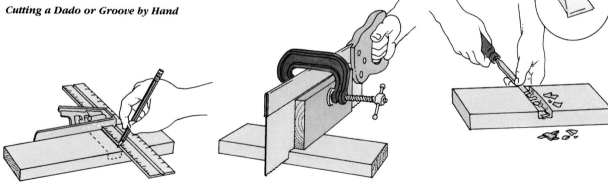

1. Mark and draw cutting lines with a square and/or a straightedge. Dado cuts should not be deeper than two-thirds of the thickness of the board.

2. Clamp on a guide board so that the amount of blade below the board equals the depth of the dado.
3. Cut the sides of the dado to the depth of the guide board.

4. Remove most of the waste by working from each side at an upward angle toward the center. Hold the chisel with the bevel side up.
5. Clean out remaining waste and smooth the bottom of the dado or groove with the bevel side down.

Miter Joint

This classic joint, in which two pieces are cut at 45-degree angles and joined together, has dozens of applications around the house. It is used for picture frames, molding, shelf corners, handrails, and any other place where you want to conceal the end grain of both boards.

The simplest and most accurate way to cut is with a power miter saw. Set the cutting angle to 45 degrees for the front cut. Then rotate the saw around to the 45-degree mark on the opposite side for cutting the second piece of wood. If you have to cut freehand, lay out a 45-degree angle on a piece of wood with a try square or combination square, which have the angle built into them. Mark the board both across the face and down the side so that you can follow accurately with the backsaw.

Two pieces of mitered wood can be joined in several ways. The simplest—and weakest—is to glue both faces, pull them tightly together with a picture-frame clamp, and drive two corrugated fasteners across the joint on each side. A method that is nearly

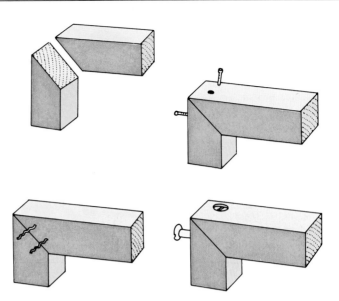

as simple but makes the joint a little stronger is to glue the faces and then nail them together. A stronger joint is made by gluing and then screwing the faces together. The strongest method of all is to use dowels.

The 45-degree cuts make this joint into a right angle, but any angle is possible simply by making different cuts. Decide the overall angle first, using a protractor to measure it. Then divide the measurement in half to get the angle for the cuts. Lay out and cut each board with the new angle, and then join them together with glue, screws, or dowels.

Dovetail Joint

This joint is used for assembling drawers and for decorative applications. It is very strong, and can have straight, fingerlike edges or the dovetail configuration shown here. You can make the cuts with a handsaw by laying them out with careful measurements on one piece, cutting it, and then tracing it onto the second piece.

An easier method is to use a router and dovetail template. With them you can do in minutes what would otherwise take hours by hand. The router should have a dovetail bit, which is shaped something like a tapered cork with the wide end at the bottom. Clamp a piece of stock onto the jig in a vertical position, butting the end up against the bottom of the fingered plate and letting the rest of it hang down in front of the jig. Then run the router back and forth across the top of the stock, using the grooves as a guide. Make each cut by pushing the router toward the back and pulling it forward again; then move the router over to the next groove and repeat the pro-

cess, all the way down the line.

When the first piece of wood is finished, clamp a second one into the jig in a horizontal position so that the end of it faces you and is flush with the front edge of the grooves. Rout it in the same matter as the first. Square off the inside of each cut with a saw and fit the two pieces together for a test. Mark the top and bottom for cutting so that the two pieces will be flush with each other at the joint. When you are satisfied with the fit, apply glue to all of the pieces and clamp them together.

Template

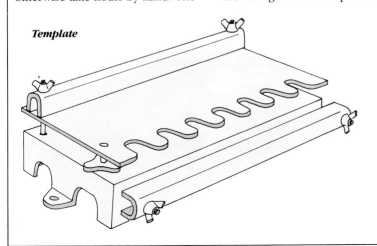

Dovetail Joint

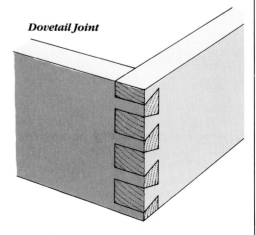

Repairing Stick Chairs

Remove any loose parts. Don't disassemble tight joints if you don't have to.

Remove all old glue from the dowels and sockets with a sharp knife, sandpaper, or a chisel. Be careful not to damage or enlarge the dowel sockets.

Test-fit the joint before gluing it. If it is only slightly loose, coat the dowel with glue and wrap it tightly with a layer of thin cotton thread. Add more glue and insert the dowel into the socket. If the joint is more than slightly loose, pack with flat toothpicks before gluing it.

Clamp the joint with bar clamps or web clamps or wrap it tightly with rope. Wipe off any excess glue; it will come off easily with water when wet, but not once it is dry. As you tighten the clamps or rope, make sure all parts remain in correct alignment.

Stick Chair

1. Tap joints apart and twist out dowels

2. Remove old glue from dowels and sockets

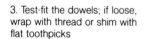

3. Test-fit the dowels; if loose, wrap with thread or shim with flat toothpicks

4. Glue and clamp the joints

Repairing Frame Chairs

The most common break in this type of chair is at the joint where the sides of the seat meet the rear legs and back. This is usually doweled. Gently spread the joint far enough to see it. If it is doweled, you will need to crack open the opposite joint and cut the dowels on that side or drive off the other side rail with a padded mallet. Do not pound directly on the furniture. Use woodblocks to protect it.

Once the joint has been disassembled, cut off the dowel flush with the surface.

Drill out the dowels on each side with a bit $\frac{1}{16}$ inch smaller than the dowel. Be careful not to drill too deep or enlarge the hole.

Clean out the dowel socket with a sharp chisel or screwdriver.

Test-fit the new dowels. If they don't line up perfectly, sand or drill the sockets to be slightly larger, then shim the dowel with flat toothpicks.

Glue and clamp the pieces, making sure that they are straight and correctly aligned.

Wipe off any excess glue while it is still wet.

Frame Chair

1. Pull joints apart; cut dowels flush and drill out

2. Clean out sockets

3. Test-fit new dowels; if loose, shim with flat toothpicks

4. Glue and clamp the joints

Repairing Table Legs

Four-legged tables are usually assembled with bolts and corner blocks. If the corner blocks are secure, loose legs can usually be fixed by tightening the bolts. If a corner block is loose, remove it, clean off the old glue, and reglue it. Use a screw or clamps to hold it in place while the glue dries. If you use a screw, predrill the corner block with a hole slightly larger than the outer diameter of the screw threads so the screw will pull the block in tight. If the block is cracked, make a new one. Use the old block as a template for cutting and drilling.

Repairing a Table Leg

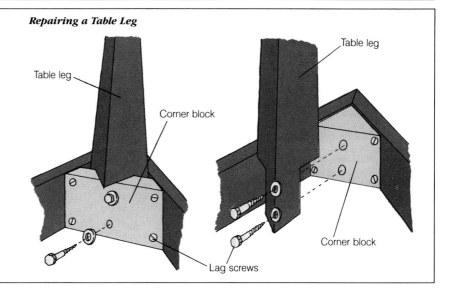

Table leg

Table leg

Corner block

Corner block

Lag screws

Repairing Drawer Joints

Disassemble the loose joints, leaving the still-tight joints connected if possible.

Clean off all old glue (glue sticks very well to wood, but not very well to old glue). Use a sharp chisel or knife, or sand it off. Try not to remove any wood.

Apply woodworker's glue to the joint, following the glue manufacturer's instructions. Secure the glued joints with bar clamps, web clamps, or rope wrapped tightly around the drawer.

While the glue is still wet, drill screw or nail holes through the joints. Install screws or nails and countersink the heads just below the surface.

Reglue any loose corner blocks. If desired, you can install corner blocks in a drawer that doesn't already have them.

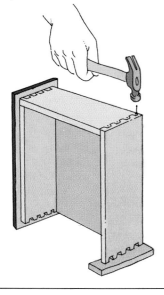

Repairing Veneers

Furniture is often covered with veneer, a thin layer of decorative wood. Veneer that is lifting at the edges can be reattached. Damaged veneer can be replaced or patched.

To reattach a lifting section, make the veneer pliable by placing a barely damp towel over the loose section and heating it with an iron or hair dryer for 5 to 10 seconds. Repeat until the wood is pliable. Note that this may damage the finish; shellac is especially vulnerable to water. Once the veneer is pliable, scrape out as much glue as possible and squeeze new glue into the crack. Press down the veneer firmly and wipe up any excess glue. Cover the loose section with wax paper and a flat woodblock, then weight it down or clamp it until the glue dries.

To repair a blister, carefully cut it open along the grain of the wood. Inject glue using a tool specifically for that purpose; these are available at stores that sell veneer. Press the veneer flat, remove the excess glue, cover the blister with wax

paper, and weigh it down until the glue dries.

Before you cut a veneer patch, use a scrap piece to practice matching the finish of the furniture. The wood may or may not be stained. With open-grained woods, such as mahogany, a paste filler may be used to smooth the surface. The final finish may be varnish, lacquer, or shellac.

Cut the patch first. Trim it to be slightly larger than the chipped-out section. Align the grain of the patch and the remaining surface.

Use the patch to mark the existing veneer. The marked area, like the patch, should be slightly larger than the chipped-out section.

If the patch is thicker than the existing veneer, sand the backside of the patch to thin it.

Test-fit the patch and recut as required.

If necessary, stain the patch to match the existing color. Apply the same final finish used on the original surface. Attach the patch with contact cement.

Hide the seam with furniture putty that matches the veneer.

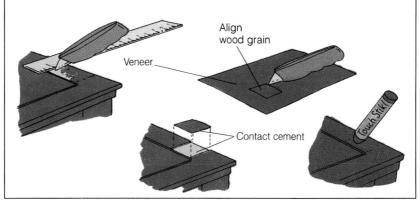

Align wood grain

Veneer

Contact cement

KITCHEN LAYOUT

The kitchen is the nerve center in most homes, with a number of appliances, fixtures, work areas, storage spaces, and traffic corridors concentrated in one room. This focus of activity, combined with a bewildering choice of available colors, materials, and styles, makes the kitchen the most complex room to plan.

Most professionals organize their planning into a series of steps that includes a survey of the available space, an inventory of the occupants' habits and needs, the development of a floor plan, and the selection of specific materials for creating the desired look. This process entails many changes and refinements, going back and forth between the steps many times. Some decisions involve functional considerations and others involve matters of taste and style, but the key to the entire process is the development of an efficient floor plan.

Whether the design involves your present kitchen or a proposed addition, develop your own kitchen layout by starting with an accurate floor plan. Then, through testing and revision, try various layouts until you find the most satisfying arrangement of appliances, furniture, and space. You will have to try many arrangements; layouts are easier to do if you sketch on tracing paper over the floor plan. Another way to experiment is to use templates, drawn to scale.

There can be several satisfactory layouts for a kitchen. The one that works best depends on a combination of your needs, your budget, the available space, and the desired effect.

Recommended Cross-References

Cabinets, Countertops, Dishwashers, Electrical System, Hoods & Vents, Lighting: Indoor, Plumbing, Ranges, Ovens & Cooktops, Sinks & Garbage Disposers, Wiring.

In the kitchen (opposite) a pantry cupboard provides generous storage space with easy access to the contents. Countertops between the stove and refrigerator and next to the cooktop are convenient places to set food while cooking or putting away groceries. The sink and dishwasher are conveniently close together, as are the refrigerator, oven, and cooktop.

Preliminary Considerations

First clarify why you need a new kitchen. Do you desire: a different stove, a different sink, more counter space, a nice window, more storage, better circulation? Be as specific as possible about your needs. Some are clear because they are prompted by nagging irritations or they are ideas that you have got from magazines or other kitchens. Other needs may be less obvious because they are dictated by habits and patterns, but they are equally important. Ask yourself:

- How many cooks are there?
- Do you like to eat in the kitchen?
- How often do you cook?
- How often do you bake?
- How often do you entertain?
- How often do you shop?
- What kind of cooking do you do?
- What equipment must be stored?
- What things will you display?
- Are your work habits flexible?
- How often do you clean?
- Does your family like to congregate in the kitchen?
- What other activities occur in the kitchen (homework, sewing, laundry, play)?
- Do you like company in the kitchen?
- How do you want the kitchen to look? (tidy, busy, warm, sleek, etc.)
- Which things require concealed storage? Open storage?
- How tall are the cooks?
- Do any of the cooks have particular physical needs?
- Are the cooks right-handed or left-handed?
- Is there access to the dining room?
- Do you need access to the garden?

Ways to Add Space

Even if you're unsure if your budget will allow them, identify all possible structural changes. You may find that moving a doorway, opening up a closet, or bumping out a bay window is feasible and that it will enable you to have your dream kitchen.

First ask:

- What assets and limitations does the existing space have?
- Can you move nonbearing walls?
- Which doorways and windows could you move?
- Which design features (moldings, finish coverings, cabinets, or fixtures) do you want to preserve?
- What are the dominant traffic patterns?

If these solutions are too drastic, consider moving or closing off a doorway to create more wall space, or converting an existing window to a bay window. (Bumping out a bay window seldom requires a structural change.) Built-in benches and tables, compact laundry equipment, and under-the-counter water heaters can free valuable space. To create the impression of space, enlarge windows, add a skylight, use light-colored cabinets, and replace some cabinets with open shelves (and keep them uncluttered).

Plumbing and Wiring

The location of pipes, wires, and ducts for all the appliances will restrict your layout. You can move a sink a few inches without changing the rough plumbing by extending the supply tubing and drain arm. A second sink or radical relocation requires roughing-in a drain, vent pipes, and water pipes. Islands require a specific venting arrangement.

You can move an existing gas stove or cooktop a few feet by lengthening the flexible supply pipe, but the shutoff valve must remain accessible.

Provide a range hood with at least 150 CFM capacity. Duct it to the outside through an exterior wall or through an attic directly overhead.

An electric range, oven, or cooktop must have its own 240-volt circuit; you cannot splice into an existing line to lengthen it. Run new wiring from the service panel or a new subpanel. Any fixed appliance, such as a dishwasher, garbage disposer, in-counter blender motor, or trash compactor, must also have its own circuit.

In addition to circuits for lighting, a kitchen must have at least two 20-amp circuits for convenience receptacles. Lights can be on an existing general-purpose circuit. Other electrical needs may include wiring for a smoke detector, telephone, intercom, and TV cable.

Also consider heating and cooling equipment. You may not be able to move existing ducts and registers.

Space Standards

Professional designers have developed standard dimensions and arrangements that users consider desirable. Try to incorporate these standards in your floor plan.

The Work Triangle. Position the three major appliances—sink, stove, and refrigerator—so that the traffic pattern between them forms a triangle. Each leg should be from 4 to 7 feet long; the total length of all three legs should measure 12 to 26 feet. The most efficient arrangement places the sink at an equal distance from the other two appliances. At the very least, try to place the sink and stove no more than three steps apart. In addition to the work triangle, think of each appliance as the center of its own work area.

The Refrigerator Area. Allow a 33- to 36-inch space for the refrigerator, whether or not your present model is that wide. The door should swing so that you can reach into the refrigerator from the sink area (most refrigerators hinge on the right side). Allow at least 15 to 18 inches of counter on the latch side, or no more than 48 inches across from the refrigerator if you prefer. Place the refrigerator at the end of a counter rather than where it would interrupt the flow of work from one side to the other. Make sure that the door does not collide with the doors of other appliances. Place other food storage near the refrigerator.

The Cooking Area. A range or cooktop should have at least 15 inches (and preferably 18 to 24 inches) of countertop on one side. As a safety requirement, the other side should have at least 12 inches of counter space to accommodate pot handles. If counters intersect near a range, allow 9 to 12 inches from the range to the corner so you do not have to lean over the stove to reach the adjacent counter. Plan to store pots, pans, utensils, spices, and other seasonings near the cooking area.

A microwave oven should have 15 inches of counter above, beside, or below it.

A built-in oven is not used as often as a cooktop; a viable layout may place it outside the basic work triangle. The oven should have at least 15 to 18 inches of counter on one side. If possible, position it near a mixing center. Like the refrigerator, the oven is tall; do not place it where it will interrupt the flow of work.

The Sink Area. The sink is the center of kitchen activity and should have the highest proportion of counter and storage space. Provide at least 24 to 36 inches of countertop on the side of the sink where you stack dishes (usually the left side). Provide 18 to 30 inches where you drain dishes. A sink should be at least 12 to 21 inches from a corner (3 inches if there is 21 inches of counter around the corner). Average sink dimensions are 24 inches for a single bowl; 36 inches for a double sink. If you have a dishwasher, allow 18 to 24 inches of counter and 21 inches of standing space on each side.

Mixing and Food Preparation. Provide 36 to 42 inches of counter for general food preparation for each cook. The mixing center may be a separate area or you may combine it with another work area. It should be near a sink. Other activity areas that may require a counter include a baking center, eating area, hobby area, and entertainment center. Each may require storage cabinets or specific fixtures (such as a bar, a sink, or cable TV hookup).

Passageways. Where counters or appliances face each other, the space between them should be at least 48 inches. To allow two people to work comfortably, allow 60 inches. There should be at least 42 inches of clearance around all sides of an island counter. The space between a table and wall should be 26 to 36 inches; allow 30 to 44 inches if the space also serves as a passageway.

The layouts (opposite) show variations on two different kitchens.

Rectangular Kitchen

Problems. Limited and inconvenient work areas and storage.

Few Structural Changes. 1. Vent and fan added above range; roll-out shelves on left. **2.** New upper and lower cabinets to right of range. **3.** New side-by-side refrigerator/ freezer, with storage. **4.** Floor-to-ceiling storage cabinet. **5.** Open shelves. **6.** Fold-up table encloses open upper shelves. **7.** Track lighting. **8.** Built-in bench. Upholstered top lifts up to reveal storage space. **9.** Doorway to dining room moves to make way for counter. **10.** Outside door replaced by desk and greenhouse window. **11.** Glass-fronted wall cabinet. **12.** Lazy susan.

Extensive Alteration. 1. Cooktop. **2.** Closing the entrance from hall allows for corner units. **3.** New wall oven and microwave. **4.** Side-by-side refrigerator/freezer, with enclosed cabinet above. **5.** Built-in bar with shallow shelves above. **6.** Pocket door. **7.** Pass-through to dining room with buffet counter. **8.** French doors to patio. **9.** Movable chopping cart with knife storage and shelves. **10.** Open shelving tops tiled counter over dishwasher. **11.** Extralarge sink. **12.** Install new lighting panel.

Corridor Kitchen

Problems. Insufficient counter and storage space. Inadequate lighting.

Few Structural Changes. 1. Increase counter to 18 inches to accommodate wider sink. **2.** Install track lighting. **3.** Widen cooktop counter to 24 inches and tile for pot landing. **4.** Move refrigerator to create long baking center. **5.** Hutch is removed and round table replaced. **6.** Reposition refrigerator. **7.** Add higher wall cabinets.

Extensive Alteration. 1. Replace half-walls near dining room with full walls; add doors to create privacy. **2.** Increase the counter depth to 24 inches and tile. **3.** Install freestanding range, with microwave above. **4.** Counter angled for refrigerator access. **5.** Recess the refrigerator. **6.** Table-height counter with track lighting above. **7.** Corner cabinet with revolving shelves. **8.** Install double sink. **9.** Expand counter width. **10.** Recessed spotlights.

Basic Layouts

The space standards, together with considerations regarding cooking habits, utility requirements, and the existing space, will determine your kitchen layout. There are four basic configurations for kitchen work areas: (1) one-wall, with work areas along the same wall; (2) L-shaped, in which traffic flows outside the work area and allows dining in the opposite corner; (3) U-shaped, which has no traffic through the work area and allows an efficient placement of appliances; and (4) corridor, with work areas along two facing walls and traffic through the middle. An island or counter opening presents variations.

Rectangular Kitchen

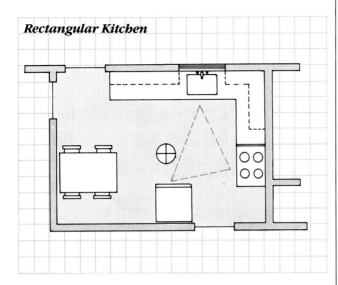

Corridor Kitchen

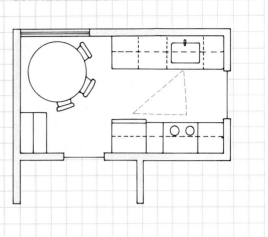

Few Structural Changes

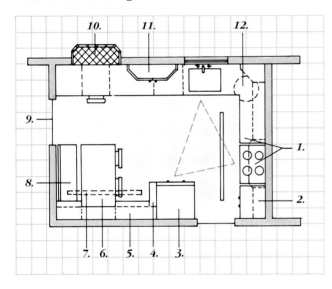

Few Structural Changes

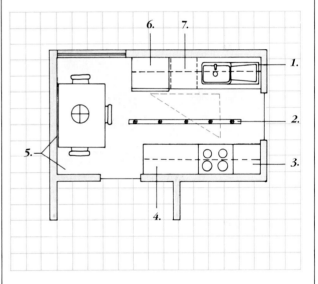

Extensive Alteration

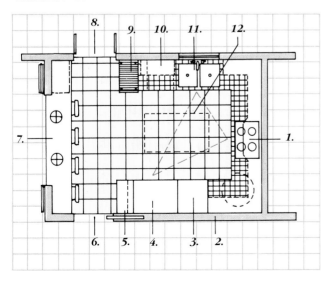

Extensive Alteration

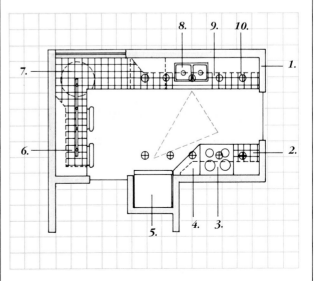

LATTICE

Lattice is an effective screening material whether used alone or in combination with fences, trellises, gazebos, shutters, screens, and overhead patio structures. Latticework creates shade, admits filtered views, provides support for plants, and forms a decorative background for any garden setting. It is easy to work with and can take on any size or shape.

Attach lattice to any kind of supporting framework. For appearance and strength, nail each lath securely on the outside edges. A frame of 2 by 4s will provide adequate nailers.

Recommended Cross-References
Fences, Gates, Gazebos, Trellises.

Latticework Structures

Fences. The spacing of fence posts depends on whether you want to nail the lattice panels to the surface of the posts, forming a continuous lattice plane on one side, or whether you want to install panels between the posts. If you install panels between posts, nail 2 by 2s to the insides of the posts and attach the panels to them. Nail 2 by 4s across the tops of the posts to frame the lattice panels.

To gain privacy and provide vines with a trellis, top an existing fence with long, narrow panels of lattice. Add a frame of 2 by 4s to the top of the fence and nail the lattice directly to it.

Overhead Shade Structures. Lattice spans should not measure more than 4 feet; spans of 2 to 3 feet are preferable. Run the supports above the lattice and attach the panels to it to maintain an uninterrupted plane of lattice below.

Trellises. Attach lattice panels to a fence or wall, using 2 by 4 blocks as spacers to hold them away from the surface. An ordinary handsaw will allow you to cut panels of different sizes and shapes, including curves.

Screens. Latticework serves well as a screen. Think of each unit as a small fence and follow the instructions for nailing panels on or between posts.

Apart from adding decorative accents, lattice panels are versatile outdoor materials. The panels can be made into walls, fences, windbreaks, or roofs. They can support vines, conceal storage, or provide shade.

Types and Finishes

Wood lattice is made of strips of lath nailed (or stapled) together in crisscross fashion. Vinyl lattice is similar in appearance, but its strips are chemically welded together. The strips can run at right angles or diagonally. Lattice is available in prefabricated panels, or you can make your own. Most wood lattice is made from $\frac{3}{8}$-inch by $1\frac{1}{2}$-inch lath, spaced $1\frac{1}{2}$ to 2 inches apart, but other sizes are also available. Vinyl lattice is available in several styles and sizes.

The spacing between laths determines the overall appearance of the lattice. If strips are close together ($1\frac{1}{2}$ inches), the lattice has a solid texture and tends to blend into the background. If strips are more than 2 inches apart, the lattice seems airy, allows less privacy, and will not shade as well.

Painted or stained wood lattice can match other architectural features (vinyl lattice is color impregnated). If you paint, cover the lattice with an oil-based primer. After the primer dries, apply a topcoat of alkyd or acrylic latex paint. (Spray applicators are fast, but waste more paint than a brush.) If you paint or stain the lattice a color different from the support structure, coat it before you install the panels—the color contrast will be crisper. Another option is not to coat at all. If latticework is of a durable wood species, it can weather naturally.

Lighting plays a key role in interior design and is a major part of any electrical wiring project. It is easy to overlook the importance of lighting and the role it plays in the comfort and ambience of a room, but it should be considered as much as any other factor in planning a room. All too often the solution is to settle for one ceiling fixture and some scattered table lamps.

Home lighting should be varied and dramatic. Fixtures should be connected to dimmer switches that can create different effects. The lighting should be flexible enough to illuminate many activities as well as be a focus of interest in itself.

Recommended Cross-References
Electrical System, Lighting: Outdoor, Switches, Wiring.

In the dining and living rooms (opposite), the light beams from recessed ceiling fixtures highlight key parts of the room and create dramatic contrasts of light and shadow. Dished sconces (above) provide side light—ideal for a bathroom mirror. Recessed fixtures set into a soffit (below) swivel so you can direct the light.

LIGHTING: continued

Types of Light

Consider the type of bulb when choosing fixtures.

Incandescent. Incandescent bulbs produce a yellowish white light that flatters skin tones and highlights warm colors. The light is easy to direct. Incandescent bulbs cost more to operate, expend more energy in heat than light, and do not last as long as fluorescent tubes.

Fluorescent. Fluorescent tubes spread light, do not overheat, last a long time, and are about four times more economical to run than incandescent bulbs. They are available in many colors, from cool blues, to full-spectrum white, to warm tones. The ini-

tial cost of the fixtures is high.

Quartz Halogen. Quartz halogen bulbs produce a brilliant white light. One powerful bulb can illuminate an entire room, cast interesting shadows, and bathe a space in "sunshine." Because they put out so much heat, these bulbs must be used in special fixtures.

Types of Lighting Fixtures

Although there are many design variations of the fixtures shown, most fall into one of the following categories.

Type of Lighting	Type of Fixture		Comments
Incandescent	Surface-mounted		Wall or ceiling; provides ambient or task lighting; attach each fixture to prewired electrical box.
	Pendant		From chandelier to simple shade; offers flexibility in placing fixture.
	Recessed		For downlighting, wall washing, or uplighting; cannisters are usually installed before ceiling is finished, but retrofit units are available.
	Track		Fixtures in a variety of shapes are snapped or clipped onto a track. Units can be positioned and directed individually.
	Strip		Tiffany-type lights or incandescent tubes provide concealed lighting or dramatic accent lights.
Fluorescent	Surface fixture		Primary lighting for bathroom or kitchen; tube or ring-shaped bulb.
	Luminous ceiling		Light fixtures attached to ceiling and concealed by translucent panels held by grid suspended below lights.
	Compact bulbs		Have screw-type bases for use in standard light fixtures in place of incandescent bulbs.
Low Voltage	Individual fixture or complete system		Incandescent or halogen bulbs; requires transformer to step down house voltage.

A Lighting Tour

With overall lighting goals in mind, focus now on each room of the house. Some specific ideas to get you started follow. They are not intended as rules or guidelines, only as suggestions for providing adequate lighting and creating special effects.

Living Room. Install lighting that can be directed to reflect off walls or ceiling. Use valances to hide fluorescent tubes near the ceiling. Install track lights pointed in particular areas. Provide light for reading or playing the piano.

There are many opportunities in a living room for accent lighting. You can spotlight artwork, light a large plant from beneath, conceal lights under bookshelves or in alcoves, or showcase a special piece of furniture with a table lamp.

Dining Room. Illuminate the dining table directly with a pendant fixture on a dimmer, or indirectly with recessed lighting reflected off the walls and ceiling. Accent china and glass with hidden spotlights. Use low-voltage minilamps, like candles, to create sparkle.

Kitchen. Light all work surfaces well. Do this with fluorescent tubes under the cabinets, low-hanging fixtures, or a luminous ceiling. Use track lights or recessed fixtures to highlight particular areas. Bounce indirect light from the ceiling for general lighting, or conceal lighting in a skylight well or other alcove.

Bedroom. Provide soft light with indirect fixtures behind valances or coves. Use wall-mounted spotlights or bedside lamps for reading lights, and place lights on each side of the mirror in dressing areas.

Bathroom. Place lights beside the mirror rather than above it. Use a recessed fixture to spotlight the tub or shower. For general illumination, consider a luminescent panel in a soffit above counters.

Precautions

Besides the normal precautions you should take with all electrical wiring, there are some safety considerations unique to lighting. Recessed fixtures generate heat that will build up if it is trapped. Do not cover such fixtures with insulation; allow at least 3 inches of clearance all around. Observe the limit the manufacturer places on the maximum wattage of a fixture.

Fire Hazards. Closet lights pose a fire hazard if clothing or other combustible material is too close. Lights should be installed on the ceiling or on the wall above the door. A surface-mounted fixture must be at least 18 inches from stored materials, and must have unobstructed clearance between it and the floor. A recessed fixture must have a solid lens and be at least 6 inches away from stored material. A fluorescent fixture must have 6 inches of clearance.

Moisture. Lights in the bathroom should have moistureproof housings. Switches should not be beside the tub or shower.

Height. The lights in children's bedrooms should be at a safe height so they will not be broken during normal play. Avoid lamps in the room of an infant or toddler.

Stairwells and Entrances. Illuminate stairwells and entrances well. Many low lights are better than one light, which may cause shadows.

Code Requirements. Observe all code requirements for locating, switching, wiring, and grounding light fixtures. These requirements were written for your protection.

The Goals of Lighting

General lighting is the overall illumination of a room—just enough to see your way around or have casual conversation. The best light source is indirect fixtures that cast a warm glow, or directional lights that wash a wall or curtains. General lighting is more effective if it is controlled by dimmer switches.

Task lighting illuminates specific areas where direct light is needed, such as counters, desks, reading areas, and work tables. You should never work in your own shadow.

Accent lighting is purely decorative, although the results will contribute to the general lighting level. Accent lighting consists of directional light aimed at specific objects or architectural features, mood lighting that washes over a wall or uplights from the floor, and light produced by lamps and hanging fixtures.

Bedroom lighting casts soft shadows and pools of light rather than a harsh glare.

Track Lighting

Track lighting consists of pieces of track, available in different lengths. The track has to be connected to a power source and, to avoid trailing wires, the usual connection is to a ceiling outlet. (You can get track that you merely plug into a wall outlet.) The individual light units that snap or clip onto the track are purchased separately.

Installing Track Lighting. Turn off the power and remove the old ceiling fixture from the ceiling box. See if the screw holes in the canopy box line up with the corner tabs of the ceiling box. If not, you can use the round box adapter as an intermediate bracket.

Thread the wires from the canopy box through the square plastic cover plate and the adapter ring, if needed. Connect them to the wiring in the ceiling box. Screw the canopy box into the ceiling box, tucking the wires carefully out of the way.

Drill holes in a section of track for toggle bolts, slide the end into the canopy box, and screw the toggles into the ceiling.

Snap the light fixtures into the track wherever you want them, and secure them in place with the locking levers. Turn on the lights and swivel and tilt them into position. If necessary, unlock the levers and slide them up or down the track until they are in perfect position. Relock the levers.

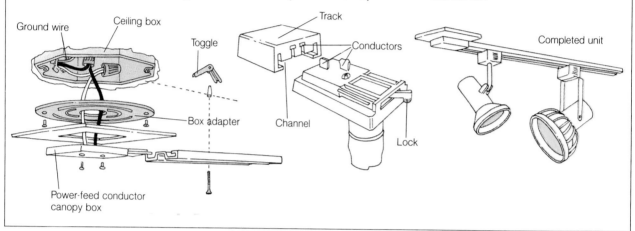

Ground wire · Ceiling box · Toggle · Track · Conductors · Completed unit · Box adapter · Channel · Lock · Power-feed conductor canopy box

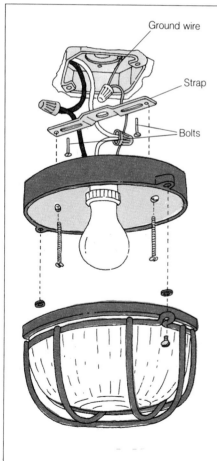

Ground wire · Strap · Bolts

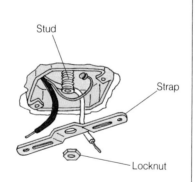

Stud · Strap · Locknut

Installing a Ceiling Fixture

Make sure the power is off. Attach the mounting strap to the ceiling box in one of two ways, as shown. The more common way is to screw the strap into the corner tabs of the box. If the box is plastic, the strap must be grounded.

Connect the wires by joining black to black and white to white. If the fixture is a metal one, run a short pigtail from the grounding screw to the grounding wire.

Screw the fixture base to the mounting bracket, tucking the wires carefully out of the way. Screw in the bulb and attach the globe.

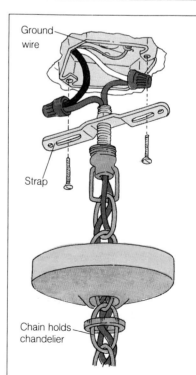

Ground wire · Strap · Strap · Chain holds chandelier

Installing Pendant Fixtures

Pendant or swagged fixtures are mounted in much the same way as ceiling fixtures. Feed wire through the center of a threaded nipple and connect it. Attach the canopy. If the fixture hangs from a chain, thread the wire through the chain to make it less conspicuous.

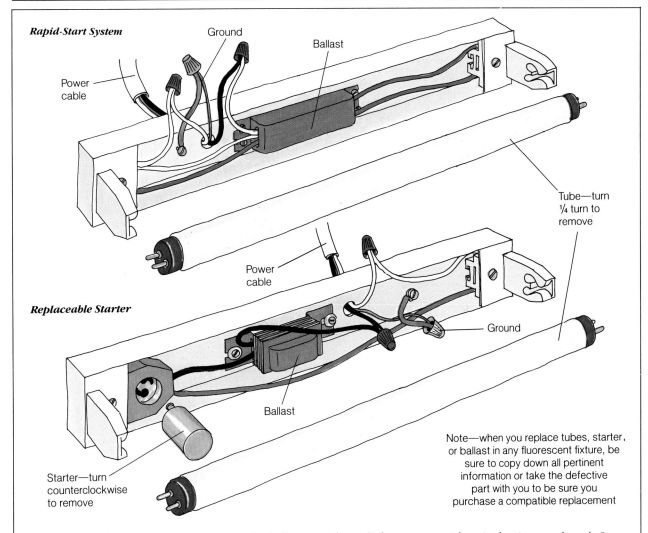

Rapid-Start System

Power cable

Ground

Ballast

Tube—turn ¼ turn to remove

Replaceable Starter

Power cable

Ballast

Ground

Starter—turn counterclockwise to remove

Note—when you replace tubes, starter, or ballast in any fluorescent fixture, be sure to copy down all pertinent information or take the defective part with you to be sure you purchase a compatible replacement

Fluorescent Fixtures

There are three types of fluorescent lamps: preheat, rapid-start, and instant-start. In preheat models, the starter is separate from the ballast and is replaceable without removing the ballast. Rapid-start lights have the starter built right into the ballast, and instant-start fixtures have no starter. The latter are less common than the other types and are distinguishable by the use of tubes with a single pin at each end. Common repairs of fluorescent fixtures include replacing burned-out tubes, replacing the starter when the tubes flicker but never brighten, and replacing damaged or corroded sockets.

Bulbs

Type A. The familiar pear shape is available in frosted or clear, from 4 to more than 200 watts. Special types include 3-way bulbs that produce varying light intensities, long-life bulbs that provide up to 200 percent more use, and silvered-bowl bulbs that have an opaque silver coating on the bottom to prevent direct glare.
Type G. A round globe with a screw-in base; from 15 to 100 watts.
Type T. A tubular bulb, 5 inches long or longer, from 15 to 60 watts. A variation is the flame-shaped decorative bulb.
Type R. A reflector bulb, shaped like a funnel, with silver coating inside.
Type PAR. Parabolic Aluminized Reflector—a floodlight that resembles an auto headlamp.
Type ER. Ellipsoidal Reflector—a variation of a reflector bulb that focuses light differently.
Tungsten-Halogen. Brilliant white light used with special fixtures.

Low-Voltage Bulbs

Low-voltage bulbs operate on direct current (DC) that requires attaching a transformer to regular house current.
Reflector Spot. Similar to Type R, but smaller—only 15 to 25 watts.
PAR. Similar to auto headlamp.
Minireflector. Like photographic projector bulb; highly focused.
Minilights. Tiny lights, such as Christmas tree lights.

Tubes

All fluorescent tubes operate similarly; a phosphorous coating on the inside of the glass glows brightly when stimulated by energy passing through mercury vapor inside the tube. Only the size and shape varies. Wattages range from 8 to 40 watts; the bulb can be tubular, U-shaped, or circular. Compact fluorescent lamps include type PL, which consists of parallel tubes, and type SL, which fits incandescent sockets. Install these in heavy-use areas, where their high cost will be paid back quickly.

LIGHTING: outdoor

Outdoor lighting is much more than a fixture for the front porch. On just the practical side, a well-designed lighting system illuminates driveways, walkways, doors, stairs, and gates. It also provides security around the house by eliminating shadows where intruders could hide. On the less practical but equally relevant side, lighting enhances a garden after dark for greater enjoyment. It makes evening outdoor activities possible, such as relaxing and entertaining, and it also brings an enchanting air of magic and beauty to your garden that can be enjoyed indoors as well as out.

Low-Voltage Lighting

Low-voltage outdoor lighting is safe, inexpensive, and easy to install. Manufacturers usually include very clear instructions with their systems. Planning the layout is often the most difficult part of the job. Be sure the total wattage of the light fixtures doesn't exceed the capacity of the transformer. If it does, you will need to install one or more additional transformers.

Recommended Cross-References

Electrical System, Lighting: Indoor, Security, Wire, Wiring.

Lighting trees (above) or water (right) can provide spectacular effects at nighttime.

Planning Your System

The goals of a complete outdoor lighting system are to provide safe lighting for activity and security, to illuminate plants, pools, and other garden features, and to create whatever moods and effects the character of the garden suggests. There are various techniques and equipment for accomplishing these goals, but they should always be used with these principles in mind:

Think Safety. Always install all wiring with proper permits and according to code. Outdoor electrical systems require special care, equipment, and materials.

Don't Overlight. A small amount of the right kind of lighting is much more effective than indiscriminate "ballpark" lighting.

Vary the Brightness. Vary the levels of brightness. In some areas the lighting should be dim; in some, medium; and in others, bright.

Use One Type of Lamp. There are many types of lamps available, such as incandescent, fluorescent, sodium, and metal halide.

Define Space. Use light to define spaces and emphasize what's important. Bright lights that contrast with dimmer surrounding lights will point out pathways, steps, and activity areas for visitors, as well as illuminate interesting focal points.

Hide the Source. To avoid glare, place lights high above the ground, use fixtures with canopies close to the ground, shield fixtures behind plants or other features, reflect the light off light-colored walls, or use fixtures that have grilles and baffles.

Keep fixtures out of the way, and match their style. They should not interfere with walking, gardening, or plant growth.

Make the System Flexible. Use several circuits, each on its own switch—use a dimmer wherever possible.

Switches. Place switches at central indoor locations. On larger systems, you should also include auxiliary switches at the point of use.

Lighting Techniques

The location of a light source, direction of its beam, and intensity of the light are three variables that can be altered for different lighting effects. The following techniques are useful for outdoor lighting.

Downlighting. This is a general term that refers to placement of the light source high enough so it shines down upon an object or a general area. It is most effective when several lights are used and you cannot see the source. Use floodlights or filtered lights, depending on the mood desired, and locate them in trees or on high walls of the house. The effect is like moonlight filtering down through the trees.

Uplighting. This is any lighting where the source aims light upward at an object. This rarely happens naturally and therefore results in a startling effect that should be used with discretion. It is most effective for illuminating a special object or feature, or for lighting a tree so that it frames a particularly dramatic vista.

Safety Lighting. Pathways, steps, and activity areas should be lighted so people feel comfortable using them. Use downlighting or low path lights, depending how large an area you want to illuminate. It should be bright enough to make hazards and heavily used areas stand out from lighted surroundings.

Security Lighting. Lighting to discourage intruders does not have to be harsh and unpleasant. A well-planned outdoor lighting system is sufficient, as long as it leaves no shadows for easy hiding. Multiple sources are much better than a single floodlight. Controls should be inside the house, and should operate different parts of the system separately. Time clocks, photocells, and wireless controls increase the system's effectiveness.

Area Lighting. Areas of activity or heavy use, such as lawns, patios, and decks, should have a comfortable level of illumination for entertaining, work, or play. You can use downlighting, either from floodlights or diffused low-voltage lamps, but it should also be combined with other techniques. Floodlights alone give a flat, dull look in which no special features are emphasized. In addition, if it is too bright it can cause irritating glare, ruin any other lighting

effects, and disturb neighbors.

Diffused Lighting. If a light source is at eye level or in a direct line of vision, it should be diffused to prevent harsh glare. Use frosted globes, plastic panels, canvas shades, or other translucent objects around a fixture to soften the glare.

Emphasis. This is light to emphasize an object. There are several ways to dramatize an interesting feature with lighting. If it has an attractive texture, such as brick, bark, or siding, you can place a light close to the object and direct its beam to graze across the textured surface.

You can use small spotlights focused on a specific plant or sculpture to highlight it. Other ways to accentuate it are to direct the light onto a wall behind the object, creating a silhouette, or to place the light so it casts a shadow of the object onto a wall behind it. A long feature, such as a path or the edge of a pool, can be accented with a series of small lights that follow its contour.

Fill Lighting. Some areas of the garden do not need direct light, but should have low-level lighting to provide a background for the main areas. If excess light from the main sources is not enough to light these areas, you can provide low-level lighting near the floor of the garden to fill in.

Lighting Water. Pools, fountains, and other water features are ideal candidates for lighting. You can place lights underwater to create a diffused glow, or merely use the surface of the water as a mirror to reflect objects on the other side that are accented with either uplighting or spotlighting.

Vista Lighting. Many homes, especially those in hilly areas, look out on a beautiful view. This may be a natural area, such as a woodland, field, or nearby mountain, or it may be a sparkling cityscape. Vista lighting is a way of protecting that view. This is done by carefully controlling the height and brightness of garden lights. For example, you may use medium-bright lighting in the garden foreground near the house, but only low-voltage lights in ground-level fixtures in the further garden areas in order to see the view beyond. Or, if tall trees frame the view, uplight them from the ground in order to emphasize the view.

Some of the numerous ways in which you can use outdoor lighting are illustrated here. The eerie shadows and dramatic pools of light make plants and trees come alive at night.

Materials for Outdoor Wiring

Electrical boxes for receptacles, switches, and wire junctions are similar to indoor types, except that they have special gaskets and covers to make them weatherproof. Conduit, required for all above-ground wiring and some underground runs, must be joined with weathertight connectors.

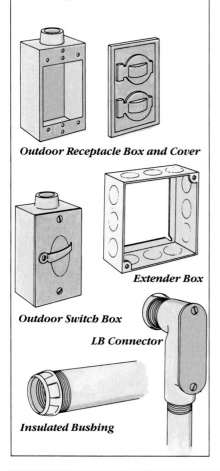

Outdoor Receptacle Box and Cover

Extender Box

Outdoor Switch Box

LB Connector

Insulated Bushing

Tapping Existing Wiring

Inside Outlets. For one or two outdoor fixtures, you may be able to tap into an existing circuit at an inside outlet. For several fixtures, it is better to wire them on their own circuit with their own switches. Any outdoor receptacles must be GFCI (ground fault circuit interrupter) protected.

A Porch Light. If a fixture is already located on an exterior wall, you can extend the wiring to additional fixtures. Any exposed wiring must be enclosed in conduit. The new fixtures will be controlled by the same switch as the porch light.

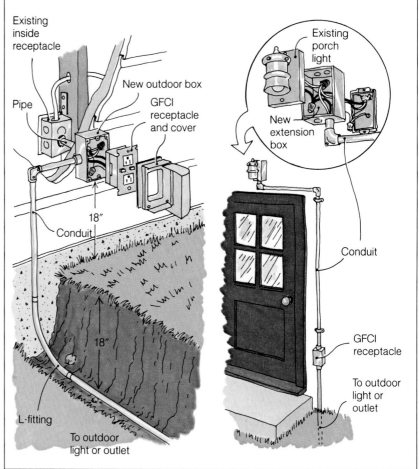

Existing inside receptacle

New outdoor box

GFCI receptacle and cover

Pipe

18"

Conduit

18"

L-fitting

To outdoor light or outlet

Existing porch light

New extension box

Conduit

GFCI receptacle

To outdoor light or outlet

Lamps and Fixtures

Your main choice for lighting fixtures involves the type of lamp, or bulb, you plan to use. The choices are incandescent, quartz incandescent, fluorescent, and high intensity discharge (HID).

Incandescent. Incandescent lamps include the "A" type bulb commonly used indoors and various types of reflector lamps. The most common reflector lamp for outdoor spotlighting and floodlighting is the PAR (parabolic aluminized reflector) lamp.

Most incandescent lighting is 120-volt, but low-voltage (12v) incandescent lamps are excellent for lighting pathways, accent plants, or areas needing fill lighting. Because of their wide availability, pleasing qual-

ity of light, and capacity for dimming, incandescent lamps are the most popular choice. Quartz incandescent lamps are a special type that give brighter light.

Fluorescent. Fluorescent lamps are more suitable for accent lighting than general area lighting because the light given off creates a somewhat flat effect. They are also not as energy efficient as the HID lamps.

High Intensity Discharge. The HID lamps include mercury vapor, high-pressure sodium, and metal halide bulbs. They all give brilliant light and are energy efficient, but cannot be dimmed easily and vary in their color rendering. The high-pressure sodium lamp is not used widely for residential systems because of the

orange hue that it casts. Metal halide lamps are very bright, with limited choice of intensities. The most versatile HID lamp for residential gardens is the mercury vapor, especially the clear, or "blue" type. If you use any of the HID lamps, you should supplement the lighting with incandescent lamps for greater warmth.

Fixtures. Once you have chosen the type of lamp each fixture will contain, you need to choose fixtures that will direct the light to where you need it. There are many types available, including simple lampholder sockets for floodlights, bullet lights that resemble canisters, well lights that are partially buried in the ground, and decorative fixtures that are meant to be seen.

Installing Outdoor Lighting

The first step is to plan the exact location of all lights and receptacles, using the lighting techniques that best suit your landscaping. Consider safety and area lighting first, and then any accents or special effects you want to include. Then, determine whether your system will provide enough lighting for security, and make adjustments for any deficiencies. Include switch locations in your planning. They should be indoors, with auxiliary outdoor switches in areas of high use.

Next, determine how many circuits the lighting system will need. Receptacles are usually kept on a separate circuit from lights. They must be GFCI receptacles, unless the entire circuit has a GFCI breaker or the outdoor portion of the circuit is protected by an indoor GFCI receptacle wired for "downstream" protection. If the garden is small and there are only a few lights, they

can probably be wired into extensions of existing circuits. For a larger system, you will want a separate circuit for every 6 to 12 fixtures, depending on the total wattage of lamps per circuit.

Plan circuits so you can group certain fixtures on the same switch, using dimmers for increased flexibility. You can also install some lights on special switches for greater security, such as timers, photocells, or sensing devices that turn on lights when they detect motion.

Once you have determined the location of all fixtures, switches, and receptacles, you should make a sketch to help you obtain necessary permits. Note all outlets, the size and type of wire, and the location of the main service panel. You probably will not need a permit to wire a low-voltage lighting system from an existing outlet. It is a good idea to have a professional electrician go over your plan first, even if you will be

doing all the wiring yourself.

All wiring runs should be buried or enclosed in conduit, except low-voltage wiring. In most code areas, you can bury type UF wire directly; in others you must run buried wiring through conduit. You may have a choice between rigid metal or PVC plastic conduit. Metal resists rodent damage and usually does not have to be buried as deeply as PVC, but it will also corrode in time. PVC is easier to work with, but must be buried at least 18 inches and is subject to chewing by rodents. For wiring above ground, use metal conduit with weathertight connectors.

If you run low-voltage wiring, all you have to do is connect the transformer to a 120-volt outlet and then run the correct low-voltage cable that is specified for the fixtures. You can attach the wiring to trees, fences, or sheds; lay it on the ground, or bury it. The outlet for the transformer should be controlled by a switch.

Anchoring Outdoor Fixtures

Fixtures and receptacles that are freestanding should be well anchored. A concrete block works very well. Make a 90-degree bend in the conduit at the point where your fixture will be, and slide the block over it. The section of conduit above the ground, and which bends down through the block, should be metal. The buried portion may be metal or PVC. After all the conduit is in place, fill the cells of the block with concrete. Then attach the junction box, run all necessary wiring, and install the light fixture or receptacle.

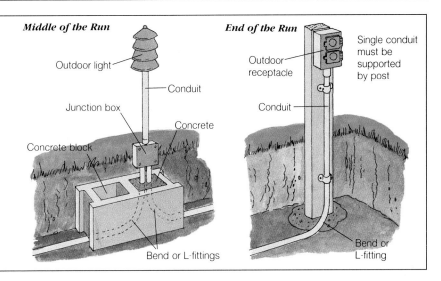

Middle of the Run

Outdoor light
Conduit
Junction box
Concrete
Concrete block
Bend or L-fittings

End of the Run

Single conduit must be supported by post
Outdoor receptacle
Conduit
Bend or L-fitting

Attaching a Fixture to a House

An outdoor fixture that is installed with all wiring indoors can be wired like any indoor light fixture, except that it must be approved for weather exposure. Simply cut a hole in the wall, install an octagon box, run wiring through the attic to the nearest outlet or junction box, wire it to a switch, and attach the exterior fixture. Be sure to caulk any gaps between the electrical box and the siding.

LOCKS

A visit to a hardware store or lock-smith will bring you up to date on all the doorknobs and locks available today. New styles are being developed continually, including electronic devices. The locks shown on this page are the most common and can be installed by any homeowner with a few simple tools.

When you install a lock, make sure that the rest of the door is sound. Replace a glass-paned or hollow-core door with a solid or steel-clad door. The jambs should be at least 1½ inches thick, with the stops milled right into them. If stops on your door are separate from the jamb, add extra nails or screws.

Door latches and dead bolts engage a strike plate that is set into the jamb. If the strike plate fails, the lock gives. Most strike plates are made of a flimsy metal that is held to the jamb with ¾-inch screws. You can buy reinforcement plates that are made of heavy-gauge metal and include long screws that penetrate all the way through the jamb and into the stud.

If the door swings outward the hinge pins will be on the outside of the house. To prevent the pins from being pulled out, open the door wide and drill through the knuckle and pin for a self-tapping screw. The screw will hold the pin in place and will be concealed when the door is shut. Do this for each hinge.

Give your back door at least as much attention as your front door. Be sure it is solid core as well, and reinforce the jambs, stops, strike plate, and hinges as needed.

Avoid double-key locks, which can only be opened from the inside with a key. They make escape very difficult in such emergencies as a fire or even confronting a trapped burglar. If you are considering installing a double-key lock because the door has glass panes that make the door easy to open if the glass is broken, either replace the door or install polycarbonate plastic in place of the glass panes. Polycarbonate plastic is virtually smash-proof, although its strength depends on the mullions in the door being strong enough to resist the force of an attempted break-in.

Recommended Cross-References
Doors, Security.

Cylinder Lock

The cylinder lock, also called a tubular or key-in-knob lock, has a wide barrel that goes through the door. The lock mechanism is in the knob. It is easy to install and fairly inexpensive, but it is also the easiest lock to force because of the rounded latch. If you have a damaged or malfunctioning lock, it is simpler to replace the entire unit than to repair it. Many styles of knob are available.

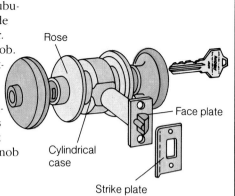

Mortise Lock

This lock has a separate latch and dead bolt in the same unit, which offers good security. However, it is also difficult to install, and the mortise also weakens the door. Many old doors have this kind of lock. The most common problem is a broken spring, which can be replaced by removing the entire lock from the door and opening it up. Whenever you look for new parts, take the lock with you. The key cylinder can be replaced with a new one.

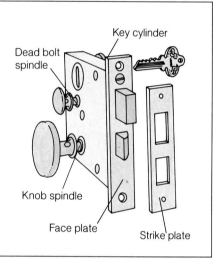

Dead-Bolt Lock

A dead bolt is intended to supplement a doorknob for increased security. The bolt should extend at least 1 inch into the jamb, since prying open a door will usually force the lock no more than ½ inch. The outside face of the lock is either flush with the door surface or protrudes out from the door on a tapered cylinder. It is installed the same way as a cylinder lock.

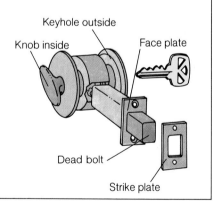

Rim Lock

Like the dead bolt, this lock is installed in addition to the doorknob. It is mounted on the inside surface of the door, with the strike plate being secured to the casing as well as to the rim of the jamb. The lock shown here features a vertical bolt that takes advantage of gravity as an additional means for holding the bolt in place.

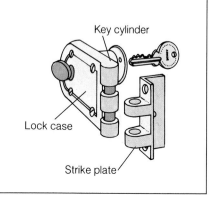

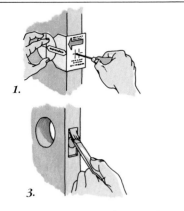

1.

2.

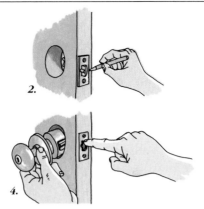

3.

4.

Installing a Cylinder Lock or Dead Bolt

Doorknobs should be centered 36 inches above the inside finish floor. Dead bolts are usually installed 3 or 4 inches above the doorknob. In measuring for locks and marking the hole centers, always work from the "high side" of the door—the edge away from the stop. Stabilize the door by wedging shims under it. Install the lock or dead bolt first, followed by the strike plate.

1. If the door does not have pre-drilled holes, you will have to drill them yourself. Begin by making a mark on the edge of the door 36 inches from the floor. Use a square to extend the mark across the edge of the door on both sides. The holes will be centered on these lines.

The lock should come with instructions that include a template. Hold it against the edge of the door at the height of your marks to establish the exact centers for drilling the holes. Drill the cylinder hole through the face of the door first, using a hole saw or dial saw set to the diameter specified. To prevent splintering the face of the door, drill only half way through the door from one side and then complete the drilling from the other side.

Next, drill the hole for the latch or bolt. Use an auger or spade bit, sized for the bolt, usually $^{15}/_{16}$ or 1 inch. It is important to drill perfectly straight, holding the bit perpendicular to the edge of the door.

2. Mark the edge of the door for chiseling out a latch mortise by inserting the latch in position and tracing its outline.

3. Chisel out the mortise so that the face plate of the latch fits flush with the edge of the door.

4. Slip the latch or bolt mechanism into the bolt hole and fit the face plate over it. Then insert the knob mechanism into the cylinder hole so that it engages the end of the latch that is already in the door. Push the other half of the knob mechanism into the other side of the door so that it lines up with the first half. Screw the two halves together, then screw the face plate to the door.

To install the strike plate, close the door and mark where the latch or dead bolt will hit against the door jamb. Trace the strike plate onto the jamb at this point, so that its hole is centered where the bolt or latch is centered. Chisel out a mortise for the strike plate. Then drill a hole into the jamb (through it if the bolt is long). Screw the strike plate over it.

Installing a Mortise Lock

1. Mark the outline of the lock on the edge of the door.
2. Drill a series of holes to the depth of the lockset and $^1/_{16}$ inch wider.
3. Chisel out the wood between the series of holes. If you have one, use a lock mortise chisel.
4. Insert the lock in the mortise and mark the outline of the face plate. Chisel enough out for the face plate to fit flush with the edge of the door.
5. Using the manufacturer's template provided with the lock, mark and bore the holes for the cylinder and spindles. Note that some holes only go through one side.
6. Assemble the lockset in the door. Then mark, drill, and mortise for the strike plate on the jamb. Screw the strike plate into position.

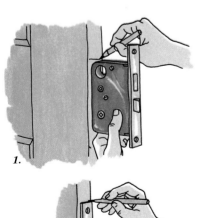

1.

2.

3.

4.

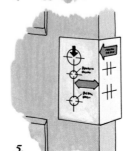

5.

6.

MANTELS

A mantel adds a touch of traditional warmth to any fireplace. It can be a massive board across the top of a rugged stone fireplace or an elegant frame that trims the joint between a brick fire box and smooth finish wall.

There are many ways to make a mantel. If you have the proper tools and skills, you can mill custom trim pieces and fabricate your own design. An easier way is to make a mantel from stock pieces of molding or order a complete mantel kit from a building supplier that specializes in finish fixtures. Consider installing a used mantel; scout salvage yards and antique stores for a rescued treasure. Installation techniques for each type vary with the design of the mantel, the dimensions of the fireplace, and the unique requirements of the room, but the steps shown are typical.

Because the mantel is a focal point for the entire room, choose materials carefully. Make sure that every piece is smooth and fits well. The materials you choose depend on how you plan to finish the mantel. If you want to paint it, make the mantel from pine. If you intend to leave the wood natural, use the same type of wood that is used throughout the room or add a different species to add a visual accent. Oak, birch, walnut, and mahogany make handsome mantels. Also consider mixing species, or using stone. Tile makes an effective border, accent, or major finish covering.

There are only a few distinctions in mantel design. The simplest mantel is a horizontal piece of lumber, usually 3 or 4 inches thick and 6 to 12 inches wide, that extends across the top of the fireplace. The mantel may rest on top

of a course of bricks, on two or three protruding bricks, or on brackets that attach to the wall. The shelf of a more ornate mantel may rest at each end on a piece of vertical trim that either sits on edge or lies flat against the brick facing. Together with the shelf across the top, these side pieces frame the fireplace. Most mantels are variations of these two simple designs, with extra molding added for decoration.

If you are not sure what kind of design to use, look through magazines and books to find one you can copy. Just make sure it is in character with the rest of the room, whether ornate, austere, rustic, or tied to a particular architectural period.

Recommended Cross-References
Fireplaces, Joinery, Moldings.

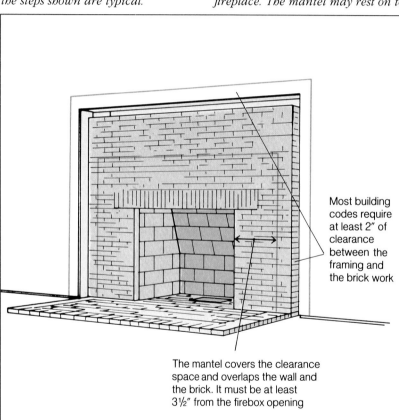

Most building codes require at least 2" of clearance between the framing and the brick work

The mantel covers the clearance space and overlaps the wall and the brick. It must be at least 3½" from the firebox opening

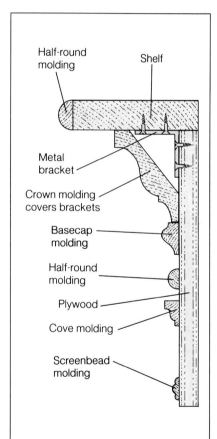

Half-round molding

Shelf

Metal bracket

Crown molding covers brackets

Basecap molding

Half-round molding

Plywood

Cove molding

Screenbead molding

Preparing for Installation
Measure the fireplace opening and draw a set of plans to scale. Most mantels attach to a backer board cut to fit around the fire box and cover the joint between brick and wall. The backer board should be made of veneered plywood because a portion will remain in view. If you do not use a backer board, be sure there are nailers behind the finish wall. You

may have to strip away some of the wall covering and install extra studs, plywood, or blocking between the existing studs.
Codes. Observe local code requirements for fireplace clearances. Wood trim should be at least 3½ inches from the fire-box opening. If the mantel has a projecting shelf, allow 12 inches of space from the fire box to the overhang.

Section View
With a little ingenuity, you can create quite ornate mantels, even if your lumberyard only stocks standard molding pieces. You can butt simple pieces together to form more complicated designs. If you use molding pieces in different woods, you will have to either stain the individual pieces so that they match, or paint the entire mantel.

Installing the Shelf

Choose a clean, straight board for the shelf and attach a piece of half-round molding or other trim to the front and side edges. Miter the trim at the corners. You may also choose to add a decorative edge on the shelf with a router. Fix the shelf to the backer board with angle brackets or wood cleats. Space the supports approximately 24 to 36 inches apart. Attach the brackets or cleats to studs behind the wall covering if you do not use a backer board. If you use metal brackets, cover them with crown molding. Some kits include a soffit that attaches to the bottom of the crown molding. The soffit allows you to attach the crown molding to the shelf before installing it.

In most installations, the shelf should be approximately 16 inches above the fire box or high enough for the top of the mantel to be approximately 4 feet to 5 feet above the floor. The length of the shelf will vary with the type of mantel and fireplace. The shelf should overhang the sides of the mantel assembly by 3 to 4 inches.

Wood Brackets. Instead of metal brackets, you may choose to attach the shelf with wood cleats. Cleats are stock items in many home centers or lumberyards; however, a jigsaw enables you to cut your own. Cleats do not have to be concealed by a crown molding. In fact, if you have cut attractive-looking ones, you will not want to cover them. Attach them to the wall by drilling pilot holes and screwing the cleats into studs. Fill all holes with wood putty.

Adding Trim Pieces. If you use wood cleats as shelf brackets, cut trim pieces to fit between them. In all cases, begin by installing the molding strips that are closest to the shelf and work down. Glue the molding to the backer board with paneling adhesive; use finishing nails to tack them in place. Miter trim that turns a corner, and be sure that the molding fits tightly before nailing it securely.

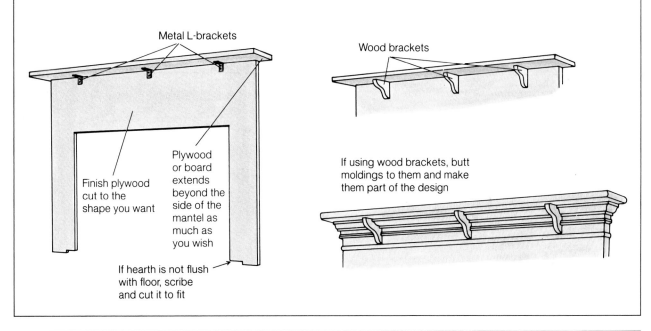

Metal L-brackets

Finish plywood cut to the shape you want

Plywood or board extends beyond the side of the mantel as much as you wish

If hearth is not flush with floor, scribe and cut it to fit

Wood brackets

If using wood brackets, butt moldings to them and make them part of the design

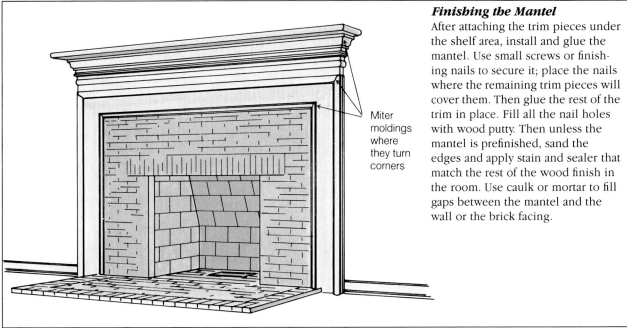

Miter moldings where they turn corners

Finishing the Mantel

After attaching the trim pieces under the shelf area, install and glue the mantel. Use small screws or finishing nails to secure it; place the nails where the remaining trim pieces will cover them. Then glue the rest of the trim in place. Fill all the nail holes with wood putty. Then unless the mantel is prefinished, sand the edges and apply stain and sealer that match the rest of the wood finish in the room. Use caulk or mortar to fill gaps between the mantel and the wall or the brick facing.

MOLDINGS

Molding, also referred to as trim, covers gaps and provides decorative relief for flat wall surfaces. In general, molding is used sparingly in contemporary architecture. However, in older homes, it is widely used and often quite elaborate. When remodeling, try to match existing moldings.

Some trim is simply standard dimension lumber, such as a 1 by 4. Most trim, however, is milled to a decorative shape. Each shape is produced by running dimension lumber through a shaper, or molding machine. Although some manufacturers have their own classification system, most use standard profiles established in 1957 by the Western Wood Molding and Millwork Producers. Ask your lumber supplier for a profile chart for the WM or WP series to see what is available. No lumberyard stocks all available shapes, but they can order many of them for you.

Most moldings are made of ponderosa pine; manufacturers also use sugar pine, Douglas fir, larch, white fir, cedar, and hemlock. Hardwood moldings are also available, chiefly oak and mahogany. The best moldings are of a single piece of wood. Choose one-piece molding if you plan to stain the trim. Short lengths of wood finger-jointed together form less expensive moldings that usually take paint. The glue in the joints is not waterproof, so use this type only indoors. Plastic moldings are also widely available. Vinyl moldings can be curved easily, but may not be paintable.

To remove trim without damage, instead of trying to pry the molding loose from the wall, punch the finish nails through the molding with a nail set to prevent splitting. If you must pry off the molding, do not remove the nails by pounding them back through the wood. Instead, pull them through from the back with nippers to prevent damage to the face of the molding. Even if you don't plan to reuse the molding immediately, saving a few of the best long pieces for future use is advisable.

Recommended Cross-References
Ceilings, Doors, Floors, Framing, Joinery, Mantels, Paneling, Stairs, Wallboard, Walls, Windows.

Typical Moldings

The most common interior moldings are: casings around doors and windows; baseboards at the bottom of walls; crown moldings at the top of walls; picture molding, usually about 1 foot below the top of the wall; and chair rail, which covers the seam between wainscot and finish wall. Most building and home center stores only carry fairly simple, basic styles but you can combine two or three different shapes to match the more ornate versions that are generally found in older homes.

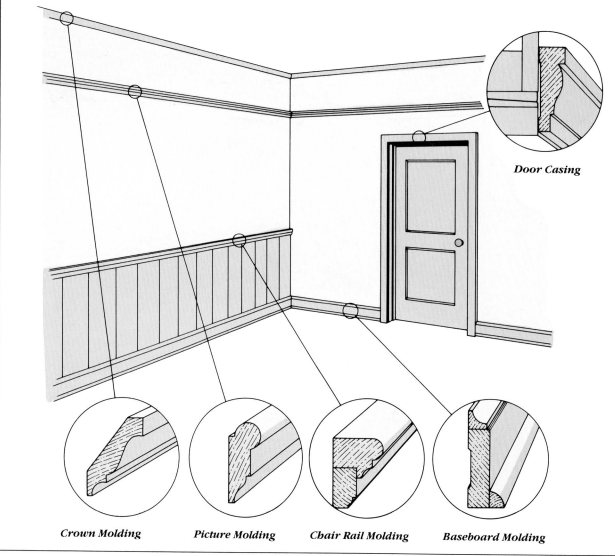

Door Casing

Crown Molding　　*Picture Molding*　　*Chair Rail Molding*　　*Baseboard Molding*

Choosing and Using Moldings

Always try to match moldings to the original style of the house. If you need to match a molding that is out of date, start by trying to duplicate the pattern with two or more pieces of stock molding. If that won't do, look for a salvage yard that stocks old materials, or see if a local lumberyard can mill a special piece. Another solution is to take a piece of molding with the same pattern from a place in the house that is less conspicuous, and replace it with the closest match you can find. When you buy moldings, order 20 percent more to allow for waste.

In rare cases, you may have to restore moldings made of plaster instead of wood. Some cities have specialty suppliers who stock some of the plaster patterns. Suppliers also sell plastic moldings that are based on older designs. As a last resort, create a new section of molding by making a template to match the pattern and fitting it over wet plaster.

Moldings make a plain house look pleasingly fancy if the moldings harmonize with the original character of the home. Avoid highly ornate moldings, such as scallops or decorative friezes, unless they obviously fit in with the rest of the design.

If you want to dress up door and window casings of simple dimension lumber (such as 1 by 4), merely add a piece of decorative molding across the tops of the head casings. Add short pieces of the same molding at each end, and miter the corners.

Another simple touch that dresses up a plain room is to run a strip of chair rail around the wall from 3 to 3½ feet above the floor or at the same height as the windowsills. Finish the wall below the rail differently from the rest of the room by using paneling or a darker paint.

Moldings tend to break up large expanses of wall and add visual interest to a room. They can make rooms and hallways seem larger through visual deception—a valuable trick with the current emphasis on smaller homes. If you want a room to appear higher, place horizontal moldings near the ceiling at a height slightly lower than the tallest pieces of furniture. The new horizontal line creates a feeling of space above the furniture. The deception works even better if you install molding around the top of the walls as well. To complete the artificial enlargement, add horizontal molding around the bottom of the wall, about 18 inches above the floor. Bottom molding enhances the definition of the walls, taking visual impact away from furniture and windows.

If a small room has a vaulted ceiling, take advantage of the expansive effect by installing molding around the walls at the same level as the top of the doors and windows. The molding accentuates the beginning of the ceiling and emphasizes the height. A similar molding around the bottom of the walls, about 18 inches above the floor, makes the room seem even larger.

If a room with low furniture has architectural features like a fireplace or alcove, use molding to outline them. Add molding to plain walls, too. Both techniques call attention to the room and can prevent furnishings or other features from overpowering the space.

Use these tricks with caution. Molding alone will not solve design problems. However, using it cleverly can create interesting effects.

There are many unconventional uses for molding, such as trimming a flush door to make it resemble a panel door or trimming posts and other structural members. In such cases, use molding sparingly, if at all. Remember that molding is most effective when it enhances existing architectural lines, not when it creates new shapes.

Exterior Moldings

As in the rest of the house, exterior molding should complement architectural design. Incompatible molding is especially noticeable with traditional styles, such as colonial and classic revival. If you have any doubt about the suitability of a molding, ask an architect or do some research at the local historical society.

Exterior trim for doors, windows, corners, and roof overhangs is usually fashioned from dimension lumber. Wood exterior moldings are usually of redwood or other durable species. Outdoor moldings include crowns and coves for joints under the eaves, brick molding for trimming doors and windows in brick or stucco walls, and one-piece corners.

When you install outdoor trim, always prime the back. If you need to join two pieces end to end, cut each piece on a bevel so they overlap. Bevel vertical trim as well as horizontal trim. Predrill the nail holes so that nailing does not split the trim. Apply a bead of caulk before installing the molding, and set all nail heads below the surface. Do not use finger-jointed moldings outdoors.

Techniques for Installing Molding

Store the molding where rough construction will not damage it. Do not install the molding until all the walls are completely dry; shrinkage could open the joints. Priming the back of moldings before installation will minimize shrinkage. If you choose to stain the trim, do so before installation.

Try to use full-length pieces wherever trim will be prominent. If you have to join two pieces end to end, cut both pieces on a 45-degree bevel so one overlaps the other. Do not use a butt joint.

Neat trim requires precision measuring and cutting. Make all your marks with a knife blade or sharp scribe. Cut with the sharpest saw blade available. If you saw by hand, use a backsaw. The most accurate power saws are the power miter saw and the radial arm saw; use one of these saws if you can. Run the blade slowly through the wood for a smooth cut. Professionals use a tool called a miter trimmer, which slices instead of saws. You may be able to rent one from a picture-frame shop.

Nail moldings with 4d, 6d, or 8d finishing nails. Always countersink the nail heads and fill in the holes with wood putty or filler. If it is necessary for the trim to bend and flex in order for it to hug close to an irregular wall, use thin moldings or moldings with recessed backs.

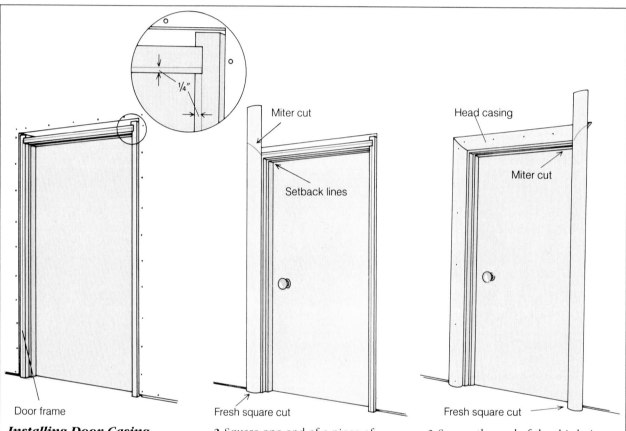

Door frame

Miter cut

Setback lines

Fresh square cut

Head casing

Miter cut

Fresh square cut

Installing Door Casing

Some casings butt into a door cap, but mitered casings are more common. The following steps show how to miter a doorway.

1. Plan the layout so the casing leaves ¼ inch of jamb exposed around the edge of the opening. This exposure is called a reveal or setback. Mark the setback on the jamb; the mark also shows where the inside edge of the casing will lie.

2. Square one end of a piece of casing, align the inside edge with the mark on the jamb, and stand it on the floor. Mark the top of the piece where the setback lines intersect, and scribe a 45-degree line upward from that mark. Cut along this line and nail the casing in place with 4d nails at the jamb edge and 6d or 8d nails along the outside edge.

Make a miter cut at one end of another piece of casing and hold it in position as head casing. Mark the bottom edge where the setback lines intersect and scribe a 45-degree line upwards from that mark. Cut along the mark and tack the head casing in place. Don't nail it securely because you may have to remove the casing to adjust the cut.

3. Square the end of the third piece of casing and stand it in place. Mark both the inside and outside edges where they cross the head casing. The line between the two marks should run at a 45-degree angle. If not, adjust the cut of the head casing so it will complement the angle of the side casing and re-install it. Then scribe the side casing, cut it, and complete the nailing.

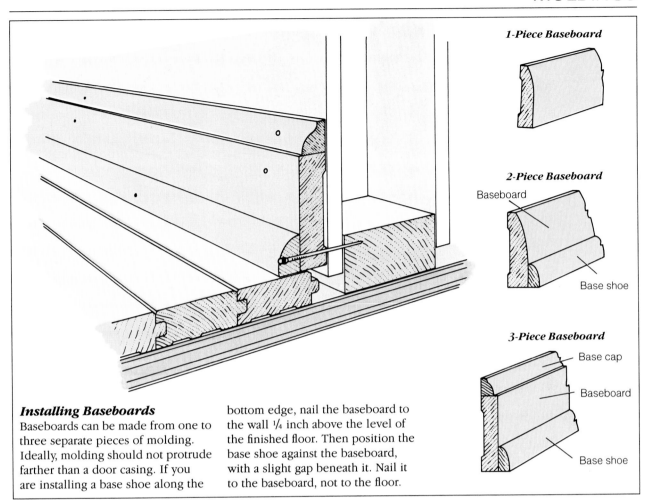

1-Piece Baseboard

2-Piece Baseboard

Baseboard

Base shoe

3-Piece Baseboard

Base cap

Baseboard

Base shoe

Installing Baseboards

Baseboards can be made from one to three separate pieces of molding. Ideally, molding should not protrude farther than a door casing. If you are installing a base shoe along the bottom edge, nail the baseboard to the wall ¼ inch above the level of the finished floor. Then position the base shoe against the baseboard, with a slight gap beneath it. Nail it to the baseboard, not to the floor.

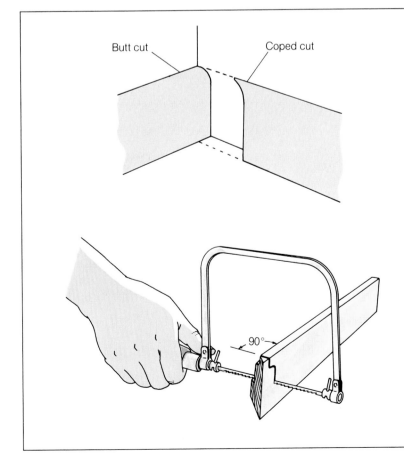

Butt cut

Coped cut

90°

Coped Joints

In most carpentry the basic joints are butt joints and miter joints. In finish work, however, the miter joint does not work very well for inside corners because it can open up easily and reveal an unattractive gap. Butt joints work better in this situation, but for moldings with a profile you need to use a modified butt joint known as a coped joint. It allows the board on one wall to butt against the board that is already installed on the adjacent wall.

Square the end of the first piece of baseboard and butt it into the corner. Cut the end of the second piece at a 45-degree angle. Use the profile created by this cut as a guide for making the final cut with a coping saw. Keep the coping saw at a 90-degree angle to the baseboard. Fit the second piece of molding against the first, then continue to combine butt cuts and cope cuts in the other corners. Tack the molding into position; do not secure it until you are certain of a tight fit around the room.

PAINT

Painting is a dramatic way to improve a home, inside or out. It is a popular project, one that most homeowners can do easily. When done carefully with high-quality materials, the process itself can be as positive as the results.

A good coat of paint will protect your home from weather and wear. Of course, you cannot expect it to disguise existing problems. Defects should be corrected before painting to prevent future damage.

Well-chosen, well-applied color has a positive, uplifting effect; a poor choice will haunt you. For this reason you should select a color scheme carefully. Avoid hasty choices, and devote time to the other important steps: preparing the surface, selecting an appropriate type of paint, and using sound application techniques.

Recommended Cross-References

Caulking, Ceilings, Flashing, Glass, Gutters & Downspouts, Insulation, Siding, Ventilation, Wallboard, Wallpaper, Weather Stripping.

A can of paint turns even a novice into an instant decorator. Dazzling effects are easily achieved for the cost of a can of paint.

Choosing Colors

Exterior. Nothing affects the overall appearance of a home as much as color. Choose colors that harmonize with the character of your home and neighborhood. To get ideas, tour the area, obtain color charts from a paint dealer, and look through magazines and books. Be sure to choose colors that are compatible with permanent features that won't change, such as

brickwork, roofing, or natural siding.

The design of your home often dictates how color should be used. If the architecture is strong enough, as in Luis Barragan's patio home, seen here, walls can become canvases for an imaginative, abstract statement. For the majority of homes, three colors are usually sufficient.

Light colors are the safest choice, but they tend to be dull and profit

from a contrasting trim color. If the foundation is distinct from the primary structure, paint it a darker tone.

Avoid bright, pure colors as well as combinations of two colors with equal intensities unless you want to make a strong statement. Muted earth tones work well for exteriors because they blend into the landscape. They also tend to last longer than pure hues.

Interior. The color of a room affects size, mood, and even temperature.

Generally, light colors seem to enlarge a room, and dark colors shrink it, although this generality does not always hold true. Some color schemes seem to effectively enlarge a room by combining a light color with a dark contrast.

To play it safe, use no more than two colors of paint, unless the colors are different intensities of the same hue. If one of the colors is off-white, choose a shade with a hint of color that matches the other colors in the room. High-gloss paints are back in style. Experiment with them for up-to-the-minute fashion statements. If two rooms are connected by a wide doorway, use compatible colors.

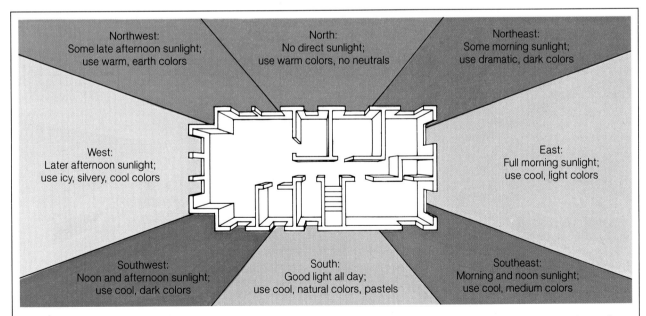

Choosing Colors by Exposure

The amount and quality of natural light in a room should affect your color choice. If a sunny room with windows facing west and southwest tends to feel hot and stuffy, use cool colors such as blue and gray. Rooms with windows facing north tend to be colder than other rooms; they will

benefit from warm colors such as red, orange, and some browns. Rooms that face east can be painted in warm or cool colors depending on whether the morning sun needs a cheery boost or a cooling contrast. The illustration shows how one designer uses these principles to arrive at specific color recommendations.

Exposure is an important factor for choosing colors, but not the only one. The use of a room should also be considered—bright yellow may not be the best color for a living room, even if it faces north. Also remember that color should harmonize with permanent features, such as a hardwood floor.

Choosing Paint

Although paint manufacturers are continually improving their products, there is no single type of paint that works for all situations. A paint may also be oil-based (alkyd) or latex (a category that includes acrylics). There are also primers and specialty paints to consider, as well as stains and sealers.

Besides the obvious distinction between exterior and interior applications (although exterior paint can be used inside), the decision is usually oil-based versus latex paints. In some cases, such as priming metal gutters or painting ceramic tile, the conditions of the job limit you to specialty paints. Most of the time, however, both oil-based paints and latex paints will do the job.

Oil-Based Paints. Alkyds penetrate wood and stick to smooth surfaces better than latex paints. They wash better and last longer. On exterior surfaces, however, the color of an oil-based paint tends to fade because the pigments are close to the surface. Use oil-based paint for trim, interior woodwork, high-traffic areas, or areas that get smoke or water stained. The disadvantages of alkyds are that they do not adhere to masonry or wallpaper. They give off fumes while you paint. Cleanup requires paint thinner or turpentine. They take from 8 to 12 hours to dry, and should not be recoated in outdoor applications for 36 to 48 hours.

Latex Paints. Latex paints are easy to use because you use water for cleanup and thinning. They dry quickly and can be repainted within an hour or two. They are particularly suitable as a covering for interior walls and ceilings where you want a flat finish. Latex paints are also available in semigloss finishes which, although not as durable as oil-based paints, wear well under normal use.

Exterior latex paints hold their color longer than alkyds because the paint forms a coating of resin over the color pigments. However, when this coating wears off, the color may change dramatically.

Latex paints also have the advantage of being semipermeable, allowing any moisture inside to escape through the exterior wall coating.

Thorough surface preparation is essential because latex adheres to the surface rather than penetrating it. Latex paints work well on masonry, such as stucco or concrete block, and can even be applied under slightly damp conditions such as on a surface covered with morning dew.

Primers. Primers can have an oil or a latex base. Choose a primer with the same basic formulation as your topcoat. Always heed the manufacturer's recommendations; primers are formulated to adhere to a specific surface and to provide adhesion for a specific type of topcoat. In some cases, primers penetrate the surface and change the composition of old paint to provide better tooth. In other cases they stick tenaciously to the surface of old paint. Painters usually use oil-based primers to repaint wood and save latex and acrylic primers for plaster and masonry.

Specialty Paints. Manufacturers formulate some paints and primers for specific applications. If your painting schedule includes metal, concrete block, new masonry with a high alkali content, areas subject to mildew, nonporous surfaces (such as ceramic tile), or appliances subject to high temperatures (such as flue pipes or radiators), ask your paint dealer for recommendations. There is an appropriate paint for each situation.

Buying Paint

Always buy a high-quality paint, which usually bears the designation "premium". Major brands are usually more reliable than lesser-known brands, although some local paint manufacturers are able to offer high-quality paints because they only distribute through their factory. Avoid discount paints, that sometimes carry the designation "professional"; they are the lowest in price and quality. Discount paints generally rely on clays and other inexpensive inert compounds for covering power.

In some cases you can compensate for the deficiencies of an inferior paint. One example is titanium oxide, a white powder that makes light-colored paints more opaque. Your dealer may be able to add this ingredient as long as he can also adjust the formula to allow for the slight change in color.

One simple way to judge the quality of paint is to to drop a stick into a well-stirred paint can and lift it straight out. Ideally, $1/8$ to $1/4$ inch of paint should cling to the stick, while the rest runs off. If too much runs off, the paint will not cover; if the paint simply sticks without running off, it is probably too thick and will require more paint than necessary to do the job.

Do not rely on your memory when choosing colors. Bring color cues (old woodwork, swatches of fabric, magazine pictures, or wallpaper scraps) with you to the paint store. Take home several color cards to see how they look in the specific room. Finally, buy small cans and paint test patches. Look at them for several days before making a final decision.

After you have decided, buy all your paint at once. Batch buying ensures a good color match. Buying in 5-gallon buckets will save money. Calculate your needs by measuring the square footage to be covered. Have the dealer convert footage to gallons. Typical coverage is 300 square feet per gallon, but this varies according to formulation. Buy extra for unexpectedly porous surfaces and forgotten nooks and crannies.

Using Paint

Buy enough paint at the beginning to complete the whole job. Also check to see if the batch numbers, printed on the can lids, are all the same. If not, they may vary slightly in color. To maintain continuity of color, mix each new can of paint with a can that is half empty, or mix the entire batch in a 5-gallon bucket. Pour paint from the large batch into a small bucket. The small bucket will be easier to move and spills will be smaller.

Paint in dry, calm weather. Do not paint the exterior if rain is threatening or in late afternoons if there is likely to be dew during the night. Try to paint in the shade. Some painters like to paint the south side in the morning and work their way around the house so that they are always ahead of the sun.

To catch missed spots, called "holidays" by painters, always look over each section before moving the ladder. Do touch ups while the paint is wet or patches will show as dark splotches.

Mixing Paint

Pour the thin top paint into a separate pail. Stir the thick paint left in the can. While stirring, slowly pour the thin paint back. Then pour the paint back and forth between cans.

To keep the groove around the top of the can from clogging with paint, pound a few nail holes in the bottom of the groove for the lid. Excess paint will drain through these holes.

Oil-based paints often develop a thick scum on the surface. Don't try to stir or mix this scum into the paint. Instead, gently lift it off the surface and pour the paint through a nylon stocking or cheesecloth strainer to get rid of any lumps.

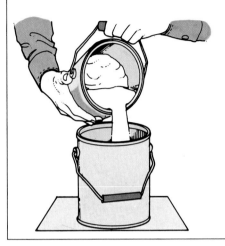

Paint Applicators

Brushes. Brushes with flagged bristles (split ends) hold paint better and produce a finer stroke. Use natural bristles with oil-based paints, varnishes, polyurethane finishes, and most chemical strippers. Use synthetic bristles for latex. A 4-inch, 3-inch, and 1½-inch brush will serve most purposes.

Rollers. Rollers are usually 9 inches wide. Choose one that turns on nylon bearings, has a threaded handle plus short and long extension poles. Roller covers come in lamb's wool, mohair, and synthetic fiber. Synthetic covers work well with most paints, especially latex. Lamb's wool covers well when you are using oil-based paints, and mohair produces good results with high-gloss enamels and clear finishes. Use a short-nap (¼-inch) cover for smooth surfaces, ½-inch nap for textured surfaces, and ¾-inch nap for rough surfaces such as stucco or concrete block.

Spreader and Trim Pads. Spreader and trim pads have become increasingly popular in recent years because they are faster than brushes and leave less texture than rollers. Pads are narrower than rollers, but make up for their size with easier handling, absence of spattering, and simple cleanup. The pads come in a variety of sizes.

Foam Brushes. These inexpensive blocks of foam on handles are handy for any painting chore. They leave no brush marks and do not require cleanup—throwing them away is cheaper than buying paint thinner.

Shown below: 1. Roller cover. 2. Plastic paint tray liner. 3. Airless sprayer. 4. Painting pad. 5. Edger pad. 6. 1½-inch natural bristle brush. 7. 4-inch synthetic bristle brush. 8. 1-inch badger brush. 9. 2-inch badger brush. 10. Glue brush. 11. Roller. 12. Steel wool.

Preparing Exterior Surfaces

Today's paints last from 4 to 7 years, depending on the exposure (sunny exposures fade more quickly), the color (darker colors fade faster), and the surface preparation. Do not paint a house too often; the thick layers of paint will peel away. Most paint wears slowly, through a process called chalking. In many cases removing the chalk by scrubbing will renew a dull painted surface.

Your house needs a new coat of paint when the existing paint has almost worn off, or if it is peeling, blistering, cracking, or alligatoring. Start by removing as much old paint as possible with a paint scraper, wire brush, or power sander. Always wear a respirator—old paint often contains lead.

Wash the surfaces with a solution of trisodium phosphate (TSP) and water or any strong household cleanser. Concentrate on soffits, porch ceilings, and areas under the eaves. Rinse the surfaces with a hose. A rented pressurized power washer can speed paint removal.

If the original paint showed signs of peeling, especially on attic walls or uninsulated walls, eliminate the cause of the problem: moisture that seeps through the wall. The solution: Provide vents in the attic or install 3/4-inch vent holes drilled near the top of the stud cavities. Also consider coating the affected walls with special primers specified as vapor barriers.

Set protruding nail heads and caulk all cracks, seams, and joints. Sand down high spots as well as shiny surfaces that need tooth (a rough surface to which coverings will adhere). You are now ready to apply the primer.

To prepare masonry, scrub the walls with a wire brush and strong detergent. As moisture evaporates from masonry over time, the remaining deposits turn into a crystal-line powder known as efflorescence. To remove powdery efflorescent salts, scrub masonry with a mixture of 1 part muriatic acid and 3 parts water. Never add water to acid; always pour the acid into water. If the wall is too slick for paint to adhere, scrub again with a stronger acid solution. If the wall is too porous, prime the surface with a block filler.

Preparing Interior Surfaces

Prepare interior walls, ceilings, and woodwork by washing them with a solution of TSP and water. Then patch all cracks and holes. Do not paint wallpaper with an oil-based paint. If the paper adheres well and is smooth, a latex primer and paint will probably cover it satisfactorily. If not, scrape off the wallpaper or rent a steamer to soak it off.

When recovering an enamel-paint surface, add some tooth for the new paint. Sometimes TSP will degloss the enamel sufficiently. Otherwise, roughen it by sanding with medium-grit paper, using a circular motion. Use an oil-based primer and either an oil-based or latex topcoat.

If layers of paint obscure details in the woodwork, you may want to strip the paint. Complete stripping is desirable if you refinish the wood with clear sealers; partial stripping will be adequate if you cover the trim with new paint. If you are lucky, you will be able to strip the wood with scrapers and sandpaper. If not, you will have to use a chemical paint remover, following the instructions on the can. You will need lots of newspapers, rags, steel wool, and ventilation. If you can find new molding with a pattern similar to the painted molding, replacing the trim may be easier than stripping.

Finish by removing all light fixtures, electrical cover plates, doorknobs, and other hardware.

Patching Deep Cracks. It is tempting to patch plaster walls and ceilings with a superficial coat of patching compound. Don't—the cracks will almost certainly open up again.

To do the job properly, widen the cracks as well as making them deeper. Using a pointed object, such as a can opener or crack-opening tool, remove enough plaster to make a V-groove approximately 1/4 inch deep. Protect your eyes with goggles and blow out all dust and debris.

Moisten the cracks with a plant sprayer and apply patching compound with a putty knife. Use a wide blade for multiple cracks. Most compounds will shrink slightly when they dry, so you will have to apply a second coat. Sand as necessary.

Patching Hairline Cracks. Where multiple hairline cracks have developed, (especially on ceilings), a fiberglass mesh will save you from having to open the cracks. Spread a thin coat of compound over each crack then embed the mesh into it. Cover it with a final layer of compound. Feather the compound at the edges so it blends into the surrounding area. Mix in some sand or texture the patch to match the rest of the ceiling.

Patching Holes. Remove all loose plaster, being careful not to separate sound plaster from the lath. Wet the lath and apply a coat of plaster or patching compound about 1/8 inch below the finish surface. Score the wet patch with a nail. After the first coat dries, apply a final coat of compound. Feather the edges, and stipple this last coat with a brush so that it matches the surrounding area.

Preparing Windows

Scrape away all loose paint with a putty knife or paint scraper. Remove loose putty around the glass, and replace it with new glazing compound. Paint the exposed wood first with linseed oil or primer.

If layers of old paint have sealed the window, cut through the paint with a putty knife or special scoring tool so the window moves freely.

Look for damaged or rotten wood. Many window frames are made of pine, which rots easily. If the damage is extensive, replace the window. If the damaged area is small, dig out the bad wood and patch with epoxy filler, smoothing it while it is pliable. Patch and sand all holes. Spot-prime patches and bare wood.

Using a Power Washer

This is one of the best methods for removing dirt and peeling paint, but don't try to use it to strip all of the old paint from wood. It will dig out the softer wood and cause ridges, as well as leaving the surface rough and fuzzy. Hold the nozzle about 12 inches from the surface to prevent damaging the wood. Most peeling paint will come off without getting so close that the wood is damaged. Try an area, then inspect your work.

Power washing is especially good for aluminum siding. After 15 to 20 years the paint chalks heavily; power washing will remove dirt, grit, and the chalk residue.

Most 2,000-square-foot houses can be washed in half a day. Some scraping or sanding may still be needed, but washing provides a clean surface that paint will adhere to. You may not even need to repaint if the paint film is still intact; power washing removes residue and rejuvenates the finish.

Power washers come with extension rods or wands for reaching high areas. Try to avoid using a ladder; the water pressure can knock you off balance and cause a fall. Be extremely careful not to work near power lines. The combination of water, electricity, and a metal wand can cause a fatal shock. Stay at least 10 feet away from any power lines. Prepare any areas around power lines by hand. Always

Gas-powered machine — Rain gear — Spray wand — Goggles — Spray nozzle

Water supply hose

Gloves

wear rubber gloves and goggles.

The following tips will make power washing easier and safer.
- Handle the power washer with caution. When you turn it on, the pressure will kick the wand back 3 or 4 feet. Never point the washer at anyone or let children use it. The water pressure is hard enough to penetrate skin. If this happens, see a doctor immediately.
- Keep the nozzle about 12 inches from the surface and at a 45-degree angle to the wall.
- Cover light fixtures and electrical outlets with plastic and duct tape.

- Put down drop cloths to collect the paint chips.
- Cover plants or bundle them and tie them back from the wall.
- Don't use the washer on windy days. The overspray will travel.
- Do not spray directly at windows from close range. The water pressure can break the glass.
- Avoid spraying up under lap siding or into openings such as eave vents.
- While you have the power washer, clean patios, concrete driveways, lawn furniture, garbage cans, or the car. It does a fabulous job.

Painting Techniques

Rollers. Dampening the roller cover removes lint and primes it. Use water if you are using latex; use thinner with an alkyd. Run the roller over a clean towel until it is dry. To load the cover with paint, roll it back and forth in a paint tray or on a grid hung in a 5-gallon bucket. The nap should be full but not dripping.

Always paint ceilings first, so that spatters will not mar newly painted areas. First use a brush or small roller to paint corners, and around trim, fixtures, and other obstacles. Then paint the rest of the ceiling. Use an extension pole on the roller and wear a billed cap to protect your eyes. When you finish the ceiling, paint the walls from top to bottom.

To apply paint with a roller, spread the first few strokes in a zigzag pattern. To cut down on paint drips, make the first stroke an upward one. Rolling slowly will cut down on spattering. Increase pressure to spread the load evenly.

Then, without lifting the roller, spread the paint across the zigzag pattern. Use even, parallel strokes; take care not to roll too fast. As the zigzag disappears, begin to feather the paint into adjacent areas, painted or unpainted. Lift the roller at the end of each feather stroke.

Brushes. Dip the brush into the paint no farther than half the length of the bristles. Lift the brush straight out of the paint and slap it lightly against the inside of the can. Don't draw the

brush across the rim, or you'll get clumpy bristles.

Hold the brush at a 45-degree angle and apply paint in long, light strokes. Work in small sections, about 3 feet square, and slightly overlap previously painted sections. Make sure the entire tip of the brush touches the surface. Always brush into the section most recently painted, which is called the wet edge, to avoid lap marks.

After laying on the paint with two or three strokes, spread it evenly. Use vertical strokes on flat walls and ceilings, horizontal on board siding. Work the paint toward uncoated areas. To produce a thin, feathered edge, finish each stroke by lightly lifting the brush from the surface.

Painting Trim

Trim usually contrasts with the color of surrounding surfaces. Therefore, a clean line between the two colors is imperative. For durability, use oil-based paint, especially outdoors. When painting trim and woodwork, paint the horizontal surfaces before working on the verticals. Follow the "inside-out" rule—work from inner sections to outer portions. When using oil-based enamels, use a roller to save time, then finish missed spots with a brush. Always use a brush when applying latex enamels.

As a general rule, paint trim before adjacent surfaces because cutting in a recessed flat surface is easier than painting a raised molding. Although you must paint the surrounding surfaces with care to avoid spatters, masking tape or shielding devices are seldom necessary. Baseboards are an exception. Paint baseboards last and, if necessary, use a shield to form a perfect edge.

To cut in on trim or adjacent wall surfaces, hold the brush so that all the bristles bend slightly (not too much) and make full contact. Then drag the brush slowly, twisting it slightly so that the leading corner glides along the boundary line between the two colors. Starting at the line and working away from it, brush on the paint with long, even strokes.

It is not always possible to paint all the exterior trim at one time. If you use scaffolds or a painter's fall, work from the top down, completing an entire section before moving the equipment. It may be necessary to cut a new color into an existing edge when it is still tacky.

Window Trim. Work from the inside out, painting the sash around the glass first. Mask each windowpane with tape unless you have a practiced, steady hand. Masking tape works well, but common transparent tape works better. Leave a hairline crack between the tape and sash so the paint seals against the glass. When painting double-hung windows, reverse the sash positions for easier access to each half.

Doors. Prime unpainted flush doors with a roller if you use oil-based paint; otherwise, brush on the primer and topcoat. Spread the paint from the inside to the outside edges, then immediately brush with long, vertical strokes. If the door is paneled, paint the panels first, then the trim. The patterned shadows cast by elaborate moldings will be much more dramatic if you paint the door in a single, light color. The latch edge of the door should match the color of the room into which it opens; the hinge edge should match whichever room it faces. Paint the stop to match the surrounding frame.

Baseboards. Use an angled sash brush or trim brush to paint the top edge of the baseboard. Use a paint shield to protect the wall or, if the wall is wallpapered, use paper tape. Then paint the bottom edge, again protecting the floor with a shield or tape. Finally, paint the center portion with a larger brush, feathering the wet paint into the top and bottom edges. Use long, horizontal strokes.

Painting a Window

Paint top half of lower window, then reverse windows and finish

Painting Order for a Paneled Door

Painting a Flush Door

Stop

Paint edge first   Paint horizontally, away from edge, then vertically

Painting a Room

Move or cover everything you don't want painted.

If the ceiling, walls, and trim are greasy, wash them with TSP or detergent. TSP must be rinsed, but some detergents don't require rinsing.

Remove switch plates and outlet covers. Mask the switches and receptacles with tape.

Patch any cracks or holes. Use sandable spackling compound except for small cracks that open seasonally. Paint these with an elastomeric primer. You can also use vinyl spackling compound, but wipe it down with a sponge before it dries because it can't be sanded.

Caulk any gaps along the baseboards or trim with paintable caulk. Wipe away excess caulk with a sponge or wet finger.

Prime sealed areas before painting. If there are large patches of sealer or areas of new wall, prime the entire surface.

Paint around doors and windows and in corners. The painted area should be 2 to 3 inches wide.

Roll on paint with a damp roller.

Paint trim with an angle brush. If you paint carefully, it won't be necessary to mask the walls. If you do mask, let the paint on the walls dry thoroughly first.

Paint wood-frame windows, starting next to the glass and working outward. The paint should just touch the glass to seal the edge of the wood. Paint around the glass, then the rest of the sash, then the jambs, then the casing, and finally the sill and apron.

Paint the panels in a panel door first, then the trim. The door can be painted in place or taken down. If you are using a sprayer, remove the door hardware and stuff the openings with paper towels.

Common Mistakes

● Not doing all the preparation before starting to paint.
● Not using a primer where it's needed.
● Buying low-quality paint or tools.
● Applying thin coats of paint and trying to cover too much area. Two thick coats will wear better than three thin ones.
● Ignoring instructions on the paint label (thinning too much, trying to paint when it is too hot or too cold).
● Painting in the wrong sequence.
● Using the wrong type of brushes for the paint base. Use natural-bristle brushes with oils and alkyds, and polyester or nylon for latex paint.

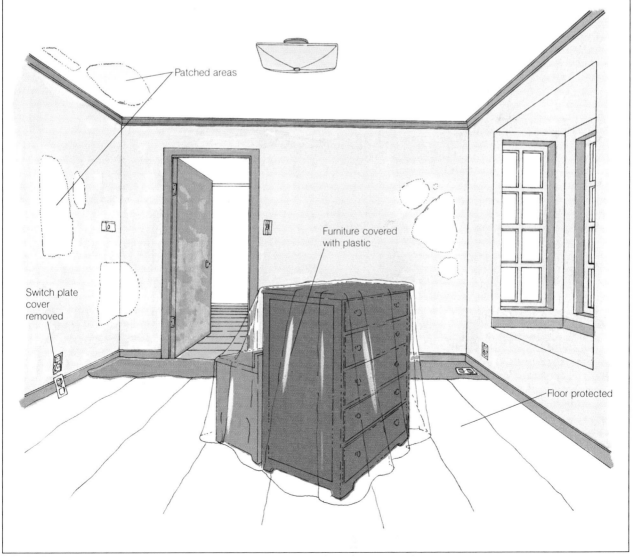

Patched areas

Switch plate cover removed

Furniture covered with plastic

Floor protected

Creating Special Effects

Creating special effects with paint dates back in history. Today many of these techniques are enjoying a dramatic rebirth. Some of these effects are simple to produce, using sponges, rollers, and stencils.

Painting With Glazes. Glazes are special liquids that cover a base paint to produce various textures and patterns. Glazes are transparent, but you can add coloring to produce streaks, swirls, or daubs, in a contrasting color. The effects range from dramatic to subtle, and can simulate clouds, fabric, leather, woodgrain, parchment, or entirely original textures.

Glazes are most effective when the base wall is fairly smooth. Paint the wall with an oil-based paint so the surface has a sheen that does not absorb any of the glaze.

If you are repainting the base wall, you may decide to tint the paint rather than the glaze. Add 1 part tint to 2 parts paint thinner. Use the thinner as you normally would to prepare the alkyd for the base wall.

Contrary to the name, glaze dries with a flat finish. For a high gloss, apply a top coat of varnish.

Wait for the painted wall to dry before glazing. Then choose one of the following techniques.

Dragging. Apply a thin coat of glaze onto the wall with a brush. Then drag a dry brush down the wall, using long vertical strokes side by side to produce a combed texture. Overlap each stroke slightly, and do not lift the brush from the wall until you reach the bottom. The overall effect is an elegant and uniform texture that resembles fine straw or hair.

Sponging. Use a natural sponge to daub glaze onto a painted wall in random patterns, resembling clouds or soft foliage. An alternate technique is to cover the wall with glaze and then remove patches of it by pressing a clean sponge onto it in a random pattern.

Crosshatching. Make a combing tool out of a rubber squeegee by cutting V-shaped notches into its edge. Apply glaze over the entire wall. Rake the wall in horizontal strokes with the comb. Comb again using vertical strokes. When the glaze dries it will resemble cracked parchment.

Marbling. Marbling should be attempted only by the adventurous—it is one of the most elegant painted finishes but also one of the most difficult to do well. Success depends on careful surface preparation.

First, repair all cracks, holes, and rough spots. Then apply at least three base coats of tinted enamel, preferably oil-based. Sand between each coat. Finally, seal the surface with shellac and buff it with fine steel wool to give it a warm glow.

Start by applying a thin coat of kerosene. Then, using a sponge, a feather, and a dry brush, create a pattern of large shapes mixed with slender veins of color. Finally, seal the wall with shellac. Use realistic colors if you want to simulate marble or produce unusual effects by using colors of your choice. For beginning, follow a simple, diagonal pattern.

Optical Effects. Some color schemes produce optical effects that can make a room seem better proportioned.

Long, narrow rooms can be shortened by using a dark-color paint on the short wall farthest from the entry.

Small rooms can be made to appear larger if they are painted with light colors.

Horizontal stripes or patterns in light colors make a room seem larger, as does using blue paint on a wall. Vertical stripes make the ceiling appear higher.

Stenciling. A favorite among enthusiasts of Early American style, stenciling is easy to do. Choose a simple design that lends itself to repetition, such as a leaf, acorn, tulip, grapevine, or geometric pattern. Transfer the design onto heavy-duty stenciling paper by tracing it over carbon paper. Darken the outline. All bridge areas in the design should be at least 1/4 inch wide. Cut out the design using a modeler's or utility knife.

Calculate how much space to allow between each painted design. Then lay the template on the area to be stenciled and mark each position with a pencil. To paint the stencil, spray adhesive on the back and attach it to the surface to be painted. Apply paint with a brush dipped into the paint no more than 1/4 inch. Repeat this process over the entire area.

Using a Sprayer

Sprayers cover large areas quickly and apply paint smoothly to ornate or textured surfaces such as fences and carved woodwork. Airless sprayers, which have small electric pumps in the unit rather than remote air compressors, are a common kind of sprayer. Airless sprayers work at extremely high pressure—up to 3,000 pounds per square inch. Should you accidentally pull the trigger while touching the opening, the sprayer may inject you with paint. Such injuries cause almost no pain or loss of blood, but they can result in severe tissue damage and blood poisoning. If you have an accident with a sprayer, seek medical attention at once.

To prevent injuries, make sure the sprayer has a safety lock and guard, as well as a protective shield that keeps your fingers away from the tip. Never point the gun toward anyone, including yourself. Unplug the sprayer before you try to unclog the tip. Store the sprayer in a locked cabinet when it is not in use.

Cover areas with drop cloths or masking paper. Nearly all sprayers produce some overspray. To use a sprayer, thin and strain the paint. Spray a large piece of cardboard and adjust the spray so that the paint will spread evenly, without spattering. To avoid lap marks, spray in an elliptical pattern that is wide in the center and tapers at the ends. Hold the gun about 12 inches from the surface and move it back and forth horizontally, bending your wrist to keep the direction of spray perpendicular to the wall. Do not spray one spot too long or the paint will sag. It is better to spray several thin coats than one thick coat. If the sprayer clogs, remain calm and unplug the cord immediately. Follow the manufacturer's instructions to release pressure and clean the tip. For cleanup, use lacquer thinner rather than paint thinner; it is a stronger solvent.

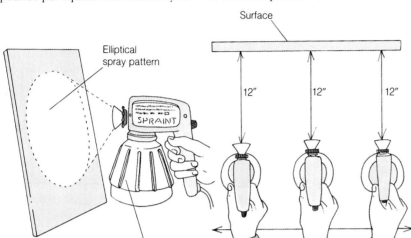

Elliptical spray pattern

Airless sprayer

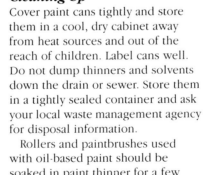

Surface

12" 12" 12"

Cleaning Up

Cover paint cans tightly and store them in a cool, dry cabinet away from heat sources and out of the reach of children. Label cans well. Do not dump thinners and solvents down the drain or sewer. Store them in a tightly sealed container and ask your local waste management agency for disposal information.

Rollers and paintbrushes used with oil-based paint should be soaked in paint thinner for a few minutes, then flushed out by working the solvent into the bristles or nap and dipping them up and down in the solvent a few times. Repeat with fresh solvent until the solvent no longer absorbs color. A special brush and roller cleaner is available that works like a child's top. It will remove moisture.

Soaking Paintbrushes. You can store brushes temporarily in liquid thinner when painting with alkyds; use water with latex paint. Suspend the brushes as shown; don't stand them on the bristles.

Drying and Wrapping Brushes. Spin brushes, as shown, to dry them. Doing this inside a box will prevent spatters. Wipe with a clean rag and wrap brushes in plain butcher paper. Store rollers upright, not on end.

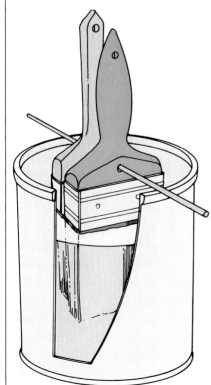

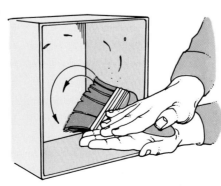

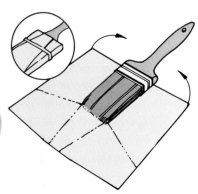

PANELING

Paneling provides a distinctive design element, and the wide range of available materials and patterns makes it extremely versatile.

Installing paneling is a relatively simple undertaking for most homeowners because the job requires few tools and skills. The most difficult steps are preparing an irregular subsurface and handling large sheets of plywood or hardboard.

There are several advantages to using paneling rather than other finish wall materials. It is extremely durable and almost maintenance-free. Once installed, it needs little if any finishing. Paneling will cover a damaged wall so long as you do some preliminary steps including smoothing the damaged surface.

The disadvantages are that, with the exception of minor scratches and blemishes, paneling is hard to repair, and a careless installation can result in shabby-looking seams and edges.

Recommended Cross-References
Caulking & Adhesives, Ceilings, Framing, Moldings, Wallboard, Walls.

How to Use Paneling
Use paneling wherever wood will create a warm accent. Use it on ceilings, as a wall covering, as a wainscot, or to cover doors and shutters. Generally, it is better to use an expensive paneling to cover a small area than a cheap paneling to cover a large area.

Board paneling is generally more expensive than sheet paneling, but it has several advantages. It works better for long runs (ceilings or two-story walls, for example), because individual boards can be joined randomly, whereas 4-foot-wide sheets can only be joined end to end. Board paneling can also be installed diagonally or in a herringbone pattern. It is easier to cut than sheet paneling, although the boards are more tedious to attach.

Most paneling has grooves, which create a strong line pattern that can have different effects depending on use. For instance, a short wall seems taller when covered with vertically grooved paneling. Horizontal paneling makes a wall seem shorter. If you panel a far wall, perspective lengthens, making the room seem longer.

The color of paneling also creates different effects. A ceiling with light paneling, such as maple or some varieties of oak, appears higher. A room with walls of light paneling appears larger and brighter. Dark paneling makes a ceiling appear lower and creates either an intimate or confined feeling.

Always choose a pattern that is consistent with the overall character of the room. Try to match existing wood trim or other details, especially in homes of a particular architectural style. Paneling with randomly spaced grooves or a coarse grain that includes worm holes or other markings should be used in casual settings. For a formal look, choose paneling that features a straight, tight grain pattern, narrow boards, and a smooth finish. If you panel a bathroom or other wet area, use real board paneling of a durable species, such as redwood or cedar. Finish it with several coats of a clear sealer.

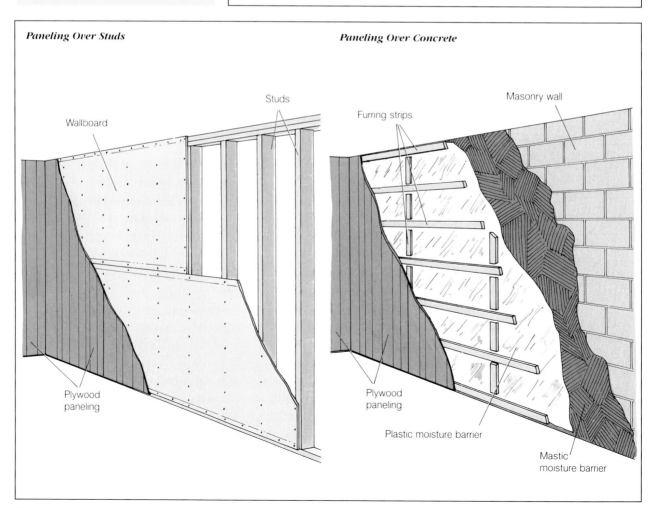

Paneling Over Studs

Studs

Wallboard

Plywood paneling

Paneling Over Concrete

Masonry wall

Furring strips

Plywood paneling

Plastic moisture barrier

Mastic moisture barrier

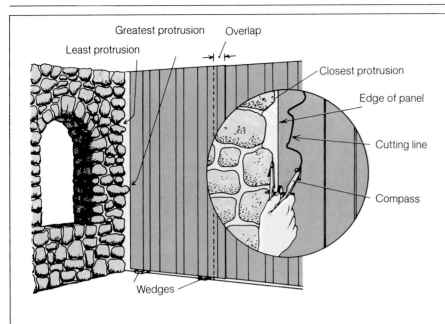

Greatest protrusion

Overlap

Least protrusion

Closest protrusion

Edge of panel

Cutting line

Compass

Wedges

Fitting an Irregular Edge

1. Where paneling fits against an irregular edge, such as a fireplace, board siding, or highly textured plaster, cut it to fit the profile of the irregular surface. To do this, place wedges under the panel and hold it so that the top jams snugly against the ceiling. The sheet should be plumb and the edge should butt against the closest protrusion of the wall. Be sure the sheet is snug enough to press against as you scribe a line for cutting.

2. Use a compass and pencil to scribe a cutting line. Set the compass so that the legs bridge the widest gap between the panel and the irregular wall. Trace the length of the panel, following the contours of the wall.

Types of Paneling

Boards. Traditionally, paneling consisted of individual boards. It can still be done using dimension lumber ranging in thickness from 1-by lumber to very thin veneers. Some boards tend to warp and buckle over time, causing gaps at the joints. You can minimize this effect by using kiln-dried lumber.

Tongue-and-Groove. Tongue-and-groove paneling is usually made of softwood—pine, redwood, or cedar—but oak and mahogany are also available. Boards vary in thickness from 3/8 inch to 11/16 inch and in width from 2 inches to 8 inches. Some are tongue-and-grooved on the ends. Often, single boards are made to look like two or three narrow boards by milling vertical grooves into the single board. Some types have a rough, or resawn, surface on one side and a planed surface on the other. Options also include unfinished boards or boards that are prefinished.

Sheet Paneling. The greatest variety of paneling is available in sheets. Paneling sheets are usually 4 feet wide by 8, 9, or 10 feet long. One type of paneling has plywood backing in thicknesses from 3/16 inch to 5/8 inch. The other type of paneling uses hardboard backing. Most hardboard is 1/4 inch thick. Sheet surface options are almost endless. In some cases real wood strips, called veneers, are glued to the plywood backing to produce a surface identical to individual-board paneling, but which is much less expensive. Some hardwood veneers are thick enough to have V-grooves, and the sheets come completely finished.

Most sheet paneling has a printed surface; some is also embossed with wood patterns and textures.

Exterior Siding. Outdoor siding, ranging from common pine to clear redwood or cedar, can also be used indoors. It can be installed vertically, horizontally, or diagonally, and comes in various patterns, such as shiplap, V-groove, and channel rustic. It can be painted, stained, or finished with a clear sealer.

Installing Paneling

To prepare a surface for paneling, locate all the wall studs and indicate their position with marks on the floor and ceiling. Then check for high spots and low spots with a long straightedge. If all areas are within 1/4 inch of a flat plane, apply paneling directly to the wall after patching holes and cracks and removing nails and other obstructions. If the wall is irregular, nail 1 by 2 furring strips 2 feet apart and wherever panel seams will occur. If the wall consists of bare studs, nail up 1/2-inch wallboard and tape it before installing paneling.

Bring the paneling indoors at least 24 hours before installation.

Hardboard paneling is particularly susceptible to expansion and contraction, but all paneling needs to acclimate to the home. Store it flat rather than standing it against a wall, and handle it carefully to avoid marring the surface.

Start by planning the layout. Use full sheets wherever possible. Locate filler pieces over doorways and windows. Place all edges directly on the wall or a furring strip. Install the first panel in a prominent corner. Use a level to make sure the sides are plumb.

The easiest way to install paneling is to apply adhesive with a caulking gun. Apply a quick-drying adhesive immediately before each sheet goes up. Some adhesives require that you push the sheet against the adhesive, then pull it away to allow the glue to set before finally pushing the panel into place. Even with adhesive, most paneling still needs to be nailed along the top and bottom.

Cut sheet paneling with a handsaw, table saw, or circular saw. If you use a handsaw, find one with fine teeth, 10 to 15 points per inch. Saw with the paneling faceup when using a handsaw, table saw, or radial arm saw. Saw with the paneling facedown if you use a portable circular saw. Clamp a long straightedge to the sheet. Start holes for electrical receptacles and other fixtures with a drill and finish them with a keyhole saw.

PANEL SIDING

In spite of the wide range of paneling styles, the actual core of most panels is the same—either plywood or hardboard. Only the veneer, or thin top layer, distinguishes panel designs from one another. In some cases it is real wood, usually cedar, redwood, or Douglas fir, and makes the panels very expensive. Less expensive panels use lower grades of wood, resin-treated paper, or embossed hardboard. These kinds of panels must be painted or stained for weather protection.

Panel siding is the easiest type of siding to install and, if it is plywood, eliminates the need for sheathing. It is applied directly over the wall framing. Siding panels are made from plywood, hardboard, or other composition materials, and include a wide range of styles. Some are plain, some resemble board siding, and others have embossed patterns on them to resemble stucco or other masonry. They can be painted or stained.

Recommended Cross-References
Board Siding, Caulking, Flashing, Framing, Shingle Siding, Siding, Stucco.

Types and Sizes
Plywood and hardboard panels are widely used for covering exterior walls because they are relatively low in price and can be installed quickly. Price depends on the type of wood used for the surface veneer—some premium grades of redwood and Douglas fir plywood are as expensive as board siding. Panel siding comes in a wide variety of patterns and designs. Some include a rabbet along the edges and others are plain. The kind of edge makes a difference in how the panels are installed.

Standard sizes are 4 by 8, 4 by 9, and 4 by 10. The bottom edge of the panel should overlap the foundation wall by at least 2 inches, but should not be any closer than 8 inches to the ground. For houses framed with standard 8-foot walls, this means using 4 by 9 panels to have the least number of joints. For a new installation, panel siding should be at least $\frac{3}{8}$ inch thick; patterned or grooved material is thicker, usually $\frac{5}{8}$ inch. When re-siding over an irregular surface, such as shingles or horizontal siding, thick, stiff $\frac{1}{2}$-inch or $\frac{5}{8}$-inch panel siding should be used. Use $\frac{3}{8}$-inch panels over smooth surfaces, such as old panel siding or board siding with battens (if any) removed.

Concealing the Joints
The main design consideration with panel siding is what to do about the joints. If the panels have decorative grooves, only the end joints will show, but for plain panels both the side joints and end joints will be visible. One way to conceal joints is to cover them with battens or trim boards. Another method is to use panel siding only on short sections of wall, so the panels will span the entire section without the need for end joints. You may also be able to order longer panels to cover a wall from top to bottom, such as 9-foot, 10-foot, or even 12-foot lengths. Finally, if you must join panels end-to-end, place the joints near the foundation or over doors or windows, where they will not be very noticeable. To disguise the joints, cover them with trim pieces that blend into the lines of the facade.

Cutting Around Openings
When working around openings, use full panels rather than making a patchwork of smaller pieces. The leading edge must always fall in the middle of a cripple stud (the short stud above or below a window). There are two ways to cut out the panels for a window or door. The first way is to nail a full panel in place as if the opening for the window or door were not there. Then cut out the opening from the back with a reciprocating saw, using the framing as a guide.

If the window or door is already installed, measure the panel carefully and cut out the opening before nailing it up. Leave a $\frac{1}{4}$-inch gap around the opening to make fitting easier. Take measurements carefully. Because you will have to make cuts with a circular saw from the back of the panel, be sure to reverse the measurements as you mark them. Lay out these measurements with a straightedge before cutting.

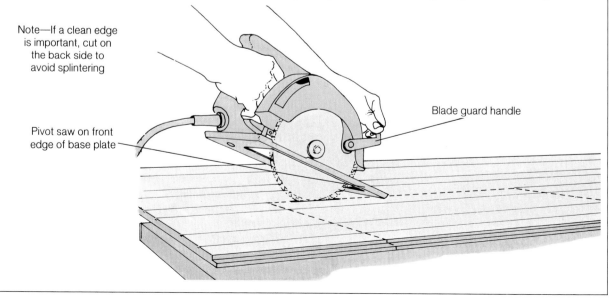

Note—If a clean edge is important, cut on the back side to avoid splintering

Pivot saw on front edge of base plate

Blade guard handle

Installing Panels

Use 6d HDG box nails for ³/₈-inch panels placed over existing siding, 8d or longer for all other thicknesses. Nail every 6 inches, on center, around the edges and 12 inches, on center, in the field. Leave a ¹/₈-inch expansion gap between panels and a ¹/₄-inch gap around windows and doors. Caulk before trimming.

In new construction there is no need to add paper between the studs and siding, but paper flashing should be applied around windows and doors. If you are covering existing siding, it is best to apply 15-pound felt or other building paper first.

Panel siding is heavy and awkward to lift, so have a helper. After the panel is positioned, one person should hold it in place while the other person nails. Panels are normally installed vertically, and all edges must be joined over a stud.

The first panel is the critical one: It must be perfectly plumb or all succeeding panels will be out of alignment. If you have difficulty getting the first one square, spread the corrections over several panels.

In new construction, install panel siding before the rafters, flush with the top of the cap plate so that you can cut the rafters to fit over it. This eliminates having to notch the panels to fit around each rafter.

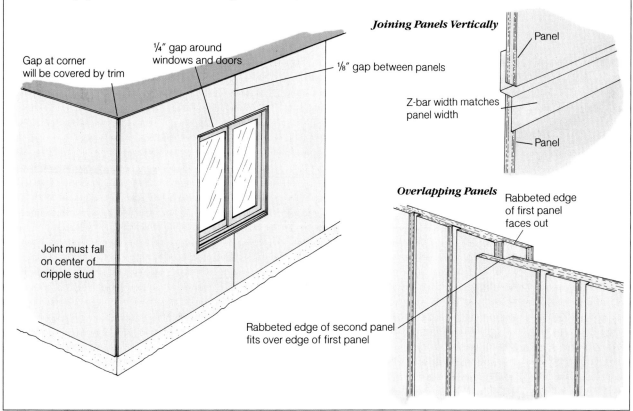

Gap at corner will be covered by trim

¹/₄" gap around windows and doors

¹/₈" gap between panels

Joint must fall on center of cripple stud

Joining Panels Vertically

Panel

Z-bar width matches panel width

Panel

Overlapping Panels

Rabbeted edge of first panel faces out

Rabbeted edge of second panel fits over edge of first panel

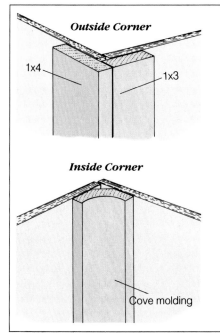

Outside Corner

1x4

1x3

Inside Corner

Cove molding

Applying the Trim

When the panels are in place, caulk all gaps and joints around doors, windows, and in the corners. Caulk again after applying the trim.

Windows and Doors. Windows and doors are commonly trimmed with 1 by 4s, with the top piece overlapping the side trim rather than mitering the corners. This minimizes the chance of water running underneath.

Outside Corners. Overlapping 1 by 4s are the most usual way to trim an outside corner. Some people like to substitute a 1 by 3 on one side for a more symmetrical look.

Inside Corners. The trim for an inside corner can either match the outside corner treatment or you can use a piece of molding.

A thick layer of pea gravel covers the paths in this easy-maintenance garden. Plastic film deters weeds from growing and a 2 by 4 edging strip keeps gravel out of the planting beds.

In spite of their humble function, paths conjure up romantic images of leisurely strolls across flower-filled meadows, warm welcomes, or mysterious adventures on walks through shadowy forests. The word path is often a metaphor for life. No wonder successful gardeners and landscape designers make frequent use of this important feature to direct both the eye and the feet toward a particular focal point, and stress the use of paths as design elements.

Paths do not have to be complicated or hard to build. The simplest are of stepping-stones or mulches such as gravel and bark. Pavings, such as stone, brick, and concrete, are also fairly easy to install. Designing a path and choosing appropriate materials may be more of a challenge than constructing it.

Recommended Cross-References
Benches, Brick, Concrete, Decks, Garden Walls, Lighting: Outdoor, Patios, Steps.

Designing Paths

Most paths serve a practical purpose; place them wherever you need access. Paths can be more than domestic highways, however, if you consider their visual and emotional impact. They lend a strong visual element that creates patterns, defines spaces, and adds texture and color. Emotionally, they offer an invitation to visit, to stroll, to explore. Professional landscape designers favor a path that leads nowhere—it travels out of sight around a corner or behind a grove of trees. An unknown destination heightens the sense of mystery in the garden.

What makes a path appealing? First, it must be safe and comfortable. Most garden paths are too narrow, especially for two people to stroll together. Important paths, such as front entries and main garden paths, should be at least 48 inches wide; 60 inches is an ideal width. Secondary paths for single-file use should be 30 to 36 inches wide. Paths in small gardens intended as borders or to meander through the garden with no apparent destination, may be narrower.

A comfortable slope for paths on an incline is between 5 percent and 8 percent (5 to 8 inches of rise for every 100 inches of horizontal distance). Provide steps if the slope is greater. Avoid single steps in the middle of a path; it is always better to have at least two steps together so they are easy to see. If a single step is unavoidable, locate it at a corner or other prominent point.

Let aesthetics take the upper hand in determining whether a path should be straight or curved, unless some compelling reason exists for a beeline between two points. Straight paths tend to be dull unless they parallel some other feature such as a house or fence, or unless they serve as borders or axes for a formal landscape. When a path is in the open, it is better to curve it gracefully or break it into intersecting segments that resemble large stepping-stones.

Color and texture are important elements that contribute to the appeal of a path. Red brick is successful in gardens with rich greenery because red and green are complementary colors. Paving materials with earth tones or neutral colors also work well because they are suitable backgrounds for most color schemes. Paths that repeat colors or use identical materials in the exterior of the house are also effective. Use only one or two materials in a given path. When mixing materials, it is better to have one color or texture dominate and to use the others as accent. When it comes to combining materials, small paving units and finely textured materials are more versatile.

Edge a path with a curb or border of contrasting material. A border keeps plants in place, defines the path more crisply, and contains loose materials such as gravel and bark. Install lights if you will use the path at night. A bench adds a final touch that will make a path even more appealing and inviting.

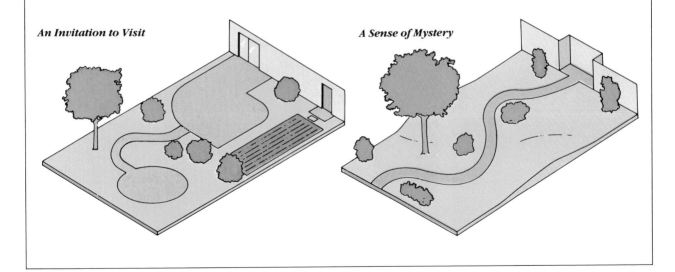

An Invitation to Visit

A Sense of Mystery

Materials

Stone. A row of stepping-stones that meanders through a garden or lawn serves as a simple and charming path for light use. Flat fieldstones, flagstones, broken chunks of concrete, cast-concrete pavers, log ends (called rounds), and short sections of railroad tie are popular choices. Also consider the use of smaller units, such as brick; mortar a few together to form each step. Individual stones should be at least 12 inches square and set so the centers are 20 to 25 inches apart. All stones should be close to the same size. If your path is a straight line, uniformly sized stones work best. Otherwise, stagger the sizes in an attractive pattern. In lawns, set stones flush with the ground to facilitate mowing. Stepping-stones surrounded with gravel or bark make an attractive path that is easy to maintain.

Loose Materials. Gravel, bark, and pine needles are inexpensive materials that are easy to install. Smaller sizes (such as 3/8-inch pea gravel) are more comfortable surfaces on which to walk. Add wood edgings to contain loose materials. Use 2 by 4s for straight paths or a double thickness of bender board for curved paths.

Choose pressure-treated lumber or heart grades of a durable species. Anchor them by pounding stakes below the top of the edging board; paving material will eventually cover the stakes. The paving should be 3 to 4 inches thick with polyethylene sheeting underneath to stop weeds.

Wood. Although they are not permanent, wooden paths may last for many years if the lumber is pressure treated for ground contact or a heart grade of a durable species. In one type of installation, thick planks or large timbers such as railroad ties lie directly on a 3-inch bed of sand. Nail the planks together to minimize the uneven edges caused by settling. In another type long 4 by 4 sleepers lie on the ground with shorter planks over them. This installation keeps the top surface flush and reduces ground contact for the planks.

Masonry. Brick, stone, thick tiles, and interlocking pavers make excellent paths. Lay them on a bed of sand, either loose or with mortared joints, or, to form a more durable path, install them over a concrete base with mortared joints. Masonry paths are expensive, but if the path is short and prominent, you might judge that masonry is worth the cost. Installa-

tions on a sand base tend to settle and shift over time especially in areas where there are a lot of tree roots or many days of frost.

Concrete. Concrete is durable, less expensive than masonry, and fairly easy to install. Concrete can also be a cold and uninteresting surface unless you do something to relieve the gray expanse. Break the path up into smaller sections with wood or brick edgings. Broom finishes, salt finishes, and exposed aggregate finishes also create pleasing textures. Some seeded aggregates add dramatic color to a path. Another way to change the color of concrete is to paint it with a latex patio paint, available in many exterior house colors. Even a plain concrete path is enhanced by attractive border plantings, especially if some plants fringe the edges.

Materials for a path should be in keeping with the landscape. Flagstone (below left) is a neutral background for colorful border plants. Stones used to terrace the yard (below) are also laid as a path. Used brick (opposite above) matches the wall in a city garden. Straightline pattern of bricks (opposite below left) is appropriate with formal planting. Wood (opposite center and right) is a natural choice for paths winding through trees.

Use bender board for gentle curves on paths that wind through the landscape. These flexible strips can be used as edging to fend off the lawn mower or as concrete forms.

Edgings

Edges can be constructed of a variety of materials, from brick to wood to concrete. They can be flush with the soil surface, below grade, or above ground. If it is a lawn that needs an edge, consider installing edging below grade, as shown, to all but eliminate the need for hand edging and trimming—a considerable weekly savings in time and effort.

Railroad ties, 2 by 4 redwood (or other types of wood treated with a preservative), and three layers of bender board are popular choices.

More permanent edges are constructed of brick or concrete. A concrete edge can be installed as many inches above grade as you want.

An L-shaped edge is one of the best configurations for eliminating the need for edging next to a lawn. Brick or a combination of concrete and wood or concrete and brick can be used for this type of edge.

1. Wood Beam. Use a wood beam or railroad tie to edge a gravel patio.

2. Raised Concrete. A raised concrete edging will give a definite curb along a path.

3. Flush Concrete. This blends into the landscaping but still provides a definite edge.

4. Wood Block. A staked board clamps wood blocks firmly between it and a brick path.

5. Brick. Decorative bricks, set on end, are an easy way to make a curved edging.

6. Wood and Concrete. The combination of wood and concrete makes a well-defined and permanent edging.

7. Flush Wood. A 2 by 4 on edge is set flush between a path and a lawn. Be sure to treat the lumber with a preservative.

8. Above Grade. Setting the 2 by 4 above grade bridges the different levels between lawn and path.

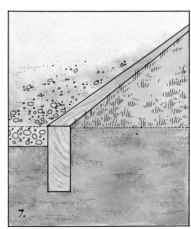

PATIOS

A patio should be more than a bald square of concrete poured behind the back door. Like a deck, it should be an extension of the house, a smooth transition that expands the activity area of a home and adds to the pleasures of outdoor living. It might be square, and it might be concrete, but it should be inviting.

The most obvious advantage of a patio is that there is no lawn to mow, and no soil to till. But, even if your wish is a low-maintenance backyard, remember that an unrelieved paved area can look awfully boring. Make it more attractive by adding curves, angles, small planting areas, freestanding planters and garden furniture, interesting paving patterns, or contrasting paving materials.

Just as the patio should be a smooth transition from the house, it should also be a smooth transition to the other areas in your backyard. In your plans, include steps or paths to lead toward the lawn or pool.

Whether you are building a new patio or improving an old one, spend as much time as possible in planning so that the space will suit your family's needs and your yard.

Recommended Cross-References

Barbecues, Benches, Brick, Concrete, Decks, Drainage, Fences, Garden Walls, Lighting: Outdoor, Paths, Planters, Tile, Trellises, Zoning, Codes & Permits.

Patience and planning were the keys to success in this patio (opposite), which converts a small space into a serene hideaway.

Planning Your Patio

You should consider many factors as you plan your patio. Start by focusing on your family's needs and life-style. List all the activities for which you might use a patio. Rank the list in terms of priorities to help you determine where to place the patio and how large it should be. Also consider the potential of your yard. What does it offer in terms of space, views, and related activity areas? What are the local zoning requirements? Weather conditions, particularly sun, shade, and wind, are important factors, too. Finally, consider what textures, colors, and shapes will harmonize best.

Choosing a Location. Consider how you plan to use the patio and place it accordingly. For instance, if you plan to use the patio for dining and entertaining, it should be close to the kitchen. If you plan multiple uses, arrange access from two or three different rooms. You may discover that two small patios will serve your needs better than a large one, or that a patio in the side yard or front yard will get more use than a backyard patio. Exposure to the sun and access play a large role in determining use.

Local zoning regulations may affect your plans regarding an overhead structure or tall screening. Regulations seldom restrict paving material, however. Keep in mind that the sun and wind will play different roles through the seasons. Weather has an important influence on the comfort and enjoyment of a patio. For instance, you may choose a location that is sunny at breakfast time in the spring, or a site that is protected from prevailing breeze when you want quiet dinners at sunset. Shade structures and windscreens alter the microclimate to some extent, but be aware of the unalterable effects of the macroclimate.

Determining Size. A typical patio is 15 feet by 25 feet—large enough to accommodate a table and chairs, a small cooking area, and one or two lounges. As a general rule, outdoor spaces should be slightly larger than indoor spaces used for the same purpose, although the area of the yard and shape of the patio also affect layout. A large, expansive patio can be uncomfortable—better to break up space with planters, fences, or barriers, or to construct two or three separate patios instead.

Choosing a Shape. Fit the patio to the available space. The shape of the patio should reflect the house, fences, and other prominent structures. Simple shapes usually work best, but that does not mean that all patios have to be plain rectangles. Arrange several rectangular shapes together to create visual interest and to define distinct areas for separate activities. If you use angles, limit the variety. All the angles may measure 45 degrees, for example, or 60 degrees. Align the angles with some prominent feature in the landscape.

Furnishings. An attractive, inviting patio is much more than a large slab of pavement. An inviting patio includes whatever amenities render the space usable and create unity. A list may include garden furniture, overhead shade structures, a barbecue, insect screens, or benches. Plan these additions carefully.

Overhead structures provide shade. Some types, such as awnings or fiberglass roofing panels, protect the patio from rain, but they may also trap unwanted heat if the area is not well ventilated.

Privacy. Use walls, screens, fences, tall plants, and the house to create privacy and a sense of enclosure. Tall barriers are particularly effective in making a small patio seem larger, as long as the height is approximately one half to one third the width of the space. Terraced planters that recede from the patio and draw the eye upward also help to make a small patio seem larger.

Even where the need for privacy does not play an important role, low barriers may be necessary to create a sense of intimacy. Benches, planters, low walls, and perimeter plants provide attractive means to define space. They can also serve functional purposes. A low wall can serve as a counter near a cooking area and benches may provide storage space.

As you consider these factors you will begin to get specific ideas about location, size, shape, amenities, and paving material. Work these ideas into a preliminary plan, changing and refining as you go. Look for ideas in magazines, in books, and in the homes of your friends and neighbors. When you have a completed plan, make a list of all the materials and the amounts you need in order to estimate the cost of the project.

Concrete Patios

Concrete is a durable patio surface that does not have to be a cold, gray slab. Texture, color, contrasting borders of wood or brick all provide interesting patterns.

Layout. To prepare the site, lay out the perimeter with string lines and drive grade stakes around the lines at 10-foot intervals. If the ground is rough, drive a stake every 5 feet. You will need reference points to guide excavation and grading. The points should fall at the same pitch as the finished surface. To establish pitch, stretch a chalk line and snap it along each row of stakes. Adjust the marks so that a line between them would slope away from the house at a rate of 1 inch per 10 feet. (Rough concrete surfaces require a steeper slope.) Attach string to stakes at the level of the slope mark. Stretch strings across the patio area to form a grid that reflects the finished slope.

Determine the elevation of the patio. The lower edge should be slightly above the ground or flush with it, not below the ground. Try to plan the patio so that the edge closest to the house falls 1 inch to 2 inches below a doorway. Allow for adequate clearance between the pad and wood siding. (Most codes require 8 inches of clearance.) If the door is too high, plan a step or two. Determine how far below the strings the paving surface will lie. Add the thickness of the concrete and sub-base to this figure. The sum represents the distance from the string grid to the bottom of the excavation.

Excavation. Remove all vegetation, debris, and soil down to the level you established. Be careful not to disturb the soil too much since the concrete slab must rest on compact earth. Excavate deeper around the perimeter—a deeper footing will reinforce the outside edge of the patio. In some areas, codes require that the footing extend below the frost line. In such cases, excavate, form, and pour the footing before pouring the rest of the patio.

When the patio is above grade you need to fill rather than excavate. The fill can be clean soil or whatever material local code requires. You

Easy-maintenance concrete patio is divided into squares by expansion strips. Some squares are left open for planting.

must always compact the fill; rent a mechanical tamper. If the area is boggy or drains poorly, install a drainage system first.

Base. If the ground is particularly firm, you can pour concrete directly on it. Generally you need to put down and tamp a 2- to 4-inch-deep sand bed. For problem areas—expansive soils or soils subject to freezing—put down 3 inches of pea gravel topped by 2 inches of sand.

Forms. Forms can be made from 2 by 4s. If they are to remain in the concrete as decorative expansion strips, use redwood, cedar, or pressure-treated lumber. Cover the top edges of the wood with masking tape to prevent concrete stains.

Drive a stake every 4 feet (or less) to hold the form. If you leave the forms in place, use redwood or cedar stakes and drive them about 1 inch below the top edge of the forms. Use the string grid to set the top of the forms at the correct height.

To engineer curved edges, cut saw kerfs halfway through one side of a 2 by 4 at intervals of about 1 inch. Bend 1 by 4s and stake them every 2 feet to create gentle curves. Three layers of $3/8$ by 4 bender board will also serve as a curved form.

Because concrete expands and contracts, a patio should have expansion joints every 8 to 10 feet. If you leave form boards in place, they will serve as joints. If not, place vinyl expansion strips in the concrete when it is wet. Also, remember to install a strip of expansion material between the house and the patio.

Although patios generally do not require steel reinforcement, it provides extra insurance against large cracks and uneven settling. Use welded wire mesh and place it on rocks or special supports.

Pouring and Finishing Concrete. Calculate in cubic yards the volume of concrete you need. A cubic yard is 27 cubic feet; 27 cubic feet of concrete covers approximately 80 square feet of patio if it is 4 inches thick ($1/3 \times 8' \times 10' = 26.67$ cubic feet). Mix batches less than 1 cubic yard with a small mixer; for more, order ready-mixed concrete.

Handle the concrete as little as possible. Drop it in place, overfilling the forms by about $1/2$ inch. Consolidate the concrete by jamming a shovel or stick up and down at various

places, especially next to the form boards. Strike off the concrete by dragging a long 2 by 4 across the tops of the forms with a sawing motion. Dragging levels the concrete, but does not smooth it.

Immediately after strike-off, use a float to bring the surface to a preliminary smoothness. You may need a bull float with a long handle to reach the center of larger patios. Use a magnesium float for air-entrained concrete. Drag the float slowly across the surface, raising the leading edge slightly. Then run the tip of a trowel about an inch deep between the forms and concrete to clean the edge. Let the concrete set before finishing it.

Finishes. Various finish surface options are available. For a rough appearance and texture, the floated surface can be left as is. Edging it with a special edging tool will add a finishing touch. Run the tool back and forth against the side forms.

A broom surface is skid-resistant and has very fine parallel lines. It is produced by dragging a damp broom lightly over the floated surface, being careful not to overlap the runs.

Steel troweling produces the smoothest and most slippery surface. An initial troweling can be done shortly after floating, but for a smoother surface, you must trowel again after the concrete stiffens and barely responds to light troweling activity.

To add color, sprinkle on a dry-shake coloring agent after bleed water has evaporated from the slab. Add more color after each troweling. You may choose to paint or stain the patio after it cures.

When using exposed aggregate, "seed" decorative stones into the surface after striking off the concrete. Wet the stones first, then spread them over the slab. Embed the stones below the surface with a float, level the surface, and wait for the concrete to set. Use a broom and fine spray from a hose to flush away the surface concrete and expose the tops of the seeded stones.

Curing. The easiest way to cure concrete is to cover the slab with plastic sheeting. Leave the plastic on for one week, making sure the edges are well anchored. You may also choose to spray on a curing agent; do this if you intend to paint the patio.

Brick Patios

Brick is a versatile paving material that looks equally at home with casual or formal settings. It comes in a variety of sizes and colors and it can be laid in numerous patterns or combinations of patterns. If laid in sand, the bricks should butt fairly tightly. When set in concrete, the grout line will become part of the pattern. (For a more detailed description of the choices that are available to you and details of the installation methods, refer to the Bricks section.)

The mark of a professional installation is a level surface and precise alignment. This is not difficult for even an amateur to achieve—it will just take longer. Although large quantities of bricks are extremely heavy, an individual brick is easy to handle. If you are laying your own brick patio, you can purchase and pick up small quantities and install a patio in stages, as your time and budget permit.

The most durable installation is one that has a concrete base and the bricks set in mortar with grout. A firmly packed sand bed yields a reasonable stable base, although you may have to relevel a few spots each year if the soil is of heavy clay or some other expansive material, or if the ground freezes and thaws. Sand-based installations require a stable edge to hold the bricks. The best edging is a concrete curb (below grade) topped with bricks. Set the bricks on the surface of the curb while the concrete is wet. Butt them together if the paving bricks butt. Otherwise, set curb bricks with the same spacing as paving bricks. Whether you choose a concrete base or sand bed, prepare the grade and the bed as you would prepare for a concrete installation.

The romantic brick patio beside a pond (above) is laid on a sand base; edging strips prevent the bricks from shifting. Stone radii (below) repeat the theme of stone walls and rock gardens. A circular pattern is not complicated to lay; start in the center and work your way outward.

Stone Patios

Flagstone and other natural stones make a suitable paving for large, rugged, earthy-looking patios. Flagstones create an uneven surface, but the durability and natural look they provide more than compensate.

Paving with flagstone is similar to paving with brick, except that flagstones go down faster and must be installed with mortar or sod in the joints. Sand alone will not hold them because of the wide space between stones. You may choose to lay stones over a concrete base or a sand bed. Sand beds must be at least 2 inches thick to accommodate the irregular shape and thickness of the stones.

Cutting Flagstone. Cut flagstone in a manner similar to cutting brick. Use a broad chisel or a brickset and hammer. Wear protective goggles because small chips of stone will certainly fly at you.

Mark the cut by scratching a line on the surface with the chisel, and score the line deeply. Repeat the process on the bottom.

Place the stone with the scored line just over the edge of a 2 by 4. Place the brickset on the line and give it a sharp rap. If the stone does not break, rap it in one or two other places along the line. Use the chisel to trim the cut.

If you need precise cuts, stone yards will use special saws to make cuts for you at a modest price.

Installing Flagstone. Prepare the ground for flagstone as you would for a brick or concrete patio—mark the area with stakes and string, then level the site. Lay a 2-inch to 3-inch sand bed; dampen and tamp it firm.

Place a border around the site. The border and the flagstones should lie flush with the ground.

After screeding the sand, lay all the flagstones in position to judge their final appearance. Place stones 3 inches apart to take mortar; space them farther apart if you will fill them with soil and grass.

A dry mortar of 1 part portland cement and 3 parts sand works well with flagstone. Mix the components in a wheelbarrow until the mortar is a uniform color.

Spray the site with water so that the flagstones and the sand base are thoroughly wet. Let the stones dry, then spread the dry mix over the area. Fill all the spaces. Sweep the mortar with a broom until it is smooth and level.

Set the hose nozzle to produce a fine spray that will completely soak the joints. After 15 minutes, spray again to ensure that the water has penetrated. Add more dry mix in areas that have settled.

After 24 hours, clean the stones of mortar stains with a mixture of 1 part muriatic acid to 10 parts water. Mix by adding acid to water. Never add water to acid. Keep the area damp for at least 5 days for a proper cure.

If you prefer to fill the spaces with soil, tamp in fill with the end of a 1 by 4; pack it tightly around the stones. Then you can lightly rake in grass seed or encourage moss to grow between the stones.

You may choose to place flagstones directly in the ground. If so, cut around their outline with a trowel, remove the stone, and dig out the soil. Place the stones on a bed of sand to stabilize them.

To create a more enduring installation, prepare a 3-inch concrete base. Lay out the stones on the base, then mix the mortar (1 part cement, 3 parts sand). Remove a few stones at a time, place the mortar, and replace the stones. Let the mortar set overnight; grout the joints the next day.

Planted tree wells are emphasized by the circular pattern of the stone paving.

PIPE

If you work with plumbing, you will most likely need to patch, cut, or join some kind of pipe. Depending on the age of your home, you may find copper, plastic, galvanized steel, or brass in the water supply system; cast iron, galvanized steel, plastic, or copper in the drain-waste-vent (DWV) system.

When you choose pipe to rough-in new plumbing, find out which types your local code allows and which are readily available. Plastic and copper pipes are easy to handle. Threaded steel pipe is convenient if the lengths are the right size and if you do not need to cut and thread new pipe. No-hub cast iron is also fairly easy to handle, but cutting it requires specific equipment. Cast-iron pipe with leaded joints and gas piping are dangerous to handle. If your plumbing project requires these materials, hire a professional. Polybutylene pipe is easy to use, but may not be accepted by your local code.

A few simple fittings allow pipe fitters to make basic connections, but there are dozens of variations. Some fittings are threaded, others have smooth hubs that slip over the ends of pipe, and others are without hubs so they clamp to pipe. Fittings for the water supply system are different from DWV fittings. Even if the fittings are made of the same material and resemble each other, they are quite different. Specialized fittings join pipes of different materials, such as plastic to cast iron or copper to steel. Whenever you join copper to steel, use an appropriate dielectric fitting or put a brass or plastic nipple between the pipes to prevent corrosion. You must also support pipe with brackets and straps of the same material.

Recommended Cross-Reference
Plumbing.

Cast-Iron Pipe

Many DWV systems use cast-iron pipe (although smaller drain and vent pipes may be galvanized steel or copper). In older cast-iron systems, molten lead seals the joints. Newer cast-iron pipe, which is called no-hub, joins with compression bands. Pipe, fittings, and bands are available in 1½-inch, 2-inch, 3-inch, and 4-inch sizes. Although most codes now allow plastic DWV pipes, some areas still require cast iron, particularly if plumbing will lie under a slab or if roots are a problem.

There are two ways to cut cast-iron pipe. The first method requires a specialized tool that has a chain that wraps around the pipe. Tighten the knob and rotate the handle, and the chain snaps the pipe. The second method uses a circular power saw with a metal cutoff blade. Sawing makes a lot of sparks but is effective. If you need only one or two pieces,

have the supplier cut them for you.

No-hub pipes and fittings join with a clamp that consists of a neoprene gasket, a stainless steel band, and two nuts. Slip the pieces into the clamp and use a plumber's torque wrench to tighten the nuts. The specified torque is 60 inch-pounds.

To make a molten lead joint, rent a plumber's furnace and ladle. Clean both pipes thoroughly. Pack oakum into the joint, leaving 1 inch of space for the lead. If the pipes are horizontal, attach a joint runner against the hub to contain the lead. Melt the lead; if a scrap of newspaper dipped into it burns, the lead is too hot. Heat the ladle before you dip it into the hot lead or the lead could explode. Ladle the lead into the joint. Be very careful; lead spatters if it hits moisture on the pipe or ladle. Because of the danger and the need for specialized equipment, you are better off hiring a professional.

Cutting No-Hub Pipe

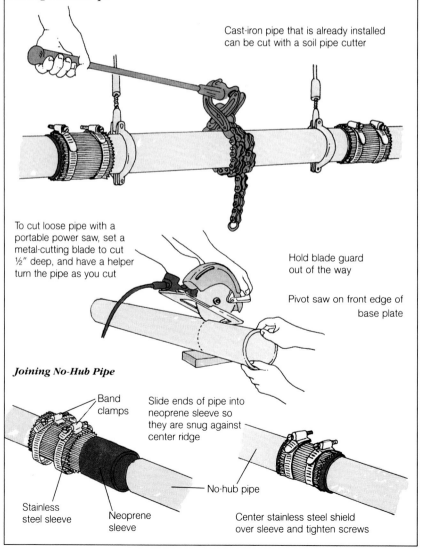

Cast-iron pipe that is already installed can be cut with a soil pipe cutter

To cut loose pipe with a portable power saw, set a metal-cutting blade to cut ½" deep, and have a helper turn the pipe as you cut

Hold blade guard out of the way

Pivot saw on front edge of base plate

Joining No-Hub Pipe

Band clamps

Slide ends of pipe into neoprene sleeve so they are snug against center ridge

No-hub pipe

Stainless steel sleeve

Neoprene sleeve

Center stainless steel shield over sleeve and tighten screws

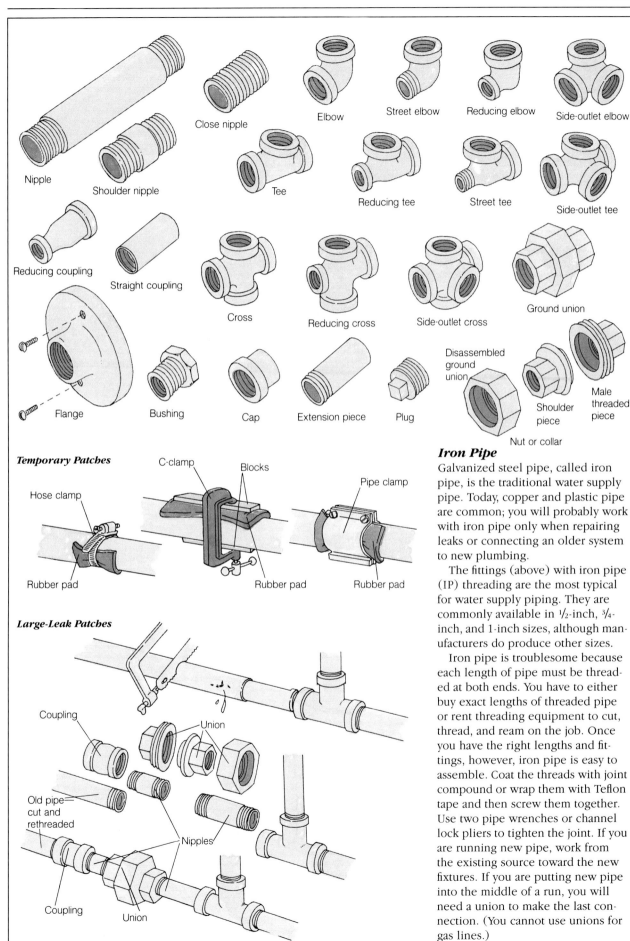

Nipple

Shoulder nipple

Close nipple

Elbow

Street elbow

Reducing elbow

Side-outlet elbow

Reducing coupling

Straight coupling

Tee

Reducing tee

Street tee

Side-outlet tee

Flange

Cross

Reducing cross

Side-outlet cross

Ground union

Bushing

Cap

Extension piece

Plug

Disassembled ground union

Nut or collar

Shoulder piece

Male threaded piece

Temporary Patches

Hose clamp

C-clamp

Blocks

Pipe clamp

Rubber pad

Rubber pad

Rubber pad

Large-Leak Patches

Coupling

Union

Old pipe cut and rethreaded

Nipples

Coupling

Union

Iron Pipe

Galvanized steel pipe, called iron pipe, is the traditional water supply pipe. Today, copper and plastic pipe are common; you will probably work with iron pipe only when repairing leaks or connecting an older system to new plumbing.

The fittings (above) with iron pipe (IP) threading are the most typical for water supply piping. They are commonly available in $\frac{1}{2}$-inch, $\frac{3}{4}$-inch, and 1-inch sizes, although manufacturers do produce other sizes.

Iron pipe is troublesome because each length of pipe must be threaded at both ends. You have to either buy exact lengths of threaded pipe or rent threading equipment to cut, thread, and ream on the job. Once you have the right lengths and fittings, however, iron pipe is easy to assemble. Coat the threads with joint compound or wrap them with Teflon tape and then screw them together. Use two pipe wrenches or channel lock pliers to tighten the joint. If you are running new pipe, work from the existing source toward the new fixtures. If you are putting new pipe into the middle of a run, you will need a union to make the last connection. (You cannot use unions for gas lines.)

Plastic Pipe

Plastic pipe is inexpensive, durable, and easy to work with. There are four types commonly used in plumbing systems: acrylonitrile-butadiene-styrene (ABS), polyvinyl chloride (PVC), chlorinated polyvinyl chloride (CPVC), and polybutylene (PB). Plastic has gained wide acceptance. Many plumbing codes now approve it, but be sure to check your local code before using plastic pipe. You may find that the code allows it in DWV systems but not water supply systems, or for outdoor use but not indoor use.

Types Used in the DWV System.
Drain-waste-vent systems use ABS and PVC piping. Both are available in sizes from 1¼ inches to 4 inches and larger. Measurements of DWV pipe refer to inside diameter (ID). Plastic DWV pipes are fairly rigid, although you can bend them slightly to make connections if runs are out of alignment. ABS disintegrates from constant exposure to the ultraviolet rays of the sun. Therefore, only use ABS indoors. You may use ABS for a vent pipe that penetrates the roof, however. Just be sure to paint the exposed portion with white paint or a reflective covering.

If plastic DWV pipe is not well supported, especially on horizontal runs, it tends to sag. Straps or brackets must be plastic, rather than metal. On 1½-inch pipe, position straps or brackets no farther than 3 feet apart. Space supports 4 feet apart when working with larger pipe sizes. The brackets must fit loosely enough for the pipe to expand and contract freely. You cannot mix ABS and PVC pipes or fittings; they are incompatible.

Types Used in the Supply System.
PVC, CPVC, and PB are acceptable for cold-water pipes. CPVC and PB, which are more expensive, are the only plastics capable of piping hot water. PB is flexible and runs almost as easily as electrical cable. It joins with compression fittings rather than solvents.

Measurements of supply pipes refer to the outside diameter (OD).

Working With Plastic Pipe.
When you measure plastic pipe for cutting, include the portion that slips inside each fitting. Mark the pipe and cut it with a tubing cutter or a handsaw. If you use a handsaw, be sure to square the cut by using a miter box. Remove burrs with a knife and clean all gloss from the surfaces with emery cloth or a liquid cleaner.

It is always a good idea to dry-fit several pieces before actually welding them together. You will not get a completely accurate mock-up, however, because the inside hubs taper slightly; the pipe will not slide all the way in until the welding solvent is applied. Nevertheless, if you compensate for the taper you can ensure that all cuts are the correct length before permanently welding them. You should also make a mark that indicates the alignment of pipe and fitting. The mark will prevent you from accidentally rotating them out of alignment when you weld.

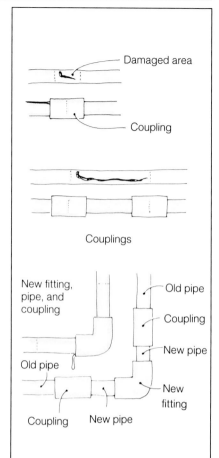

Couplings

New fitting, pipe, and coupling — Old pipe — Coupling — New pipe — Old pipe — New fitting — Coupling — New pipe

Repairing Plastic Pipe

To repair a pinhole or small leak, turn off the water, drain the pipe, and let it dry for a few hours. Force some plastic solvent cement into the hole and wrap the area tightly with plastic electrical tape.

For larger holes or leaky joints, cut out the damaged section and install new pipe and fittings. New pipes usually bend enough to fit.

Joining Plastic Pipe

Plastic pipe is one of the easiest plumbing materials to work with. It is lightweight, cuts easily, and the fittings are quite cheap. You still must work carefully, however, to ensure a good joint. To weld a joint, apply solvent cement to each surface—a heavy coating on the pipe end, and a light coating inside the hub of the fitting. Use the brush supplied with the can. The solvent is not a glue; it actually dissolves the plastic so both pieces fuse together when they join. When both pieces are coated, quickly join them and twist the pieces into alignment. You have only a few seconds to make any adjustments before the joint is hard.

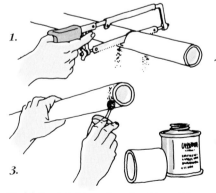

1.

3.

Hold the joint together for 10 to 15 seconds. Wait about 2 minutes before handling it again. Wait until the next day before testing it with water.

Solvent cements are airborne contaminants and combustible liquids.

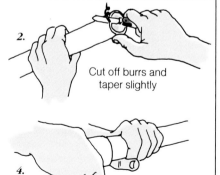

2.

Cut off burrs and taper slightly

4.

Work in a well-ventilated space.

Plastic may be joined to copper, cast-iron, or iron pipe with adapters or no-hub clamps. Use Teflon tape on plastic screw fittings. Do not use pipe dope on plastic pipe.

Copper Pipe

Both water supply systems and DWV systems use copper pipe and fittings extensively. Copper is easy to work with but is fairly expensive, especially for use in DWV systems. Most copper pipe is rigid, but coils of flexible tubing are available for use in slabs or in installations where pipes turn without fittings.

Copper pipe comes in the same sizes as iron pipe—from ¼ to 2½ inches. The outside diameter of the tubing is ⅛ inch larger than the size by which it is classified, and the inside diameter varies with the thickness of the tube wall. Copper tubing for supply lines is available with three wall thicknesses, which are designated by letters—"K" for the thickest wall, "L" for a medium wall, and "M" for the thinnest wall. Unless your local code specifies otherwise, M is adequate for home water supply systems. DWV pipe comes in larger sizes that cannot be used as water supply piping.

Working With Copper Pipe. To measure pipe for cutting, measure the length between the faces of the fittings and add the length of pipe that will go into each fitting. If you are working with flexible tubing, it is a good idea to route the tubing before you cut it. Secure the starting end temporarily and run it exactly where you want it. Mark the cut, then allow a little bit of extra length before cutting. The extra length will allow you to make fine adjustments when you actually make the connection.

A hacksaw cuts copper pipe, but a tubing cutter works faster, more easily, and more accurately, and is inexpensive. The tool has a small cutting wheel that scores the pipe deeper and deeper as you tighten the handle while rotating the cutter around the pipe. Apply the pressure slowly or you will distort the tubing and the tubing will not go inside the fitting. When the pipe is cut, remove any burrs with a reamer or sharp knife. If you must use a hacksaw, it should have 32 teeth per inch. Saw with a miter box for a clean, straight cut.

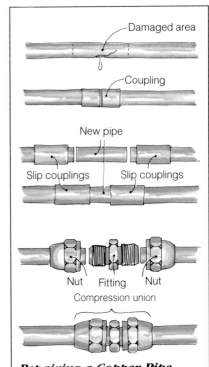

Repairing a Copper Pipe

To fix pinhole leaks, clean the area, apply flux, and solder. For larger leaks, cut out the damaged section.

Joining Copper Pipe

Copper pipe can be soldered or joined with solderless compression fittings. The process of soldering copper joints is called sweating. Clean the pipe and fitting thoroughly. Use emery cloth or steel wool to polish the copper until it is bright. Apply a thin coat of flux to both surfaces and slip the tubing into the fitting. Rotate tubing and fitting to distribute the flux evenly; wipe away any excess.

Set the assembled pipes in a stable position so the joint is accessible and away from combustible material. Do not attempt to hold the pipes while you solder; they heat up quickly. Heat the joint with a propane, MAPP gas, or acetylene torch. Direct the flame to the fitting rather than to the pipe, heating from both sides. When the flux begins to bubble, touch the end of the solder to the joint. Use lead-free solder. When the solder melts, capillary action will suck it into the joint.

If you solder existing pipes that have had water in them, be sure to drain the system thoroughly. Even a few drops of water in the pipe will cause steam that prevents the solder from taking. Leave a nearby faucet open so that steam can escape safely. If water is still a problem, stuff some white bread up into the pipe to dam it while you solder. The bread will dissolve and flush out naturally.

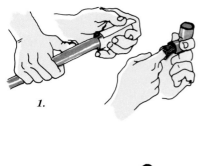

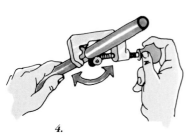

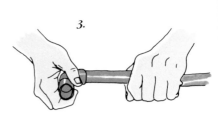

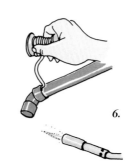

PLANTERS

Raised planters are a marvelous way to display plants, raise them out of the way, and improve drainage where soils are poor. Permanent planters can be made from brick, stone, concrete block, poured concrete, railroad ties, or rough planks. Select a material that blends with your house.

Construct a planter in the same way you would a garden wall; but do not make the sides higher than 3 feet high or you may have to construct a costly retaining wall. If a planter wall is around 18 inches high, cap it with a plank at least 12 inches wide to provide a bench for informal seating.

Bear in mind that there are only a few permanent shrubs that remain less than 24 inches wide for any length of time. Make a planter slightly larger than you think you'll need. Large shrubs and small trees require widths up to 10 feet.

If you use the house wall as one side of a planter, do not place soil directly against the house. Coat the house wall with a bituminous sealer and place crushed rock against it. A better idea is to build a completely separate back wall for the planter. Leave at least 1 inch of space between the siding and planter wall to allow for proper drainage and air circulation. Cover the space with flashing to divert water into the planter. Provide weep holes at the base of the front wall so that excess water drains away from the house.

Building a planter around a tree may look good—until the tree dies. Most trees are highly sensitive to extra soil against the trunk. A safe way to achieve the same effect is to build a planter with good drainage that merely disguises the fact that the bushes are already in containers.

Recommended Cross-References
Brick, Concrete, Garden Walls, Joinery, Wood.

Container gardening allows you to enjoy plants on paving, a rooftop, a balcony, or even a fire escape. The planters can be moved to wherever you need some color.

Tub Planter

This planter is not difficult to make. However, you do need a table saw with blade-angle adjustment and dado attachments.

1. Cut 20 rough redwood staves (15 at a length of 8 inches; 5 at 11 inches) and dado to match the drawing. Cut an 18-inch-diameter base out of ½-inch exterior plywood. Drill drainage holes in it.

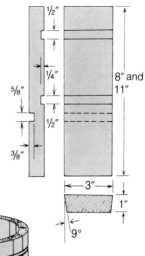

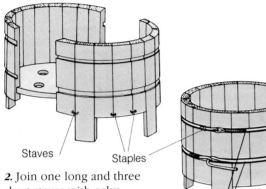

Staves   Staples

2. Join one long and three short staves with galvanized staples. Place the groups around the base and strap with banding material.

Strapping

Banding Materials. Tack metal or plastic strapping to one stave, pull it tight around the others with pliers, and tack it again. Or ring the staves with wire or metal clothesline two or three times and staple the ends. Cinch plastic clothesline tight by making a loop at one end, running the line around the staves, through the loop, and pulling back hard.

Octagonal Planter

Make use of scrap lumber from another project and build a collection of these handsome containers.

1. Cut 105 five-inch lengths of 1 by 2.

2. Cut a 15-inch-diameter base from ½-inch plywood. Drill drainage holes.

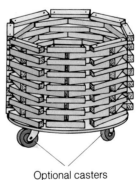

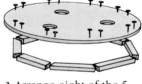

Optional casters

3. Arrange eight of the 5-inch pieces into an octagon. Nail on the base. Turn this over and nail on a second tier of 5-inch pieces. Add successive tiers in the same manner. Create different patterns by varying the relationship of the tiers.

Random   Spiral

Basket

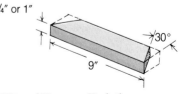

¾" or 1"   30°
9"

Mitered Hexagon Variation.
Cut 98 nine-inch lengths of 1 by 2. Cut 30-degree miters at both ends. Create a hexagon with six of the pieces and nail the base to it. Turn this over and nail on successive tiers.

PLANTERS: continued

Vertical Planter

This wooden version of a strawberry pot is lined with plastic. The plastic holds in the earth and becomes obscured by the plants.

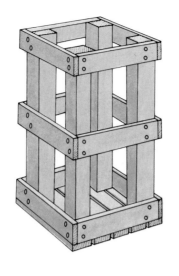

1. Using finished redwood, assemble the sides by nailing three 8-inch-long pieces of 1 by 2 between two 16-inch lengths of 2 by 2. Join the sides with 9½-inch crosspieces.

2. Assemble the base by nailing five 9½-inch 1 by 2s across one end.

3. Line the planter with black plastic film and fill with soil mix. Make slits in the plastic to insert plants.

Pagoda Planter

A table saw with dado attachments is a prerequisite for making this planter—unless you have a lot of patience.

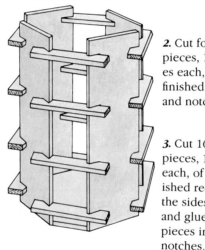

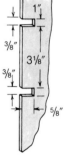

1. The base is an 8¼ by 8¼ piece of ¾-inch finished redwood.

2. Cut four side pieces, 13 by 5 inches each, of ½-inch finished redwood and notch as shown.

3. Cut 16 crosspieces, 1 by 5 inches each, of ⅜-inch finished redwood. Nail the sides to the base and glue the crosspieces into the notches.

4. Line with black plastic film and fill with soil mix. Make slits in the plastic to insert plants.

Display Pedestal

One end is recessed for pots, the other flush for display.

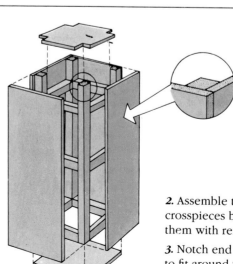

1. Using finished 2 by 2s, cut four 48-inch corner posts and twelve 10-inch crosspieces. Make end and side pieces of sheathing. Cut two ends, each 13¼ inches square; two sides, each 48 by 13¼ inches, and two sides, each 48 by 13¾ inches plus two thicknesses of sheathing for overlap at corners.

2. Assemble two sides by nailing three crosspieces between corner posts. Join them with remaining crosspieces.

3. Notch end piece for the recessed end to fit around the corner posts.

4. Paint or cover with adhesive vinyl.

Tray Garden

Built to the size shown, this planter will hold four or six 1-gallon cans or 6-inch plastic pots.

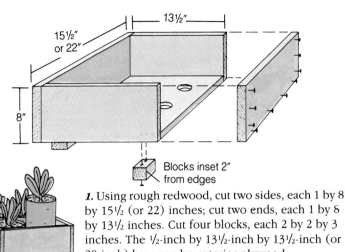

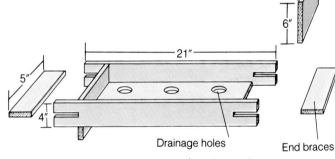

Blocks inset 2" from edges

1. Using rough redwood, cut two sides, each 1 by 8 by 15½ (or 22) inches; cut two ends, each 1 by 8 by 13½ inches. Cut four blocks, each 2 by 2 by 3 inches. The ½-inch by 13½-inch by 13½-inch (or 20-inch) base can be exterior plywood.

2. Drill drainage holes in base. Nail sides, ends, and base. Add block feet.

Narrow Box

Define the edge of a deck or patio with a line of these simple-to-build planters. You can either fill them with earth and plant directly, or use them to hide the containers of plants that are already potted.

Drainage holes

End braces

1. The sides, ends, and braces are ½-inch rough redwood. Two sides are 4 by 21; two ends are 4 by

6; two end braces are 2 by 5. The ½-inch by 4-inch by 16-inch base is exterior plywood.

2. Drill drainage holes. Assemble side, ends, and base with nails. Cut ½-inch by 2-inch notches in sides to accept end braces. Glue in end braces.

Mitered Box

Mitered corners give a more tailored look than the box-end planters.

45° miter

Drainage holes

Blocks inset 2" from edges

1. From finished redwood, cut two sides, each 2 by 6 by 18 inches, and four blocks, each 2 by 2 by 3 inches. Cut the 15-inch square base from exterior plywood. Miter all ends.

2. Drill drainage holes. Nail sides to base. Inset blocks 2 inches from edges.

PLUMBING

Even if you don't plan to do the work yourself, it is a good idea to have a working knowledge of the plumbing system in a home and the strict code requirements that apply. Most plumbing work relies on common sense, and simple repairs have probably introduced you to the concepts that are *fundamental to the system as a whole. A home plumbing system has four components: the building sewer, the drain-waste-vent system (DWV), the water supply system, and the fixtures. Different functions, different rules, and different plumbing techniques characterize each component.*

Recommended Cross-References
Bathroom Layout, Bathtubs, Dishwashers, Faucets & Valves, Framing, Pipe, Pumps, Showers, Sinks & Garbage Disposers, Toilets, Washbasins, Washers & Dryers, Water Heaters.

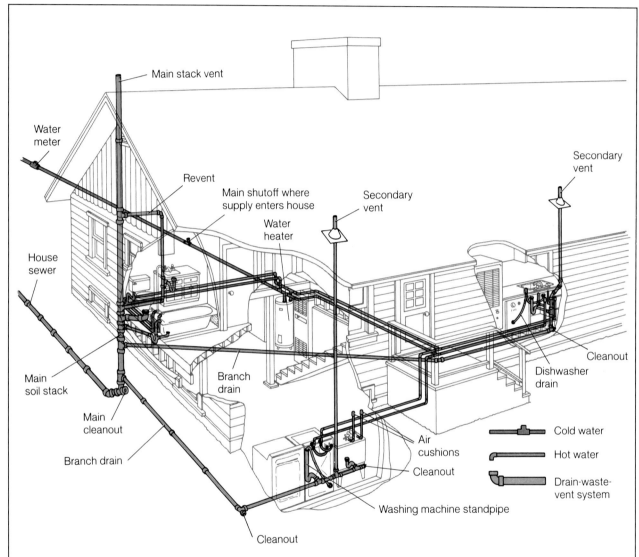

Main Drain

The House Sewer. All the drains in the house connect to the main drain, which is called the house sewer once it is outside the foundation. The main drain connects to a septic tank or to a public sewer stub at the property line. Most local codes specify the size of the connecting pipe. The pipe size for a single-family dwelling is usually 4 inches ID (inside diameter). Codes also specify the type of pipe—usually vitrified clay, cast iron, plastic, or bituminized fiber. Clay pipe must join with nohub bands or by compression. Mortar joints, which were common in

older homes, no longer meet code specifications. The house sewer must be at least 10 feet away from the water supply pipe or 12 inches below it if the two are in the same trench. The depth of the trench depends on the climate and the location of the septic tank inlet or public sewer stub. The sewer pipe must slope ¼ inch per foot.

The DWV System. Sometimes called the sanitary system, the DWV system includes all the drains and waste pipes in and under the house as well as the vents. The DWV system is completely independent of the water

supply system and contractors usually install it first. The DWV system is not pressurized; water and waste move because of gravity. For this reason the DWV system requires careful installation. "Upstream" and "downstream" are important locations; keep your position in mind.

The regulations and standards for the DWV system are strict. Precise local codes protect public health. All the requirements concerning pipe size, fitting orientation, trap location, slope, and fixture height are strategies that keep contaminants—liquid, solid, or gas—out of the house.

Water Supply System

The water supply system brings cold water to the house, heats some of it, and distributes the water to various fixtures. The supply system is pressurized so pipes can run directly and do not have to slope or have vents. Normal "street pressure" is 40 to 55 psi (pounds per square inch), but may range as low as 30 psi or as high as 80 psi. If the street pressure is above normal, install a pressure reducer near the main valve. The main shutoff valve should be near the foundation line. Supply systems in cold climates should include a bleeder valve that allows the homeowner to drain the whole system.

The size of most water pipes is ½ inch or ¾ inch. You will find a larger main if street pressure is lower than normal or if the house is taller than two stories. Use a ¾-inch line to feed the water heater and for all runs that feed more than one fixture. If a water softener is included in the system, the pipes should be one size larger than normal to make up for the drop in pressure it causes. If you install a water softener in an existing system, you may be required by the local building code to run a bypass around it to maintain pressure.

All fixtures except dishwashers and toilets have both hot- and cold-water supply pipes. (In humid areas the toilet may have both to prevent condensation.) Cold water is on the right and hot water is on the left. The pipes stub out and terminate at

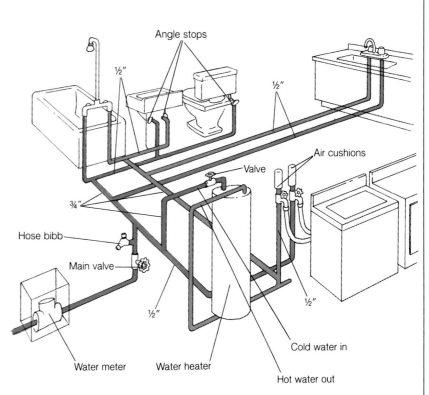

valves, called stops, which are located under the fixture.

Sometimes pipes bang and chatter when you turn off a faucet; the noise is called water hammer. To prevent it, many codes require air chambers. Air chambers are short, capped-off pipes above the supply stub tees of a fixture. They are usually 12 inches long and one size larger than the supply pipes. The chambers trap air and cushion the shock of water hammer. Dishwashers and washing machines need them because they use electric valves that snap shut. In addition, install air chambers for the kitchen sink and for the highest fixture in the bathroom. Strapping the pipes and nailing straps to the joists will also prevent water hammer.

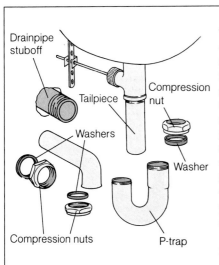

Traps

The part the P-trap plays in saving contact lenses and wedding rings makes it a familiar fixture. The P-trap is an ingenious device that also plays a vital role in the DWV system. The under-the-sink P-trap is a valve with no moving parts. Water and waste flow through it easily, but gases from the sewer cannot pass because the water that is left in it after each use forms an airtight seal. If this water were siphoned out, which may happen with improper installation, sewer gases could enter the house.

Every fixture must have a trap. Some are visible (sink traps), while others are under the floor (bathtub and shower traps), in the wall (washing machine traps), or even in the fixture itself (toilet traps). Codes specify the maximum vertical distance between the fixture outlet and trap; the distance is usually 18 to 24 inches (toilets are an exception). The trap size should be the same as the drain size for the fixture. Codes do not allow a fixture to have more than one trap.

P-traps, which have a short horizontal arm at the outlet, are the most common traps. Codes do not allow S-traps and bell traps; nor can traps concealed in a wall or under a floor have cleanout plugs or slip joints.

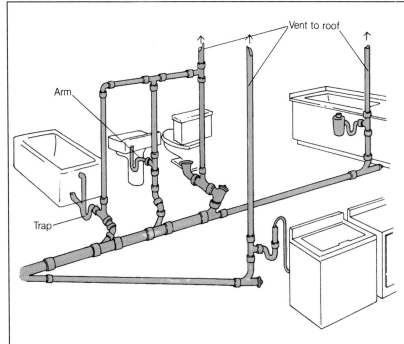

Vent to roof

Arm

Trap

Alternates for Toilet

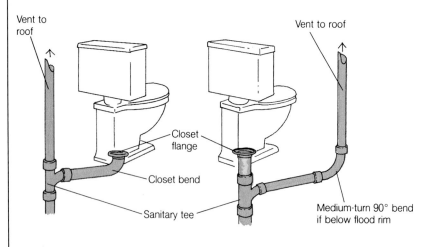

Vent to roof

Vent to roof

Closet flange

Closet bend

Sanitary tee

Medium-turn 90° bend if below flood rim

Fixture Venting

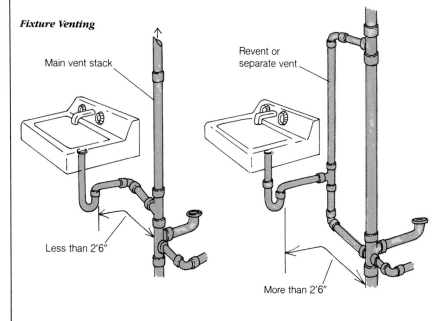

Main vent stack

Revent or separate vent

Less than 2'6"

More than 2'6"

Cleanouts and Vents

Cleanouts. Cleanouts provide access to clogged pipes and should be built at the upstream end of every horizontal run. Codes may contain more specific rules. They may require a cleanout where the house sewer connects to the public sewer, where the main drain joins the house sewer, and after every 50 feet of straight run. In addition, most codes specify a cleanout immediately upstream of any combination of horizontal and vertical changes of direction that exceed 135 degrees. Fixtures and roof vents qualify as cleanouts.

All cleanouts must be accessible. Cleanouts that serve underground drains must extend to an accessible location. There must be at least 18 inches of space behind any cleanout on a 3-inch line; 12 inches on smaller pipe. If a cleanout is under the house or in an enclosed area, it must be within 15 feet of an access door.

Vents. The DWV system includes a number of pipes called vents that do not carry water. Vents prevent vacuum siphoning of the traps. They also release sewer gases away from living areas, and ensure proper flow by equalizing air pressure in the system.

Each trap must have a vent near the outlet before the drainpipe reaches another fixture or a vertical drain. Codes always specify the distance between trap and vent. For a sink, this is usually 3 to 5 feet.

All vents terminate on the roof. The area of all cross sections must equal or exceed that of the main drain. A vent terminal must be at least 3 feet above or 10 feet away from a window, door, or air intake.

In general, a vent pipe extending up from a trap arm cannot change to a horizontal direction within 6 inches of the flood rim of the fixture. Codes specify the distance for some fixtures—42 inches from the floor for sinks and washers, 24 inches for toilets and tubs.

A vent pipe that connects to a horizontal drain from the side must connect above the center of the drain. A vent that serves a vertical drain must extend at a 45-degree angle, not at 90 degrees. Horizontal vent pipes should maintain the same slope as drainpipes (1/4 inch per foot) so that trapped moisture will drain. Many codes do not allow drains to tie into vent lines.

DWV Fittings

Fittings for the DWV system are different from those for water supply pipes, even if they look the same. For one thing, DWV pipes are usually larger and the inside surface of the pipe fits flush with the inside of the fitting. This design ensures the smooth flow of material past the joint. Also, DWV fittings have "direction" built into them; they can be installed only one way so that waste and water flow only one way (as long as there is a proper slope). The angles in DWV fittings are not the same as the nominal angle of the bend. For instance, if you need a 90-degree change in direction, the fitting is actually slightly more or less in order to account for the slope.

Fittings differ in material, pipe size, and shape. In spite of dozens of variations, you need to know only a handful. However, it is still important to use the correct fitting for each situation, because where two or three types may actually fit, only one is the correct type. The ¼ bend (or

90-degree bend) and the sanitary tee (both single and double models) are used where the direction of flow changes from horizontal to vertical. This is the only situation where codes allow these fittings.

When the flow direction changes from vertical to horizontal, you must use fittings that have a gradual bend. For this situation, learn about long sweep ¼ bends, and the combination Y-branch. You will negotiate corners by using ⅙ bends, ⅛ bends, 1/16 bends, or the 45-degree Y. Use fittings with the most gradual bends when a pipe changes direction on the same horizontal plane. The closet bend for toilets is an exception. The closet bend must fit within the floor joists, so codes do not require a sweep, or elongated, fitting.

In all cases the size of the fitting must match the size of the pipes it is connecting. In some fittings all of the outlets are the same size, and in others they vary. You can use reducers to change the size of an outlet to a smaller size, if necessary.

Cross Connections and Backflow

Beware of connections that could allow contamination of the water supply from an external source. Contamination can develop from a submerged hose, from a faucet spout that is lower than the overflow rim of a sink, from a dishwasher drain hose that flows backwards, and from lawn sprinklers. Install air gaps on hose bibbs and sprinkler systems to prevent contamination.

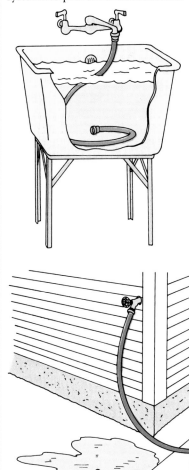

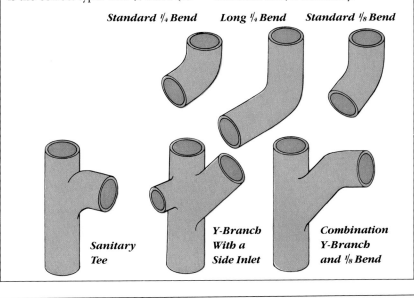

Standard ¼ Bend   *Long ¼ Bend*   *Standard ⅛ Bend*

Sanitary Tee   *Y-Branch With a Side Inlet*   *Combination Y-Branch and ⅛ Bend*

Pipe Sizes

Codes specify the exact size of all drainpipes; the sizes are not minimums. The size of fixture outlet, trap (outlet and trap must be the same size), and vent depends on the amount of water flowing through the fixture. Codes measure the flow in *fixture units*. The chart summarizes typical code requirements. Remember that codes specify pipe sizes in fixture units, not by fixture type.

Typical Code Requirements

Fixture	Fixture Units	Trap Size (in inches)	Vent Size (in inches)
Toilet	4	3	2
Washing machine	3	2	1½
Shower	2	2	1½
Bathtub	2	1½	1¼
Kitchen sink	2	1½	1¼
Washbasin	1	1¼	1¼
Kitchen or laundry	varies	2	1½
Bathroom	varies	3	2
Whole house	varies	3 or 4	total = drain size

Planning an Installation

Before you install new plumbing, plan the location of fixtures carefully. Diagram all the pipe runs and include the sizes of fittings and pipes. Planning ensures that the materials are on hand before you start, makes it easier to get a permit, and expedites your work. If possible, hire a plumber for an hour or so to help you plan the job, calculate runs, and estimate materials. Most plumbers do this quickly, and can visualize the necessary components, as well as note problems and solutions.

Drain and waste pipes are the most critical consideration because they must maintain required slope and connect to existing drains with proper fittings. Position cleanouts upstream of long horizontal runs and make sure the cleanouts are accessible. (Remember that sinks and tubs qualify as cleanouts.) Start planning from the existing main drain and work upstream toward the fixtures.

Vents. Vents are easier to run than drainpipes, but give careful thought to two special cases. Venting a sink that sits in a kitchen island can be difficult. See if the local code permits the use of a venting loop. Venting a basement can also cause headaches if upstairs walls do not align and if first-floor windows limit venting options. Consider these vent arrangements:

• An individual vent serves one fixture. In some cases two adjacent fixtures can use the same vent if their traps are the same height.
• A common vent consists of individual vents tied into one stack of a size appropriate for the total fixture units.
• A combination waste and vent stack is used in a home with more than one story. Downstairs vents are revented into the stack above the highest fixture.
• A wet vent is used when one fixture with a low unit rating vents through the drainpipe of a vented fixture upstream. Some codes do not permit wet vents.

Water Supply Line. Planning the water supply line is not as complicated as planning the DWV lines. Water supply lines follow the general path of the drain lines and easily run around obstacles. Keep hot-water lines short—you will save energy and not have to wait for hot water at the tap. If necessary, insulate hot-water lines.

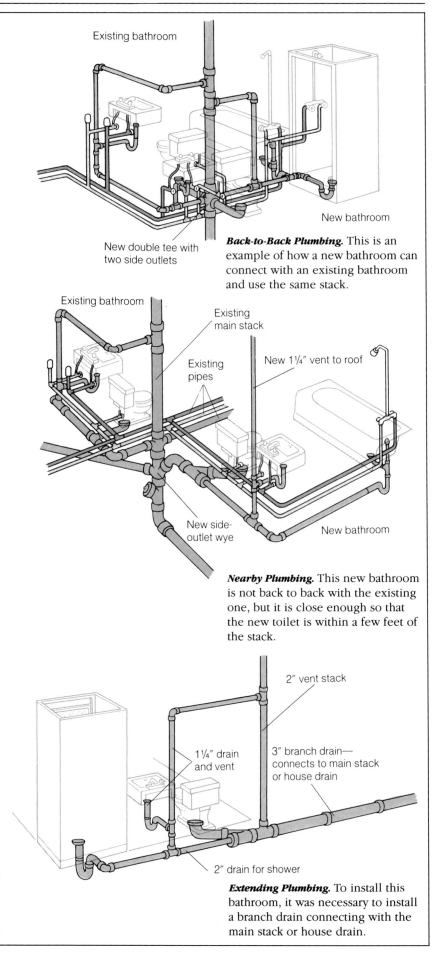

Back-to-Back Plumbing. This is an example of how a new bathroom can connect with an existing bathroom and use the same stack.

Existing bathroom

New double tee with two side outlets

New bathroom

Existing bathroom

Existing main stack

Existing pipes

New 1¼" vent to roof

New side-outlet wye

New bathroom

Nearby Plumbing. This new bathroom is not back to back with the existing one, but it is close enough so that the new toilet is within a few feet of the stack.

2" vent stack

1¼" drain and vent

3" branch drain— connects to main stack or house drain

2" drain for shower

Extending Plumbing. To install this bathroom, it was necessary to install a branch drain connecting with the main stack or house drain.

Fixture Clearances

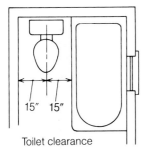

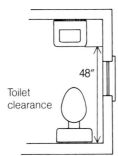

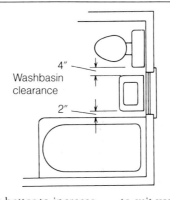

15″ 15″

Toilet clearance

48″

Toilet clearance

Washbasin clearance

4″

2″

24″ to 30″

Shower clearance

Positioning Fixtures

A crawl space or unfinished basement under the floor allows you much more flexibility in placing fixtures and running pipes. Upstairs floors and slabs can limit system design. Position new fixtures close to existing plumbing. Attach a new fixture to the back of a wall that already has plumbing or next to closets or utility chases that have room for new pipes. Conceal horizontal drainpipes between floor joists. If a drainpipe runs perpendicular to the joists, hang it below them rather than weakening the joists by notching. Conceal the pipes in a soffit.

Try to place bathroom fixtures so plumbing runs will be uncomplicated, although an efficient layout for the user is also important. Plastic is cheaper and easier to work with than cast iron or copper. Use plastic DWV pipes if your code allows. If not, place your new fixtures (especially the toilet) near the main stack. The waste pipe should be no longer than 6 feet unless it vents separately. If other fixtures drain into the same waste pipe, the drain must connect upstream from the toilet or the toilet must vent before the connection.

Clearances. When you place bathroom fixtures, consider the clearances between various fixtures and walls. Codes specify minimum dis-

tances; it is always better to increase the distance as much as possible.

Rough-In Dimensions. Know the rough-in dimensions for pipe stubs when you plan your installation. In some cases the dimensions are a matter of convenience or convention. Sink shutoffs, for example, probably won't give you any problem. On the other hand, other dimensions depend on the size of fixture you use. If you buy new fixtures, such as a toilet, shower base, or bathtub, get a manufacturer's specification sheet so you can plan the plumbing accordingly. In the case of floor drains, be sure to check whether dimensions measure from the framing or the finish wall. Use these guidelines, along with any drawings, to determine rough-in dimensions:

Toilet. In most cases the center of the flange should be 12 inches from the finish wall; some toilets require 14 inches. The shutoff valve is always on the left side, low enough to connect the supply tube to the tank.

Washbasin. Drain stubs are usually 15 to 17 inches from the floor. Supply stubs are usually slightly higher, but if they are inside a vanity you might place the stubs lower so they are easier to reach.

Shower. There are standard heights for the faucet and showerhead, but you may want to adjust the fixtures

to suit your personal preference.

Bathtub. Drain location depends on the tub model; most center 14 or 15 inches from the back wall and 8 to 10 inches from the end wall. You will need to cut a larger hole in the floor for access to hook up the tub from below. If you use the tub more often as a shower, you may want to locate the faucet at shower height to avoid having to bend over so far.

Kitchen Sink. The drain stub should center 15 inches from the floor and the supply stubs should center 19 inches from the floor. Installed stubs are usually 8 inches apart, unless the sink faucet is offset considerably or unless the hot-water stub must be close to a dishwasher.

Dishwasher. Most dishwashers connect to the sink fittings, but in some cases you may need to rough in a separate hot-water stub for a shutoff valve. A separate stub comes up through the floor under the dishwasher, either at the front or back. If you have access from below, it is easier to locate the valve under the floor and run $3/8$-inch flexible copper tubing to the dishwasher.

Washing Machine. Pipe usually terminates about 3 feet above the floor. Place the trap between 6 and 18 inches above the floor, and install hose bibs from 33 to 42 inches above the floor, 4 to 12 inches apart.

Rough Plumbing Dimensions

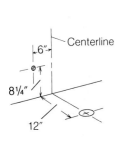

6″

Centerline

8¼″

12″

Toilet

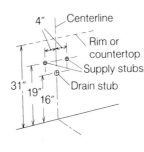

4″

Centerline

Rim or countertop

Supply stubs

Drain stub

31″ 19″ 16″

Washbasin

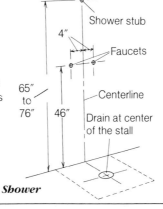

Shower stub

4″

Faucets

Centerline

Drain at center of the stall

65″ to 76″

46″

Shower

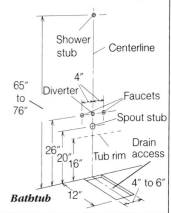

Shower stub

Centerline

4″

Diverter

Faucets

Spout stub

Drain access

Tub rim

65″ to 76″

26″ 20″ 16″

12″

4″ to 6″

Bathtub

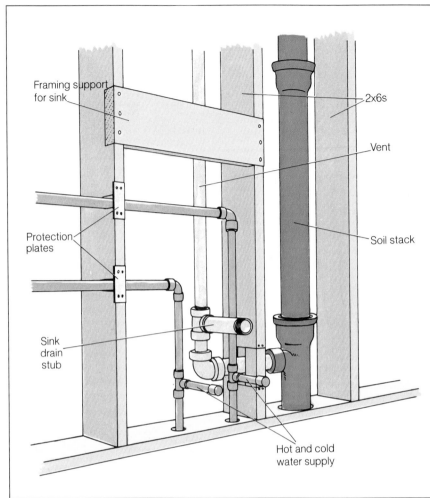

Framing support
for sink

2x6s

Vent

Protection
plates

Soil stack

Sink
drain
stub

Hot and cold
water supply

Installing Rough Plumbing

Obtain a plumbing permit if you add new fixtures or extend pipes. List all fittings and pipe lengths you think you will need and make arrangements with your supplier to return unused materials, then buy extra fittings. (There is nothing worse than running out of materials.)

Always install DWV pipes first, then water supply pipes. Do not cover any pipes until they have been inspected. Stub the pipes up through the floor and cap them off. Extend them after framing and subflooring.

All horizontal runs of the DWV system should slope ¼ inch per foot. Avoid steeper slopes because liquids will outrun the solids and cause them to accumulate. Be careful not to install fittings backwards, especially for vent fittings, and to observe fitting rules for changes of direction.

Hot- and cold-water pipes usually run parallel, 6 to 8 inches apart. Do not let them touch or the hot water will cool drastically. At places where they cross or make close contact, insulate the hot-water pipe or place a piece of rubber between the pipes. Try to engineer runs that are perpendicular or parallel to framing members. Avoid diagonal runs.

Running Pipes Through Framing

Whenever you notch or drill holes in framing, observe these guidelines to prevent weakening the structure. When working under floors, do not notch or drill girders. When working with joists, do not cut notches in the middle portion. Codes allow notches in joists at either end (within one third of the joist length), but drill holes instead. Most building codes permit holes anywhere in a joist, as long as they are not within 2 inches of either edge and their diameter does not exceed one third of the depth of the joist.

Notches in exterior and bearing walls should not exceed 25 percent of stud width. Holes should not exceed 40 percent of stud width. In nonbearing walls the notches may be as wide as 40 percent of the stud width; holes may be as wide as 60 percent of the stud width. If the studs are 2 by 4s, some pipes (stack, for example) are too large. To widen a plumbing wall, use 2 by 6 studs or use 2 by 8 plates with a row of 2 by 4 studs turned sideways along each edge. The cavity that you create in the middle of the wall will accommodate the pipes.

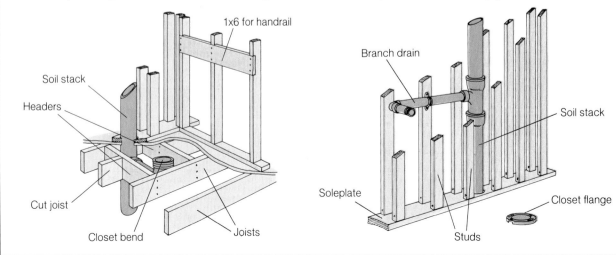

1x6 for handrail

Soil stack

Headers

Cut joist

Closet bend

Joists

Branch drain

Soil stack

Soleplate

Studs

Closet flange

Completing Runs

When you install DWV pipes, start from the main stack or drain and work upstream toward the fixtures. The whole process will go much more smoothly if you draw a schematic first, including each fitting and the direction of all runs. As you work, check that the slope is a consistent $1/4$ inch per foot. Make up assemblies of two or three fittings and install them as a unit, especially in areas where several assemblies cluster. As you get closer to each fixture, set the fixture trap or stub in place and begin to work downstream from it toward the drain. The art of plumbing—and it is an art—is to lay pipes from both ends of the run so they line up perfectly when you join them. Making the final connection at an intersection is easier than making the connection in the middle of a run. Take your time and do a dry layout of pieces before gluing, soldering, or clamping them.

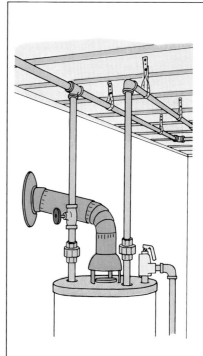

Main Drain and Sewer Connections

If you tie a new drain line into an existing cleanout, attach a new Y fitting to maintain a cleanout at that location. Stuff a rag inside the new Y fitting to block sewer gases while you finish the rest of the plumbing. Retrieve the rag through the cleanout hole after you finish roughing-in the DWV pipes.

If you run a new house sewer, you will have to dig a trench between the foundation and the stub of the public sewer. The pipe must be under at least 12 inches of soil, but should not drop below the sewer stub. Pipes parallel to the foundation should not lie within 2 feet of the building. If they lie deeper than the foundation, they must not be within a 45-degree arc of the corner of the footing. Don't fill the trench until the inspector has approved the piping.

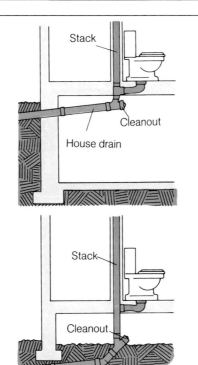

Stack

Cleanout

House drain

Stack

Cleanout

House drain

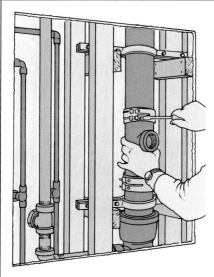

Tying Into a Soil Stack

If you cannot tie into an existing drain or cleanout in the main stack, you will have to install a suitable fitting. Before cutting the pipe, attach brackets above and below the fitting. Cut the soil stack and remove the unwanted section. If the pipe is cast iron, clamp a no-hub cast-iron fitting into place. The brackets hold the stack in place. Similar fittings and bands are available to make it possible to attach plastic to cast iron or to attach plastic to plastic.

Tapping Supply Lines

Water lines are much easier to tap and extend than DWV pipes. You can run supply lines through walls, around corners, past obstacles, and just about anywhere. Joining pipes of different metals is problematic, however. Galvanic action transfers molecules from one metal to the other, leading to corrosion and clogging. The effect is increased in most underground locations. This has occasionally led to breaks in lines in a year or less.

The traditional solution is to insert a dielectric coupling between the copper and galvanized steel pipe. This technique has had mixed results, sometimes causing a mineral buildup at the union.

The condition varies in different localities. Check your local building code and follow its recommendations.

Caution. If you come upon an electrical ground wire clamped to a pipe that must move, treat it as a live wire until you clamp it safely to another well-grounded pipe. The wire is probably inert, but it would carry a full charge if the electrical system would suddenly short-circuit. Handle the wire with rubber insulated tools and rubber gloves.

No matter the size of your garden, a pond adds immensely to the appeal. Water has a soothing effect, especially water that gently splashes from a fountain or cascades in a small waterfall. Neither of these effects is hard to achieve. With a helper and some careful planning you can create a pond in one afternoon that should last for several years. Build a permanent pool using concrete, tile, or brick, and complete it with lighting and a circulating system. Whichever you build, the pond will only be as effective as the plants, setting, and amenities that enhance it.

Recommended Cross-References
Brick, Concrete, Garden Walls, Lighting: Outdoor, Patios, Pipe, Plumbing.

If well placed and well landscaped, even a small pond can add a delightful dimension to a stroll along a garden path.

Quick Ponds
Make an attractive pond quickly by digging a shallow hole and lining it with a container that will hold water and not disintegrate. Start with a thick layer of newspaper to protect the plastic liner from punctures. The newspaper will form a clay-like layer as it decomposes and can be easily disposed of if you decide to remove the pond. Cover the newspaper with plastic. Four-mil black polyethylene sheeting serves as an effective liner. Double the plastic two or three times in case the first layer is punctured. A more durable liner is an elastomeric membrane of the type used beneath mortar bed shower pans. Seams in this material are joined with easy-to-make solvent welds. Cut it to fit the hole, allowing a few extra inches on all sides. Set the liner in the hole, lapping the edges over the rim. Place rocks, bricks, or gravel around the edge to hold the plastic in place. Fill the pond, add aquatic plants that can grow in submerged containers, then landscape.

Any serviceable container that will look attractive can serve as a liner. In addition, garden centers often sell pool liners. If you use a metal container, coat the outside with an asphalt sealer and use epoxy paint to change the color of the inside. Plug the drain hole with a rubber stopper.

Concrete Ponds
Build a permanent pond with concrete. It can be flush with the ground or have walls that rise a few inches above a patio. The easiest shape is a free-form bowl where the edges are flush with the ground; you will not have to build forms for the concrete. Raised edges, vertical sides, and square corners require forms.

To cast a pond without forms, excavate a hole of any shape to the depth of the pond plus 6 inches. The ground around the rim should be level. Excavate a slight depression at one end to serve as a spillway when the pond is full. An alternative overflow is a length of plastic pipe embedded in the concrete near the rim of the pond. If you want the outside edge of the pond to be straight and clean, make a form from bender board. Wrap it around the edge of the hole and stake it so the top is level and flush with the finished grade. Backfill against the concrete after you remove the form.

For best results, place steel reinforcing wire or curved rebar in the bottom of the hole, 3 inches off the dirt. Then mix the concrete and shovel it in. The mix should be stiff so the concrete will stay in place. Mix enough to do the entire pond in one pour. Consolidate it as you fill, but not to the extent that it all slumps to the bottom of the bowl. The concrete should be about 6 inches thick. Screed it with a wood float to the shape you want, then finish it. Make the rim more attractive by embedding bricks or stones in the wet concrete. In cold weather areas, do not install the stones so they hang over the edge. Otherwise the frozen pond water might dislodge the stones.

You may want to install a drain at the bottom of larger pools. Connect 2-inch-diameter plastic pipe and a standard shower drain to a dry well or other low spot. Install a gate valve close to the pond. If you install a fountain or waterfall, either embed the inlet pipe in the concrete or run plastic tubing over the rim of the pond.

Planning
Your pond does not have to be deep or large. A dark color such as navy blue, deep green, or black can make it appear deeper. The requirements of the fish or plants that you plan to include may determine the depth of the pond. Twelve inches is usually sufficient, but check with your nursery. Create depressions in the bottom of the pond for plants that require more depth. A shallow pool, 4 to 12 inches deep, needs little water, provides calm reflection, and is reasonably safe if small children are around (although you cannot assume that any pond is absolutely safe).

If your winters are severe, slope the sides of the pond up toward the edge so ice will have room to expand harmlessly. Expanding ice could shove against and damage straight sides. A pond with sides that slope like a saucer also has the advantage of being easier to build.

The water source needn't be anything more than an ordinary garden hose. With plastic pipe, however, it is an easy project to run an underground line to the pond. Terminate the pipe with a hose bibb staked beside the pond or close enough for easy access. If you hook up any water lines for your pond, even a hose attachment at the bibb, install a vacuum breaker at the connection. This breaker will prevent the water from siphoning back into your plumbing system should the pressure in the water pipes suddenly drop.

A waterfall or fountain is easy to incorporate. These effects do not need a continuous stream of water from your plumbing, only a pump that circulates the pond water. Hide the pump outside the pond, or submerge it and conceal it with rocks. The falling water will aerate the pond and prevent stagnation, as well as provide a pleasant background sound for your garden.

Place the pond wherever you need a focal point, accent, or cooling feature. It can be rustic and informal, surrounded by rocks, plants, or lawn, or it can be part of a formal patio with paving to the edge. Choose shapes that reflect forms already in the landscape. Get help for complex ponds and a permit for ones deeper than 24 inches.

POOLS

Installation of a new in-ground swimming pool is best left to professionals. Maintenance, on the other hand, is an ongoing project that requires diligence to preserve your investment and ensure pleasurable use.

Whether your pool is plaster-coated concrete, fiberglass, or vinyl-lined, the same procedures keep the water clean and maintain the systems.

Recommended Cross-References
Decks, Hot Tubs & Spas, Lighting: Outdoor, Patios.

Pool Covers
The primary source of heat loss in a swimming pool is evaporation. A swimming pool cover reduces most of the evaporation, traps the heat, and keeps debris out of the water. Of the wide variety of pool covers available, a simple hand-winch mechanism is easy to install and operate. Electrically operated units are more expensive to install but even simpler to use. Whatever your choice, a pool cover is a very worthwhile investment.

Whether free-form with natural boulders (below) or rectangular, surrounded by brick (opposite), a pool demands regular attention to keep it attractive to swim in.

Maintenance
During the Swimming Season. Some pool companies offer year-round maintenance at a set fee. Because pool care can be time-consuming—8 to 10 hours a week at the height of the season—professional maintenance may be worth the cost.

Daily Maintenance Program.
• Skim leaves and debris from the surface of the water and the bottom of the pool.
• Clean out strainer basket.
• Check filter pressure. Clean filter if the water is not clear.

Weekly Maintenance Program.
• Test the water with a water-test kit and add recommended chemicals.
• Brush all tile and walls with a nylon brush. Use a stainless steel brush to loosen algae on concrete walls.
• Check walls or vinyl liner for cracks or tears, and repair. Use an underwater patching compound on concrete, a fiberglass repair kit on fiberglass, and a vinyl repair kit on a vinyl liner.
• Hose off the deck, aiming the water away from the pool.

During Winter. Where the winter is mild, continue your summer maintenance program on a reduced schedule, adding extra chlorine to help keep the water clear. Test the water and clean out debris once a month. Run the filter pump about half as often as during the swimming season. A pool cover will greatly reduce the amount of maintenance your pool will require during the winter months.

Prepare a pool for a severe winter by following these steps:
• Run the filter for several hours to remove dirt and debris. Vacuum the pool thoroughly.
• Clean the filter according to manufacturer's instructions. Remove the cartridge from a cartridge filter and store it in a warm, dry place.
• Lower the water level until you can reach the outlets. Empty supply pipes, return pipes, and water lines of as much water as possible. Plug the outlets with adjustable rubber plugs. Drain water from the heater, filter, and pump.
• Turn off all gas and electricity to the system.

Reopening the Pool in Spring. Have a professional start your heater and pump and treat the water at the beginning of the season. Prepare for the service visit by hosing off the deck and cover, and removing the plugs from the outlets.

PUMPS

Pumps play an important role throughout the house. You find small pumps for dishwashers and washing machines, circulating pumps for garden pools, sump pumps for keeping a basement dry, and a well pump for providing water for the entire home. One out of five American homes depends on a well for water. Local codes usually require that a licensed professional install this kind of supply system. You may be able to maintain, repair, or replace an existing pump, however. Many homeowners can install their own sump pumps. Other pumps, such as pumps for decorative fountains and pools, simply plug into an outlet.

Recommended Cross-References

Hot Tubs & Spas, Pipe, Plumbing, Ponds, Pools.

Well Pumps

Most residential wells are drilled very deep and require a pump to bring up the water. The pump for a domestic water supply may be at the well head, in the house, in a special well enclosure, or submerged in the well. The underground pipe from the well is called a suction line, and must be at least 1 inch in diameter and slope slightly back toward the well.

The jet and the submersible are the most common types of pumps. A jet pump is located in the house or at the well head. It works by centrifugal action and is good for well depths up to 100 feet or so. The submersible pump can be used in much deeper wells—as deep as 450 feet or more. It requires a 4-inch well casing and must be checked and maintained periodically. It usually has a chain or rope attached to enable you to pull the pump to the surface.

The pump does not operate all the time. Instead, it pumps water into a pressurized storage tank, which stores water and delivers it as needed. As the pump forces water into the tank, the water compresses the air in the tank. When a faucet is on, the compressed air forces water into the house plumbing. Therefore, the pump does not have to operate constantly. Most tanks can discharge about 9 gallons before the pump turns on again.

Diagnosing Pump Problems

There are some problems, such as those listed below, that you can diagnose yourself, even if you are not able to fix them. If you have any doubt about your diagnosis, consult a professional.

Pump Won't Start. Check the circuit breaker. If it is on, check all wires for loose connections; shut off the breaker before you tighten them. If the pump still won't run, or if the breaker trips when the pump starts, call an electrician.

Pump Won't Quit. Look for the pressure switch and change the setting. If the pump doesn't respond, shut off the circuit breaker; then take the switch apart to see if any contact points are stuck. If the points aren't stuck, the water level may be too low. If the pump is submersible, try lowering it deeper into the well, but make sure it doesn't hit sand.

Pump Runs Too Often. The pressure tank may leak. Spread soapy water over the surface and look for bubbles. If there are none, check the setting and contact points on the pressure switch. Then check the air-control valve and check for leaks in the house plumbing, particularly a running toilet. Finally, switch off the breaker; then attach a pressure gauge to any fitting on the well side of the pump. Attach a bicycle pump to the nozzle of the gauge and pump up the pressure to 40 or 50 psi. If the gauge does not hold the pressure for 15 minutes, there is a leak in the suction line. Examine all visible piping and repair any leaks. If necessary, dig up the line all the way to the well to fix or replace it.

Sewage Ejector

A sewage ejector makes it possible to install toilets and other plumbing below the level of the house sewer or main drain. In some cases it serves an entire house that is downslope from the public sewer. The unit is costly but worthwhile if it enables you to add living space.

A sewage ejector consists of a tank with a pump inside. It has an inlet that receives waste from a standard waste pipe. The ejector pumps the waste up as many as 10 feet into the main drain or up into a branch line that leads to the public sewer.

The tank is about 30 inches high and 20 inches in diameter. The 4-inch inlet pipe enters the side of the tank about 10 inches from the bottom, and a 4-inch discharge pipe comes out the top to connect with the sewer line overhead. Because the ejector tank inlet must be below the toilet discharge, there is no way of installing one of these units for a basement toilet without excavating below the basement floor.

Some codes permit up-flush toilets and up-flush sinks that operate as sewage ejectors. The pump in an up-flush fixture serves only that fixture.

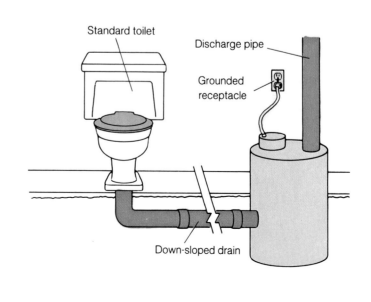

Standard toilet

Discharge pipe

Grounded receptacle

Down-sloped drain

Sump Pumps

Control groundwater, rainwater, or gray water—water from a washing machine, bathroom sink, shower, or bathtub—with a sump pump. The waste water runs into a concrete or plastic-lined sump pit. The pump starts automatically when water reaches a certain level in the pit. In some cases, when the water is uncontaminated underground seepage, you may terminate the outlet pipe in a dry well or in a street gutter.

If seepage or rainwater flood the basement, the sump pit should be at the lowest point of the floor. Place a sump pit for a sink or washer anywhere that is convenient for a drainpipe. The size and kind of pump you choose will determine the size of the pit. There are two kinds of sump pumps: the pedestal pump and the submersible pump.

Pedestal Sump Pump. The oldest, most common, and least expensive sump pump is the upright type that consists of an electric motor on top of a pedestal. The base of the pedestal contains the pump and discharge pipe and rests on the bottom of the pit. A ball float in the pit connects to the motor switch by a rod. When the water in the pit reaches a predetermined level, the float flips on the switch. When the pump lowers the water level, the ball descends and turns off the switch. The water level that stops the pump is usually about 6 inches; the pump can be damaged if it empties the pit and runs dry. The pit for an upright sump pump should be 12 to 24 inches deep and 12 inches or more across. It may be either round or square.

Submersible Sump Pump. The submersible pump is more expensive but generally more satisfactory than the upright type. Flooding cannot damage the submersible pump and it requires less maintenance. The submersible pump can run with a lower water level than the upright pump. Two kinds of switch mechanisms are available. One works with a float and is similar to the switch in an upright pump. Float switches may jam if dirt or debris accumulates in the sump pit. The more desirable type of switch is activated by water pressure. The amount of pressure that cues the switch is adjustable. The sump pit for a submersible pump should be 12 to 15 inches deep.

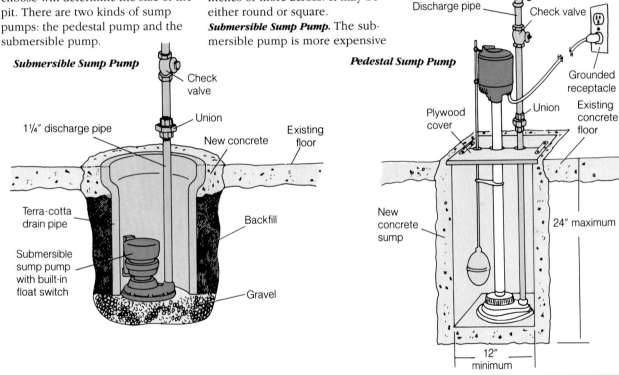

Submersible Sump Pump

Check valve
Union
1¼" discharge pipe
New concrete
Existing floor
Terra-cotta drain pipe
Backfill
Submersible sump pump with built-in float switch
Gravel

Pedestal Sump Pump

Discharge pipe
Check valve
Grounded receptacle
Plywood cover
Union
Existing concrete floor
New concrete sump
24" maximum
12" minimum

Installing a Sump Pump

First prepare the pit, which should have a level concrete bottom. The sides may be of concrete or terracotta pipe 12 inches or more in diameter. Plastic liners are available, and, if your code allows it, you can even use a 5-gallon plastic pail.

Break a hole in the basement floor and dig a hole a little wider and 3 or 4 inches deeper than the pit will be. Put 3 or 4 inches of gravel in the bottom and set a wooden form, a pipe section, or a plastic pan into the hole. Pour concrete in the bottom of the hole and around the form.

Smooth and level the bottom, and smooth the concrete around the edge so it is flush with the floor.

When the concrete has set, position the pump and make the necessary connections to the sewer or seepage pit. Install a check valve so water will not flow back toward the pump. Install a union below the valve so you can disconnect the pump easily. The pump should have its own grounded electrical outlet, with no other outlets or appliances on the same circuit.

Make a cover for the sump pit from ¾-inch exterior grade plywood. Drill three holes in the cover for an upright pump, one for the pedestal, one for the float rod, and one for the discharge pipe. Submersible-pump covers need only a hole for the discharge pipe. Saw the cover in half, cutting through the middle of the hole or holes. Fit the halves around the projecting pieces. Hold the cover together with straps of aluminum or wood held with screws.

Maintenance. A sump pump may sit idle for months and then suddenly be needed. Therefore, check it every three months. Once a year, remove it, clean it, and clean out the sump.

RAILINGS

The railing is a finishing touch to most deck and outdoor stair projects. But you have to consider safety requirements as well as the visual impact.

Code Requirements

Most codes specify a railing for any deck over a certain height—usually 30 inches but sometimes 18 inches—and for any stairway that includes four risers (some codes specify two risers). Codes require railings on both sides of open stairways, and sometimes require a center railing if the stairway is wider than 4 feet.

The required height for deck railings is usually 36 inches, although codes vary. Stair railings must be from 30 to 34 inches high, as measured from each tread nosing. A screening requirement pertains to decks and high stairways. Screening refers to the distance between railing members. To prevent children from falling between the railing members, codes usually require that they be no more than 6 to 9 inches apart. Codes also specify that a railing be strong enough to withstand 15 pounds of horizontal pressure per lineal foot. Codes may also contain specifications on finishing the ends of handrails.

Design Criteria

Your first consideration should be the aesthetic character of the house and landscape. Is it formal? Does it accentuate horizontal or vertical lines? Are angles prominent? Such questions will help you determine which railing designs fit better than others.

While considering aesthetics, be aware of functional requirements. Is wind a factor? Will you want to set food and drinks on top of the railing? Do you need privacy? Will low flower pots or other small objects be placed next to the railing—objects that could slide under the bottom rail and fall?

By the time you have answered these questions, the railing will have designed itself. Your final task is to evaluate pictures and actual railings for ideas to satisfy your needs.

Recommended Cross-References
Benches, Decks, Fastening Hardware, Fences, Footings, Framing, Gates, Joinery, Lighting: Outdoor, Steps.

As long as they meet code and safety requirements, railings can be as ingenious and varied as your imagination allows. They should suit the architecture of your home. the landscaping of your yard, and be placed wherever the need exists and the look demands.

Railings for Decks

Posts. Baluster posts may be extensions of the deck posts. Or build a separate post by bolting 4 by 4s to the rim joists with two ⅜-inch carriage bolts per post. For a more finished appearance, notch the bottoms so they lap over the deck framing.

Handrails. Cut 2 by 6 handrails to length, using the longest lengths possible. Make sure that any necessary joints in the handrail will occur above a post. Cut joints at a bevel so they overlap slightly. Miter the corners. Rout a groove that measures ⅜ inch by 1½ inches on the underside, then nail the rail to the posts with 12d HDG casing nails.

Middle Rails. Cut the middle rails to fit between posts, but do not attach them yet. Use a bevel gauge to mark cutting angle for a stairway.

Assembling. Assemble baluster sections. Use the middle rail and a length of ⅜-inch lath for the bottom and top members, respectively, and 2 by 2s for balusters. The lath should be long enough to overlap both of the posts. Space the balusters evenly.

Installing. Fit the lath of each baluster section into the handrail groove. Toenail the middle rail to the posts.

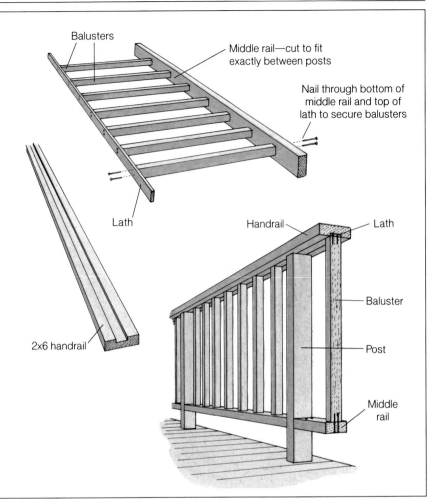

Balusters

Middle rail—cut to fit exactly between posts

Nail through bottom of middle rail and top of lath to secure balusters

Lath

2x6 handrail

Handrail

Lath

Baluster

Post

Middle rail

Railings for Steps

Railings for low steps can be a simple, open design or match other more solid railings. The posts are set directly in the ground like fence posts. Wood should be pressure-treated 4 by 4s suitable for ground contact. Post anchors set into concrete footings avoid direct ground contact. Bolt the posts to the anchors after the concrete sets.

To mark the angle that you need to cut, clamp a board across the sides of the post and adjust the level until the board is at a uniform height above all tread nosings. Allow 1½ inches for the cap rail. Mark, then cut the posts. Cut a 2 by 4 or 2 by 6 cap rail. Toenail it through each post with 12d HDG casing nails.

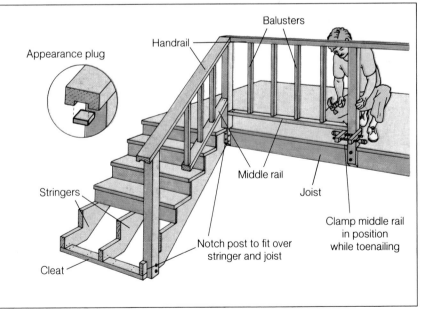

Appearance plug

Handrail

Balusters

Middle rail

Joist

Stringers

Cleat

Notch post to fit over stringer and joist

Clamp middle rail in position while toenailing

RANGES, OVENS & COOKTOPS

From a cast-iron pot on the hearth to the latest microwave unit, the variety of cooking options seems endless. Stoves, ranges, ovens, cooktops—where to begin?

Begin with a basic question: gas or electric? Assuming that both types of hookups are available, your choice is largely a matter of preference. Gas appliances are responsive; cooks can fine-tune the temperature. Traditionally, cooks prefer gas appliances as demonstrated by their wide use in commercial kitchens. Electric ranges and cooktops now heat quickly, however. A cook can set and reset a temperature by pushing a button. In terms of energy efficiency, gas is slightly superior although cooking preference is certainly a more impor-

tant consideration. Gas does have a significant drawback in terms of indoor air pollution. Gas units should always have a venting arrangement, either a range hood or internal downdrafting unit. The cost of gas and electric units is comparable. The final decision may boil down to choosing the type of hookup that is already in your kitchen.

With one decision behind you, ask yourself another question: Should you buy a range or separate cooktop and oven units? The higher cost of a separate oven and cooktop may determine your decision. Convenience is another consideration. A built-in oven is at eye level (only a few freestanding ranges have overhead ovens). A separate cooktop presents the

advantage of convenient storage underneath, and you do not have to stand in front of a hot oven to cook. If your work triangle is cramped, a separate cooktop may provide more storage space; move the oven, an appliance that you use less often, somewhere else. A slide-in range is prone to collect grease and debris in the crack between the counter and stovetop, but this type of unit does have a distinct advantage: You can take it with you when you move.

Recommended Cross-References
Cabinets, Countertops, Hoods & Vents, Kitchen Layout, Receptacles, Wiring.

Gas Slide-In Ranges

Get the installation specifications for your new range and make sure the gas cock will fall in the recess in the back panel. The range will be flush against the back wall only if the two features align. To install the range, simply connect one end of a length of flexible gas tubing to the gas cock and the other end to the range stub. Slide the range into position. Most ranges also have a 120-volt electric cord for the clock, lights, and pilotless ignition, so be sure there is an outlet handy.

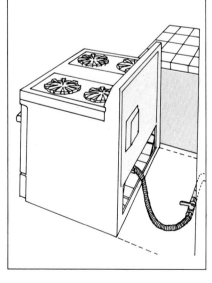

Electric Slide-In Ranges

The advantage of a slide-in range is the ease with which it can be installed. You merely strip off the packing carton and slide it into place. Take care not to scratch your floor when you position the range—slide it on a piece of the cardboard carton.

A freestanding electric range has its own pigtail cord for plugging into a separate 220-volt circuit.

To install this type of range, all you have to do is to plug in the unit and slide it into place.

Hood

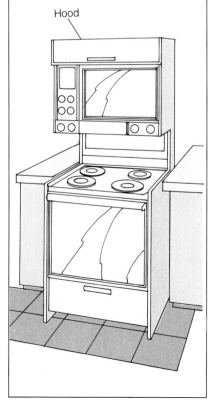

Installing a Drop-In Range

Drop-in ranges require a low base cabinet with a cutout in the front. The counter must also have a cutout for the range and be in position. Some drop-in ranges have a flange around the cooking surface that rests on the counter and supports the weight of the range. This type of unit requires no additional anchors to hold it. Other ranges have flush edges at the top; screws hold them in place, either in the base or along the sides.

To install either type of drop-in range, connect the gas or electric line first. Rest the range on the cabinet lip so you have room to reach behind and make the connections. Use flexible tubing for gas. A gas range also needs a 120-volt receptacle for the lights, timer, and pilotless ignition.

An electric range has a heavy-duty cord that fits into the 240-volt outlet. Some ranges have a flexible armored cable instead of a plug.

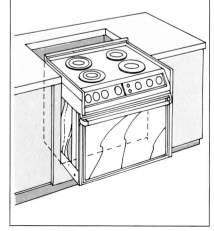

Fastening Methods for Drop-In Ranges

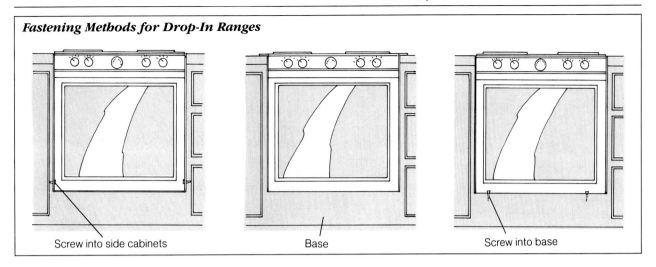

Screw into side cabinets

Base

Screw into base

Installing a Built-In Oven

If you do a lot of baking, have a separate baking oven; install a double oven or two separate ovens. You also have the options of radiant, microwave, and convection cooking. Choose an oven that combines two or even all three of the modes, or buy separate units.

To install a built-in oven, you need a cabinet unit with cutouts and shelves of the right size. Most ready-made cabinet suppliers stock such cabinets. Installation is simple; just slide the oven into the opening. Some ovens require screws to hold them in place. If there is a storage space below, you can connect the gas or electricity when the oven is in place.

Oven models differ, so be sure that the specifications you have for roughing in gas and electric lines refer to the oven you plan to install.

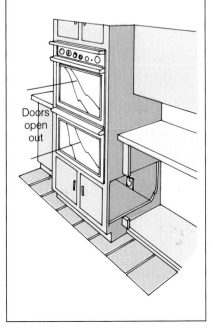

Doors open out

Installing a Cooktop

Cooktops use either electricity or gas. As a result, you could choose an electric oven and a gas cooktop. Most cooktops simply drop into a cutout in the counter and can have a regular base cabinet located beneath them. Cooks often use commercial gas cooktops in their homes. Commercial cooktops have a pedestal base and need to sit on a dropped section of counter so the

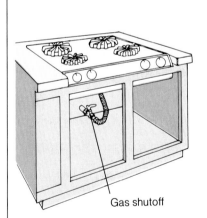

Gas shutoff

cooking surface is flush with the rest of the counter. This type of installation requires custom cabinetry and tile or other nonflammable surfacing material around the recessed section of countertop as well as on the wall behind the cooktop. Commercial cooktops are available as 2-burner, 4-burner, and 6-burner units; a small cooktop is a useful extra, especially when it is set into an island away from the main cooking area.

Electrical plug

Downventing Cooktops

If you do not want a hood over your cooktop, buy a gas or electric unit with a down-drafting vent. This option is offered mostly on electric appliances. The vent must be ducted outside, either through the cabinets to an exterior wall or through the crawl space below the floor.

The hookups for a cooktop are the same as for a gas or electric range. Unless you are replacing an existing unit, bear in mind that you will have to make a cutout in your countertop.

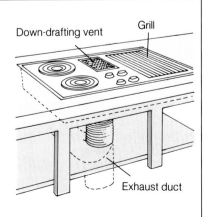

Down-drafting vent

Grill

Exhaust duct

RECEPTACLES

Our homes are full of silent workers that we never give much thought: the duplex receptacles, commonly called electrical outlets—some homes may have as many as fifty or sixty of these. They are always ready for a plug; we demand that they be convenient, that the plug fit, and that the connected circuit not overload. If you are doing any wiring, know the types of available receptacles and the techniques for installing them.

Recommended Cross-References
Electrical System, Lighting: Indoor, Switches, Wire, Wiring.

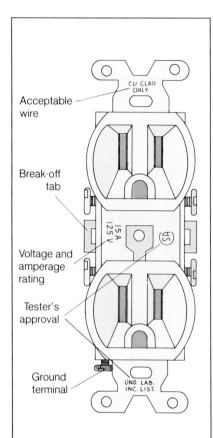

- Acceptable wire
- Break-off tab
- Voltage and amperage rating
- Tester's approval
- Ground terminal

Reading a Receptacle

Like switches, receptacles bear important markings. First look for the UL approval. Then make sure that the amperage of the receptacle is compatible with the circuit. (Twenty-amp circuits can use receptacles rated at fifteen or twenty amps.) Finally, be sure your receptacle can accept the wire you are using. Copper wire can be used with any receptacle. Copper-clad aluminum is compatible with receptacles marked CU/AL, but you must only use aluminum wire with receptacles marked CO/ALR.

Types of Receptacles

Most house circuits are 15-amp or 20-amp, 120-volt general-purpose circuits. They include one hot wire, one neutral wire, and one ground wire. The receptacles have the same amperage rating and have three slots connected to the three circuit wires. Most people recognize the hole for the grounding prong, but many do not realize that the other two slots are different sizes. The shorter slot is connected to the hot wire and the longer slot to the neutral wire. This distinction is important with the increased use of electronic equipment in the home. Many of the plugs for this type of equipment are "polarized," meaning that one prong is wider than the other because internal switches and other components must connect to the current in proper sequence. Ungrounded two-pronged receptacles can be replaced with GFCI receptacles.

Besides maintaining polarization, matching plugs and receptacles ensure that no appliance connects to a circuit with a different amperage or voltage rating. Cords for all heavy-duty appliances have prong configurations that match only receptacles of the same amperage and voltage. Specific configurations make it impossible to plug a 50-amp range into an outlet intended for a 30-amp clothes dryer. There are over thirty-five configurations of plug and receptacle, ranging from 15-amp duplex receptacles that we all recognize to 55-amp kitchen ranges that have four prongs.

The duplex receptacle, which is the workhorse of a house wiring system, has an important feature that increases its usefulness. On each side is a break-off tab that connects the top and bottom receptacles. By breaking this tab you can isolate one receptacle from the other. You may choose to wire the receptacles on separate circuits, to wire one into a switch and keep the other hot all the time, or to deaden one to prevent overloading the circuit. Both tabs break off, but common practice is to break only the hot side and to attach the neutral side to a common wire. This practice is only acceptable, however, if the common neutral wire is a pigtail and is not wired "through" the receptacle.

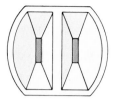

**Ungrounded Two-Prong
(120 volts)**

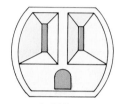

**Grounded Three-Prong
(120 volts—15 amps)**

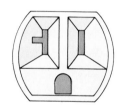

**Grounded Three-Prong
(120 volts—20 amps)**

**Grounded Three-Prong
(120/240 volts—30 amps)**

**Grounded Three-Prong
(120/240 volts—50 amps)**

**Grounded Three-Prong
(240 volts—30 amps)**

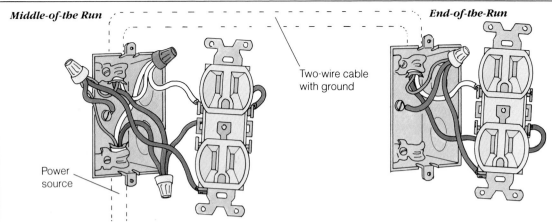

Middle-of-the Run

End-of-the-Run

Two-wire cable with ground

Power source

Installing Receptacles

After installing boxes and running wire to outlet locations, test with a low-voltage continuity tester. If the test shows that all is correct, install the receptacles. The diagram shows wiring for both middle-of-the-run and end-of-the-run installations. To attach the wires, strip $1/2$ to $5/8$ inch of insulation off the ends. If the receptacle is a backwiring type, push the wires into the rear holes. If not, bend them around the screws clockwise and tighten the screws. Be sure that the receptacle has a ground.

If a circuit has a single receptacle, the receptacle must have the same rating as the circuit. If the circuit has multiple receptacles, no receptacle rating can be higher than the rating for the circuit. The receptacles may have a lower rating, however. For example, on a 20-amp circuit, you may use a 15-amp receptacle.

Keep the number of receptacles on a circuit to a minimum. The NEC (National Electrical Code®) does not restrict the number of outlets on a circuit. Many local codes do, however. Always consult your local code

when planning circuits. Common practice is to install only 3 to 6 outlets on circuits for small appliances and 9 or 10 outlets on general-purpose circuits. In your installation, strive to divide the outlet load among as many circuits as possible.

Notice the color of the screw terminals. Silver-colored screws take neutral (white) wires, brass-colored screws take hot (black) wires, and green screws take ground wires. If the colors are not obvious, remember that the longer slot is for the neutral connection.

Surface Wiring

Raceways and plug-in strips add capacity to an existing receptacle. Be sure that a protective conduit covers all wires.

Some metal raceways match the height and thickness of the baseboard. To install these raceways, remove as much baseboard as you will replace with raceway. Try to locate

one end of the raceway directly under an existing outlet, which will serve as the power source. Make sure the power is off. Then pull the wires from the raceway through the wall and into the receptacle. Connect the wires at both ends, screw the raceway frame into the desired position, and snap on the cover plate.

If you use an extender box with

a raceway, you do not have to drill through the wall. Turn off the power, remove the wallplate and the receptacle, and attach an extender box to the outlet. Then measure, cut, and attach the raceway backing to the wall so that it joins the extender box. Connect the wiring to the existing outlet, replace the receptacle, and attach all the covers.

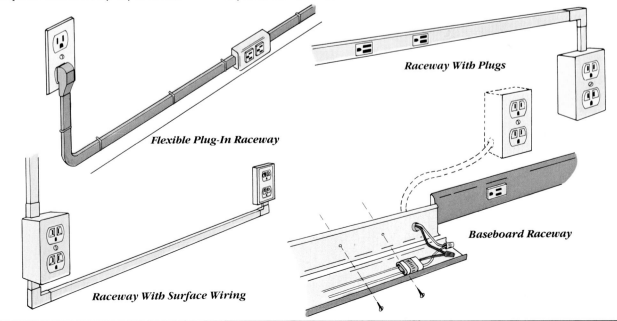

Flexible Plug-In Raceway

Raceway With Plugs

Raceway With Surface Wiring

Baseboard Raceway

RESILIENT FLOORING

Resilient flooring is both practical and elegant. It is easy to install, and the patterns and textures range from glossy to matte, from lightly mottled to highly textured, from monochromatic to marbleized; and all are available in almost any color imaginable.

Most resilient flooring is made of vinyl or a vinyl composition; rubber sheet, cork tiles, and wood tiles finished with polyurethane are also available. Solid vinyl and vinyl-covered cork are the most expensive and have the highest resiliency and sound-insulating qualities. Vinyl-composition flooring is generally less expensive; the resiliency varies with the thickness of the material.

While your own color preferences and design needs will guide you in selecting a pattern, keep in mind a few general guidelines:

● Do not use patterns that simulate natural materials in places where the real material would never be used. For instance, do not curve a Spanish floor-paver pattern up a wall.

● Avoid patterns that will overwhelm a room. The bigger and more intricate the pattern, the larger the room should be. If you like an intricate pattern for a small room, but fear that it may appear too busy, check to see if it is also available in neutral, monochromatic tones.

● If sheet materials need to be seamed in prominent places, conceal the seams by choosing a pattern with straight lines, such as simulated tile with grouted joints.

Resilient flooring is suitable for any room of the house, as long as the floor on which it is laid is perfectly smooth. Because seams are vulnerable to moisture penetration if they are not fused properly, sheet materials rather than tiles are usually recommended around plumbing fixtures.

Most tiles measure 12 inches square and are sold by the piece. Resilient sheet is sold by the square yard. It usually comes in 6- or 12-foot-wide rolls, although 9- and 15-foot widths are sometimes available. Plan to in-

stall sheet flooring so that seams fall in the narrowest part of the room or away from highly visible, heavily trafficked areas. When you measure the dimensions of a room to calculate square footage, include toe spaces under cabinets, spaces under movable appliances, any closets you want covered, and at least half the distance into every doorway. Add about 3 inches of extra length beyond the actual dimensions of a room for trimming and fitting. If you need to seam two or more pieces together, add another 8 to 10 percent for pattern matching. Always bring a floor plan with accurate dimensions with you when you consult with your dealer.

Recommended Cross-References
Floors, Subfloors.

Do not feel that it is necessary to stick to the traditional placement of tiles. With a little careful cutting and artful positioning, dramatic effects can be achieved with just simple black and white squares.

Preparing the Floor

Resilient materials are thin and therefore reveal any dents, bumps, cracks, or depressions in the sub-surface, including recessed nail heads. They must be installed over a surface that is entirely free of potential moisture. Whereas other floorcoverings are porous enough to allow small amounts of moisture to evaporate through, a resilient floor traps it. The result is deterioration of the adhesive bond and, eventually, even the underlayment or subfloor. In humid climates, use stable underlayment materials.

Use the chart (right) to plan your floor preparation. Follow the chart directions after making sure that the existing floor structure is sound and after correcting any moisture problems. If the chart indicates that an existing floorcovering must be removed, do so; then refer to the chart for the additional steps required to prepare the newly exposed subsurface.

Sheet flooring needs to "relax" before being installed. At least 24 hours before you install it, unroll sheet flooring in the room for which it is intended or in a room heated to 70° F. When you are ready to install it, reroll it face side in. It tears easily, so roll carefully.

Adhesives

Different types of resilient materials and subfloors require different adhesives. Use the type of adhesive recommended by the flooring manufacturer. The most common is water-soluble paste, which can be used for wood floors or concrete floors above grade. Asphalt emulsion or cut-back asphalt can be used above grade as well as below. It cannot be mixed with water. Other types include latex adhesive for moisture-causing situations; epoxy for places where extra strength and moisture resistance are needed; and adhesives for cove bases, rubber stair treads, and other specialty applications.

Always follow the manufacturer's instructions carefully, and use caution with flammable adhesives. The room should always be well ventilated and have no pilot lights on. Avoid using equipment that may cause sparks, and do not smoke.

Preparation Steps for Resilient Sheet and Tile

This chart summarizes the preparation steps required for installing resilient flooring materials over various existing floors and floor systems.

Existing Floor	Preparation for Resilient Sheet or Tile
Exposed Joists	• Install ¾" tongue & groove CDX plywood subfloor. • Install ¼"–½" particle-board underlayment, or underlayment-grade plywood. • Fill joints and underlayment nail- or screw-head depressions, and sand surface smooth.
Bare Concrete	• Make surface repairs to slab as needed.
Wood Floor or Subfloor *Over Wood Frame*	• Make surface repairs as needed. • Install ¼"–½" particle-board underlayment, or underlayment-grade plywood. • Fill joints and underlayment nail- or screw-head depressions, and sand surface smooth.
Over Concrete Slab	• Remove all wood materials to expose the concrete. • Make surface repairs to the slab as needed.
Resilient Sheet or Tile *Over Wood Frame*	• If existing resilient is cushioned or springy, remove it and make surface repairs as needed. • If existing resilient is embossed, not tightly bonded, or has wax or surface sheen, install ¼" particle-board underlayment, or underlayment-grade plywood. • Fill joints and underlayment nail- or screw-head depressions, and sand surface smooth.
Over Concrete Slab	• If existing resilient is cushioned or springy, or not tightly bonded, remove it and make surface repairs to exposed concrete as needed. • If embossed, smooth the surface with a liquid-type underlayment. Otherwise, remove wax and roughen the surface.
Ceramic Tile *Over Wood Frame*	• If possible, remove existing tile; otherwise, smooth and even out the surface with a liquid-type underlayment. • After removing existing ceramic tile, make surface repairs to exposed subfloor as needed. • If subfloor is very rough, install ¼"–½" particle-board underlayment, or underlayment-grade plywood. Fill joints and underlayment nail- or screw-head depressions, and sand surface smooth.
Over Concrete Slab	• If possible, remove existing tile; otherwise, smooth and even out the surface with a liquid-type underlayment. • After removing existing ceramic tile, make surface repairs to exposed slab as needed. If surface is very rough or uneven, smooth it with a liquid-type underlayment.
Carpet *Over Wood Frame*	• Remove existing carpet. • Make surface repairs to exposed subfloor as needed. • If subfloor is very rough, install ¼"–½" particle-board underlayment, or underlayment-grade plywood. Fill joints and underlayment nail- or screw-head depressions, and sand surface smooth.
Over Concrete Slab	• Remove existing carpet. • Make surface repairs to exposed slab as needed.

Caution: Existing resilient floors may contain asbestos fibers, which are harmful if inhaled. When removing old flooring, wear a respirator and avoid breaking pieces up.

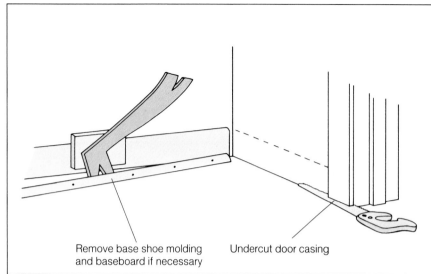

Remove base shoe molding and baseboard if necessary

Undercut door casing

Preparing for Installation

When you have prepared the sub-floor and are ready to begin installation, remove the baseboards or base shoes and undercut any vertical door casings to enable you to slide the resilient material under them. This method is much easier than trying to fit the flooring around such obstacles. Sweep the room very carefully. Even a grain of sand will make a noticeable bump if it gets trapped under the flooring.

Laying Out Resilient Tile

Use the quadrant method shown below for laying out resilient tiles. Cork, wood block, and parquet tiles follow the same installation procedures as resilient tiles. If the room has an irregular shape, has alcoves, or has protruding obstacles such as cabinets, prepare the layout in the largest rectangular portion of the room. To begin, measure and mark the midpoints along the two shortest walls opposite each other; snap a chalk line between them. Do the same for the other two walls; but before you snap this line, be sure that it is square with the first chalk line. Check this measurement by making a 3-4-5 triangle: Measure 3 feet from the intersection along one chalk line and mark it. Going back to the intersection, measure 4 feet along the intersecting chalk line and mark it. If the distance between the two marks is exactly 5 feet, the intersecting lines are perpendicular.

If you are laying out a diagonal pattern, first establish the guide lines just described. Then measure 5 feet out from the intersection along each axis and make a mark. Find the midpoints between these marks, and snap a chalk line through two opposite midpoints so that the line also intersects the center. It should extend to the walls in both directions.

This line should be at a 45-degree angle to the original quadrant lines. Stretch the chalk line across the remaining two midpoints, making sure it is square with the first diagonal. Make adjustments as needed.

These layout techniques, which average the distance between walls, work well for most rooms. However, if one wall is noticeably out of square, the whole layout will skew toward that wall and make the pattern out of square with the rest. In that case, establish the line running in the same direction as this wall by measuring from the opposite wall rather than by connecting midpoints along the walls at each end.

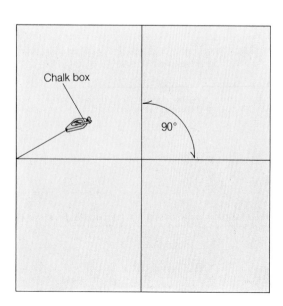

Chalk box

90°

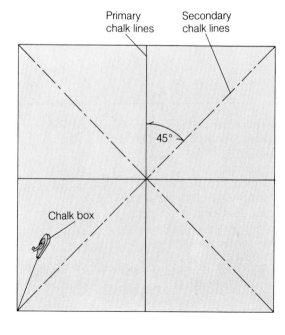

Primary chalk lines

Secondary chalk lines

45°

Chalk box

Installing Resilient Tile

1. Making a Test Run. Without applying adhesive, lay dry tiles along both axes of one quadrant, starting at the center and working toward the walls. Adjust the guidelines until the borders have full tiles or pieces at least half a tile wide. For the sake of durability and appearance, it is advisable to compose the border, or first row, in front of a doorway or an opening out of full tiles.

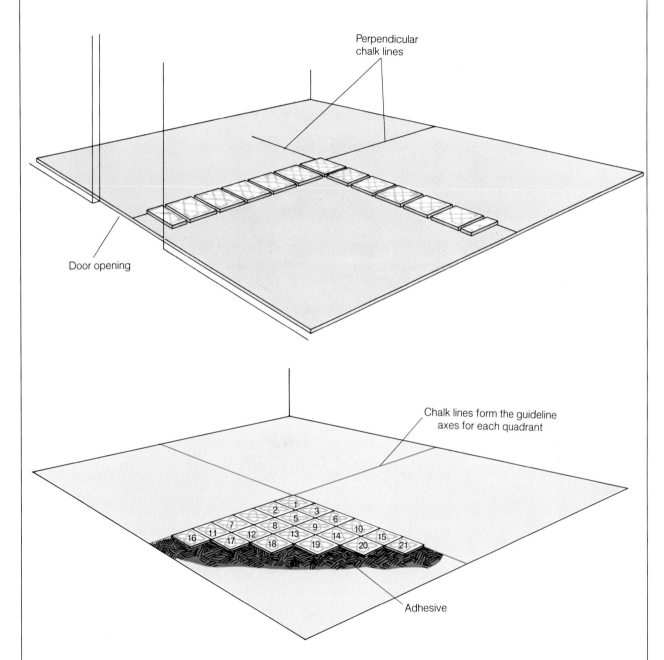

Perpendicular chalk lines

Door opening

Chalk lines form the guideline axes for each quadrant

Adhesive

2. Installing Quadrants. Sweep and vacuum all dirt from the floor. Read the label to see if the adhesive is applied with a roller, brush, or toothed trowel. All adhesives have a specified open time—the period during which tiles can be laid before the adhesive becomes too dry. When working with some adhesives, you will only have enough time to set six or seven tiles; with others, you will have enough time to set most of a quadrant in one application.

Begin spreading adhesive in the center of the room, being careful not to cover up the chalk lines. Avoid spreading the adhesive too thick, causing the adhesive to ooze between the tiles, or too thin, preventing a good bond. Carefully position the first tile so that it aligns perfectly with both chalk lines. Build out from that tile and avoid sliding tiles into position. Work carefully; minor errors can cause major alignment problems later on. Cut the tiles to fit as you come to walls or other obstacles. After you finish laying the first quadrant, do the remaining quadrants in the same way. As you proceed you will have to walk or kneel on newly laid tiles. Use a scrap of plywood to distribute your weight over them. Immediately wipe off any adhesive that oozes up between joints with a rag and compatible solvent. After you have laid all of the tiles, wait the specified time for the adhesive to set before walking on them.

3. Marking and Cutting Tiles. To cut tiles to fit against a wall, mark each one in position. Set the tile to be cut exactly on top of the last full tile. Place a second tile on top of it, butting it against the wall and allowing a ⅛-inch gap for expansion. Mark the cutting line on the first tile, then either cut it with a knife or score and break it if it is too heavy to cut. Tiles are difficult to cut if they are too cold and brittle. To make cutting an easy job, warm them briefly in an oven or over a furnace before cutting.

4. Making a Template. If you have to fit tiles around an obstacle, such as a pipe, mark the tiles from a template made out of cardboard. You may have to draw the template several times before it fits correctly. Use dividers to duplicate intricate shapes.

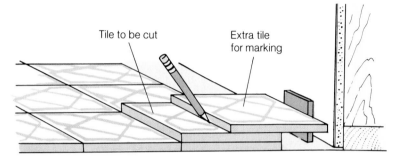

Tile to be cut

Extra tile for marking

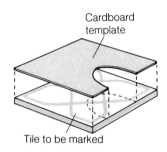

Cardboard template

Tile to be marked

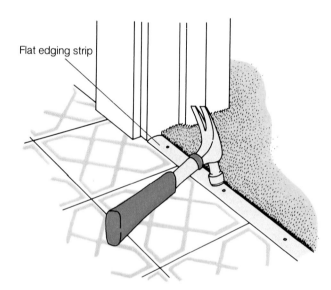

Flat edging strip

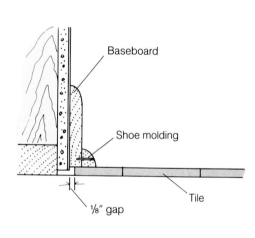

Baseboard

Shoe molding

⅛" gap

Tile

5. Metal Edging Strip. Cover the joint where resilient tile and other flooring meet with a flat edging strip. Be careful not to dent it with your hammer.

6. Installing a Wood Baseboard. After the resilient tile is completely installed, nail baseboards around the edge of the floor to cover the gap required for the tile to expand. Raise the board slightly above the flooring so that the resilient material can move freely.

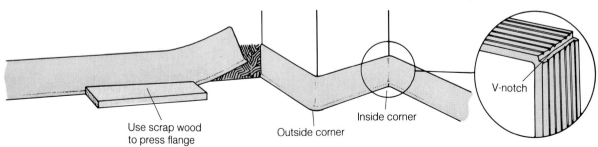

Use scrap wood to press flange

Outside corner

Inside corner

V-notch

7. Installing a Cove Base. A vinyl cove base is an easy and attractive way to finish a resilient floor. It is sold in precut lengths. Cut the strips to fit and glue them to the walls with the specified adhesive. At inside corners, cut a V-notch in the flange and score the back of the strip. Simply wrap the base around an outside corner; the flange will stretch. Apply adhesive to the grooved back only; do not glue the flange to the flooring.

Installing Sheet Flooring

Sheet flooring is a sensible choice for rooms with plumbing fixtures or other potential sources of moisture. In the past, sheet materials required professional installation because they were so heavy and hard to work with. Now they are lightweight and quite flexible, making it possible for most homeowners to do their own installation in a few hours.

Three options are available for adhering resilient sheet: gluing it fully, gluing just the perimeter, and laying it loose with only a few staples around the edge. The method of adhesion depends on the material you choose. Some types are not intended to be laid without adhesive. Installations with seams should at least be glued around the perimeter and at the seam. The best installation is full adhesion.

The most difficult part of any installation is cutting the material to fit cleanly around the edges. One way to minimize problems is to install a baseboard over the edge when you are finished.

1. Cutting the Sheet. There are two approaches to cutting. One is to make a paper pattern that exactly fits the room and use it to trace an outline onto the sheet flooring where you have room to roll it out and cut it. Pieces of butcher paper work well; trim and tape them together so that they form a continuous pattern around the edge of the room. Leave a ¼-inch gap at the walls. Some manufacturers supply a kit for this procedure.

If the material is flexible and easy to handle, a more direct cutting method is first to rough-cut the sheet 3 inches larger than room dimensions, then do the final trimming after putting the sheeting in place.

Make the cuts with a utility knife, shears, or a rotary power cutter.

2. Making the Relief Cuts. After you cut the sheet to its rough dimensions, roll it so that the face is inside, the edge for the longest wall free. Position that edge so that it curls up the wall slightly. Unroll the sheet, tugging and adjusting it so that it is centered and the pattern is square.

To get the sheet to lie flat, make relief cuts at all the corners. To make a relief cut, slit the curled margin with a knife, just to the point where the floor intersects the corner. Do not cut beyond this point.

To fit resilient sheeting around a pipe or post, cut a slit in from the edge of the flooring to make the sheet separate and close around the obstruction. Continue to make small relief cuts until the sheet lies flat on the floor and the two halves of the slit join back together again.

Resilient sheet flooring is attractive, inexpensive, durable, and easy to apply.

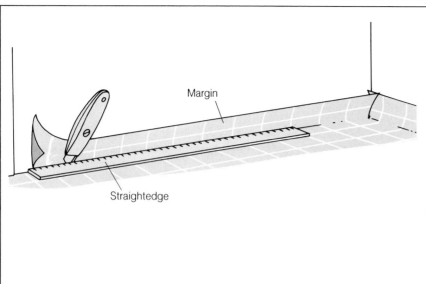

Margin

Straightedge

3. Trimming the Edges. Some manufacturers supply a marking tool with their sheet goods that makes it possible to draw accurate lines along the edges for trimming. Without this tool, you may need to trim twice, first to remove most of the margin and then to perfect the fit. Heating the flooring with a hair dryer will make it more flexible. Make freehand cuts with a knife, feeling for the exact edge of the floor with the blade; or push a straightedge tightly against the folded edge of the flooring. Leave a $\frac{1}{8}$-inch expansion gap. At doorways without a threshold, trim the flooring at the centerline of the closed door.

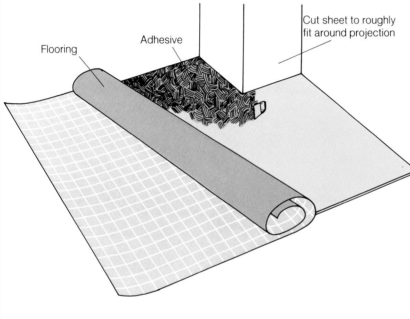

Flooring

Adhesive

Cut sheet to roughly fit around projection

4. Gluing the Sheet. To apply adhesive, carefully lift the sheet along one edge and fold it back on itself so that half of the floor is exposed. Apply adhesive to the floor with a toothed trowel, according to the manufacturer's directions. Work from the corners to the center of each length of wall if you are adhering only the edges. If you are gluing the sheet fully, cover all of the exposed floor up to the folded sheet. Then unfold the sheet into place; walk on it to press it into the adhesive. Repeat the process for the other half of the room. To ensure a tight bond, press the adhesive down with a rented floor roller.

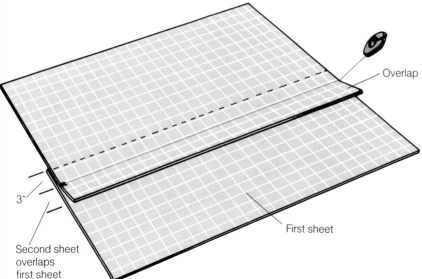

Overlap

3"

Second sheet overlaps first sheet

First sheet

5. Seaming Two Sheets. Cut out, trim, and fit the first sheet in place, leaving a 3-inch margin at the seam. Glue this sheet down, stopping 8 or 9 inches short of the actual location of the seam.

Next, cut and fit the second piece so that it overlaps the first by 3 to 6 inches. If the flooring has a pattern, be sure to position the second sheet so that it matches up perfectly. Glue down the second sheet, applying the adhesive only to within 5 or 6 inches of the first sheet and letting the unglued edge of the second sheet overlap the first.

6. Cutting the Seam. Use a straight line in the flooring pattern as a cutting guide, or snap a chalk line along the seam location after squaring it to the two side walls. Cut along the line with a sharp utility knife, using a straightedge to guide the blade. Press hard so that you cut through both layers of flooring at the same time. Retracing the cut can cause slivers and unsightly slits. Remove the scrap pieces and clean under the seam thoroughly, making sure there is no dust or debris on the floor.

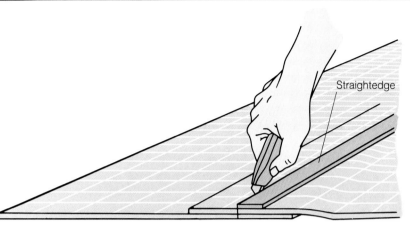

Straightedge

7. Adhering Each Piece. Test the seam by dry fitting the two pieces together. They should abut without pushing the seam up or leaving a crack. Although you will probably not have to, you can trim away any irregularities, again using the straightedge. Glue the seam by pulling back both edges of flooring and spreading a band of adhesive along the floor. Then join the two edges together and press the seam into the adhesive. Immediately wipe off any adhesive that oozes up, and clean the seam with a compatible solvent.

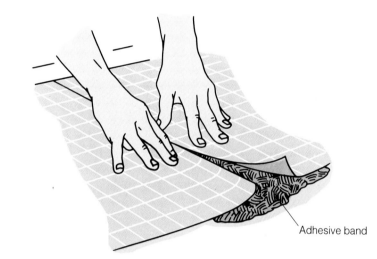

Adhesive band

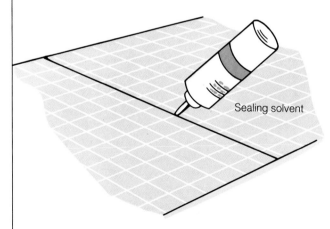

Sealing solvent

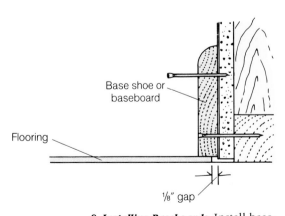

Base shoe or baseboard

Flooring

⅛" gap

8. Fusing the Seam. After the adhesive has set, seal the seam with a special solvent that melts the seam edges enough for them to fuse together. The solvent comes in a bottle that includes a special applicator spout. Run the spout along the seam, according to directions, applying the sealer to the seam, not the flooring. The seam is now waterproof.

9. Installing Baseboards. Install baseboards or base shoes around the room so that it covers the gap between the flooring and walls. Leave a slight space, about the thickness of a matchbook cover, between the bottom of the baseboard and the surface of the floor to allow for movement.

ROLL ROOFING

Roll roofing is inexpensive and easy to apply, although it must be replaced sooner than most other roofing materials and usually has a Class C fire rating (A is the most fire resistant). It is particularly suitable where cost is more important than appearance or for low-slope roofing that you want to install yourself. It can be used for roof slopes down to 2 in 12 with the exposed-nail method, or down to 1 in 12 with the concealed-nail method. Each method can be used with full-width mineral-surface (single-coverage) rolls or selvage-edge (double-coverage) rolls. Double-coverage roofs last much longer, up to fifteen years or more.

As a rule, because roll roofing can crack in cold weather it should not be applied when the temperature is below 45° F. If the job must be done anyway, store the rolls in a warm place prior to application, or unroll and cut them into strips no longer than 18 feet and let them lie on the roof until they are flat. If possible, install roll roofing over a smooth plywood deck, either perpendicular or parallel to the slope. The roofing should overhang the eaves by ½ inch, except when you install drip-edge flashing on top of the roofing along the rake edge. An underlayment of felt roofing is optional. You will need $\frac{1}{10}$ gallon of lap (not mastic) roofing cement for every roll, and 2 pounds of roofing nails for every square. (In roofing, one square equals 100 square feet.) Use 1-inch nails for new roofing; they are long enough to penetrate the sheathing. Use 1¼-inch nails for reroofing. Enlist the aid of one or two helpers to handle the long strips.

Valleys will be open, so flash them beforehand with metal or with two layers of roll roofing, the first an 18-inch-wide strip and the second 36 inches wide. Install the first strip upside down. Nail along one edge first, spacing nails ¾ inch in from the edge and 6 inches apart. Then nail the opposite edge. Make sure to overlap all end joints at least 6 inches.

Recommended Cross-References
Flashing, Roofs.

Concealed-Nail Application
The key to a tight roof is applying the roofing when it is warm enough for full expansion and staggering the nails along the top edge of each course so that the 4-inch band that gets covered with lap cement is sure to lie perfectly flat.

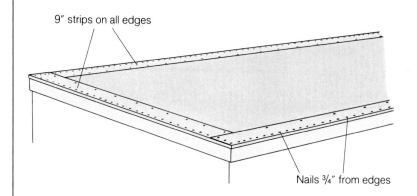

9″ strips on all edges

Nails ¾″ from edges

1. Install valley flashing if necessary. Cut 9-inch-wide strips and place them along the rakes, nailing ¾ inch from the edge every 4 inches.

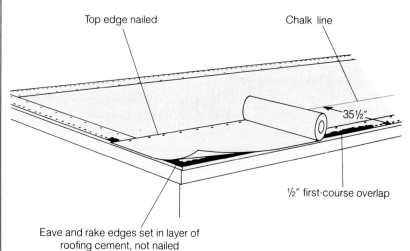

Top edge nailed

Chalk line

35½″

½″ first-course overlap

Eave and rake edges set in layer of roofing cement, not nailed

2. Snap a chalk line, position the first sheet, and nail it across the top every 4 inches. For maximum stability, stagger the nails along the top edge. Set the bottom and side edges with lap cement.

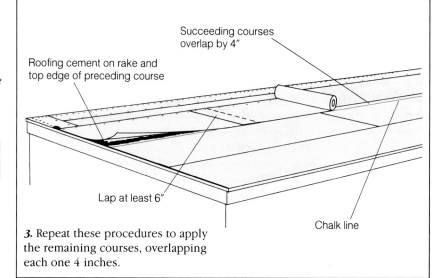

Succeeding courses overlap by 4″

Roofing cement on rake and top edge of preceding course

Lap at least 6″

Chalk line

3. Repeat these procedures to apply the remaining courses, overlapping each one 4 inches.

Exposed-Nail Application

Install each course of roofing as shown on the previous page. As you work your way up the roof, take measurements between each chalk line and at various points along the eave and ridge to make sure the courses will come out evenly. Nails along the bottom of each course should be 2 or 3 inches apart, according to the manufacturer's specifications. Keep nails aligned neatly.

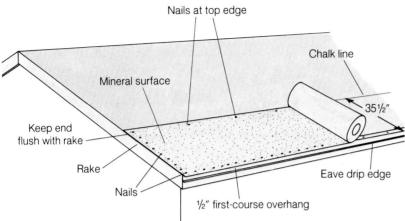

1. Snap a chalk line 35½ inches above the eave. Position the first sheet, tack the top edge every 2 feet, and nail the rake and eave edges every 3 inches, keeping the nails ¾ inch away from the edge.

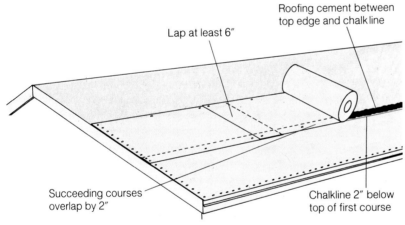

2. Snap a chalk line on the top of the first piece 2 inches below the edge. Tack the upper edge of the second strip. Then spread a 2-inch band of roofing cement under the bottom edge. Nail every 2 or 3 inches.

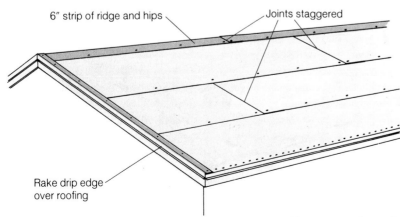

3. Install the rest of the sheets in the same way, staggering end joints. Apply ridge and hip caps and metal drip edging along the rakes.

Hips and Ridges

For hips and ridges, cut the roofing so that it meets but does not overlap the joint. Snap a chalk line on each side 5½ inches away from the center of the hip or ridge. For exposed-nail applications, spread a 2-inch-wide strip of roofing cement from each line back toward the center; then cut a 12-inch strip of roofing the length of the hip or ridge, gently bend it, and nail it in place. For long hips that require more than one strip, work from the bottom up, lapping end joints 6 inches or more. When using the concealed-nail method, apply lap cement to the entire area between the chalk lines and then embed the 12-inch strip in it. Only use nails in the top two corners.

Vent Flashing

Cut a hole in the roofing just large enough for the vent pipe and lay the strip in place. Then install metal vent flashing over the pipe, coating the roofing with mastic first so that the metal flange is embedded in it completely. Nail around the flange every 2 inches. For maximum strength, install blocking under the roof in places where the nails will penetrate the sheathing.

Double Coverage

Selvage-edge roofing is installed the same way as full-width roll roofing, except that each course overlaps the previous course 19 inches instead of 4. This technique will also work with full-width rolls if you cannot find selvage-edge roll roofing in your local store.

ROOFS

Most roofing materials eventually wear out and need replacement—some sooner than others. Those who are comfortable walking around on a roof can usually perform simple roof repairs. However, if you are installing new roofing on a room addition or replacing an entire roof, weigh several factors before choosing roofing materials and deciding whether or not to do the work yourself.

In most cases, the roof must go up quickly in case of rain. To estimate the time for an inexperienced person, allow 2 hours for the first square (100 square feet) of shingles, which you might be able to reduce to 1 hour after having some experience. Compare that speed with about ½ hour per square usually taken by a professional roofer.

Also consider the type of roofing. Certain roofs, such as tar and gravel, slate, and metal with standing seams, should be done professionally. Roll roofing, composition shingles, tile, and wood shingles or shakes can be installed by homeowners who are handy and have enough help with lifting roofing materials to the roof.

Recommended Cross-References
Dormers, Flashing, Framing, Roll Roofing, Roof Tiles, Roof Shakes, Roof Shingles: Composition, Roof Shingles: Wood.

Removing an Old Roof
If you are roofing over an existing roof, check to see how many layers it already has. Codes usually allow a total of three roof layers. You can tell how many layers your roof has by inspecting along the eave of a gable end (not a regular eave, which has double courses of starter shingles). If there is only one roof and it is not made of shakes, you can reroof over it. In some cases, you can reroof over two layers. But if there are three layers already or if you are installing a heavy material such as tile, tear off the old roofing before installing the new. This involves renting a debris box or large truck, scraping off all the roofing with shovels and crowbars, and pitching it in. Work carefully, standing above or behind the debris to keep from sliding on it. This is a perfect job for strong and enthusiastic helpers.

Getting materials up on the roof is one of the biggest challenges of roofing any home. This supplier delivers materials to the roof with a conveyor mounted on the delivery truck.

Roof Slope
First you need to know the slope of your roof. Slope, also called pitch, is the number of inches of rise for every 12 inches of horizontal distance; it is expressed as "something in 12." The simplest way to measure slope is to place a short board on the roof, rest a level on it, and measure down to the board from a point on the level exactly 1 foot from the end of the board.

These are the minimums required by most codes.

Type	Slope
Tar and gravel	0 in 12
Roll roofing	1 in 12
Metal panels	2 in 12
Composition shingles:	
Double underlayment	2 in 12
Regular installation	3 in 12
Tile	3 in 12
Wood shingles	4 in 12
Wood shakes	4 in 12

Roofs steeper than 6 in 12 are difficult to install roofing on, especially if there are also a number of dormers, hips, and valleys. Either hire professionals for such a roof or plan on a long and tedious job.

Preparation
You will need at least one sturdy ladder and roof jacks if the slope is steeper than 6 in 12. Be prepared for rain by having a roll or two of plastic sheeting handy. Wear soft-soled shoes, such as sneakers, that will not damage the roofing material. Most roofing can be done with basic carpentry tools, although a roofer's hatchet is one tool to buy if you are installing wood shingles or shakes.

The easiest way to estimate the area of your roof for ordering materials is to take measurements on the roof itself, then calculate the total square footage. If the roof is steep or complex, you may have to make an estimation from the ground. To do this, measure the ground-floor area of the house and add the area for eaves and overhangs. To account for the slope, multiply the total by one of the following coverage factors:

Slope	Coverage Factor
2 in 12	1.02
4 in 12	1.06
6 in 12	1.12
8 in 12	1.20
10 in 12	1.30
12 in 12	1.41

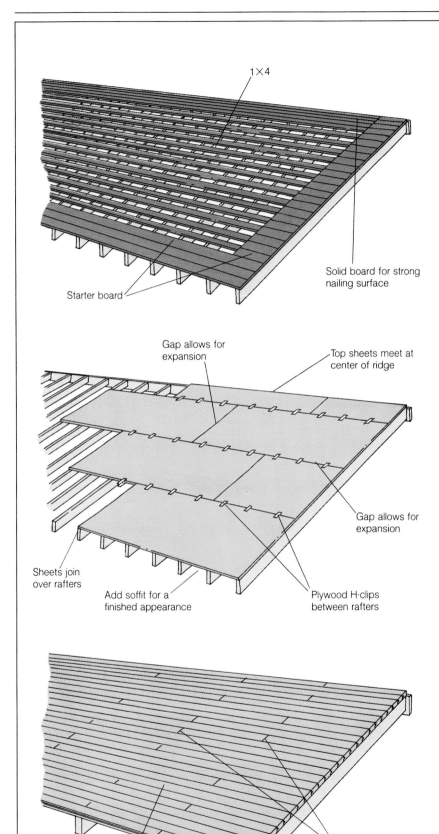

1×4

Solid board for strong nailing surface

Starter board

Gap allows for expansion

Top sheets meet at center of ridge

Gap allows for expansion

Sheets join over rafters

Add soffit for a finished appearance

Plywood H-clips between rafters

Staggered joints

Tongue-and-groove sheathing

Sheathing

Spaced Sheathing. Generally made with 1 by 4s, this is commonly put under wood-shingle, wood-shake, tile, and metal-panel roofs. Sometimes the slats may be installed over a plywood roof deck for purposes of insulation or shear strength. In most cases, however, they are nailed directly to the rafters, spaced according to the required exposure of the roofing material. For instance, if wood shingles are applied with a 5-inch exposure (the bottom part of the shingle that is exposed to the weather), the sheathing must be spaced exactly 5 inches, center to center, or the shingle nails will not align. Where appearance is important, use an attractive starter board, such as V-rustic, for the eaves and rakes, or install a soffit underneath. On shake and shingle roofs, cover the 18 inches just below the ridge with solid boards for an adequate nailing surface.

Plywood Sheathing. Use plywood sheathing for composition shingles, roll roofing, and slate, as well as for the base for spaced sheathing when the roof requires diagonal strength or a solid wind barrier for materials such as tile. Plywood sheathing is usually $1/2$ inch thick. Install the panels perpendicular to the rafters. Leave gaps at the ends and edges to allow for expansion; the requisite distances are usually stamped on the plywood panels. Double these measurements in a humid climate. Stagger end joints by 4 feet. Special clips are available that can be slipped between the panel edges to lock them together where they span between rafters. Nail plywood with 8d nails spaced every 6 inches along the edges and 12 inches in the field.

Tongue-and-Groove Sheathing. If the sheathing is visible from inside the house, as in cathedral ceilings, use 2 by 6 tongue-and-groove roof decking. Install the first board along the eaves with the tongue edge facing toward the ridge. Use a scrap piece of tongue-and-groove about 2 feet long as a hammering block to knock successive boards into place. Stagger butt joints so that they do not line up over the same rafter, and leave $1/16$ inch for expansion. Some decking is manufactured with tongue-and-groove ends as well, so you can place butt joints anywhere.

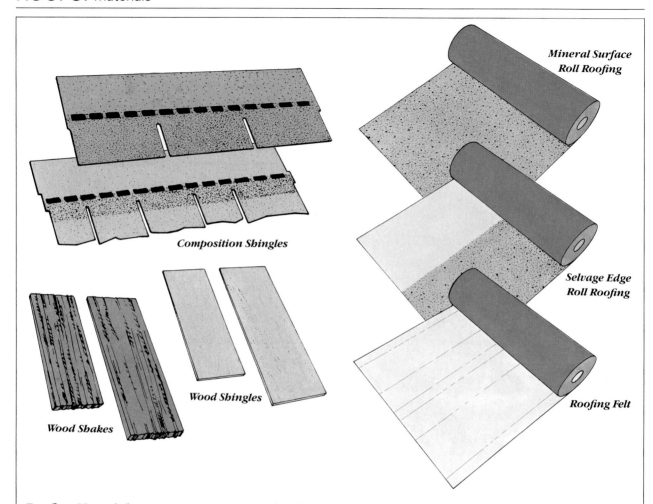

Composition Shingles

Wood Shakes

Wood Shingles

Mineral Surface Roll Roofing

Selvage Edge Roll Roofing

Roofing Felt

Roofing Materials

Composition Shingles. Composition shingles, also called asphalt shingles, come in a staggering array of colors, weights, tab sizes, textures, and edge configurations, but the easiest to apply are three-tab shingles, which are 12 inches wide and 36 inches long. Shingle weight and the fabric used for the central core determine durability. Shingles weigh from 215 to 300 pounds per square and last from 15 to 30 years. The most durable have a fiberglass rather than felt core. Fiberglass-core shingles also have a Class A fire rating (felt shingles are Class C), which makes them desirable in areas where forest or brush fires are common. Laminated fiberglass/ asphalt shingles are gaining popularity. The lower half of each shingle is a double thickness. Most are designed to create shadow lines and to imitate the look of random wood shingles. They are also known as dimensional, heavyweight, and architectural shingles. They last up to 40 years and are more expensive than standard shingles.

Most shingles come with strips of roofing cement to seal the tabs of the course applied above them. After the shingle is installed, the heat of the sun bonds the shingles.

Wood Shingles and Shakes. These two materials are made of wood, usually western red cedar, but the similarity ends there. Shingles are smaller, thinner, and lighter than shakes, and are sawn on both sides. Shakes are split by hand; some are resawn on one side only. Shakes cost more because they are thicker and are manufactured by hand. Each material is installed in a different manner.

Shingles and shakes are graded by number: 1 (the best), 2, and 3. Only number 1 should be used for roofs, because it is cut from heartwood and free of knots. Number 1 shakes and shingles may last 20 to 25 years. Shakes last longer than shingles. Make sure your local fire code allows the use of wood shakes or shingles.

Wood-Fiber Shingles. Resembling wood shingles, this material is made of compressed hardboard and comes in panels 4 feet long. It is much less expensive than wood shingles and

shakes, and is usually guaranteed for 25 years. The panels are installed the same way as shingles, but go on more quickly because they have alignment marks that make it unnecessary to measure each course.

Roll Roofing. Roll roofing is essentially the same material as composition shingles. It does not last as long because there is only one layer covering a roof, compared to the three created by overlapping shingles.

There are two basic types of roll roofing: full-width mineral surface and selvage edge. A roll of mineral surface, which weighs 90 pounds, is 3 feet wide and 36 feet long. It will cover one square. It can also be used as flashing and is commonly put in valleys under metal flashing.

Selvage-edge rolls are also 3 feet wide and 36 feet long, but it takes two rolls to cover a square.

Roofing Felt. This paper is used for underlayment with such materials as composition shingles, shakes, and tile. Rolls are classified by weight, usually 15 pound, 30 pound, and 45 pound. One roll covers either two or four squares, depending on the size.

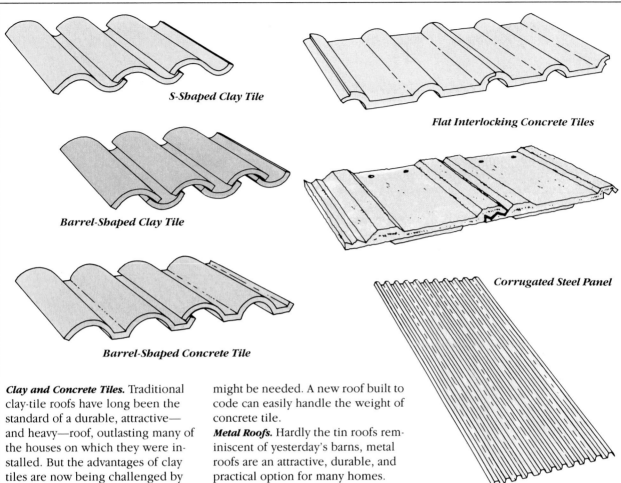

S-Shaped Clay Tile

Barrel-Shaped Clay Tile

Barrel-Shaped Concrete Tile

Flat Interlocking Concrete Tiles

Corrugated Steel Panel

Clay and Concrete Tiles. Traditional clay-tile roofs have long been the standard of a durable, attractive—and heavy—roof, outlasting many of the houses on which they were installed. But the advantages of clay tiles are now being challenged by tiles made from concrete. They are lighter, weighing from 750 to 900 pounds per square, compared with over 1,000 pounds for clay tiles (even more when they are wet). Concrete tiles cost less than clay tiles, as well as other roofing materials such as shakes and some metal materials. The tiles are also easier to install because each one is molded with a ridge on the back that simply hooks over spaced sheathing, sometimes called battens.

Concrete tiles come in many shapes: They can be flat, barrel shaped, or resemble shakes. They come in a wide choice of colors, from traditional reds and browns to glazed surfaces of bright blue, red, or green.

If you are installing tile on an existing roof, consider the weight factor, especially if the tiles are being laid over existing roofing. Some distributors will send a sales representative to your home to evaluate the roof for you if you are considering purchasing their tile. They will recommend any additional framing, such as purlins or extra joists, that

might be needed. A new roof built to code can easily handle the weight of concrete tile.

Metal Roofs. Hardly the tin roofs reminiscent of yesterday's barns, metal roofs are an attractive, durable, and practical option for many homes. Some corrugated panels are suitable for installation by the homeowner, but the most durable roofs are flat sheets joined by a standing seam and should be installed by professionals. Some metal roofs, made either of aluminum or steel, are manufactured to resemble shingles and shakes; they should also be installed by professionals. One particular metal roof made in Sweden is strong enough to span between rafters without wood sheathing. This saves one complete step in building a new roof.

Tar and Gravel. Used primarily on slopes ranging from a flat roof to a 3-in-12 slope, this kind of roof is made of alternating layers of roofing felt and hot tar. It is also called a hot mopped or built-up roof. The tar is covered with a layer of gravel to prevent direct sunlight from evaporating the solvents in the tar. When a tar-and-gravel roof becomes worn, usually in less than 15 years, another one can be put directly over it, to a maximum of three roofs. To inspect your roof, look for cracked and brittle areas, as well as seams that are pulling apart.

Cold Mop Roofing. Cold mop roofing is an inexpensive method of applying a built-up roof, but it is less effective than hot tar. The material is a liquid with an asphalt base. It does not have to be heated because it lacks the clays and other hardening agents that are part of a hot tar roof. This type of roofing is little used today except for repair work; standard roofing materials such as composition shingles, shakes, and tile are better choices.

Elastomeric Roofing Membranes. Many roofing materials have been developed for commercial and industrial use that have specific residential applications, such as flat roofs with a deck built over them. Local roofing suppliers will advise you on the products suitable for your area, but most of them are tough membranes that are applied in liquid form or solid sheets. Some systems include a fiberglass mesh. They are usually applied in stages—a primer coat plus two or three follow-up coats.

Repairing a Roof

While some roof problems need urgent attention because they cause obvious leaks, many can go undetected for years until they have caused serious structural damage—surprisingly, near the foundation or inside walls where you would least suspect trouble. It is prudent to inspect your roof once a year, looking for cracked shingles, rusted flashing, open joints, or brittle mastic. The prime areas for problems are valleys and chimneys. Other likely places are ridges, hips, vent flashing, and other flashing.

When you repair composition shingles, choose a warm day so the shingles will lift and bend easily. On a cold day, heat them with a propane torch. Repair cracked or curled shingles, and replace broken ones.

Split or broken wood shingles must be replaced. A bowed shingle, caused by installing it without a proper gap, can be repaired by carefully splitting a thin strip down the middle with a chisel so that it will lie flat. Make sure the new split is not directly over a joint in the underlying course. If you replace several rows of shingles, remove the top course first and work down. Then install new shingles from the bottom up, making room to insert the top row under the overlapping course by hacksawing off all the nails.

Flat roofs can develop air blisters that eventually leak. Repair them by slitting blisters down the middle, inserting roofing cement, and patching. Fix holes in a similar way. Cover new patches with gravel to shade them from damaging sunlight.

Metal roofs are not prone to leakage, but if you discover a small hole you can patch it by first cleaning the area with steel wool and then filling the hole with epoxy resin. Pack larger holes firmly with steel wool, then cover with epoxy. Cover with a second coat after the first one dries.

Spotting a Leak. Rarely does a leak in the ceiling come from a spot directly above it on the roof. If you have access to the attic, you can trace the leak during a rain storm. Mark with bright chalk on the rafter where the water is coming through the roof, so that you can go back during better weather and poke a long nail or straightened coat hanger up through the roof. If you cannot search for the leak during a storm, have someone spray the roof with a hose while you look for the leak.

Sealing Valleys

Closed Valleys. In some valleys the shingles butt together to conceal the metal flashing. This method is not as effective as a full-lace valley, because water can rush down one side of the roof fast enough to overshoot the valley and seep under the shingles of the opposite side, especially along the center seam. To repair leaks, slip diamond-shaped pieces of flashing under each course of shingles, starting at the bottom. Cut the few nails you run into with a hacksaw blade. Nail each shingle and coat the head with mastic.

Open Valleys. First, sweep away all debris from the valley. Then make sure the roofing material is cut in a smooth, straight line on each side and that the distance between the shingles on each side widens from ridge to eave at a rate of $1/8$ inch per foot of valley. Trim the shingles accordingly. Lift the shingles, one by one, and coat the area where they lie on the valley with roofing cement. Then use a cartridge gun to run a bead of roofing cement down the valley tin next to the shingles. If the shingles are made of wood or other inflexible material, run a bead of roofing cement down the edges.

Roofing paper

Metal

Shingles butted

Slide diamond-shaped pieces of aluminum under shingles. Overlap at least 2″

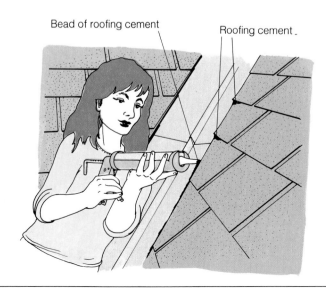

Bead of roofing cement

Roofing cement

Composition Shingles

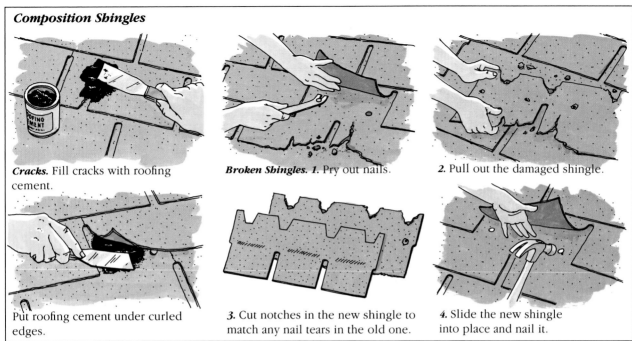

Cracks. Fill cracks with roofing cement.

Broken Shingles. 1. Pry out nails.

2. Pull out the damaged shingle.

Put roofing cement under curled edges.

3. Cut notches in the new shingle to match any nail tears in the old one.

4. Slide the new shingle into place and nail it.

Tar & Gravel Roofing

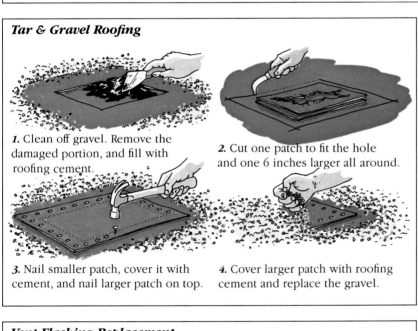

1. Clean off gravel. Remove the damaged portion, and fill with roofing cement.

2. Cut one patch to fit the hole and one 6 inches larger all around.

3. Nail smaller patch, cover it with cement, and nail larger patch on top.

4. Cover larger patch with roofing cement and replace the gravel.

Wood Shingles or Shakes

Pull out damaged shingle, and saw off nails with a hacksaw blade.

Slip flat pry bar under shake and on top of nail, then hammer on bar to drive nail.

Vent Flashing Replacement

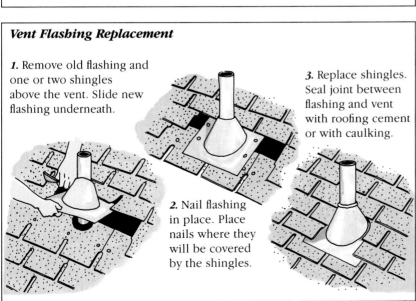

1. Remove old flashing and one or two shingles above the vent. Slide new flashing underneath.

3. Replace shingles. Seal joint between flashing and vent with roofing cement or with caulking.

2. Nail flashing in place. Place nails where they will be covered by the shingles.

ROOF SHAKES

The rustic charm of a shake roof has made it a traditional favorite for both casual-looking and formal-looking homes. Cedar shakes are a remarkable natural roofing material that resists decay much longer than other woods; a shake roof has been known to last more than 100 years. The one drawback is that it is not fireproof; for this reason, many codes do not allow shakes in certain wooded areas or on homes with a fireplace. Shakes that have been treated for fire resistance—some with a Class A rating—fulfill most code requirements.

Recommended Cross-References

Flashing, Framing, Roofs, Shingles: Wood.

Kinds of Shakes

The most common types of shakes are taper split, hand split, resawn, and straight split. Except for the straight split, they are thick at the butt end and taper to a thin end.

Straight-split shakes are equal in thickness at both ends and are not suitable for most roofs because they are so bulky. Hand-split shakes are the most expensive but are also the thickest. Tapered resawn shakes are not as thick, but they give the roof a more even profile because one face is smooth and flat.

Exposure

Shakes function best on roofs with at least a 6 in 12 slope, particularly in wet and humid climates. Shakes measuring 18 inches are overlapped 10½ inches, leaving an exposure of 7½ inches; 24-inch shakes are overlapped 14 inches, exposed 10 inches. This amount of overlapping provides standard 2-ply coverage. However, you will have a markedly better roof with 3-ply coverage, which means a 12½-inch and 16½-inch overlap, respectively. Nail the same as you would for wood shingles. Allow ½ inch of space between shakes.

Preparing the Roof

Shakes are normally laid over spaced sheathing, either 1 by 4s or 1 by 6s. However, because shakes are irregularly shaped, air can still circulate underneath them—essential for wood roofs—when they are installed over solid sheathing or an existing composition roof. Solid sheathing should be used in areas that get wind-driven snow or in earthquake areas where plywood is needed for lateral strength. To cover an existing roof, cut back all roofing at the eaves and rake edges to make room for 1 by 6 trim boards. The trim boards provide solid edges for the shakes to rest on and conceal the unsightly existing roof.

Flash all valleys with ribbed valley flashing, sometimes called W-metal, before applying roofing felt. Unlike wood shingles, 30-pound roofing felt, in strips 18 inches wide, must be interleaved between the courses of shakes. The underlayment assures that any water that penetrates under the shakes will quickly be carried out to the roof surface again. If you cannot locate 18-inch-wide felt in your area, cut a full roll in half by cutting it around and around with a circular saw, using an old blade or an abrasive cut-off wheel. Either apply the felt as you install each course of shakes or prefelt the area you plan to install in one day.

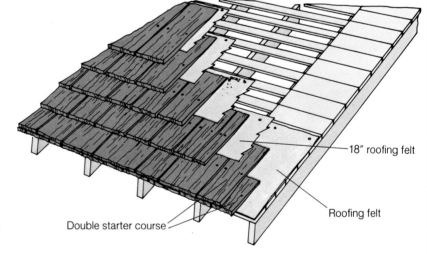

18″ roofing felt

Roofing felt

Double starter course

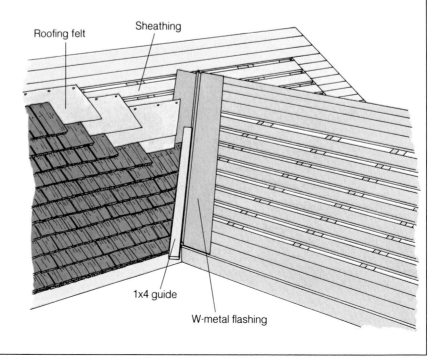

Roofing felt

Sheathing

1x4 guide

W-metal flashing

Roofing Around Vents

To apply shakes around a vent, carry the course to the vent pipe. With a keyhole or saber saw, notch shakes to fit on each side of the pipe so that they line up with a standard gap of ½ inch. Slip the flashing over the pipe, and lap the next course of shakes over the top edge of the flashing, notching the shakes to fit around but not touch the pipe collar. If you don't want the metal of the vent flashing to show through, paint the metal (before applying it) so it blends with the roof. If you try to conceal the flashing with shakes on the bottom, they will dam the water and cause problems. If the vent interferes with the bottom edges of the next course of shakes, notch them to clear the pipe. If there is too much of a gap between the shakes and the pipe, slide one shake down to cover the gap and prevent leaking.

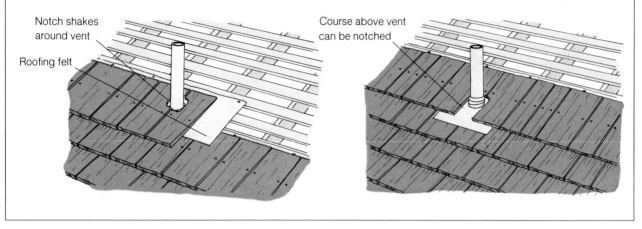

Notch shakes around vent

Roofing felt

Course above vent can be notched

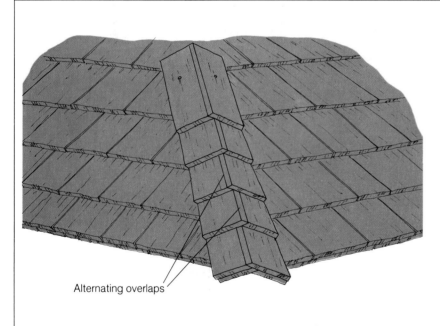

Alternating overlaps

Applying Hip Shakes

As you run each course of shakes to a hip, cut them with a saw so that they end at the center of the hip. The shakes for covering hips and ridges are factory prepared with mitered edges. They require 8d nails or longer. Place one hip shake at the bottom of the hip and one at the top, and snap a chalk line between them along one edge as a guide for placing the rest of the hip shakes. Apply a double hip shake at the eave, cutting the first one so that its top edge butts against the next course of shakes. Proceed up the hip, alternating the overlaps of the mitered corners. For more protection, lap the courses of roofing felt from the side applied last over the hip, trimming felt before applying the hip shakes.

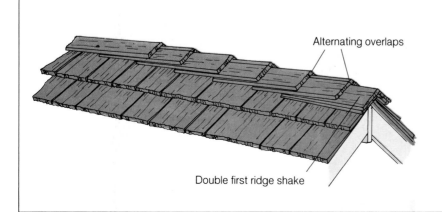

Alternating overlaps

Double first ridge shake

Applying Ridge Shakes

Apply ridge shakes the same way as hip shakes. Snap a chalk line to guide alignment after placing a ridge shake at each end. Work from the end of the ridge that receives the worst storms, or for a symmetrical design work from both ends toward the middle. You can create another interesting effect by using more than two shakes to start each end, thus giving the roof a sway-backed look. Cover the last two nail heads with mastic cement.

ROOF SHINGLES: composition

Composition shingles, also called asphalt shingles or comp shingles, are the roofing material most homeowners are likely to install themselves. Seventy to eighty percent of the homes in this country have them. These shingles come in a wide range of colors and styles, and some are guaranteed up to 30 years.

Installation includes preparing the roof deck, applying a felt underlayment, flashing the valleys, applying the shingles, and covering the hips and ridges. The only difficult parts

are keeping the lines straight and enduring the tedium of repetitive nailing.

Arrange for rooftop delivery to avoid having to carry 90-pound bundles up a ladder. If necessary, rent a ladder hoist (which works like an elevator) to carry the shingles to the roof. Besides the shingles, you will need 15-pound roofing felt, metal-drip edges, flashings for valleys and vents, and 2 pounds of roofing nails per square (100 square feet). Nails should be long enough to penetrate the roof

decking ¾ inch. If available, use a roll of starter strip instead of upside-down shingles for the first row. Although you can easily do all the work from the roof for slopes up to 4 in 12, provide scaffolding along the eaves for steeper roofs, so that you can get the first few courses up in a comfortable and safe way.

Recommended Cross-References
Flashing, Framing, Roofs, Roof Shakes, Roof Shingles: Wood.

Preparing the Roof

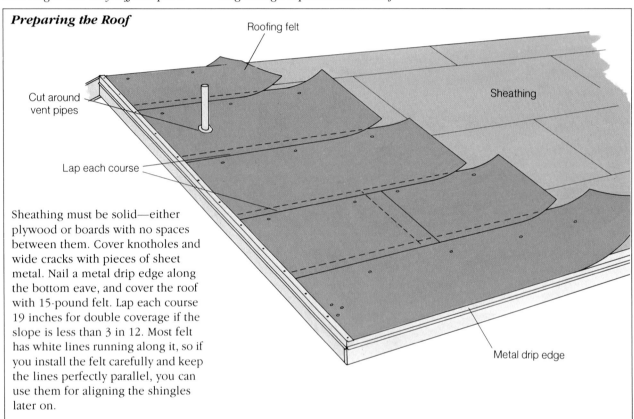

Roofing felt

Cut around vent pipes

Lap each course

Sheathing

Metal drip edge

Sheathing must be solid—either plywood or boards with no spaces between them. Cover knotholes and wide cracks with pieces of sheet metal. Nail a metal drip edge along the bottom eave, and cover the roof with 15-pound felt. Lap each course 19 inches for double coverage if the slope is less than 3 in 12. Most felt has white lines running along it, so if you install the felt carefully and keep the lines perfectly parallel, you can use them for aligning the shingles later on.

Choosing a Shingle Pattern
Gaps between the shingle tabs create a strong pattern on the roof. On 3-tab shingles the tabs are 12 inches wide; if they are staggered evenly, the gaps between each course would be offset by 6 inches. This is called a 6-inch pattern and is the easiest to install, although deviations show up clearly.

A 4-inch pattern creates a strong diagonal look. It wears better than a 6-inch pattern and is recommended for slopes less than 4 in 12. The most random-appearing pattern is 5 inch, which many professionals use. Save the cut-off ends for finishing courses. Start new courses by cutting off shingles; never use scraps. Cut on the back with a utility knife.

4-Inch Pattern

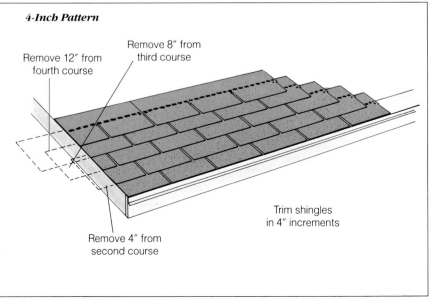

Remove 12″ from fourth course

Remove 8″ from third course

Remove 4″ from second course

Trim shingles in 4″ increments

Applying Shingles

Start with a row of solid roofing along an eave, using either starter-strip material or 3-tab shingles turned upside down. Snap a chalk line to keep the top edges straight. Overlap the starter course ⅜ inch beyond the edge. Then apply the first row of shingles over the top of the starter strip, making sure the ends do not line up over the gaps below. Work from one end toward the other as far as you can reach, then start the next course without changing your position. Start as many courses as you can reach, and then move over and repeat the process. The weather exposure for composition shingles is 5 inches. To keep the courses from drifting out of line, measure up from the eave at several points along the course you are applying. Or snap vertical chalk lines every 3 feet to keep the gaps in perfect alignment.

Nailing Pattern. Nail each 3-tab shingle with four nails, nailing each one ¾ inch above the top of the tabs. Leave a slight gap between shingles.

Flashing an Open Valley. An open valley—where shingles terminate instead of cross over—should have metal valley flashing installed over roofing felt. Painting the flashing before applying shingles makes it blend in better with the roof. To trim the shingles in an even line, snap chalk lines on each side of the valley. The lines should taper together toward the top, at a rate of ⅛ inch per foot, causing the shingles to flare apart from top to bottom and eliminating any edges that might catch water or debris.

Full-Lace Closed Valley. To create a smoother valley with no breaks for flashing, you can interweave shingles of alternating courses so that they cross over the valley and extend at least 1 foot up the opposite side. The valley should be flashed first with a full sheet of roll roofing, which is turned upside down to minimize cracking.

In applying the final shingle of each course, it is important that you "dub" (trim) the corners about 2 inches so that no sharp corners can trap errant water and debris under the shingles as they rush down toward the valley and cross over it. Embed dubbed corners in a patch of mastic about 3 inches wide.

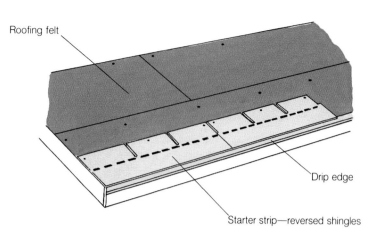

Roofing felt

Drip edge

Starter strip—reversed shingles

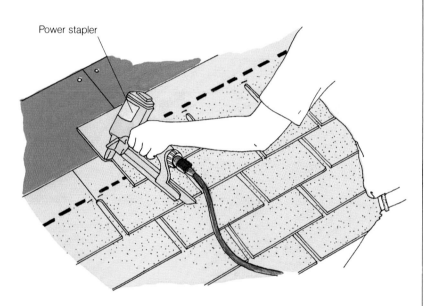

Power stapler

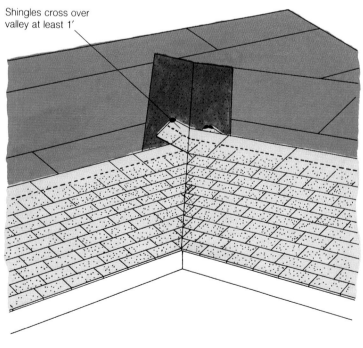

Shingles cross over valley at least 1′

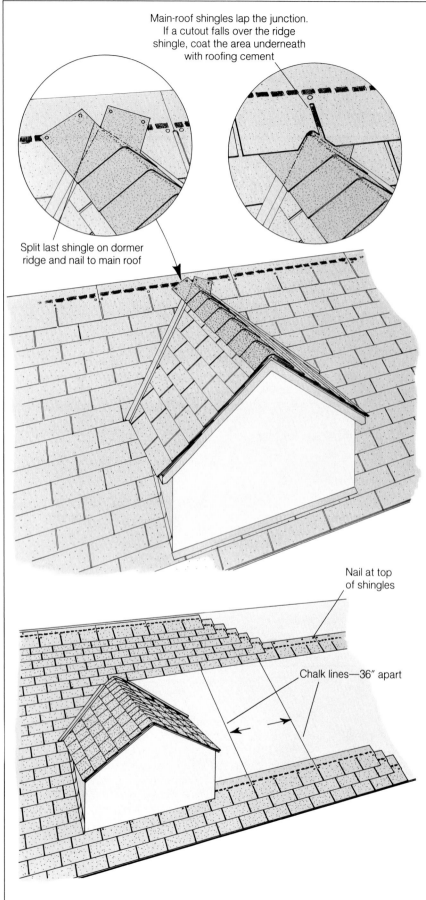

Main-roof shingles lap the junction. If a cutout falls over the ridge shingle, coat the area underneath with roofing cement

Split last shingle on dormer ridge and nail to main roof

Nail at top of shingles

Chalk lines—36″ apart

Shingling a Dormer

Shingle dormer roofs when the courses on the main roof reach the eaves of the dormer roof. Shingle dormers in a standard manner, protecting the valleys with the full-lace method. Apply ridge shingles to the dormer before nailing the course of shingles on the main roof that will eventually cross the dormer ridge shingles. Begin applying ridge shingles from the outer edge, working toward the main roof. When you reach the main roof, split the top of the last ridge shingle and carry it at least 4 inches onto the main roof. Shingles from the main roof should lap that junction.

Tying In. This is the process of working around a dormer to assure that the cutouts between tabs are vertically aligned on both sides of the dormer. To tie in a roof, shingle the roof upward toward the main ridge while at the same time extending the courses toward the dormer. Carry the lower courses across the bottom of the roof to the other side of the dormer. When you reach the dormer roof, shingle it, then bring the main roof shingles over to it and complete the left valley either with flashing or a full-lace valley.

For the actual tie in, carry the course immediately in line with the top of the dormer roof to a point about four shingles beyond the right side of the dormer roof. Nail only the tops of the shingles so that the course that is eventually brought up to it can be slipped underneath.

Continue roofing above this line all the way to the ridge. Now, using the gaps between tabs of these upper courses as guides, snap a chalk line from the ridge to the eave near the right edge of the dormer. Snap another one 36 inches further, and so on. Then complete the shingling, sliding the last course under the tabs of the top course. As you complete each course at the dormer, install step flashing along the side. Also, it is a good idea to snap horizontal chalk lines on the right side of the dormer to keep that side aligned. When measuring from the eaves for these horizontal lines, be sure to add the amount of shingle overhang at the eaves.

Applying Hip Shingles

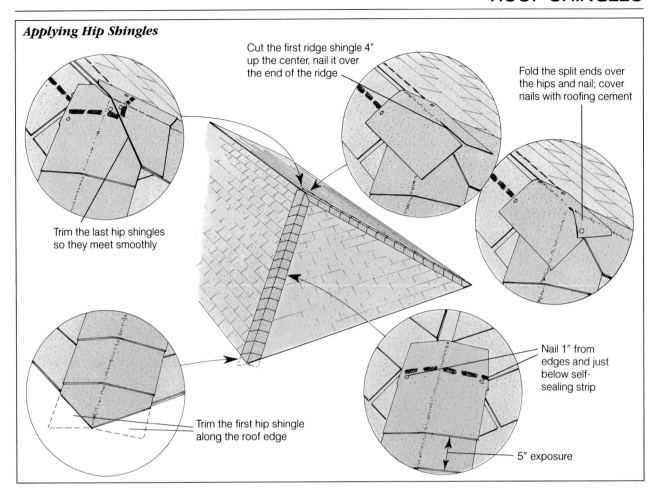

Cut the first ridge shingle 4" up the center, nail it over the end of the ridge

Fold the split ends over the hips and nail; cover nails with roofing cement

Trim the last hip shingles so they meet smoothly

Nail 1" from edges and just below self-sealing strip

Trim the first hip shingle along the roof edge

5" exposure

Covering an Old Roof

If your present roof has only one or two layers of roofing, you can probably roof right over it. However, if it is not fairly smooth, the new roof will reveal all the bumps and depressions. Be sure to remove protruding shingles and patch low spots first.

When covering an existing roof of composition shingles, try to match the shingle pattern that is already on the roof. Apply the starter strip along the eaves, but make it the same width as the first course of existing shingles—usually 5 or 6 inches. Then install the first course of new shingles, trimming the width to 10 inches so they will butt up to the third course of existing shingles. Complete the roof in the same way as for a new roof, butting each course of new shingles up to an old course. Remember to use 1¼-inch nails, not staples.

If the existing roof is tar and gravel, remove it. If it is wood shingles, use the same method of butting shingles up to existing courses, as long as the exposure is the same. For shakes, remove the roof.

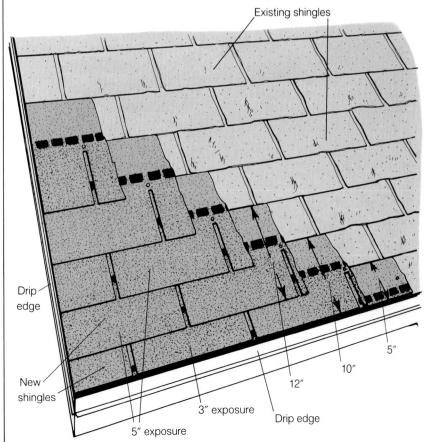

Existing shingles

Drip edge

New shingles

5" exposure

3" exposure

Drip edge

12"

10"

5"

ROOF SHINGLES: wood

Wood shingles, like shakes, are rigid, long lasting, and easy to apply, but they also are lighter in weight and give a smoother, more uniform appearance. Shingles come in lengths of 16 inches, 18 inches, and 24 inches. They are sold in bundles. Four bundles will cover a square (100 square feet) if they are applied with a 5-inch exposure. (It takes 5 bundles of 24-inch shakes to cover a square, applied with a 10-inch exposure.) The minimum allowable slope for shingles is normally 4 in 12, although they can be applied on 3-in-12 slopes if the exposure is reduced. You must use grade 1 shingles for roofing.

Wood shingles and shakes have two drawbacks: combustibility and discoloration from fungi. Both can be alleviated with chemical treatments, which should be applied commercially before installation for best results. Codes in some areas with extreme fire hazard may still not allow wood roofs, even after they have been treated.

Recommended Cross-References
Flashing, Framing, Roofs, Roof Shakes, Roof Shingles: Composition.

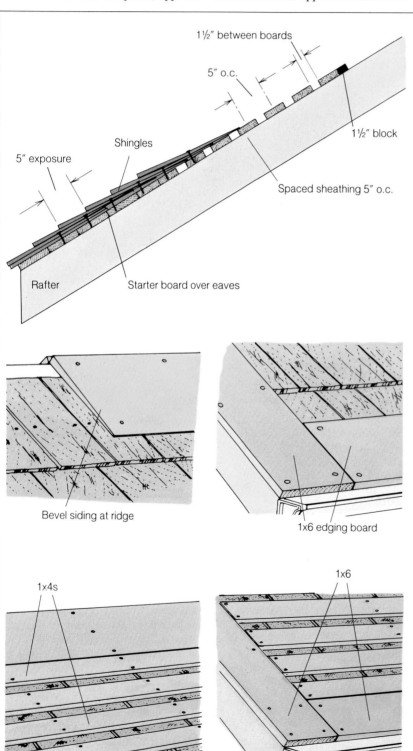

1½" between boards

5" o.c.

1½" block

Shingles

Spaced sheathing 5" o.c.

5" exposure

Rafter

Starter board over eaves

Bevel siding at ridge

1x6 edging board

1x4s

1x6

Preparing for Installation

Preparing the Deck. Wood shingles last a long time only when they are allowed to breathe: when air can circulate both beneath and above them. Therefore, they must be installed over spaced sheathing and the attic space must be well vented. Sheathing is usually made of 1 by 4s, spaced the same distance as the shingle exposure. In this example, the exposure is 5 inches, so the gap between 1 by 4 boards (which are actually 3½ inches wide) is 1½ inches. Sheathing along the eaves may be solid for the sake of appearance, and should be solid for 18 inches next to a ridge to allow for changes in nail spacings. Install ribbed valley flashing before shingling. Do not use drip edges with wood shingles.

Preparing an Old Roof. If the old roof is laid with wood shingles that are in reasonably good shape, you can apply new shingles directly over them. Just nail down or replace any warped shingles. Remove shingles along the eaves, rakes, and ridges to make room for 1 by 6 edging boards. Cut a clean line by setting a circular saw to just the right depth; cut only the shingles and not the sheathing. Use an old blade since you may be cutting through nails. Nail bevel siding to the ridge, and install new flashing in the valleys.

If the roof is made of composition shingles, tar and gravel, or roll roofing, nail spaced sheathing directly over it. Remove ridge and hip shingles first, and replace them with a strip of paper flashing (used for windows). Trim back the shingles with tin snips where they overhang eaves and rakes. Nail 1 by 6s along these edges and 1 by 4s for the rest of the spaced sheathing. At valleys, nail 1 by 4s down each side and run the regularly spaced sheathing up to them, leaving a ½-inch gap. Then install valley flashing.

Exposure

The amount of shingle or shake that can be exposed to the weather varies with the length and the roof slope. You want three layers of wood at any point on the roof.

It is important to keep shingles and shakes in a straight line as you nail. Mark the handle of your hammer or set the gauge on your hatchet to the correct exposure, so that you can measure for each shingle. Also measure up from the eave or down from the ridge from time to time along the course you are nailing to make sure the course is even. If you are drifting, do not try to make up the difference in one course. Instead, gradually work your way back into line over the next few courses.

This table lists recommended exposures, but check with your local building department:

Shingle Size	3 in 12 Roof	4 in 12 or Steeper Roofs
16-inch	3¾"	5"
18-inch	4½"	5½"
24-inch	5¾"	7½"

Applying Wood Shingles

The First Course. Do not use a felt underlayment with shingles. Instead, nail them directly over spaced sheathing or existing wood shingles. To start, nail a shingle at each end of the eave so that they overhang the eave 1 inch and the rake ¼ to ⅜ inch. Drive a nail into the butt of each shingle, and stretch a line between them to use for the rest of the starter course. Leave a ⅛- to ¼-inch gap between shingles. Double the first course of shingles, staggering gaps by at least 1½ inches. Then start the second course of shingles at the recommended exposure.

Nailing. Use HDG box nails, figuring that you will need a little more than 2 pounds per square. Use 3d nails for 16- or 18-inch shingles and 4d nails for 24-inch shingles. Nail shakes with 6d nails. Use longer sizes for reroofing as well as for nailing hip and ridge shingles.

You can nail with any hammer, but a roofer's hammer has the right heft for so much nailing and includes measuring gauges. To find the right placement for each nail, measure up from the butt of the shingle you are nailing a distance equal to the exposure plus 1 or 2 inches. To find this distance easily, mark the handle of your hammer with tape or a notch. Nail snugly, but not so hard that heads break the wood fibers. If a shingle is crooked, don't try to align it after two nails have been hammered in; it is better to pull it out and replace it.

Stagger gaps between shingles at least 1½ inches between courses; they should not line up over gaps in the courses below.

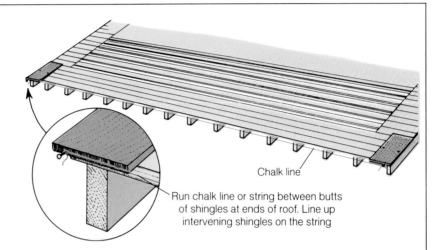

Chalk line

Run chalk line or string between butts of shingles at ends of roof. Line up intervening shingles on the string

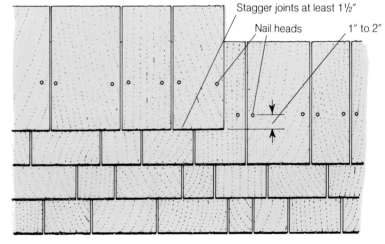

Stagger joints at least 1½"

Nail heads

1" to 2"

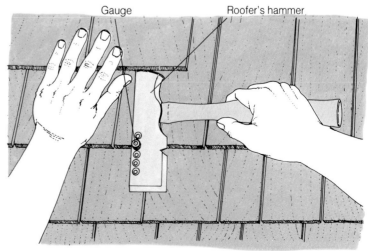

Gauge

Roofer's hammer

ROOF TILES

Tile roofs are fireproof, beautiful, long lasting, and, at least for many new styles, surprisingly easy to install. Roof tiles are suitable in any climate, although those permeated with color tend to last longer in regions used to snow. Tiles can be installed on both low-slope and high-slope roofs.

Installation techniques vary with the type of tile and the manufacturer. Some clay tiles require that a hot mop roof be installed underneath, while others can be laid over spaced sheathing. One of the easiest types to install is interlocking flat tile, shown here.

Recommended Cross-References
Flashing, Framing, Roofs.

Preparing the Roof

Sheath the roof with 1/2-inch exterior-grade plywood or, for an exposed ceiling, with 2 by 6 tongue-and-groove decking. Some tile has air pockets that provide an R-11 insulation value. Increase this value markedly by covering the sheathing with 1/2-inch foil-covered, rigid insulation. Or, apply roofing felt.

Some tiles are nailed to the sheathing; others have lugs to hook over wood battens. For the battens, use redwood or pressure-treated 1 by 2s, spacing them according to the exposure required. Consult the manufacturer's recommendations, but 14 inches is a typical exposure.

Install metal drip flashing along the eaves under the felt and along the rake edges over the felt. Flash valleys with W-metal flashing at least 25 inches wide laid over 90-pound mineral surface roofing. Cover hips and ridges with a double layer of felt that overlaps at least 6 inches on both sides.

Nail a 2 by 2 board along the center of every hip and ridge to support the cap tiles. Nail the board to the framing so that the plywood sheathing butts up to it. Also nail a 1-by board along the outside edges of the rake rafters to hold the rake tiles away from the rafters. Finally, nail a 1 by 2 starter board along the edge of the eaves. If the tiles are not flat, this starter strip can become a dam for water blown under curved tiles. Cut drainage notches. For tiles with an irregular profile, such as barrel tiles, manufacturers offer special metal edgings over which the tiles fit flush.

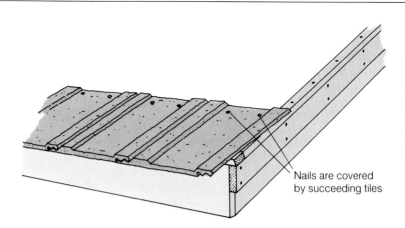

Nails are covered by succeeding tiles

Installing Roof Tiles

1. The First Course. Install the first course so that each tile overhangs the starter strip, beginning at the right-hand rake edge. Nail the tiles with HDG common nails long enough to penetrate the roof sheathing 3/4 inch. Snap a chalk line to align the top edge of the tiles.

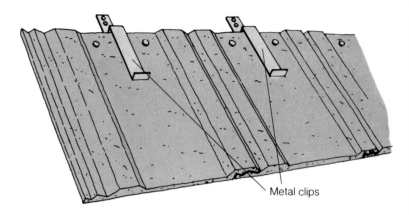

Metal clips

2. Clips. For roofs steeper than 6 in 12, use clips on every fourth row in addition to nails; use clips on every row for roofs steeper than 10 in 12. These clips are provided by the manufacturer to fit the particular type of tile and are nailed into the sheathing. Clips are also available for installations in high-wind areas; they hold down the side of each tile, near the bottom, where it will be covered by the next interlocking tile.

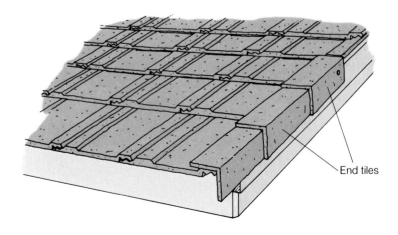

End tiles

3. Trim Tiles. Cover the rake edges with special tiles or use metal trim provided by the manufacturer. Some of these metal trim pieces are designed so that a fascia board will conceal them along the side.

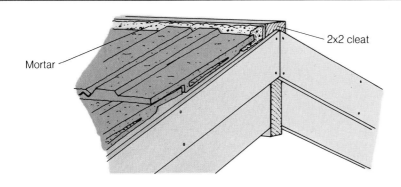

Mortar

2x2 cleat

4. The Final Course. For ridge and hip tiles, cut the final course of tiles so that they stop short of the 2 by 2 cleat by 1½ inches. Use a circular saw with an abrasive blade. Then lay a bed of mortar against the 2 by 2 and embed each tile in it as you nail it in place. Cover the nail heads with mastic. Some manufacturers recommend a ½-inch gap between the ridge cleat and the tile; some specify mastic instead of mortar.

5. Cap Tiles. Cover the hips and ridges with cap tiles. They come in various shapes, either angled or rounded, and should cover at least the top 3 inches of each side. Nail the cap tiles into the hip or ridge cleat, and apply mastic over the nail head and end of tile that will be covered by the next cap tile. Start the installation at the bottom of a hip and at the end of the ridge from which prevailing storms come.

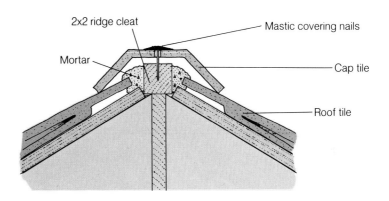

2x2 ridge cleat

Mastic covering nails

Mortar

Cap tile

Roof tile

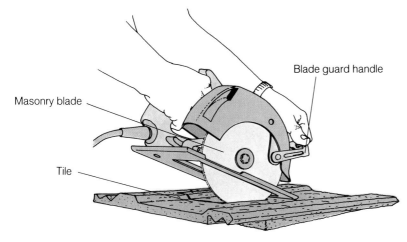

Blade guard handle

Masonry blade

Tile

6. Cutting Around Vents. Cut the tiles to fit snugly around the vent pipe, using plunge cuts with a circular saw. Lift the blade guard out of the way and bring the saw down slowly into each tile while it is running, keeping the front edge of the shoe steady against the tile. The saw blade will not cut into the corners, so just rap it out with a hammer.

7. Vent Flashing. Flashing for tile roofs must be specially made from lead at a sheet-metal shop. After you place a cut-out tile over the vent, apply mastic around the pipe and onto the tile. Then drop the flashing down over the pipe and shape the lead flange to conform to the profile of the tile pattern by pressing it into place. The next course of tiles should lap over the top edge of the flashing, just like vent flashing for shingles and shakes.

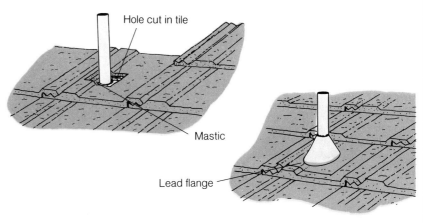

Hole cut in tile

Mastic

Lead flange

SAFETY

Safety should be the highest priority for improving any home. Some hazards, such as those contributing to fire, falls, or electrical shock, are obvious and can be identified with a quick home inspection. Others, such as structural deficiencies, asbestos hazards, radon, and lead paint, are not so obvious and require professional help to locate and remove.

Use the checklist to perform your own safety inspection. Include all family members in your tour. You can take care of many problems immediately. Other improvements, such as installing lights, should move up to the top of your to-do list. As you tour your home, keep in mind that the most common household accident, by far, is a fall, and that two thirds of all home fires start in the kitchen.

Recommended Cross-References
Bracing, Chimneys & Stovepipes, Doors, Electrical System, Fireplaces, Garages, Glass, Lighting, Pools, Railings, Security, Stairs, Telephones, Ventilation, Windows, Wood-Burning Stoves, Zoning, Codes & Permits.

Accommodating Specific Needs

For those who have physical disabilities or who intend to stay in their home as they age, foresight can make life more comfortable, convenient, and safe. The best time to make major changes is during a remodeling project.

For people in wheelchairs, make doorways 2 inches wider than standard. Place electrical receptacles in the faces of cabinets below counters. Equip doors with levered knobs, drawers with easily grasped handles, and slide-out cutting boards with one-touch latches.

For people with limited vision, incandescent lighting is better than fluorescent lighting because it causes less glare and color distortion. Areas where levels change, such as steps or landings, should be highlighted with borders of contrasting color or texture to prevent falls. Edges of countertops should also be highlighted.

For those who have difficulty moving about, an intercom system is a major convenience.

Designing for a Wheelchair

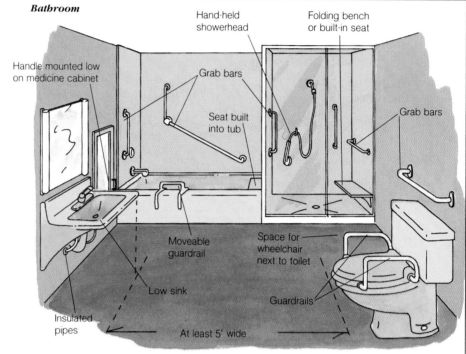

Bathroom

- Hand-held showerhead
- Folding bench or built-in seat
- Handle mounted low on medicine cabinet
- Grab bars
- Seat built into tub
- Grab bars
- Moveable guardrail
- Space for wheelchair next to toilet
- Low sink
- Guardrails
- Insulated pipes
- At least 5' wide

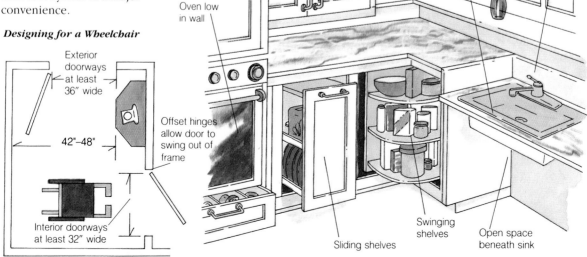

- Exterior doorways at least 36" wide
- 42"–48"
- Offset hinges allow door to swing out of frame
- Interior doorways at least 32" wide

Kitchen

- Low countertops
- Faucet with single handle
- Low cabinets
- Oven low in wall
- Sliding shelves
- Swinging shelves
- Open space beneath sink

A Home Safety Checklist

Note: Asterisks denote recommendations for homes with children.

Entry. _ Is the floor nonslippery?
_ Are rugs secure?
_ Is there adequate lighting?

Stairs. _ Is a light over the stairs, with switches at top and bottom?
_ Are handrails secure and no higher than 32 inches above each riser?
_ Are balusters close enough to prevent a baby from falling through (4 inches maximum opening)?*
_ Are stairs free of clutter?
_ Is a smoke detector at the top?
_ Are tread and riser dimensions safe? (Maximum height for main stairs is 7½ inches; minimum width is 9 inches.)
_ Does a door open outward over stairway? If so, the door should be 3 feet from the top stair or reversed to swing inward.
_ Is there a second, lower handrail?*

Living Room/Family Room/Den.
_ Are there any one-step changes in floor level? If so, are they marked prominently with a change of flooring material or with accent lighting?
_ Do all windows within 18 inches of the floor have tempered or safety glass?*
_ Are sliding glass doors marked?
_ Does the fireplace have a fire screen or glass doors?*
_ Is a fire extinguisher easily accessible near the fireplace?
_ Does the fireplace hearth extend at least 20 inches into the room?
_ Has the chimney been cleaned within the past six months?
_ If there is a wood-burning stove, was it installed with a proper permit?
_ Are there enough electrical outlets?
_ Do extension cords avoid runs under carpet or across doorways?
_ Are valuables in a fireproof safe?
_ Are ashtrays convenient?
_ Are light bulbs the correct wattage for each fixture? Use 60-watt bulbs if you're not sure.
_ Are dangling cords tied up?*
_ Are electrical outlets childproof?*
_ Are tippy lamps, furniture secure?*
_ Are any houseplants poisonous?*
_ Are all choking hazards—anything small enough for a youngster's throat—removed?*

Hallway. _ Is there adequate lighting, with switches at both ends of the hall?
_ Is the hallway free of clutter?
_ Are rugs secure and skid-proof?

Kitchen. _ Are key telephone numbers (emergency, family doctor, poison control center) handy?*
_ Is a Class B:C fire extinguisher handy and visible? (It should not be next to the cooktop.)
_ Have curtains above or behind the cooktop been removed?
_ Are utensils handy so you don't have to reach over the cooktop to get them?
_ Are large lids close to the cooktop to use for smothering a grease fire?
_ Is there a smoke detector between the kitchen and living areas?
_ Is the cooktop away from doors that swing inward and windows that open over it?
_ Are main traffic paths away from the main work area?
_ Are floors and work surfaces well lighted?
_ Is a first-aid kit handy?
_ Are tablecloths that toddlers might pull removed?*
_ Are cleaning supplies and caustic materials in locked storage?*
_ Are cooktop controls childproof?*
_ Do cabinet doors and drawers have childproof latches?*
_ Does the garbage disposer have a safety switch?*
_ Are sharp tools (knives, scissors) safely stored and out of reach?*
_ Is there a play space for toddlers close to the kitchen, but not in the main work area?*

Bathroom. _ Does the bathtub have a nonskid bottom?*
_ Do electrical outlets have GFCIs?
_ Are light and fan switches out of reach from the tub or shower?
_ Do rugs have nonskid backing?
_ If there is a portable heater, is it approved for "wet" locations?
_ Does the shower door have safety glazing (tempered, laminated, or hard plastic)?
_ Are towel racks securely mounted?
_ Does the tub or shower have an antiscald faucet?*
_ Does the shower have a grab bar?
_ Can the door be unlocked from the outside with a nail or common object?
_ Does the medicine cabinet have a locked section?*
_ Does the toilet lid have a latch?*

Bedrooms. _ Does each bedroom have safe egress—an openable window with a clear opening at least 20 inches wide by 24 inches high and a sill within 44 inches of the floor?

_ Does each second-story bedroom have access to a secondary escape?
_ Is there a clear path to safety, unhindered by furniture or clutter, for quick exit in the dark?
_ Is a lamp or wall switch within reach of each bed? A flashlight?
_ Is smoking in bed prohibited?
_ Does the phone have emergency numbers displayed or on speed dial?
_ Are smoke detectors installed? (There should be at least one per floor, outside sleeping areas; they should be UL approved; test monthly with smoke and replace batteries yearly.)
_ Is the crib safe (no doodads on top of corners; slats no more than 2⅜ inches apart; lead-free paint; mattress fits snugly against sides; bumper pads around the inside of the crib, attached by snaps)?*
_ Are windows childproof (cannot be opened more than 5 inches and no climbable furniture nearby)?*
_ Are light switches in the bedroom and bathroom low enough to reach?*

Garage/Basement. _ Does automatic garage door have safety reverse?
_ Is the floor dry and free of debris?
_ Are gasoline and flammables stored in approved containers?
_ Are they stored away from appliances with pilot lights?
_ Is a fire extinguisher handy?
_ Are all ladders safe and solid?
_ Are appliances with pilot lights at least 18 inches above the floor?
_ Does the furnace have adequate air intake and flue?
_ Is the dryer vent in good repair?
_ Is the water heater temperature lowered to 120 degrees if children or older persons live in the home?*
_ Does everyone know how to shut off gas and electricity to the house?
_ If there's a fuse box, are extra fuses of the right amperage handy?
_ Are workshop areas well lighted?
_ Do workshop areas have enough receptacles? GFCI protection?
_ Are power tools locked up?*
_ Are hazardous materials locked?*

Outdoors. _ Do electrical receptacles have GFCI protection?
_ Are walkways, entrances, and steps well lighted?
_ Do decks and stairs have railings?*
_ Are spaces between deck-railing members no wider than 4 inches?*
_ Is swimming pool or spa fenced, with a door alarm on patio doors?*
_ Are any of the plants poisonous?*

SCREENS

A screen door in need of repair may not seem like a major home improvement. However, if you consider the frustration and nuisance it causes, repairing it may endear you to your loved ones. A screen door is fragile compared to a solid-core or sliding glass door and, with everyday use, it is to be expected that the screen will tear, break, sag, or simply come out. The only trick to replacement is to make sure that the new screen is taut.

Recommended Cross-References
Doors, Windows.

Wood Doors

On a wooden screen door, start by removing the door. Lay planks over a pair of sawhorses to provide a clamping platform. Lay the door on the sawhorses.

1. Pry up the molding around the screen, being very careful not to break it. (If you do, you may be able to find a replacement piece at a lumberyard that carries a full line of moldings. It is called screen bead.)

2. Use a screwdriver or the corner of a putty knife to remove all the staples that hold the old screen.

3. Cut a new piece of screen so it overlaps the opening by 1 inch all around. Attach the screen across the bottom edge of the door only, using a staple gun. Be sure the screen is straight and the staples are snug.

4. There are two ways to stretch the screen. One is to bend the door frame slightly by placing sticks under each end of the door and clamping the middle down to the sawhorse planks. Staple the top of the screen in place, release the tension slowly, then staple both sides. Do not staple the center rail until last. Trim the excess screen with a sharp knife and replace the molding.

The second method requires a lot of extra screen at the top. Leave the door frame flat and wrap the excess screen around a board so that you can apply tension. As you hold the board down, staple the top of the screen to the door frame.

5. Staple the sides, then the center of the screen to the door.

6. Replace the molding over the edge of the screen.

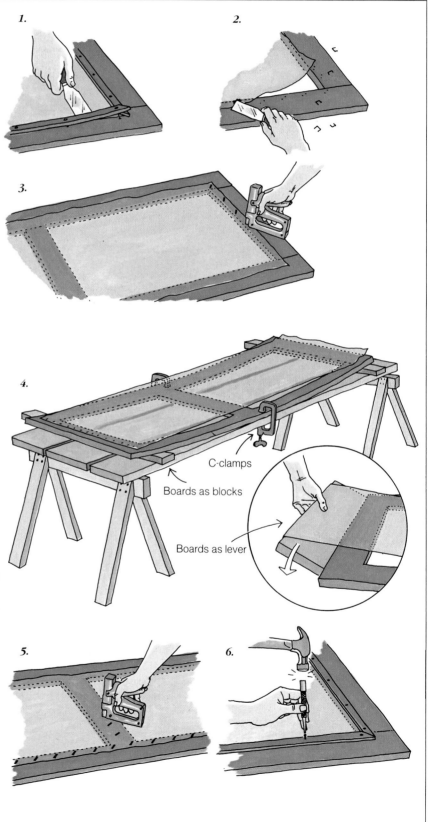

C-clamps

Boards as blocks

Boards as lever

Strengthening Screen Doors

To strengthen corners, countersink long wood screws through the stiles into the ends of the rails.

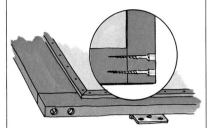

To correct a sagging door, run a wire or light cable from the top on the hinge side to the bottom on the latch side—tighten with a turnbuckle. In order to keep it taut, run the wire through the turnbuckle in a figure eight pattern.

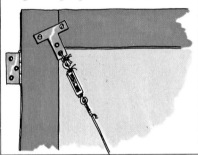

Aluminum Doors

Aluminum screen doors and windows are easier to work on than wood ones because they have flexible plastic or metal splines that hold the screen. To remove the old screen, use a screwdriver to pry up one corner of the spline from its channel. Work your way around, being careful not to bend the spline. Cut the replacement screen so that it fits the outer edge of the door.

Next, using a special roller tool, put the screen in the bottom channel and replace the spline. Keeping the aluminum door perfectly square, work your way up one side with the spline and all the way around the screen. The combination of pressure from the tool and the spline compressing into the channel will pull the screen taut. Finally, trim off all the excess screen using wire cutters or a utility knife.

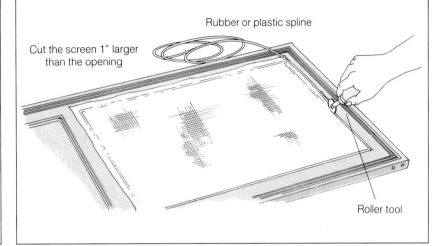

Rubber or plastic spline

Cut the screen 1″ larger than the opening

Roller tool

Screening Materials

Suppliers sell screen by the square foot, usually from rolls that are 24, 26, 28, 32, 36, 42, or 48 inches wide. The mesh comes in three typical sizes: 16 by 16, 16 by 18, and 18 by 18. The classifications refer to the number of wires per inch; the higher the number, the tighter the screen. All three sizes keep most insects out, but if you are particularly concerned about mosquitoes, you should buy 18 by 18 mesh.

Screening for windows and doors is available in four different materials: plastic, galvanized steel, bronze, and aluminum. If you replace a screen, use the same kind of material for the new screen. Be certain that you are not combining metals that are incompatible, or the screen will corrode more quickly than normal. Use plastic or aluminum screen with aluminum doors, not bronze or galvanized steel. If you attach screen to a wood door frame, use copper nails for bronze screen, aluminum nails for aluminum screen, and galvan-

ized nails for galvanized screen. Use staples on plastic or galvanized screen only if they are corrosion resistant or protected from direct exposure to the weather. Each type of screen has certain advantages and disadvantages.

Galvanized Screen. Galvanized screen is usually the least expensive screening and the least resistant to corrosion. The zinc coating wears off fairly quickly, allowing the steel to rust and cause stains. When galvanized screen is new, it is the strongest screening.

Plastic Screen. Plastic screen is resistant to corrosion and stains. The individual strands are larger than equivalent screen sizes, so the screening tends to be denser. A plastic screen is somewhat flexible; it has more impact resistance than bronze or aluminum screen. Plastic screens melt at the touch of a candle or lighted cigarette, however. Plastic screens cost slightly more than galvanized steel screens. The main disadvantage of plastic is that it must be

stretched very tightly for proper installation. Fold all edges before you staple them.

Aluminum Screen. Slightly more expensive than plastic, aluminum screening is stronger and almost as resistant to corrosion. The wire consists of a high-strength alloy core coated with a more corrosion-resistant aluminum. Aluminum will corrode near salt water and tends to turn a dark color in smoggy areas. In most cases, soapy water cleans aluminum effectively.

Bronze Screen. Bronze screen is the most expensive and the most durable. Bronze screen is available with one of two finishes: bright and antique (the antique finish is dark brown). A coat of varnish covers the finish and prevents staining, although the varnish wears off in a few years. At that point, the screen may stain the floor or nearby surface. A new coat of varnish or lacquer will renew the screens. If you coat bronze screens, thin the coating so it will not clog the spaces.

SECURITY

Most of the precautions you can take against intruders are common sense, beginning with the recognition of where dangers exist. About half of all burglaries occur between 8 a.m. and 5 p.m. In more than 25 percent of burglaries, there is no forced entry, although smash-and-grab techniques are more common than sophisticated lock picking. When forced entry does occur, it is usually done by kicking in a door or destroying a lock cylinder with a pry bar or large wrench. Front doors are not often attacked if there is another option, because they are usually visible from the street. Once inside, burglars generally search the master bedroom first, because this is where they expect to find valuables and cash.

Recommended Cross-References
Doors, Electrical System, Fences, Garages, Gates, Glass, Lighting: Outdoor, Locks, Railings, Stairs, Steps, Windows, Wiring.

Lighting

Outdoor lighting is another deterrent to burglars. In many cases the actual burglary is committed during the day, but only after the burglar discovered the location of unlocked doors and windows on a previous night.

Bright searchlights are not necessary to maintain adequate security; rather, pick a lighting system that is suitable for all your outdoor needs: a variety of intensities coming from a variety of sources. Nor is it necessary to leave lights on all night. Switches are available that are sensitive to motion or sound. They will automatically turn on the lights if a person moves into their range or if they detect a sharp sound, such as the clinking of a tool. After a short time, usually 10 to 15 minutes, they shut off automatically. Some packaged units include this kind of switch, together with one or two floodlights.

Alarm Systems

Although no home is completely burglarproof, you can go a long way toward securing your home from intruders by investing in a home-security device. However, keep in mind that security is more than something you simply buy at a store and install. A few fundamental, common-sense precautions can be as effective a deterrent as equipping your home with elaborate security equipment.

Alarms vary widely in effectiveness, sophistication, and price, but the two basic systems are perimeter protection, which trips an alarm whenever an outside door or window is opened, and space protection, which trips an alarm whenever motion is detected inside the house. Both types consist of sensors, a central control panel, and the alarm. In some systems the parts are hooked together with wires, which must be concealed and protected against cutting but which are also very reliable. In other systems the sensors transmit radio signals to the central control panel located in the house. The signaling system relies on sophisticated electronics, and should be checked thoroughly and installed by a professional. Locate the sensors at doors, windows, or central locations where they can scan the interior spaces.

Both kinds of system have a circuit that connects the central panel to one or two alarms, in some cases to a telephone that automatically dials a predetermined number and gives coded messages. This option is the most successful if the phone is hooked up to a home security service. The service will have phone numbers of neighbors and friends to contact, as well as the ability to determine from the coded message which police, fire, or other emergency personnel should be notified. It also inspects your system to see how reliable it is before taking you on as a subscriber.

You can install most alarm systems yourself if you have basic wiring skills, but get professional advice from several sources before you buy and install the system. Many insurance companies reduce their premiums with the installation of a security alarm.

Locks

Most burglaries are committed in homes with unlocked doors or windows, so install locks and use them. A locksmith can recommend the best ones, but they are expensive. Have solid doors with two locks each. Fit basement and ground-floor windows with sash locks or similar devices.

Sliding glass doors should have security bars and pin locks. Garage and cellar doors should be locked, and windows near a back door should contain shatterproof glass.

Secure upstairs windows, especially those close to climbable trees and trellises. Some police departments have programs where they will send an officer to your home to advise you about potential entry points and make security recommendations.

Dead-Bolt Lock

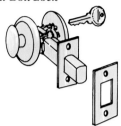

Maximum-security dead bolts have keys in both sides. Make sure inside keys are not removable, or are kept handy for exit in case of fire

Doorknobs for Inside Rooms

Locked from one side, insertion of a screwdriver or ice pick into the hole or slot in other side allows exit in case of emergency

Window Lock

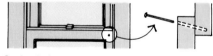

Sash window
pin latch

Sliding window
pin latch with key

Sliding Doors

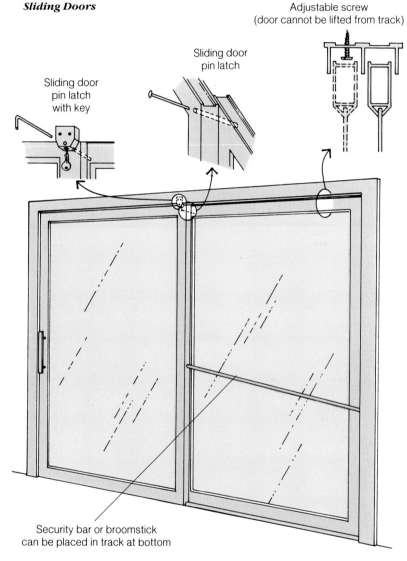

Sliding door
pin latch
with key

Sliding door
pin latch

Adjustable screw
(door cannot be lifted from track)

Security bar or broomstick
can be placed in track at bottom

Good Housekeeping

Keep up the yard and exterior of your home to show that someone cares. Trim back shrubs that create hiding places near the house or that obscure your door from the street. Make arrangements for mail and newspaper pickup, housesitting, and police surveillance whenever you go on vacation. Set timer switches to turn on a light and TV or radio at night. These precautions should deter burglars who are on the lookout for an easy target.

Protecting Valuables

Provide extra protection for valuables such as money, jewelry, keys, art objects, and silverware. Buy a home vault or find good hiding places. Engrave your ID on all electronic equipment, power tools, small appliances, and other valuables. Many police departments loan engraving tools, or you can buy one cooperatively with your neighbors. Inventory your possessions and store the list in a bank deposit box.

With a Little Help From Your Friends

A neighborhood watch is extremely effective. Contact your local police department for information about starting a program in your area.

What about getting a dog to keep burglars away? Experts agree that they will deter an intruder, especially when you are at home. However, unless they are trained, they generally make poor security guards. (But don't tell your dog.)

SHEDS

The right shed to buy is the one that works best for you on three different levels: It should fit in with your overall storage plan; it should involve expending the amount of time, effort, and money you choose to invest; and the structural design and appearance should be appropriate to your site.

It is important to clarify your reasons for needing a shed, then plan it carefully so that it accommodates them. Consider not only how the shed will look, but also the size, the location, the position of the doors, interior amenities, utility hookups, and other possible uses.

Your choices for a shed include building your own structure or buying a fabricated shed or a construction kit. Each has its own advantages. If you are limited in time and construction skills, buy as complete a kit as possible. If you want the shed a particular size or shape and you enjoy a challenging outdoor project, design and build it from scratch.

Be sure to locate the shed where the access is convenient and where there is good drainage. You should also check with local building codes before starting any construction.

Recommended Cross-References
Concrete, Doors, Foundations, Framing, Roofs, Siding, Storage: Outdoor, Windows.

A shed can be large and concealed behind a fence (below) or integrated into the landscape (opposite top and center). It can also be a small structure just large enough for garbage cans (opposite below).

Design Considerations

Changing the design elements of a shed can affect how it functions as well as how it looks. The storage capacity and access to things being stored inside are largely set by where you place doors and window openings and any interior partitions or walls.

Door and Window Placement. Doors and windows can go anywhere, as long as they are properly framed with headers, side jambs, and sills. Modifying a plan to add a window or shift a door isn't difficult. Having them in the right place is important, though, because it will affect the way you enter, move around in, and use the shed.

Choosing the right place is, of course, up to you. By experimenting with sketches of your shed plans, you'll be able to see whether a proposed arrangement will let the building function as you want.

Interior Walls. If your shed is to serve more than one purpose, interior walls can help it do so. They define spaces clearly and separate activity areas that you don't want to mix. For example, you could run a solid wall through the middle of the shed and place a door to the outside at each end of the structure. This way, you can create a playhouse for the children on one side that keeps them safely away from the tools and chemicals that are stored on the other side.

Interior walls can be put up wherever you'd like them. In a space as small as a shed, they act as partitions rather than as load-bearing walls. Frame them in the same way as the framing for the exterior walls, and nail them to the floor and the wall framing.

Built-Ins. It is much easier to keep a shed neat and organized if there are specific places for the items stored. Plan storage cabinets to house general equipment and supplies. Make wall racks for storing tools, fishing rods, and the garden hose. Install hooks in the rafters for hanging ladders or the canoe. Make individual bins for each of the children so that they can keep track of their toys. Customize the interior of your shed so that you get the most benefit from the storage space.

Lean-To

This small lean-to shed is attached to the back wall of a house. There is good access close to the back door and the location is ideal for storing patio furniture, cushions, the barbecue, and other furnishings that need shelter in bad weather.

This shed can be built deeper, longer, or higher than shown just by changing the dimensions. Choose proportions that relate to the architecture and suit the wall on which it is placed. Finish materials for the lean-to should match those used on the main house.

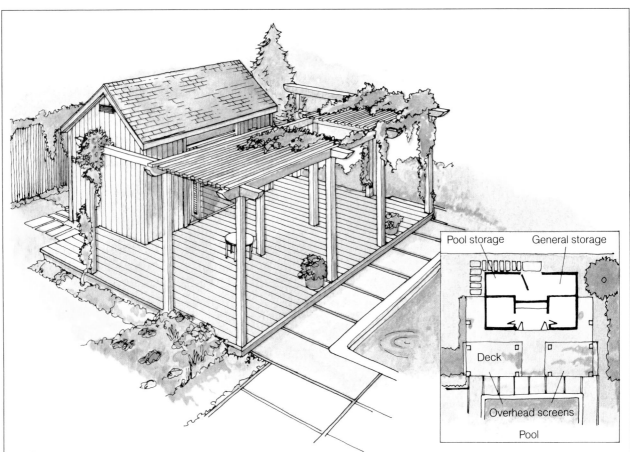

Cabana

This poolside cabana is walled through the middle to create two distinct spaces. The front half has dressing rooms with benches for changing. The high windows provide light, yet ensure privacy. Between the dressing rooms, there is a cabinet for towels and water toys.

The back area has its own entrance. In one half, the mechanical equipment for the pool hums away out of sight; the other half houses general household or garden storage. There's also room for chemicals and long-handled pool tools.

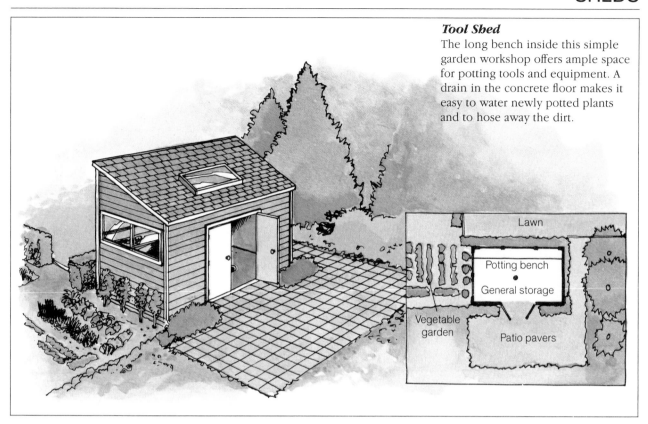

Tool Shed

The long bench inside this simple garden workshop offers ample space for potting tools and equipment. A drain in the concrete floor makes it easy to water newly potted plants and to hose away the dirt.

Lawn

Potting bench

General storage

Vegetable garden

Patio pavers

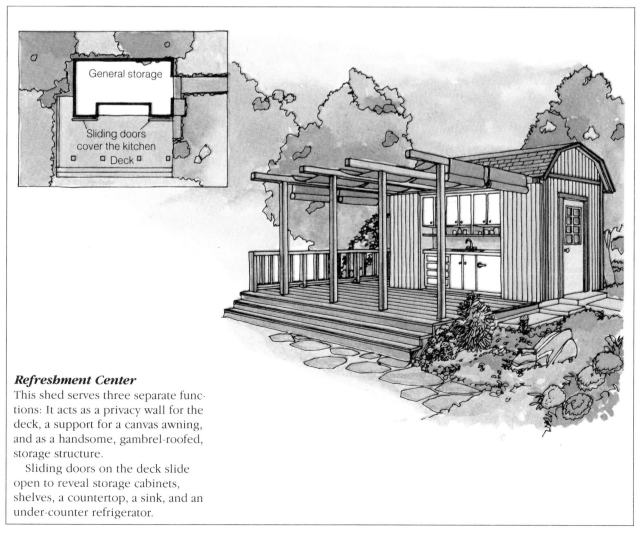

General storage

Sliding doors cover the kitchen

Deck

Refreshment Center

This shed serves three separate functions: It acts as a privacy wall for the deck, a support for a canvas awning, and as a handsome, gambrel-roofed, storage structure.

Sliding doors on the deck slide open to reveal storage cabinets, shelves, a countertop, a sink, and an under-counter refrigerator.

Basic Shed

This shed is a simple and versatile freestanding structure that can be used solely for storage or for storage combined with a workshop, a garden center, or a child's playhouse.

An experienced builder with one other person to help could put the shed up in a day or a day and a half. A novice without help should plan on at least six days or three weekends.

To simplify construction and elimi-nate a lot of cutting, use building materials in common sizes. The di-mensions of this shed are 12 feet by 8 feet. If you wish to alter the size, it is practical to make all changes in 4-foot increments.

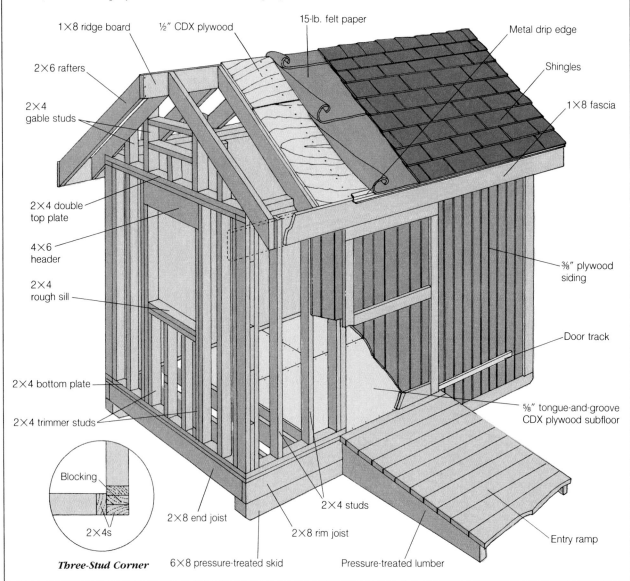

1×8 ridge board · ½" CDX plywood · 15-lb. felt paper · Metal drip edge · 2×6 rafters · Shingles · 2×4 gable studs · 1×8 fascia · 2×4 double top plate · 4×6 header · ⅜" plywood siding · 2×4 rough sill · Door track · 2×4 bottom plate · ⅝" tongue-and-groove CDX plywood subfloor · 2×4 trimmer studs · Blocking · 2×4s · Three-Stud Corner · 2×8 end joist · 2×4 studs · 2×8 rim joist · Entry ramp · 6×8 pressure-treated skid · Pressure-treated lumber

Choosing the Right Location

In the right spot, a shed is a conve-nience and a beneficial addition to the landscape. In the wrong place, it can be a nuisance and an eyesore.

Convenience. Pick a location conve-nient to the area where the stored items will be used: near the vegeta-ble garden if it will contain garden tools; near the play area if it will contain the kids' outdoor toys.

Access. Make sure that there are no sharp corners that have to be negoti-ated in order to get a lawn tractor, for example, from the shed to the lawn. Also think about how often you will need to go to the shed in bad weath-er. If you will use it a lot, situate it close to the house.

Terrain. Choose a spot that is flat, firm, and dry. Avoid soft ground. In addition to causing excessive or un-even settling of the structure, it may indicate that the site is damp. If necessary, regrade the site so that any runoff flows away from the building.

Siting. Carefully consider the effect that the shed will have on your back-yard. Not only should you make sure it blends in with the landscape, but also that it will not cast shadows over your rose garden.

Check Building Codes

Building codes regulate how far from the lot line your shed must be, how tall it can be, and what percentage of your total lot can be covered with construction.

Inquire about permits before you begin building. Requirements vary considerably from place to place. In some areas you don't need a permit for a shed that will be less than 120 square feet; in others, you need one for any sort of construc-tion. To obtain a permit, you must submit copies of your plans to the building inspector for approval.

Metal Sheds

Metal sheds have the advantages of being inexpensive and easy to erect. They come in a variety of sizes, but with limited design options. If you live in an area that gets strong winds or heavy snowfall, realize that metal sheds can dent and rust.

A metal shed tends to stand out more prominently in the environment simply because the material isn't common to gardens. By taking care to integrate it purposefully and thoughtfully into the surroundings, with pathways, plantings, and other landscape elements, a metal shed can share your outdoor living spaces discreetly and serve your storage needs well. In most cases you will have to construct the floor for the shed—either a concrete slab, a temporary wood floor, or a permanent wood floor on its own foundation.

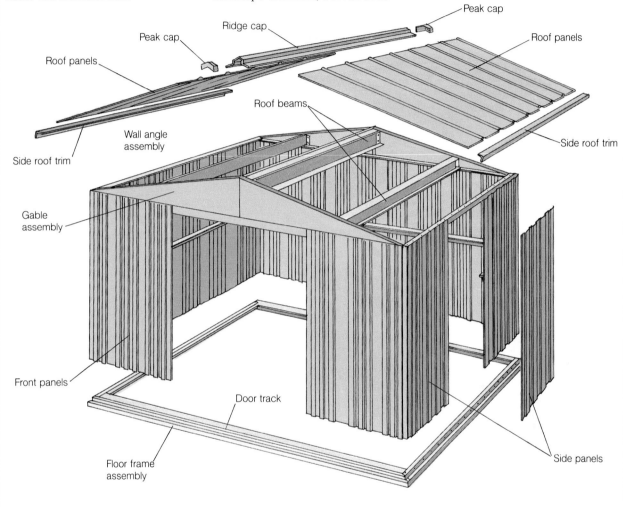

Prefabricated Sheds

Prefabricated wood structures are available in a variety of shapes and sizes. They do not come ready to use—they have to be assembled. The package includes parts, materials, and instructions. The amount of labor, skill, and tools required can vary greatly.

Precut Kits. This type of kit includes precut framing, precut sheathing, hardware, trim, and instructions. All you have to supply is the paint and incidental finish materials.

You need very few tools, and the assembly is generally quite simple.

Partially Precut Kits. With this kind of kit you will get precut wood framing, uncut sheathing, precut trim, and hardware. In some cases the framing components may be metal.

The precut pieces are often numbered to make assembly easier, but you still need to do some measuring. Sheathing materials need to be cut to fit.

Uncut Kits. An uncut kit generally includes cardboard templates and uncut framing and sheathing materials. Necessary hardware may or may not be supplied.

Cardboard templates are used like a dress pattern to guide measuring and cutting procedures. Sometimes the templates are sold separately with instructions and a lumber list so you can choose your own materials.

Foundations. No matter what type of kit you select, you'll have to do some site preparation and lay a foundation. The site should be a level, firm, and well-drained spot, so the shed will sit squarely, settle evenly, and be impervious to dampness.

Depending on local building codes, you have several choices for a foundation: a layer of patio blocks, a bed of gravel, a concrete slab, a pier foundation, or pressure-treated lumber skids. Whichever base you use, the shed has to be firmly anchored.

Some prefabricated sheds come with flooring, but most do not. Therefore the foundation will be your floor unless you opt to construct a finish floor on top of it.

Shelves can be a wall of cubbyholes (above), separate units that flank a fireplace (opposite above), or act as a room divider suspended from the ceiling (far right). They can house decorative objects or a collection of good-looking kitchenware (right).

There always seems to be a need for more shelves in a home, both for storing items that should not be seen and for showcasing those collections of things that you want on view. You need shelves in cabinets, shelves in storage areas, shelves in closets, shelves for books, shelves for records and tapes, shelves in the kitchen and the bathroom—the list is endless.

Building your own shelves is an excellent way to practice carpentry and create something that is useful. To make your efforts worthwhile, use good materials and techniques. It is surprising how simple it is to build complicated-looking shelves, and how good simple shelves can look when they are built from quality materials.

Recommended Cross-References

Cabinets, Closets, Fastening Hardware, Joinery, Paint, Storage: Indoor & Outdoor, Vanities, Wood.

SHELVES: continued

Shelf Material

Most shelves are of dimension lumber, plywood, or pressed board. Lumber, especially hardwood, is a solid and attractive choice, but it may be expensive. Hardwood also tends to warp unless it is kiln dried. Plywood edges need to be concealed, but the material is dimensionally stable and ranges from inexpensive grades that require paint to expensive panels with fine hardwood veneers. Various kinds of pressed board, all inexpensive, have limited use because they tend to sag, don't hold screws or nails well, and the edges are rough. Hardboard, a type of pressed board, works well as a backer board to hold bookcases square. In addition, you can buy prefinished shelves in different sizes.

Various Shelf Supports

If you don't have the tools or the skills to make accurately spaced grooves, there are several alternative shelf supports that are stocked in almost every hardware and home center store. These include rails, standards, brackets, and clips of all kinds. Choose whichever system suits your purposes and your design scheme. Even if your skills are not in question, these supports will enable you to change the shelf arrangement.

Metal shelf standards are simple to use. Merely screw them in place (making sure that you screw into studs) and snap in one of the various brackets that fit in the slots. To recess the standards, rout grooves into the panels. For shelves that will bear heavy loads, install several standards. Another flexible shelf system is to drill a series of holes in the side panels. Then plug in dowels, metal clips, or pieces of pipe, depending on the weight of the objects that the shelf has to support.

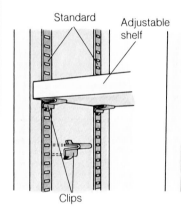
Standard / Adjustable shelf / Clips

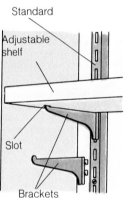
Standard / Adjustable shelf / Slot / Brackets

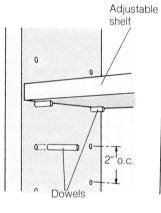
Adjustable shelf / 2" o.c. / Dowels

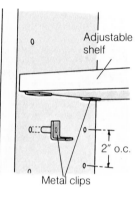
Adjustable shelf / 2" o.c. / Metal clips

Basic Bookcase

The shelves in this freestanding bookcase fit into dadoes in the uprights. This type of connection provides stability and an interesting edge detail. Notice the toe space beneath the bottom shelf; toe space is usually 3 inches high. The top shelf is rabbeted into the sides. Glue reinforces all joints.

An alternative to rabbeted joints is to use simple butt joints. Secure with glue and screws for maximum strength.

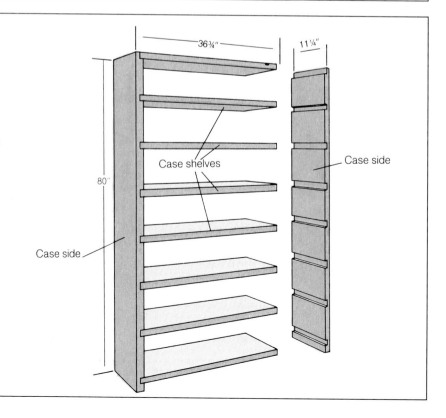
36¾" / 11¼" / 80" / Case shelves / Case side / Case side

Bookcase With Face Frame

This shelf features face frames on the front and back so it can serve as a room divider that is attractive and accessible from both sides. The face frame also hides the edges of the main case, making it possible to use veneered plywood such as cherry, oak, mahogany, birch, or other fine woods. The shelves are adjustable and ¼- by ¾-inch strips hide the plywood edges.

The dimensions given here are for a modest unit that sits on top of a cabinet. Adjust the dimensions to suit your purpose. Backless shelves of ¾-inch plywood should be no longer than 40 to 42 inches. Shelves that will hold books should be no longer than 36 inches, 32 inches if the books are heavy. To alter this design so the case will stand on the floor, construct a simple pedestal out of 1 by 3s and attach it to the bottom.

To build the unit, cut all the pieces and drill holes in the sides. Assemble the top and bottom shelves with butt joints. Use clamps to hold the glue if you do not nail. Assemble the face frames with doweled joints and glue them to the case, using clamps or nails. The outside edges of the frames should be flush with the outside edges of the case. Sand all inside edges smooth. Glue the edge strips to the shelves, making sure they will clear the face frame. After the glue sets, sand and finish all components and install the shelves.

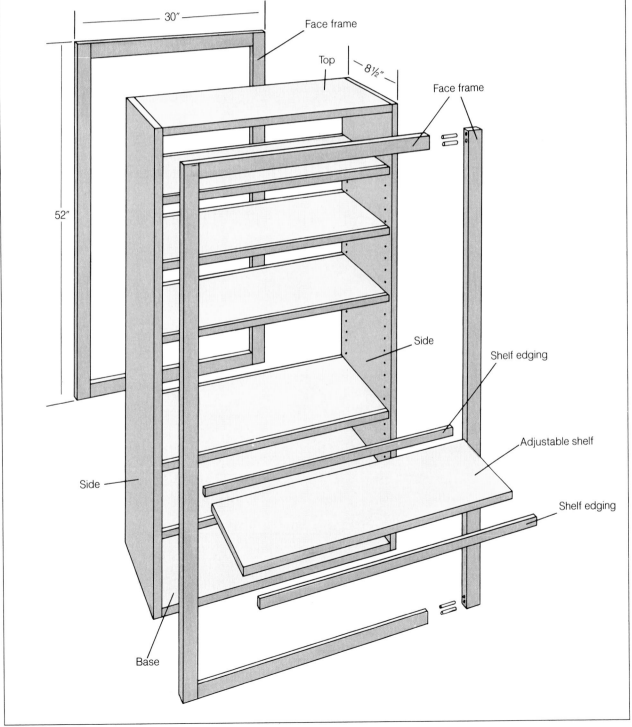

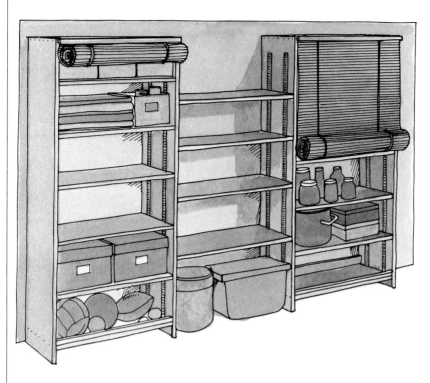

A Shelving Unit

This unit, suitable for outdoor storage, consists of two freestanding cases with additional shelves hung between them. Shelf track and clips allow easy adjustment of all the shelves, but they could also be attached permanently to the uprights. Some tracks have a top and bottom, so be sure you do not mount them upside down. Use a level to align marks for the first horizontal row of screw holes, or measure up from the floor an equal distance for each screw. Also use a level to make sure the tracks are plumb.

Stabilize the unit by installing 1 by 4 cleats across the back edge of the top and bottom shelves and screwing them to the wall or by gluing and nailing thin plywood to the back.

To obscure the contents, without going to the trouble or expense of hanging doors, attach roll-up blinds to the tops of the cases.

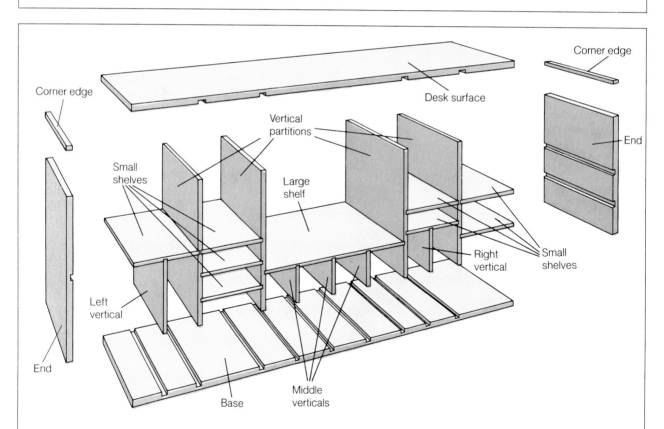

Cubbyhole Shelves

The cubbyhole case for this simple desk requires patience and accurate measurements rather than a high level of carpentry skill. The shelf is most effective when it is suspended about a foot above the desk surface.

This unit is 10 inches deep and is made of ½-inch plywood with a walnut veneer, though it could be shallower or deeper. The best saw for the project is a table saw or radial arm saw. Either will saw the pieces to length and cut grooves with a dado blade. Dadoes on both sides of the same vertical partition weaken the partition until all pieces are assembled, so handle the partitions carefully during construction. An optional plywood backpiece makes the case stronger and easier to hang.

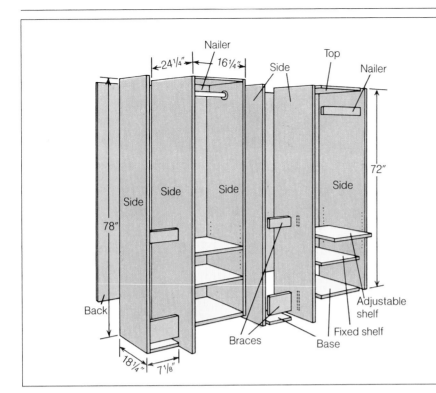

Sports Closet

There is often a lot of air space beneath garments in a closet with a single hanging pole. All too often, this space goes unused. These lockerlike modules are simple to make and will house a variety of sports equipment as well as clothes. Attach the separate units together with braces, and use the thin space created for storing items like hockey sticks and tennis rackets.

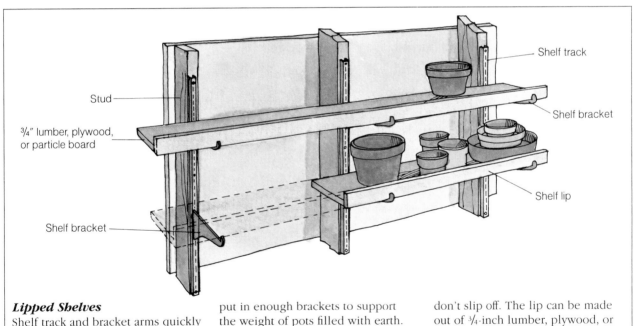

Lipped Shelves

Shelf track and bracket arms quickly create open shelving. For storage above a potting area, make sure to put in enough brackets to support the weight of pots filled with earth. Also, glue and nail a lip to each shelf to make sure that the stored items don't slip off. The lip can be made out of ¾-inch lumber, plywood, or particle board and should be securely glued and screwed to the shelf.

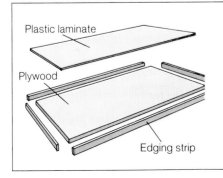

Desk Shelf

A shelf can act as a desktop when it is integrated into a wall system. It can also be supported on cleats fastened at each side of an alcove. If you want a freestanding desk, rest the shelf on two-drawer file cabinets.

Cover a length of plywood with plastic laminate, and glue and screw on an edging strip.

SHINGLE SIDING

Wood shingles have been a popular siding material for decades. They are attractive and long lasting, and lend themselves both to traditional and contemporary architecture. They are more expensive than most other sidings, but have the advantage of saving on maintenance. They can also save on installation because they are *very easy, although tedious, to apply.*

Avoid painting wood shingles. It traps moisture inside, causing early decay. You will also have to repaint them, whereas natural shingles require little or no maintenance. If you want them to have color, choose a light-bodied, oil-based stain; consult with your local dealer for other rec- *ommendations. Beware: Linseed oil adds to their life, but makes them extremely flammable.*

Recommended Cross-References
Board Siding, Caulking, Doors, Flashing, Framing, Insulation, Shakes, Shingles: Wood, Windows.

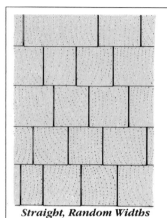

Straight, Random Widths

Staggered, Same Width

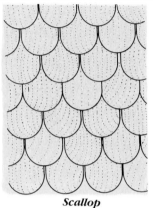

Scallop

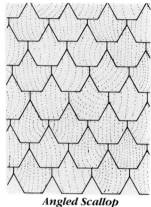

Angled Scallop

Types and Sizes

Two types of cedar shingles are commonly used: white cedar, which weathers to a silvery gray, and red cedar, which weathers to a silvery gray, a medium brown, or a dark brown, depending on local climatic conditions. Shingles are sold in three grades: No. 1, premium shingles, usually used for roofs; No. 2, with some sapwood, used for most sidewall shingling; and No. 3, with sapwood and knots, mostly used for utility buildings or interior walls.

Fancy-Cut Shingles. With fancy-cut shingles you can create a variety of accent patterns, even cover an entire wall. They are generally No. 1 grade and quite expensive; the distinctive touch makes them worth it. They are useful for topping off gables, as an accent band along the center of a wall, or for filling the space between two windows. Apply them as you would standard shingles.

Exposure. The maximum weather exposure for shingles and shakes is greater for sidewalls than for roofs. For the sake of appearance, you can double the shingles of each course to get longer exposures. A variation of this technique is to install the top shingles of each double course with their butts 2 inches above the underlying shingles, creating alternating bands of narrow and wide exposures. The maximum exposures that comply with most codes are:

Shingle Length	Single Course	Double Course
16 inches	7½ inches	12 inches
18 inches	8½ inches	14 inches
24 inches	11½ inches	16 inches

Preparing Walls

For new construction, install ½-inch plywood sheathing to the wall framing. Install the doors and windows, along with paper flashing and any casings. Then cut and fit metal flashing over the door and window casings, as needed, extending it 4 to 6 inches up the wall. As you shingle, install building paper on each wall, wrapping it around the corners. Most installers use 15-pound building paper, but try to find what is called red resin paper. It is similar to 15-pound felt, but does not contain as much asphalt, allowing the shingles to breathe while still blocking the wind. Install corner trim after wall shingles are in place. It is a good idea to paint corner, door, and window trim before shingling.

Prepare existing walls that are flat and sound in the same manner as plywood sheathing. For rough walls, such as stucco or existing shingles, nail 1 by 3 horizontal furring strips to the wall and jamb extenders to the windows. Space the strips at the same interval as the shingle exposure you plan to use. It is a good measure to apply panels of 1-inch rigid insulation to the walls before nailing up the furring strips.

In many cases you are better off removing the old siding (except stucco) so that you can add insulation to the walls.

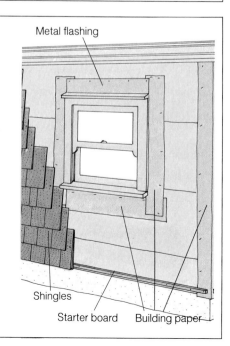

Metal flashing

Shingles

Starter board   Building paper

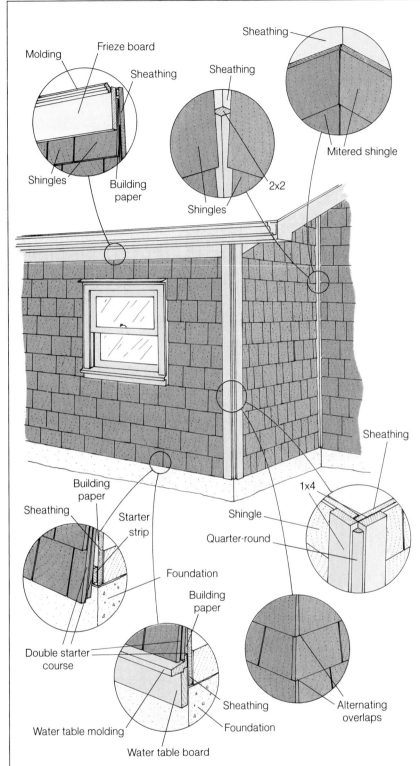

Molding
Frieze board
Sheathing
Shingles
Building paper

Sheathing
Sheathing
2x2
Shingles

Sheathing
Mitered shingle

Building paper
Sheathing
Starter strip
Double starter course
Water table molding
Water table board

Foundation
Building paper
Sheathing
Foundation

Shingle
Quarter-round
1x4
Sheathing
Alternating overlaps

Installing Shingles

To make measuring easier for keeping the courses straight, prepare a story pole: a piece of 1 by 4 or other lumber tall enough to stand against the wall. Mark all the shingle spacings on it. Plan your layout so that butts will align with the tops and bottoms of window and door frames, thus minimizing the number of shingles you will have to cut to fit.

The first shingle course across the bottom should be doubled and should have a water table board or a starter board behind it. To keep this course level, nail a shingle at each corner of the building with the butt 1 inch below the starter board. Tack a small nail to the bottom of each shingle and stretch a string line to align the rest of the starter course.

For all successive courses, tack a straight 1 by 4 across the shingles in line with the story pole marks and align the shingle butts on it.

If you are shingling an old house that is not level, the first course should follow the slant of the house rather than be level; otherwise it will emphasize the irregularity. Adjust each successive course by 1/8 inch until the courses are level. This slight change will not be noticeable.

If a place is too narrow for you to tack on the guide board, snap chalk lines between the story pole marks.

Where shingles must be cut to fit around obstructions, measure and cut with a handsaw or coping saw. Use a block plane to smooth a cut that fits along casings or trim boards. Apply caulk at the joints.

If you must shorten shingles to fit above a window or door opening, cut from the butt end so that the shingles will maintain the same profile as the rest of the course.

Nailing. Use 3d HDG or aluminum box nails (5d for double courses), two per shingle. Nail them approximately 3/4 inch from each edge. Space shingles to allow for expansion. Normal spacing is 1/8 inch, but many shingles are now being sold "green" and may shrink to this dimension, so check with your dealer. Gaps should be offset by at least 1 1/2 inches between courses, and no two gaps should line up with less than three courses between them. When nailing a course above a door or window, do not let a gap line up with the window or door edge.

Corner Treatments. The fastest way to shingle corners also gives the most effective weather protection: Use trim boards for both the inside and outside corners—2 by 2s for the inside and at least 1 by 3s for the outside. Pick redwood or cedar if you want the boards to weather with the shingles; plan to paint other types of lumber.

If you shingle all the way to the corners, the easier method is to "weave" the corner so that each course of shingles alternates in overlapping the edge. To mark each shingle for cutting, hold it against the edge of the corner and score it on the back. Cut with a power saw. Mitering the edges will give you a very tailored look. However, this kind of cutting is a painstaking job, and the edges are prone to leak.

SHOWERS

There are two basic choices when it comes to installing a new shower: buying a prefabricated shower stall unit or building a custom-made stall from scratch.

When making your choice, consider available space, ease of installation, availability of materials or units, cost, and personal preference. There is no reason why a new shower should be dark and cavelike, unless you choose to have it so. Even if you have limited space, you can transform a simple shower stall into a luxurious spa by adding a skylight overhead, lowering the partition walls so they do not go all the way to the ceiling, installing a fan and light unit overhead, or installing a small window near the top of the stall. If you have enough space, you can make the shower large enough for two or more people, install additional faucets and showerheads, or even tile the entire bathroom floor and install the shower drain at one end. Installation techniques will vary with your choice, but the basic plumbing is all the same.

Recommended Cross-References
Bathroom Layout, Bathtubs, Tile, Faucets, Framing, Plumbing, Wallboard.

Custom-Built Showers
A shower built from scratch offers greater choice of size, shape, color, and materials, but also takes more time and effort. It can be as small as 32 inches square or as large as a complete room with several shower-heads and faucets. The walls can be ceramic tile, plastic panels, synthetic marble panels, or wood.

Before your imagination runs wild, however, you should recognize a limiting factor: the shower pan. Although it is possible to make the floor any size or shape imaginable and then cover it with tile, this process requires that an elaborate waterproof pan be under the tile. An easier installation is to use a molded plastic or fiberglass shower pan for the floor and other materials for the walls. The size and shape of the stall will then depend on the pan.

Most custom-built shower stalls are tile, because it is readily available, comes in many attractive designs, is easy to clean and maintain, and can be installed over awkward shapes. The only drawback is that the grout lines are not waterproof, but this is not a problem if the backing is sound.

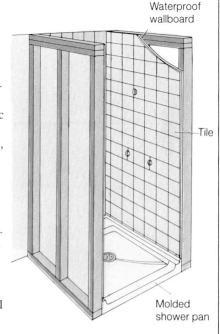

Waterproof wallboard

Tile

Molded shower pan

Prefabricated Units
The advantage of prefabricated shower stalls is their simplicity of installation. They include everything except the plumbing fixtures. Costs vary widely with the quality of materials and design. A prefabricated stall is not as durable as a custom-built shower, and it must be maintained and used carefully to avoid scratches, chips, and dulling.

Three types of ready-made shower stalls are available: freestanding, one piece, and sectional.

Freestanding Units. A shower that is freestanding can be placed in a corner, along a wall, or even away from any walls. Some are made from enameled steel, which is noisy and prone to rusting and chipping. Others are made from plastics, such as polypropylene or ABS, or from fiberglass with an aluminum frame. The drain pan may be made of the same material as the walls or from a heavier material that resembles marble. These units come in a variety of sizes and shapes, including 32- or 36-inch

squares, corner units with a rounded or angled front, and circular units for installation away from walls. Most come in sections (fixtures not included) and need to be assembled.

One-Piece Alcove. This type of shower is molded from fiberglass or plastic and must be installed in a framed opening. Some are square, with either 32, 36, or 40 inches on each side. Others are rectangular, usually 32 by 48 inches, or 5-sided corner units, either 36 or 40 inches on the long sides. Before you buy one, be sure you can get it through the house and into the bathroom. Try to have the unit on the site before framing the opening, or get accurate specifications from the manufacturer.

Sectional Units. These come in 3-piece or 5-piece shapes, and can be ordered with a drain pan, or without one if you are using the stall for an existing shower. The sections can be carried through any doorway. Some panels are designed so that the size of the assembled unit can be adjusted to fit an irregular opening.

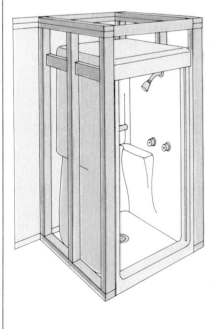

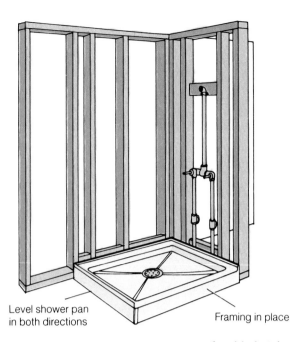

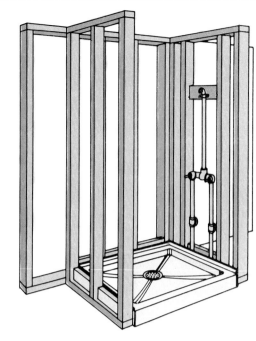

Level shower pan in both directions

Framing in place

Installing a Custom-Built Shower

1. Shower Pan and Plumbing. Shower bases, or pans, usually come in 32-, 36-, and 40-inch squares, 32- by 48-inch rectangles, and 5-sided corner showers. Other sizes and shapes may be available. They are molded to slope toward a drain hole that receives a standard shower drain. If a drain fitting is not included with the pan, get the kind with an internal compression sleeve for connecting to the rough plumbing stub. Before installing rough plumbing, frame the back wall and faucet wall.

Use 2-inch pipe and fittings for the rough plumbing. The trap should be below the floor, with the trap inlet positioned directly in line with the shower pan drain hole. If you have not done so already, cut a hole in the floor for the shower drain to fit through, then connect a short stub to the trap just long enough to slip the drain fitting over. Next, install the drain fitting in the base. Put a ring of plumber's putty around the hole first, insert the fitting into the hole, and screw the tightening ring snugly against the bottom of the base. Then set the base in position so that the drain fitting slips down over the stub-out. Tighten the neoprene compression sleeve by turning the tightening ring with a screwdriver and a special tool that comes with the drain assembly.

The supply pipes are usually 1/2 inch wide. Install the faucet at a comfortable height, normally 42 to 48 inches above the pan. Some local codes require shutoff valves for the hot and cold supply lines, which must be accessible from a small door behind the wall. They may also require air chambers, which are short pipes with caps installed just above the faucet. The riser pipe for the showerhead should be from 54 to 78 inches above the floor, depending on your preference. When you strap the pipes to the framing, putting carpet scraps or pieces of foam rubber under the straps will eliminate vibration.

Test the shower for leaks at this time, since corrections will be much harder to make later on.

2. Framing. Use 2 by 4s to frame in the rest of the shower. Studs should be a minimum of 16 inches on center, and the walls should have a soleplate and top plate. If it is new construction, you can assemble the walls on the floor and raise them into place. Otherwise, it is easier to nail the soleplate and top plate into position and toenail each stud between them.

If you want a low ceiling in the shower, nail 2 by 4 cleats to the walls at the level of the new ceiling and put short 2 by 4 joists between them. If you want the top of the stall to be open, build the partition wall so that it does not go all the way to the ceiling. However, you will have to brace it somehow. One way is to add a header across the top of the door opening, which can either be exposed or covered with finish material. Another bracing technique is to tie the wall into an adjacent counter or closet.

All of the corners should have a stud or some blocking on each side to back up the wallboard. Install blocking to back up any towel racks, grab bars, or door enclosures. Then nail 2 by 4 blocks between the studs around the top of the shower base. Secure the base by nailing the flange to the studs or by following the manufacturer's instructions.

Be sure the shower stall has proper clearances. There should be at least 18 inches (preferably 24) between a stall with a shower curtain and any plumbing fixture on the opposite wall. If the stall will have a door, there must be at least 28 inches of clearance for the door to swing open. The minimum floor area of a shower is 32 inches square; some codes require more.

When installing a tile floor rather than a prefabricated base, build a short curb across the doorway out of 2 by 4s. Nail 1/2-inch plywood to the inside of the curb and around the bottom of the walls. Fabricate a shower pan from a code-approved material: hot mop roofing, copper sheet with soldered seams, or a continuous rubberized membrane. The shower pan should lap over the curb and up the walls at least 3 1/2 inches higher than the curb. It should also slope toward the drain.

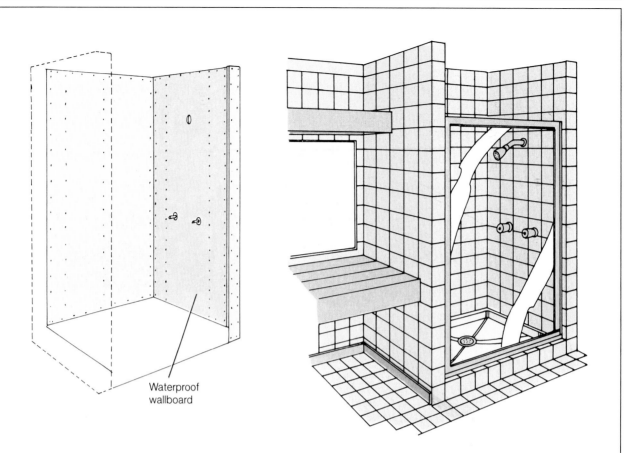

Waterproof wallboard

3. Wallboard or Tile Backing. To provide a backing surface for ceramic tile or other finish material, install panels of moisture-resistant wallboard (if code allows) or tile-backing board over the wall framing. Do not use regular wallboard.

The wallboard panels should not extend all the way down to the lip of the base. Leave about a ¼-inch gap above the base so that any water that might seep behind the tile will not wick up into the wallboard. The space will be covered with tile and sealed with caulking or grout. Before you install the panels, seal all cut edges with a special sealer or the joint compound that is specified for moisture-proof wallboard. Cut holes for the faucet stems and shower arm so there is approximately ¼-inch clearance. Do not put a vapor barrier behind moisture-resistant wallboard. Nail the panels directly to the studs with coated wallboard nails, 8 inches on center. Then tape and fill the joints and cover all the nail heads. Use compound specified for the type of wallboard you are using.

Although moisture-resistant wallboard is widely used as a backing for tiled showers, it will not hold up indefinitely if water seeps into it

through cracks, grout joints, or any other path. A more durable type of panel is now available for tile backing that will not disintegrate as easily. It is a sandwich panel with a lightweight concrete material on the inside and mesh reinforcing cloth on each face. You cut and nail it like wallboard, attach it with roofing nails, and tape the joints with fiberglass mesh tape.

4. Finishing. Tile is by far the most common finishing material for custom-built showers. Tiles can be installed directly on wallboard or mesh-reinforced backing board.

Start the tile layout at the bottom. Lap the first course of tiles over the flange, but leave a ⅛-inch gap above the base itself for sealing with caulking. The tile should extend at least 6 feet above the floor. If it terminates before the ceiling, use bull-nosed tiles or radius trim pieces for the top row, or trim with wood molding. Cut the tile for the faucet stems and shower arm with nippers or a saw. Then grout the joints. To ensure proper curing, cover the grouted tile with plastic sheeting for a few days or spray it with a fine mist of water 2 or 3 times a day for 5 days. When completely cured and dry (approxi-

mately 2 weeks) apply a joint sealer.

Panels of plastic or synthetic marble can also be used to finish shower walls. Kits are available for standard-sized showers and tubs, although you may need to cut panels to size with a power saw. Use adhesives to glue the panels to the wallboard. Seal the joints with caulking.

It is also possible to finish shower walls with wood siding, but this requires sealing the backing and using naturally durable woods such as redwood or cypress. Several coats of penetrating sealer must be applied to the wood surface, and it must be maintained diligently.

The final step is to install faucet handles and a showerhead. Fill the gaps around the faucet stems with caulking, slip the cover rings over them, and attach the handles. If the shower valve is a single-handled unit, remove the temporary plastic tile spacer from the valve, apply a bead of caulking around the back of the cover plate, and screw the plate into the valve. Then attach the handle. For the showerhead, screw the arm into the elbow behind the wall. Use a rag to prevent pliers from scratching the finish. Then screw the showerhead to the arm.

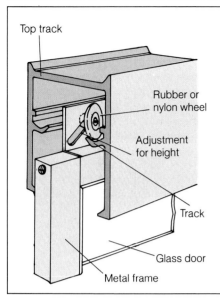

Top track

Rubber or
nylon wheel

Adjustment
for height

Track

Glass door

Metal frame

5. Installing a Door or Enclosure. Several styles of shower doors and tub enclosures are available. They all have aluminum frames, although the color of the metal may be gold, bronze, or silver. The glass used in the doors must be tempered, and may be either clear or opaque. The glass doors are usually trimmed with a metal frame, but some styles come without it.

Installation methods vary, depending on whether the door rolls on a track or swings on a hinge, but several techniques are the same for all installations. First, be sure to install blocking behind the rail locations when you frame the walls. You can use expansion bolts when installing doors for an existing shower.

A common technique for cutting the metal framing to fit the opening is to use a hacksaw and a miter box to keep the cut square.

Most installations also require drilling through tile so that the side rails can be screwed into the walls. If possible, locate screw holes in the grout joints because they are easier to drill through. In any case, use a masonry bit with a carbide tip, and be patient.

Supply Plumbing

This exploded view illustrates the supply plumbing for a combination bathtub/shower installation. Water can be diverted from the spout to the showerhead either with a third handle on the valve or a diverter on the spout. A valve for a shower stall does not include a diverter.

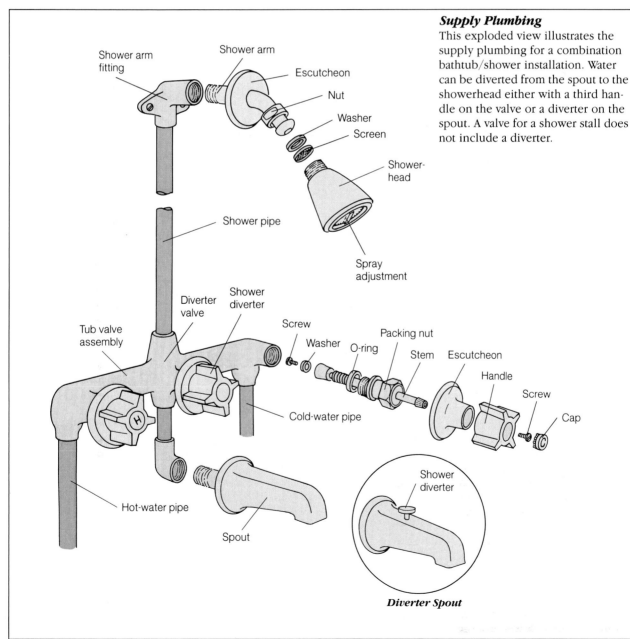

Shower arm fitting

Shower arm

Escutcheon

Nut

Washer

Screen

Shower-head

Shower pipe

Spray adjustment

Diverter valve

Shower diverter

Screw

Washer

O-ring

Packing nut

Stem

Escutcheon

Handle

Screw

Cap

Tub valve assembly

Cold-water pipe

Hot-water pipe

Spout

Shower diverter

Diverter Spout

SIDING

Whether you are doing new construction or planning a major face-lift for your existing home, you should choose siding with all the care and consideration you give to the interior of your home. Factors to consider are: your own taste, the style of your house, the prevailing styles of homes in the neighborhood, durability, cost, and ease of installation.

Most sidings are versatile enough to fit many kinds of architecture, although some traditional styles almost dictate a choice—a saltbox seems to demand shiplap, a ranch house may call for vertical siding with stone veneer, and a restrained Georgian facade seems to resist natural wood shakes. The choice you make should take into consideration the prevailing styles and color combinations in the neighborhood; your home should blend in with the houses around it.

The roofing material is another factor to consider. The safest choice is to install siding that contrasts with the roof in both texture and color, although sometimes a pleasing effect is to make them similar.

Shingles, board siding, and panel siding are easy to apply. Other sidings, such as stucco, brick, vinyl, and aluminum, are more difficult to work with. In all cases new siding is expensive. For that reason alone, it is best to choose a material that will stay attractive for a long time and not require constant maintenance.

Recommended Cross-References
Board Siding, Caulking, Doors, Flashing, Framing, Insulation, Paint, Panel Siding, Shingle Siding, Stucco, Ventilation, Windows, Wood.

The Weatherproof Exterior

Siding is an important part of the exterior "skin" of your home—the protective layer that keeps water and other harmful elements out of the structure of the house. Siding basically works by shedding water away from the house at every point on its downward journey, from roof to foundation. The materials must be sound and have a waterproof surface. More importantly, the joints, gaps, and seams must be constructed to repel the water. A place that traps water or diverts it inward becomes a weak link in the chain of protection.

The following pointers are things that you should keep in mind when installing siding:
- Joints should be staggered so that a vertical row does not create a channel for sustained water flow.
- Caulk long, vertical joints so that water flowing down the face of the siding will not be wicked into joints.
- Wood, which can absorb and hold water, should always be backed by building paper or a similar material to prevent trapping water against another wood surface. For maximum protection, prime or seal the back surfaces as well as the ends of boards before installing them.
- Surfaces should either be vertical or slope away from the house.
- Nails, flashing, and all metal should be corrosion resistant, either made of aluminum or high-quality galvanized steel.
- Securely nail boards and other components, preferably into framing members, so they do not work loose.
- Make sure the walls, crawl space, and attic have adequate ventilation so that moisture does not accumulate and cause rotting from within.
- Gutters and downspouts carry away much water and can damage siding quickly if they leak; keep them in good repair and clear of debris.

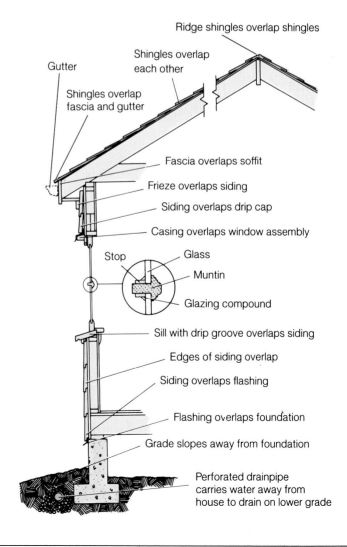

Ridge shingles overlap shingles

Shingles overlap each other

Gutter

Shingles overlap fascia and gutter

Fascia overlaps soffit

Frieze overlaps siding

Siding overlaps drip cap

Casing overlaps window assembly

Stop

Glass

Muntin

Glazing compound

Sill with drip groove overlaps siding

Edges of siding overlap

Siding overlaps flashing

Flashing overlaps foundation

Grade slopes away from foundation

Perforated drainpipe carries water away from house to drain on lower grade

Manufactured Siding

Several materials besides wood are used for siding. They include vinyl, aluminum, and steel. Each has advantages and disadvantages.

Vinyl. The use of vinyl siding has been increasing rapidly, due in part to low cost as well as improvements in the material. A wider choice of colors and trim, together with its low maintenance requirements, will probably help vinyl remain the most popular nonwood siding.

Vinyl has several advantages.
- High resistance to dents.
- The color permeates the material.
- It is lightweight and easy to install.
- It is not affected by salt air.
- It is quieter than other siding materials in wind.

Vinyl also has disadvantages.
- It is likely to buckle or crack if installed incorrectly.
- It may sag when very hot.
- It becomes brittle and may break when very cold.
- The color is more likely to fade than that of other siding materials.
- The textures are shallower than on metal siding.
- It is not fireproof.
- Unevenness in walls shows through vinyl more than through other types of siding.

Aluminum Siding. This is the second most popular nonwood siding. Its colors range from whites and pastels to deep rich tones, and it can be repainted. It is lightweight and fireproof. Available textures range from smooth to rough-sawn.

Aluminum siding dents easily, and the dents are difficult to repair. Its finish is also easily scratched. Abrupt temperature changes or wind can cause it to make noise (although insulated backing will help). Aluminum siding conducts electricity and must be grounded in some areas. As with any painted surface, the paint may fade or chalk.

Steel Siding. Steel siding has the same advantages as aluminum, but has greater resistance to dents. For this reason, it is sold in areas where hail is likely. If it is scratched, its paint must be touched up to prevent rust. It is more vulnerable to salt air or acid than aluminum or vinyl, and is heavier and more difficult to install than the other types.

Vinyl siding (top) and hardboard siding (bottom) are applied in panels over sheathing.

Like everything else in a kitchen re-modeling project, choosing the sink is not as simple as it used to be. Besides the basic color and size, you need to select the number and size of bowls, the type of material, the mounting detail, and the number of holes for the faucet and accessories. Even a single sink comes in over ten sizes. In spite of the number of options, installation procedures are the same.

Your choice is a matter of prefer-ence and, in some cases, available space. A single-bowl sink is suitable for any installation that requires a sink less than 28 inches long. Double-bowl sinks offer more flexibility. The bowls in some sinks are the same size, while others have one large bowl and one smaller one. Three-bowl sinks in various depths are also available.

To select a size that will fit your needs, consider how often you fill large pots, whether you like to keep one bowl free, and how often other members of the household interrupt the cook to use the sink.

Kitchen sinks are usually of enam-eled cast iron and stainless steel, al-though acrylic, synthetic marble, and porcelain-coated steel are also avail-able. Stainless steel is durable and inexpensive, but it looks institutional in some settings. Stainless steel sinks come in various gauges, or thick-nesses, usually 18 gauge, 20 gauge, or 22 gauge. Lower numbers represent thicker gauges. Choose 20 gauge or lower to minimize vibration from the disposer. Shiny stainless steel is diffi-cult to maintain; brushed and matte finishes are more practical.

Enameled cast iron is durable, heavy, and expensive. A rainbow of colors is available; choose a color that blends into your kitchen or one that stands out as a major accent.

Sinks come with three, four, or five holes on the back rim for mounting faucets and other accessories.

Drain holes are identical on most sinks and accommodate a standard strainer drain or garbage disposer.

Garbage disposers require a dedi-cated 20-amp circuit, and the switch location may be specified by the local building code.

Recommended Cross-References
Cabinets, Countertops, Dishwash-ers, Faucets & Valves, Kitchen Lay-out, Plumbing, Tile.

Types of Sinks
Self-Rimming. This type of sink is easy to install. First, lay a bead of caulk around the opening. Set the sink into it and install clamps every 4 or 5 inches from underneath. Wait for the caulk to set, then score around the edge of the sink with a knife to remove any caulk that oozed out from under the rim.

Surface Mounted. A surface-mounted sink comes with a separate stainless steel mounting rim. Lay a bead of bathtub caulk or similar sealant around the cutout opening. Set the sink into the opening, support it temporarily, and insert the rim around it. Install clips every 4 to 6 inches around the sink from under-neath. Use a screwdriver to tighten the clips against the sink.

Recessed. Single-wall stainless steel sinks expand and contract more quickly than surrounding tile. As a result, a good seal around the edge is difficult to maintain. Because of this problem, a knowledgeable contrac-tor does not usually recommend a single-wall stainless steel sink for recessed installation. A recessed in-stallation is similar to the installation of a self-rimming sink without the clips. The tile will hold the recessed sink. Sometimes a bullnose edging surrounds the sink. Other sinks have a rim that allows the installation of full tiles with tops flush with the top of the sink.

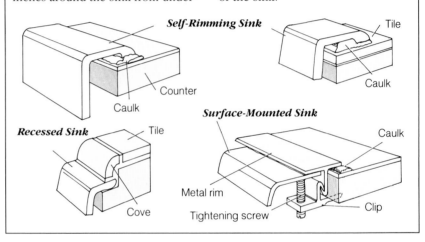

Self-Rimming Sink — Tile — Caulk — Counter — Caulk

Recessed Sink — Tile — Cove

Surface-Mounted Sink — Caulk — Metal rim — Tightening screw — Clip

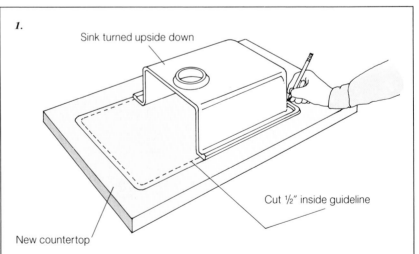

1.

Sink turned upside down

Cut ½" inside guideline

New countertop

Installing a Sink
1. Marking for the Cutout. Almost all kitchen sinks are installed in coun-tertops, some after the countertop is installed and others in a plywood deck ready for tile or some other covering. Place the sink upside down on the countertop or plywood deck and set it in position. Be sure to center it over the sink cabinet so the bowl edges will clear the sides of the cabinet. Leave at least 1½ inches at the front edge. Leave more space if your counter is wider than 24 inch-es, as is the case if your sink lies in an island or peninsula. Place it no farther back than 3 to 4 inches. Pen-cil a line around the edge of the sink and lift it off. Then draw a second line ½ inch inside the first outline.

2. Cutting the Opening. Drill a hole at each corner of the inside line. Each hole should be large enough to accommodate the blade of a saber saw or jigsaw. Saw between the holes along the inner line, supporting the cutout toward the end so the weight does not crack the countertop as you free it. If you do not have a saber saw, use a handsaw for the straight runs and a keyhole saw for the curves. The edges do not have to be perfectly straight nor smooth—the rim of the sink will cover them.

Before you install the sink, attach strainer assembly, faucet, and all accessories. Attachment is easier if you set the sink on a pair of sawhorses.

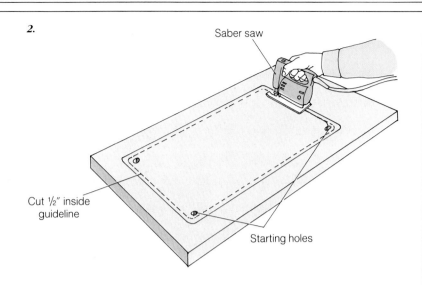

3. Hooking Up the Faucet. Connect the faucet to each angle stop with a length of supply tubing. Tighten all the nuts with flat wrenches.

4. Hooking Up the Drain. Apply plumber's putty around the drain opening, install the strainer bowl, and tighten the locknut. Hook up the

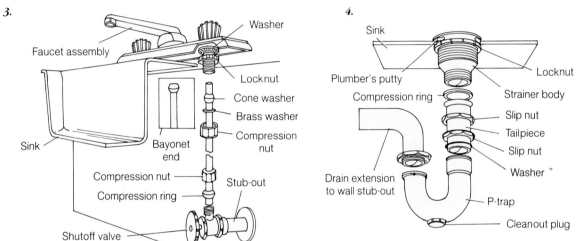

P-trap assembly, connecting it to the drain stub-out with a slip nut and to the strainer tailpiece with another slip nut. Tighten the nuts by hand.

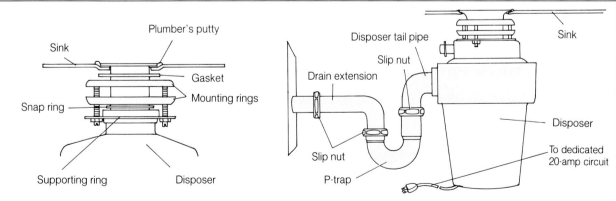

Installing a Garbage Disposer
The disposer includes a mounting bracket that detaches from the unit. Apply a bead of plumber's putty around the drain opening. Then install the bracket in the drain hole before you position the sink.

After installing the sink consider the P-trap. The P-trap connects to a curved tailpiece on the disposer. Install the P-trap before you mount the disposer under the sink. Hook up the P-trap the same way that you would hook up a regular drain.

Now attach the disposer to the mounting bracket. Most units are held by mounting screws. Some have a quick-mount feature; you merely twist the lock ring onto the bracket. Connect the hose from the dishwasher air gap with a clamp.

SKYLIGHTS

Building a skylight is an excellent project for bringing about dramatic change with only a modest investment. A skylight brightens any space in the home, especially those areas that otherwise tend to be drab and forgotten: hallways, bathrooms, stairwells, back bedrooms, even closets. A skylight can admit five times as much light into a room as a window of the same size; therefore, it does not have to be large to make a difference.

Consider the following factors as you plan the size, type, and location of your skylight.

Glare and Heat Gain

Direct sunlight through a skylight can be a problem. Furnishings fade, the room heats up, and the strong light creates an uncomfortable glare. Here are some solutions:
● Make the skylight opaque. Bronze and translucent-white openings admit light without causing direct glare. However, they also block the ability to gain solar heat.
● Install a retractable shade screen. Many manufacturers include this option, and homemade variations are possible.
● Utilize deciduous foliage. Plant a fast-growing tree or take advantage of a tree that already shades part of the roof during the hotter months.
● Locate skylights on the north side of the roof. This will cut out most glare, except during June and July.
● Design around the glare. If direct sunlight is your goal, make the most of it by reducing some of the uncomfortable side effects. Make the skylight openable to exhaust excess heat.

Heat Loss

Heat loss is a more serious problem than excess heat gain. Skylights can lose enormous amounts of valuable heat to the cold night sky. How can this be prevented?
● Install a double- or triple-glazed skylight. The insulating values of R-2 to R-4 are much better than the R-1 rating for single-glazed skylights although, compared with a ceiling insulated to R-30, they still lose heat.
● Locate skylights near the eaves rather than near the ridge of the roof. Heated air will not escape as readily.
● Provide movable insulation to put up each night. Buy quilted shades or make shutters out of rigid insulation.

Overall Effect

Skylights enhance a space in other ways besides adding light. If you are installing a clear skylight, consider the view: the night sky on warm evenings when stars and moon etch their paths across the sky, clouds illuminated by city lights, the changing patterns of the daytime sky.

The larger the skylight, the stronger the focal point it creates. But be careful: A skylight can add a feeling of tension to a room by competing with some other dramatic effect. To preserve balance, build a smaller skylight or set it in a less prominent location. Another alternative is to make the skylight so large that it clearly dominates the room.

Recommended Cross-References
Flashing, Framing, Insulation, Roofing, Windows.

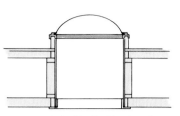

Straight Shaft/Flat Roof

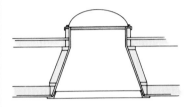

Flared Shaft/Flat Roof

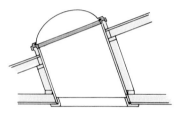

Angled Shaft/Pitched Roof

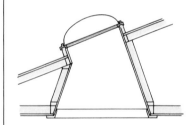

Flared Shaft/Pitched Roof

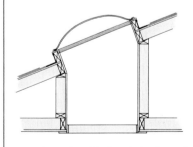

Combination Shaft/Pitched Roof

Choosing a Skylight
Skylights come in an array of sizes, shapes, and styles. The differences are the type of glazing, the type of frame, and optional features. The least expensive skylights are usually acrylic domes, which come in clear, white, or bronze. Polycarbonate is a more durable and more expensive plastic. Both types are available single, double, or even triple glazed. Plastic skylights are usually domed because plastic expands and contracts. The domed shape allows this movement to occur without affecting the waterproof seal around the edges. Acrylic and polycarbonate plastics are also available in flat sheets, even double glazed, for customized, homemade skylights. Glass skylights offer a flat profile and do not scratch or turn color. They are also more expensive. Codes require that safety glass be used.

Frames can be made of wood or metal, but they are usually aluminum. Features include shades, screens, insulating devices, and opening mechanisms. The more elaborate opening mechanisms are operated electrically with a thermostat control.

Skylights range in width from 16 inches to 4 feet, and in length from 2 to 6 feet. Sizes correspond to standard rafter spacings.

Light Shaft Variations
You do not need a light shaft in an attic or room with a cathedral ceiling. However, in a room with a dropped ceiling, you will. The shape is a matter of design preference and how much you want to maximize the light. Generally, the smaller the skylight, the more you should flare the shaft.

Skylights can be more than practical; this one (above) bathes the bed in dramatic beams of light. Hanging plants (left) thrive when they get sufficient top light. Skylights installed in humid locations should include gutters in the skylight frame to collect condensation.

Preparation

Check with your building department about code requirements and obtain the proper permits. Some codes specify maximum sizes for skylights, usually figured as a percentage of the floor area. Codes may also require adding a curb to roofs with a slope of less than 45 degrees; specify how close a skylight can be to the property line, and may require insulated skylights.

Most skylights are designed for easy installation. The most difficult installations are on flat roofs. If you install your own, hire a professional to seal around the curb with hot mop roofing. The best installers add an expandable waterproof membrane at the corners.

Installation takes anywhere from half a day to three days, depending on how many interior alterations are involved and the type of roofing material that you are patching. If the room has a sloped ceiling, installation will go quickly. If not, you need to build a light shaft. If the skylight is large, you may also need to shore up some of the roof rafters before installing the headers. If the roof is framed with trusses, consult a professional before you cut any framing members.

The key to an easy installation is preparation, since you will be making a hole in the roof. It is possible to install a skylight even in rainy weather if all the materials are on hand and the preparatory framing is completed. You can break through the ceiling and install the framing for the light shaft and the skylight itself before you cut the hole in the roof. Then you can cut the hole in the roof once the weather clears.

Skylight Framing Patterns. From the illustrations you can see the different patterns of framing an opening, depending on your particular needs and where the opening will be positioned. The simplest way is to use existing rafters rather than building in one or more jack rafters.

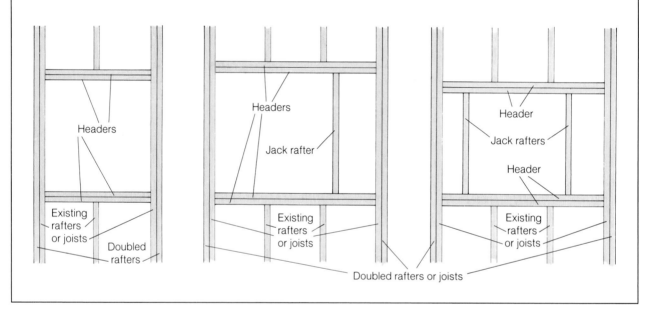

Headers — Existing rafters or joists — Doubled rafters

Headers — Jack rafter — Existing rafters or joists

Header — Jack rafters — Header — Existing rafters or joists

Doubled rafters or joists

Installing a Skylight

1. Laying Out the Opening. After determining the position of the skylight, drive a nail through the ceiling at the center of where the light shaft will be. In the attic, drop a plumb bob from the underside of the roof deck to the nail in the ceiling to find the center of the roof opening. Mark that point. Then use a tape measure and carpenter's square to lay out the dimensions of the roof opening on the underside of the roof. The size of the opening should equal the inside dimensions of the skylight, less twice the thickness of curb material, and ⅜-inch clearance in each direction.

Nail marks center of ceiling opening

2. Framing the Opening. After laying out the opening, add 3-inch allowances for the double headers at the top and bottom of the layout and mark the rafters for cutting. If you are cutting more than one rafter, brace them above and below the skylight location by nailing 2 by 4s between the rafters and the closest possible point to a bearing wall. Cut the rafters with a handsaw or reciprocating saw and nail the jack rafters and headers in place, as shown.

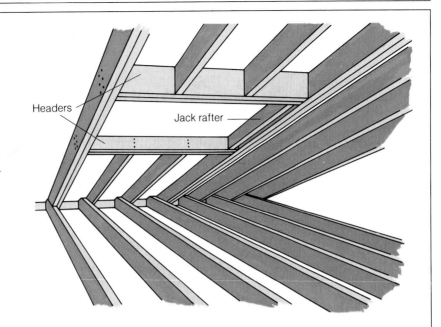

Headers

Jack rafter

3. Cutting the Opening. Be sure no wiring in the attic or obstructions on the roof will interfere with cutting. If the roof is steep, you may be able to cut the opening from the attic side with a reciprocating saw, using the headers and rafters as a guide. Otherwise, make the cut from the roof side. Lay out the cut by drilling holes or driving nails up from the attic at the four corners of the opening. On the roof, snap chalk lines between the holes. Cut through the roofing first and then the sheathing. If the blade gets gummed up from asphalt shingles, remove the shingles by hand and just cut through the sheathing.

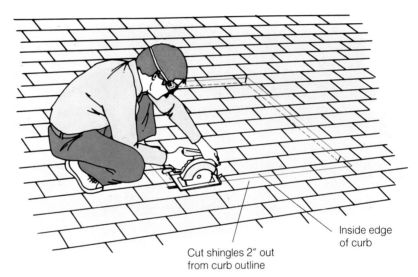

Cut shingles 2" out from curb outline

Inside edge of curb

4. Installing a Self-Flashing Skylight. Because this type of skylight requires no curb, the opening equals the net inside dimensions of the skylight. Remove the shingles around the sides and top of the opening so that the flange lies flat on the roof sheathing. Coat the edges of the opening with roofing cement and lay the skylight in place, lapping the bottom flange over the shingles along the bottom edge of the opening. Make any adjustments in alignment and nail the top and sides of the flange with roofing nails spaced every 6 inches. Coat the top of the flange with roofing cement and replace shingles around the skylight.

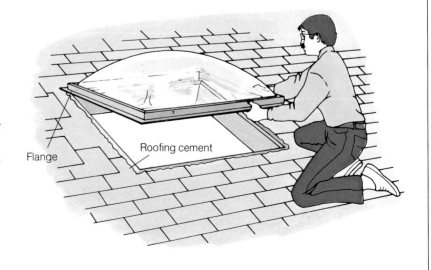

Flange

Roofing cement

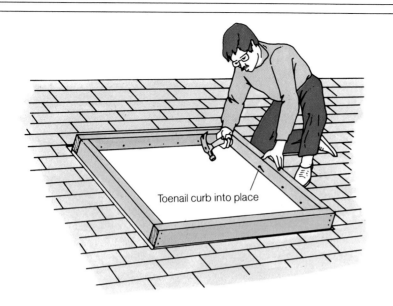

Toenail curb into place

5. Installing a Curb. Most skylights are mounted on a curb. Build a simple frame of 2 by 4s, making the outside dimensions equal to the inside dimensions of the skylight, less ³⁄₈ inch in each direction. Remove enough shingles around the roof opening for the curb to sit directly on the sheathing. Using 8d nails, toenail the curb down through the sheathing into the rafters. Be sure to square the curb first, measuring both diagonals. Also make certain that the top surface is on a flat plane. Correct any sagging corners with shims.

Caulk

6. Installing the Skylight. The curb should be flashed with step flashing on the side collars for the top and bottom, made by a sheet-metal shop. Install the bottom collar first, then put the step flashing on both sides, followed by the top collar. Repair any roofing that was damaged around the edges. Then lay a bead of caulk around the top edge of the curb and set the skylight down on it. Foam weather stripping also makes a good seal. Drive nails through the sides of the skylight into the curb, using special aluminum nails with neoprene gaskets. Most skylights have holes drilled in the sides for this purpose.

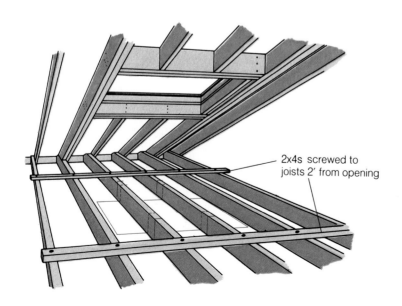

2x4s screwed to joists 2' from opening

7. Cutting the Ceiling Joists. Lay out the opening for the ceiling by dropping a plumb bob from each corner of the framed roof opening. These locations define the inside edges of the headers and tail joists you will be installing in the ceiling.

Provide temporary bracing for the ceiling joists by positioning two 2 by 4s that extend for at least two more joists in each direction. Set the 2 by 4s far enough back from the opening to leave room for you to work. Screw, rather than nail, them to the joists in order not to disturb the ceiling below. If the joist spans are particularly long, make the braces permanent strongbacks by attaching a 2 by 6, on edge, to the side of each one and connecting the strongbacks to all the joists with metal hangers.

8. Framing the Ceiling Opening. Carefully cut through the joists. Be careful if you use a power saw because the saw will tend to bind if the cut causes the joist to sag. If you use a reciprocating saw with a long blade, you can avoid this problem by beginning the cut under the joist and cutting upward. After cutting, install headers and double up the side rafters, as shown. If you are cutting through only one joist, single headers should be sufficient. Double up the side joists when they are longer than 8 feet or if you are cutting through two or more joists.

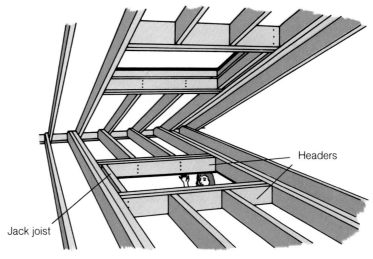

Headers

Jack joist

9. Framing the Light Well. Use 2 by 4s, spaced no more than 24 inches apart, to frame the walls of the light shaft. If you have installed a wide skylight and therefore added intermediate rafters and joists, they will line up with each other. Toenail the tops of the 2 by 4 studs to the rafters, and toenail the bottoms to the joists. To mark them for cutting, hold them in place against the rafter and joists at whatever angle you want the light well to be. You may have to cut them to approximate length first for them to fit for marking. Mark each stud separately.

Mark the angle where 2x4 crosses rafter and joist

2x4 slightly shorter than distance from roof deck to ceiling

10. Finishing the Light Well. If the rafters and joists do not align with each other, which is usually the case for small skylights, you will have to nail the 2 by 4 studs to whatever surface is most convenient to keep them plumb. If you are facenailing one end of the 2 by 4 to a rafter or joist, mark it in the same manner as for toenailing, but cut far enough away from the line to leave room for facenailing. When the framing for the shaft is complete, install blanket insulation between the studs, facing inward. Then staple a plastic vapor barrier to the inside of the framing, install wallboard, and finish the shaft with paint and trim.

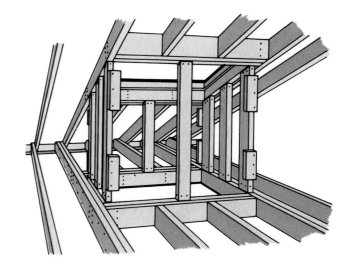

SOLAR ENERGY

Having large expanses of glass on a south-facing wall (top) is one of the simplest and most efficient ways to trap warmth from the winter sun. A deep overhang prevents the ground floor from becoming too warm during the summer months. A wall of solar panels (bottom) uses the sun's energy to heat water, which can then be circulated to warm the house or stored for cooking and bathing. Careful attention to architectural design is necessary to keep this type of system from being visually obtrusive.

Direct sunlight is a benign, abundant, and free source of energy that can be put to many uses in a home. Solar energy is not a new technology, but an ancient idea that has been revived. During the last few decades we relied on other sources of energy for all heating, cooling, and lighting needs. The volatility of cost and limited availability of these sources prompted the search for alternatives. Initial experiments and exploration of solar energy produced many residential applications. They ranged from off-the-shelf hardware to complete homes designed around the solar potential of the site. Some resemble space-age fantasies, but most strive to integrate solar features into traditional home design. The two most viable applications of solar energy to an existing home relate to direct space and water heating.

In the minds of many, solar energy involves high-tech hardware and futuristic house design. Energy research may involve these elements, but the greatest impact has been the simple rediscovery of the sun. Solar energy is nothing new to any of us—we experience it when the interior of our car warms up in a sunny parking lot, when we gravitate toward sunny rooms in the winter, or when our west-facing dining room is too uncomfortable for dinner during the summer. What is different now is that we consciously design houses to take into account the position of the sun at various times of the day during different seasons. A solar home is a home in harmony with the sun, whether we want sunshine to heat and cool or simply to enjoy.

Recommended Cross-References
Cooling, Furnaces, Glass, Greenhouses, Heating, Insulation, Skylights, Solariums, Ventilation, Water Heaters, Windows.

The Path of the Sun

Although it is the sun that is stationary and the earth that moves, we perceive the sun as rising and setting. The course of the sun changes gradually, and the extremes occur on the winter solstice in late December, when the sun rises and sets quite a bit south of due east and west, and on the summer solstice in late June, when it rises and sets at the northernmost point. How far north or south depends on geographic perspective, the differences being more extreme the farther north you go.

Not only does the sun appear to rise and set at different positions during the year, it also travels a higher or lower arc through the sky. In the winter it travels a low arc; the highest point at noon may be only a few degrees above the southern horizon. When viewed from the northern hemisphere, the lowest arc occurs in late December. In late June the arc is highest. Of course these positions are a matter of perspective; in the southern hemisphere the highest arc occurs on the winter solstice.

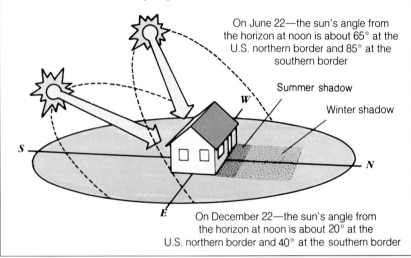

On June 22—the sun's angle from the horizon at noon is about 65° at the U.S. northern border and 85° at the southern border

Summer shadow

Winter shadow

On December 22—the sun's angle from the horizon at noon is about 20° at the U.S. northern border and 40° at the southern border

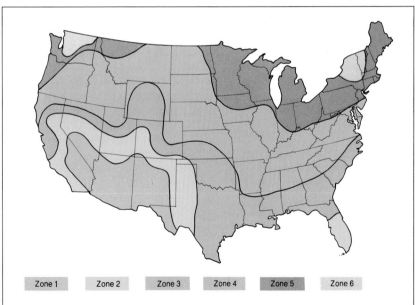

Zone 1   Zone 2   Zone 3   Zone 4   Zone 5   Zone 6

Solar Bands

While sunlight falls on all parts of the United States, more useful sunlight for solar heating falls in some places than in others. The map divides the continental United States into six principal sunfall zones. More sunlight falls in Zone 1, where it is feasible that solar heating can satisfy practically all annual home heating needs. The least sunlight falls in Zone 6, where it is optimistic to think that solar heating could satisfy more than about 35 to 40 percent of the heating requirement. The amounts do not relate directly to average daily temperatures; they reflect latitude and cloud cover.

Solar Space Heating

Solar energy is an untapped heat source that your home should take advantage of in every possible way. The easiest way to tap the sun is with windows, thanks to the seasonal change in the solar path. Just when you need heat the most, the sun is at a low position in the sky that allows the rays to penetrate far into the home through south-facing windows. In the summer the sun is far enough overhead that eaves and simple overhangs block sunlight that would cause overheating.

In the summer windows on the east and west sides of the house receive the full blast of morning and hot afternoon sun. Windows on the north side rarely receive direct sun.

One way to tap solar energy, then, is with plenty of south-facing windows. The other way is with collectors that absorb heat from the sun and distribute it into the home. Again, the optimum orientation is due south. Both methods have drawbacks, and controlling them is what solar design is all about. In the case of windows, the drawbacks are heat loss, limited heat distribution, and overheating. In the case of collectors, they are cost, appearance, and sufficiency of heat. Appropriate design overcomes these drawbacks to various extents. Even if you have to make compromises, the fact that you can meet from 20 to 70 percent of your annual heating needs with solar energy may make them worthwhile.

Although simplistic, a useful definition of solar heating is: making full use of the south-facing portions of your house. This does not mean total glazing, which has proved unnecessary, but it does mean orienting windows as much toward the south as possible and placing collectors efficiently. There are three types of solar heating systems that do this: direct gain, indirect gain, and isolated gain.

Direct Gain

One way to heat living space is with direct sunlight. The obvious requirements are south-facing windows and direct solar radiation (there is useful radiation through most types of cloud cover, although full sunlight is preferable). This type of heating is not feasible if the windows are blocked from the sun by trees, hills, or buildings between 10 a.m. and 2 p.m. during the winter months.

Any room with unobstructed southern windows will receive direct heat. The more rooms along the south wall of the house, the more space that can be heated directly by the sun. An elongated house with the longest wall facing south is ideal for direct gain, although clerestory windows (windows between roof sections) do admit sunshine into interior or north rooms. It is best to concentrate on installing windows in rooms that are used during the day, so that the total glazing area is approximately 15 percent of the floor area you are heating.

This free heat could easily satisfy all your heating needs except for two problems: The source disappears at night and during heavy overcast—the times you are most likely to need it—and the windows that admit heat are also notorious heat losers. If you want to heat only with the sun, there are two ways to overcome these problems: abundant thermal mass (masonry floors and walls) inside the living space that absorbs heat during the day, and heavy insulation for the windows at night. The problem is that you need more glazing to heat up the extra mass, and the added glazing requires more insulation. In most climates you are better off without the extra thermal mass so you can keep the glazing area small—around 10 to 15 percent of floor area—to minimize insulation. A house seems to contain enough mass to modulate temperature swings, and the absence of the extra mass makes it easier for a room to heat up quickly when the sun does pop out. In the sunny Southwest, however, where maximum solar gain is possible with minimum glazing, thermal mass works efficiently.

It is just as important to shade south-facing glass from the summer sun. Overhangs work well, although there are cool days in the fall and spring when they inhibit solar heating. Awnings that can be adjusted offer a good solution.

The abundance of glass may also create problems with glare, fading fabric, and undesirable views. One solution is to concentrate the direct gain in one room, called a solarium, which you can close off from the rest of the house when necessary. A solarium will only heat adjacent rooms but provides a very enjoyable living space. If lack of privacy or pleasant views makes south-facing windows or a solarium undesirable, install the windows at a height higher than normal. Having windows higher up is actually an asset for rooms farther from the south wall because the sunlight penetrates deeper into the house. If the problems of the southern exposure are insurmountable, confine direct gain to the attic.

Indirect Gain

An indirect gain system also utilizes south-facing glass, but immediately behind the glass is a barrier of masonry, water tubes, or other thermal mass. Indirect systems solve the problem of heat loss at night by capturing the solar heat during the day and distributing it into the house when it is needed. The windows themselves are closed off from the house at night, so that they do not rob heat from the living space, the thermal wall, the water tubes, or the other thermal material.

The wall or water containers must be a dark color on the window side to capture the maximum amount of solar heat. Dark blue or dark green are effective, but not as effective as black. Water stored in tubes or in any other type of container must be treated for algae, which diminishes heat-absorbing capabilities. The water must not fill the container completely so it has room to expand.

Thermal walls do not have to be obtrusive. A thermal wall made of masonry can be covered with tile or a brick veneer. A conventional framed wall can be finished to match any other wall in the house. Thermal walls do monopolize the south windows, however. For that reason they are best suited for homes with a large south wall with room for conventional windows as well, or for homes that already have a masonry wall or exposed basement wall that can easily be enclosed with glazing.

Trombe Walls

The name of the thermal wall derives from the name of the Frenchman who invented it. A trombe wall is 12 to 16 inches thick and has vents at the top and bottom which open into the living space. As sunlight penetrates the glass, it heats the dark-colored wall and the air trapped behind the glass. The air escapes through the top vent into the living space and is replaced with air from the lower vent. At night the vents are shut, and the wall radiates heat.

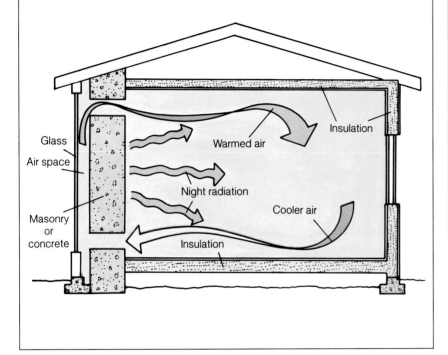

Glass
Air space
Masonry or concrete
Warmed air
Night radiation
Insulation
Cooler air
Insulation

Tube Walls

Tubes filled with water absorb solar heat during the day. At night they heat the air around them, which enters the living space through the top vent and is replaced by cool air from the lower vent. The vents must be shut when the tubes cool, or warm air will escape.

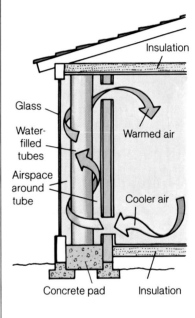

Insulation
Glass
Water-filled tubes
Airspace around tube
Warmed air
Cooler air
Concrete pad
Insulation

Isolated Gain

It may not be feasible to install large areas of windows in the south wall because of structural, economic, or aesthetic limitations, or because the wall receives insufficient sunlight. In such cases it is possible to capture solar energy with an isolated collector, which then distributes heated air into the house. The collector captures only half as many BTUs as a window of equivalent size, but unlike a window it is not a thermal hole and does not need insulation.

Some systems use collectors that heat fluid that is then piped to the house and used in a hydronic radiant heating system. The most successful isolated gain systems use air collectors. A window box is the easiest to install. The system consists of a metal box with a glass window and an absorber plate that fits below an openable window. The plate is usually black sheet metal. As sunlight strikes it, the air in the box heats up and escapes into the room. It is replaced by cooler air from the floor. The air circulates by a process known as thermosiphoning, and does not need a fan. In order to apply thermosiphoning, the box must be below the window and it should be sealed from the room at night with a flap or small door.

A similar device, but much larger, is a thermosiphoning air panel (TAP). It is a flat air collector that attaches directly to a south wall rather than fitting under a window. Most are 3 to 4 feet wide and 8 feet tall. A TAP heats air the same way as a window box. Air circulates into the house through an upper vent in the house wall and is replaced by air entering a lower vent. The large size of this type of collector enables it to heat a whole room on sunny days and several rooms when two or three collectors are ganged.

It is possible to build your own window box, but manufactured units are usually more reliable and easier to install. TAPs are usually built on the site, but you may be able to find a manufactured unit in your area. If not, plans are usually available through solar organizations.

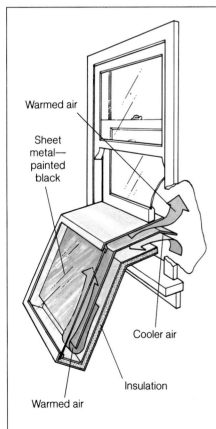

Warmed air
Sheet metal—painted black
Cooler air
Insulation
Warmed air

Solar-Heated Water

Solar energy has been used in many parts of the world for decades to heat water for domestic use, and is an increasingly popular energy source in the United States. To meet all your hot water needs with solar energy is infeasible because you would require an immense storage tank. It makes much more sense to design a system to meet only 40 to 80 percent of your annual need. This percentage may justify the cost of a solar system because hot water can account for as much as a third of your monthly heating bill. The payback period for a solar hot water system is very short compared to elaborate space heating systems. In some arrangements the solar system only preheats the water before it enters a conventional heater. In others the solar-heated water is hot enough—anywhere from 120° to 160° F—to be used directly.

The basic systems for heating water are flat-plate collectors and batch heaters. The flat-plate system uses a pump; it is also known as an active system to distinguish it from thermosiphoning, which uses heat, rather than a pump to circulate water. Batch heaters and flat-plate systems require a storage tank, valves, and controls, as well as a means of protecting the collector and pipes outside the house from freezing.

Flat-Plate Collectors. Collector panels vary in size, shape, and components, but a typical panel is an enclosed metal box with clear glazing on top and a black absorber plate inside that has tubes attached to it or in it. The tubes flare out in an array across the absorber plate and converge, or manifold, at the top and bottom. Fluid enters a single pipe at the bottom of the collector, flows into the smaller risers where it is quickly heated by the absorber, and reconverges into another pipe at the top through which it leaves the collector. Circulating fluid can reach 120° to 160° F. Water that stagnates inside the collector can easily reach temperatures as high as 400° F.

Most collectors heat 1 gallon of water a day for every square foot of glazing surface. If one person uses from 10 to 20 gallons per day—a typical amount in a home with a clothes washer and dishwasher—then a typical household of four people requires two 4 foot by 10 foot

Banks of flat-plate collectors can be located anywhere but are usually mounted on a roof with a southern exposure. This location keeps them out of sight and out of the way.

panels to satisfy 40 to 80 percent of their annual hot water needs.

Although it is possible to make your own collectors, considering the loads and stresses they must endure, it is better to buy them. Besides freezing and extreme heat, they must also resist corrosion from the mating of dissimilar metals, endure snow and wind loads, and resist leaks. They can be installed anywhere that the sun will shine on them all year, but are usually mounted on roofs to receive maximum exposure and to be out of the way.

Collectors should face within 20 to 30 degrees of due south. The angle of tilt should be the same as your latitude, which ranges from roughly 25 degrees near the southern border of the continental United States to approximately 50 degrees at the northern border. At certain times of the year the solar arc will not coincide with this angle, but it is a compromise that maximizes year-round heat gain. In determining the tilt of your collector, remember to compensate for the tilt of your roof. A slope of 4 in 12 equals 18½ degrees.

The greatest danger to a collector is freezing. Even when the air temperature at night is well above 32° F, idle fluid in the collector can freeze because it radiates all heat up to a cold, dark sky. You can prevent this by using antifreeze instead of water. It circulates in a closed loop and transfers heat to the storage tank in a heat-exchanging coil. It is important to use propylene glycol rather than ethylene glycol and test it every two years; ethylene glycol can poison you if the exchanger leaks.

A second way to prevent freezing is to design the system so the collectors and exterior pipes drain back into a holding tank whenever the circulating pump is not on. In milder climates this automatic draining function can be substituted with a simpler system that drains all the water on command from an automatic temperature-controlled valve. In very mild climates you may prevent freezing simply by allowing the water to circulate through the collectors on cold nights. The water loses heat, but the alternative, a freeze, could ruin the system. These three methods are vulnerable to a power failure, so you must have a warning system with manual backup valves.

Flat-plate collector systems include a storage tank. The typical tank has a 100 gallon capacity and holds water from the domestic water system. Cold water enters the inlet, circulates to the collectors, and returns to the tank.

Batch Collectors. The batch collector incorporates the storage tank with the collector, and usually consists of a black tank enclosed in a box with glazing. The nonglazed surfaces of the box have a reflective coating to concentrate the solar energy onto the tank from as many sides as possible. The large size of the tank and dual glazing help prevent the water from freezing at night.

Thermosiphon System. This system uses flat-plate collectors, but they must be mounted below the tank so that the heated water will naturally rise toward the storage tank without the assistance of a pump. It is best to locate the collectors on or near the ground so that the heavy storage tank does not have to be on the roof.

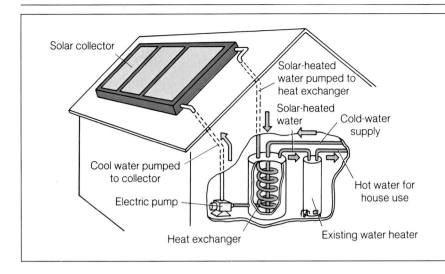

Flat-Plate Collector System

A small pump pushes fluid up into the collectors where it is heated by absorber plates. The heated fluid flows down through a heat exchanger inside a storage tank, then back to the pump.

Sensors are located at the collector outlet and the pump inlet. When the main control senses that the temperature in the collector is higher than the outlet of the heat exchanger, it kicks on the pump. The system should also include an air vent and a pressure relief valve (PRV) at the highest point of the system.

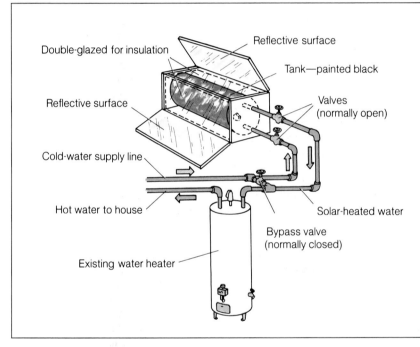

Batch Heating System

Because the batch collector holds water all the time, it is not suitable for climates subject to extreme cold unless it is used seasonally or has insulated covers for night.

A batch heating system does not heat water as quickly as a flat-plate system, but it does heat the water all at once. It relies on intermittent rather than continuous use.

Water, under pressure from the domestic water system, circulates through the batch collector and into a conventional water heater. That's it.

The appearance of batch systems has been a major drawback, but units are now available that fit into the roof structure and resemble a skylight. Others can be enclosed within interior spaces so they are less obtrusive and are protected from freezing.

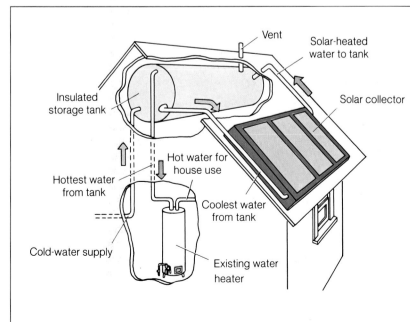

Thermosiphon System

Like other solar systems, a thermosiphon system works best when you schedule hot water use around periods of greatest availability—late afternoon and early evening.

This system combines the efficiency of flat-plate collectors with the simplicity of a batch system. However, it only works if the tank is at least 1½ feet above the top of the collectors. Considering that a 120-gallon tank of water weighs 1,400 pounds, this can be a problem.

The advantage of this system over a batch heater is that water can be recirculated constantly through the collectors, raising the temperature in the storage tank until it is needed. Water is tapped from the top of the tank, where it is warmest.

SOLARIUMS

Solariums, also called sunrooms or sun spaces, are very popular architectural elements in many homes. They combine the unique appeal of an indoor-outdoor living space with the benefits of solar heating and cooling. Some solariums are separate rooms added on to the house, and others are integrated into the main living space of the home. Of all the ways to apply solar technology to existing residential space heating, adding a solarium is probably the most effective and the most harmonious in terms of aesthetics. Although a solarium is not likely to heat an entire home, it can certainly heat the rooms immediately adjacent to it and contribute significantly to meeting total home heating and cooling demands each year. It is also a delightful living space.

Recommended Cross-References
Cooling, Greenhouses, Heating, Insulation, Skylights, Solar Energy, Window Coverings, Windows.

The bow window in this solarium allows an expansive view of the hills and bay. Woven blinds may be lowered to prevent excessive heat gain.

Planning a Solarium

The notion of using solar energy to heat homes is ancient and well developed in many regions of the world, but the idea of a glass-enclosed room for this purpose is fairly recent. The first designs were often experimental, but those pioneering efforts have led to refinements and simplifications that make a solarium an efficient heating device.

A solarium is a room with a great number of south-facing windows that receive direct sunlight. Most often it is a modular greenhouse attached to the house, but it can also be an ordinary room with a large expanse of windows. Whatever the form, a solarium must have a way for the solar heat to circulate to other parts of the house as well as a means to control the extreme heat gain and heat loss that accompany so much glass. The goal of a solarium is a balance where the heat gain from direct sunlight is sufficient to offset the amount of heat loss through the glass at night or on overcast days.

Orientation. In the northern hemisphere a solarium must be on the south side of a building for proper solar exposure. It does not have to face due south, but can be skewed up to 30 degrees to the east or west and still absorb over 90 percent of the solar heat a south wall receives. For minimum winter heating it should receive full sunshine for at least four hours on the winter solstice, the day in late December when the sun dips closest to the horizon.

Location and Size. Ideally a solarium should be adjacent to the living spaces of the home that are used during the day—the living room, dining room, family room, or kitchen. In this configuration the solarium expands living space as well as adds heat where it is needed most. A solarium also makes an excellent airlock entry if it contains a door to the house as well as to the outside.

Attics are another good location, because they are likely to receive uninterrupted sunlight. A solarium can be any size, but a room 12 feet long and 8 to 12 feet wide is typical for most homes. If you desire more heating or a larger space, it would be more effective to have two separate solariums than one large one.

Glazing. Early solarium designs featured a vast area of glazing, usually on all three walls as well as the roof. Contemporary designs, which strive for the most efficient balance between heat gain and heat loss, have glazing only on the south wall. This balance usually amounts to only 15 percent of the total floor area of the solarium and immediately adjacent rooms. This figure varies depending on the area of other south-facing windows and whether the solarium can be isolated from the main living areas. It is important, however, that the east and west walls be solid instead of glazed so they can be insulated. Glazing on the east and west walls is desirable if you grow plants that need morning sun.

Roof glazing, such as skylights or a greenhouse roof, is an optional rather than a necessary component of solariums. Roof windows may leak, allow tremendous heat loss during the night, and are not necessary for optimum solar gain during winter days when the sun swings a low arc. They also cause overheating during the summer months if they are not shaded. If you plan to include roof windows, place them along the ceiling directly adjacent to the south wall. This allows you to insulate the rest of the roof.

In some designs the south wall is slanted so the windows will be perpendicular to the sun during certain heating seasons. This slope is only necessary when you are trying to squeeze the maximum amount of solar energy out of every inch of glazing. When the windows are vertical, some of the sunlight is deflected rather than absorbed. Sloped glazing does not recover enough of this deflected sunlight to warrant the correspondingly high heat gain during the summer, the difficulty of insulating slanted windows, and the possibility of leaks. Furthermore, vertical windows actually absorb more heat than sloped windows in areas and times when it is needed most; they capture sunlight reflected from snow.

The windows should have a short cripple wall beneath them rather than extend all the way to the ground. The cripple wall protects the window from snow piles, provides more insulating area, and places windows where the sunlight can penetrate most effectively.

Most solarium windows are dual-glazed, although dual glazing admits only 18 percent as much solar heat as single glazing. On the other hand, dual glazing provides 50 percent more insulation.

With the addition of glazing, you can turn a deck or screened porch into a solarium.

Thermal Mass

Some solarium designs include heavy mass, such as brick, concrete, or water-filled containers, to absorb heat from the sun and radiate it back during evening hours. Thermal mass is most effective in climates such as the Southwest, which are subject to excessive heat gain during winter months. These climates receive enough sunlight to heat both the house and the mass during the day. In cooler climates the thermal mass can actually prevent the solarium from heating the house during the day because it takes so long to heat itself. For this reason, as well as the fact that the mass should be a dark color, it is not a necessary or even desirable component of all solarium designs. If your design does include thermal mass, you can usually incorporate it in the structure of the solarium as a masonry floor or a masonry wall against the house.

The purpose of thermal mass is to capture and store as much solar radiation as possible. Heavy materials work best. Water is the most efficient but many materials that are already used in conventional construction, such as brick, concrete, and concrete block, will retain heat. If you use containers of water for thermal mass, add a small amount of algaecide to the water in each container. Containers painted black retain the most heat, but any dark color will also absorb high percentages of available solar heat.

Solariums should be open to the house, ventilated, or equipped with blinds to prevent excessive heat gain.

Distributing the Heat

On sunny days a solarium collects great quantities of heat. Due to a greenhouse effect, the energy that comes in through the glass in the form of light and heat cannot escape as readily. Heat accumulates and can be used to heat other rooms in the house. There should be access between the solarium and the rest of the house through a door or several windows; some of the heat can flow into the house naturally through these openings.

The best arrangement has windows or vent openings near the ceiling and others near the floor so the warm air that flows upward and into the house through the high vent is immediately replaced by cooler air from the floor of the house. Vents in these two locations create a convective flow much more readily than a single door. However, it is best to install a fan in one of the high vents to draw heat more efficiently into the house. The fan should be large enough to move from 2 to 4 CFM (cubic feet per minute) for every square foot of south-facing glass. Combine the fan with a duct that directs the heat down to the floor or to remote parts of the house.

Controlling Heat

Heat Loss. The easiest way to control heat loss is to close off the solarium from the rest of the house at night and during overcast days simply by shutting doors and windows. The exterior windows of the solarium, as well as windows between the solarium and the house, should be dual-glazed. If the solarium contains plants that are vulnerable to cold nights, you may have to leave the door open and sacrifice some heat from the home to protect them. Direct heating devices provide a better way to protect plants. Electric heating tape or warm-water pipes buried in the soil will heat the plants, not the entire space.

If the solarium is part of your living space and you live in a cold climate, provide window insulation. Thermal blankets, insulating shutters, and heat-radiating shades are some of the devices you can use. It is much easier to attach them to vertical windows than sloped or overhead windows.

Some other factors may prevent a solarium from heating as much as it should, even on sunny days. Too many plants can affect heating efficiency. Plants can monopolize much of the available heat in normal transpiration. Water in the solarium also uses up energy as it evaporates, turning plants, soil, and uncovered hot tubs into energy liabilities.

Overheating. Solariums overheat very easily in the summer, and even on clear winter days. One way to control overheating, particularly in the winter, is to have one or two vents near the ceiling that open to the outside. As the air becomes too hot it escapes out the vent instead of into the house. A good design also does not have too much glazing. Local solar designers or energy departments can advise you about the best ratio between glass area and floor area for your region.

Two simple measures will control overheating during the summer. Shading devices, such as overhangs, awnings, deciduous plants, or window films, are all effective ways to block sunlight.

The other way to control overheating is to allow sunlight into the solarium and then put the collected heat to use. Do this by having ample vents—about one sixth of the floor area—at the top of the solarium to exhaust the overheated air to the outside. When you open the upper vents between the house and solarium at the same time, the heated air escapes, pulling warmed house air with it. Cooler air enters low vents or windows along a shaded side of the house, and the solarium acts as a fan that moves air through the house. This scenario depends on a significant difference in temperatures between the heated air of the solarium and the outdoor air. In the absence of a significant difference, place a fan near the solarium roof vent in order to aid air movement.

Building a Solarium

The easiest way to add a solarium to your home is to buy a prefabricated kit and install it. Although you can modify a greenhouse kit to build a solarium, it is better to buy a kit specifically for solariums.

The floor of most homes lies over a crawl space or basement. Build a floor platform for the solarium at the same level, or build on a concrete slab or masonry floor at floor level to make construction easier and to take advantage of natural convective currents.

You will have to provide your own foundation and possibly the base wall for any solarium. The foundation should be the same as for a room addition, with rigid insulation around the outside of the wall below grade. The base wall can be an extension of the foundation wall or a short stud wall framed with 2 by 6s with sufficient insulation. The stud wall is better because it can be insulated, although a masonry wall can provide indirect thermal mass if you insulate it completely on the outside. Cover rigid insulation board with flashing or covering material.

East and west walls should be 2 by 6 stud walls joined to the framing of the house. Insulate them with fiberglass blankets between the studs and, in very cold climates, an additional layer of rigid insulation outside the sheathing. In addition, east and west walls support the solid portion of the roof if there are no posts on the south wall or if there is a curved roof.

Insulate a roof without skylights or windows to the R-value specified for your area. Some kits have rafters supported by a beam over the top of the south-facing windows, others have laminated wood trusses, others have a metal grid. In all cases attach the roof to the house at a ledger bolted into the house studs or rafters.

If you install your own windows, take precautions against expansion and contraction of the sealing components as well as settling and movement of the framing. If the windows are vertical, install them as you would fixed panes. If they slope or include roof windows, consult a local glazing specialist or have them installed professionally.

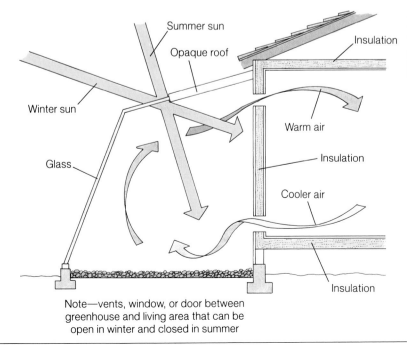

Note—vents, window, or door between greenhouse and living area that can be open in winter and closed in summer

SOUND CONTROL

There are two principal ways to reduce unwanted sound: generate less and transmit less.

Sound travels by vibrating molecules of solids or gases in waves, like a pebble tossed into a pond makes ripples. When sound waves radiate through the air and strike a solid object, such as a door or wall, they cause it to vibrate as well. If the object is rigid and there is enough sound energy, the far side vibrates and transmits the sound, passing it almost unaltered into the next room.

Recommended Cross-References
Framing, Wallboard.

Reducing Sound Transmission

The airborne transmission of speech through walls or ceilings is measured in STCs (sound transmission class). Transmission through walls and floors is rated in IICs (impact insulation class). For either measurement, a higher number indicates that less sound is being transmitted. A rating of 45 to 50 is reasonable; at this level, loud speech is barely heard as a murmur.

The ideal materials for deadening sound transmission are heavy and nonrigid, such as lead or water. The heaviness keeps sound from vibrating the material; the resiliency keeps the material from resonating.

The lower the pitch of the sound, the more difficult it is to block. If high-pitched sounds are transmitted from room to room, there are probably air gaps that let the sound through. A one-inch gap in a wall can reduce the STC rating from about 50 to about 30.

Wood-frame buildings need interrupted assemblies to stop the transmission of sound from the structure to the air. This is easy with walls, since double-row stud walls are effective in preventing sound transmission. It is harder with ceilings, especially in an existing house that is being remodeled.

Relationship of Sound Transmission Class to Speech Privacy

STC 25	Normal speech intelligible
STC 30	Loud speech intelligible
STC 35	Loud speech blurred but intelligible
STC 40	Loud speech rarely intelligible but still audible
STC 45	Loud speech unintelligible and barely audible
STC 50	Loud speech almost inaudible
STC 55	Loud speech inaudible

Reducing Sound Generation

Appliances, duct work, furnaces, pipes, furnishings, and other sources produce sound that can be reduced.

Hammering water pipes can be quieted with arresters, which act like shock absorbers. They can be installed throughout the house or at a single appliance. Rattling water pipes can be supported with hangers. Plastic pipes that rub against the frame of the house and squeak can be silenced by stuffing fiberglass insulation between the pipe and the framing members. Cast-iron drains are much quieter than plastic, but this is an expensive project to do separately. If you are remodeling, however, specify that the second-floor drains be cast iron (the vents can still be plastic).

Low-noise toilets are quieter than standard ones, but more expensive. If the local building code requires ultralow-flow toilets, test one before you buy. Some are very noisy.

Appliances can be supported on rubber vibration pads. You can also use sheets of foam or fiberglass sound deadener to reduce some of the higher-frequency noise. Air space between appliances and walls or cabinets will also muffle noise.

Appliances have noise ratings, although they are not usually included in the sales literature. The information is on file with the manufacturer's specifications.

Air-conditioning will let you close the windows when it is noisy outside. Whole-house units are quieter than room units.

Heat ducts can act like sound tunnels, transmitting fan, wind, and room-to-room noise. They may also creak and pop. Oil the furnance pulleys and replace filters and fan belts to quiet the furnace. Reroute straight ducts so they have bends and install a flexible rubber boot at the furnace output and cold-air return plenums. Readjust sections of duct work that pop. If that doesn't work, lightly score the surface of the duct in an X pattern. This allows the metal to flex without popping.

For room-to-room sounds, replace interior hollow-core doors with solid doors, and weather-strip them like exterior doors. Use sound-deadening furnishings, such as stuffed furniture, fabric wallcoverings, rugs, and drapes.

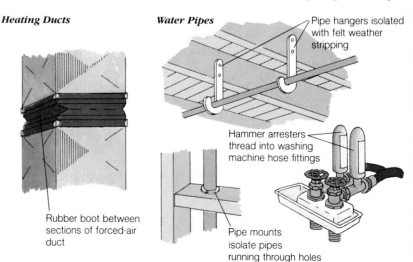

Heating Ducts

Rubber boot between sections of forced-air duct

Water Pipes

Pipe hangers isolated with felt weather stripping

Hammer arresters thread into washing machine hose fittings

Pipe mounts isolate pipes running through holes

Quiet Walls

A wall 6 to 8 inches thick and filled with sand would give an STC rating of about 60. Only the beat of loud music can penetrate something like that. However, the cost and the structure needed to hold the weight make it impractical. More realistic solutions include covering a standard stud wall with ½-inch sound-deadening board on both sides, then finishing with ⅝-inch wallboard on both sides. This will give an STC rating of about 45.

Another method is to use resilient channel on the studs and cover the wall with ½-inch wallboard. This will give an STC rating of approximately 50.

A third method is to build a double-row stud wall. Stagger the studs, weave fiberglass insulation between the walls, and cover each wall with ½-inch wallboard. This will give a rating of about 50.

In all cases, the number of electrical receptacles and heating ducts should be kept to a minimum.

Storm windows, either the exterior or interior type, will reduce the transmission of sound through exterior walls a great deal.

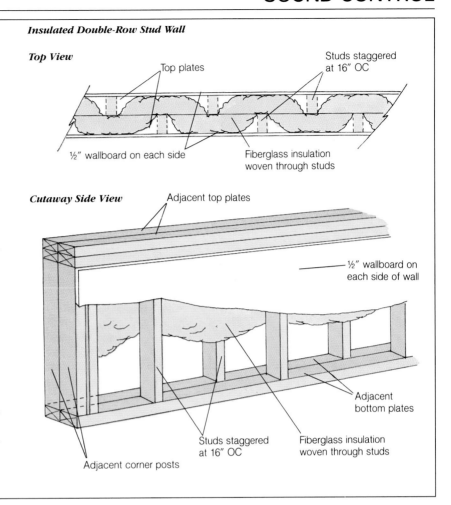

Insulated Double-Row Stud Wall

Top View

Top plates
Studs staggered at 16″ OC
½″ wallboard on each side
Fiberglass insulation woven through studs

Cutaway Side View

Adjacent top plates
½″ wallboard on each side of wall
Adjacent bottom plates
Studs staggered at 16″ OC
Fiberglass insulation woven through studs
Adjacent corner posts

Quiet Floors and Ceilings

The easiest, most cost-effective way of quieting floors is to install a thick pad and carpet. A more expensive method, if the structure can support the weight, is to build them up with wallboard or, better yet, lightweight concrete.

If they are made of fiberglass panels or mineral-fiber tiles, suspended ceilings added to existing ceilings will reduce sound transmission.

Another method is to use resilient channel on the ceiling joists. All the material must be removed from an existing ceiling so the resilient channel can be attached directly to the joists (it won't work if you attach it to wallboard or plaster). If you can't attach the channel directly to the joists, add more layers of wallboard to the ceiling if the structure can support the weight. Resilient channel must have at least 3½ inches of air space above it to be effective. The larger the air space, the better it performs.

When you attach resilient channel, be careful not to use screws

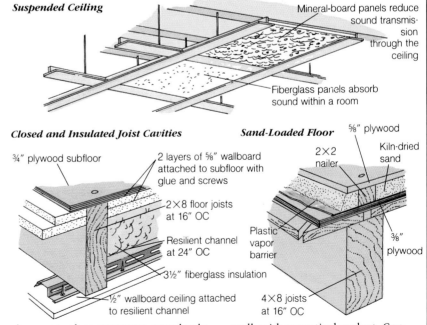

Suspended Ceiling

Mineral-board panels reduce sound transmission through the ceiling
Fiberglass panels absorb sound within a room

Closed and Insulated Joist Cavities

¾″ plywood subfloor
2 layers of ⅝″ wallboard attached to subfloor with glue and screws
2×8 floor joists at 16″ OC
Resilient channel at 24″ OC
3½″ fiberglass insulation
½″ wallboard ceiling attached to resilient channel

Sand-Loaded Floor

⅝″ plywood
2×2 nailer
Kiln-dried sand
Plastic vapor barrier
⅜″ plywood
4×8 joists at 16″ OC

long enough to penetrate completely through the ceiling joists. Only a few such penetrations will significantly reduce the effectiveness of the channel.

Seal the edges of the wallboard at the walls with foam backer rod, and caulk with acoustical sealant. Conceal the joints with molding that doesn't quite touch the ceiling. Seal any openings, such as those for light fixtures, with acoustical caulk or nonhardening sealant, such as butyl or silicone.

SPRINKLER SYSTEMS

*A sprinkler system is a convenient
and effective way to water large
lawns or garden areas. A good system
represents a considerable investment—of both money and time—but,
once installed, it will save you time,
conserve water, and provide convenience. You can even make your system fully automatic, vary the type of
sprinkler heads, or install a drip irri-
gation system for areas that are planted sparsely where broad coverage
from spray heads would waste water.
If you are installing a sprinkler system
in a yard with mature landscaping,
consider having it put in by professionals. They use a pipe-pulling machine to avoid digging trenches, which
disrupts soil and plants.*

Recommended Cross-References
Pipe, Plumbing.

Calculating Flow Rate
A sprinkler system depends on a
certain amount of water pressure to
ensure smooth operation and adequate coverage. Water pressure is
measured as flow rate in gallons
per minute. To determine the water
pressure, measure how many seconds it takes to fill a 1-gallon container from an outside faucet, with
the tap wide open. Divide that
number into 60 to determine your
flow rate in gallons per minute. (If
it takes 5 seconds, your flow rate is
12 gallons per minute.)

To make sure this flow rate is
adequate for your sprinkler plan,
write the required flow rate next to
each sprinkler head on your plan.
Catalogs will give you this information. Then add up the flow rate for
each circuit. The total should be
from 60 to 75 percent of the flow
rate for your home. (In operation,
only one circuit is turned on at a
time.) If necessary, adjust the number or size of heads on each circuit
so the demand will not exceed the
available flow rate.

Designing the System
Locating Sprinkler Heads. First draw a
site plan that includes all the lawns
and planting beds you need to water.
Then choose appropriate heads for
your watering needs: pop-up or stationary heads for lawns, heads on
risers for shrubs, bubbler heads for
trees, and rotating heads for large
expanses of lawn or ground cover.
Planning the Circuits. Plan the circuits so all the areas that need to be
watered at the same time and for the
same duration are together. All heads
on a given circuit should be of the
same type; otherwise one type may
monopolize the water pressure. As
you cluster the heads into various
circuit patterns, consider where the
connecting pipes will run. Avoid
runs where pipes are close to trees
or must be tunneled under paths.

Each circuit will be controlled by
its own valve. On a manual system,
locate the valves close to one another for convenient operation.

A manifold—a junction of several
pipes that allows distribution of the
water from the main source to the
various circuits—should be planned
wherever several circuits converge,
or, in the case of manually controlled
valves, where valve locations are the
most convenient. The system should
also have a main valve to isolate the
sprinkler system from the house water supply system and an antisiphon
valve, also known as a vacuum breaker or backflow preventer. This prevents water in the sprinkler system,
which may be contaminated from
ground contact, herbicides, or insec-
ticides, from flowing back into the
main water system should there be a
loss of pressure in that system. The
antisiphon valve must be installed at
a higher point than all the other
valves, pipes, and heads.

If you live in an area where the
ground freezes, you will also have to
provide a bleeder valve or other
means of draining the system.

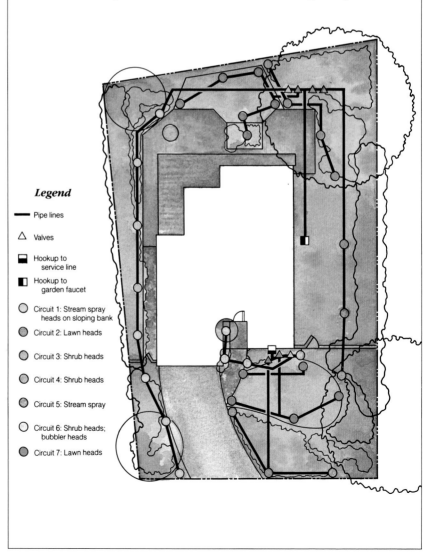

Legend

— Pipe lines

△ Valves

▭ Hookup to
service line

▮ Hookup to
garden faucet

○ Circuit 1: Stream spray
heads on sloping bank

◔ Circuit 2: Lawn heads

○ Circuit 3: Shrub heads

○ Circuit 4: Shrub heads

◑ Circuit 5: Stream spray

○ Circuit 6: Shrub heads;
bubbler heads

◔ Circuit 7: Lawn heads

Pipes and Valves

Sizes. The pipes and valve for each circuit should accommodate the required flow rate (gpm) for that circuit. Most systems use ¾-inch pipe for 14 gpm, 1-inch pipe for 25 gpm, or 1¼-inch pipe for 40 gpm.

The main feeder line from the house to the manifold should be no smaller than the largest circuit pipe. If the feeder line is longer than 100 feet, it should be one size larger, even if this makes it larger than the house service to which it connects.

Types of Pipe. You can use any kind of pipe, but the lighter gauges of PVC pipe (class 315, 200, and 160) and some of the other plastics, such as polybutylene and polyethylene, are easy to work with. They resist corrosion, an important feature if they are going to be buried. Where water pressure is high, such as main feeder lines, use pipe with a stronger rating, like PVC, Schedule 40.

Valves. The best type of valve for the main shutoff is usually a gate valve, the same size as the main feeder line. It is used only once in a while,

and must be either completely on or completely off. Locate an antisiphoning device near the main shutoff valve or buy special antisiphon valves for the circuit control valves if each circuit will be turned on manually. Antisiphoning devices prevent potentially contaminated water in the sprinkler heads from flowing back into the domestic water system. The antisiphoning unit must be installed higher than the heads. Automatic valves are buried in a valve box at the beginning of each circuit.

Automatic Control Panels. Units with solid-state components can operate all your circuits independently, allowing you to program watering times for different watering needs. They also allow you to set watering times when the pressure is likely to be greatest and evaporation and wind conditions minimal.

Moisture Sensors. These can be inserted in the ground at various depths and wired to the control panel. They indicate when water is actually needed, eliminating wasteful automatic watering.

Installing the System

Tap into the house water supply and install a main valve for the sprinkler system. Run a line from the valve to the manifold location and assemble the manifold from conventional fittings and sections of pipe, starting at the upstream end. Attach the circuit valves to their manifold stubs, turn them off, and open the main valve to test for leaks in the manifold.

Drive a stake in the ground at each head location. Indicate the pipe runs with agricultural lime or similar marking material. Dig trenches at least 12 inches deep, carefully cutting and removing sod if the lawn is already established. Assemble pipes, fittings, and risers, but not the heads. Work back to the manifold or circuit valve. When the assembly is complete, turn on the water to flush out the pipes. Attach the heads. Test the entire system to make sure the water coverage is adequate before backfilling the trenches. Install a drain valve to protect the system from freezing.

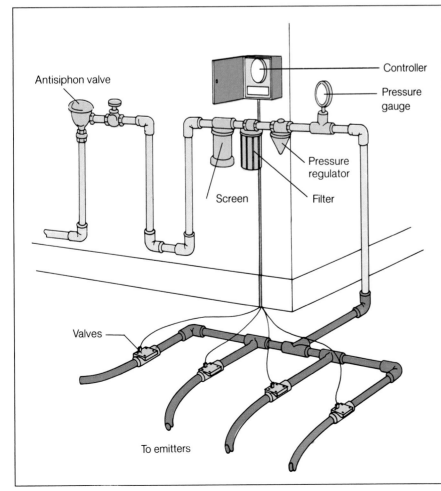

Antisiphon valve

Controller

Pressure gauge

Screen

Pressure regulator

Filter

Valves

To emitters

Drip and Soaker Systems

The key element in a drip system is the emitter, which releases water one drop at a time no matter how much pressure is in the supply lines. Emitters are sized by the rate of delivery, from ½ gallon to 5 gallons per hour (1 gallon is common). Some emitters deliver a fine mist.

The emitters are connected to flexible plastic pipe, connected with compression fittings.

The simplest drip systems merely attach to an outdoor faucet. To ensure correct pressure and a safe and clog-free system, there should be a filter to prevent the emitters from clogging. A pressure regulator may be necessary to reduce the ordinary household pressure (about 40 to 50 psi) to the lower level used by most drip systems (about 15 psi). More sophisticated systems tap directly into the plumbing system and may include electronically controlled valves. A variation of the drip system is the porous soaker hose. This attaches to outdoor faucets and works well in heavily planted, level areas. Install an antisiphon device on any sprinkler system.

STAIRS

Installing a new stairway is not a casual weekend project. The job demands thorough planning, numerous mathematical calculations, and careful carpentry. Most homeowners with some carpentry experience are able to build a conventional, straight-run stairway for an attic or basement access, but a more elaborate, hardwood stairway requires the same skills as fine woodwork.

Before you launch in and take on the building of a complete stairway yourself, investigate the following options: Perhaps it would be worth getting a local manufacturer to prefabricate and deliver the stairway as a unit? Maybe this same manufacturer

would install the stairs, or you could do it yourself. A second option is to hire a contractor to install prebuilt stairs or to custom build them on site. The third possibility is to take your stair dimensions to a building supplier or a stair specialty company and order precut parts. Prefabricated decorative balusters, posts, and railings are readily available.

If you plan thoroughly and work carefully, however, you can build a simple flight of stairs.

Recommended Cross-References
Attics, Basements, Framing, Joinery, Railings, Steps.

Where to Locate a Stairway

Convenience should be the primary consideration when placing a new stairway. It should be easily accessible from as many rooms as possible. Another major consideration is the amount of structural work that will be necessary.

Make sure that there will be enough headroom, especially for attic stairs. If the stairway is too close to the eaves, there will be no room to stand up when you reach the top. Also consider noise, which travels all too freely up and down stairs. For instance, a room for formal entertaining or quiet retreat should be away from a stairway that would pipeline noise from other rooms.

Finally, if you are designing new space such as a room addition, regard the stairs as a major design

element rather than a utilitarian afterthought. Going up and down stairs is a dramatic transition. Try to arrange for an appealing view at the top—a window or attractive alcove rather than a stark hall or blank wall. Also consider the view as you descend. Place a window or an inviting room where the steps terminate.

The most logical place to locate a new stairway is directly above an existing stairway. Place a new set of attic stairs above the main stairs or basement stairs, for example. If this isn't practical and you are forced into cutting a hole in the floor or ceiling, try to position the flight so the steps run parallel to the joists. If the steps must run perpendicular to the joists, position the stairway along a bearing wall or add a new wall or posts to support the trimmer joists.

Optional Configurations

Stairways take up a lot more space than most people realize. A typical straight-run stairway from one floor to the next requires almost 40 square feet of floor space (3 feet wide by 12 to 13 feet long), not to mention an additional 9 square feet of floor space for a landing at the bottom. The well opening eliminates another 36 feet of floor space upstairs. Such a stairway occupies approximately 84 square feet. Other configurations, such as L-shaped stairways or stairways that turn 180 degrees, require an even larger area.

Space-saving configurations include steeper, spiral stairs and the use of winders. Making stairs steeper

to save room is safe only to a point. The preferred angle of incline is from 30 degrees to 35 degrees. A 9-foot stairway within that range requires a run of 13 feet 5 inches. A steeper stairway angled at 38 degrees would require only 10 feet 7 inches. Winders save space by eliminating the level platform where the stairs change direction. Codes have strict requirements regulating the size of winders, however. In some areas the local code does not permit them. Prefabricated spiral stairs come with diameters ranging from 4 feet to 6 feet. Most codes specify that a spiral stairway serve only as a secondary flight if the upper story contains more than 400 square feet.

Code Requirements

Building codes are strict about stairs. Check your local code before you start building. Most codes require that main stairs be at least 32 inches wide between handrails and allow a minimum headroom of 80 inches. If you have room, increase the width to 36 inches and the headroom to at least 7 feet to enhance comfort and convenience.

Most codes require a handrail on at least one side of the stairway. You will probably need one on both sides if the stairway is open or is wider than 4 feet. The rail should be a consistent height of 30 to 34 inches as measured from the nosing of each tread. The handrail should terminate at both ends in such a way that cuffs and loose clothing will not catch. Allow at least 1½ inches of clearance between the handrail and the wall.

If there is a doorway at the top of the stairs, it must swing away from the stairs or there must be a 3-foot landing on the stair side. Landings must be the same width as the stairs and at least 3 feet deep. No stairway should rise more than 12 feet without a landing.

Rise and Run. Local codes specify the acceptable height (the unit rise) and depth (the unit run) of each step.

To a significant degree, the rise and run determine the safety of a stairway. Most codes specify the maximum rise as 7½ inches and the minimum tread width as between 10 and 11 inches. Added together, the tread and riser should total between 17 and 18 inches. This relationship must be constant because a higher riser requires a narrower tread—an 8-inch riser with a 10-inch tread, for instance. A gentler slope calls for wider treads—a 6-inch riser with a 12-inch tread, for example.

Codes also specify that an individual riser may not deviate by more than ³/₁₆ inch in height from the others in the run. If you build an enclosed stairway (or enclose the space beneath an existing stairway), you must use ⅝-inch wallboard and provide fire blocking between all studs.

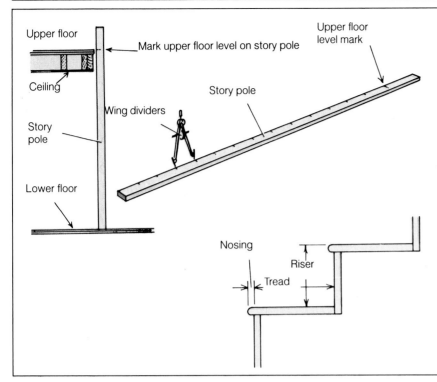

Riser Height and Tread Width

Measure the total distance from floor to floor allowing for the depth of finish flooring. Divide the total distance by 7½ to get the approximate number of steps. Round up the answer to the nearest whole number, then divide the round number back into the total rise. The answer should be 7 and a fraction, and it represents the height each riser must be for the stairway to fill but not exceed the allotted space. To find the tread width, subtract the riser dimension from 17½ inches.

For example:

$$108'' \div 7\frac{1}{2} = 14.4 \text{ steps}$$
$$108'' \div 15 \text{ steps} = 7.2''$$
$$\text{Riser} = 7\frac{3}{16}''; \text{ tread} = 10\frac{5}{16}''$$

You can arrive at the same answer by using a story pole. Mark the total rise on the pole. Through trial and error, divide the distance into equal segments with dividers.

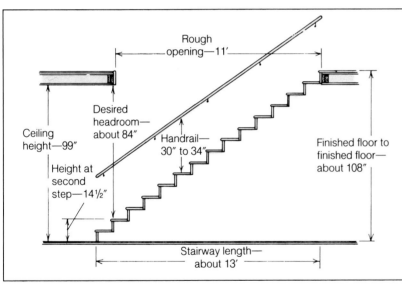

Length of the Opening

From the previous calculation you know the number and width of the treads in the stairway and the height of each riser. Determine the total length of the stairway by multiplying the tread width times the number of treads minus one. To find the length of the stairwell opening, subtract the headroom from the ceiling height and determine how many risers and treads will fit. Then subtract the combined width of those treads from the total length of the stairway.

If there is not enough room for the opening or for the total length of the stairs, try another design that uses higher risers and narrower treads.

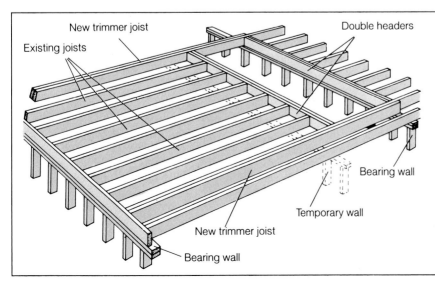

Preparing the Rough Opening

If the opening runs parallel to the joists, you just need to cut through only one or two joists. If the opening is perpendicular, support the joists temporarily with shoring, then install trimmers, a new wall, or a beam.

To frame the opening, nail trimmer joists to the end joists with 16d nails 12 inches on center. Make sure the joists are supported at both ends. Mark the cut for the opening. Allow room for framing, finish materials, and handrails. Remove ceiling and flooring within the opening, erect shoring or new walls as needed, cut the joists, and install double headers.

Installing a Stairway

Use straight 2 by 12 stock for the stringers. To mark the cuts for the first stringer, set a framing square so the tongue (the short leg) indicates the riser dimension and the blade (the long leg) indicates the tread width. These two lines that intersect at the nosing should meet at the edge of the stringer. Scribe the outline of the square onto the wood. Continue this process until you have marked all risers and treads. Mark carefully; the height of each finished riser must measure within $3/16$ inch of every other riser.

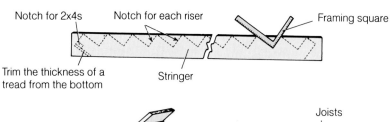

Notch for 2x4s   Notch for each riser   Framing square

Trim the thickness of a tread from the bottom   Stringer

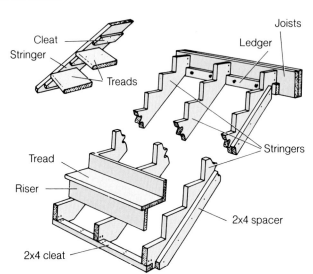

Cleat
Stringer
Treads
Ledger
Joists

Tread
Riser
Stringers

2x4 spacer
2x4 cleat

To make the bottom step the same height as the others, trim the bottom of the stringer by the thickness of one tread, and cut a notch for a cleat made from a 2 by 4. Place the stringer in the rough opening to see if it fits properly. Adjust it if necessary. Then use it as a pattern to cut another stringer. If the stairway is wider than 32 inches, you need to cut two more stringers. Install the stringers, using a ledger or joist hangers at the top. If you nail one stringer to wall framing, add a 2 by 4 spacer for wallboard and finish trim. Install two or three risers at a time. Then starting from the bottom, attach the treads. Affix them with construction adhesive and 8d nails. In addition to facenailing, drive nails from the back of the risers into the treads.

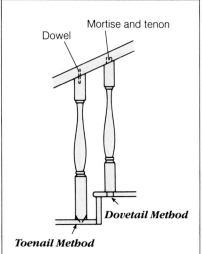

Dowel   Mortise and tenon

Dovetail Method

Toenail Method

Attaching Balusters

Traditional carpenters dovetail balusters into treads and cover the joint with molding. An easier method employs pilot holes drilled at an angle into the baluster. Screw or toenail through the holes and into the tread. Position and fasten the handrail to the posts and balusters with dowels or mortise-and-tenon joints. There should be two balusters per tread.

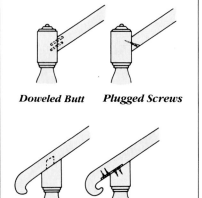

Doweled Butt   Plugged Screws

Mortise and Tenon   Metal Straps

Attaching a Handrail

A handrail can be attached in several different ways, including doweled butt joints, mortise-and-tenon joints, countersunk and plugged screws or bolts, and metal straps.

Holding the handrail in position, mark the location of each baluster on it by dropping a plumb bob to baluster marks on the treads. Also mark the correct angle to guide you when drilling dowel holes or cutting mortises. Drill the holes and install the handrail.

Tightening a Handrail

To tighten a loose handrail, squeeze glue into the gap and predrill the baluster for countersunk screws. Tightening the screws should tighten the handrail.

If the gap is too large to repair with screws, drive a glue-coated wedge between the rail and the baluster.

Repairing Loose or Squeaky Stairs

Apparently, Japanese rulers used to surround their sleeping quarters with specially designed porches and stairs that creaked loud warnings if anyone set foot on them. For most of us, however, things that go squeak in the night are annoying and alarming rather than reassuring.

Squeaks are caused by two pieces rubbing against one another, so treat them just as you would a squeak in your car: Locate the problem, then, using a small tube of graphite powder, shoot in some lubrication. Repeat the application until the problem is solved.

If your problem is loose stairs, the solution requires a little more work. Because of warps or settling, the edge of the tread sometimes separates slightly from the riser. You can live with squeaks, but a loose step is downright dangerous and should be fixed at once.

Whenever possible, make repairs on a staircase from underneath. This allows you to use heavier bracing and any mistakes you might make will be hidden. The bracing can be metal brackets or a glue-coated block positioned tight against the tread and screwed to the riser. It is a good idea to have someone stand on the tread while you are working. The weight will press the tread and the riser firmly together.

If you must make repairs from above, be sure to predrill nail and screw holes to avoid splitting the wood. Use nails, screws, or wedges depending on which will perform best and show the least.

With Nails. Angle the nails in opposite directions. Set heads and fill holes with putty.

With Screws. Drill pilot and countersink holes. Tighten screws and fill holes.

With Wedges. Remove any trim molding and drive small, glue-coated wedges between the tread and the riser as shown. Note that the direction of the wedge depends on the type of construction.

After the glue dries, cut off the wedges flush with the surface. Cover the gaps with decorative molding.

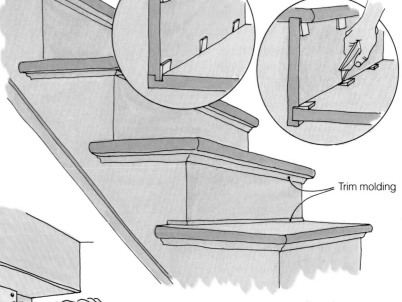

Trim molding

With Cleats. Get someone to stand on the loose step while you are working. From underneath, position a glue-coated cleat against the tread and screw it into the riser.

STEPS

Access and convenience usually demand at least a few steps in the garden or near the house. When you plan steps, your major consideration should be safety. Select nonskid paving materials. Risers should be at least 4 inches high, and all risers and treads in the same flight should match. Provide a handrail if there are more than four steps in a flight and install lighting nearby.

Be aware that your local building code probably specifies riser and tread dimensions. A typical code prescribes a maximum rise of 7½ inches and a minimum tread of 11 or 12 inches. The most comfortable relationship, especially for long runs, is a 6-inch riser and a 15-inch tread, but a ratio as low as 4:19 or as high as 7:13 is suitable for a few steps. Because outdoor space is usually less restricting, outdoor steps can be more luxurious than indoor steps.

Steps that lead to outdoor areas should be wide enough to permit easy passage and to relate to the scale of the total area. Eight feet is a suitable minimum width. Also, consider how to treat the edges of the steps. Will they remain bare or will you line them with planters or other barriers?

Recommended Cross-References
Brick, Concrete, Decks, Paths, Paving, Railings, Stairs.

Whether they lead from the back door to the yard or a deck to the ocean, steps should be planned to look attractive, fit with the landscaping, and be safe to use.

Layout

To determine the best riser-tread relationship, you first need to find the total vertical rise and total horizontal run. Use a long 2 by 4 to find these dimensions, leveling it for accurate measurement. If the distance is too great for a single board, take a series of measurements between intermediate points along the slope. Draw these measurements carefully on graph paper to give you a cross section of the slope to scale.

After you have plotted the total rise and run on graph paper, experiment on paper with different riser heights and tread widths until you find a ratio that conforms to the slope without being too steep or too flat. The risers should divide the slope into equal segments so all the steps are exactly the same height and width. Arriving at a standard is usually easier with outdoor steps than with indoor stairways because you can adjust the grade level at the top or bottom of the slope to create a full step if necessary. In some cases, however, an outdoor flight presents at least one fixed point, such as an existing path, sidewalk, deck, patio, or driveway. If steps terminate at a sidewalk or some other kind of public access, you may be required to get a building permit.

In planning riser and tread dimensions, keep in mind points where landings are necessary or desirable. Avoid single steps; cluster two or three together so they are easy to see. Plan a slope of 1/4 inch per foot for each tread to provide drainage.

Choosing Materials

Many materials work well as outdoor steps, including brick, stone, concrete block, poured concrete, railroad ties, timbers, and lumber.

Some materials, such as railroad ties, block, and timbers, will dictate the height of each step because each riser consists of a single member. Other materials are more adaptable, especially brick and concrete. Generally, the easiest type of stairway to build over a long run is a wood one supported by continuous stringers. Although stepping-stones or individual paving logs may seem easier to install, excavating the slope is a matter of trial and error.

Brick Steps. Excavate to accommodate a concrete footing, or build the new steps over an existing concrete stairway. If you pour a new base, make sure that the brick layout fits the chosen riser height or you will have to cut the bricks. Start laying the bricks at the bottom and work up. Set the risers in place, then lay the treads on a mortar bed. Grout all the joint spaces.

Loose Fill. Use wooden boards, timbers, or concrete blocks as risers and then backfill with a contrasting material for an interesting effect. The riser should be wide if the backfill is a soft paving material that easily gives way. The tread area should be well drained, preferably with a gravel base. Drive pipes or pressure-treated stakes below the level of the tread paving to hold riser boards.

Stepping-Stones. Where conditions permit, set concrete blocks, heavy log rounds, thick flagstones, or similar materials directly in the soil. The slope must be gentle and the soil stable. Pour a concrete landing at the bottom of the steps to anchor them and prevent the entire stairway from slipping. Excavate to accommodate a gravel or sand sub-base that will stabilize each paving unit.

Platforms. If you need only one or two steps, the simplest way to build them is to construct small platforms using 2 by 6s or 2 by 8s as joists. A 2 by 6 is 5 1/2 inches high; a 2 by 8 is 7 1/2 inches high. Both heights are common for risers. If you use one step to separate two deck platforms, run the decking boards perpendicular to each other. Define the edge of the platform with a fascia board to make the step easy to see. Some codes do not permit a single step on a deck.

Railroad Ties. Select ties of a uniform thickness. Most ties are 7 to 9 inches thick and 8 feet long. To excavate a bench for each step, stretch a level string line above the stairway. Determine the point at which each nosing will lie, and measure down the distance to the step plus the thickness of the tie. Dig a level bench from this point back into the hill. Start at the bottom of the stairway and work up, one tie at a time. Take measurements from the string line, then double-check by measuring from one tie to the next. Drill a 3/4-inch hole at both ends of each tie with a 1/2-inch electric drill bit or a brace and bit. Pound a 30-inch length of pipe or rebar into each hole to secure the step.

Make treads by laying two or three ties together, or use ties for the risers and backfill with brick, gravel, or a ground cover such as grass or dichondra. Some plants will not grow well because of the creosote in the ties. Check with your local nursery.

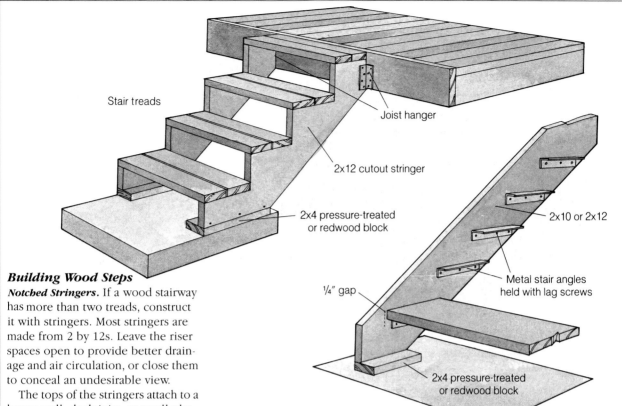

Stair treads

Joist hanger

2x12 cutout stringer

2x4 pressure-treated or redwood block

¼" gap

2x10 or 2x12

Metal stair angles held with lag screws

2x4 pressure-treated or redwood block

Building Wood Steps

Notched Stringers. If a wood stairway has more than two treads, construct it with stringers. Most stringers are made from 2 by 12s. Leave the riser spaces open to provide better drainage and air circulation, or close them to conceal an undesirable view.

The tops of the stringers attach to a house wall, deck joist, or small platform. The base should rest on a concrete pad. If the stringers are not of a durable species or of pressure-treated lumber, don't set them directly on concrete. Place them on 2 by 4 blocks so the bases won't decay.

To build stringers, calculate the exact riser dimension that will produce an even number of steps. Determine the best tread width to go with the riser size. For outdoor steps the total of riser height and tread width should be 20 to 21 inches.

Use a framing square to lay out each step on the 2 by 12. Position the

square so that the mark showing riser height and tread width end at the edge of the stringer. Cut out the stringer. Check that it fits; when it does, use it as a pattern.

Install all the stringers and make sure they are level. For protection against decay and splitting, coat all the stringer edges with sealer or primer. Then attach treads with outdoor construction adhesive or 16d HDG box nails. If you use risers, the tread nosings should overhang them by 1½ inches.

Solid Stringers. The treads, which

should not be wider than 3 feet, are suspended between two solid stringers by wood or metal cleats. The stringers can be 2 by 8s, but should be at least 2 by 10s for spans longer than 10 feet. Rough lumber will provide more strength. Mark risers and treads on the stringers as if you were going to cut them. Use the marks as a guide for attaching cleats. Fasten cleats with lag screws or carriage bolts, or use nails long enough to clinch after they penetrate the stringer. Each tread should overhang the one below it by 1½ inches.

Constructing Concrete Steps

Build concrete steps on level or sloping ground. The footing portion of the stairway, below the steps themselves, should be at least 6 inches thick—or thicker to reach below the frost line.

Use 2 by 6s to build forms for 5½-inch risers; use 2 by 8s to build 7½-inch risers. If the steps are on level ground, build the sides using a series of stacked horizontal pieces. If the steps are on sloping ground, set 2 by 10s diagonally along the sides at the same angle as the slope. Nail vertical cleats on the inside of each diagonal to support the crosspieces. The crosspieces, or riser forms, may an-

gle back to provide more toe room. Cut the forms with a 45-degree bevel on the bottom. The cut will enable you to reach to the inside corner with finishing tools in order to smooth the concrete surface of the tread. Forms must be sturdy and well braced, especially at the corners and along wide portions.

Place ⅜- or ½-inch reinforcing bars in the forms so there is a horizontal piece along the width of each step near the nosing. Set diagonal pieces 6 to 10 inches apart along the length of the stairway slab. Every 12 inches place crosspieces between horizontal and vertical bars.

After you build the forms, fill them

with rocks, bricks, and broken concrete to reduce the amount of concrete required for the pour. Keep the fill away from the top and edges so it won't be exposed or weaken the surface bond of the concrete.

Aggregate for the concrete should not be bigger than 1 inch, and the mix should be stiff when you place it. Begin placing it in the bottom step, then work your way up. As you consolidate the concrete, work a trowel up and down between the concrete and the forms to smooth the sides. Float each step after you fill it. When the top step is filled, strike it off, then float it. Finish with a broom for a nonskid surface.

STORAGE: indoor

Today, with the emphasis on smaller living areas, open space, and streamlined interiors, a project that increases storage space has top priority in almost any home.

The key to increasing storage is utilizing space. You may be surprised at the usable space in nooks, insets, gaps, and "next-tos" (next to the door, next to the stove).

Distinguish discrete activity areas and traffic corridors. Draw diagrams and floor plans to help you organize the spaces efficiently. Separate quiet activities from noisy ones. Arrange areas devoted to related activities close to each other; place the relaxing area close to the reading area, the area for bill paying close to the area for correspondence, and the entertaining area close to the dining area. By clustering similar activities and defining traffic corridors, you enhance harmony and free existing space for storage.

Defining activity areas also helps you determine where the items in your home belong. List the things you need or would like to have nearby each activity area. Inventory all the items you presently store in that area, and make particular note of those that belong elsewhere. This process will take some time, but it is much easier to write than to move items around the house. From this process you will probably discover a number of items that you needn't keep. Donate, sell, or dispose of these things as soon as possible.

Before you begin a storage project or purchase ready-made products, identify the items you plan to store in them and the available space. Keep the following criteria in mind as you choose a component:

- *Does the shape suit the space?*
- *Should shelves be stationary or adjustable?*
- *Is it strong and stable enough?*
- *Is it versatile enough to serve other purposes later?*
- *Is it easy to maintain and replace?*
- *Does the design complement the style and color of the room?*
- *Is the cost reasonable?*

Store things near the area where they are used. Look at the ideas that follow to find and adapt space.

Recommended Cross-References
Cabinets, Closets, Drawers, Kitchen Layout, Shelves, Storage: Outdoor.

Where to Find Storage

Where there's a will, there's a way; and where there's a need, there's a space. It may take some finding, but there is nearly always a corner you can convert into extra storage.

Dormers. You can usually fit a purchased or custom built storage bench under a window.

Eaves. Install cupboards along a wall where there is insufficient headroom to use the floor space.

Fireplaces. The fireplace is a focal point. Make it worth looking at by surrounding it with shelves.

Unfinished Ceilings. Use a hammock to store yard equipment. In the summer, it can move outside along with its contents.

Garage Space. A garage is the ideal spot for a workshop. It doesn't matter if you make a mess.

Beds. A standard double bed takes up almost 30 square feet of floor space. Put this to use by placing a mattress on top of drawer units. Hide-a-bed kits are available in many designs. They can be used in a guest bedroom or for a child who has gone to college but still comes back often. The kits are attractive and relatively simple to install.

Bathroom Cabinets. Add roll-out shelves under the sink. They do not have to be full depth if the plumbing gets in the way.

Kitchen Cabinets. Make use of the space between wall and base cabinets with extra shelves or bins.

Countertops. Solve the problems of clutter and trailing cords by installing an appliance garage.

Under Counters. A roll-around cabinet provides extra counter space when pulled out and tucks neatly away when it is not in use.

Under Sinks. If it stands on a pull-out shelf, the garbage can be close at hand and out of sight underneath the kitchen sink.

Utility Room. Mount shelves or cupboards above the washer and dryer. These will house supplies and be convenient for storing linens.

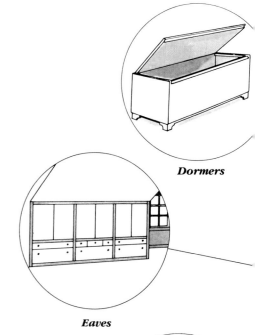

Dormers

Eaves

Fireplaces

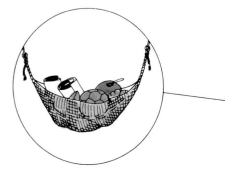

Unfinished Ceilings

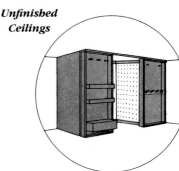

Garage Space

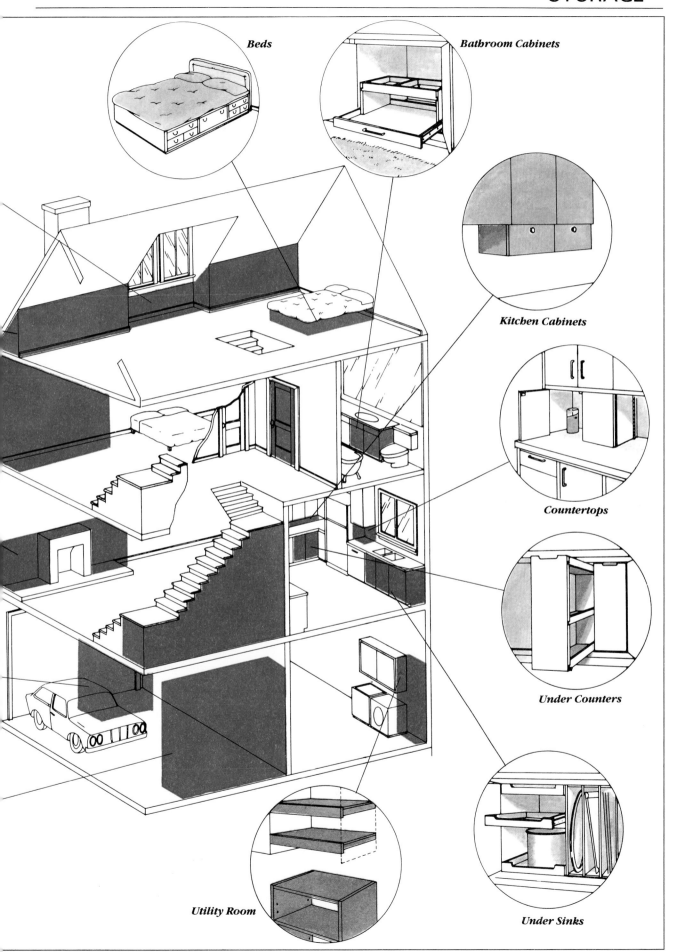

Beds

Bathroom Cabinets

Kitchen Cabinets

Countertops

Under Counters

Utility Room

Under Sinks

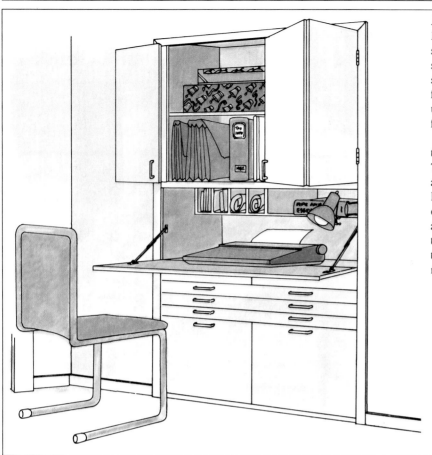

Built-In Desk

Many homes have alcoves that once served as storage areas, closets, or seating nooks. This built-in desk and storage unit utilizes such a space from floor to ceiling. When not in use, doors and drawer fronts close to form a sleek facade.

The plywood case and drawers on the bottom slide into the opening. The sides, back, and interior pieces are paint grade. Use a finish grade or laminate for the drawer faces and doors. Build the overhead shelves and doors as a separate unit, and trim the outside of the unit with molding that harmonizes with the rest of the room.

Under-Sink Rollout

Are you wasting the under-sink in your bathroom and kitchen? Make use of it by building a lipped roll-out platform to fit the cabinet. Build a small shelf just wide enough to fit on the platform and low enough to clear the plumbing. Screw the shelf to the platform.

The platform will slide on one of two types of standard drawer hardware—a partial-extension slide or a full-extension slide. A partial-extension slide will stop the platform with about 4 inches inside the cabinet. They cost less than full-extension slides, are easier to install, and are sufficient for light loads of towels and paper products.

Sewing Closet

Open this standard closet and find a whole workroom. The closet door has been removed to accommodate a cabinet that rolls on casters. A hinged panel attaches to the cabinet and unfolds to form a work surface. Another cabinet on casters supports the work surface at midspan.

The tabletop is 3/4-inch plywood topped with plastic laminate. Length depends on available space. The leaves are joined by piano hinges, which extend the full width.

Construct the rolling cabinets from 3/4-inch paint-grade plywood with 1/2-inch plywood inserts and sides. The rollout bin for storing fabric is made out of three pieces of 3/4-inch plywood mounted on full-extension drawer rollers. Pieces of fabric hang on 5/8-inch dowels.

The upper part of the doorway consists of swing-out shelving. The sides and dividers are 1/2-inch plywood; the back is 1/4-inch plywood. A piano hinge allows the upper section to close until the back is flush with the opening. The upright on the latch edge angles inward so that the unit clears the door frame.

Shelves on the inside of the closet complete the work space. Shelf track enables you to adjust the heights. One shelf should be at the same height as the tabletop or between 30 and 36 inches high.

Before renovation

Hammock Storage

Increase garage storage by suspending a net or hammock over the hood of a parked car. Into the hammock throw bulky, soft things that would not mar the car if they fell.

If the garage walls are too far apart to serve as attachment points, tie the hammock to ropes that travel through an overhead pulley. The pulley allows you to raise and lower the hammock to any height.

Platform Bed

Most people slide boxes and loose items under a bed, but built-in storage is far more efficient. These units eliminate dust and clutter, make good use of the space, and may even eliminate the need for a dresser.

Create the storage platform by building several smaller units of the same height and clustering them together. Small units are easier to transport. The drawers need not extend under the entire width of a large bed. Support the mattress with a large sheet of plywood that rests on top of the storage chests. Flush drawers create a clean profile. It is a good idea to include a toe kick.

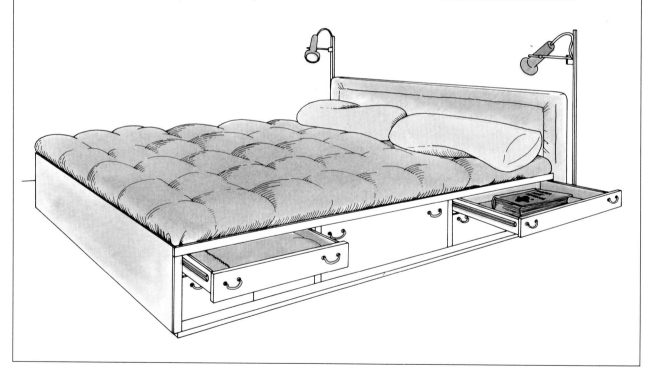

Kitchen Storage

Storage systems are utilitarian, but they should also be consistent with the dominant style of the room.

Kitchen styles generally fall into four categories: open shelf, an informal look, where what you store is what you see; traditional, where cabinets, usually of wood, are the prominent feature and there is a wealth of concealed storage; contemporary, featuring clean lines, with all equipment tucked away; and high tech, seen here. The style of this kitchen is high tech, which simply means that appearance is subordinate to function. The tools, equipment, and storage facilities are the style. See it, reach it, use it, clean it, and put it away. That's the style, and everything fits into the theme of instant access. The shape of each component is simple and focuses attention on the items it contains. All the storage components utilize grids, modules, or repetitive elements to suggest organization and order.

Vinyl coated steel grids have become very popular and are available in most hardware and home center stores. These grids provide flexible storage possibilities. Add S-hooks and hang kitchen utensils directly on them. Add shelves or baskets and fill them with spice jars, coffee mugs, or items you want near at hand.

A different style might emphasize a streamlined look. Cabinets would have simple lines. Colors would be muted. The cracks between doors, the edges of the counters and cabinets, and the shapes of the appliances would create lines that are a major design element.

Kitchen Cabinet

In a kitchen, a base cabinet with fixed shelves is inefficient. The back of each shelf is inaccessible and there is usually wasted space above the stored items. Transform such a space waster into a storage unit with double the usefulness. A cabinet that used to have two shelves now contains four shelves and a work area.

A cutting board that glides on rollers frees valuable counter space. Face a slab of butcher block with a drawer front. Install vertical dividers that enable you to store cookie sheets, large lids, and other flat items on end. Rout mortises into the bottom of the cabinet deck and insert ¼-inch plywood to serve as vertical dividers.

A bank of roll-out trays increases storage space and makes every item easy to find. A lip keeps items from sliding off the front. Dividers provide more organization.

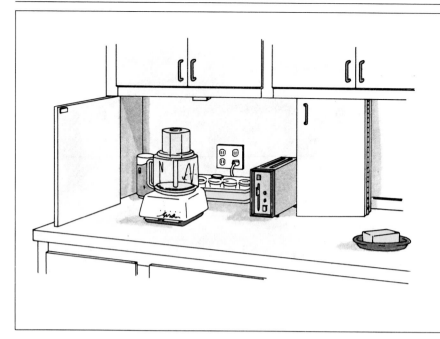

Appliance Garage

In some cases you do not have to create new space to improve storage, you only have to conceal it. This appliance garage keeps the countertop from appearing cluttered. Even though the counter remains the same size, it seems larger.

Most kitchens have a herd of appliances that need corralling. Line them up to see how much space each one needs and decide which ones you use the most.

Install the garage close to an electrical receptacle. Pulls and doors should match the rest of the cabinets. Order door replacements for your cabinets and cut them to size or use plywood and coat it to match. Use piano hinges at the joints and magnetic catches on the doors.

Linen Rack

Linens stay fresh and uncreased when you hang them on a lift-up door-back frame. The rack also makes it possible to spot linens easily, rather than rifling through a stack on a shelf.

The frame is made of 1 by 3 clear lumber. Use a ½-inch drill bit to bore holes on 4-inch centers in—not through—the sides. Glue ½-inch dowels into the holes before attaching the top of the rack. A continuous piano hinge connects the rack to a 1 by 3 cleat on the back of the door.

When the door is closed, the rack lies flat. The rack should be 6 inches narrower than the door. Mount it at a height convenient for reaching as well as seeing.

Door Pockets

Doors for cabinets and small closets represent potential storage space. Construct pockets of any size or shape. Keep these factors in mind when you plan them: the number and size of the items you plan to store, clearance for the door swing, and shelves or other features that might get in the way. If the door has a hollow core, attach ½-inch plywood to serve as backing.

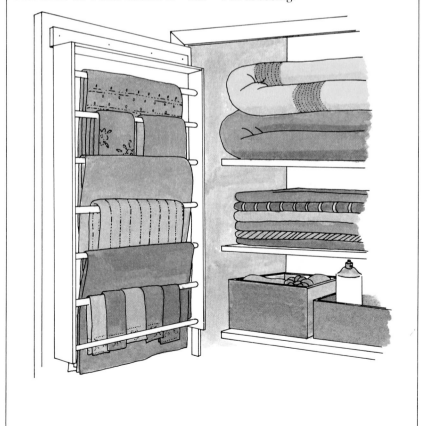

Storage Wall

A large entrance hall makes a pleasant welcome but it can also be a place to find extra storage space. As this is an area that seems to gather clutter regardless, why not accept the fact and plan for it?

What was once a plain wall with a door in the center has become a hall closet for coats and boots, a mail center, and a place to store rarely used bulky items such as suitcases and sleeping bags.

This unit consists of three plywood cabinets that surround and top the door. Organize and store items needed every day within easy reach and place the lesser-used items overhead. On one side is a hanging closet with shelves above. On the other side are two large cabinets with adjustable shelves. The upper cabinet door is covered by a mirror so you can check your hair before flying out of the house. Between these two storage units is a compartment with a drop-down shelf. This makes an ideal place to store letters, stamps, envelopes, keys, and all those bits and pieces that you remember you need just as you are going out of the door.

Install this unit in a bedroom, hall, garage, or wherever there is a suitable wall.

Build the lower cabinets by cutting four sides out of ¾-inch plywood and two backs out of ¼-inch plywood. Install bases cut from ¾-inch plywood and make a pedestal for each one out of a 2 by 4 frame laid flat. Install shelves, dividers, and closet poles as needed. Cut 1 by 2 or 1 by 4 lumber in half to form door frames. Within the frames, use hollow-core flush doors or make your own doors out of ¾-inch plywood of lumber-core construction. Hang them on 2-inch butt hinges.

The upper cabinet has a ¾-inch plywood base. Install plywood sides and back or a frame of 1 by 2 stock that attaches between the ceiling and lower cabinets. Match the lower cabinets, and install molding around the edge of the frames to match the style of the room.

The goal of an outdoor storage system is to provide well-organized space for all the equipment, materials, and articles we use outdoors or cannot find room for indoors. Too often, these items are piled randomly in whatever sheltered area is available, or even left scattered around the yard. (How many garages do you know of where there is enough room for the car?) A good storage system eliminates the clutter, simplifies the flow of household and outdoor activities, and cleans up the yard. Designing and filling it involves careful planning and sorting of all the items to be stored.

Recommended Cross-References
Cabinets, Sheds, Shelves.

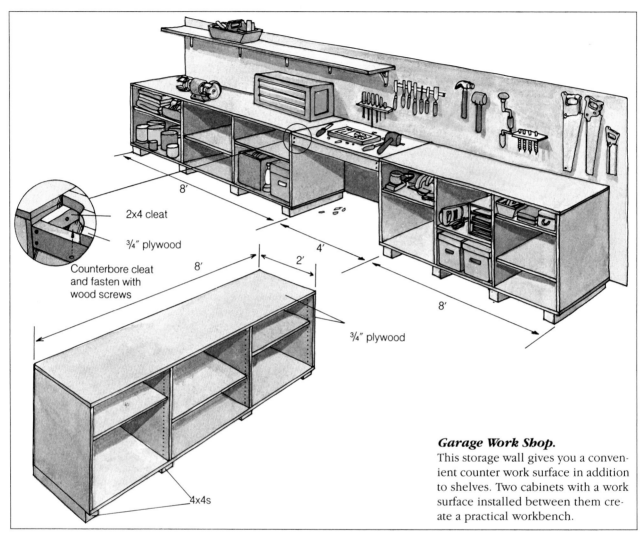

2x4 cleat

¾" plywood

Counterbore cleat and fasten with wood screws

8'

2'

4'

8'

8'

¾" plywood

4x4s

Garage Work Shop.
This storage wall gives you a convenient counter work surface in addition to shelves. Two cabinets with a work surface installed between them create a practical workbench.

Suspended Platform
This platform turns high, otherwise wasted space into a place for storing light loads.

To make the platform, assemble two slings (3-sided frames) out of 1 by 3s. Tack one of the uprights to the joist with a single nail. Hold a level on the crosspiece to determine the correct position for the second upright and tack it in place. For permanent fastenings, use nails, screws or lag bolts. Hang the second sling in the same way using a level and a long straightedge to make it level with the first one. Slide a piece of ¾-inch plywood between the two slings and tack it in place.

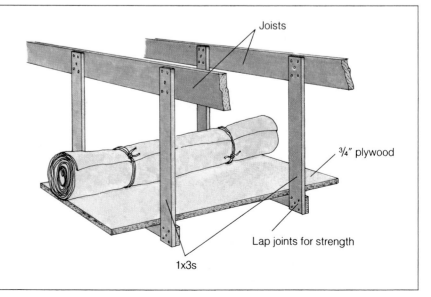

Joists

¾" plywood

Lap joints for strength

1x3s

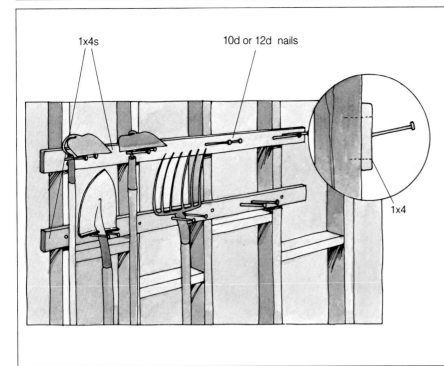

1x4s

10d or 12d nails

1x4

Tool Racks

A simple solution to the problem of where to keep long-handled garden tools is to hang them. These simple racks are merely lengths of 1 by 4 nailed or screwed across the studs.

The hangers can be nails or dowels installed in pairs. If you use nails, mount the 1 by 4s to the wall and drive 10d or 12d nails in at a slight upward slant, far enough into the wood for the nails to be stable.

You may prefer the look of wooden dowels. Four-foot lengths of hardwood dowel are available at most hardware and home center stores. Cut these into appropriate lengths. As with the nails, the dowels should have a slight upward slant. To make sure that the angle is always the same, make a drilling template out of a block of wood. Drill all holes using the template as a guide.

Bins

Bins such as these can house a multitude of items. They can prevent balls from rolling around on shelves, bicycles from toppling over, or keep scrap pieces of lumber conveniently sorted by type or size. Small bins holding gardening supplies can be carried to where they are needed.

Make the bins out of ¾-inch plywood with ¼-inch plywood or hardboard for the back pieces. Cut all the individual pieces to size and glue and nail or screw them together.

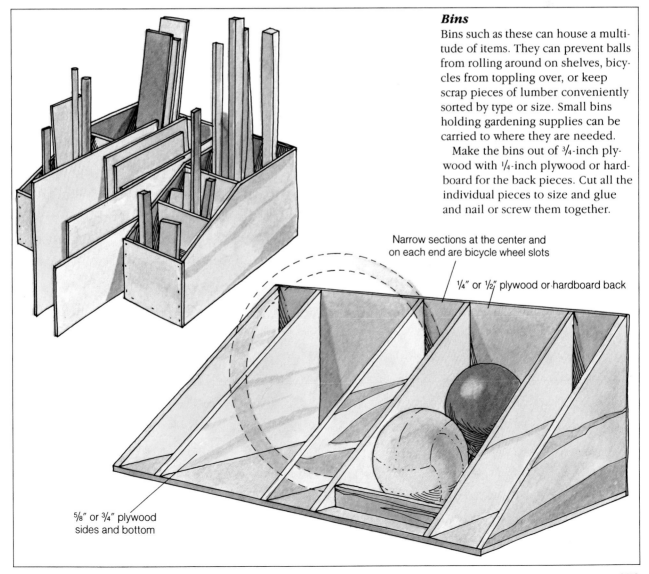

Narrow sections at the center and on each end are bicycle wheel slots

¼" or ½" plywood or hardboard back

⅝" or ¾" plywood sides and bottom

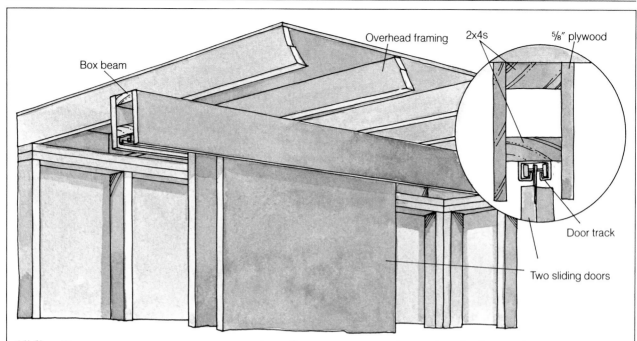

Box beam
Overhead framing
2x4s
5/8" plywood
Door track
Two sliding doors

Sliding Doors

Even if they're organized, a collection of objects of different sizes, shapes, and colors presents a cluttered look. A wall of sliding doors can section off a storage space and conceal it at the same time.

Build a box beam to provide a sturdy mounting surface for the double-channel sliding-door track. Use a length of 2 by 4 fastened to the ceiling framing members, lengths of 5/8-inch plywood for the sides, and another 2 by 4 on which to mount the track. Assemble as shown.

Enclosed Deck

A deck that is high above ground level offers the benefits of outdoor living space on the top and enclosed space beneath. Enclosing the understructure provides generous storage space but, in order to prevent water dripping through, you will have to install roofing under the decking.

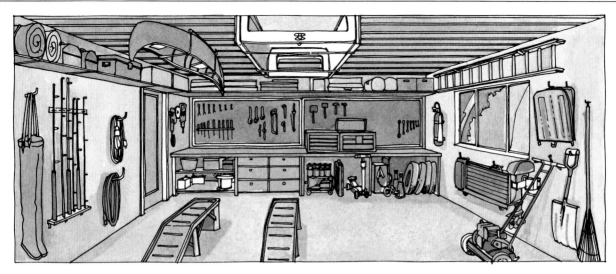

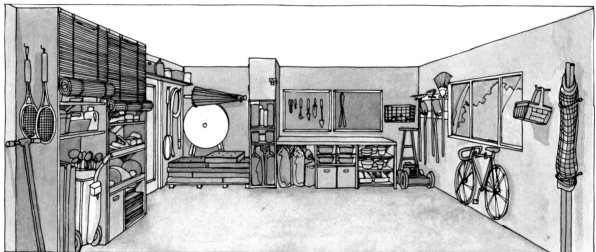

Organizing a Garage

A garage can be used to store a lot more than just a car, but it has to be well organized or, as often happens, the paraphernalia displaces the car. Use wall space: Racks, hooks, and shelves prevent sports equipment from getting damaged, hoses from getting tangled, and bikes from falling over. Large items, such as canoes, can be suspended on a hook and pulley system.

Organizing a Carport

Although the interior space in a carport is exposed to the weather, you can install cupboards around the perimeter that will protect items you wish to store. While very large, heavy objects can't be stored here, most of the automobile, gardening, and sports equipment will find a home.

STUCCO

Stucco is a popular siding because it is durable, weathertight, and inexpensive to maintain. Stucco does have drawbacks, however. Stucco requires careful application—without it, the finished surface is liable to crack. It will also crack if the house is subject to settling. Nonetheless, if you are a careful worker with one or two strong helpers and have professional advice to get you started, applying stucco is not that difficult to do.

Recommended Cross-References
Framing, Siding.

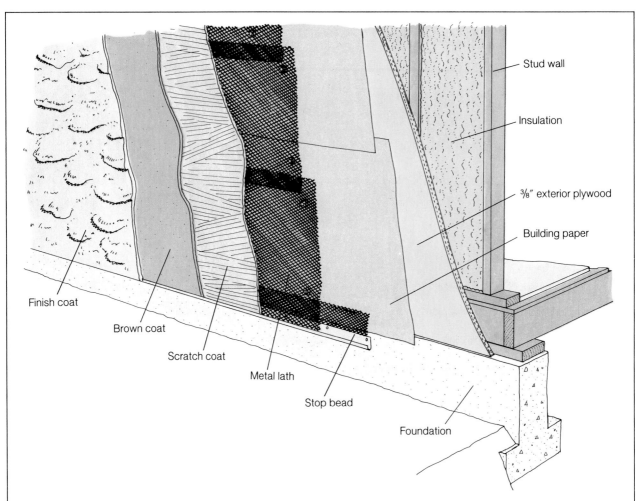

Stud wall

Insulation

⅜" exterior plywood

Building paper

Finish coat

Brown coat

Scratch coat

Metal lath

Stop bead

Foundation

How and Where to Use Stucco

Stucco is a mixture of cement, sand, lime (lime keeps the mixture plastic), and water. Buy premixed sacks of the dry ingredients for small patch jobs or mix your own bulk ingredients for a large job. A finished wall consists of three separate coats over metal lath. The lath is either an extruded screen or a wire similar to chicken wire. Nails pass through the lath, a layer of building paper, and into the sheathing. The nails, called furring nails, are specialty fasteners with fiber washers. The washers hold the wire away from the building paper. Some lath is self-furring and attaches with roofing nails.

The first coat, called the scratch coat, is about ¼ inch thick. It is supported by the lath. Before this coat dries, a rake-like trowel called a scarifier is used to score the surface. The rough texture of the first coat helps the next coat to adhere. The second coat, called brown coat because it used to contain brown sand, is about ⅜ to ½ inch thick. This coat must be smooth because the final finish coat, which is no more than ¼ inch thick, won't hide irregularities.

Weather is an important consideration in applying stucco. If hot afternoon sun bakes the wall, the stucco may dry too rapidly, then shrink and crack. Rapid drying does particular damage to the thick second coat. Plan to stucco when direct sun will be minimal, or hang shade cloths from the eaves. The best temperature range for applying stucco is 50° to 80° F. Do not apply stucco when the temperature drops below 40° F; the mixture will be too stiff.

Do not apply stucco until after the interior wallboard is nailed into position. Otherwise, the hammering could easily ruin a freshly stuccoed wall by jarring the material loose.

The best base for stucco is ½- or ⅜-inch plywood sheathing. Apply 15-pound felt or kraft paper over the sheathing. To trim windows and doors, use stucco mold, also called brick mold. Stucco mold is of redwood and has a groove for locking the stucco into place.

Stucco should not extend down to the ground. A stop bead, also called a weep screed, must edge the bottom of the sheathing. A stop bead supports the stucco and allows moisture to escape. Stop bead comes in 10-foot lengths; install it before the lath. Cut it with tin snips. Some types attach to the concrete foundation with nails; others have a flange that nails into the wood sheathing. The paper laps over the flange. The lath, extruded or wire, must be far enough away from the paper for the stucco to adhere behind it.

Large expanses of stucco and glass plus a tile patio evoke the warmth and charm of the Mediterranean. Stucco can be applied with numerous textured finishes to adapt to different architectural styles. Here, the smooth finish emphasizes the strong, sleek shapes.

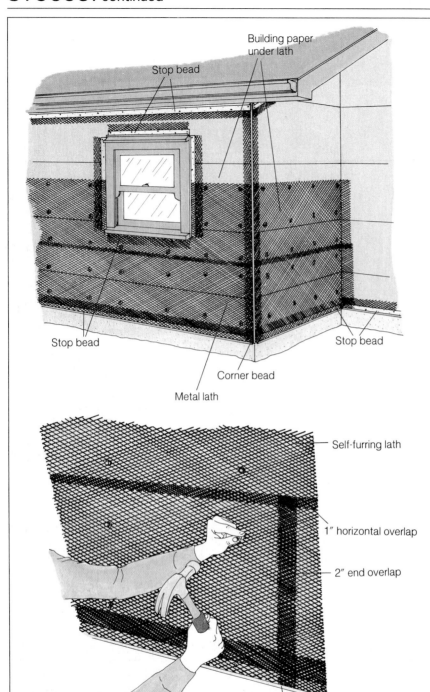

Building paper under lath

Stop bead

Stop bead

Stop bead

Corner bead

Metal lath

Self-furring lath

1″ horizontal overlap

2″ end overlap

Lath fits into stop bead

Preparing Wood Walls

Installing Lath. Start from the bottom at one corner and work up. The first lath sheet rests in the stop bead. Stretch the wire mesh each time you hook a nail, working out from the center of the panel. At the corners, nail a strip of corner bead. The metal strip should protrude from the edge by ¾ inch. Use a level to plumb the bead, and if you use more than one length, align the ends carefully. Double-check that the placement is accurate—the beads serve as important guides when you stucco.

Installation of self-furring lath takes less time. It comes in rolls that include the building paper. Horizontal wires on the back enable you to install the lath directly over studs, although plywood sheathing provides better backing. Self-furring lath attaches with roofing nails, and extra paper along one edge laps over the previous course.

Overlap the strips 1 inch where they meet horizontally; overlap them 2 inches at the ends. Place furring nails every 6 inches on the lath. The nails have washers close to the nail head. Push the washers away from the head, hook the wire between the nail head and washers, and drive the nail home. To make it easier on your fingers, hold the nails with needle-nose pliers, although the process is time-consuming. Remember to stretch the mesh each time you hook a nail and to work out from the center of a panel. The job goes faster with a helper who pulls on the lath as you nail.

Apply masking tape to door and window casings to protect them as you stucco.

Mixing and Applying Stucco

To mix stucco easily, buy premixed ingredients and rent a mixer. What you pay in rent you save in time.

If you buy and combine bulk ingredients, mix 3 parts building sand (different from finer mortar sand), 1 part portland cement, and ¼ part lime. The amount of water depends on how wet the sand is.

Mixing. Put all the dry ingredients in the mixer or mortar box and turn.

Mix until the stucco is an even color. Slowly add water until you think you have almost enough. Then mix some more. The mixture should now be a soft, plastic consistency that you can squeeze and hold in your hand without it dripping.

Have at least one helper and a wheelbarrow. If you work slowly, cover the wheelbarrow with plastic so the stucco will not dry.

Loading the Trowel. Chop the stucco

with the edge of the trowel and spread it evenly around the center of the hawk. Simultaneously tilt the hawk down while you scoop the slice of mortar onto the trowel.

Applying Stucco. Start at the top of the wall and work down. Press each trowel of mortar into the lath with an upward motion, tilting the top edge of the trowel toward you slightly. Blend adjacent areas with smooth horizontal strokes.

The Scratch Coat

The first coat should be ⅜ to ½ inch thick, with most of the stucco behind the lath. Check carefully for pockets and bulges and correct them. Before the stucco dries, score it horizontally with a rakelike scarifying tool. The tines should bite deep enough to almost touch the lath, but not expose it. Allow this coat to dry overnight before proceeding.

The Brown Coat

Preparation. Ensure the evenness of the brown coat by taking two prepa-ratory steps: First, stretch strings hor-izontally across the wall. Do this by attaching strings to nails placed be-yond the corners. The strings will be held out ⅜ to ½ inch from the scratch coat by the protruding stop bead nails. Place one string near the top of the wall, one near the bottom, and one (or more, if the wall is high) at the center. Then drive a roofing nail every 5 feet along the string so the head is flush with the inside of the string. They will be reference marks for ensuring a level coat of stucco. When the nails are in, re-move the strings.

Applying Screeds. Trowel on screeds (narrow vertical strips of stucco) just thick enough to cover the nail heads. After you apply each strip, run the edge of a straight board over the screeds and smooth out high and low spots. Allow to dry for 24 hours, then fill in the areas in between using the screeds as levelers.

Applying the Brown Coat. Spray the wall lightly with a mist, dampening only as much wall as you can coat in 1 hour. Apply the brown coat from top to bottom. Feather the stucco into the screeds with smooth, even strokes so no joint is visible. Smooth the mortar over the corner beads and stop beads.

Allow each section between a pair of screeds to dry for about an hour; then go over it in circular motions with a wood float. Rub lightly until you feel the sand at the surface.

Allow to dry for at least 24 hours, misting with water every 4 hours.

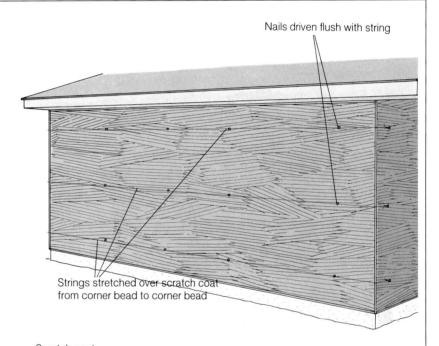

Nails driven flush with string

Strings stretched over scratch coat from corner bead to corner bead

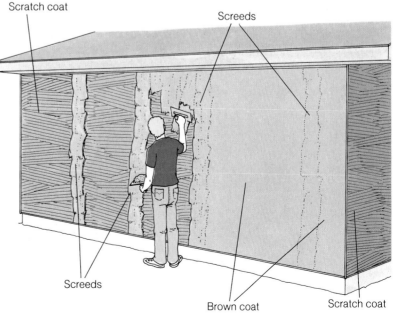

Scratch coat

Screeds

Screeds

Brown coat

Scratch coat

The Finish Coat

Color and texture the final coat to your tastes. To achieve shades of brown, tan, or off-white, mix a pigment available from your stucco supplier with the final coat. To achieve a white finish, use white cement and white sand. You may choose to paint the final coat. Coat with a primer formulated for stucco, and use a compatible latex paint.

Standard Smooth Finish. While the stucco is still wet, smooth the surface with a wood float. Repeat the process while the stucco is still damp, working the float in a circular motion that does not leave a pattern.

Modern American Finish. Apply a float finish to wet stucco, and let it set slightly. Scrape the finish coat in vertical strokes with a 2 by 4 block just after surface moisture disappears. Press firmly to roughen the stucco without tearing it.

Old English Finish. This finish style requires a thin finish coat. After the finish has dried for about an hour, use a round-nosed trowel to apply irregular gobs of mortar. Work quickly for a spontaneous, rugged look.

Spatter Finish. This style, also called a dash finish, is often seen on houses over 30 years old. To create it, mix a small batch of stucco that is thinner than normal, dip a large brush in the mixture, then snap it against a stick to spatter stucco onto the wall. Spatter the wall as evenly as possible. Let it dry for about one hour, then repeat the spattering process to ensure an even effect.

Travertine Finish. First, float the finish coat. Then jab the bristles of a whisk broom into the finish while it is still damp, working horizontally. After the stucco sets up slightly, go back over the surface with a steel trowel. Smooth using long, horizontal strokes, so that the top of the rough ridges flatten but the valleys and craters remain. The overall effect will resemble marble or other types of natural stone that have texture showing behind a smooth surface.

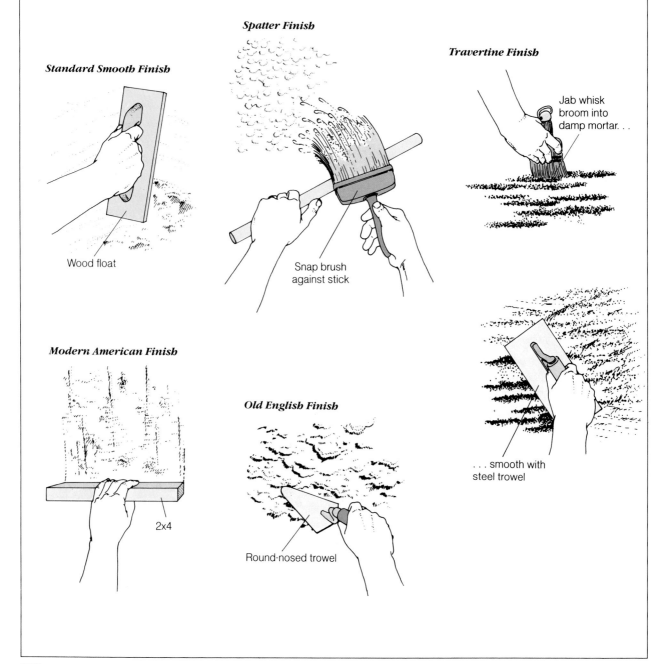

Standard Smooth Finish

Wood float

Spatter Finish

Snap brush against stick

Travertine Finish

Jab whisk broom into damp mortar. . .

. . . smooth with steel trowel

Modern American Finish

2x4

Old English Finish

Round-nosed trowel

Stuccoing Masonry Walls

Stucco is an excellent way to finish a concrete block wall. It produces a clean, uniform surface that you can texture and color almost any way you can imagine.

Preparing the Wall. If you cover concrete block or old stucco with new stucco, scrub the wall first with a wire brush to remove all dirt and loose material. Spray the wall with a hose. After it dries, use a brush or roller to coat the wall with a masonry bonding agent. Bonding agents are available at hardware and paint stores. Let the coating dry overnight.

Applying the Stucco. Combine pre-mixed stucco or dry ingredients with water. Apply the scratch coat directly to the wall after the bonding agent dries, using the same spreading technique as for wood-framed walls. The block is porous enough for the stucco to adhere. Scarify the scratch coat before it dries. Because the block provides a very rigid and stable base, you can apply the finish coat directly to the scratch coat without an intermediate brown coat. The finish coat should not be applied until the scratch coat dries thoroughly. You can add a coloring agent to the mix for permanent color. Although you can use any texturing pattern to finish the stucco, a heavy texture works very well for rustic outdoor walls.

Repairing a Crack

Clean with a wire brush.

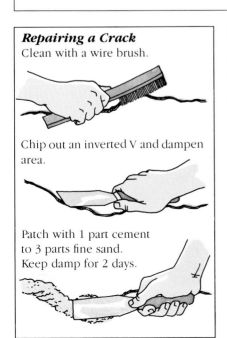

Chip out an inverted V and dampen area.

Patch with 1 part cement to 3 parts fine sand. Keep damp for 2 days.

Repairing a Hole

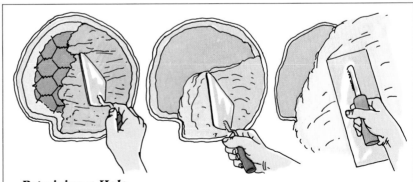

Weave in new wire lath. Wet the area, then apply the scratch coat. When it begins to set, score with a scarifier or nails in a board. Keep damp for 48 hours.

Apply the second layer, which should come within ⅛ inch of the surface. Keep damp for two days, then cure for four or five more days.

Dampen the wall before applying the finish coat complete with colored pigment. Keep damp for two days.

SUBFLOORS

Typical floor construction includes a subfloor installed over the joists. In older homes it consists of 1-inch boards. They may be installed diagonally or perpendicular to the joists. Newer homes have oriented strand board (OSB) or plywood subfloors. It is stronger and easier to install, especially if the edges are tongue and groove (T&G).

Most plywood subfloors are rough, with knotholes and other depressions in their surface. If the finish floor requires a smoother surface, one side of the plywood is plugged-and-touch-sanded (PTS), or a separate underlayment is nailed over the subfloor when the floor covering is installed. This is called a double-wood floor.

Some homes have very thick subflooring, either 1⅛-inch-thick plywood or nominal 2-inch tongue-and-groove decking boards. The subflooring is supported by girders spaced 4 feet apart rather than joists on 16-inch centers. If an upstairs subfloor is built with 2-inch decking, it can also function as the finish ceiling material for the rooms below, in the same way as an exposed-beam ceiling.

Subfloors are vulnerable to rot caused by moisture from plumbing leaks or spills, or from excessive humidity under the house. Repairing a rotted subfloor involves removing the finish floor over the affected area and replacing the decayed subflooring with new plywood. When remodeling a kitchen or bathroom, inspect under the house carefully beforehand so that you can make such repairs during the rough carpentry phase of the project. If the boards are tight and sound, you may be able to sand and finish them for an attractive softwood floor.

If you are building a new floor, all underfloor utility lines must be installed and inspected before you cover them with subflooring. It is also easier to install underfloor insulation before the subfloor goes in.

Recommended Cross-References
Basements, Carpet, Floors, Framing, Resilient Flooring, Tile, Wood Floors.

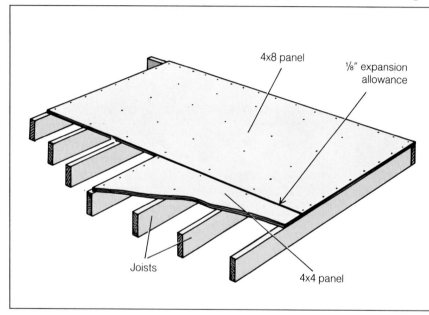

4x8 panel

⅛" expansion allowance

Joists

4x4 panel

Installing a Plywood Subfloor

Be sure the joists are spaced on 16-inch centers to support the end joints. Use OSB or tongue-and-groove plywood, minimum ¾ inch thick, either CDX grade if you want a rough surface or PTS for a smooth surface.

Start by snapping a chalk line across the joists 4 feet in from the outside edge of the rim joist. Install a full panel first. To prevent a squeaking floor, apply construction adhesive to the joists with a caulking gun before laying each panel. Nail with 8d nails every 6 inches along the edges and every 10 inches inside. After finishing the first row, stagger the joints 4 feet on all of the remaining rows.

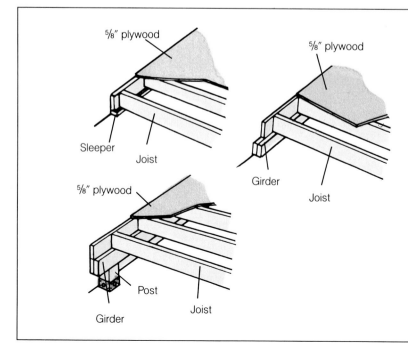

⅝" plywood

Sleeper

Joist

⅝" plywood

⅝" plywood

Girder

Joist

Post

Girder

Joist

Constructing a Subfloor Over a Concrete Slab

Usually, a wood floor is built over a concrete slab by using 2 by 4 sleepers laid directly on the concrete. This is typical for most basements and main floors.

There are times when you may want to raise a wood floor higher, such as in a garage conversion when you want the new floor to match the level of the rest of the house. To do this, build a joist system on whatever sleepers, shims, or posts are needed to raise it to the required height. Then install a plywood subfloor over it, placing insulation between the joists first. Be sure to correct any moisture problems with the concrete before building such a floor.

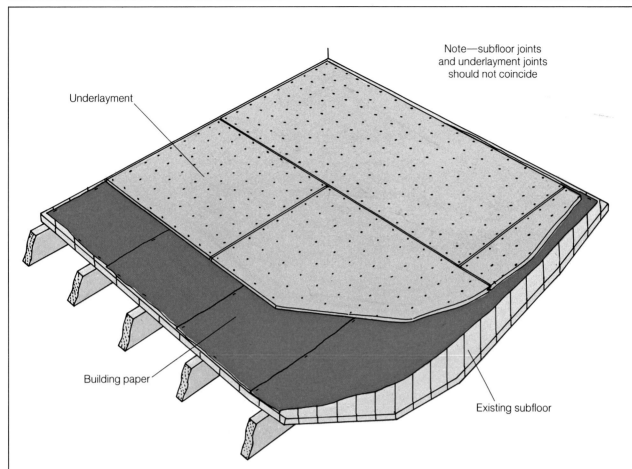

Underlayment

Note—subfloor joints and underlayment joints should not coincide

Building paper

Existing subfloor

Installing Underlayment

A wood underlayment smooths out a rough subfloor. Three types of material are used for underlayments: plywood, particleboard, and hardboard.

Plywood. Plywood is the strongest material and is good for bridging cracks and holes. Exterior grades resist moisture well. However, it is expensive if a smooth surface is required, and, unless it is a particular underlayment grade, it contains voids that are subject to collapsing. Plywood is used primarily for tile installations, usually ⅜ inch thick (⅝ inch for epoxy).

Particleboard. This is also known as chipboard and waferboard. It is a popular underlayment material, usually ⁵⁄₁₆ inch thick. The surface is smooth and free of voids, and it is quite resilient. It is not strong enough to bridge large cracks and holes, and moisture makes it expand and even disintegrate. It is not recommended for use in bathrooms.

Hardboard. Hardboard is denser and smoother than particleboard. It is not as vulnerable to moisture and is used when a very smooth surface is required. However, it does tend to break or chip easily.

Install the underlayment over a vapor barrier, or building paper if the floor is over unfinished space. Tack down the underlayment with nails, then staple it with a rented staple gun. The staples may be as close together as 6 inches on center in the middle of the panels and closer on the edges (use up to 150 staples per sheet).

Curing Subfloor Squeaks

A squeaking floor is generally caused by individual boards rubbing together. If the finish floor is wood, it is likely that some of the boards are loose and need to be tightened. Nail them into the subfloor (drill pilot holes first) or drive screws up into the boards from below.

If the subfloor itself is squeaking, nail it to the joists from the top or drive wedges between the joists and the subfloor.

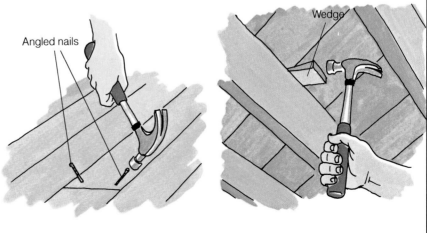

Angled nails

Wedge

SWITCHES

All switches may look similar, but they have significant distinctions. Furthermore, identical switches are wired differently in different situations. The main distinction is the number of switches controlling a particular light or group of lights, and whether wiring from the electricity source goes first to the switch or to the fixture. In spite of all the variations in style and the addition of certain features on some switches, there are really only four basic types, and only two are generally used in residential wiring.

Recommended Cross-References
Electrical System, Lighting: Indoor, Receptacles, Wire, Wiring.

How to Read a Switch

Look for the UL approval, then check the amperage rating. Most lighting circuits are 15 amps. If you have a 20-amp circuit, you need a 20-amp switch, unless the local code allows an exception. A switch also specifies the type of current; residential wiring is always AC. Finally, check for which type of wire has to be used. All switches can be used with copper wire (shown by the marking CU). Switches marked CO/ALR are to be used with aluminum wire. The National Electrical Code recommends replacing switches marked AL/CU with switches marked CO/ALR.

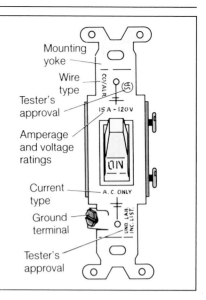

Wiring Switches

Connect wires to a switch using screw terminals. Strip ⅝ inch insulation from the wire, loop the bare end around the screw clockwise, and tighten the screw. Always loop the wire around the screw clockwise. Another method is to connect terminals by pushing the bare end of the wire into the designated hole in the back of the switch. Use the wire gauge on the switch to strip the end of the wire to length.

Be sure to connect the wire to the correct screw and terminal:

Black Wire to brass-colored screw
White Wire to silver-colored screw
Green Wire to green or dark-colored screw
Bare Wire to box (ground)
Red Wire to brass-colored screw.

Specialty Switches

Clock. Includes a digital clock that always runs.
Dimmer. Some dimmers have a built-in rheostat to reduce the flow of current to the light, although they throw off extra current as heat. Other dimmers are genuine energy savers because they control the amount of current coming to the switch. Both types extend the life of the light bulb significantly. Fluorescent fixtures require special dimmers.
Time Delay. This switch goes off after about 45 seconds. It is useful in a garage or laundry where you often have your hands full when you leave.
Time Clock. A switch with a time clock can be set to go on and off at any time. When you are going away, you can wire a time clock into circuits that supply lamps to make it appear that someone is home.
Key Operated. Prevents the unauthorized use of power tools or other appliances—recommended if you have young children. The key fits into a slot and moves the switch toggle up and down.
Pilot Light. Shows whether a light in another location—such as the basement—is on or off.
Remote Control. This is a handy, low-voltage switch that operates a full-current switch located elsewhere. Wiring for a remote-control switch is 16 or 18 gauge.
Door Operated. A push-button switch activated by the opening of a door. You see them in cars and refrigerators. They are also handy for closets and storage areas.

Types of Switches

Single Pole. Use a two-way, or single-pole, switch as the only switch operating a fixture. A single-pole switch has on-off markings on the toggle and two terminals (besides ground).

Double Pole. Use for 240-volt equipment or to operate two circuits at the same time. Has on-off markings and four terminals.

Three-Way. Use in pairs, when two switches control the same fixture.

The toggle can be on or off in either position. Has three terminals.

Four-Way. Use with two 3-way switches when three switches control the same fixture. Toggle is on or off in either position. Has four terminals.

Single Pole

Double Pole

Three-Way

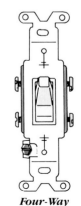

Four-Way

Basic Principles of Switching

There are many configurations for wiring connections involving two-way, three-way, and four-way switches. It is more important to understand connection principles than to memorize the hookups. This way you will be able to adapt to any installation.

The most important principle is that a neutral wire is never switched. A switch interrupts the flow of current to a fixture, never from it.

The path of the current is always the same: from the source to the switch(es) to the fixture and then back to the source. All wires leading to the fixture are hot; all wires returning from the fixture to the source are neutral. If you are wiring with cable, remember that a cable is a cluster of individual wires that serve different functions.

Wires should be color coded properly. If you are wiring with cable, there are times when you may need to use the white wire as a hot conductor (the switch loop seen below is an example). In such cases, always blacken both ends of the white wire to indicate that it is hot. Use electrician's tape or paint.

Use switches with the correct terminals and cable with the appropriate number of conductors.

The switch-fixture connections are only part of larger circuits; the boxes may also be junction boxes for extending the circuit in other directions. There may be other wires in the same box you are working in, so always be aware of their function.

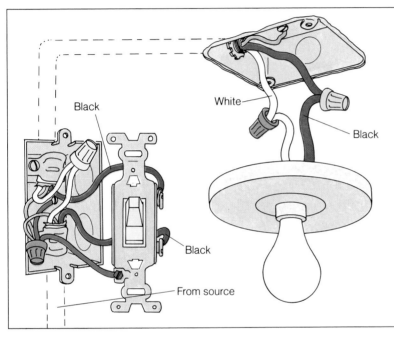

Black

White

Black

Black

From source

Two-Way Switch: Source Through Switch

The cable from the source has a black conductor, white conductor, and ground. The black conductor is wired to the switch but the white conductor is wired through the box. This switch could control an additional light simply by running another two-wire cable from the first light to another box. Join the hot wires of both fixtures in the first box. Do the same with the neutral wires and ground wires of each fixture, then pigtail each connection.

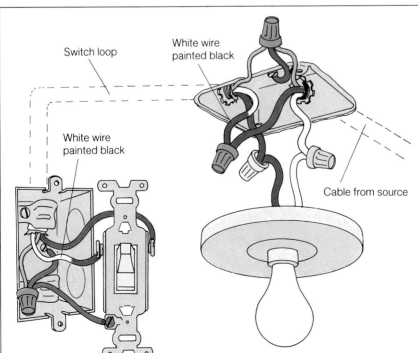

Switch loop

White wire painted black

White wire painted black

Cable from source

Two-Way Switch: Source Through Fixture

If the black hot wire from the source cable were connected directly to the light fixture, the light would always be on and the switch would do nothing. Instead, the hot wire is looped through the switch before it connects to the light. This is called a "switch loop." Notice that the wire leaving the switch to feed the fixture is a hot wire and must be color coded as such. This switch has no neutral wire.

Three-Way Switch:
Source Through Switch

Three-way switches do not interrupt the current, they simply direct it from one wire to the other. In the three-wire cable that proceeds from the first switch, either the red or the black conductor is always hot; the other one is "idle." For the light to go on, the current from the first switch must pass along the same wire with which the second switch is aligned. The current heats the common terminal of the second switch, which is linked to the light fixture by a black conductor.

Notice that the second switch in this system is on a switch loop. It has no neutral wires, and the white conductor is black.

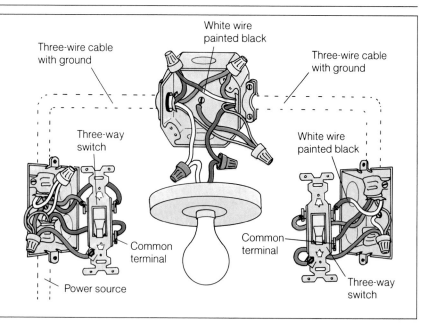

Three-wire cable with ground
White wire painted black
Three-wire cable with ground
Three-way switch
White wire painted black
Common terminal
Common terminal
Three-way switch
Power source

Three-Way Switch:
Source Through Central Fixture

The hot lead from the source is not wired directly to the fixture. It is wired through the fixture box to the common terminal of one switch. The two wires leaving this switch, called traveler wires, are wired through the fixture box all the way to the second switch. The common terminal of the second switch is wired to the hot side of the fixture. Both switches are switch loops and they do not have neutral wires.

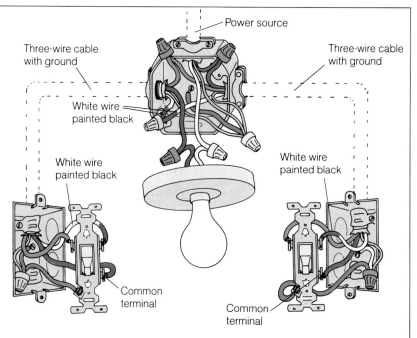

Power source
Three-wire cable with ground
Three-wire cable with ground
White wire painted black
White wire painted black
White wire painted black
Common terminal
Common terminal

Three-Way Switch:
Source Through Fixture

Again, the hot wire from the source cable is wired into the switches rather than the fixture. Both switches are part of a single switch loop, with no neutral wires in their boxes. Notice that a two-wire cable (with ground) is sufficient for the leg between the light and nearest switch, but the leg between the switches requires three-wire cable.

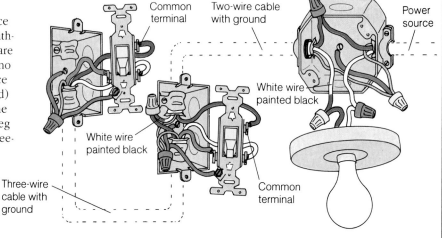

Common terminal
Two-wire cable with ground
Power source
White wire painted black
White wire painted black
Three-wire cable with ground
Common terminal

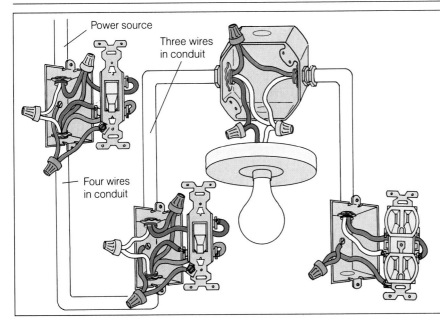

Three-Way Switch: Source Through Switch and Receptacle Beyond

This shows how switch and fixture boxes serve as junction boxes for circuit wiring to other demand points. Current from the hot wire of the source cable must serve both the switch and the light system, but also travel through to the receptacle without being switched. To wire this type of switch, use a four-wire leg (plus ground) between the two switches. If you use conduit, pull white, black, red, and blue wires and use the blue conductor as a continuous feed for the receptacle. With cable, use two two-wire cables (plus ground).

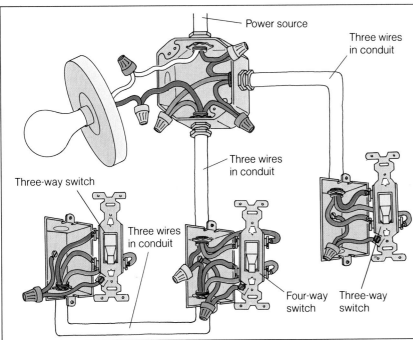

Four-Way Switch: Source Through Fixture

To control a light from three points, use a four-way switch and two three-way switches. The four-way switch is always in the middle and has four terminals. The hot source conductor connects to the common terminal of the first three-way switch, which then sends two travelers to the four-way switch. The travelers connect to the top two terminals. Travelers of the same color connect to the bottom two terminals of the four-way switch and proceed to the second three-way switch. The four-way switch simply redirects current between travelers.

In this example, all the wiring is in conduit, which provides a continuous ground. If you wire with cable, use three-wire cable, with ground.

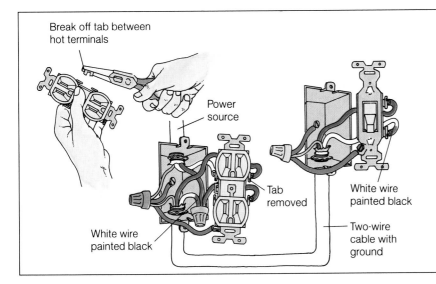

Split-Circuit Receptacle

In some rooms the switch controls a receptacle instead of a permanent light fixture. This diagram shows how to wire the receptacle so only half of it is controlled by the switch and the other half is always hot. All receptacles have a breakable fin on the hot side for split-circuit wiring. If there is one on the neutral side, do not break it or there may be no return path for the electricity and a serious ground fault could occur.

TELEPHONES

Since the court-imposed breakup of AT&T, many people have found out how simple it is to buy and install their own telephone equipment. To tempt you to do the same, there is an ever increasing variety of instruments offered, many with novel convenience features.

Installing a new telephone jack is one home improvement that you can probably complete in an afternoon. Installing a jack is well within your capabilities, and you will certainly save money if you do it yourself.

Planning a telephone installation is easy because the modular connectors for all new phones are the same size. Standard jacks allow you to move the telephone from one room to the next simply by unplugging it from one jack and into another.

Make sure all your equipment works properly before you disconnect or extend wiring. Otherwise you will be unable to determine if new problems result from faulty connections or malfunctioning equipment.

Although there should be no danger of electrical shock, most phone companies recommend a few precautions: Don't work during thunderstorms. Avoid touching bare wires or screws, and use tools with insulated handles. If possible, disconnect the house system from the company network before you patch into an existing outlet. If disconnection is impossible, unplug all the phones in the house or remove their handsets. Do not work on telephone wiring if you wear a pacemaker. These precautions protect you from the remote possibility of shock, and they protect your equipment as well.

Recommended Cross-Reference
Wiring.

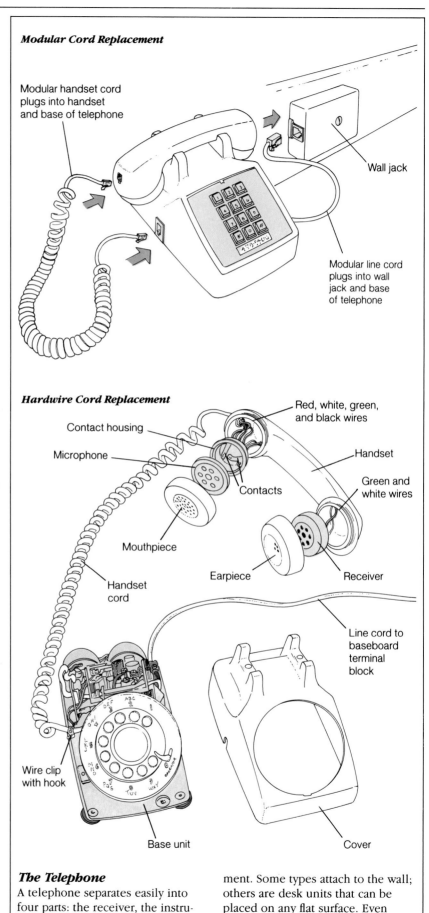

Modular Cord Replacement

Modular handset cord plugs into handset and base of telephone

Wall jack

Modular line cord plugs into wall jack and base of telephone

Hardwire Cord Replacement

Contact housing

Microphone

Red, white, green, and black wires

Handset

Green and white wires

Contacts

Mouthpiece

Earpiece

Receiver

Handset cord

Line cord to baseboard terminal block

Wire clip with hook

Base unit

Cover

The Telephone

A telephone separates easily into four parts: the receiver, the instrument, the casing, and the cord connecting the receiver to the instrument. Some types attach to the wall; others are desk units that can be placed on any flat surface. Even cordless telephones must have a wall jack to plug in the control unit.

Installing a New Jack

To install a modular jack in a new location, you need a jack and a length of wire that will reach from the proposed location to an existing jack or junction box. In some cases, the new jack will be so close to the old that all you need is a T-adapter that plugs into an existing modular jack. Otherwise you need to run new wire, either along baseboards, behind walls, or under floors.

Begin by making sure that neither wires nor plumbing lie behind the wall or baseboard where you will install the new jack. Then drill pilot holes where the jack will fasten. Screw the base to the wall or baseboard. Strip 3 inches of sheathing from the length of wire and 1 inch of insulation from each conductor. Attach the appropriate conductors to the color-coded screws.

Run the wire along the top of the baseboards, behind them, or under the house to the nearest modular jack. Secure the wire with rounded staples every 8 to 12 inches; do not let the staples penetrate the wire.

To attach the new wire to an existing modular jack, first remove the cover from the existing jack. Strip 3 inches of sheathing from the new wire, then strip 1 inch of insulation from each conductor. Attach the conductors to the color-coded screws in the same manner as the existing wire connects. If the jack is not modular, now is a good time to convert it.

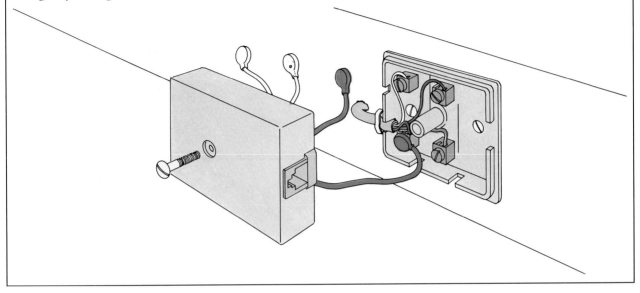

Converting to Modular Wiring

Phone sets that are not modular are hardwired into an existing jack—you can't unplug them. If you have a new telephone with a modular plug, all you need is a new modular cover; you do not have to replace the base. Remove the old cover. Identify the incoming wires so you don't disconnect those, then snip the wires that connect the telephone. Snap color-coded caps of the new cover onto the screw terminals. Screw the cover to the base.

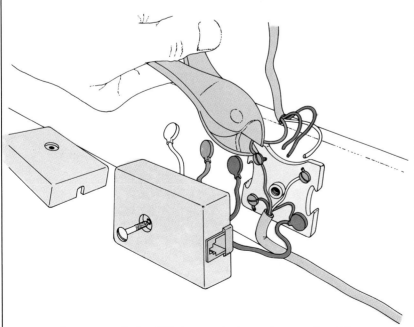

Adapters

Some jacks have four round holes that accept a prong-type plug. All you need to update the jack is a plug-in adapter available wherever telephone parts are sold. New wiring is unnecessary.

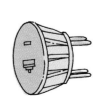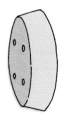

Plug-in adapter converts
4-prong jack to modular

Running Telephone Cables

Telephone cable within a house can be installed easily by a homeowner.

Types of Cable. There are three main types of telephone cable. Standard cable is the general-purpose cable used to wire houses. It can be used to connect phones to jacks. It includes four wires: red, green, yellow, and black. Normally, only the red and green wires are used, with the yellow and black reserved for a second phone line.

Modular cable is a flat cable used only to connect phones to jacks.

Multiwire cable consists of wires arranged in pairs and twisted together.

Concealing Cable. Besides the obvious ways to conceal cable (running it under the floor, through the walls, or through the attic), there are other methods. These methods are safe only for low-voltage telephone cable, however; do not use them for wires that carry house current. Run cable as follows:

• under the edge of wall-to-wall carpeting, between the tack strip and the wall

• under the bottoms of cabinets, through the cabinets at the back, or under the toe kick

• through the backs of closets next to the baseboard

• through a heating-system cold-air return or alongside pipes in plumbing chases

Practices to Avoid. Never run telephone cable in electrical conduit or in a junction box with electrical wiring. Do not run phone lines in wet locations or where they will contact hot pipes. Do not splice telephone cable; it causes noise on the line.

Fishing Cable. When running telephone cable through closed walls, choose interior partition walls if possible. They are not insulated and usually don't contain fire blocks.

Measure carefully or drill a small marker hole in the stud bay where the new jack will go. Drill the marker hole 1 inch from the wall, into either the attic or basement. Push a clothes hanger or a long piece of wire through the hole so it will be easy to find.

Find the marker hole under the floor or in the attic and measure to the center of the wall. Drill a hole at least ⅜ inch in diameter through the top or bottom plate into the stud bay.

Cut the hole for the phone jack to fit a remodeling box.

If you are running the cable from the attic, hang a weighted string down past the jack opening and hook it with a fish tape or bent clothes hanger.

If you are running the cable from beneath the floor, a fish tape is very useful because it is stiff enough to reach up into the wall. If you don't have one, suspend a weight on a string from the phone-jack opening and hook the string from below (have someone help with this).

Once the string is hooked, pull it through the jack opening. Securely tape the phone cable to the string and pull it through.

Install the electrical box and attach the jack.

Wire the jack. Connect the other end of the wire to the phone block or another jack, and then test.

Testing. After the jack is connected, test it with a line tester or a working phone. The tester can be used on one-line or two-line working installations. Simply push it into the jack with the No. 1 side up to test the red and green wires, or the No. 2 side up to test the yellow and black wires. A green light indicates correct polarity. A red light indicates that the wires are reversed. No light indicates a wiring fault. Open up the jack and look for a loose wire; if there isn't one, check at the other end of the wire run.

If you test with a phone, plug it into the jack. If there is a dial tone, try to call a number. If the dial tone won't stop, the wires are reversed. If there is no dial tone, follow the wire run and look for a short or open connection.

In very rare cases there may be an interior break in the wire. Either substitute the yellow and black wires for the red and green or replace the wire.

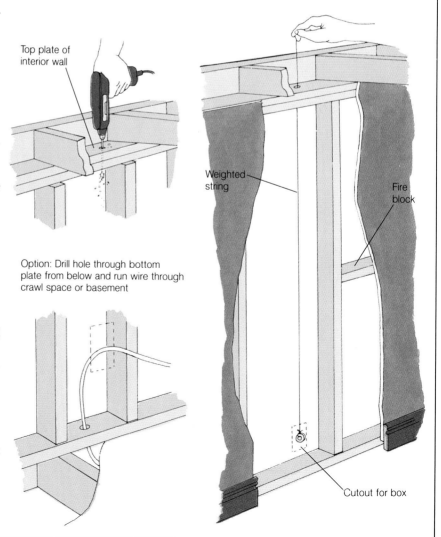

Top plate of interior wall

Option: Drill hole through bottom plate from below and run wire through crawl space or basement

Weighted string

Fire block

Cutout for box

Troubleshooting and Repairs

Homeowners are responsible for telephone repairs from the main wiring block into the house. Fortunately, many common problems are easy to diagnose and fix.

When a problem occurs, first determine whether it is inside or outside the house (if it is outside, the telephone company will repair it). Test the jack nearest the wire coming into the house. Check at the point where the line enters the house; you will find either a lightning protector or a modular connection with a test jack. If there is a modular connection, plug a working phone into the jack. If the problem still exists, it is outside the house. If not, it is inside. If there is a lightning protector and no test jack, either devise one or find the jack nearest the lightning protector and use it to test.

If the problem is inside the house, follow the wires and look for loose connections.

Noise. If there is a noticeable hum but the phone works, try reversing the red and green wires at the jack. If the noise becomes louder, switch the wires back to their original connections. Follow the wire and look for places where it touches a metal water pipe or conduit. Lift the wire and staple it away from the metal. If the wire has any bare spots, wrap them with electrician's tape. Repair any loose splices. If the problem persists, replace the run of wire.

Sizzling sounds may be caused by wet connections. Dry the connections with a hair dryer and remove the source of moisture.

Dead Phone. Try the phone at another jack to determine whether the problem is with the phone or the wiring.

A common problem is with the cord that connects the handset to the base unit. If it appears damaged, replace it. Look inside the jack. If the ends of the wires are touching each other, gently separate them with a knife blade and trim the excess wire.

If the phone unit works properly, the line has a break or a bad connection (open circuit) or a short circuit. Check the jack for wire ends that touch, as you did with the phone. If you can't repair the jack, replace it. If a wire is broken (usually because it was nicked when the insulation was stripped), splice it or run a new length of wire.

No Bell. If the bell doesn't ring but the phone works, the striker may be jammed. Open up the phone unit and look for the clapper. Free it with a small screwdriver or a knife.

Dialing Problems. Few dialing problems can be repaired at home, whether the phone is a rotary or touch-tone type. If the dial tone won't stop and the phone is a touch-tone type dating from the early 1980s, you may be able to fix it by reversing the red and green wires in the jack. If not, the phone must be repaired by a professional or replaced.

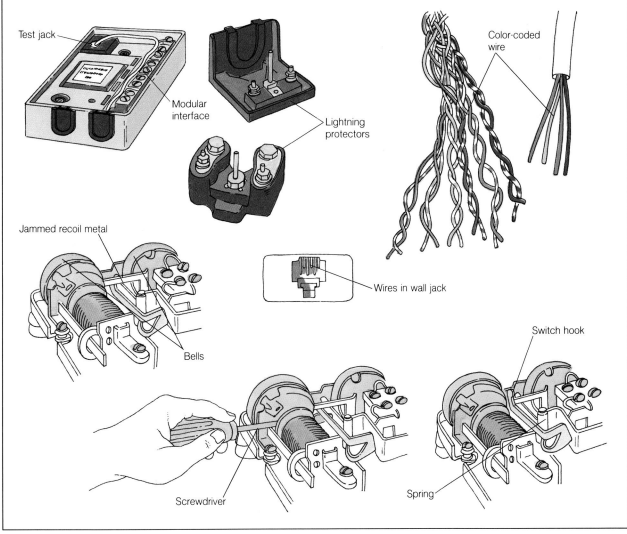

Test jack

Modular interface

Lightning protectors

Color-coded wire

Jammed recoil metal

Bells

Wires in wall jack

Switch hook

Screwdriver

Spring

TILE

Tile is a versatile and attractive surface material for walls, floors, ceilings, countertops, tub backs, showers, and hearths. The wide range of colors, textures, sizes, and shapes makes it suitable for installations that vary from simple and angular to warm and textural. Tiles can cover a large area or they can be used in small panels combined with other materials to provide contrast and interest.

Installation can be easy or difficult, depending on the shape of the surface to be covered and the type of backing required. Most homeowners can do their own installations using thin-set techniques, although wet areas like showers, tubs, and sinks require careful attention.

A tile installation is not automatically waterproof. Tiles themselves vary in their absorption characteristics, from nonvitreous (highly absorbent) to semivitreous to vitreous (low absorption) to impervious (won't even absorb dye). The grout can be even more vulnerable to water absorption than tile. Most portland cement grouts include waterproofing additives, but joints in wet areas should still be sealed after curing. An extremely waterproof grout system is a rubberlike material made from silicone or polyurethane. It is used to pregrout sheets of tile at the factory, and is applied to ungrouted joints on the job site with a caulking gun. Waterproof grouts with resin or epoxy bases, used for industrial installations, are also used in some residential applications.

Recommended Cross-References
Bathtubs, Countertops, Floors, Showers, Sinks, Vanities, Wallboard, Washbasins.

Ceramic tile is available in a wide range of colors, sizes, shapes, and textures. It can cover floors, walls, ceilings, and counters.

Types of Tile

There are many ways to classify ceramic tile, but common designations are glazed wall tile, mosaic tile, quarry tile, and pavers. Glazed wall tiles are the standard type used for walls, tubs, showers, vanities, and kitchen countertops. Glazing makes most tiles waterproof. Some handmade tiles have soft glazing, which is not suitable for tubs, showers, or counters. Sizes of imported tile vary; standard domestic sizes are 4¼ inches and 6 inches square.

Mosaic Tile. Mosaic tiles are small, usually 1 or 2 inches across, although some are as small as ⅜ inch square. They come affixed to sheets of paper or mesh, usually 1 foot square, for easy installation. Mosaic tile comes glazed or unglazed, and is particularly ideal for curved or intricate surfaces.

Quarry Tile. Quarry tile is intended for floors and hearths. It usually comes unglazed and is vitreous to semivitreous. Most kinds of quarry tile are manufactured by an extrusion process that is not as meticulous as the dust-press process used for most wall and mosaic tiles.

Pavers. Pavers are quarry tiles made by the dust-press method. They can be either glazed or unglazed, and are quite durable. They are generally 12 inches square, and they tend to be quite thick. Pavers are intended for patios and floors. If used indoors, they should be sealed. Beware of using them outside in areas with severe winters; expansion and contraction due to freezing and thawing may cause them to crack.

Marble and Granite. These are popular floor and accent tiles. In addition to natural stone, there are composites made of marble or granite and epoxy resin. They must be cut with a water-lubricated power tile saw, not a standard tile cutter. This tool can be rented; some full-service tile stores have one on the premises.

Glazed Wall and Floor Tile. These standard ceramic tiles range in size from 2 to 12 inches square. The glazing on floor tile is harder than on wall tile. Floor tile can be used on walls, but wall tile shouldn't be used on floors.

Preparation

Tile must have a firm, smooth base that will not shift and settle. Tile in wet areas needs a backing that will not deteriorate if moisture seeps through the tile or grout. Common backing materials are a bed of mortar, wallboard, plywood, and glass-mesh mortarboard—panels of cement material sandwiched between two membranes of fiberglass mesh.

Walls. In areas that are dry or that are exposed to a limited amount of moisture, tile can be installed over any smooth wall surface with thin-set organic adhesives. Some surfaces, such as new wallboard, should first be sealed with a primer that is compatible with the adhesive to be used. Existing wall surfaces must be free of wax, grease, efflorescence, or other residue, and should be roughened by sanding if they are glossy or painted. Install a new backing material, such as wallboard, over walls with cracks or irregularities.

Wet locations, such as tub and shower enclosures, require a waterproof backing. The most reliable is a professionally installed mortar bed; but if the tiles and grout are properly sealed, you can expect satisfactory results with glass-mesh mortarboard. If you install glass-mesh mortarboard, tape the joints with fiberglass-mesh tape, fill them with an appropriate compound, and use dry-set or latex–portland cement.

Floors. Tiles can be installed over concrete or wood, but the floor must be prepared properly. For new construction over wood framing, install a subfloor of ⅝-inch plywood and put an underlayment of ⅜-inch plywood over it (⅝ inch for epoxy adhesives). For heavy materials, such as thick pavers, or for any installations over a mortar bed, add extra joists, making sure that the surface of the finished tile floor will be flush with other floors.

Before installing tile in an existing room, it is best to remove the finish floor to reduce thickness and then nail ⅜- or ⅝-inch plywood over the subfloor. If the existing floor surface is noncushioned vinyl laid over plywood (not particleboard), you can leave it on if you remove all wax and roughen the surface so that the adhesive will bond. Tile can also be installed over old tile if the floor is solid and you are able to roughen the surface to ensure tight bonding. Applying a liquid type of underlayment (if you are using mastics) or epoxy mortar will level any irregularities.

Concrete floors make an excellent base as long as they are dry, smooth, and level. Remove any old floor materials first and roughen the surface to ensure adhesion. If the floor is cracked, damp, or otherwise unstable, repair it before installing tile. Concrete slabs should be sound, well cured, and free of any wax, oil, or curing compounds. Tile will adhere directly to a steel-troweled slab with the use of organic adhesives or dry-set mortar. Epoxy or portland cement mortar is appropriate for rougher surfaces.

Countertops. For thin-set organic and epoxy adhesives, use plywood at least ¾ inch thick. However, it may deteriorate in wet locations if the tile is not well sealed. A better backing for dry-set and latex–portland cement mortars is glass-mesh mortarboard installed over plywood. The best installation is a reinforced mortar bed floated over plywood or 1-inch boards.

Adhesives and Mortars for Tile Installations

Adhesives and Mortars	Composition	Conditions for Use	Comments
Type I Mastic	Solvent based.	For damp areas.	Thin-set, ready to use, flammable, may irritate skin and lungs.
Type II Mastic	Latex based.	For dry areas only.	Easy to clean up, nonflammable.
Dry-Set Mortar	Portland cement mixed with sand, additives, and water.	For concrete or glass-mesh mortarboard. Not recommended over wood or resilient floors.	Not water-resistant, nonflammable, easy to clean up, rigid, impact-resistant.
Latex–Portland Cement Mortar	Portland cement mixed with sand and liquid latex, sometimes diluted with water.	For concrete or glass-mesh mortarboard, not recommended for use over wood or resilient floors.	More water-resistant than dry-set mortar and easier to work with, less rigid, tends to move.
Epoxy Adhesive	Epoxy resin mixed with hardener.	Preferred adhesive for moisture-prone areas. Use over plywood or old resilient floors.	Expensive, toxic to skin, works best between 70°–85° F.
Epoxy Mortar	Epoxy resin mixed with hardener, sand, and portland cement.	Preferred adhesive for moisture-prone areas. Use over concrete or existing ceramic tile.	More body than adhesive. More chemical resistance than adhesive; levels uneven subsurfaces.
Portland Cement Mortar	Traditional mortar bed—portland cement mixed with sand and water.	Preferred adhesive for moisture-prone areas or where subfloor is uneven.	Thick bed (¾" to 1¼"), reinforced with wire mesh, long lasting, waterproof, offers structural strength, requires careful installation.

Cutting Tile

Whether you have just one or two cuts or a great many cuts, it is easiest to pay the extra charge and have the tile supplier make perfectly smooth cuts with a water-cooled cut-off saw. If you wish to cut tiles yourself, use the following techniques.

Cutting With a Tile Cutter. This tool, which can be rented, makes straight cuts quickly and accurately. The handle has a small cutting wheel that scores the tile when you pull the handle across the tile. An extension arm on the handle forces the sides of the tile down to snap it.

Round Cut. 1. Mark the diameter of the circle to be cut out, then score and cut the tile along this line. On each half tile, score around the half circle. Also make crosshatch scores all over the area to be cut away. ***2.*** Using pliers or nippers, break out waste in small chips.

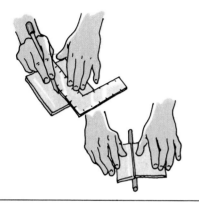
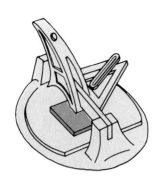
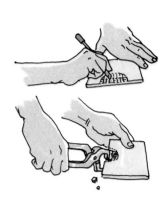

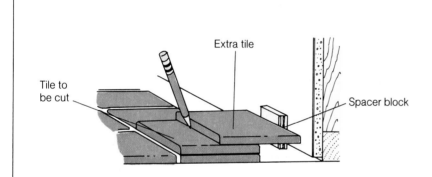

Tile to be cut — Extra tile — Spacer block

Marking for Cutting

When laying out a tile installation, strive for the fewest cuts. Try to adjust the layout so that rows end with full tiles. However, short rows look better if they are equal on both sides of the centerline. When a row must be ended with a cut tile, use the method shown here to mark the tile for an accurate cut. Mark for each cut tile in case there are variations in the wall. The spacer accounts for grout lines on both sides of the cut tile.

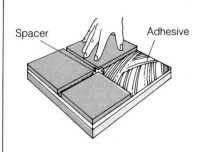

Spacer — Adhesive

Setting Tile

Spread adhesive over an area approximately 3 feet square, using a notched trowel. If the floor tends to get damp, apply a preliminary coat of adhesive over the entire surface with a smooth trowel, let it dry, then apply a second coat. Set tiles into the wet adhesive with a firm, twisting motion. Insert spacers between tiles and wipe off excess adhesive immediately.

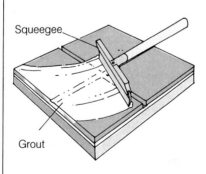

Squeegee — Grout

Applying Grout

Remove spacers and let the adhesive dry. Be sure the adhesive does not fill any of the grout spaces. Mix cement-based grout according to the type of tile: stiff for mosaic tile, loose for most white-bodied tiles, and runny for red-bodied tiles. Force grout into the cracks by spreading it diagonally across the tiles with a rubber float or squeegee. Work it into joints.

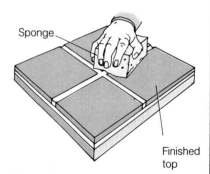

Sponge — Finished top

A toothbrush handle is a good tool to use for doing this.

Remove as much excess as possible, and wipe off the remainder with a wet sponge. Wait 30 minutes, let a haze form, and polish the surface with a soft cloth. To cure, keep the grout moist by covering the tiled area with plastic sheeting or spraying it at regular intervals for two or three days. Seal after two weeks.

Tiling Floors: Method 1

With this method you establish tile location from preliminary lines drawn through the middle of the room. This method is effective for rooms with large doorways that make the floor clearly visible from other parts of the house.

Starting the Layout. Snap a chalk line down the center of the room, perpendicular to the doorway. Snap another chalk line perpendicular to the first. Then, starting with a full tile at the doorway, lay a dry run of tiles along the first line. Use spacers between every tile for uniform grout spaces. If you do not have enough space for a full tile at the end, decide whether to have a cut tile at one end or at both ends; another solution is to widen the grout spaces. Repeat the process along the second chalk line, readjusting both lines so that they intersect at a tile corner.

Installing Temporary Straightedges. Draw a line on the floor to mark the outside edge of the last full tile at the doorway. This line must be perpendicular to the first chalk line and perfectly straight, even if the wall is not. Extend the line along the length of the wall. Repeat this process for the other walls. Set long boards on the outside of each line and nail them to the floor. Use 1 by 2s or 1 by 3s so that you can straighten them as you nail. Use a 3-4-5 triangle to square the boards. Measure 3 feet out from the corner along one board and 4 feet along the other. If the two points are exactly 5 feet apart, they are square.

Setting the Tiles. Starting in the corner where the boards intersect, spread a small area of adhesive with a notched trowel. Then gently press the corner tile into place with a slight twisting motion. Continue setting tiles in the order shown, inserting spacers between them to keep the alignment straight. Use molded plastic tees, scraps of plywood, or similar material for spacers. Tamp down uneven tiles with a rubber mallet or beat on a cushioned 2 by 4 with a hammer. Wipe any excess adhesive off of the tile surface immediately. Allow the adhesive to set, remove the straightedges, and install cut tiles along the edges leaving a $1/8$-inch gap along the wall.

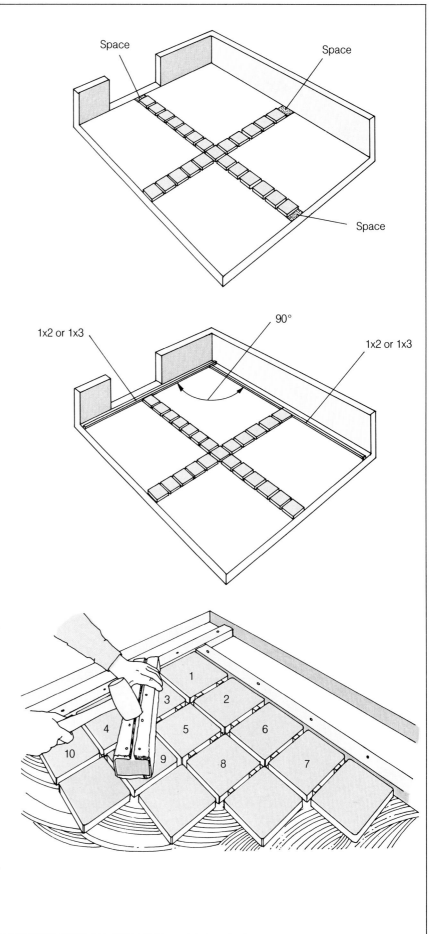

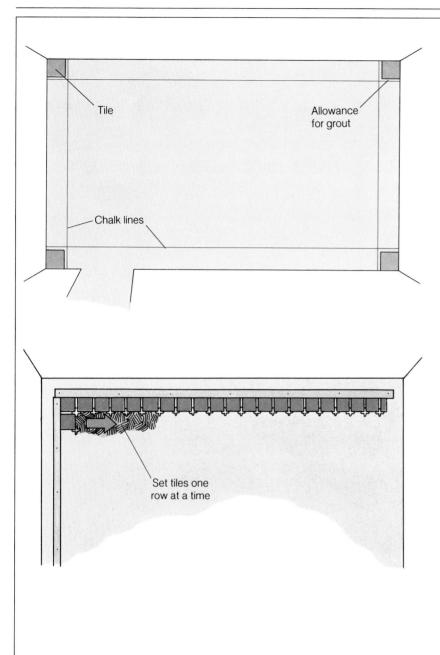

Tile

Allowance for grout

Chalk lines

Set tiles one row at a time

Tiling Floors: Method 2

Begin the layout along a prominent wall and establish perimeter lines. Use this method if you want a border of contrasting tiles or if cut tiles will not be too noticeable.

Starting the Layout. Decide which is the most prominent wall—the one where it is most important to have full tiles. Lay two tiles, one in each corner of the chosen wall allowing for grout. Snap a chalk line between the tiles. Repeat this process for the other three walls, using a framing square or a 3-4-5 triangle at each corner to keep the lines perpendicular. Double check for square by measuring both diagonals to be sure they are equal. Then make a dry run, as described in Method 1, to decide where any cut tiles should go. You may want to have full tiles on the prominent wall and finish with cut tiles on the wall opposite.

Setting the Tiles. Nail straightedges along two intersecting chalk lines. Spread a small amount of adhesive according to the manufacturer's instructions. Be sure to wear gloves if you are working with epoxy. Spread adhesive right up to the boards, but not over the working lines.

Set the first tile in the corner, abutting it to both straightedges. Complete the starter row, inserting spacers as you go. Then start the second row from the same end and complete all subsequent rows in the same order. If the spacing is regular, you can prepare the cut tiles needed to finish the rows ahead of time. After the last row, wait for the adhesive to set, remove the straightedges, and set the remaining tiles.

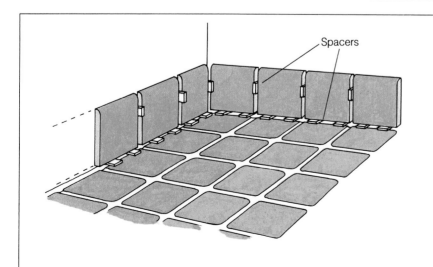

Spacers

Tile Base Trim

Instead of a wood baseboard, you may wish to use tile that matches or coordinates with the floor. If you do, use bullnosed trim tiles so that the visible edge (the top of the tile) is a finished one. After the floor has been installed, cut and fit the first border piece so that the rest will align with the existing grout lines of the floor. Set each tile by applying adhesive on the back. Use spacers between and under border tiles.

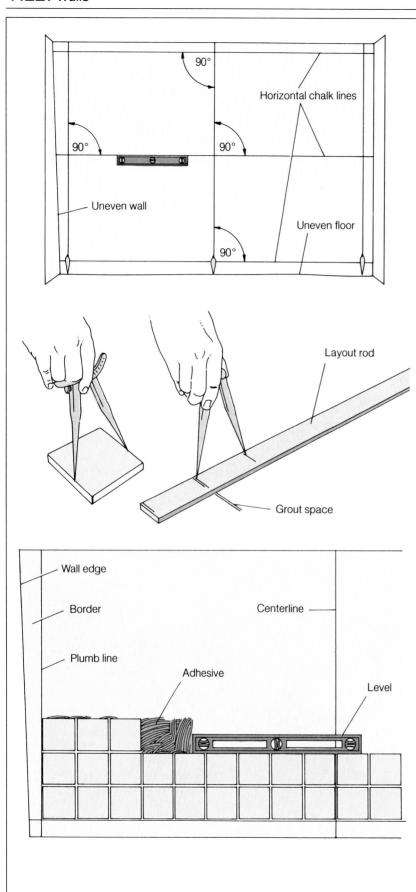

90°

Horizontal chalk lines

90°

90°

90°

Uneven wall

Uneven floor

90°

Layout rod

Grout space

Wall edge

Border

Centerline

Plumb line

Adhesive

Level

Tiling Walls

Laying Out Walls. In order to do a layout for a wall installation you will have to simulate a dry run on a special stick called a layout rod. First, find the center point of the wall and snap a plumb line from the ceiling to the floor. Snap two more plumb lines close to the edges of the wall. Then snap an exact horizontal chalk line across the center of the wall. Check the angles between this line and the three vertical lines to be sure they are all square. Then snap two more horizontal lines as close to the floor and ceiling as possible. Check the angles. This array of lines will show you where tapered tile cuts are needed because of uneven walls and give you centerlines for starting the installation.

Making Layout Rods. Cut two 1 by 2s to the height and width of the wall. Mark a tile layout along each rod, adjusting grout spacing and the location of cut tiles until you are satisfied the layout will look right. If you need to start over again, turn the rod around. If you are using special tiles or trim pieces as a border, be sure they are included at the proper ends of the rods. Transfer the marks from each layout rod to the wall by holding the rod against two of the plumb lines or horizontal lines. These marks will guide the installation.

Setting Wall Tiles. Begin the installation on the bottom row, starting at the centerline. Apply enough adhesive for the first few tiles, but leave the baseline and centerline visible for accurate alignment. Set the first tiles in place and insert spacers between them. For a thinner grout line than the one allowed by a spacer, use matchbook covers, toothpicks, or any other suitable thin material.

When the tiles are set, let the adhesive dry for a day or two before grouting the joints. For wide joints, use cement-based grout with sand added for bulk. Grout narrow joints with cement, epoxy, or elastomeric grouts. Use a toothbrush handle to pack it in tightly. If you are grouting a bathtub or shower, plug the drain with a rag to keep grout out of the plumbing. To cure the grout, keep it damp for at least 72 hours by covering it with plastic sheeting or spraying it periodically.

Installing Mosaic Tile

Mosaic tile is available in a wide array of colors and sizes, either glazed or unglazed. Tiles are assembled into sheets, usually 1 foot square. They are held together with paper on the face or mesh on the back. Some are bonded together with rubberlike elastomeric grout, and the joints between the sheets are grouted with the same material applied with a caulking gun. This kind of grout is excellent for tub and shower enclosures, but should not be used for surfaces where food is prepared. Mosaic tiles usually require less cutting because the units are smaller and more likely to fit. Use the same subsurface preparation techniques and laying out guidelines as described for floor and wall tile installations.

1. Check the layout by setting sheets of tile in place. Avoid tugging on corners and distorting the spacing. Instead, set one edge of the sheet down and unroll the rest. The space between each sheet edge should equal the space between each tile.

2. When you fit a sheet of mosaic tile around an obstruction, use a utility knife to cut the paper or mesh and remove full tiles. Cut individual tiles to fit any remaining spaces, using nippers to notch out corners.

3. To fill border spaces, turn the sheet over, slide it over the space, and mark it, allowing for an expansion gap. Cut along the line with a mechanical tile cutter, or cut single tiles with nippers or a hand cutter.

4. Spread adhesive with a notched trowel, embedding sheets of tile in it. Unroll the sheets to prevent sliding them around in the adhesive. Press them in place. If the tiles are attached with paper glued to the top surface, soak the paper with warm water and gently peel it off.

After the adhesive dries, grout mosaic tile the same way you would other kinds of tile. Force it into the cracks with a rubber float or squeegee, working on the diagonal. Bear in mind that you will need a lot more grout to fill the joints around mosaic tile than you would for an equivalent area covered with larger tiles.

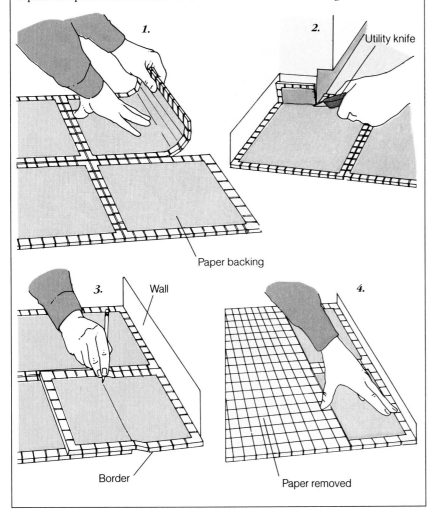

1.

2.

Utility knife

Paper backing

3.

Wall

Border

4.

Paper removed

Replacing Grout

1. Chisel out old grout. Clean and dampen joint.

2. Apply new grout. Smooth with your finger. Clean off excess.

Replacing Tile

1. Break up the cracked tile and remove pieces of tile and grout.

2. Scrape off old adhesive.

3. Apply adhesive and set new tile. Hold it in place with toothpicks.
   The next day, remove toothpicks, dampen the joints, and apply grout.

Tiling Countertops

Tile is a popular surface for bathroom and kitchen counters. It is clean and attractive, more durable than a lot of other materials, and it is not difficult to install. There are two main drawbacks. The first is that, being a hard surface, glasses, dishes, and other fragile objects can break if they are put down too sharply. The second drawback is that the grout joints tend to collect dirt and stains, although less so if the grout is colored and well sealed. Even so, it is advisable to avoid using mosaic tiles for a kitchen countertop.

A countertop is subject to moisture penetration and impact from falling objects. Even so, you do not need the thick tiles required for floors as long as you select high-quality tiles that are not likely to chip.

Install glazed or semivitreous tile around sinks, food preparation areas, and where water splashes—unglazed tile tends to stain.

When the surface is properly prepared, tile can be installed over many different materials. If you are attaching it to ¾-inch plywood, make sure the tile and grout are waterproofed. Also cut slots in the plywood, 2 inches apart, to provide for expansion. Mounting glass-mesh mortarboard over the plywood deck makes a more reliable installation.

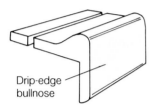

Drip-edge bullnose

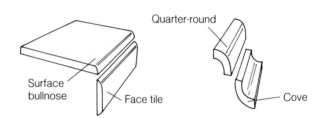

Surface bullnose
Face tile

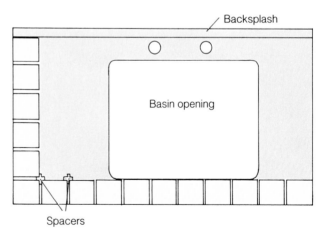

Quarter-round
Cove

1. Various trim pieces are available for the edges, corners, backsplash, and sink opening of a countertop. These are usually sold by the linear foot. When you select tile, be sure that whatever pieces you need are available in the same pattern and color, or in one that harmonizes. Be sure to buy a few extra pieces so that, should you break or damage any, they can be replaced.

It looks much neater if a countertop is tiled with only complete tiles. If this doesn't work out naturally, you can install a self-rimming sink instead of a sink mounted below the tile. (The rim will cover the cut edges.) You can also trim the edge of the counter with wood, such as an attractive hardwood stained and finished to blend with the tile. The trim can be painted to match the cabinets or other details in the room. The backsplash can be a piece of wood instead of tile. Or the splash can be tile that is extended all the way up to the wall cabinets or other fixtures.

2. Lay out the tile pattern and test it with a dry run. Start with trim pieces or bullnose tiles first, continuing with full tiles. If possible, plan the width of the counter to avoid narrow cuts along the back. If the counter is L-shaped, start the layout at the inside corner and work outward both ways. The corner piece should be a full tile. All trim pieces should be laid out so the grout lines follow the grout lines of the rest of the tiles.

3. When you are satisfied with the layout for the front and back edges, lay out the tiles around the sink. If the sink is self-rimming or has a metal rim, mark tiles for the sink cutout by laying each one in place and scribing them from beneath. Use a tile cutter or nippers to cut them back. The sink will cover the raw edges. If you have a recessed basin, set it in place and cut tiles and trim pieces to fit around it. Mark and cut tiles for any faucet holes, as well.

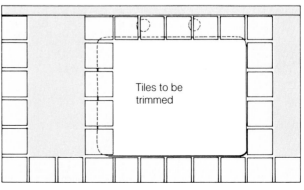

Backsplash

Basin opening

Spacers

Tiles to be trimmed

4. When you know where all your tiles will go, mark tiles, counter, or both to guide you in tricky areas. Make all your cuts before starting installation. Apply adhesive over a small area with a notched trowel. Hold the trowel at about a 45-degree angle to achieve maximum coverage. Different adhesives take different amounts of time to dry, so check the manufacturer's specifications for the one you use. Also check the safety precautions regarding adequate ventilation and open flames such as pilot lights. Start the tile installation with bullnose tiles or trim pieces at one of the corners, using spacers between tiles. Start at the inside corner of an L-shaped countertop.

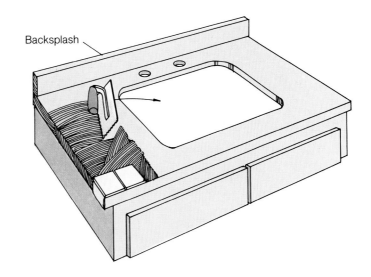

Backsplash

5. Continue installing tiles on the surface of the countertop, using spacers to keep the alignment even. Work in small areas to prevent the adhesive from drying before setting tiles into it. Place each tile carefully and press it down with a twisting motion. When necessary, use nippers to cut tiles to fit around obstructions. As you finish each row of tiles on the surface, work your way up the backsplash or wall. End with a row of bullnose tiles or full tiles edged by moldings. When you finish setting tiles, remove excess adhesive from the tiles as quickly as possible. Then let the work dry for one or two days.

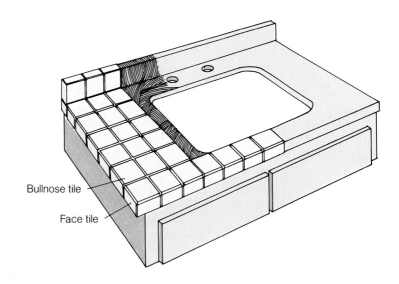

Bullnose tile

Face tile

6. Use a rubber float to spread grout into the joints, according to the manufacturer's specifications. Spread grout diagonally across the tiles. Be sure to force it firmly into the joints, using a small tool such as a toothbrush handle where necessary. Remove excess with a damp sponge, cleaning the sponge frequently. Let the surface residue dry to form a haze, and polish the tile with a soft cloth. Cover the countertop with plastic sheeting for two or three days to let the grout cure properly. After two weeks or so, apply a grout sealer that includes mildew protection.

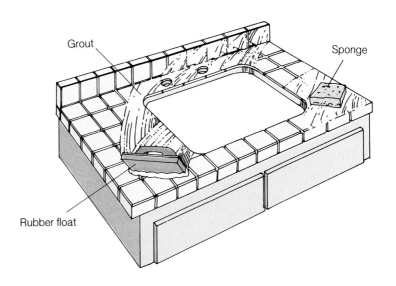

Grout

Sponge

Rubber float

TOLETS

If you intend to replace a toilet or install a new one, you will find techniques for removing and installing toilets on the following pages. If you wish to upgrade an older toilet or solve chronic problems common to most toilets, these pages describe repairs you can do without removing the toilet.

Many people are reluctant to even work on a toilet because they think it is complicated and requires the skills of a professional plumber. However, this is not the case. Even replacing a toilet or installing a new one is well within the capabilities of most homeowners. Most household toolboxes contain the necessary wrenches and screwdriver, and repair parts are readily available at hardware stores and home centers.

Recommended Cross-References
Bathroom Layout, Plumbing.

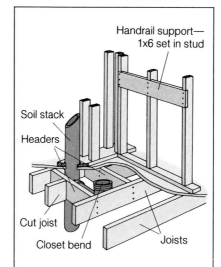

Framing for a Toilet
When the closet bend runs perpendicular to the joists, cut and support one of the joists. A toilet vent must be a minimum of 2 inches in diameter. Studs for a soil stack wall must be either 2 by 6 or double 2 by 4s to accommodate the 4-inch pipe.

Choosing a New Toilet
Each manufacturer's product has its own features, but all toilets are variations on the following:

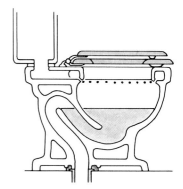

Reverse-Trap Toilet. Deeper trap and more of bowl is covered by water.

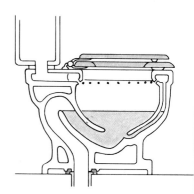

Siphon-Jet Toilet. Identifiable by a small hole below the waterline used to direct a jet of water into the trap, starting a quick, powerful siphon that pulls water and waste from the bowl. Quieter and uses less water than the reverse trap.

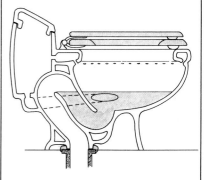

Siphon-Action or One-Piece Toilet. Quietest, most efficient, and most expensive toilet. Instead of a small hole and a jet of water, it has an elongated hole at the side of the bowl. Water swirls to create a siphon. The sides of the bowl are steeper and the bottom rounder.

Low-Flow Toilets
Plumbing codes in some areas require ultralow-flow (ULF) toilets. These toilets may use no more than 1.6 gallons of water per flush (GPF). Standard toilets use 3.5 to 7 GPF. ULF toilets work in most cases like a standard toilet, using steeper sides and higher tanks to increase the velocity of the water and to get more flushing action. Replacing standard toilets with low-flow toilets can save between 8,000 and 21,000 gallons of water per household per year. This conserves water and reduces the load on septic-tank leach fields and municipal sewage systems.

Most low-flow toilets use the same principles as standard toilets. One uses air compressed in the tank by water pressure to speed the flow of water. If your system has low water pressure, this model will take a long time to recharge and may not generate enough force to work efficiently. It is also noisy, but it does use less than 1 gallon per flush. Similar models use compressed air from a conventional compressor to flush. Listen to these before buying.

Some plumbers insist that low-flow toilets are trouble. In the early 1980s some poorly designed toilets were marketed that did cause prob-

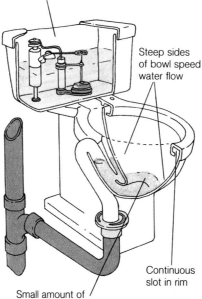

lems. Major advances have eliminated those problems, however. Low-flow toilets have been used in Europe for more than twenty years with no sewer problems traced to them. They will soon be standard in the United States. When you buy, be sure the toilet is a "low-flow" or "ultra-low-flow" type, not a "water saver," which is just another name for the standard 3.5-GPF toilet.

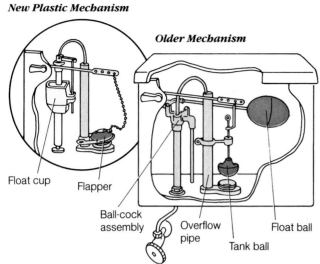

New Plastic Mechanism

Older Mechanism

Float cup

Flapper

Ball-cock assembly

Overflow pipe

Tank ball

Float ball

How a Tank Toilet Flushes

Pushing the handle down raises the flushing lever. The lever is attached to the tank ball (or flapper), and lifts it to allow the water in the tank to rush down into the bowl. As the tank empties, the drop in water level causes the float ball (or float cup) to lower. This ball is attached to an arm that operates the intake valve located in the ball-cock assembly, automatically opening the valve when water leaves the tank and closing it when the tank refills. While the tank is refilling, water is squirting through a tube into the overflow pipe. It flows down the pipe into the bowl, rinsing and refilling after the initial flushing.

Water Running Periodically

If the intake valve of the ball-cock assembly shuts on and off when no one has flushed the toilet, the problem is a leaking tank ball or flapper. The leaking water causes a gurgling sound, and the intake valve must let new water into the tank periodically to replace the lost water, which flows harmlessly into the bowl. To correct this, flush the toilet to empty the tank. To keep the tank from refilling, temporarily tie the float ball up with a piece of string. Then unscrew the tank ball from its guide rod, clean the valve seat, and replace the tank ball with a new one. Better yet, replace it with a flapper. Flappers are less prone to misalignment and they are very simple to install. Just clip the flapper around the base of the overflow pipe and attach the chain to the flushing lever.

Water Running Constantly

If water continues to run into the tank after the tank fills, the problem is the float ball or a defective valve. To find out what's wrong, pull up on the float ball. If the water shuts off, the problem is the float ball: It is either set too high or has water in it. Unscrew the ball and shake it. If it contains water, replace with a new one. If it does not contain water the rod needs to be lowered. Some mechanisms have an adjustment screw on the ball cock. If there is no adjustment screw, bend the rod to lower the ball. The ball should be adjusted so that the water level is $1/2$ inch to 1 inch lower than the top of the overflow pipe or at the waterline stamped on the inside of the tank.

If, when you pull up on the float ball, you feel resistance but the water still doesn't shut off, the problem is the intake valve itself. The problem may just be a worn washer, which you can change like the washer in a faucet. If the valve is corroded or appears to be broken, don't try to fix it or even to replace it with the same type of valve. Instead, replace it with a new, plastic flush mechanism.

Replacing Valve and Tank Ball

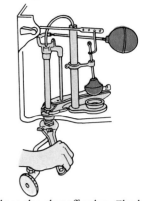

1. Close the shutoff valve. Flush to empty the tank and sponge out any remaining water. Loosen the nut beneath the tank that connects the supply tube to the ball cock.

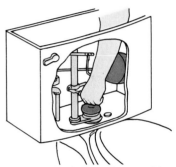

2. Remove the ball-cock assembly and the old rubber washers.

3. Install the new valve according to the manufacturer's directions, making sure the rubber washers are seated tightly.

4. Reconnect the supply tube and turn the water back on.

Overfilling

If, after flushing, the water seems to run for an unusually long time before shutting off, the tank may be filling too high. First, remove the cover. Flush the toilet and watch the tank refill. If the water rises to the top of the overflow pipe, the intake valve did not shut off soon enough. Since the intake valve is controlled by the float ball, you can adjust the point at which it shuts off simply by bending the float ball rod with your hands. Bend it so that the ball is lower than before.

Condensation

Moisture may build up on the outside of a tank when cold water flowing into the tank cools it enough to condense vapor in the warm air. This is called sweating, and it can be more than just a nuisance. Constant sweating causes water to drip onto the floor, which can loosen tiles and soak the subfloor, causing rot. If the water coming into the tank is not extremely cold, the easiest solution is to line the inside of the tank with a layer of insulating foam. Half-inch-thick Styrofoam or foam rubber works quite well. First, remove the cover from the tank and put it in a secure place; it can break easily. Then drain the tank by turning off the shutoff valve and flushing the toilet. Sponge up excess water and wipe the tank completely dry. Then, use epoxy resin cement to affix the insulation to all four sides. It should reach well above the waterline and not interfere with the mechanisms. Make sure the cement is completely dry before refilling the tank.

If the tank still sweats, the incoming water can be warmed by tapping into a nearby hot-water line. Put a reducing tee in both the hot-water and cold-water supply lines. Then connect them to a mixing valve, using pipe that is one size smaller than the existing supply lines. Connect the supply tube for the toilet to this valve.

Another solution is to buy a replacement tank unit. This will cost you less in the long run than it will to heat the extra water. Tank units come already insulated and complete with all internal mechanisms.

Removing an Old Toilet

Replacing or removing an old toilet is more time-consuming than it is complicated.

1. Turn the water off at the shutoff valve under the tank and then flush the toilet. Use a sponge to remove as much of the water as you can from the tank and the bowl.

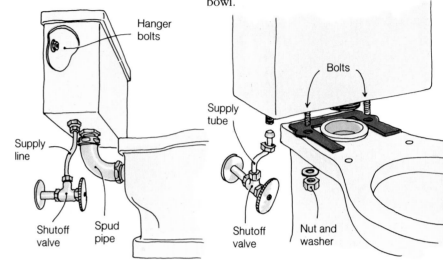

2. Disconnect supply tube from intake valve at the bottom of the tank.

If the tank is wall-mounted, remove the spud pipe or elbow connecting it to the bowl. Then, unscrew the nuts inside the tank and lift it off the wall. If the tank is mounted on the bowl, remove connecting bolts and lift the tank off the bowl.

Installing a New Toilet

First, be sure the rough-in dimensions for the flange and shutoff valve are correct for the new toilet. The center of the flange is usually 12 inches from the wall framing; the valve is usually centered 8 inches above the floor and 6 inches to the left of the centerline of the toilet. The flange should be screwed securely to the subfloor.

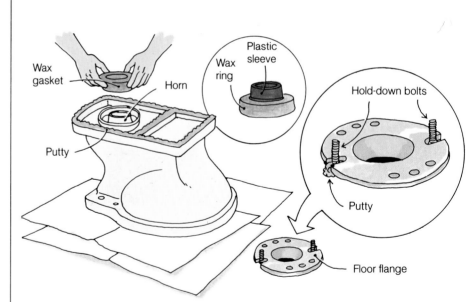

1. Place a new wax gasket around the horn of the outlet opening, pressing it firmly in place. If the closet flange is recessed, use a wax ring with a plastic extension. Apply a bead of bathtub caulk or plumber's putty around the bottom edge of the bowl.

Slip closet bolts into the slots on the floor flange. If necessary, press plumber's putty around the heads of the bolts to hold them steady.

3. The bowl is connected to the closet flange with two bolts. There may also be bolts at the front of the bowl, which are screwed directly into the subfloor. Be sure that the new toilet you are buying has the same rough-in dimension; on most toilets it is either 12 or 14 inches.

4. After removing the nuts from the closet flange bolts, you are ready to remove the bowl. Straddle it and rock it from side to side. This will loosen the wax seal.

5. When the bowl is free, lift it straight up so that water doesn't spill from the trap.

With a putty knife or other tool, scrape all wax and debris from the closet flange. You are now ready to install a new toilet or to remove the flange and cap the soil pipe.

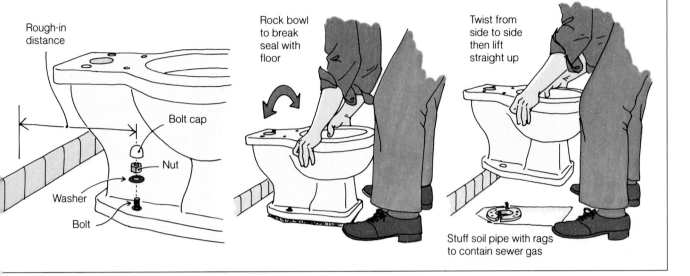

2. Set the toilet in place on the flange. Twist it back and forth and then sit or lean on it to force the wax ring down into the flange. Make sure it is level both from front to back and from side to side. If necessary, slip thin shims under the base. When tightening the nuts on the flange bolts, be careful. You want the nuts to be tight, but not too tight or you will crack the bowl.

3. Place the rubber cushion on the bowl so that it lines up with the bolt holes. Push the cone-shaped rubber gasket over the flush outlet and set the tank in place on the bowl. Put the rubber washers on the ends of the bolts and screw on the nuts. Tighten the bolts but, for the same reason stated above, not too much.

4. If the new tank requires lowering the shutoff valve, add an elbow, then a 4-inch to 6-inch nipple and another elbow to the stub. Then attach the shutoff valve.

Hook up a supply tube between the shutoff valve and the tank. Several types are available, including tubes of solid or flexible metal and reinforced plastic. Be sure the diameter of the tubing and that of the connecting fittings match the outlet of the shutoff valve.

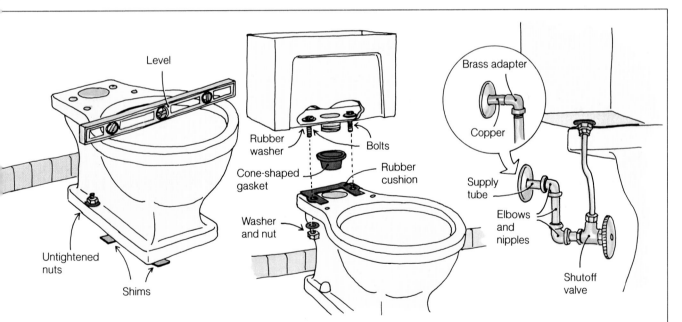

TOOLS

There is no sense owning a tool that you will use only once, but you should equip yourself with basic carpentry tools. Buy the best that you can afford: replacing ineffective or poor quality tools ends up costing you more.

Recommended Cross-References
Most entries.

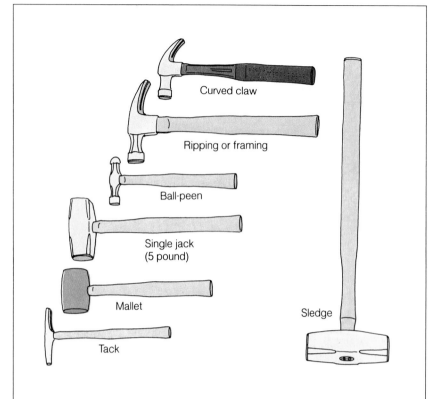

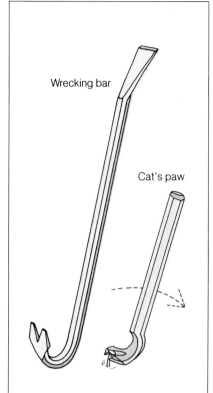

Hammers
Eventually you will need several hammers for different uses, but start out with a 16-ounce claw hammer. It can be used for light finishing work and some heavier framing, although you will soon want to buy a framing hammer (at least a 20-ounce one) for extensive building. Most framing hammers have a ripping claw, which is more useful for heavy work than a curved claw.

Nail Pullers
A nail puller is essential for removing nails already driven completely into the wood. A wrecking bar pulls nails easily once the heads are clear of the surface.

Screwdrivers
There are two general types of screwdriver tips—single slotted and cross-slotted known as a Phillips. In order to do even the most basic work you will need a medium-size slotted and a No. 2 Phillips. Eventually you will want at least three sizes of each, as well as handles and shanks of various lengths, which could mean a large collection. Specialty screwdrivers speed the fastening process and also have interchangeable tips so you do not need to have a large collection of ordinary screwdrivers.

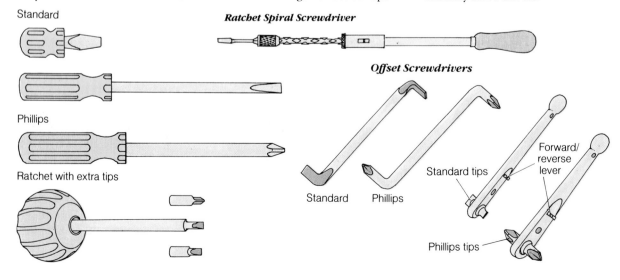

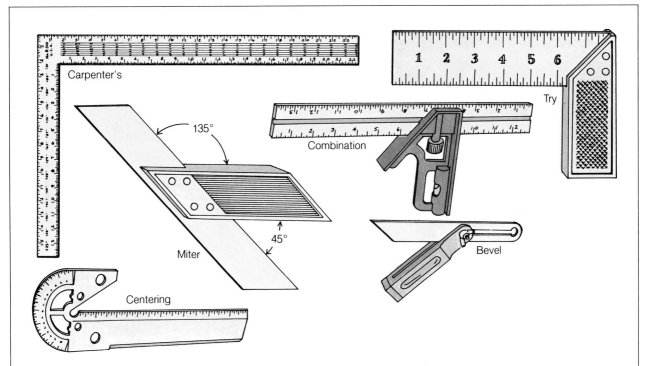

Carpenter's

135°

Try

Combination

45°

Miter

Bevel

Centering

Squares

A carpenter's square helps you check corners, but it has countless other uses ranging from laying out stair stringers to calculating rafter lengths. Usually, one leg is 24 inches, the other 16 inches long. A combination square enables you to scribe 90-degree or 45-degree marks for cutting boards, and a bevel gauge makes it possible to duplicate any angle and transfer it to a board you want to cut.

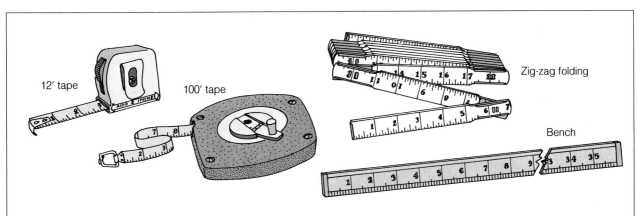

12' tape

100' tape

Zig-zag folding

Bench

Tapes and Rulers

A 12-foot steel tape measure is adequate for general household use, but choose a 25- or 30-foot tape measure with a 1-inch wide blade for any large projects. You may also need a 100-foot tape measure for laying out a room addition or landscaping project. Rulers are seldom used except for fine carpentry and cabinetry.

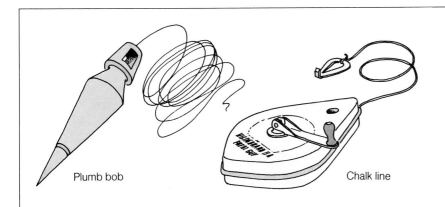

Plumb bob

Chalk line

Markers

A plumb bob hangs from a length of string and gives you a true vertical. It is widely used to locate the corners of a foundation as well as a starting line when hanging wallcovering.

A chalk line consists of a piece of string wound inside a container of colored chalk. The chalk-coated string is stretched taut between two points, then snapped to quickly mark a long straight line. Most chalk lines can double as plumb bobs.

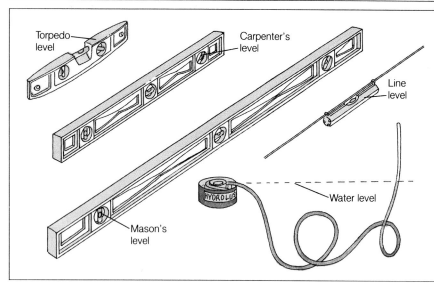

Torpedo level
Carpenter's level
Line level
Water level
Mason's level

Levels

A 24- or 30-inch carpenter's level will handle most jobs around the house, but if you are doing extensive framing or working with brick or concrete block you should also have a 4-foot level. A metal level works well for carpentry and light masonry work. A heavy wood mason's level costs more, but survives drops much better. A small torpedo level is handy for your tool apron, especially for plumbing and formwork. Use a line level for layout, fences, and footings where a transit is not available.

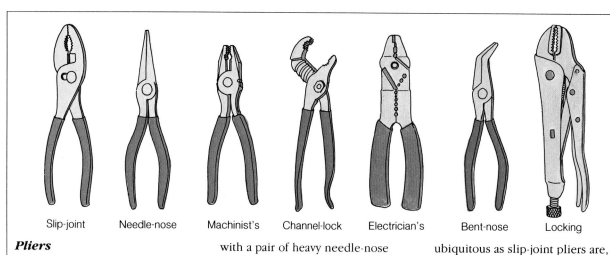

Slip-joint Needle-nose Machinist's Channel-lock Electrician's Bent-nose Locking

Pliers

At some time or other you will need almost all the pliers shown, but start with a pair of heavy needle-nose pliers and then a smaller pair of adjustable channel-lock pliers. As ubiquitous as slip-joint pliers are, they are not nearly as useful as the other specialized types.

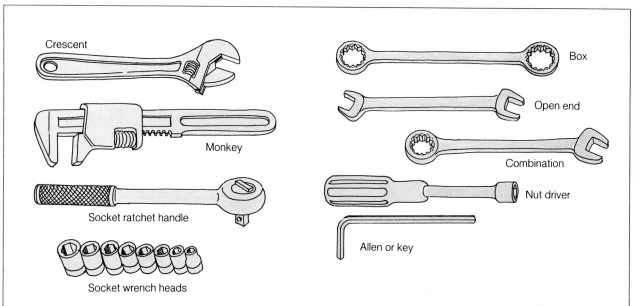

Crescent
Monkey
Socket ratchet handle
Socket wrench heads
Box
Open end
Combination
Nut driver
Allen or key

Wrenches

If you already have wrenches for automotive work you will not need another set for household carpentry unless you want to keep them separate. Wrenches are used most often for bolting beams and mud sills, but they are also handy for plumbing and installing appliances.

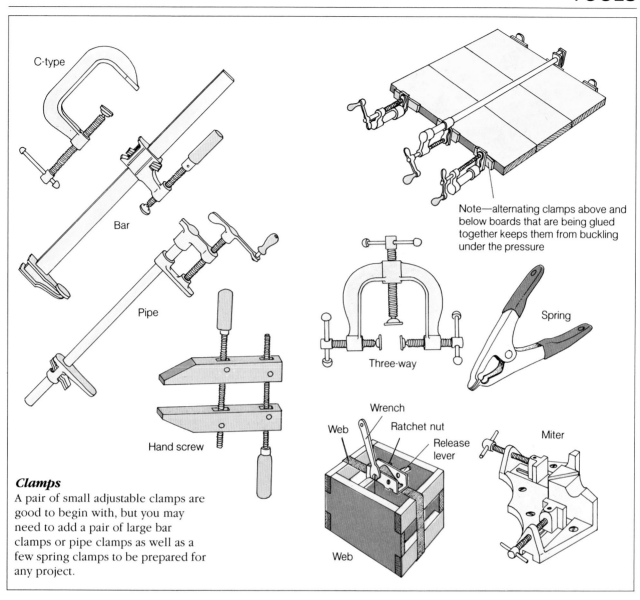

Note—alternating clamps above and below boards that are being glued together keeps them from buckling under the pressure

Spring

Wrench

Ratchet nut

Web

Release lever

Web

Miter

Three-way

Hand screw

Clamps

A pair of small adjustable clamps are good to begin with, but you may need to add a pair of large bar clamps or pipe clamps as well as a few spring clamps to be prepared for any project.

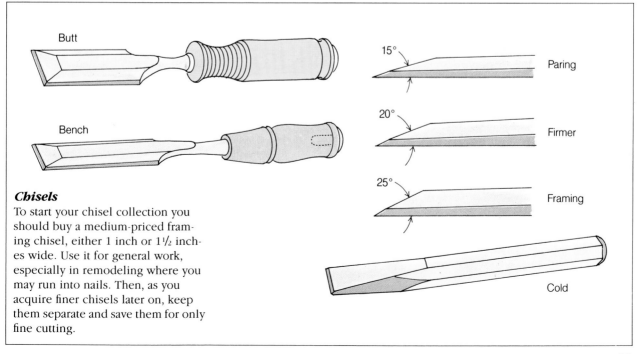

Butt

Bench

15° Paring

20° Firmer

25° Framing

Cold

Chisels

To start your chisel collection you should buy a medium-priced framing chisel, either 1 inch or 1½ inches wide. Use it for general work, especially in remodeling where you may run into nails. Then, as you acquire finer chisels later on, keep them separate and save them for only fine cutting.

Files and Rasps

These tools smooth metal or wood surfaces to give professional-looking results to your projects. The 4-in-1 file is easily carried in your tool belt and has a variety of textures for smoothing wood. Rasping planes, good for preliminary smoothing, come in several sizes.

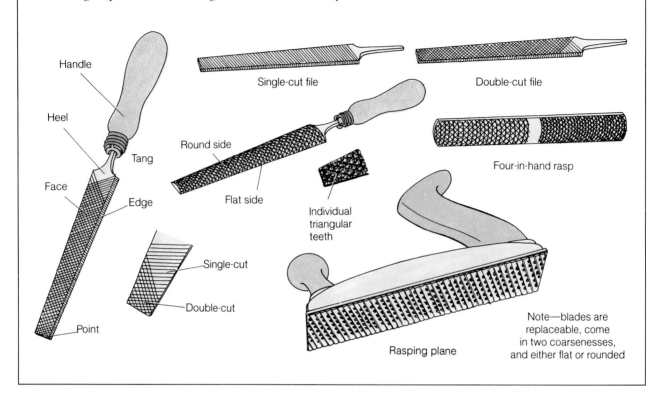

Handle
Heel
Tang
Face
Edge
Point

Single-cut file

Double-cut file

Round side
Flat side

Single-cut
Double-cut

Individual triangular teeth

Four-in-hand rasp

Rasping plane

Note—blades are replaceable, come in two coarsenesses, and either flat or rounded

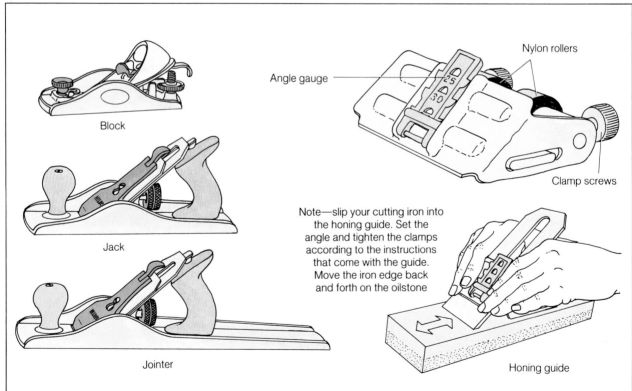

Block

Jack

Jointer

Angle gauge

Nylon rollers

Clamp screws

Note—slip your cutting iron into the honing guide. Set the angle and tighten the clamps according to the instructions that come with the guide. Move the iron edge back and forth on the oilstone

Honing guide

Planes

A medium-sized jack plane will be sufficient for most projects unless you plan to do extensive fine wood-working or cabinet work. A plane is used for final smoothing work, and requires a very sharp blade for best results. The double plane iron (the beveled cutting piece), the level cap, the depth-adjustment screw, and the lateral-adjustment lever must all be carefully set for the plane to function properly. Choose a plane with high-quality steel and buy a stone for honing it periodically.

Handsaws

A good all-around saw, for cutting boards across the grain where extremely fine cuts are not necessary, is an 8-point crosscut saw (it has 8 teeth per inch). You are not likely to need a ripsaw if you own a power circular saw. A compass, or keyhole, saw comes in handy for many remodeling tasks, and a backsaw with at least 12 points is essential for making fine cuts. Have a hacksaw with 18-, 24-, and 32-tooth blades for cutting metal. A hacksaw is also good for cutting wood moldings.

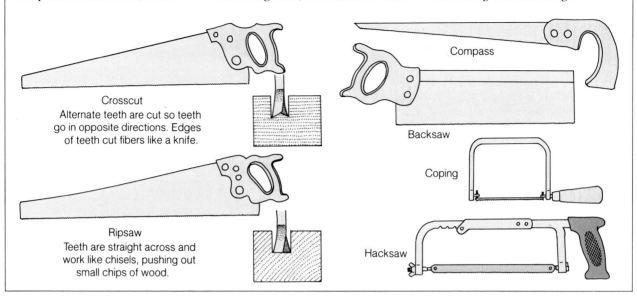

Crosscut
Alternate teeth are cut so teeth go in opposite directions. Edges of teeth cut fibers like a knife.

Ripsaw
Teeth are straight across and work like chisels, pushing out small chips of wood.

Compass

Backsaw

Coping

Hacksaw

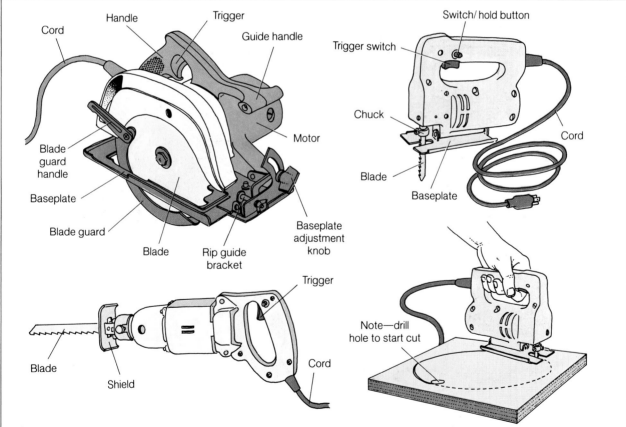

Cord

Handle

Trigger

Guide handle

Blade guard handle

Baseplate

Blade guard

Blade

Rip guide bracket

Motor

Baseplate adjustment knob

Switch/ hold button

Trigger switch

Chuck

Blade

Baseplate

Cord

Trigger

Blade

Shield

Cord

Note—drill hole to start cut

Electric Saws

Circular Saw. A circular saw saves time and makes more accurate cuts than a handsaw. A heavy-duty model is less likely to buck or kick back, and is safer to use, but always choose one that feels comfortable to you.

Choosing the proper blades and keeping them sharp is just as important as selecting the best machine.

Saber Saw. The small blade of this saw is ideal for cutting out circles or making curved cuts. Different kinds of blades are available for cutting wood, plywood, plastic, and metal.

Reciprocating Saw. This saw is essential for demolition or for doing extensive work on an existing structure. It works like a saber saw, but is much more powerful and makes very rough cuts. Blades are available for various types of cuts, as well as other materials besides wood. It makes an excellent power hacksaw.

Power Drill

A ³/₈-inch variable speed drill will bore holes through wood, metal, or plastic, drive screws, mix paint, sand, and bore holes into some types of concrete. You can increase its adaptability with various attachments such as a drill press stand or a doweling jig. Some drills that are battery operated are truly portable.

If you plan to bore large holes for plumbing or to connect heavy beams together, you will eventually need the more powerful ¹/₂-inch drill. It turns at a slower speed than smaller drills, but enables you to cut wide or deep holes many times.

Even more important than the drill are the bits. For small diameters, up to ¹/₄ inch, you can use high speed twist drills, which also work with metal. A spur drill is a variation of the twist drill that is shaped to make holes that are not tapered at the end. For holes from ¹/₄ inch to 1¹/₂ inch in diameter, use a spade bit. For larger holes, use a dial saw or similar attachment for your drill, or special heavy-duty bits for a ¹/₂-inch drill.

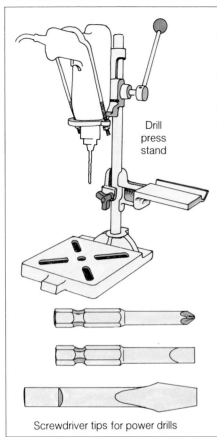

Screwdriver tips for power drills

Routers

Once you use a router, you'll wonder how you ever got along without one. The router consists of a motor that drives a shaping bit at tremendous speeds enabling you to make decorative edges on furniture, cut dovetails, trim plastic laminates, and perform a host of other tasks.

Routers range in horsepower from ¹/₂ hp to 3 hp. The smaller the motor, the harder it has to work, and the sooner it will wear out.

Router with bits

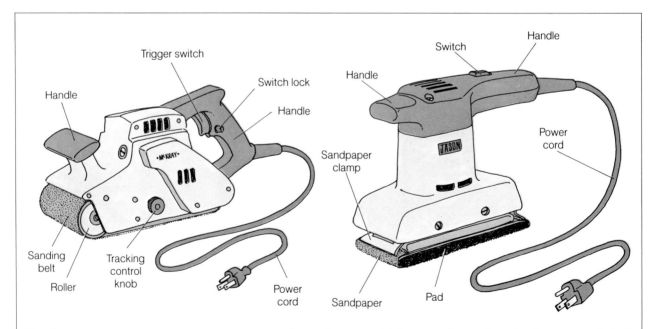

Sanders

Sanding is an essential part of all finish carpentry. You can plane or file wood smooth, but only expert sanding will give a project a professional look. Although you can sand by hand, power sanders do the job just as well and considerably faster.

Belt Sander. The belt sander has an abrasive belt that is stretched be-

tween two drums that turn at high speed. It removes uneven and rough material, and prepares the work for finish sanding. Always keep a belt sander moving while working. If you hold it in one place, it will quickly cut grooves in the wood.

Orbital Sander. An orbital sander is the most common for finish sanding. It has a pad on the bottom that

vibrates in a circular manner. A similar type of sander is called "in-line", which moves back and forth with the grain rather than in a circle.

Always sand with rougher grits of paper first, using progressively finer grits. Before giving wood its final sanding, wipe it down with a damp rag. This removes sanding dust from between the grain lines.

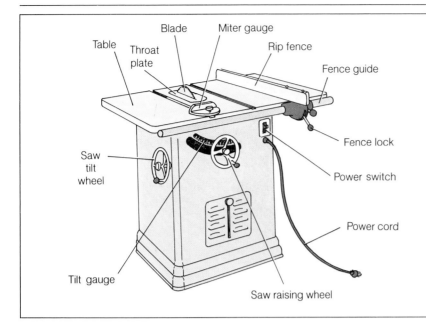

Table · Blade · Miter gauge
Throat plate · Rip fence
Fence guide
Fence lock
Power switch
Saw tilt wheel
Power cord
Tilt gauge
Saw raising wheel

Table Saw

This is particularly effective for cutting plywood or paneling, and for ripping long boards to length. It must be placed in the center of the floor so you can work around it, which means you must have ample shop space.

Blade sizes range from 6½ inches to 12 inches in diameter, but the two most popular sizes for the home are 9- and 10-inch blades.

The blade can be moved up or down, and set at any angle up to 45 degrees. A miter gauge is a separate accessory that allows you to make cross cuts through a board at various angles. A ripping fence attachment acts as a guide for making accurate, long cuts repeatedly.

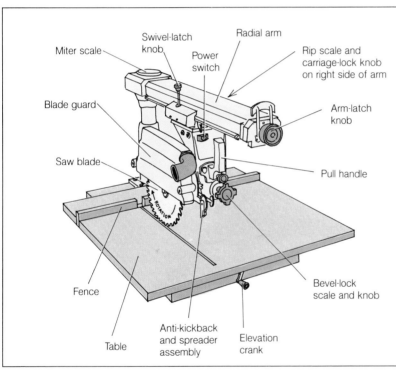

Miter scale
Swivel-latch knob · Radial arm
Power switch
Rip scale and carriage-lock knob on right side of arm
Blade guard
Arm-latch knob
Saw blade
Pull handle
Fence
Bevel-lock scale and knob
Table
Anti-kickback and spreader assembly · Elevation crank
ROTATION

Radial Arm Saw

This saw performs many of the same functions as a table saw, as well as making crosscuts. The radial arm saw with the right attachments can also function as a drill, a router, a saber saw, and a sander. It also takes up less space because it fits against a wall. It does not cut large sheets of plywood easily, however, and is not as portable as many table saws.

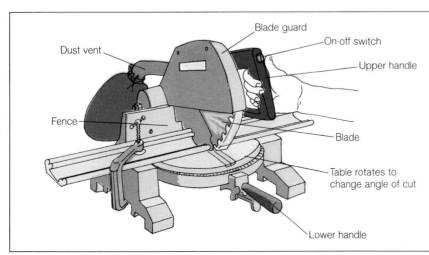

Dust vent
Blade guard
On-off switch
Upper handle
Fence
Blade
Table rotates to change angle of cut
Lower handle

Power Miter Saw

This tool performs many of the functions of the radial arm saw but is more portable. It is ideal for cutting trim; it can make perfect miter cuts, including compound bevels, and remove paper-thin pieces from the end of a board. With a metal-cutting blade, it can be used to cut aluminum tubing and L-metal. The principal limitation of the power miter saw is the size of material it can cut. Most models will cut stock up to 2 by 6.

Working With Metal

Metal is used in a number of building materials, such as flashing and framing connectors. Windows, doors, and many other items include metal parts that may need modification. Working with metal building materials requires many basic metalworking skills.

Most metals used in construction are alloys. The most common are steel, aluminum, and brass. Iron and copper are the only ones commonly used in pure form and even they may include small amounts of other metals to improve specific characteristics.

Sheet metal is simply flat metal up to ³/₁₆ inch thick. Thicker flat metal is called plate. Bar metal may be round, T-shaped, L-shaped, flat, or other more unusual shapes, but all would be less than 12 inches wide if flattened out.

Safety

Whenever you work with metal, observe the following precautions:
• Wear goggles or safety glasses when cutting, drilling, sawing, or soldering.
• Clamp metal pieces securely.
• Wear heavy leather gloves when cutting metal or installing sharp pieces; the raw edges can cause serious cuts.
• File off any burrs or sharp edges after cutting or drilling.
• Use any safety features, such as shields, included with your tools.
• Keep cutting tools sharp. Don't force cutting tools into metal.

Measuring and Marking

Plan metal assemblies carefully. Create cardboard templates for the pieces you will need or cut the pieces oversized, then trim them to fit. In either case, allow extra time.

In addition to common measuring tools, you may need a gauge tool. The thickness of sheet metal is measured in gauge numbers, according to several standards. The only thing the standards have in common is that larger gauge numbers indicate thinner metal. Each standard has its own gauge tool.

Metal can be marked with scribes, engraving tools, knives, center punches, or felt-tipped pens. A sharp nail will work in a pinch.

Cutting Metal

The most common metal-cutting tools are the hacksaw and sheet-metal snips, also known as aviation snips. Snips come in straight cut, right-hand cut, and left-hand cut configurations. Straight snips are colored yellow, right-hand snips are red, and left-hand snips are green. Snips may damage one side of the piece of metal. If you need both pieces, a saw may be a better choice.

For extensive cutting, you can buy or rent power snips, or use a metal-cutting blade mounted in a jigsaw or circular saw.

Using Snips. Wear gloves. Open the jaws fully, but don't close them completely because they will leave small bumps or burrs on the metal. Cut from the side that allows you to bend the work away from the cut, making room to operate the snips.

To make an inside cut, score the line and drill a hole to start the cut. Make a rough cut at first, then trim to the line.

After making a cut with snips, file the edges and hammer them flat.

Scoring. Thin metal can be scored several times with a utility knife and bent back and forth until it snaps. Clamp it securely and wear gloves while bending.

Using a Cold Chisel. This technique works for rough cuts. The chisel should be sharp.

Score the cut line and clamp the piece to be cut over a wood or metal support. Hammer the chisel along the entire line. Repeat several times until the cut is done. File or grind the edges as needed.

Using a Hacksaw. Use a sharp blade. Clamp the piece to be cut. Rotate oddly shaped pieces so the blade doesn't bind.

Drilling

Mark the location of the hole with a V or X. Make a small indentation at that point with a center punch or a sharp nail. If you don't, the drill will tend to wander.

Clamp the piece before you drill. Use a twist bit and apply a small amount of oil to the indentation.

Hold the drill bit perpendicular to the metal. If the bit slips off, stop drilling and make a small groove with a cold chisel back to the correct point. Other approaches are to restrike the hole location with the punch or to drill a pilot hole with a smaller bit.

As you drill, keep the hole lubricated with oil. Pull the bit out to let it cool and keep adding drops of oil as needed. Bits dull very quickly if they get too hot.

In thick sheet metal or metal plate, it is much faster to drill a hole in stages, starting with a small bit and working up to the final size. For example, to drill a ½-inch-diameter hole in ⅜-inch-thick steel, start with a ¼-inch bit, enlarge the hole with a ⅜-inch bit, then finish with a ½-inch bit.

Holes larger than 1 inch can be cut with a hole cutter or fly cutter, but it may be easier and cheaper to take the metal to a shop.

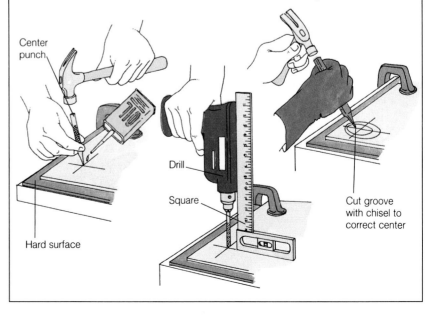

Center punch

Hard surface

Drill

Square

Cut groove with chisel to correct center

Bending Sheet Metal

Sheet-metal bends can be made with homemade jigs or specialized tools.

Simple Bend. Clamp the metal between two pieces of wood so one edge of the metal is exposed and the edge of the wood is along the line of the bend. Hammer the exposed edge over. Use a long wood-block on wide pieces of metal.

Curved Bend. Cut pieces of wood to the desired curve and clamp the metal between the pieces. Tap the metal over the wood to form the curve.

Rounded Edge. Make a 90-degree bend along the edge to be rounded, about ⅜ inch in from the edge. Press a piece of ⅛-inch plywood or sheet-metal scrap against the bend, then bend the edge to 180 degrees. Remove the plywood or metal scrap, then continue bending the edge down to the surface.

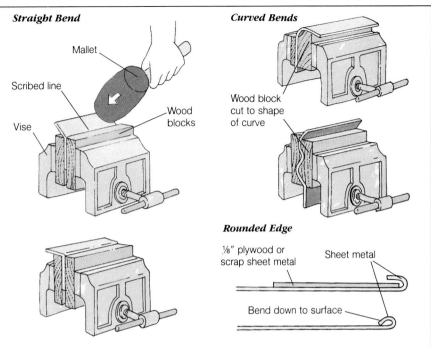

Straight Bend

Mallet

Scribed line

Vise

Wood blocks

Curved Bends

Wood block cut to shape of curve

Rounded Edge

⅛" plywood or scrap sheet metal

Sheet metal

Bend down to surface

Bending Tubing or Pipe

Bend tubing with a tubing bender or spring. These come in various sizes and should fit the tubing snugly. Make the bend by hand, if possible; a vise may dent the tubing.

Bend conduit, thin-wall pipe, and rigid pipe with a conduit bender. Place the pipe in the bender and pull the handle to bend the tubing just past the desired angle. Release the bender, and the tubing should return to the desired bend.

Bend copper or aluminum tubing by packing it with sand, then forming it around a jig.

Hollow Rivets

These are made of aluminum or stainless steel and installed with a specific tool. Tools meant for stainless steel rivets can be used with aluminum rivets, but those meant for aluminum rivets can't be used with stainless steel.

Drill holes for the rivets. Line up the pieces to be riveted and hold or clamp them together securely.

Open the rivet tool all the way and insert the rivet. Put the free end of the rivet through the holes in both pieces. Squeeze the rivet-tool handles several times until the rivet stem snaps off. If the stem slips out of the tool, open the handles all the way, slip the tool over the rivet stem, and hold the rivet down while squeezing the handles.

Soldering

Soldering can be done with a soldering iron or a torch. A torch is useful for large or heavy work, such as sweating joints in copper pipe, whereas irons are better for temperature-sensitive or fine work.

Using a Soldering Iron. The tip of the soldering iron must be tinned and clean. If the tip is new or corroded, file it down to new metal.

Brush flux on the tip, clamp the soldering iron, and plug it in. Once the iron heats up, touch solder to the tip to coat it lightly.

The pieces to be soldered must be clean; use a file, sandpaper, or steel wool if necessary.

Test the pieces for fit and make any corrections.

Coat the area to be soldered with flux. Do not touch it with fingers.

Clamp or position the pieces to be soldered. Hold the iron against the work (not to the solder). When the work is hot enough to melt solder, touch the solder to the joint. It will flow toward the heat.

Continue to move the iron along the edge of the work. When the entire edge is visibly soldered, let it cool, then wipe it clean with a damp sponge or rag. If staining is a concern, wipe off any last traces of flux.

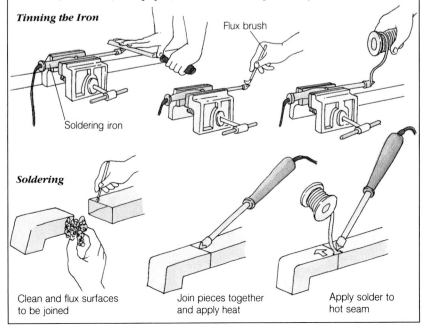

Tinning the Iron

Flux brush

Soldering iron

Soldering

Clean and flux surfaces to be joined

Join pieces together and apply heat

Apply solder to hot seam

TRELLISES

A trellis is a vertical or horizontal structure that shades a house or deck, supports a vine, screens a view, or shelters an open patio. Also called arbors, bowers, pergolas, shade shelters, or overheads, they define space, can make a small home appear larger, and certainly add appeal to any outdoor setting.

Trellises take many shapes and forms. The simplest are lattice grids that attach to the side of a house to support climbing plants. More elaborate overhead structures consist of heavy posts and beams covered with shading material. A trellis may be painted to match the house or stained to achieve a rustic effect.

If you build an overhead structure, you will probably need a building permit. Construction is fairly easy, although posts must be well supported. The size of the lumber must suit the spans involved, and connections between all members must be strong. Well-anchored posts and strong connections are especially important to freestanding structures because the frame lacks diagonal bracing.

Lightweight shade cloth and reed fencing are effective trellis coverings that are easy to remove each year, and they create a casual effect. Wood covering, usually 2 inches by 2 inches or larger, imparts a more substantial look and allows more air circulation. Lath has limited use as a covering; it is subject to severe warping. Lattice is much better. Solid material such as corrugated fiberglass offers protection from the rain but no air circulation. It also looks somewhat industrial. Greenery provides the most dramatic and versatile covering. Choose an attractive annual vine or perennial.

Recommended Cross-References

Barbecues, Benches, Cooling, Decks, Fences, Footings, Framing, Gazebos, Lattice, Patios, Sheds, Wood.

Whether you call them trellises, arbors, pergolas, or shade structures, these additions to a backyard provide coolness, tranquillity, and privacy.

Planning a Trellis

First, determine the size and location of the proposed trellis. If the trellis will attach to the house, trellis proportions should reflect the proportions of the main structure and echo some architectural feature. The trellis could span the entire length of a wall, for example, or start and end at a prominent point such as a corner, window, or doorway. A trellis usually attaches just below the eave, so the height of the trellis probably depends on the height of the eave. If the eave is too high, however, attach the trellis to some other feature. If there are no features, attach the trellis 12 inches above the window line.

A freestanding trellis should relate in size to a patio or deck. The trellis need not mirror the shape of the patio or deck, but the effect is more harmonious if at least two edges of each structure align.

Choosing Materials

Use a durable wood species for your trellis. Cedar, cypress, redwood, or pressure-treated lumber are all wise choices. Use untreated lumber only if you plan to paint it. Even with a coating, however, untreated wood will require maintenance and be subject to rotting.

Four-inch by 4-inch stock will serve as an adequate post, but the proportions of larger stock seem more appropriate for an open structure. Use 4 by 6 or 6 by 6 lumber or sandwich a 2 by 6 between two 2 by 4s to create an interesting variation. Remember that sandwiched members will trap moisture, and take appropriate precautions. To create a rustic effect, use posts made of logs or poles for the construction.

The beams that rest on the posts and support the superstructure are usually 4 by 8 timbers or larger. If you want to pair the beams, choose 2 by 8 lumber or larger and bolt two members to the side of the post. Beam size depends on span. Remember, however, that larger sizes seem to look better in open structures. Another guideline maintains that, if beams rest directly on posts, the effect will be much better if the widths of the members match.

The trellis may consist of 2 by 6s spaced 16 to 24 inches apart or of larger members spaced farther apart that hold up a grid of cross-members. Two-by lumber is more prone to warping and checking than larger stock. Determine how much shade you need and at what time of day. Slats that run east to west shade the sun at noon but allow some direct sunlight in midmorning and midafternoon during the hottest season. Slats that run north to south admit sun at noon but block it during the rest of the day. By using wider boards, you will create more shade.

Building a Trellis

Freestanding. A freestanding trellis requires a minimum of four posts. Also, shear bracing in two directions is necessary to prevent the structure from swaying.

Center posts from 6 to 12 feet apart, depending on the size of beams. A 4 by 8 beam requires a spacing of 8 feet, for example, and a 4 by 10 beam requires a spacing of 10 feet. A rectangular structure, each side with three posts, spaced 6 to 8 feet apart, has pleasing proportions.

Attach posts to concrete footings or bury them directly in the ground if the lumber is pressure treated and specified for ground contact. To bury posts, excavate to the frost line, set them on a gravel base, and pour concrete around them.

There should be at least 7½ feet of headroom, so cut the posts at approximately 7 feet. Make sure the cut marks are level and aligned with one another before trimming the posts.

Attach beams to the posts with T-straps or metal brackets and add knee braces to provide diagonal support, if needed. Paint metal brackets to match the wood, and cut knee braces out of 4 by 6 stock.

Rafters can be any size, although the greater the spacing the larger they should be. Toenail the rafters with 16d HDG common nails or attach them with metal brackets. Decorative cuts on the ends of beams and rafters create interest. Add crosspieces to form a grid, either under or above the rafters.

Attached. An attached trellis has the advantage of being supported by the house. This enables you to cut down on the amount of support posts. Nevertheless, it should be built securely and be strong enough to support a couple of hundred pounds just in case you want to add a roof later.

Bolt a 2 by 6 (or heavier) ledger to the studs with 5½-inch lag bolts 6 to 12 inches above the window line so trellis rafters clear eaves and gutters.

Install posts in a straight line parallel with the house wall. The size of the rafters determines the distance of the posts from the house. For example, 4 by 6 rafters spaced 36 inches on center can span 10 to 16 feet depending on species. Pour footings for untreated limber. Bury pressure-treated posts. If there is a concrete footing, attach the post directly to it with a surface-mounting metal anchor. Bolt the anchor to the concrete with a ½-inch expansion bolt.

Cut the posts and install the beam so that the rafters slope gently away from the house. If you use double beams that bolt to the side of the posts, include spacers every 3 feet to keep the beams from warping. Use joist or beam hangers at the ledger end and toenail the rafters into the beam at the other end. Trim the ends with decorative cuts. Install gridwork or cross-members as shading.

If the lumber is not kiln dried, do not paint or stain for 60 days; if it is, stain before assembling.

Cantilevered. This is merely a version of an attached trellis. Generally, it is either hung off a ledger or it is an extension of the roof.

If the rafter tails of the house are exposed, extend them by bolting 2 by 4s onto them. Attaching a 2 by 4 to each side of the rafter results in a more balanced look. Most rafters are strong enough to support a trellis about 3 feet wide. If you have any doubt about the capacity of your rafters, get professional advice rather than risk damage to the roof.

An alternative method is to use horizontal 2 by 4s. One end of the shade trellis attaches to a ledge bolted into the house wall. The rafter ends or fascia board supports the trellis at midpoint.

Use 2 by 2s for the screening. Stain or paint it to match the house. To increase shading during the hot months, plant deciduous vines over the trellis.

VANITIES

A bathroom vanity provides the washbasin with an attractive base and creates valuable storage space. Many sizes and styles are available, and installation is a relatively easy project. Most cabinets are open in the back; they simply fit around the plumbing in the wall.

Most vanities are 18 to 21 inches deep and from 18 to 72 inches wide.

Combine two or more cabinets to create a wider vanity. The standard height, including countertop, is 30 inches. The addition of spacers provides more height, if desired. If you want two basins, the vanity should be at least 48 inches wide. Many manufacturers offer other bathroom accessories to match their vanities. Dealers often sell a package that includes a

specific countertop. In many cases, however, you can specify a countertop to suit your bathroom.

Recommended Cross-References
Bathroom Layout, Cabinets, Countertops, Plumbing.

Recessed washbasins are installed flush with the tiles on this expansive vanity.

Types of Materials

Although you can build your own cabinet from plywood and finish it either with paint or a stain and sealer, it is much easier to buy a prefinished cabinet and attach the countertop of your choice. You can also have a custom cabinet built to your exact specifications.

The most commonly used countertop materials are tile, plastic laminate, marble, or synthetic marble. Many synthetic marble countertops have washbasins that are molded into the slab. Better quality synthetic marble materials are colored throughout the material. This means that if the surface is scratched or eroded from scouring, it can be repaired by sanding away the blemish.

Tile is an excellent countertop material and is fairly easy to install yourself. The trickiest part is making clean and accurate cuts. Check with your tile supplier; often they will make the cuts for you if you bring back a marked tile.

Installing a Vanity Countertop

The easiest type of countertop to install is the synthetic marble type with a washbasin molded into it. All you do is run a bead of silicone caulk around the top edge of the cabinet and set the countertop into place. Using any other material, such as a plywood base for tile or laminate, will involve cutting a hole for the washbasin and attaching a backsplash before mounting the countertop to the cabinet.

To cut the hole, trace an outline of the basin on the countertop. Drill a starting hole inside the cutout and use a power jigsaw to make the cut. To make sure the hole is small enough to support the rim of the basin, make the cut about 1/2 inch inside the outline.

Attach plywood backsplash and sidesplash pieces to the countertop with silicone sealant and screws, first drilling pilot holes through the edge of the countertop. If the pieces are synthetic marble, use a sealant recommended by the manufacturer. You cannot use screws. Set the completed countertop in place and drive screws into the underside through the corner cleats of the cabinet.

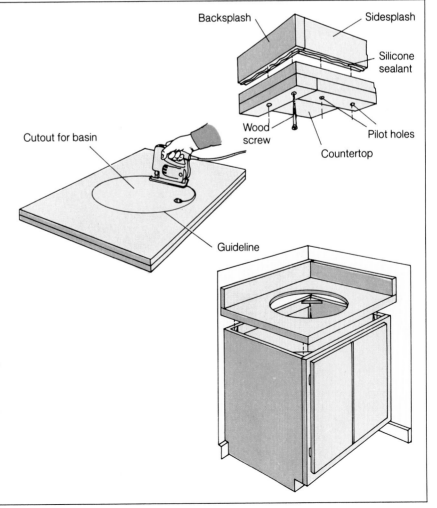

Backsplash

Sidesplash

Silicone sealant

Wood screw

Pilot holes

Countertop

Cutout for basin

Guideline

VENTILATION

Proper ventilation performs two important functions: comfort control and moisture control. Living space must have fresh air to cool it in hot weather, and also to remove steam, smoke, cooking odors, and other indoor pollutants from the home. Windows and natural air infiltration help to provide this ventilation, but every home should also contain mechanical ventilators—bathroom exhaust fans, range hoods, and dryer vents. All should be ducted to the outside.

With the advent of well-insulated homes comes the need for more extensive ventilating systems. When a home is tightly insulated, all of the air leaks and drafts are sealed off that normally keep it ventilated. Windows cannot be opened for fresh air, because the resulting drafts would defeat the purpose of the insulation. In response to this need, some manufacturers have devised heat exchangers. A heat exchanger admits fresh air into the house through a system of tubes that absorb heat from the structural duct system, hot water system, or other source of heat.

Most health experts recommend one complete air exchange in the house every thirty to sixty minutes. If your house is not insulated, the air is probably exchanged twice every hour. A house with vapor barriers and other devices for stopping infiltration may not get a complete exchange of air for at least two or three hours unless you install a ventilating system.

How Vents Work

Vents simply provide an access between interior and exterior spaces. Their effectiveness depends on the movement of air, whether from natural breezes, fans, or convective currents produced by warm air rising and being replaced by cooler air. The most effective venting utilizes cross-ventilation.

Recommended Cross-References
Cooling, Fans, Flashing, Hoods & Vents, Insulation.

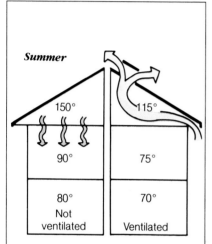

Summer

What Ventilation Does
In hot weather, proper ventilation prevents the attic from becoming a hot box that spills unwanted heat down through the attic floor (even if the attic is insulated) into the living area.

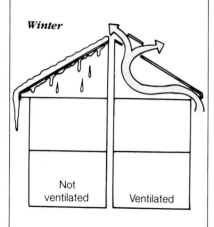

Winter

In cold weather, proper ventilation helps prevent moisture from condensing in the insulation, structural members, shingles, or on the roof.

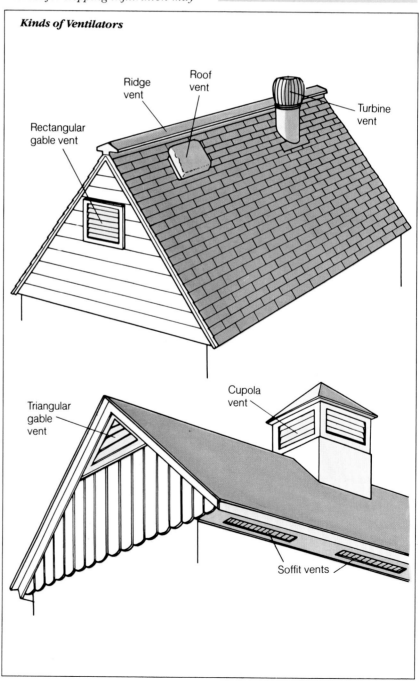

Kinds of Ventilators

Ridge vent

Roof vent

Turbine vent

Rectangular gable vent

Triangular gable vent

Cupola vent

Soffit vents

Structural Ventilation

Ventilation should control heat and moisture buildup in the attic, crawl space, and uninsulated wall cavities. Good ventilation helps to cool the house during hot weather, and helps prevent structural damage caused by condensation.

Attics. Codes and standard practices vary, but you should figure on 1 square foot of free vent area for every 150 square feet of attic. A 2¼-square-foot gable vent, with louvers and screening, would have 1 square foot of free vent area. You can reduce the required vent area by half (1:300) if half of the vents are soffit vents in the eaves and the other half are at least 3 feet off the attic floor.

Roof and gable vents are easy to install. You need only measure and cut out a piece of the roof or wall and then insert the vent into the hole. You should frame any hole cut into the roof or wall with a system of 2 by 4s, and use caulk or flashing to seal the hole around the vent after it's installed.

Crawl Spaces. Locate foundation vents for the crawl space on every wall, close enough together so there is at least 1 square foot of free vent opening (area unobstructed by screens, louvers, or other material) for every 25 linear feet of foundation. Heated crawl spaces and basements do not need these vents.

Rafters. If the rafters are insulated, such as in an occupied attic or a vaulted ceiling, the rafter space must be ventilated at the eave and ridge. A continuous ridge vent is best here.

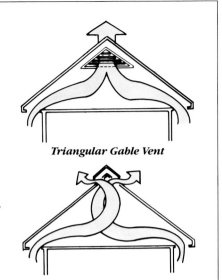

Triangular Gable Vent

Ridge Vent With Undereaves Vents

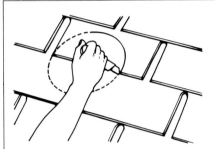

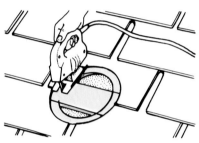

Installing Rooftop Ventilation

1. Measure and cut a hole, the size of the vent base, through the shingles, roofing felt, and sheathing. Be sure the hole is centered between rafters.

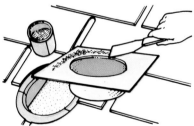

2. Apply roofing cement or caulk to the underside of the base flange and slide it under the surrounding shingles. Center the base over the hole.

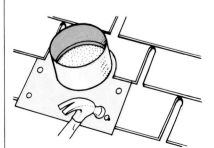

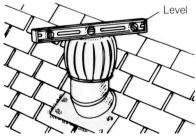

3. Nail the flange in place. Replace shingles if necessary and caulk the edge of the flange and nail heads.

4. Set the turbine (or other vent top) on the base. Level and secure it as shown on its instruction sheet.

Installing Gable Vents

1. Cut a hole to the size indicated by the manufacturer. Be sure to allow for the 2 by 4 header.

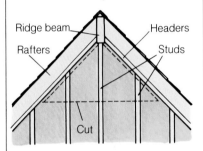

2. Nail in the header.

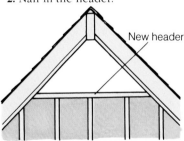

3. Install the vent according to the instruction sheet provided by the manufacturer.

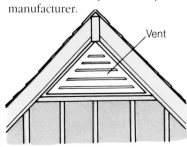

4. Caulk all the outside edges.

WALLBOARD

It is hard to imagine any home improvement project that does not involve working with some wallboard. Wallboard, also called drywall, gypsum board, gypboard, and Sheetrock (a brand name), is a versatile and inexpensive building material. It is easy to install, although it is more difficult to finish properly. It is dimensionally stable, it can be fireproofed and moistureproofed, it cuts easily, and it creates an excellent surface for texturing, painting, wallpapering, paneling, or tiling. It can be doubled up to provide thermal mass. It can even go on the outside of buildings for fire-resistant sheathing. When damaged, it is easy to repair or replace.

So, what disadvantages can wallboard possibly have? It can be monotonous as a finish wall if used without relief. It is sometimes heavy to handle, though not prohibitively so. And it takes some skill to tape and finish joints to an absolutely smooth surface. In spite of these limitations, wallboard is still the universally recommended wallcovering for interior walls.

Planning

One of the first planning decisions to make is how much of the work you are going to do yourself. Most people find it fairly easy to install wallboard themselves, as long as help is available for handling the heavy panels. If the final appearance is important or there is a large area to cover, it is best to have at least the taping and texturing done professionally. If you choose to tape and texture yourself, start with a closet and other out-of-the-way areas so that you can develop your proficiency before tackling the most visible walls.

Another early planning step is to calculate the placement of panels so that you can order the types and sizes you need. For a large project, calculate the total square footage, allow a small percentage for waste, and order an equivalent square footage in the largest size panels you will be using. For a small project, draw a layout diagram and figure the exact number of panels you will need. It is a good idea to order extra, especially since wallboard is so inexpensive.

You may also need to buy, borrow, or improvise a few specialized tools. You can use a regular hammer with some practice, but for large projects you should get a wallboard hammer. The rounded head prevents breaking through the paper, and the angle of the handle keeps your knuckles clear of the wall. You will also need extra blades for your utility knife, a wallboard saw, and a wood or metal straightedge. A foot lever helps you snug panels up against the ceiling.

Recommended Cross-References
Ceilings, Framing, Paint, Walls.

Preparation

When you are ready to start work, stack all the wallboard in a place that is convenient to the walls and ceilings you are installing, but out of the way of any jacks or bracing you will use for ceiling panels.

Examine the framing. Make sure it is on 4-foot centers, so that each joint will have a stud or joist for backing. Remove any nails. On walls, check for crooked or bowed studs. Straighten them by sawing halfway into them and then nailing short pieces of lumber or plywood on each side, or by planing if they are not too bowed. Check the corners carefully to make sure they have backing to nail both intersecting panels into, unless you are using wallboard clips.

Check the alignment of the ceiling joists to be sure they form a smooth, flat plane. If they do not, and you have access above them, install a strongback—a 2 by 8 laid on edge across the tops of the joists, with all the joists toenailed up into it. Push the low joists against the strongback before nailing them. Correct crooked joists with solid blocking nailed between joists at several points. Make sure nailers are at the tops of walls that run parallel to the joists.

Plan the layout for each room before you begin work on it. Aim for a minimum number of joints. Decide whether wall panels should be installed vertically or horizontally and where joints should go.

If you are installing wallboard over existing plaster walls, first remove all door and window casings, picture moldings, corner moldings, and baseboards. Then remove any bulges in the plaster. If there are holes in the plaster at any of the studs or ceiling joists, nail in some wood shims to provide a continuous backing along the length of the stud or joist. You do not have to shim holes between the framing members. Next, remove the cover plates from all electrical outlets and switches, unscrew each outlet from the electrical box, and pull it out enough so that it can be fed through the hole you will need to cut in the new wallboard panel. Be sure to turn off the power first.

Types of Wallboard

Wallboard is a manufactured panel made of gypsum or similar material that is sandwiched between two layers of heavy paper. One side is smoother than the other, and the two long edges are beveled slightly to create a recessed cavity when two panels butt together. This cavity makes it possible to cover the joint with a special tape and layers of taping compound. When done properly, the result is a smooth, flush wall with no visible joints.

The three types of panels are: regular, fire resistant, and moisture resistant. Building codes specify where fire-resistant and moisture-resistant panels must go. Typically, fire-resistant panels must be used in residences for common walls between the garage and living space, for enclosed closets under stairs, and in closets containing gas water heaters. Moisture-resistant panels must be used behind bathtubs, sinks, and similar moisture-producing areas; they provide a good backing for tile in these locations. Moisture-resistant panels require the use of a special joint compound and a sealant for coating all cut edges.

Most walls and ceilings are covered with $\frac{1}{2}$-inch-thick panels. Thinner panels, either $\frac{1}{4}$ inch or $\frac{3}{8}$ inch thick, are used to cover existing plaster walls or for special applications such as round corners. Panels $\frac{5}{8}$ inch thick are also sold; they are used for wider stud spacings, fire resistance, or a more solid wall.

All panels are 4 feet wide. Most are 8 feet long, but the commonly used $\frac{1}{2}$-inch-thick panels are also available in 9-, 10-, and 12-foot lengths.

Installing Ceiling Panels

Always install ceiling panels first. They can be either perpendicular to or parallel to the joists. Try to avoid joints at the ends of panels. Use long panels that span wall to wall. If that is not possible, plan the layout so that the end joints are as far from the center of the room as possible.

If you are installing more than one or two panels, you should rent a wallboard jack to do the ceiling. This device cradles a full sheet of wallboard and raises or lowers it with a simple crank. It also has wheels so that you can position the wallboard easily as you raise each panel into place. With a jack, one person can install ceiling panels, although the work goes more smoothly when there are two or more people. If you are not using a jack, improvise a T-brace that is 1 inch longer than the height of the ceiling.

Begin by marking all the wall plates where joists cross over them, so that you will know where the joists are when you cover them up. Lift the first panel into place and attach it to the joists with 1¼-inch ring-shank wallboard nails or 1¼-

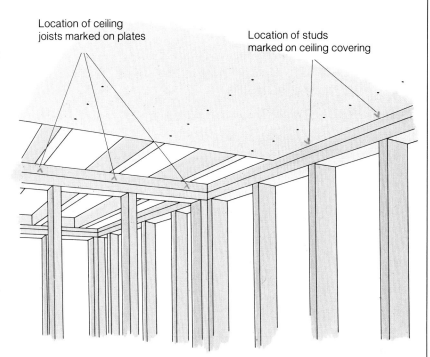

Location of ceiling joists marked on plates

Location of studs marked on ceiling covering

inch type W screws. Begin in the center and work outward.

Install the remaining panels, measuring and cutting them to fit. Stagger any end joints at least 16 inches. If you cut any panels full length, place the cut edge against the wall and leave a slight gap.

Installing Wall Panels

Wherever wiring or plumbing pass through studs, make sure they are protected by at least 1¼ inch of stud or a metal protector plate. Mark stud locations on the floor and ceiling.

If you are installing panels horizontally, place the top panel first so that it is snug against the ceiling. Then install the bottom panel so that it touches the top panel. Fill any space below the bottom panel, up to 2 inches, with strips of wallboard.

If the filler space is more than 2 inches, it is better to install panels vertically. Snug them up against the ceiling with a foot lever.

Attach wall panels with screws or nails that penetrate the studs ¾ inch. Cut panels carefully so that you do not have to force them into place.

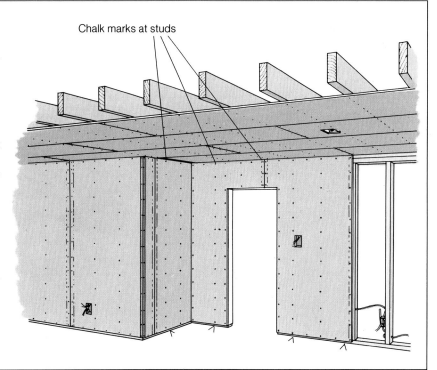

Chalk marks at studs

Cutting Techniques

Wallboard does not have to be cut for a perfect fit because the joints will be covered up. In fact, it is better to cut the wallboard slightly short so that a gap of ⅛ inch or so is between panels.

Cuts can be made with a knife or a saw. Use a utility knife for long, straight cuts, and have plenty of extra blades on hand for big jobs. Use a saw for the first leg of L-shaped cuts and for holes. The best kind of saw is a wallboard saw or a keyhole saw with coarse teeth. The sharp tip on this kind of saw makes it possible to start a cut in the middle of a panel by plunging the saw through the board without having to drill a hole first.

Cutting wallboard is a simple task. Most mistakes are due to errors in measuring, not cutting. To minimize such errors, make a simple sketch of the shape you need to cut. Then write in all the dimensions, measuring twice for each one. Be especially careful with ceiling pieces, because it is easy to reverse the dimensions when measuring something over your head and then writing it down on something in front of you.

Scribing

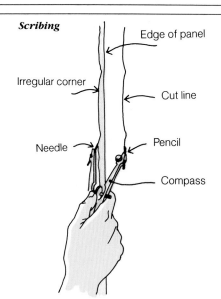

Edge of panel

Irregular corner

Cut line

Needle

Pencil

Compass

Scribing. Scribing is a technique for marking panels that must fit against an irregular surface, such as a brick fireplace or an old plaster wall. The technique is used more often with wood paneling than wallboard, because wallboard joints are usually covered. However, there are times when a perfect fit is desirable.

To scribe a panel, set it in place next to the irregular corner. Then adjust a compass or pair of dividers so that the wings are 2 or 3 inches apart. Draw it down the length of the joint, following the contour of the corner and holding the compass firmly enough to make a clear pencil mark. Cut the edge with a wallboard saw and dress it with a rasp.

Cutting Holes With a Wallboard Saw

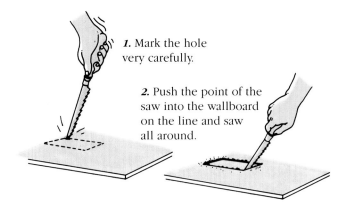

1. Mark the hole very carefully.

2. Push the point of the saw into the wallboard on the line and saw all around.

Straight Cuts

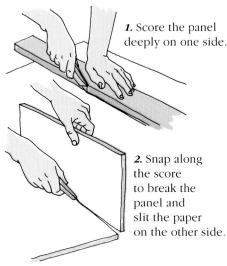

1. Score the panel deeply on one side.

2. Snap along the score to break the panel and slit the paper on the other side.

Cutting Holes with a Knife and Hammer

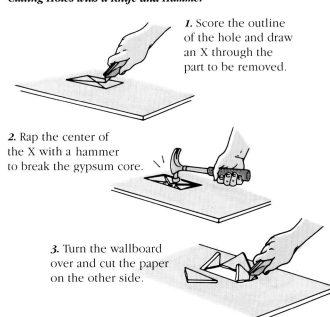

1. Score the outline of the hole and draw an X through the part to be removed.

2. Rap the center of the X with a hammer to break the gypsum core.

3. Turn the wallboard over and cut the paper on the other side.

L-Shaped Cuts

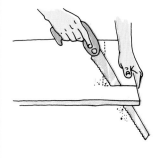

1. Cut the short leg of the L with a saw.

2. Cut the long leg with a knife, as you would a straight cut.

Attaching With Nails or Screws

Nails are the most convenient and familiar fasteners, but are subject to "nail pops" and rust stains if they are not specially treated. Screws are the strongest fasteners and can go in as quickly as nails, but are fairly expensive and require a "screw gun" or variable-speed drill with a Phillips-head bit. Screws are particularly effective for ceilings and for applying wallboard to a wall that has lath and plaster on the other side that could be jarred by hammering.

Nails. It is important to use the right kind of nail: The best type is ring shank (annular ring) specified for wallboard. Choose a length that will penetrate the framing at least ¾ inch. It is best to nail into framing that has had time to dry out and shrink somewhat. In new construction, try to close doors and windows and keep the area to be worked on at about 72° F for a week or two before nailing up the wallboard.

Nails should be placed 7 inches apart for ceiling panels and 8 inches apart for walls. An alternative pattern, called double-nailing, is to space nails 2 inches and 12 inches apart at one edge, then 12 inches and 2 inches apart at the next edge. This method reduces the possibility of nail pops, especially when nailing into green framing lumber.

Screws. Space 1¼-inch type W screws 12 inches apart on ceiling panels and up to 16 inches apart on wall panels.

Positioning Fasteners. Both nails and screws must be no closer than ⅜ inch to panel edges. If the head of a nail or screw breaks through the paper, place another nail or screw next to it. Embed all nail and screw heads far enough into the paper for compound to cover them.

If there are no nailers behind a corner, use a device called a drywall backup clip. This eliminates the need for extra studs or blocking.

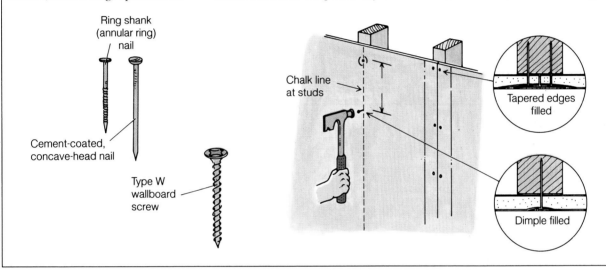

Ring shank (annular ring) nail

Cement-coated, concave-head nail

Type W wallboard screw

Chalk line at studs

Tapered edges filled

Dimple filled

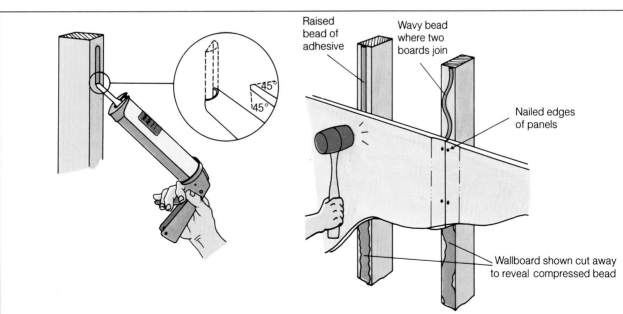

Raised bead of adhesive

Wavy bead where two boards join

Nailed edges of panels

Wallboard shown cut away to reveal compressed bead

Attaching With Glue

Adhesive also makes a strong wall, especially when combined with nails. It eliminates most of the nail holes that have to be covered with joint compound, and helps a wall absorb sound better. Adhesive is expensive but saves time. Cut the nozzle of the cartridge with two 45-degree cuts. Apply a bead of adhesive along each stud, one panel at a time. Then position the panel and press it firmly against the studs. Nail or screw the outer edges only. To ensure contact and to spread the adhesive, hold a 2 by 4 over each glue line and strike it with a hammer, or use a rubber mallet.

Taping and Filling Joints

Whether you nail, screw, or glue wallboard to the frame, you have to hide the joints and dimples. Vinyl-covered, predecorated wallboard may have a flap to cover the joint, but standard wallboard must be taped and filled, a process sometimes referred to as mudding. Even walls that will be covered with paneling or that are not important visually (such as garage walls) need one layer of tape and filler, called fire-taping.

To tape and fill joints, use three sizes of putty knives, usually 3- or 4-inch, 6-inch, and 10- or 12-inch sizes; an angled knife for corners; a tray for holding compound, a sanding block, sandpaper, wallboard tape, and joint compound. All-purpose compound is adequate for small jobs. For larger jobs, use bedding compound for the first coat and topping compound for the second and third coats. All types come either powdered or premixed in containers of up to 5 gallons. If you buy in large quantities, scoop a small amount into a tray and work from it, rather than from the bucket or box. Mix some water into the compound so it is the consistency of mayonnaise. Clean out your tray often; otherwise dust and dried-out compound will make it difficult to get a smooth surface.

1. Spread a layer of compound along the entire length of a joint.

2. Lay tape into wet compound and smooth with a 3- or 4-inch putty knife. Wetting the tape keeps it from binding.

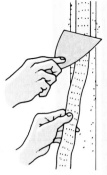

3. With a 4-inch knife, apply a thin layer of compound. Feather the edges carefully.

4. Fill and smooth all dimples with a layer of compound.

5. Let compound dry thoroughly, then sand. Or, moisten the compound with a wet sponge and smooth it with a 4-inch knife.

6. Apply a second coat. Smooth and feather with a 6-inch knife. Sand when dry. Apply a third coat and sand lightly when dry. (Two coats are sufficient under wallcoverings.)

Texturing

Texturing is done after joints are taped and filled. There are many ways to get a textured finish on wallboard, all of which require some skill. It is a good idea to experiment on scraps of wallboard before tackling a whole wall. Or, call in a professional.

First, mix compound to a consistency that will give the roughness or smoothness of texture desired. Then apply it randomly to the wallboard surface, using a sponge, roller, or trowel to get the right effect. If you want a rough, bumpy finish, leave it alone at this point or swirl patterns into it with a sponge. If you want a "knock-down" finish, drag a wide trowel over the wet compound to flatten the high spots and produce a uniform texture. Adding a small amount of sand to the compound before applying it helps to keep the trowel at the same distance from the wall.

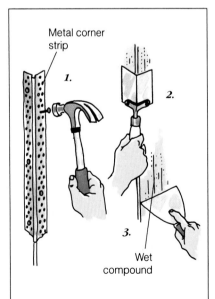

Metal corner strip

Wet compound

Outside Corners

1. Nail on a metal corner strip, making sure it fits smoothly and tightly.
2. Apply compound with a putty knife or a corner trowel.
3. Finish as for a taped joint.

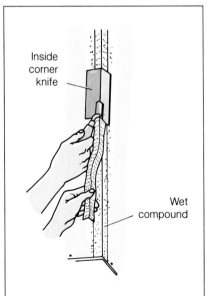

Inside corner knife

Wet compound

Inside Corners

Fold the tape in half and press it into the wet compound. Apply one or more coats of compound. Let each coat dry and sand it lightly before applying the next coat.

Repairing Small Holes

Using Tape. Holes that are too large to spackle but no more than 2 or 3 inches across can be patched with wallboard tape and compound.

1. Use paper tape or fabric mesh tape to cover the hole.

2. Spread a layer of compound around the hole and press short pieces of tape into it, covering the hole. Smooth compound over the tape, oozing it into the hole as much as possible.

3. Feather the edges and let it dry. Then sand it smooth. If drying causes cracks or shrinkage, smooth another layer of compound over the patch, let it dry, and sand it.

Using Cardboard. An alternative method is to use a piece of cardboard cut slightly larger than the hole. Thread a knotted string through it, push the cardboard through the hole, and pull on the string to hold it in place. Next, apply fast-setting patching compound, pushing it so that it oozes around the edges of the cardboard and binds it in place. The compound should be about ¼ inch below the surface. In a few minutes, when the compound sets, cut the string and score the fresh compound so that another coat will adhere to it better. Finish the patch with a second coat of compound, smoothing or texturing it to match the surrounding wall surface.

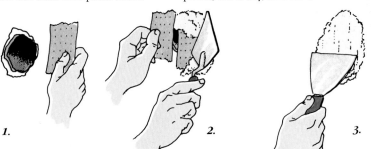

1.　　**2.**　　**3.**

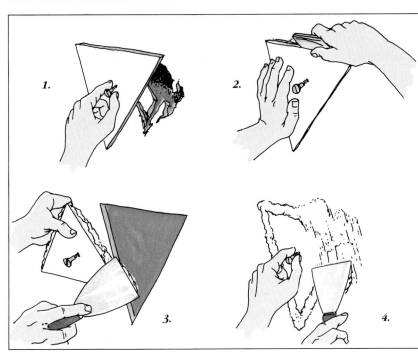

1.　　**2.**　　**3.**　　**4.**

Repairing Large Holes

Use a triangular plug for holes that are too large to span with tape but not large enough to require cutting the wallboard back to studs.

1. Cut a patch, beveling the edges toward the back side of the piece. Then trace the outline of the patch around the hole and cut the wallboard to match. Be sure to bevel these edges also, so that the patch will nest into the opening but not fall through.

2. Use a large wood screw as a temporary handle.

3. After spreading compound around the edges, push the patch into the hole until it is recessed about ¹⁄₁₆ inch, and smooth out the compound.

4. After the compound dries, tape and finish the patch so that it matches the surrounding wall.

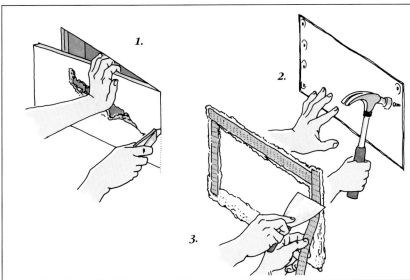

1.　　**2.**　　**3.**

Patching Very Large Holes

Holes that span most of a stud cavity, usually 14 or 15 inches wide, are best patched by removing a rectangle back to the centers of the studs.

1. Use a saw or utility knife to make the horizontal cuts (be careful in case there is wiring behind the wall) and a knife to cut the sides. If the hole is close to the floor, cut the rectangle all the way to the floor to eliminate taping the bottom joint.

2. Measure the hole and cut a new piece of wallboard to fit. Nail it to the studs.

3. Tape and fill the joints. When dry, sand and texture the patch so that it matches the surrounding wall.

WALLCOVERINGS

Wallcovering may add the crowning touch to any room. It adds richness and interest whether the pattern is subtle, dramatic, traditional, or contemporary. Applying a wallcovering is easy; the most difficult aspect may be choosing from among the thousands of patterns, colors, and styles.

First consider the design requirements. Is the character of the room formal or informal, contemporary or period, subdued or forceful? What style are the furnishings? Do you al-

ready have wallcoverings in other rooms? If so, do you want to keep the same mood or colorings? Do you want to cover all four walls or only one, as an accent?

Also consider the condition of the room. Are the walls bumpy? Are the corners or ceiling lines irregular? If so, stay away from stripes, straight-line patterns, and shiny materials such as foil. Are you stuck with floor-coverings or other permanent features that you can't change? Choose a

design that includes some of the same colors as well as another color that will provide the basis for a new complementary scheme.

Recommended Cross-References
Paint, Paneling, Wallboard.

Coordinating wallcovering, fabric, and paint results in a soft, tailored look. Drapes and wallcovering in a two-tone, small-scale pattern harmonize with the window shade that is made in a companion fabric.

Types of Wallcovering

Commonly available wallcoverings are machine-printed in widths ranging from 18 inches to 27 inches. Most are pretrimmed and many are prepasted. As a general rule, the more colors used to print the material, the higher the price.

Vinyl wallcoverings are the most durable. They are resistant to stains and dirt and can be scrubbed if necessary. The best vinyl coverings are entirely vinyl rather than vinyl-coated paper. Both types tend to stretch when stressed, but will not tear. Because they are not porous, mildew can develop in the underlying paste, but fungus-resistant adhesives will help prevent this.

In addition to vinyl, wallcoverings may be foil, cloth, and cork veneers. They can be flocked, embossed, or multistrip murals. Consult with your dealer about any special installation techniques or adhesives that are required for the covering you choose.

Estimating Needs

Always buy more than you think you'll need in case you make mistakes or in case you need extra for patches later on. If you don't buy enough, not only will you have to stop in the middle of the job, but you might find it difficult to get extra rolls from the same dye lot. As color differences can be quite noticeable, and as many dealers will let you return unused rolls, it is not worth skimping.

The easy way to figure your needs is to sketch your room, jot down all the dimensions, and take the sketch to a dealer. Let them make the estimate, based on the design that you choose. To make your own estimate, figure that most rolls cover 36 square feet. Assume coverage of 30 square feet to allow for damage and waste. European rolls are a little smaller—generally 28 square feet. Allow for 22 square feet per European roll. If you choose a pattern with a large repeat, allow for even less coverage.

To make your estimate, calculate the total wall and ceiling area that you want to cover. Divide the total area by the coverage provided by one roll. This will give you the number of single rolls (most wallcoverings are sold in double rolls).

Check your estimate against the table below, which shows total number of standard rolls needed for patterns with a short repeat.

Single Standard Rolls

Distance around room in feet	Single rolls for room with 8-foot walls	Single rolls for room with 10-foot walls	Single rolls for ceiling
36	9	11	3
40	10	13	4
44	11	14	4
48	12	15	5
52	13	16	6
56	14	17	6
60	15	19	7
64	16	20	8
68	17	21	9
72	18	22	10

Patching

Fixing a stained or damaged area is easy as long as you have some scraps from which to make a patch.

Cut a patch larger than the damaged area and adjust it to cover the damage and match the pattern. Tack the patch in place with masking tape. Using a metal straightedge and a utility knife or razor blade, cut through both layers of wallcovering. Remove the masking tape and the patch. Lift out the damaged section of wallcovering and clean the underlying wall area with a putty knife. Apply paste or glue to the patch and position it in the cutout. Smooth it into place, recheck the match, and sponge off excess paste.

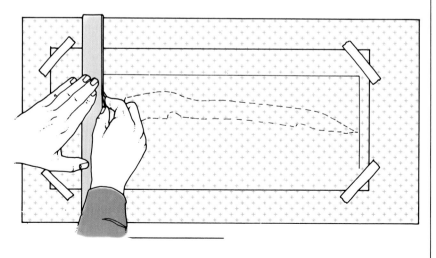

Preparing Walls

Preparing a wall or ceiling involves filling holes and cracks as you would to prepare for painting. There are, however, two considerations unique to wallcovering. First, the wall must be as smooth as possible; texture or roughness may show through. To smooth a rough wall you may have to remove existing paper or attach a special underlayment. The second requirement is that the wall must be sealed so that it neither draws too much moisture from the paste nor permits alkalis or corrosive elements to leach to the surface and discolor the wallcovering. Remember to paint the trim and ceiling before starting,

overlapping the area that will be covered by about ¼ inch.

Be careful if you are applying new covering over old covering. Go ahead only if the old covering is still sticking tightly to the walls. How can you tell? Listen while you run the tips of your fingers over the surface. If you hear a crackling noise, the covering is too loose—you should remove it. Another test is to flick the edges of a strip with a broad-bladed putty knife. If huge areas peel off easily, remove all the old covering. If not, scrape the covering back until you find an area offering resistance. Apply joint compound to the section of wall that you exposed and, when

the compound dries, sand it smooth. Glue the peeled covering back into position and do the same to isolated corners or small pieces that have come away from the wall. Remove wax or grease stains with trisodium phosphate (TSP) or other strong cleanser, and finish the entire wall with an oil-based enamel undercoat before you apply the new covering.

If the old covering is not sound enough to cover over, you have little choice but to remove it. Strippable wallcoverings are easy to remove from primed or unprimed surfaces. If the covering is not strippable, you will have to resort to steaming or some other method.

Removing Existing Wallcoverings

Strippable Coverings. Many modern wallcoverings are strippable; it is possible to pull off the surface layer, if not all, of the covering. To strip the wall, lift up a bottom corner with a scraper, then pull up and away from the wall. Remove all the covering, wash the walls with warm water, and scrape off the remaining glue with a broad knife. Rinse the walls with clear water and allow them to dry thoroughly.

Chemical Removers. Chemical removers, available from your wallcovering dealer, soak covering off the wall by dissolving the underlying paste. Removers may be sold as a ready-mixed solution or you may have to mix them with water. Be sure to follow the manufacturer's instructions about wearing gloves, safety glasses, or other protective clothing. After soaking the wallcovering with remover, use a broad knife to lift the covering away from the wall. Flush the walls with a TSP solution, rinse, and allow to dry before continuing.

Steamers. Rent a steamer from your dealer if you do not have a chemical remover or if you need to remove several layers of wallcovering. Lift the covering away as you steam, working a small section at a time. If the wallcovering is vinyl, it will lift more easily if you score it first.

Strippable Coverings

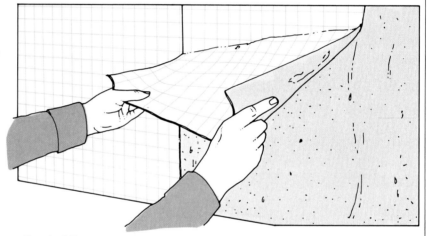

Chemical Removers

Steamers

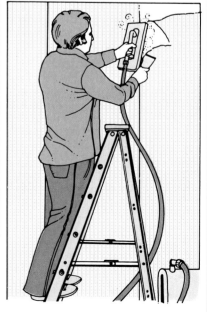

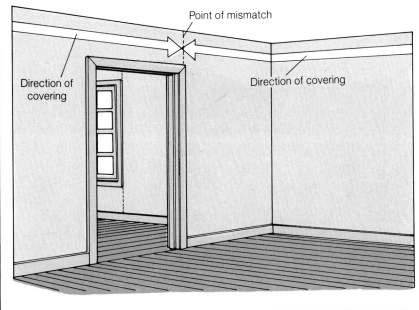

Point of mismatch

Direction of covering

Direction of covering

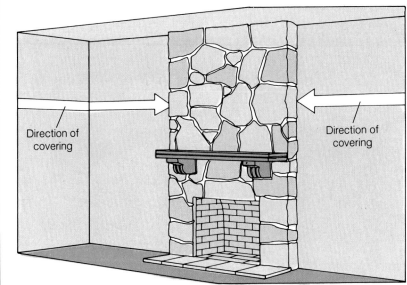

Direction of covering

Direction of covering

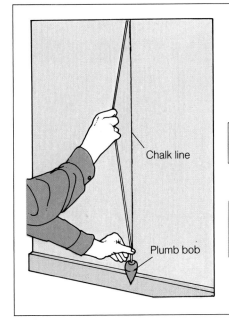

Chalk line

Plumb bob

Straightedge

Where to Start

Unless you are extraordinarily lucky, there's little likelihood that the area you want to cover is exactly divisible by the width of your wallcovering. Therefore, if you plan to cover all four walls, you will almost certainly wind up with a mismatch. Because of this, you should plan your hanging pattern so that full matching strips fall where they get the most attention—in the center of a wide space, for example.

If you think it is worth it, you can draw a line around the room and carefully mark where the edge of each strip will fall. However, if you have to lap a seam in order to stay plumb, this will throw off your layout. A simpler and easier method is to choose a point from which to start and finish where the mismatch will not be glaringly obvious.

One of the best places to start is down one side of a door frame. This way the join will occur above the door—a not very noticeable spot.

Another inconspicuous place to start is where bookcases, fireplaces, or other features that will not be covered jut out into the room. If a bookcase or mantel extends from floor to ceiling, start on one side and finish on the other.

Laying Out Plumb Lines

Individual strips of wallcovering must be hung perfectly plumb. Even if the pattern is forgiving, crooked seams will look unsightly. Correct alignment is especially important for the first strip because this will affect all the subsequent strips. (Being off by a little on the first strip can become several inches by the end.) To get the first strip plumb, snap a chalk line or use a straightedge, a level, and a pencil. (You can improvise a chalk line by tying a weight to a string, hanging it from a pushpin near the ceiling, and rubbing chalk along the string.) Your chalk line should be about ¼ inch away from the edge of your first strip so you can see it when you place the strip.

Pasting Wallcovering

Set up a work surface that is about 6 feet long, prepare the paste and let it sit according to the directions on the package. When pasting, work with one strip at a time. Cut a length from the roll equivalent to the length to be covered plus a couple of inches. Place the length pattern down on the table and clamp the top. Using a paste brush or thick-nap roller, apply paste to the strip. Spread it evenly, holding the covering down with your free hand. Work the roller or brush out toward the edges. Use a damp sponge to wipe up excess paste. When you've finished the top half, fold the strip back against itself until the end is at the middle of the strip. Turn the strip, clamp the unpasted end, and paste the other half.

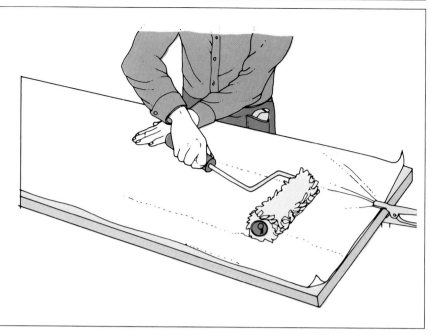

Booking and Curing Coverings

When you've finished pasting the strip, unclamp and lightly fold the second half so the ends meet—but do not overlap—near the middle. Align the edges, but do not crease the folds. This folding process, called booking, helps spread paste evenly and reduces water evaporation while the paper cures. Curing takes about 10 minutes and allows the paper to soften and expand. If the covering has a selvage, trim it off while the paper is booked, using a straightedge and a razor knife. Use a fresh blade every time.

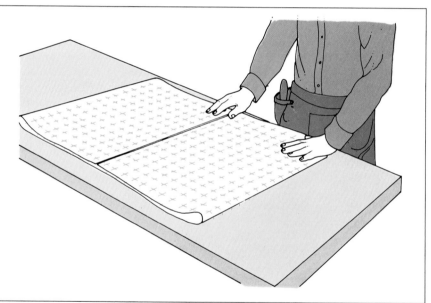

Using a Water Box

Prepasted coverings require moistening, which can be done in a plastic or metal trough. Fill the trough halfway with lukewarm water, then place it on the floor in line with the area to be covered. When you measure out covering from the roll, always add 2 inches of excess at the top as well as at the bottom of a strip. Cut a strip and reroll it, from bottom to top. Immerse it, soaking according to the manufacturer's directions, and pull it out from the top.

Some professionals use paste even with prepasted coverings to guarantee long-term adhesion. To do this, mix 2 parts premixed vinyl adhesive with 1 part water.

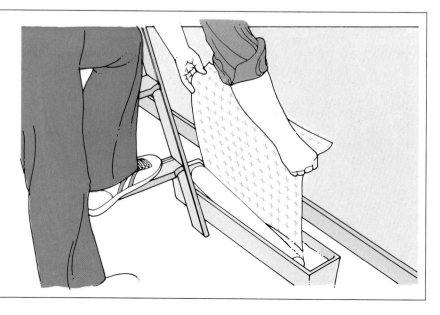

Hanging the First Strip

1. Standing on a stepladder, unfold the top section of your booked covering and gently push it against the top of the wall. Tack only the top section in place by wiping it lightly with a damp sponge or brush; do not smooth it flat. If the paper is flocked or embossed, pat it lightly with a folded cloth. Adjust the edge of the strip so it aligns with the plumb line.

2. Stroke the aligned strip flat against the top of the wall with your smoothing brush. Then smooth the covering with downward strokes, working from the center outward in both directions. Smooth out all wrinkles.

When you reach the center of the strip, release the fold and slide the strip into position.

3. Recheck the alignment and make any necessary adjustments. Smooth the remainder of the strip with your brush, working out from the center.

4. After you have brushed the strip smooth, go over it with a damp sponge to remove flecks of paste and to force out air bubbles trapped beneath the paper. Work from the center to the edges, being as neat as you can. Wait until the second strip is hung before you trim the top and bottom edges of the first strip.

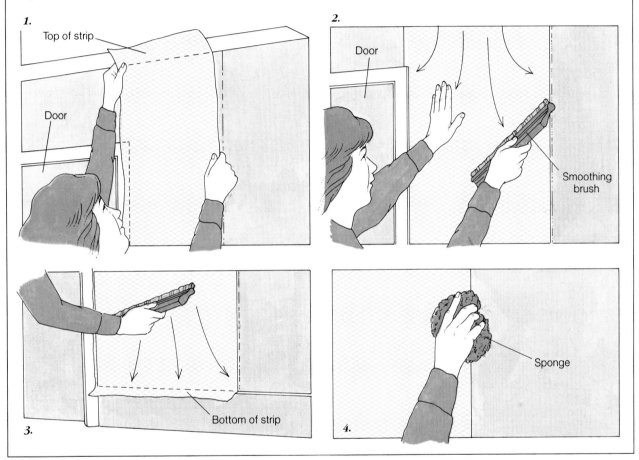

1. Top of strip / Door

2. Door / Smoothing brush

3. Bottom of strip

4. Sponge

Trimming the Edges

To trim the strips use a 6-inch broad knife as a guide and make the cuts with a razor knife. Hold the razor knife in your right hand (unless you are left-handed), and the broad knife in your other hand. Pressing the broad knife flat against the wall and into the corner, pull the razor knife along the edge of the broad knife. Then, without lifting the razor knife from its cut, leapfrog the broad knife to the next position. Continue leapfrogging until you complete the cut. Remember to change blades after every long cut. Expect to use 30 to 40 blades per room. Changing blades is a lot cheaper and less frustrating than tearing wallcovering.

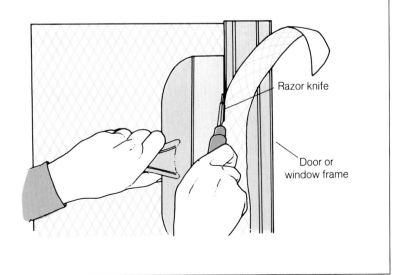

Razor knife

Door or window frame

Seams

Butting the Panels. Generally individual panels of wallcovering are joined with butt seams. To make a butt seam, slide the new strip tightly against the first until the edges form a tight ridge but do not overlap. Be sure the pattern matches, and don't stretch the paper.

Rolling the Seam. Flatten the seam with a seam roller. Use a cloth or sponge on flocked or raised coverings to prevent crushing the raised pattern. Press the roller lightly to avoid a glossy streak. Sponge away excess paste and air bubbles. Trim the top and bottom edges before or after rolling the seam. Use the broad knife and razor knife, and be sure to continue the cut from one strip to the next without interruption.

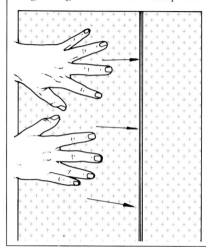
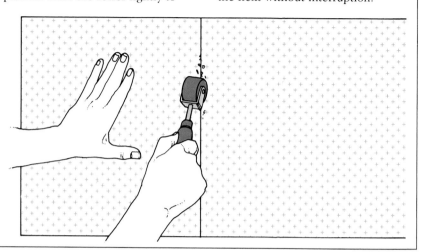

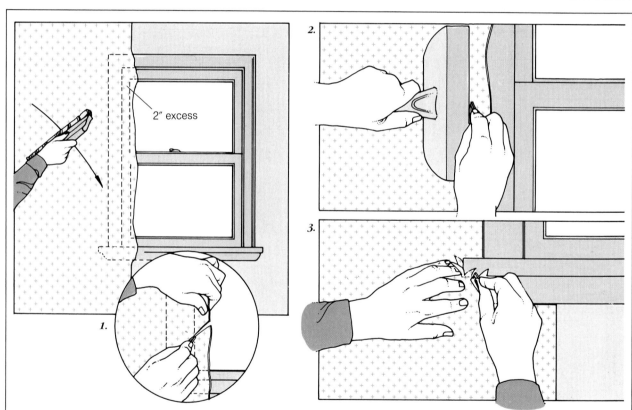

2" excess

1.

2.

3.

Trimming Around Windows

Fitting a wallcovering around any obstacle—a door, a cabinet, a built-in bookcase, or a window—is easiest when you trim after the covering is up rather than precutting the strip.

1. Hang a full strip letting it overlap the window frame. Smooth it so that it fits loosely onto all wall areas.

Cut away all but a few inches of any part that covers the window.

Then cut 45-degree diagonal slits at the top and bottom corners of the molding. Feel for the edge of the corner so you do not cut beyond it. This cut releases the covering so it lies flat against the wall.

2. Press the covering against the window molding with the smoothing brush. Use the broad knife and razor knife to trim away excess. Trim as close as possible to the window frame. On older, uneven frames, it is better to follow the irregular contours by hand.

3. Shape the covering around the rounded edge of the bottom sill by making a series of small cuts in the covering and pressing it tightly against the wall with your fingers. Trim flush to the molding. Cover the areas above and below the window making sure the pattern matches.

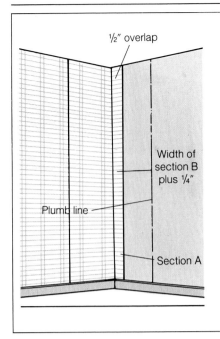

½" overlap

Width of section B plus ¼"

Plumb line

Section A

Covering an Inside Corner

Because corners are rarely plumb, take special care when covering around one. In most cases it's a bad idea to wrap a full width of wallcovering around a corner; you're likely to end up with wrinkled covering and an edge that is severely out of plumb. You can make a slit in the panel where it fits into the corner and overlap wherever necessary or you can cut corner panels lengthwise into strips A and B and hang the two strips separately. Follow these steps:

First, measure the distance between the last strip hung and the corner at both top and bottom. If you are working around an inside corner, add ½ inch to the wider dimension. Cut a strip of covering, strip A, to the sum dimension. If the remaining strip is wider than 6 inches use it to continue covering the wall beyond the corner. If it is narrower, continue with a new strip.

Apply paste and press strip A into the corner so it aligns with the previous strip. Smooth the ½-inch excess around the corner onto the next wall. Before you cut and hang the second strip, determine the width of section B and add ¼ inch. Measure the sum distance from the corner. At that point, snap a vertical chalk line on the wall. Align strip B between the corner and the new plumb line, producing an overlapping seam. There will be a slight mismatch unless the corner is perfectly plumb. Use an overlapping seam except with all-vinyl wallcoverings. On this type, make a double-cut seam.

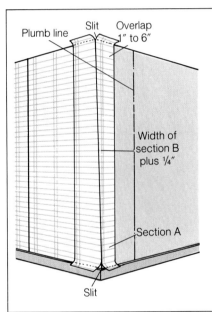

Plumb line   Slit   Overlap 1" to 6"

Width of section B plus ¼"

Section A

Slit

Covering an Outside Corner

Measure the distance from the last strip to the corner at both top and bottom. Add 1 inch to that distance; add 4 to 6 inches if the covering is particularly stiff—this is true of some vinyls and foils. Cut a strip of covering to the sum dimension, using a new razor blade and a straightedge to achieve a clean cut.

Paste and hang section A, smoothing it into place on the first wall. Use your razor knife to slit the excess at the top and bottom of the strip so you can bend it around the corner.

After you fold the covering around the corner, smooth it and trim the excess from top and bottom.

Measure section B. If it is narrower than 6 inches, use a strip of full width to cover the far side of the corner. Add ¼ inch to the width measurement of section B, then measure this distance from the corner. At that point snap a new plumb line. Hang section B so the edges lie ¼ inch from the plumb line. Double-cut the seam if the covering is all-vinyl as this type of covering does not adhere to itself.

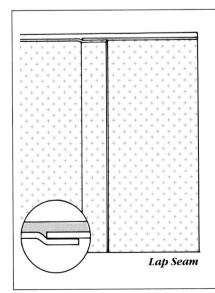

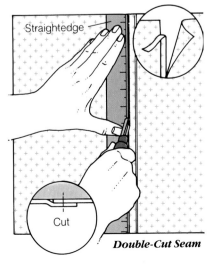

Straightedge

Cut

Lap Seam

Double-Cut Seam

Alternate Seams

A butt seam is unsuitable in corners and with all-vinyl wallcoverings.

Lap Seam. To do this alternative to the butt seam, simply overlap the first strip with the second. This produces a vertical mismatch, but prevents the gap that might appear later.

Double-Cut Seam. Use a double-cut seam for a vinyl wallcovering, which won't stick to itself. Overlap the two strips about ½ inch. Then, using the broad knife, cut through both layers. Lift up both edges, remove the waste, then flatten the seam with a roller. Never make a double cut over already papered walls—it may cause the old covering to lift.

WALLCOVERINGS: continued

Covering Around Obstructions

Around Beams. Position the wallcovering at the ceiling with the normal 2-inch excess and smooth it against the side of the beam or rafter. Make a

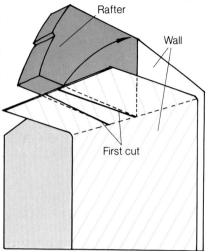

slit in the covering, cutting from the lowest edge to the top edge at a slight angle. Smooth the covering into place against the wall, but do not open the strip if it is booked. Slit

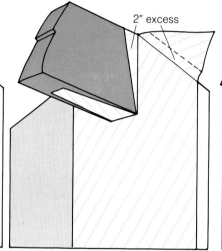

the covering at the other side of the beam (a mirror image of the previous cut). Smooth the entire panel into place, then trim off excess bits of wallcovering around the beam.

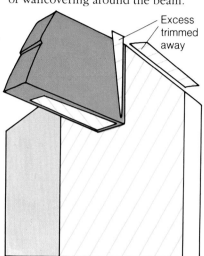

In and Around Arches.
Cover the area above and around the arch as you would any wall, allowing the strips to hang into the archway opening. When the full width of the arch has been covered, trim the excess so

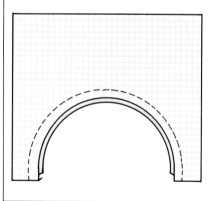

it overlaps the edge by 2 inches. Make small triangular snips all around the edge, spacing the snips more closely where the arch is sharpest. Turn the edge under, smoothing the "teeth" firmly against

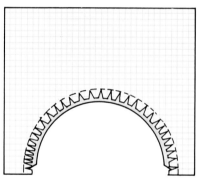

the inside of the arch. Using a new razor blade, trim them off to a length of 1/2 inch. Cut a strip of wallcovering slightly narrower than the width of the arch (to avoid peeling). Paste it into place, covering all of the teeth.

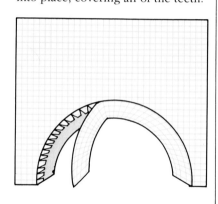

Covering Switch Plates

If the switch plates are too prominent against your new wallcovering, it is a simple job to cover them. First, remove the plate before covering the wall, covering right over the switch or outlet box. With a new razor blade, cut an X across the box, stopping about 1/4 inch from the corners. Cut off the flaps to make a hole slightly smaller than the opening.

Choose a scrap of wallcovering that is large enough to cover the switch plate and match the pattern on the surrounding wall. Cut it slightly larger than the plate, fold it lightly over the top of the plate and

match the top edge to the covering on the surrounding wall. Slide the plate down 1/8 inch and fold the wallcovering cover around the bottom. (This 1/8-inch allows for the curve of the plate, which would produce an obvious mismatch.) Repeat this procedure to make side folds.

Place the covering face down and paste it. Center the cover plate inside the folded lines, cut away the corners, and wrap the plate, pressing firmly. When the plate is dry, cut X's for the switch and outlet openings, pasting the untrimmed flaps onto the back of the plate. Use a pin to punch through the screw holes.

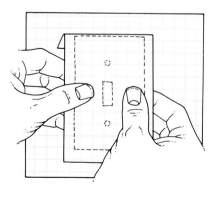

Recessed Windows

1. Try to plan your layout so that the first panel overlaps the window by the depth of the recess plus a couple of inches. Cut two triangles to fit the corners of the recess and paste them in position, as shown.

2. Smooth the first strip onto the wall next to, above, and below the window. Using your fingers, feel through the paper and locate the upper outside corner of the window opening. With a fresh razor blade, cut a 45-degree slit from the corner to the edge of the covering. Do the same at the bottom corner of the window opening. Tuck and smooth the wallcovering into the recess, pressing it firmly against the casing.

3. Hang the second panel as if you were covering a solid wall. Cut away the center portion, being careful that you leave enough to line the top and the bottom of the recess plus a couple of inches.

4. Smooth the strip into the recess and against the casing. (Hang as many strips as needed to reach the far side of the recess.) The third panel is a mirror image of the first.

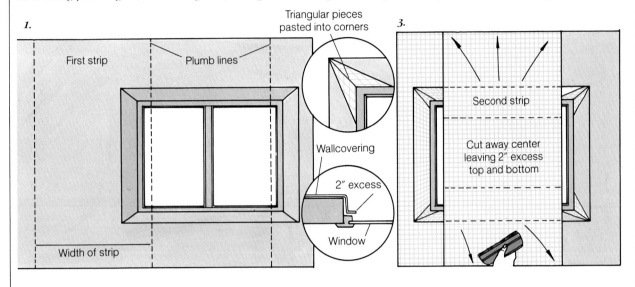

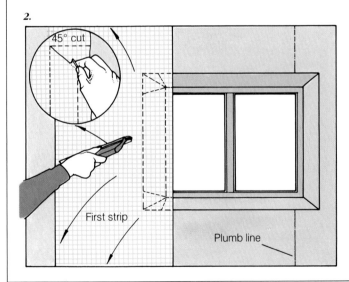

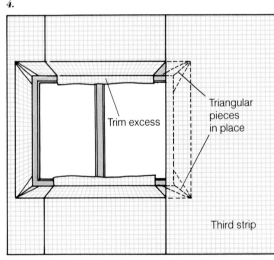

Ceilings

Covering most ceilings is as simple as covering an unobstructed wall and it is done in exactly the same way. Follow all the same steps regarding preparation, plumb lines, cutting, pasting, smoothing, and trimming.

There are two considerations that apply specifically to covering a ceiling. The first is a physical difficulty—you will be working above your head. Not only is this tiring, but it is hard to keep a tacked-down strip in place while you check the pattern match. To cover a ceiling, you will have to enlist the aid of a helper. This way, one person can hold the booked end of the panel against the ceiling with a T-brace or broomstick while the other person matches the pattern and positions it.

The second decision concerns the direction in which you should run the strips. Most important is how the pattern on the ceiling will relate to the walls. With a small-scale, all-over pattern the direction may not matter. But with a stripe, there will definitely be one way that looks better. Generally it is best to cover a ceiling with the fewest possible seams. Therefore, if the pattern looks good and the strips don't get so long that they are unmanageable, apply the strips with the seams running parallel to the longer walls.

WALLS

Walls define interior spaces. They also get in the way—if you have other plans, that is. Maybe there are lots of small rooms in your home and you would prefer fewer and larger. If your project involves altering walls, you will need to know some basic techniques for opening them up, removing them, or building new ones.

If you have always considered walls permanent and inviolate, as most people do, you may be apprehensive about tearing into a wall and changing it in any way—especially removing it altogether. It may encourage you to know that operations on walls require more common sense than technical skill, more finesse than brute strength, and more knowledge of fundamentals than answers for every situation that comes along.

Whenever you deal with an existing wall, there are two basic questions to ask: How will changing this wall affect the structure of the house? What's inside the wall?

Cutting a simple opening in a wall to install a medicine cabinet or a small pass-through will have no effect on the structure of the house as long as you do not cut into any studs. Cutting a large opening, such as a window or door, or removing a wall can have a major impact on the structure of the house if you are tampering with a bearing wall or a shear wall. Find out whether the wall is bearing or nonbearing before you start cutting through any framing, so that you can take proper precautions. You will also need to know if the wall has diagonal bracing or plywood sheathing for shear strength. If you interrupt the bracing, you have to replace it.

A wall always has studs and other framing inside. To locate where the studs are, use a magnetic stud finder or drive pilot nails near the baseboard until you hit a stud. Find the center of other studs by measuring 16 inches from the center of the stud you have located. Check your measurements with the stud finder or nails, since you cannot rely on regular stud spacings especially in older homes.

Recommended Cross-References
Attics, Closets, Doors, Framing, Wallboard, Windows.

Inside a Wall
Before opening up a wall or removing it, try to have some idea of what to expect. Although it is impossible to predict exactly what you'll find until you find it, try to find clues before starting work.

Look for electrical outlets, switches, and fixtures. It is not difficult to reroute wiring, but be prepared for the delay it will involve. Even if the wall has no visible outlets on either side, look in the attic or basement for wires that disappear into it.

Also look for plumbing pipes and heating ducts. Even though the wall does not have fixtures on it, check in the attic or basement to see if any lines run up through the wall. While these lines can be rerouted, they are not as easy to move as electrical wires and can be more complicated and expensive than you first imagined. It may, in fact, be easier to change your plans and leave the wall intact. A wall containing insulation is more of a nuisance than a complication.

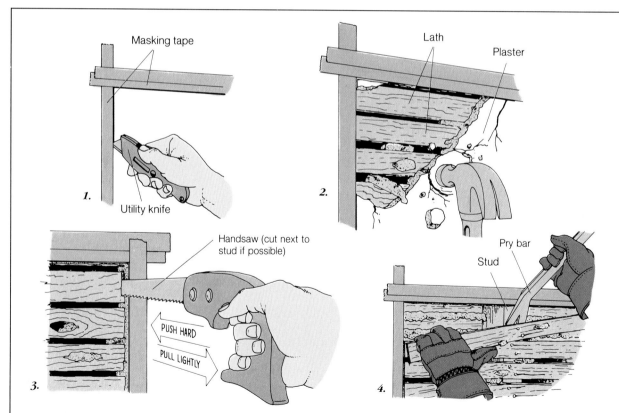

Cutting Into Lath and Plaster
Although wallboard has all but replaced the lath-and-plaster wall, if you are remodeling an older home, you may come across it. To cut an opening, follow these steps:

1. Put masking tape around the area to be cut and score with a knife.
2. Gently break up the plaster with a hammer and remove loose pieces.

3. Cut through each piece of lath with a sharp handsaw.
4. Pull off individual pieces of lath with a pry bar or claw hammer. Neaten the hole with a handsaw.

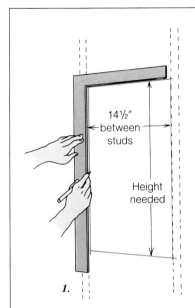

14½" between studs

Height needed

1.

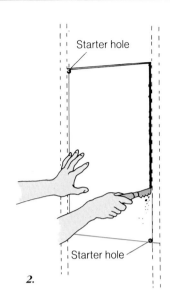

Starter hole

Starter hole

2.

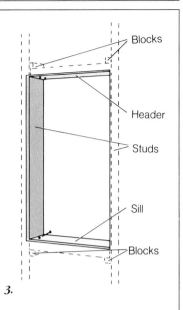

Blocks

Header

Studs

Sill

Blocks

3.

Cutting Into Wallboard

In order to install a small cabinet or an electrical outlet, you will have to cut into the wall.
1. Locate the studs and mark an out-

line for the cutout between them.
2. Use a wallboard saw to cut out the opening. Start it by drilling pilot holes or by plunging the point of the saw into the wallboard.

3. Nail small blocks or drive nails into the studs, against which you will hold the blocking. Cut blocking to fit between the studs, set it against the small blocks, and toenail it in place.

Recognizing Bearing Walls

In simplest terms, bearing walls hold up parts of the house and nonbearing walls merely enclose and divide interior spaces. All exterior walls should be considered bearing walls.

To determine whether or not an interior wall is a bearing wall, look for clues in the attic or basement. If ceiling joists run perpendicular to the wall, it is probably a bearing wall, especially if the joists are overlapped or spliced. If you can only inspect the wall from under the house, look for the main girders. Walls located directly over them are most likely bearing walls. Also, double joists probably support bearing walls. Posts and footings within the perimeter of the foundation usually support bearing walls as well.

Short sections of wall around a closet may be perpendicular to the joists, but are not necessarily bearing walls. If a central hallway runs the length of your house, only one wall is the bearing wall. Look in the attic to see where the ceiling joists overlap. Also look in the attic for strongbacks: beams or 2-by lumber set on edge to hold joists. Strongback ends bear on walls that actually run parallel to the joists, but that are bearing walls because they hold up the ends of the strongback.

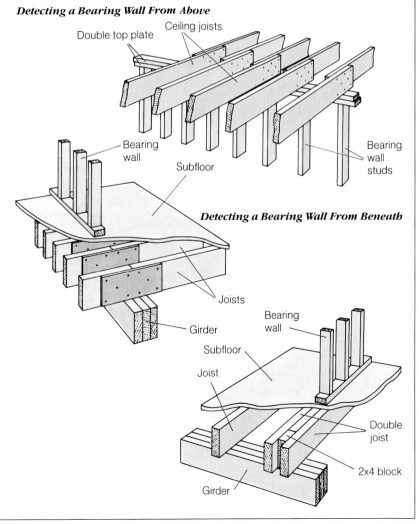

Detecting a Bearing Wall From Above

Double top plate

Ceiling joists

Bearing wall

Subfloor

Bearing wall studs

Detecting a Bearing Wall From Beneath

Joists

Girder

Bearing wall

Subfloor

Joist

Double joist

2x4 block

Girder

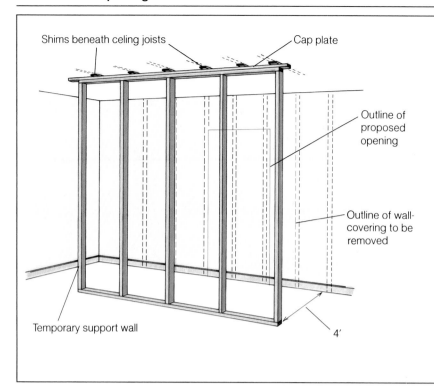

Shims beneath celing joists

Cap plate

Outline of proposed opening

Outline of wall-covering to be removed

Temporary support wall

4′

Opening Up Bearing Walls

If you are creating an opening for a door or window in a bearing wall that involves cutting more than one stud, you will need to support the ceiling temporarily until the new header is in place. Erect a stud wall that is 4 feet longer than the opening, with one top plate and a sole-plate. Lift the stud wall into place about 4 feet from the wall and slip a cap plate above it. Drive shims between the top plate and cap plate under every joist to snug the shoring into place. The cap plate will not mar the ceiling if it does not slip; if ceiling damage is a concern, allow a little extra room to put cushioning material between the cap plate and ceiling. If the bearing wall supports a particularly heavy load, such as two floors and a roof, erect shoring on both sides of the wall and provide support under the floor.

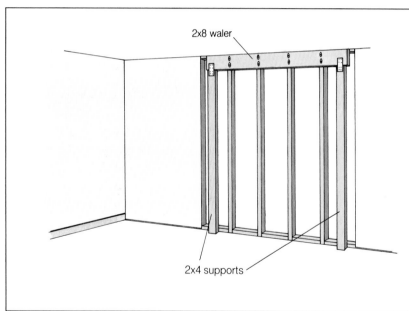

2x8 waler

2x4 supports

Shoring Balloon-Framed Walls

Remove the finish wall from the rough opening area. Tack a 2 by 8, called a waler, against the exposed studs so that it fits tightly against the ceiling and reaches completely across the planned opening. Drill holes through the waler at each stud, and tighten it in place with 3/8-inch by 4-inch lag screws. Support the waler with a 2 by 4 at each end, cut to fit snugly beneath it. Use metal connectors for extra strength. Now you are ready to cut the studs and install the permanent header. When you install new trimmer studs for the header, you will have to remove the fire blocks between existing studs and extend the trimmers all the way down to the foundation.

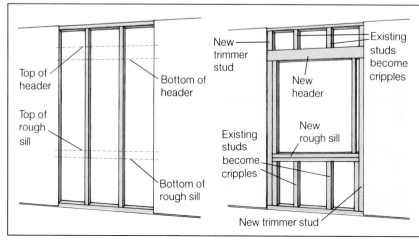

Top of header

Top of rough sill

Bottom of header

Bottom of rough sill

New trimmer stud

Existing studs become cripples

New header

New rough sill

Existing studs become cripples

New trimmer stud

Framing a Window Opening

Mark the rough dimensions of the window on the inside wall and cut away the finish wall back to the studs beyond the marks. Choose one of the exposed studs to be the king stud. Then mark the studs for the header and sill. Measure down from the header mark for the sill, allowing for sill material as well as the rough opening of the window. Cut away the studs and install a new header, trimmer studs, and sill.

Framing a Door Opening

Before cutting an interior wall, try to locate the hinge side of the door against an existing stud. When you have located a stud, snap a plumb chalk line along the inner edge of the stud. Now measure across the wall the width of the door unit, including the jambs. Find the closest stud beyond this point, and remove the finish wall between this stud and the hinge stud. Using a circular saw with a carbide blade to cut through nails, cut the finish wall back to the center of the studs. Wear goggles; there will be a great deal of dust. Making sure the hinge stud is plumb, nail an 82-inch trimmer stud to it. Measure for the width of the rough opening, and install new king and trimmer studs on the opposite side. Stabilize them with a horizontal block, install the header and cripple studs, and remove the soleplate.

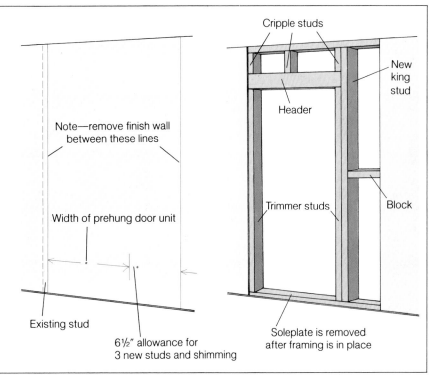

Note—remove finish wall between these lines

Width of prehung door unit

Existing stud

6½" allowance for 3 new studs and shimming

Cripple studs

New king stud

Header

Trimmer studs

Block

Soleplate is removed after framing is in place

Rerouting Utility Lines

Wiring. Before cutting into any wall, make sure the power to that area is shut off. If you are framing a fairly high window, the wires may be in the lower section of the wall where you will not be removing any studs. If you are framing a door or low window, you will have to reroute the wires over the header. Code forbids splicing wire inside walls or even in junction boxes that are not accessible to the outside. The easiest way to make the splices is to install an outlet on either side of the opening.

Plumbing. You can reroute plumbing pipes in much the same way as electrical wires. However, be absolutely certain that you are dealing with water pipes and not gas pipes. If you are not sure, call a professional. If you are sure it is a water pipe, shut off the water to that area. Cut the pipe and use elbow fittings to route it up and around the header area. You may also be able to run the pipe down into the basement or crawl space. Wherever wires or pipes are within 1¼ inches of the face of a stud, protect them with a metal plate.

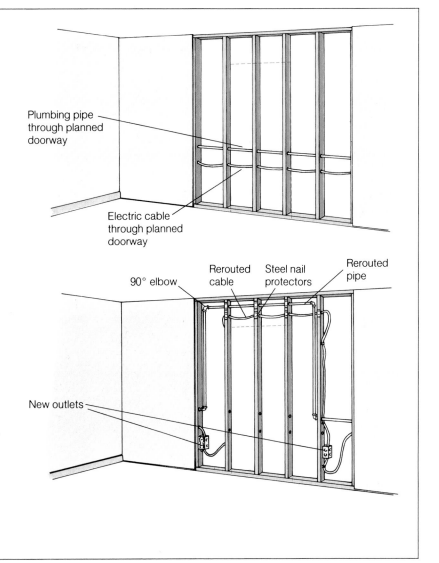

Plumbing pipe through planned doorway

Electric cable through planned doorway

90° elbow

Rerouted cable

Steel nail protectors

Rerouted pipe

New outlets

Removing Walls

Determine ahead of time whether or not the wall is a bearing wall. If it is, you will have to replace it with a beam or a strongback in the attic to support the weight it is holding. Whether it is bearing or nonbearing, you will have to take care of any wiring and plumbing lines, as well as determine whether there are any gas pipes in the wall that should be moved professionally.

Nonbearing Walls. If the wall is not a bearing wall, simply dismantle it and haul away the debris. Be sure all power to the area is shut off and that there are no gas lines in the wall. Remove trim pieces first, saving any that you can reuse. Then remove the finish wall material. If it is lath and plaster, knock down the plaster with a hammer and pull the lath away from the studs with a pry bar and a heavy claw hammer. Be sure to wear goggles, a respirator, and protective clothing. Also cover the floor with a heavy plastic sheet to make it easy to remove the debris. After clearing away all the finish wall material, re-route or remove any utility lines. Then remove the framing.

Bearing Walls. The first step is to remove the finish wall material and reroute any electrical or plumbing lines. Then erect temporary shoring to hold up the overhead ceiling or floor joists, setting it 2 or 3 feet out from the wall. Put shoring on both sides of the wall if it supports a floor, especially if the floor joists are lapped over the wall. The shoring should run the length of the wall and be supported underneath the floor with temporary posts if the floor feels at all springy. With shoring in place, remove the wall framing. Leave the cap plate in place if you are installing a beam under it that will have enough headroom below. You need at least 7 feet.

Size the beam according to the load and the span. It can be solid 4-by lumber or a built-up beam using three thicknesses of 2-by lumber. There are several ways to support the beam. One way is to cut away the wallcovering at each end and install posts inside the walls. Another way is to leave the posts on the outside of the wall, which saves having to open up the walls but leaves the posts exposed. Or you can leave short sections of the original bearing wall at each end and use them to support the new beam. Finally, if you can get a beam into the attic, you can use it as a strongback to support the ceiling joists from above. Support the ends by posts, just as for a regular beam.

End stud

Remove wallcovering back to the nearest stud

Backsaw

Stud

Toenails

Soleplate

Cat's paw

Soleplate

Wrecking bar

Removing Framing

If the studs are toenailed into the soleplate, you may be able to preserve them by pulling out the nails with a cat's paw or other pulling device. If they are not toenailed, the easiest way to remove them is to saw through them close to the bottom in order to save the longest lengths possible. Angle the saw cut slightly so that the stud can be pushed aside easily and pulled downward from the top plate. You can also cut the nails with a reciprocating saw fitted with a bimetal blade.

After the studs are removed, saw through the soleplate at both ends. If the floor should not be scratched, use a short backsaw and work carefully. You can use a reciprocating saw to speed up the cutting. After you have cut the soleplate, cut the top plates in the same way.

Pry up the soleplate from the floor and remove it. Then remove the top plate and cap plate in the same way. If you leave the cap plate in place, cut off the exposed nails with a hacksaw or heavy nippers. Fill any cavities with material to match the surrounding area, or cover them with plywood that is flush with the adjacent surfaces, to be finished later.

Replacing a Bearing Wall With a Beam

1. Erect a temporary stud wall to shore the ceiling or floor joists supported by the bearing wall. The stud wall should run the full length of the bearing wall and be on both sides if it supports a floor.

2. Remove the bearing wall. Then remove the finish wall and ceiling in the adjacent area. Take out the corner stud assembly at each end of the bearing wall in order to make room for new posts.

3. Install the beam. Notch it at both ends to fit around the top plate. Allow 7 feet of headroom under the beam. Set one end in place first and shove the post up under it. Then set the other end in place and position the top of the post under it. Use a sledgehammer to tap the bottom of the post into place.

4. The posts should have support under the floor all the way to the foundation or to new footings and posts installed under them. Always attach the tops of the posts to the beam with toenails and metal straps. Cover the wall cavities. Finish the beam with stain or a sealer or cover it with wallboard and paint.

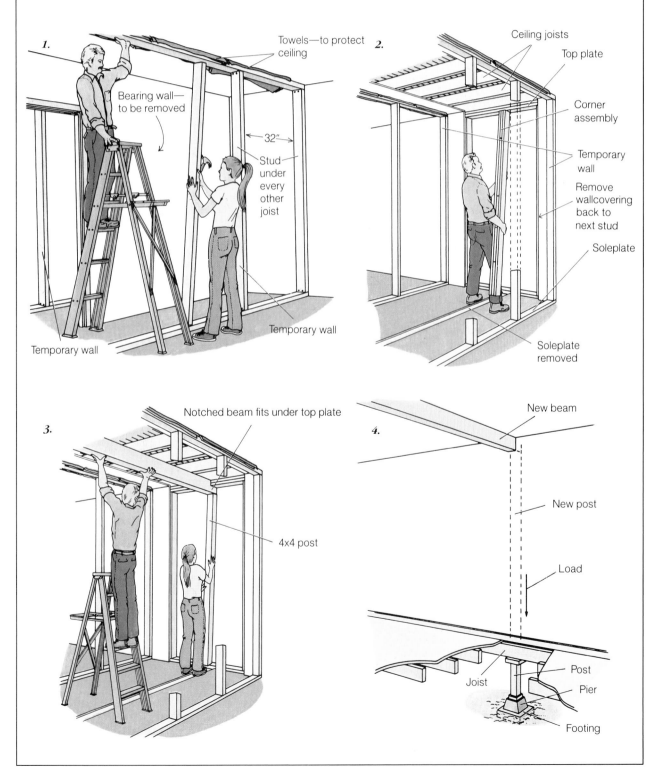

1. Towels—to protect ceiling
Bearing wall—to be removed
32"
Stud under every other joist
Temporary wall
Temporary wall

2. Ceiling joists
Top plate
Corner assembly
Temporary wall
Remove wallcovering back to next stud
Soleplate
Soleplate removed

3. Notched beam fits under top plate
4x4 post

4. New beam
New post
Load
Joist
Post
Pier
Footing

Building Partition Walls

To build interior partition walls, follow the same framing principles as for walls in new construction. The techniques for raising them are a bit different because the existing ceiling makes it impossible to tilt full-sized walls up into place. There are several methods for building an interior partition wall in an existing room, depending on how much space you have to work in and whether or not the new wall is a bearing wall. Always begin by stripping away the finish wall where the new wall intersects an existing wall, so that you can nail the new wall to an exposed stud or horizontal blocking set in place.

Erecting a Bearing Wall. If the new wall is a bearing wall, it should have a double top plate. Start by stripping away enough of the finish ceiling for a channel in which to set the new cap plate. Set a 2 by 4 cap plate in the channel and nail it to each joist with two 16d nails. Lay out and make marks for the stud spacings along one edge of the cap plate.

Cut the soleplate and set it on the floor directly beneath the cap plate. Align it with a plumb bob. Measure for the top plate and cut it to length. Then set it on top of the soleplate so that you can measure for the studs.

Using a plumb bob, transfer the layout marks of the cap plate to the edge of the top plate below it. With a try square, scribe each mark onto the soleplate as well. Then measure the distance between the cap plate and top plate for each stud, keeping the top plate stacked directly on top of the soleplate.

Cut the studs to length. Number each one to keep them sorted out. Then set the top plate and soleplate far enough apart on the floor to nail the studs between them. Use two 16d nails for each end of the stud, facenailing through the plates. When the studs are in place, lift up the wall and slide it into place beneath the cap plate. Nail the soleplate to the floor and the top plate to the cap plate, making sure the wall is plumb.

Erecting a Nonbearing Stud Wall. Remove baseboards and ceiling moldings where the new wall intersects an existing wall, or chisel out a channel for it. Then remove the finish wall material so that the new wall framing can be attached directly to the framing in the old wall. If the new wall intersects at an existing stud, you can nail it to that. Otherwise, use existing fireblocking or nail horizontal blocking between the adjacent studs to provide attachment

for nailing. To attach a nonbearing wall, it is not necessary to strip away ceiling material unless you are replacing the ceiling anyway.

There are three methods for building a nonbearing wall. The first method is to cut the top plate and soleplate to length, stacking them on the floor where the wall will be located. Then lay out the stud locations and measure between them and the ceiling for each stud. Cut the studs to length and nail them only to the top plate. Tilt the wall up and slide the soleplate beneath the dangling studs. Attach the top plate to the ceiling and nail the soleplate to the floor. Then toenail all the studs to the soleplate, making sure each one is plumb.

A second method is to cut the studs ¼ inch short and assemble the entire wall on the floor. Then tilt it into place; the studs are short enough to clear the ceiling. Fill the space between the top plate and ceiling with shims.

The third method is to nail the top plate and soleplate in place. Then measure, cut, and toenail each individual stud. This method should be used if you do not have enough space to assemble the complete wall on the floor.

Erecting a Nonbearing Stud Wall

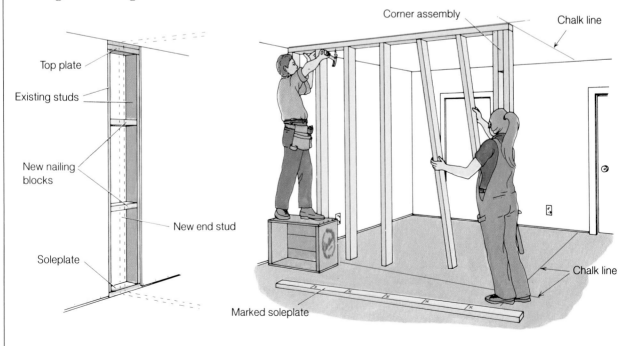

Top plate

Existing studs

New nailing blocks

New end stud

Soleplate

Corner assembly

Chalk line

Chalk line

Marked soleplate

Blocking With Finish Ceiling Removed

If the new wall runs parallel to existing joists and is located between them, you will have to provide a means for attaching it to the ceiling.

If you are removing the finish ceiling material, install blocking between the joists from below. Toenail the blocking into the two joists, high enough to attach a 1 by 6 board below it.

Nailing Board. The 1 by 6 board attached to the blocking will provide a nailing surface on both sides of the new wall for attaching wallboard to the ceiling later on. The bottom of the 1 by 6 should be flush with the bottoms of the joists.

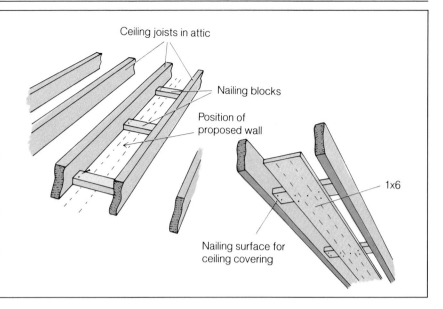

Ceiling joists in attic

Nailing blocks

Position of proposed wall

1x6

Nailing surface for ceiling covering

Blocking With Finish Ceiling in Place

If you are not removing the finish ceiling material, install blocking between the joists from above. This is possible only if there is access to an unfinished room above.

If there is no access to the ceiling joists from above, install blocking between the joists from below by removing small sections of the finish ceiling. Cut 3-inch-wide openings along the ceiling where they will be covered by the new wall. Then cut 2 by 4 blocks 1 inch shorter than the joist cavity. Insert the blocks through the openings, turn them perpendicular to the joists, and hold them in place by driving wallboard screws up through the ceiling material. Fill the screw heads. The new top plate will conceal the openings.

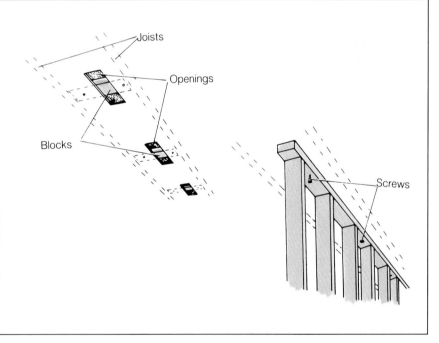

Joists

Openings

Blocks

Screws

Attaching a Wall With Toggle Bolts

If the new wall is short or is intersected by another new wall that is nailed firmly into joists because it runs perpendicular to them, you can use toggle bolts to attach it to the ceiling. First, remove the bolt from the toggle, place a large washer on it, and screw it back into the toggle. Then drill a hole through the top plate and ceiling, large enough to accept the toggle. Fold the toggle, insert it through the hole, and let it snap open above the ceiling. Finally, tighten the screw to pull the toggle against the upper surface of the finish ceiling.

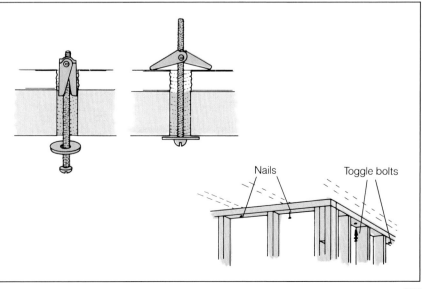

Nails

Toggle bolts

WASHBASINS

There are almost as many ways to describe a washbasin as there are types to choose from: these fixtures are often referred to as lavatories, vanities, or sinks. Some washbasins are one-piece units. They are mounted on the wall or they stand on a pedestal. On a wall-mounted sink, the plumbing lines will show, but access is convenient. With a pedestal type washbasin, the plumbing is hidden. Both types can be made of vitreous china, enameled cast iron, or enameled steel.

Other basins are mounted in a vanity. The countertop and basin can be molded in one unit, or the basin can drop into, or be mounted underneath a separate countertop that may be tile, marble, or laminated plastic. Flanges support flush-mounted and self-rimming basins.

Whatever style you choose, the plumbing is likely to be the same. In most cases, you will be able to connect the new basin without modifying the existing stub-outs. However, if you are prepared to relocate the plumbing, you will be able to include a larger or different type of washbasin. If you wish to install two basins in a vanity that presently has only one, you can usually install the two new washbasins on the existing stub-outs.

Choosing a Washbasin

When choosing a washbasin, first decide what type you want: freestanding pedestal, wall-mounted, set into a countertop, or a one-piece molded basin-countertop.

If you want to set a washbasin into a counter, you have three types from which to choose: self-rimming, flush mounted with a metal rim, and recessed. See the illustrations below.

The next decision is shape. Generally, washbasins are oval or round, but you can also get rectangular, triangular, and small corner units.

All of the above are available in a variety of sizes and colors.

Recommended Cross-References
Bathroom Layout, Countertops, Faucets & Valves, Plumbing, Sinks, Vanities.

Types of Washbasins

Type	Material	Comments
Wall-Mounted	Vitreous china Enameled cast iron Enameled pressed steel	Wall-mounted basins can be flush with the wall or have a ledge back. Plumbing lines show beneath this type of basin but the cost is relatively low, and the style might be just what you want. Install drain and faucet fittings before fixing basin to the wall. Supporting legs are rarely required.
Inset *Flush mount with metal rim*	Enameled cast iron Enameled pressed steel	Cost ranges from low to moderate. Aluminum rims are purchased separately. Frequently used with plastic laminate countertops.
Recessed	Vitreous china Hand-painted china Pottery Enameled cast iron Enameled pressed steel	This type of basin is installed from beneath the counter and is generally used with tile or marble countertops. It can, however, be used with plastic laminate tops as well. With tile tops, the basin is set on top of a plywood base, then tile is set over and around the basin edges.
Self-rim	Vitreous china Hand-painted china Enameled cast iron Enameled pressed steel	This type comes with its own rim, is easy to install, and offers a broad range of styles and sizes. Many of the larger and odd-shaped basins are self-rimming.
Molded	Cultured marble Vitreous china (small sizes only)	This basin comes molded with the countertop, and is made to fit on top of the vanity as one piece. Cultured marble varies in quality, look, and price. Comes with predrilled holes for fittings.
Pedestal	Vitreous china	These basins are regaining their popularity. Unlike wall-mounted basins, their plumbing is concealed in the pedestal. A variety of styles is available. Because there is no vanity, storage must be considered separately.

Washbasin Materials

Type	Comments
Vitreous china	Easy to clean; scratch and chip resistant; acid and stain resistant; vast array of colors; heavy.
Enameled cast iron	Easy to clean; scratch and chip resistant; many colors; very heavy; sturdier and more expensive than vitreous china.
Enameled pressed steel	Easy to clean; many colors and sizes; fairly durable; very light; low price.
Cultured marble	Many different brand names with varying degrees of quality; vast array of colors, patterns, and basin/countertop configurations; easy to clean; heavy; warmer to the touch than vitreous china, cast iron, or steel.
Hand-painted china	Not as resistant to chipping as other choices; different shapes and painted designs; can be expensive.
Pottery	More rugged than china but vulnerable to chipping; available in earth colors.

Washbasin Fittings

The two main types of washbasin fittings are spread-fit and center-fit. Styles vary considerably, and price depends on both style and material. The most common materials are polished or brushed chrome, brass, and gold. The least expensive are the polished chrome fittings.

Type		Comments
Spread-fit (8 inches)		Spread-fit faucet fittings have one spout and two handles, each independent of the others. Slightly more expensive than center-fit type.
Center-fit (4 inches)		Center-fit faucet fittings have one spout and two handles mounted together on a single plate.
Single control (4 inches)		Offered on center-fit models, a center control operates hot and cold and on and off.
Drain assembly		Most faucet-fitting sets can be purchased with or without a pop-up drain assembly. If without, the drain-hole ring and rubber stopper are purchased separately.

WASHBASINS: continued

Removing the Old Basin

Turn off the supply stops. Set a bucket under the P-trap, then disassemble the trap. Remove the supply tubes from the angle stops by loosening the slip nuts with a wrench that has flat jaws. Save the nuts. After disconnecting the plumbing, you should be able to lift a wall-mounted basin right off the bracket—in most cases, the weight of the sink holds it in place. The same is true of pedestal basins. Enlist the aid of a helper, if possible; the sink may be much heavier than you realize, especially if it is cast iron. Ask your helper to support the sink as you disconnect the pipes. If the wood behind the mounting bracket has rotted, the pipes will be carrying the weight of the basin, and disconnecting them may cause the sink to fall.

Installing a New Basin

1. Install the faucet and supply tubes before setting the basin in place. Be sure the basin has the arrangement of holes that your faucet requires. Most basins have three holes to receive a 4-inch center-set faucet. A faucet with separate handles usually needs 8 inches of space between the outside holes. Even if the faucet includes a sealing gasket, put plumber's putty around the base of the faucet before you set it in place. Under the basin, thread the washers and retaining nuts onto the faucet stems. Be careful not to crack or chip the basin when you tighten the fasteners. Connect the water supply tubes to the faucet.

2. Install the drain and tailpiece. Apply a bead of plumber's putty to the rim of the drain hole before you insert the fitting. Insert the drain post into the hole from the top of the basin and screw the tailpiece onto

it from below. Jam a block of wood into the drain fitting to hold it steady as you tighten. If you are installing a pop-up drain assembly, the tailpiece will be a tee. Tighten it so the side outlet aims toward the back.

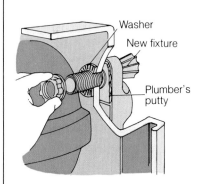

Washer
New fixture
Plumber's putty

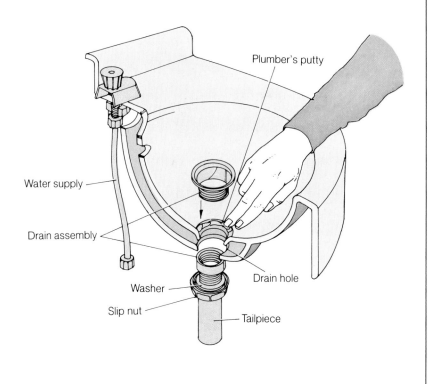

Plumber's putty
Water supply
Drain assembly
Drain hole
Washer
Slip nut
Tailpiece

3. If you are installing a countertop basin, run another bead of putty around the rim of the cutout. Set the basin into the cutout, supporting it from beneath if it is mounted with a separate rim. Use a level to align the basin. From underneath slide 6 to 12 mounting clips under the rim so they are evenly spaced, then tighten them. If the basin is self-rimming cast iron or if you purchased it as a basin-countertop unit, the weight of the basin and a bead of putty or caulk should hold it in place.

4. Hook up the plumbing under the sink. Place nuts and washers or ferrules on the supply tubes and bend the tubes gently to enable you to insert them into the outlets on top of the angle stops. Tighten the nuts onto the stops.

Install the linkage mechanism for the pop-up assembly, adjusting the height of the clevis (the fastening device) on the control rod so that the drain plug will rise far enough when you push down the plunger.

Attach the P-trap by inserting the drain section into the stub-out. Place an escutcheon around the stub and slide both washers and nuts onto the drainpipe. Do not tighten the nuts yet. Slide a nut and washer onto the tailpiece and install the P-trap. When all the pieces align, tighten them by hand, then use a flat-jawed wrench for the final quarter turn.

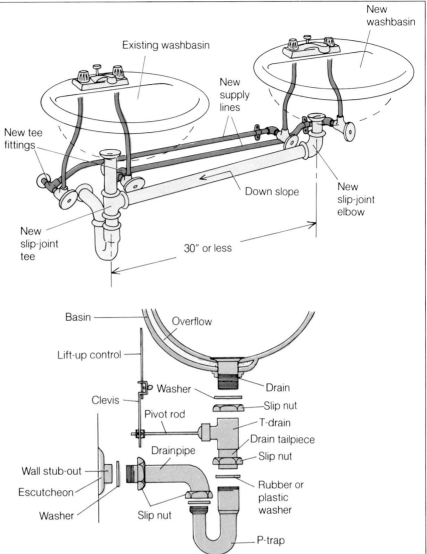

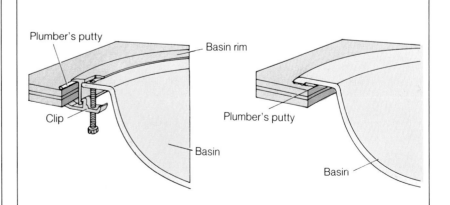

Angle Stops and Supply Tubes

Your angle stop and supply tube connect in one of three ways; be sure you have fittings of the right size and type before you begin. One type, a compression fitting, connects metal tubing. The nut squeezes a malleable brass ring around the tubing and into a beveled seat inside the outlet. Another connection, a slip joint, uses a rubber cone washer instead of a brass compression ring. The threading on the nut is different from the threading on a compression fitting, and the outlet has a larger seat. The third type of fitting is a simple nut and washer similar to the type of fitting that is found on a garden hose. The nut is permanently attached to a flexible plastic tube.

Installing a Second Washbasin

Some codes allow you to extend the plumbing from an existing washbasin to a second one. The second washbasin requires separate angle stops but the two of them can share the same P-trap. The distance between drain inlets must be 30 inches or less, and the drain extension must slope ¼ inch per foot.

WASHERS & DRYERS

Installing a new washer and dryer requires only basic plumbing and wiring skills. The difficult part is finding the space for the appliances.

When deciding on the location, weigh the benefits of convenience against the annoyance of noise and clutter. The ideal is a separate utility room close to the bedroom, but you may find space in a bathroom, hall-way, or the kitchen, as long as utility lines are close at hand.

Allow a space approximately 5½ feet wide for full-sized units. Use stacked units ranging between 24 to 30 inches wide for a small space.

Recommended Cross-References
Electrical System, Plumbing, Wiring.

Installing a Washing Machine

Plumbing for a clothes washer includes a 2-inch-diameter drain line and a hot and cold water supply. The standpipe for the drain should be 33 to 36 inches tall and have a trap in it between 8 and 16 inches above the floor. The drainpipe should be vented within 3 to 5 feet of the trap. (Local codes vary, so check with your building department.)

The supply stops should be 33 to 42 inches above the floor, and anywhere from 8 to 18 inches apart. Local codes may require air chambers or shock absorbers on the stops.

Prefabricated laundry boxes are available that include the hose bibbs and drain inlet in one tidy package that you simply recess into the wall. Some boxes also include 240-volt and 120-volt electrical receptacles. Just run the wiring and water lines to this box after it is in place, get them inspected, and then cover with wallboard or other finish material.

To hook up the washer, clamp the drain hose onto the outlet at the bottom of the machine and insert the J-bend into the standpipe. Then screw the hot- and cold-water hoses onto the washer inlets and onto the hose bibbs. Each hose should have a filtering screen where it attaches to the hose bibb, which you can clean periodically.

To complete the installation, plug the washer cord into a grounded 120-volt laundry receptacle. In some areas you may be required to have the washer and dryer (if gas) on separate circuits.

Repairing a Washing Machine

Machine Won't Fill Properly. Make sure the hose bibbs are turned on all the way. Also check the hoses to see if the filtering screens are clogged. If they are not, close the hose bibbs and unplug the machine. Locate the solenoid—the electric valve where the hoses connect to the machine. With the electricity off, disconnect the wires from the terminals. Check the solenoid with a continuity tester.

If the solenoid is working, check the water-temperature switch. It usually has three terminals: one ground, one for the wire to the cold-water solenoid, and one for the wire to the hot-water solenoid. Attach one probe of your continuity tester to the ground terminal. Turn the switch to "cold," and touch the second probe of the tester to the cold-water terminal. The tester should light up. Do the same for the hot-water side. This time your tester should not light. If the tester does not respond properly, replace the temperature switch.

The timer is the only other switch that might be causing the problem. This is very hard to test; call a professional.

Water Won't Shut Off. First, pull the power cord. If water continues to run into the machine, the problem is the mixing valve where the hoses are connected. Replace it.

If water stops flowing when you pull the cord, the problem may be the timer. Plug in the machine and advance the timer knob. If the water stops, the timer is bad and should be replaced. If not, the problem is most likely the water level switch. Call a professional.

Water Won't Drain. Unplug the machine and check the drain hose to see if it is clogged. Be careful; it will be full of water. If the hose is not clogged, plug the machine back in and turn the timer to "spin." If the machine still does not drain, turn it off and bail out all the water. Refill it, turn it on, and turn the timer to "spin." If it still does not drain, the problem is the water pump. Unplug the machine and bail out all the water. Take off the access panel and inspect the belt. If it is loose or missing, tighten or replace it. Otherwise, the water pump is probably damaged.

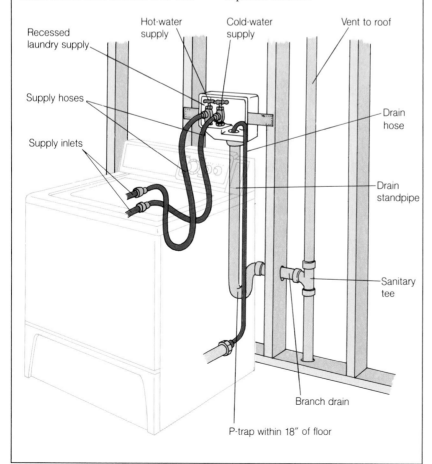

Recessed laundry supply

Hot-water supply

Cold-water supply

Vent to roof

Supply hoses

Supply inlets

Drain hose

Drain standpipe

Sanitary tee

Branch drain

P-trap within 18" of floor

Installing a Clothes Dryer

An electric dryer requires a dedicated 240-volt circuit that terminates in either a NEMA Type 10-30R receptacle (if the dryer has a cord and plug) or a junction box next to the dryer location (if it has a pigtail of flexible conduit). Try to place the outlet on the side of the dryer to make the hookup easy. Otherwise, place the receptacle behind and above the dryer so you can reach it.

To install an electric dryer, attach the power cord to the terminals behind the dryer, following the wiring diagram provided by the manufacturer. Attach the wires of the cord to the corresponding terminals in the dryer, and tighten the screw on the clamp that holds it in place. Next, connect the vent outlet to the wall duct with a length of flexible vent tubing. Make sure the circuit breaker is off, then plug the cord into the 240-volt receptacle. Slide the dryer into position. If the dryer uses gas, have a professional rough in a line

that terminates with a gas cock at the dryer location. The size of the line must be in accord with the BTU rating of the dryer and the length of the run. The run may contain left-right nipples, but it cannot have any unions. There should also be a drip nipple in the line directly under the shutoff cock for the dryer.

To hook up a gas dryer, use a flexible gas line at least 36 inches long. Use pipe-joint compound when you attach the line to the gas cock and the dryer, and use two wrenches to tighten the nuts. Then attach a length of 4-inch duct hose to the vent. Plug the electrical cord into the 120-volt laundry receptacle. Make sure the receptacle is properly grounded, or attach an isolated ground wire from the dryer to a metal cold-water pipe. Follow the manufacturer's instructions for bypassing the electric ignition long enough for air to clear out of the gas line. You will also need to adjust the air vent.

Repairing a Clothes Dryer

Whether they are powered by gas or electricity, all dryers operate in much the same way.

Smells of Gas. Close the gas shutoff valve immediately if you ever smell gas. Never smoke or light a match when working around a gas dryer.

Doesn't Dry Properly. The problem may lie in the fuel adjustment to the burner. This is usually located at the bottom of the dryer; pull out the bottom panel. On some models you may have to depress a release spring first.

With the dryer running, check the flame. If the flame has yellow tips, it is receiving too little air; if it is light blue and seems to be roaring, it is getting too much air. To adjust the burner, turn it off and let it cool. Loosen the thumb screw on the heating element and adjust the air vents. Turn them to one extreme and then the other, and then settle for the place that gives a steady blue flame with no roaring sound.

Dryer Won't Start. The rotating drum, even on a gas dryer, is powered by electricity, so make sure it is plugged in. Is the door completely closed? This is necessary to engage the door switch. This switch is a safety device that keeps the dryer from running. If this is not the problem, check the fuse or circuit breaker.

Drum Rotates, But No Heat. This can be caused by too much lint in the screen, a faulty thermostat, or by the pilot light having gone out. If the pilot light is out, follow instructions on the panel for relighting, and try again. If it goes out again, clean the orifices with a fine wire and slide paper between the contacts to clean the thermostat.

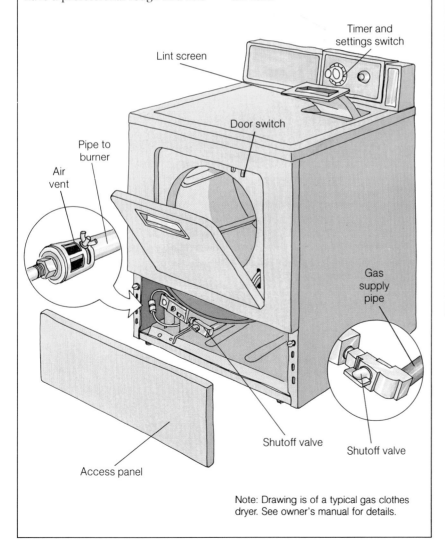

Note: Drawing is of a typical gas clothes dryer. See owner's manual for details.

WATER HEATERS

If your water heater is leaking, working erratically, or not working at all, you probably need to replace it. If it is more than 10 years old, replace it before serious problems develop.

Replace or Upgrade?

It is always easier to replace an old heater with one of the same kind. There may be reasons, however, for changing to a different size or type of water heater:

● *You may have an increased hot-water demand due to a room addition or a new washing machine.*

● *You may want to relocate the water heater when doing extensive remodeling. The new location may demand a different size or a change from electric to gas or vice versa.*

● *Your old heater may be in violation of codes and need to be changed in some way. For instance, a gas heater in a garage is usually required to be installed on a platform that is 18 inches above the floor. Gas heaters are usually not allowed under stairways or in bedrooms or bedroom closets.*

● *You may want to install a more energy-efficient water heater.*

The most likely candidate for more efficient water heating is a solar system, which many people are now installing. Solar heating requires favorable climatic conditions, but can take advantage of abundant free energy. Another energy saver is a heat-pump water heater. It operates by electricity, but uses only half as much as conventional electric heaters. Another option is a tankless water heater, which is very popular in Europe and Japan. Instead of heating water and storing it in a tank, it only heats water as it is needed. These alternatives are more expensive than ordinary gas and electric heaters, but may be worth it in the long run.

Recommended Cross-References
Gas, Insulation, Plumbing, Solar Energy, Wiring.

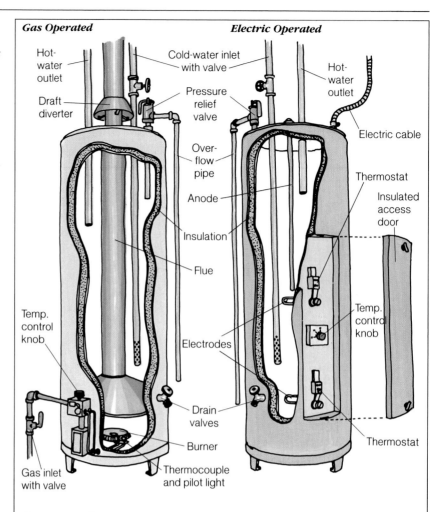

Gas Operated   **Electric Operated**

Hot-water outlet — Cold-water inlet with valve — Hot-water outlet — Draft diverter — Pressure relief valve — Overflow pipe — Electric cable — Anode — Thermostat — Insulation — Insulated access door — Flue — Temp. control knob — Temp. control knob — Electrodes — Drain valves — Burner — Thermostat — Gas inlet with valve — Thermocouple and pilot light

Anatomy of a Water Heater
These cutaway diagrams show the components of two standard water heaters. The one on the left is gas operated; the one on the right uses electricity. Positions of valves and temperature control knobs vary depending on the model.

Valves

Temperature Pressure Relief Valve. Be sure to install a temperature pressure relief valve (TPRV) in a water heater to prevent the tank from overheating. This valve must be connected to a drainpipe that terminates no more than 8 inches above the ground.

Unless you have had any indication of problems, the TPRV on the old tank can be reused on the new one as long as it fits. To check it, pull up or push down on the handle, depending on the style.

Drain Valve. The drain valve is located at the base of the water heater. It is a good idea to drain off sediment every few months.

Temperature Pressure Relief Valve

Drain Valve

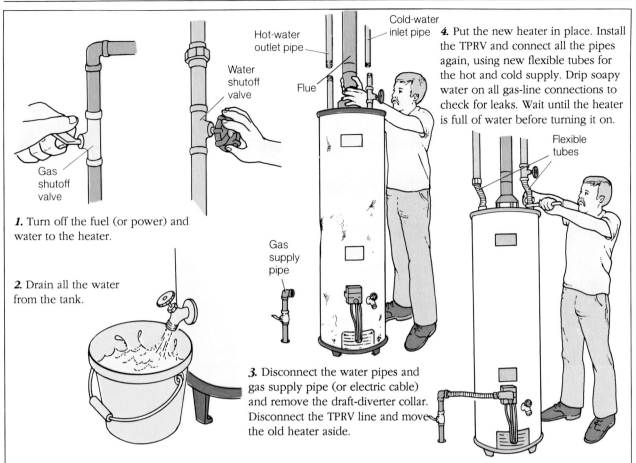

Hot-water outlet pipe

Cold-water inlet pipe

Water shutoff valve

Flue

Gas shutoff valve

Gas supply pipe

Flexible tubes

1. Turn off the fuel (or power) and water to the heater.

2. Drain all the water from the tank.

3. Disconnect the water pipes and gas supply pipe (or electric cable) and remove the draft-diverter collar. Disconnect the TPRV line and move the old heater aside.

4. Put the new heater in place. Install the TPRV and connect all the pipes again, using new flexible tubes for the hot and cold supply. Drip soapy water on all gas-line connections to check for leaks. Wait until the heater is full of water before turning it on.

Installing a New Water Heater
How to Shop for One. If you are buying a gas or electric heater, call around for prices. Markups for residential heaters are usually high. However, you must know exactly what kind of heater you want or you may end up comparing apples and oranges. These are the normal specifications for a heater, all of which you can get from the name plate of the old heater you are replacing:

- Gallon capacity (usually listed as 30, 40, or 50).
- BTU rating (for gas heaters).
- Voltage, amperage, and/or wattage rating (for electric).
- Recovery rate (generally, however many gallons per hour).
- Dimensions (especially height).

Installing a Water Heater Yourself. A handy homeowner is capable of installing most water heaters, but you might want to get some telephone quotes from professionals first. This way you will be better able to answer these questions:

- Do you have the time?
- Are you able to dump or get rid of the old heater?
- Do you have the specialized parts, fittings, and tools, or easy access to them if you are missing something and have to make a trip to the store?
- Will you be able to lift, carry, or drag both heaters?

Relocating a Water Heater
An electric heater will go almost anywhere as long as there is an adequate power source and a place for water to drain if it should leak.

Gas Water Heaters. Codes prohibit installing a gas water heater in a room that has normal home use and that is usually kept closed to outside air, such as a bathroom or interior laundry room. If it is located in a closet or other enclosed space, the space must be ventilated, usually with a vent opening at both the top and bottom of the space. Each opening must be 100 square inches, and twice as wide as it is high. Codes also prescribe clearances between a gas heater and combustible materials, usually 1 inch at the sides and back, 6 inches in front, and 18 inches on top. A gas heater in a garage must be raised 18 inches above the floor, and all gas heaters must have a flue to the outside.

Gas pipe must be fitted with an easily accessible shutoff valve and the heater must be connected to the pipe with a flexible connector that meets code requirements.

Plumbing. When planning the piping, remember that the cold-water-supply pipe to the water heater must be at least 3/4 inch, and it must have a shutoff valve in an easily accessible location near the heater. The pipe carrying water from the heater may be as small as 1/2 inch, but 3/4 inch is customary. Both the hot- and cold-water-supply pipes should have a flexible pipe or union fitting where they connect to the heater.

WEATHER STRIPPING

Caulk can seal most cracks that admit unwanted drafts, but you cannot seal the edges of doors and windows—they require weather stripping. Weather stripping is easy to install and may be one of the most cost-effective home improvements. Besides increasing the efficiency of your heating and cooling systems, weather stripping keeps out dirt, dust, noise, and moisture. It also absorbs some of the shock when you slam a window or door, keeps win-dows and doors from rattling in high winds, and cuts down on uncomfort-able drafts.

You don't need complicated meters or gauges in order to tell whether a window or door needs weather strip-ping. All you need do is to look for cracks that you can see through and feel for drafts when a breeze is blow-ing. Hang a piece of tissue paper from a coat hanger, and hold it at various places in front of the window or door, *watching for a telltale flutter. A light-ed candle also indicates drafts.*

Install weather stripping on all the offending doors and windows. Don't forget those doors that lead to en-closed but unheated spaces, such as the garage, porch, basement, or attic.

Recommended Cross-References
Caulking, Doors, Insulation, Thresholds, Windows.

Types of Weather Stripping

The type of weather stripping you choose depends on cost, durability, appearance, and installation. All are fairly easy to install, but some types last longer or are more attractive. Paying extra for a more permanent type may save money in the long run. Whatever type you choose, be sure you have the tacks, compatible brads, or other hardware you need. Many types are precoated with adhe-sive and do not require additional fasteners. Weather stripping is avail-able in many forms:

Felt. Inexpensive. Attaches with glue, nails, or staples. Door or window should press against it, not slide. Should not get wet. Cannot be paint-ed. Lasts for one to two years.

Reinforced Felt. Aluminum band holds and preserves felt. Use the same way as regular felt; it has the same limitations.

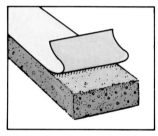

Foam Tape. Usually an adhesive ure-thane or vinyl strip. Lasts for one to two years. Adhesive may fail sooner. Temporary but quick solution.

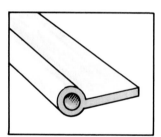

Tubular Gasket. Can withstand fric-tion. Window or door compresses tube to form a tight seal. It is visible, but can be painted. Some types stick on. Others need to be nailed.

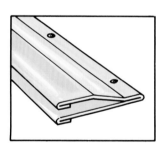

Tension Strip. The most durable, ef-fective weather stripping, although it does not bridge uneven gaps. Vinyl strips with adhesive backs come in various colors. Nail on metal strips.

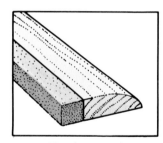

Rigid Strip. Wood or metal strips with a foam edge. Best for doorjambs; they do not withstand friction. Paint wood strips, but not foam ones. In-stall with nails.

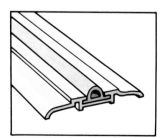

Gasket Threshold. Efficient, but traffic abrades gasket. Vinyl is replaceable. Doors require no new attachments.

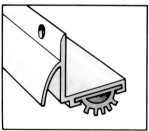

Door Shoe. Concealed from view. Need to remove door to install. Vinyl ones are replaceable. Requires solid threshold in wood or metal.

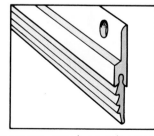

Door Sweep. Attach on side toward which door opens. Some automati-cally lift to clear carpet. Visible.

Preparation

Preparation means cleaning surfaces to which weather stripping will attach and ensuring that they are dry and sound. If necessary, prime and paint wood sashes or jambs. Double-hung windows present a unique problem: the channels on each side that contain the sash weights. Although weather stripping will seal cracks and remedy the loose fit of the sashes, the uninsulated channels will continue to allow significant heat loss. Solve this problem before you weather-strip by installing replacement channels—wood devices that fit on the sides of the window and hold the sashes in place with friction. They eliminate the need for the sash weights. Fill the empty channels with insulation.

If condensation continually forms on the inside of a storm window, weather-strip the window to prevent warm air from escaping. If condensation forms on the outside, weather-strip the storm window to keep cold air out.

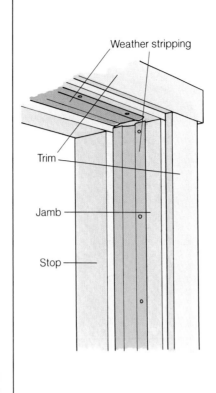

Weather-Stripping Doors

The most common ways to weather-strip doors are with material that fits between the door and the jamb (such as tension strips), between the door and doorstop (foam padding), or against the face of the stop (gasket material). Although the gasket type is very effective, it is quite conspicuous. Tension strips do not show, and are very durable. Foam padding lasts only a few seasons.

If a door hangs unevenly causing wide gaps, adjust the hinges. Tack up weather-stripping material, test the door to make sure it doesn't stick, then nail the weather stripping in place. You should also attach a strip behind the strike plate.

If you install tension strips, the open side of the V should be set against the doorstop. Attach the gasket type of weather stripping with the door closed. Push the material firmly against the door to seal all gaps, and fasten with tacks or small brads. With padded weather stripping choose a size that will compress enough to allow the door to close.

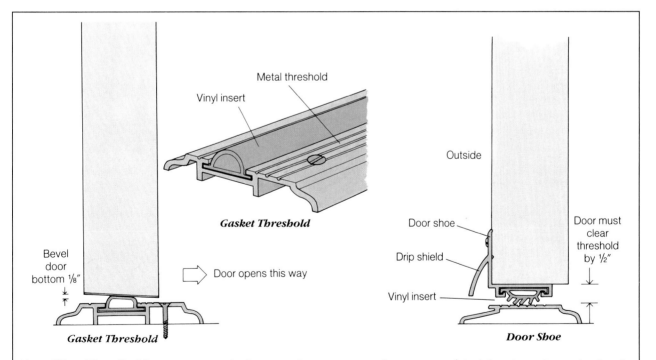

Installing Thresholds

Weather-stripping the bottom of the door is critical. A crack only ¼ inch wide can funnel tremendous drafts. There are three types of threshold weather stripping. The easiest but least effective is the door sweep: You just screw it to the door, near the bottom edge. Some types have retractable sweeps that raise automatically when the door opens.

Gasket thresholds or door shoes require removing and, most likely, trimming the door. Close the door and mark the top edge of the gasket. Scribe the cutting line, then make a ⅛-inch bevel cut. Screw the threshold into the floor so the door aligns over the center of the gasket.

To install a door shoe, close the door and scribe ½ inch above the threshold. Remove and trim the door. Cut the shoe to length and screw it to the bottom of the door.

Tension Strips

1. Measure strips to fit both side channels and the horizontal rails at the top, middle, and bottom. One strip is sufficient where the top and bottom sashes overlap.

2. Open the bottom sash completely. Attach a strip in each channel so it protrudes 2 inches above the bottom edge of the sash or cut it flush if the appearance is objectionable. The V should open toward the outside.

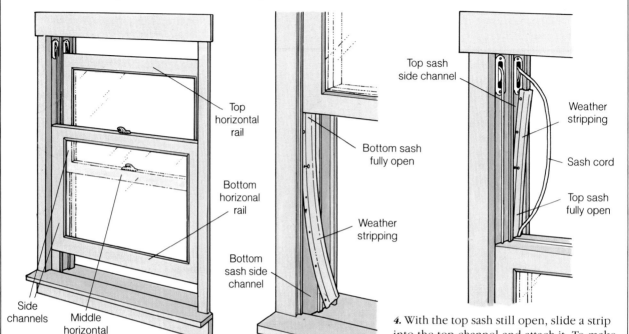

Top horizontal rail

Bottom horizontal rail

Bottom sash side channel

Side channels

Middle horizontal rail

Bottom sash fully open

Weather stripping

Top sash side channel

Weather stripping

Sash cord

Top sash fully open

3. Lower both sashes and place strips in the channels of the top sash. They should protrude 2 inches below the bottom edge of the top sash when it is closed. Do not cover the pulleys.

The weather stripping should tighten the fit of the sashes but they should still move freely. If the windows were already so snug that the weather stripping won't fit, install it only on the side that seems looser.

4. With the top sash still open, slide a strip into the top channel and attach it. To make it less noticeable, attach it to the top of the sash instead. You must cut the strip flush with the edges of the sash, so the corners will not seal. Do the same on the bottom of the lower sash.

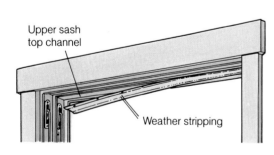

Upper sash top channel

Weather stripping

Weather stripping

Sill (outside)

Stool (inside)

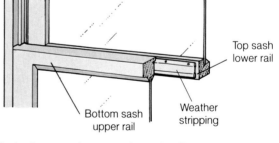

Top sash lower rail

Bottom sash upper rail

Weather stripping

5. Attach the last strip between the rails of both sashes where they overlap. The strip will be visible from the inside of the house when the window is open if you attach it to the bottom rail of the top sash; it will be visible from the outside when the window is open if you attach it to the top rail of the bottom sash.

6. Check the weather stripping for fit. Adjust metal strips simply by widening the V with a putty knife. Be sure the strip is snug and that all nails are tight.

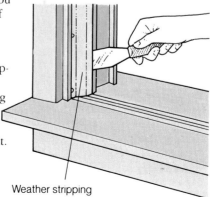

Weather stripping

Wood Sliding Windows

Seal a wood sliding window as if it were a double-hung window lying on a long side. Attach a tension strip or tubular gasket to the top channel. If only one side of the window opens, seal the fixed panel with caulk. Then attach strips to the end channels or to the sides of the sliding panels, whichever looks better. Where the two panels overlap, attach a tension strip between them. Or attach a tubular gasket to the edge of the outside panel so it presses against the inside panel when the window is closed.

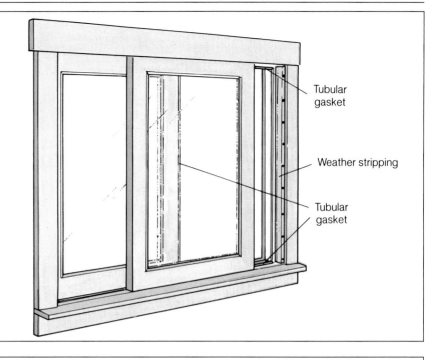

Tubular gasket

Weather stripping

Tubular gasket

Casement Windows

Wood. Attach a tension strip to the frame in a place where the window will cover it. Attach with the V opening toward the stop.

If you prefer, use a tubular gasket instead. Attach it to the stop so the window shuts against it. It creates a snug fit, but is highly visible.

Metal. Use a special vinyl gasket that is grooved down the middle. Fit the groove over the metal edge of the window frame. If necessary, attach with a rubber or vinyl glue.

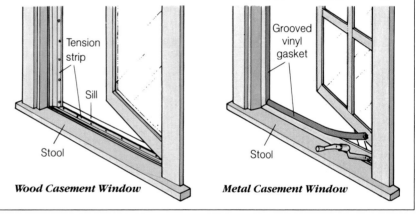

Tension strip

Sill

Stool

Wood Casement Window

Grooved vinyl gasket

Stool

Metal Casement Window

Double-Hung Windows

Gasket Strips. Nail these so the tubular portion covers the joint. The stripping will be less visible if you attach it to the outside of the window and paint it to match the window. Also attach strips to the frame on the sides and to the sash along horizontal rails. On the top and bottom rails leave room for the sash to fit into the window frame.

Foam Tape. The adhesive-backed type is the easiest weather stripping to apply, but also the most temporary. Simply peel off the backing and stick the tape where the window or door will compress it against the frame.

Strips. Neoprene strips usually last longer than polyurethane, vinyl, or felt. Do not apply felt or tape where the window slides against the frame. Felt strips do not withstand moisture. Foam strips are also vulnerable to prolonged exposure.

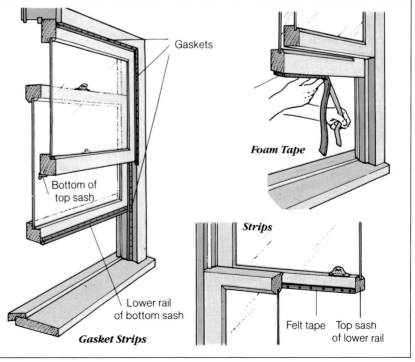

Gaskets

Bottom of top sash

Lower rail of bottom sash

Gasket Strips

Foam Tape

Strips

Felt tape   Top sash of lower rail

WINDOW COVERINGS

Window coverings have important practical functions in addition to their acknowledged decorative function. When choosing window coverings, you should consider all of the following: appearance, privacy, light control, glare and sun control, insulating value, and ease of operation. Unfortunately, few window coverings meet all of these requirements; you may have to settle on some priority characteristics or use more than one covering on a window.

Blinds, shades, and draperies are the most common window coverings. Shutters, screens, films, and special coatings are additional options.

Recommended Cross-References
Cooling, Insulation, Windows.

Blinds

The number of available styles provides a clue to the popularity and versatility of blinds. All blinds, whether standard venetian blind, miniblind, microblind, roll-up blind, or pleated blind, impart a crisp look. They control light well and provide privacy. Open blinds admit light that is bright but without harsh glare.

The drawback? Blinds do not improve winter heating efficiency. They lack insulating value and are not airtight. Blinds are more effective in summer, because they can block direct sunlight. Even in summer, however, the insulating effect may be negligible. Blinds are on the inside of the window and let in a significant amount of heat. Blinds reflect some heat if they are light in color, however. If you want blinds that are a dark decorator color, get what insulating value you can by ordering duplex blinds with the dark color on the inside and a reflective color on the outside.

Vertical blinds pivot open and shut like louvers. Some fit into permanent tracks and others gather along a rod like draperies. The latter work especially well on sliding glass doors.

Clean blinds by dusting or vacuuming. If they don't have tapes, dip them in a bathtub filled with water and ammonia.

Repairing Blinds. Replace worn tapes and ropes by untying the rope at the bottom, sliding out all the slats, threading new tape, and returning the slats. Then attach a new lift rope to the old and pull it through the mechanism into position.

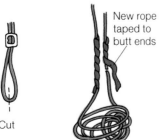

Cut

New rope taped to butt ends

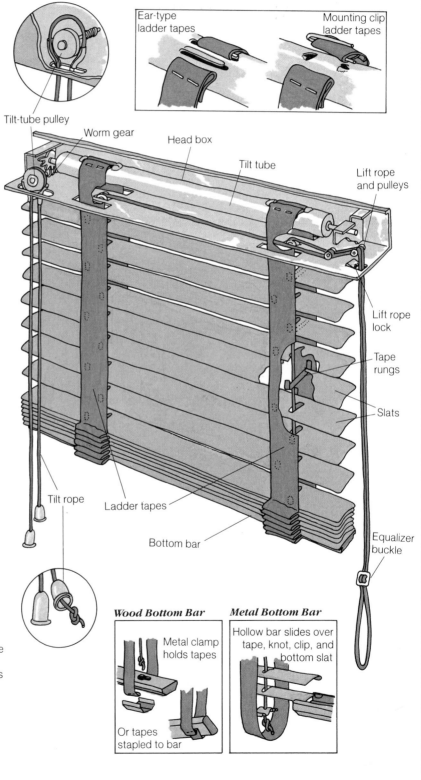

Ear-type ladder tapes

Mounting clip ladder tapes

Tilt-tube pulley

Worm gear

Head box

Tilt tube

Lift rope and pulleys

Lift rope lock

Tape rungs

Slats

Tilt rope

Ladder tapes

Bottom bar

Equalizer buckle

Wood Bottom Bar

Metal clamp holds tapes

Or tapes stapled to bar

Metal Bottom Bar

Hollow bar slides over tape, knot, clip, and bottom slat

Shades

The familiar white roller shade provides privacy and control of light. Use it effectively with curtains or dress it up with borders or decorator fabrics.

Shades are convenient. New insulating materials enhance convenience by making shades practical, too. Some shades use quilted fabrics with a core of fiberglass to maximize heat retention in the winter. Others use aluminized polyester, which works like a one-way mirror by reflecting light and heat, but allowing visibility. Shades with this material enhance summer cooling as well. Some achieve high R-values through the use of multiple layers.

Insulating shades lose value if the edges do not fit closely to the window jamb. Use self-sticking fasteners or a permanent track mounted in the window jambs to ensure a close fit.

Repairing a Roll-Up Shade. To replace a broken rope with a new rope of the same size, lower the shade completely and remove the broken rope. Starting at the back, tie the new rope to the broken end. Pass the rope down the back of the shade, up the front, through the pulley, and across to the pulley on the other side. Make a long loop for the equalizing buckle, then continue passing the rope down the front of the shade and up the back. Tie it off at the top.

Adjusting a Roller Shade. If a shade snaps up, correct it by taking it down and unrolling about 24 inches of shade. Then put it back up.

If a blind is sluggish, pull it down about 24 inches, remove it from the brackets, roll up the shade by hand, and return it to the brackets. If the mechanism unwinds accidentally while the shade is off the brackets, turn the flat pin clockwise with a pair of pliers until it is fairly tight, then repeat the operation.

Pulleys

Equalizing buckle

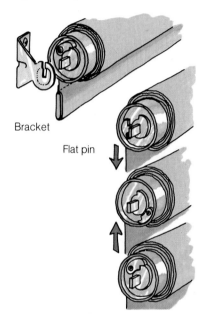

Bracket

Flat pin

Draperies and Curtains

A wide range of styles, colors, and fabrics await you when you choose draperies and curtains. The options vary widely in their ability to control sunlight or insulate the windows. Your choice of rods will be simpler—there are two basic styles: stationary and traverse.

Traverse rods tend to develop problems involving the slides and pulleys. The cord may break or come loose from one of the master slides, for example. To restring the cord, study the drawings of two-way and one-way rods. The one-way draw is straightforward; the two-way draw requires a loop in control slide B.

If only one side of your draperies moves, probably the cord has come off the hook on control slide B.

To readjust the cords, pull on the cord to open the curtains and bring control slide A to the edge of the rod. Holding the cord so it won't move, push control slide B to the other end of the rod. Loop the cord

Traverse Rod Draperies

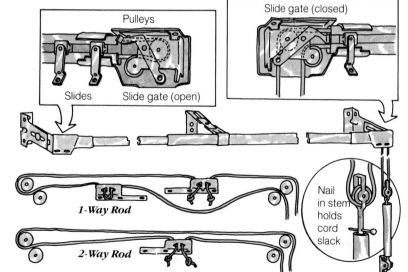

Pulleys

Slides   Slide gate (open)

Slide gate (closed)

1-Way Rod

2-Way Rod

Nail in stem holds cord slack

through the opening and over the hook. Both sides should now move. A loose cord on the tension pulley on the floor may cause inconvenience. Tighten the cord by pulling the stem of the pulley up 2 inches or more. Hold the pulley there with

either its built-in latch or by temporarily inserting a nail through the hole in the stem. Pull the rope out on the right-hand side of control slide A and tie a knot to take up the slack. Snip off the excess cord and release the stem of the floor pulley.

WINDOWS

Installing or replacing a window used to be a large project. Today, prehung window units have become widely available and have made this improvement significantly easier. All you have to do is frame an opening and attach the complete window within it, taking precautions to guard against leakage and air infiltration. Choose new units carefully; the style and material of the windows will have a considerable impact on the overall look of both the interior and exterior of your home.

Window Styles

To a great extent, the window frame determines the overall appearance of the window. Windows with aluminum, bronze, or painted frames have a sleek, bold appearance. Wood and vinyl-clad window frames create a more substantial effect.

Inside casings also contribute to the architectural and decorative style. They may be ornate moldings, slim strips of wood, or wide lumber.

The number of panes (these are called lights), as well as the size of the panes, will also affect the style. Diagonal muntins or windows arranged in a cluster may also contribute toward the effect you desire.

Ordering Windows

Cost and taste are primary considerations in choosing a particular style. You must also decide on the glazing. Would tinted glass, reflective glass, or some other innovative glazing be appropriate? Should you choose a single-pane or dual-pane unit?

There are two more variables to ponder before making your decision. Consider the size of the window. Manufacturers usually specify three of the four dimensions: the size of the glass, the size of the sash, the size of the window unit, and the recommended size of the rough opening. The dimensions of the rough opening will be of primary importance since you will be framing the opening to match. Manufacturers specify sizes in feet and inches, and list the width before the length. For example, a manufacturer would specify a rough opening as: 3 feet 11½ inches by 4 feet 5⅜ inches.

Tell the supplier the thickness of your exterior wall. You may need a jamb of nonstandard width.

Finally, you will need to specify the type of casing. If your siding is wood, the casings should have smooth edges. If your siding is stucco or brick, specify brick-mold casings. Brick-mold casings have grooves in the outside edges into which mortar or stucco locks.

Recommended Cross-References

Caulking & Adhesives, Doors, Flashing, Framing, Glass, Greenhouses, Insulation, Moldings, Screens, Security, Siding, Solar Energy, Solariums, Ventilation, Walls, Weather Stripping, Window Coverings.

The shapes of windows are as noteworthy as their placement in the house. This bow window gives a feeling of horizontal spaciousness; the semicircular window above it blends with the peak of the ceiling and opens the room to the sky. The result is a simultaneous sensation of openness and coziness.

Types of Windows

Fixed-Pane. Any window that does not open is a fixed-pane window. It does not permit ventilation or easy cleaning, but the sealed edges provide excellent protection against air infiltration. Fixed-pane windows are available in almost any shape or size. Large sizes should be dual-glazed for energy conservation; the best have two separate sealants that hold the panes and a dessicant around the edge of the enclosed space that absorbs trapped moisture. Most suppliers sell dual-glazed glass without a sash; the sealing material holds the panes in place. As a result, the glass requires careful handling.

Casement. The casement window opens in the same way as a door. Most casement windows swing outward, but models that open inward can be ordered. Casement windows provide excellent ventilation because both halves open. Older models swing on hinges; newer models have a pivot mechanism that facilitates cleaning; the entire exterior surface is accessible from indoors.

Double-Hung. These are probably the most familiar type of window. They provide less ventilation than the casement style because only one half opens. Older windows with weight-and-pulley systems tend to stick or rattle. Newer windows with spring-tension devices tend to work better.

Single-Hung. Only the bottom sash of some models opens; suppliers refer to these as single-hung units.

Sliding. A sliding window is the least expensive, especially if the frame is aluminum. Only half the window opens at one time. The inner sash disassembles for easy cleaning.

Awning. An awning window, also called a hopper window, swings like a casement window, but it is hinged on the bottom or top instead of on the side. Some units swing inward, others swing outward. An awning window is easy to clean and affords more security than other types.

Rotating. A rotating window pivots. Either side can face the inside or outside, so cleaning is simple. Reflective coatings may cover one side of the glass. The homeowner pivots the glass to reflect heat inward or outward as the season demands. Some windows rotate a full 360 degrees, others rotate partially.

Jalousie. Glass louvers form the panes of a jalousie window. Jalousie windows allow ventilation, but they do not seal well. They are not energy efficient and may represent a security risk. Many codes no longer allow jalousie windows.

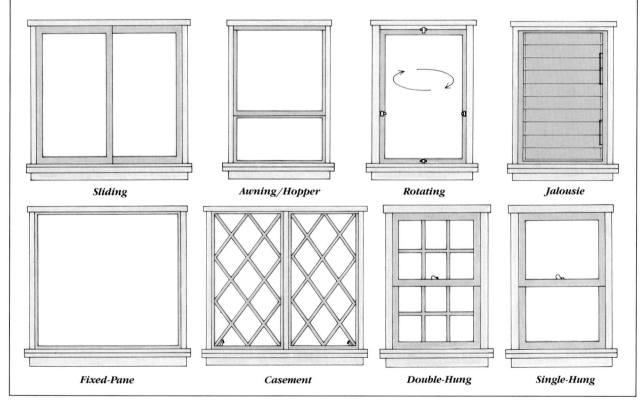

Sliding — *Awning/Hopper* — *Rotating* — *Jalousie*

Fixed-Pane — *Casement* — *Double-Hung* — *Single-Hung*

Window Frames

Aluminum	Thermal-break variety eliminates transmission of heat or cold, which can cause condensation problems. Painting not needed, but color selection limited. May not satisfy energy code.
Steel	Uninsulated steel transmits cold and heat, which may result in condensation problems. Excellent durability if painted regularly to prevent rust. May not satisfy energy code.
Wood	Excellent insulating qualities. More expensive than other frames because of individual craftsmanship required. Tighter seal than metal frames. Must be painted regularly.
Vinyl-Clad Wood	All the advantages of wood frames plus a protective vinyl coating, so no periodic painting is required. Vinyl is brittle in extreme cold. Wide variety of colors available.
Vinyl	Limited variety of colors available; energy efficient, durable, low maintenance requirements.

Removing a Wood Window

In some cases, new window units fit inside old jambs. However, if the old window is a double-hung unit with counterweights, replace the entire unit—hollow sash weight channels allow significant heat loss.

Determine the dimensions for the new window by removing only the inside casings and stool and measuring the distance from side to side between studs and from top to bottom between the header and rough sill. Since the opening may not be square, take several measurements. Order the largest window that will fit in the opening, or have a window custom-built to fit. You may also want to enlarge and reframe the opening for a larger window.

If the window is small, 2 feet by 3 feet, for instance, remove it as one unit. If it is larger, take out the sash before removing jambs and sill.

1. Start from the inside. Remove the interior casings and stool so that you can measure the rough opening and specify a new window. When it is time to remove the existing window, cut the sash cords and remove the sash weights separately. If the window is small, you can leave them in, if it is easier. Remove the apron.

2. If you plan to reuse the unit, cut all the nails that hold the jambs to the studs, then pry the casings away from the exterior wall. The entire window will come with them. The unit is intact and ready for reuse. If you are not reusing the unit, pry off the exterior casing before cutting the nails.

3. Use a hacksaw to cut the nails that hold the jambs to the trimmer studs. These nails may be easier to reach from the inside.

Without the nails, the window should swing out when you pull on it. Be very careful if you are on a ladder. Be sure you removed the sash weights. You may even want to remove the sash.

Inside casing · Cord pulley · Sash cord · Upper sash · Muntins · Inside stop · Meeting rails · Stile · Lower sash · Rail · Stool · Apron

Parting bead · Inside casing · Outside casing · Jamb · Stool · Apron · Sill · Siding

Head jamb · Weight pulleys · Weight pulley · Sash cord · Lower sash weight · Lower sash · Upper sash weight · Side jamb · Parting bead · Sill · Stool · Apron · Outside stop

1.   2.   Pull forward carefully   3.

Removing a Metal Window

Nails through flanges or fins hold metal windows to wall framing or sheathing. Exterior siding covers the flanges, so you have to remove it before you can pull the nails and remove the window.

Unless you are removing a large area of siding anyway, you will need to cut away enough to expose the flange all around the window. Start by removing all the exterior trim. Pry it off carefully so you can reuse it. Most flanges are 1½ inches wide; snap chalk lines around the window at a distance of 1¾ inches from the edge of the window.

Then set the blade of a circular saw so it will cut ⅛ inch deeper than the thickness of the siding. Use a carbide-tipped blade since you may hit nails. Cut along all four lines, and save the siding scraps if you plan to install new siding over the old. Use them to shim a new window.

Remove the nails from the flange and lift out the existing window.

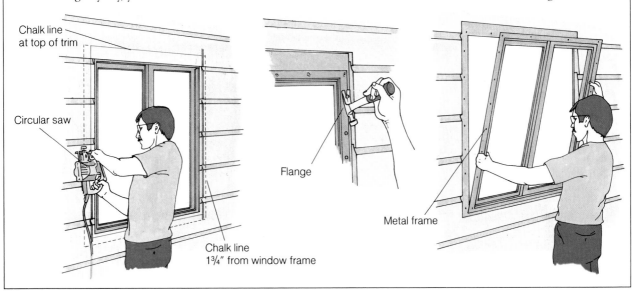

Chalk line at top of trim

Circular saw

Chalk line 1¾" from window frame

Flange

Metal frame

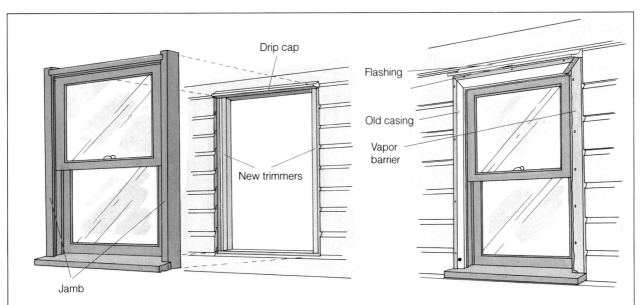

Drip cap

New trimmers

Jamb

Flashing

Old casing

Vapor barrier

Installing a Window in an Existing Opening

Measure the rough opening—there should be ¼- to ½-inch clearance all around. If the opening is too large, nail spacer boards to the studs. Use 2 by 4s as spacers.

If there is no building paper around the opening, loosen the siding boards, and tuck flashing paper under them as far as you can. Trim the paper flush with the opening or wrap it around the studs. If the new window does not come with pre-formed flashing or drip cap, cut a piece of aluminum flashing to fit across the top of the window, and tuck it 3 or 4 inches under the siding. Bend it outward so it covers the drip cap or the top casing of the new window. Nail the siding boards back in place.

Some windows have thick casings that fit against the framing or sheathing. If you have such a window, cut back the existing siding so the new casings fit snugly. Should you prefer this sort of installation, you may apply it to other units with standard casings. With horizontal, grooved-board siding, trim the ends on both sides of the opening until you can install 1 by 1 or 1 by 2 strips as an edging around the opening. The edging prevents drafts and insects from entering through the grooves. Add insulation between the window and studs, and cover it with a plastic vapor barrier.

Framing a Window Opening

Using dimensions provided by the manufacturer, mark the rough opening; then remove enough wall covering to expose existing framing (usually floor-to-ceiling) that needs to be removed or altered. Provide shoring, if necessary. Cut and remove the studs. Install the header, king studs, and trimmer studs as a unit, if possible. A pneumatic nailer makes toenailing easier. Install a rough sill and fill in cripple studs above and below the opening where needed. Cut out the exterior sheathing and siding.

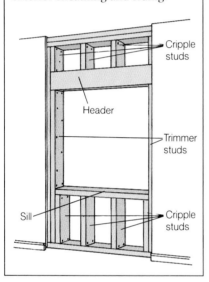

Cripple studs

Header

Trimmer studs

Sill

Cripple studs

Low-E Glass

Much of modern window technology has centered around the glass itself. One common term is *low-E*, meaning "low emissivity." The low-E characteristic is provided by a microscopically thin layer of metal oxides. This can be coated onto the glass or suspended between the panes of a double-pane window. The coating allows most visible light to pass through, while heat is reflected back into the house.

Short-wavelength solar rays, which provide visible light, pass through the low-E coating. When these waves strike the floor, furniture, or other objects, they break into longer waves, which provide heat. The longer waves are reflected back into the room by the low-E coating. This works conversely in the summer. The long-wave heat radiating up from sidewalks and driveways is reflected back off the windows instead of passing through them into the house.

Low-E glass in a double-pane insulated unit is a formidable energy saver. Manufacturers also claim that low-E glass stops a certain amount of ultraviolet (UV) radiation (which causes fading). However, there are other coatings that are designed especially to cut down on UV rays, and also to cut back on visible light. You may have seen bronze-coated windows. Gray-tinted windows are also very popular; they still cut back on light, but they don't look as dark or affect the quality of the light passing through them as much as the bronze ones.

Manufacturers have found that insulating quality, or R-value, can be increased by removing the air from between the panes of an insulated unit. Argon, a dense, inert gas, is usually injected into the space. Some manufacturers use insulating gels; others use a soft coating on a thin polyester film suspended between the two panes.

Each manufacturer uses slightly different combinations of these processes and features. Be sure to compare figures for R-value. Look for coatings designed to block UV rays, and check test results for the windows. Ask what kinds of tints are available. Be sure to see a window that has exactly the combination of features you are considering in order to make sure that the quality of light that comes through is just what you expected.

Installing a Metal- or Vinyl-Framed Window

Most vinyl-, aluminum-, and steel-framed windows have a nailing flange instead of the exterior casing found on wood-framed windows. Flash and position the metal window as for a wood-framed window. When you place the window, make sure the drain holes are on the bottom edge. On steel frames, drill a pilot hole into the flange every 12 inches to facilitate nailing.

Keep the sashes closed and locked while you are installing the unit. Run a bead of caulk around the back of the flange. Set the window in place. From inside, use shims to raise or level the window. Then, holding the window firmly, nail it from the outside with an 8d HDG box nail every 12 inches. Install a drip strip across the top of the window frame. Finally, staple the last piece of paper flashing so that it overlaps the top flange or drip strip. The wall is now ready for siding.

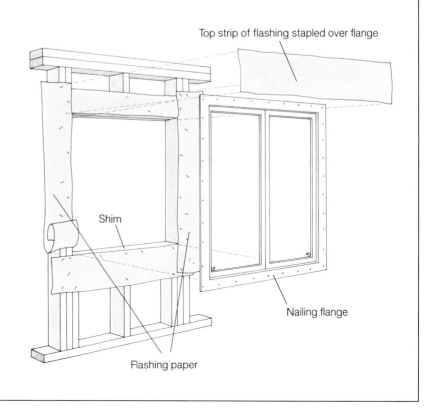

Top strip of flashing stapled over flange

Shim

Nailing flange

Flashing paper

Installing Prehung Units

The same installation procedures apply to almost all types of windows. The glass fits in a frame called the sash. Some windows have one sash, others have two. The sash, in turn, is held in a frame composed of head jamb, side jambs, and a sill. This entire assembly rests in a rough opening defined by the framing in the wall. Prehung units, which are the easiest to install, are entirely assembled beforehand. It is possible to install the sill, jambs, and sash separately, but consider doing so only if you have some old window sashes you want to recycle.

In New Construction. Most windows, whether wooden or metal, are installed after the sheathing, if there is any, and before the siding. Be sure the dimensions of the framed opening match the specifications for the rough opening, not the nominal size of the window. If there is sheathing, cut so the edges are flush with the framing. Always measure both diagonals of the rough opening to see if the opening is square. Variations up to ¼ inch are acceptable, but if the window is out of square by more than that, adjust the framing. The most critical member is the rough sill, which must be level.

The specialty paper for flashing window installations is a heavy-duty building paper reinforced with synthetic fibers. A layer of asphalt or other waterproof material coats one side. Window flashing comes in rolls 6 inches wide that you apply before installing the window and before applying the siding paper.

Most prehung wooden windows include the exterior casing. Therefore, they are easy to install. Some units do not include casings—you add them after installing the siding. To do so, extend the exterior edge of the jamb beyond the framing or sheathing until it is flush with the siding. The casings bridge the gap between jamb and siding.

1. Prepare the window by priming all the surfaces that will be concealed once the window is in position. Then staple paper flashing across the bottom of the rough opening and along both sides, so the side pieces overlap the bottom and all inside edges are flush with the opening. Do not apply flashing over the top until after the window is in position.

Caulk the back of the window casings. Get a helper to assist in positioning and attachment. Set the window into the opening, resting it on the rough sill. The person inside levels the window frame with shims. The new window should now be the same height as all the other windows. Once the frame is level, the person outside drills pilot holes in the casing, then drives enough 12d HDG casing or siding nails through the holes and into the studs to hold the frame in place.

2. From inside, place shims between the side jambs and the studs. If the manufacturer requires, drive nails through the jambs and shims into the studs, toenailing from the edge of the jambs rather than through the face. Be sure the sill is shimmed and blocked securely. Pack insulation between jambs and studs.

3. From outside, finish nailing the casings. Position the nails at least every 12 inches. Install a drip cap and metal flashing above the head casing. Staple the final piece of paper flashing so that it overlaps the side pieces and covers the vertical flange of the metal flashing.

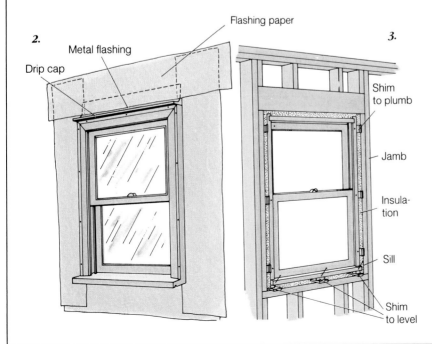

Ready-made window unit with exterior casing in place

Flashing paper

1.

Flashing paper across bottom

2.

Drip cap

Metal flashing

Flashing paper

3.

Shim to plumb

Jamb

Insulation

Sill

Shim to level

Improving Existing Windows

Double-glazed, low-E windows make sense in new construction, even if they aren't required by the building code. However, installing them in an existing house may be too expensive to justify the cost.

There are three ways to improve the efficiency of existing windows with simple techniques and inexpensive materials. In combination, they can increase the R-value to nearly that of high-quality, double-glazed windows, as well as reduce sound transmission.

Window Films. These films have improved greatly over the years. True low-E films that offer the same benefits as those installed by window manufacturers are available. They come in varying degrees of clarity and reflectivity.

Applying the films is fairly easy, but practice first on small windows. Don't try to apply the film in temperatures below 40° F or above 90° F, or when the window is in direct sunlight. Tinting film clouds for a few weeks while it cures, but it will clear by itself. The film can be removed with a solution of water and ammonia and a razor blade.

Clean the window thoroughly, using a razor-blade scraper, and dry it with a lint-free cloth.

Cut the film 1 inch oversized.

Wet the window according to the film manufacturer's instructions.

Separate the backing from the film at a corner. Be careful not to crease the film. Pull the backing away from the film while a helper wets the adhesive side. If the film sticks to itself, it will probably be ruined.

Carefully place the film on the window, avoiding creases and wrinkles. Overlap the film on the window sash.

Spray the film with water, then smooth it with a squeegee. Wipe the squeegee across the top, then down the center, then along each side.

Trim the excess film, leaving a $1/16$-inch gap.

If there are bubbles in the film, spray it with water and slowly work the bubbles out with the squeegee.

Combination Storm Windows. These windows are added to existing windows. They can be left up all year around because they can be opened. They have adjustable screen and glass panels that can be worked from the inside. Combination storm windows are made of aluminum and require no maintenance. They work only on sliding, single-hung, or double-hung windows. Color selection is limited.

Check the existing window frames for square before you order. If an existing window frame is badly out of square, order the unit about ¼ inch larger than the window in each direction, then trim the flange to fit the opening. Don't distort the frame of the storm window to make it fit.

Measure the existing window along the outside edge of the exterior stops.

Drill attachment holes in the storm window flange, spacing them according to manufacturer recommendations.

Test-fit the storm window and make any needed adjustments.

Caulk along the exterior stops.

Position the storm window and attach it with screws.

Interior Insulating Windows. These are attached to the inside of existing windows with magnetic or Velcro strips. They are easy to use, provide considerable resistance to air infiltration, and reduce sound transmission. They also minimize condensation and offer protection from broken glass. The plastic glazing is almost unbreakable. However, they can be scratched.

Nail wood stops onto the top and sides of the window jamb.

Test-fit the steel strapping. Remove the backing from the double-stick tape and press it into position.

Measure the insulating-window material carefully and cut it to size following the manufacturer's instructions.

Adding an Interior Insulating Window

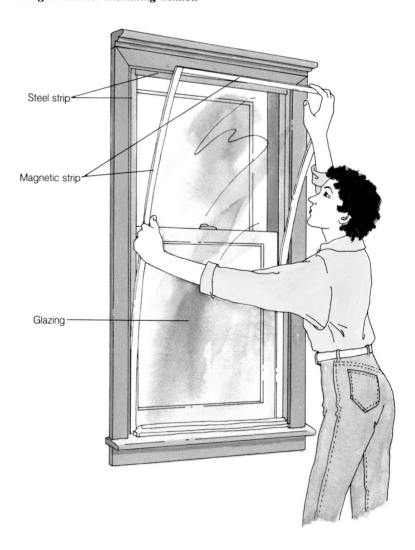

Steel strip

Magnetic strip

Glazing

Applying Tinted Window Film

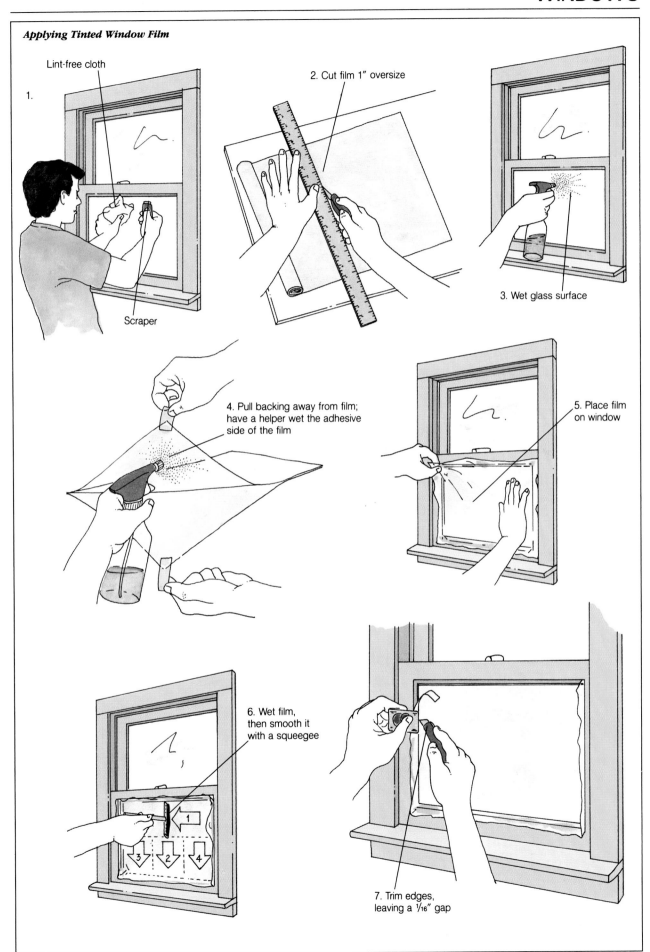

1. Lint-free cloth / Scraper

2. Cut film 1″ oversize

3. Wet glass surface

4. Pull backing away from film; have a helper wet the adhesive side of the film

5. Place film on window

6. Wet film, then smooth it with a squeegee

7. Trim edges, leaving a ¹⁄₁₆″ gap

Repairing Windows

Old double-hung windows, after years of use and numerous paint jobs, are prone to problems and are not energy efficient. However, many people consider them worth keeping because they add style or because they are expensive to replace. Your first project should be to add weather stripping. If the window is broken or the sash has deteriorated, look for an inexpensive replacement at recycling yards or contact an installer who replaces old windows.

Repair small areas of rot with epoxy compounds. A casement window may present a crank that doesn't operate properly or a loose hinge. If you have a jalousie window that needs repair, replace it with an awning or double-hung window.

Loosening Stuck Windows

1. Drive the blade of a wide putty knife between the sash and stops all around the inside and outside.

2. Drive a wedge, hatchet, or prybar between the sash and sill on the outside to force the sash up. Work slowly and gently, trying the pry in several different places. Exert the most pressure at the corners.

3. Scrape paint or hardened dirt from the window channels.

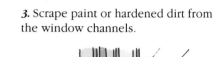

4. If the sash moves but binds inside the channel, you need to widen the channel. Cut a block of wood that is slightly wider than the channel and tap it into the channel to force the stops apart.

5. When the sash moves but doesn't slide easily, lubricate the channels with candle wax, paraffin, or silicone lubricant.

Spring Balance

1. Replace sash weights and cords with a spring balance. The adapter hooks onto the steel tape.

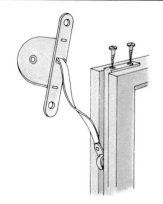

2. Remove the old sash pulleys and screw the new spring balance into the same slots.

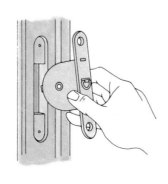

3. With the sash out of the frame, hook the tape of the sash balance to the adapter on both sides.

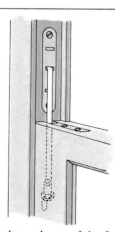

Repairing a Double-Hung Window

Replace broken sash cords with reinforced cord or chain. If you live in a cold climate, consider filling the sash-weight channel with insulation and installing replacement channels.

1. On the side with the broken cord, pry off the stop that holds the sash. Ease the lower sash out of the frame, release each knotted cord from the groove, and slowly let the sash weight pull the cord toward the pulley until the weight stops. Repair the upper sash in the same way.

2. Loosen and remove the access panel at the bottom of the window.

Take out both of the sash weights.

3. Fish new cord down through the pulley and retrieve the end through the access hole. Tie this end to the sash weights. Use wire to attach the end of a chain to a weight. Then place the weights back in the cavity and replace the access panel.

4. Attach the free end of the cord to the sash. Set the sash into the window in a closed position, pull on the cord until the sash weight is at the top, and cut the cord. Remove the sash and attach the cord.

Replace the parting strip and set the sash back into the opening. Make sure the window works smoothly.

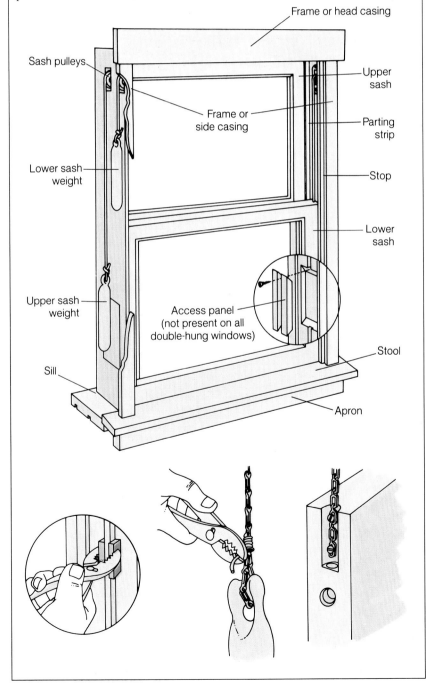

Frame or head casing

Sash pulleys

Frame or side casing

Upper sash

Parting strip

Lower sash weight

Stop

Lower sash

Upper sash weight

Access panel (not present on all double-hung windows)

Sill

Stool

Apron

Sash Spring Lift

The mechanism for this device is in a metal tube that runs up the channel. In order to adjust the speed with which the window moves, tighten or loosen the spring inside.

Casement Crank

To inspect, clean, or replace a casement crank, remove the screws that hold it in place. Disengage the arm and slide out the crank.

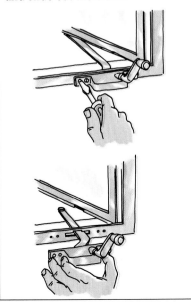

WIRE

Electricity is carried by wires that range in size from small lamp cords to high-voltage lines running across the country. The size of the wire affects the efficient flow of electricity. If it is too small for the amperage, the wire will overheat. Therefore, the National Electrical Code® (NEC®) stipulates what type and size of wire can be used in all wiring projects.

Most residential wiring is done with copper wires, except that aluminum is sometimes used for the main service-entrance conductors. There was a time when houses were wired completely with aluminum, but numerous fires have restricted its use. The problem is that aluminum expands as it heats up, causing connections to work loose. Special materials are available for making proper connections, but it is safer to do all circuit wiring with copper. Most codes now require it.

Size

Wire sizes are controlled by the American Wire Gauge System (AWG). A larger number means a smaller wire. A No. 18 wire, then, is very small and a No. 2 wire is very large. Note on the chart that wires are numbered evenly up to No. 2, and that sizes larger than No. 1 are designated 1/0 (one ought or 0), 2/0 (two ought or 00), and so on.

Most house wiring is done with No. 12 wire, although No. 14 is still used in some areas for 15-amp lighting circuits. Larger sizes are used for 240-volt appliances and for the main conductors into the service entrance.

Cable

Cable is numbered by the size and number of insulated conductors, exclusive of the ground wire. Thus, 12/2 means two No. 12 conductors. If there is a ground wire the proper designation is 12/2 w/G.

Recommended Cross-References
Electrical System, Lighting: Indoor, Wiring.

Caution
When working with aluminum wire, use only the proper connectors. Wire nuts marked CU/AL can be used with copper-wired fixtures. However, receptacles and switches marked CU/AL should be replaced with newer ones marked CO/ALR.

Types of Wire and Cable

Technically a wire is an individual conductor, either solid or stranded, wrapped in its own insulation. A cable is a cluster of two or more wires, each with its own insulation, wrapped together in plastic or metal sheathing. The most common types of wire and cable are:

Type T Wire. Used for general indoor wiring, the thermoplastic (T) insulation protects against a wide spectrum of temperature differences.

Type TW Wire. This wire provides heavy insulation for weather resistance. It is used for outdoor wiring (but not direct burial) and for wiring in damp places such as basements.

Type THW Wire. Type THW wire is similar to Type TW, but it is more heat resistant.

NM Cable. This nonmetallic cable is the type of wiring that is most commonly used in residential installations. It is widely known by the trade name Romex™. It consists of two or more individually insulated Type T wires and a bare copper grounding wire, all wrapped in jute and paper spacers and sheathed in plastic. This cable must not be used where it will be exposed to dampness.

NMC Cable. This type of cable is made specifically for damp areas like basements or laundry rooms. It often has a glass wrapping on each wire. The wires are embedded in a solid plastic sheath to keep out moisture. If NMC cable is not available in your area, use UF cable.

UF Cable. This cable is so durable it is recommended for underground burial. The wires are embedded directly in tough plastic that keeps out all water. It is an excellent choice for outdoor wiring or wiring in a barn or garage where there is always a lot of moisture. SE is another type of cable that can be buried.

Armored Cable. Known by the trade name BX, this cable has heavy paper and metal spiral sheathing. The ground wire is aluminum because the metal sheathing also acts as a ground. It should not be used in damp areas. Some local codes require armored cable in places where wiring will be exposed to potential abrasion, such as in crawl spaces or along the insides of garage walls.

Copper Wire: Sizes, Ampacity, and Use
For aluminum, use two sizes larger.

Number	Ampacity	Use
18	7	Flexible cords, low-voltage systems
16	10	Doorbells
14	15	Lighting circuits
12	20	Small-appliance lighting circuits
10	30	Individual appliances
8	40	(120 volts)
6	55	Individual appliances
4	70	(240 volts), ground wires
2	95	Service entrance
1	110	Ground wires
1/0	125	Service entrance wires
2/0	145	
3/0	165	
4/0	195	

Note: Outlets and switches have ampere ratings that are to be matched to the type of wire being used. Most of them are stamped "15 amp," which means they should be used with No. 14 wire. However, the NEC® permits you to use 15-amp switches and outlets with No. 12 wire, which has an ampacity of 20 amperes.

Stripping Cable

Nonmetallic Cable. The sheathing of nonmetallic cable should be stripped away at the end before or after it is fed into a box. Strip enough so that 8 to 12 inches of unsheathed wire is inside the box. With a knife, slit the sheathing along the length. Do not cut any wire insulation. Strip the sheathing back and cut it off. You can also use a cable stripper. Slide it onto the cable, squeeze the stripper, and pull it to the end of the cable. This slits the sheathing, which you can pull back and cut off with a knife.

Armored Cable. The flexible metal sheathing of armored cable must be cut with a hacksaw. Saw sheathing at an angle, taking care not to cut into the wire insulation inside. When you have barely broken through the metal armor, stop sawing and twist the sheathing apart.

Stripping Wire

While it is possible to strip the insulation from the end of a wire with a sharp knife, if you plan to do much wiring, invest in a multipurpose tool or a wire stripper. They work like cutters, but only cut the insulation and not the copper wire. The multipurpose tool has a separate groove for each size of wire, usually up to No. 10, as well as crimping jaws. A wire stripper has only one cutting groove, but it can be adjusted to any size.

Determine how much insulation must be removed. Then place the wire in the proper size groove and rotate the tool back and forth. When you have cut through the insulation, pull it off. Be very careful about cutting into the copper. Even an incidental nick is a weak point that may break if the wire is subject to any movement.

Testing Wires

If you want to check new wiring before turning on full house power, use a continuity tester. It has its own battery and light bulb, and indicates if a circuit is complete. Make sure the circuit is not connected to any live wires, or the current will damage the tester and possibly injure you. Then, temporarily twist wires together that will later be attached to electrical devices. Leave one connection unjoined, and touch the two wires of the connection to the tester. It should light up. Some electricians improvise their own continuity tester out of a 6-volt battery and bell. They connect it to the circuit, then touch wires together at other locations, listening for the bell.

A voltage tester does not have a battery, but lights up only when the wires have full house current.

Nonmetallic Cable

Most residential wiring is done by running nonmetallic cable through exposed framing. The NEC requires that it be stapled with approved nail-on staples at least every 54 inches. It should also be stapled within 12 inches of any metal boxes and within 8 inches of any plastic boxes. If you are fishing it behind walls, secure the cable as well as possible.

When the cable changes direction, bend it softly, giving it a radius of 5 times the diameter of the cable. Avoid kinks. Keep the cable flat, without spirals or twists. The best way to assure this is to unroll the cable from the outside of its coil rather than pull on it from the inside. If you drill holes in order to run the cable through the framing, center the holes so that the cable will be at least 1¼ inches from the edge of the stud or joist.

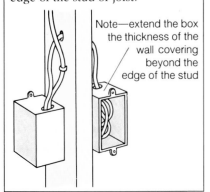

Note—extend the box the thickness of the wall covering beyond the edge of the stud

Splicing Wire

These illustrations show various wire-splicing techniques. Wire nuts are the easiest to use; they come in different sizes depending on the size and number of wires you plan to connect. Connections for household circuits must always be made inside a junction box or other electrical box, never in the middle of a run.

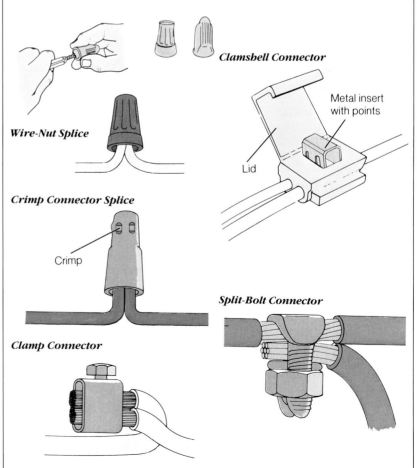

Wire-Nut Splice

Crimp Connector Splice

Crimp

Clamp Connector

Clamshell Connector

Metal insert with points

Lid

Split-Bolt Connector

WIRING

Most electrical wiring projects have two phases: rough wiring and finish wiring. Rough wiring is the process of running wires to various locations for receptacles, switches, light fixtures, and appliances. Finish wiring involves the installation of the actual fixtures. Installing the fixtures is a phase that may be accomplished several weeks after the rough wiring—after installing finish walls and ceilings. Some projects will also include a third phase: installing a new service entrance. This will be the case if you are installing a completely new electrical system. It will also be necessary if you are updating the wiring in an older home.

The following pages describe techniques for rough wiring, whether you are adding an outlet to an existing circuit, rewiring large areas of your home, or installing new wiring. Techniques vary, depending on whether the wiring is done in new construction or behind existing walls, but the principles are the same. The basic steps are planning the layout, installing electrical boxes, running wires to all boxes, and testing the installation.

Wiring should be done according to code and with proper permits. Unlike other building codes, there is only one standard code for electrical work, called the National Electrical Code® (NEC®). Requirements for local cities and counties are based on the NEC®, but may include additional restrictions. Many local code authorities publish a sheet of these variations, which you should obtain before starting work. You should also obtain a guide to the NEC®—the Code itself is not very useful to the homeowner. An electrical permit is usually required whenever you add new wiring, but not when you replace wiring.

Recommended Cross-References
Dishwashers, Electrical System, Lighting: Indoor & Outdoor, Ranges, Ovens & Cooktops, Switches, Washers & Dryers, Water Heaters, Wire.

Planning the Layout
First, plot the location of all new light fixtures and outlets on a floor plan. Use code requirements and anticipated needs to choose legal and convenient locations.

Next, group fixtures and outlets into circuits. If you are adding only one or two outlets, you can wire them into an existing circuit. If you are doing extensive wiring, start by assigning a circuit to each permanent appliance, such as a refrigerator or clothes washer. Then group outlets needed for small appliances that will be used in the kitchen, dining room, and laundry. Finally, group the general-purpose outlets. The NEC® does not specify the number of outlets allowed on a single circuit. Common practice is to install no more than 6 receptacles on a 20-amp small-appliance circuit, no more than 13 outlets on a 20-amp general-purpose circuit, and no more than 10 fixtures on a 15-amp lighting circuit.

Minimum Code Requirements for Electrical Fixtures
The following specifications will help you to locate light fixtures, switches, outlets, and appliances. These specifications are based on the National Electrical Code®; consult with your local building department for additional restrictions. Code requirements are minimum; when going to the trouble and expense of installing new wiring, it is good practice to increase the number of fixtures and outlets in anticipation of your future needs.

Lights. Every room, hallway, stairway, outdoor entrance, and attached garage must have at least one permanent light fixture controlled by a wall switch located at each entrance. The light can be mounted on the ceiling or any wall, and can be as many individual fixtures as you wish. The following list includes some exceptions to this rule:
- A wall receptacle controlled by a wall switch at the entrance to a room may be substituted for a permanent light fixture in any room except the kitchen or the bathroom.
- Light fixtures for utility rooms, crawl spaces, and attics without stairs can be controlled by pull chains.

- Lighting for hallways, stairways, and outdoor entrances can be activated by specialized switches. These include remote, central, or automatic switches.

Additional Recommendations. Lighting fixtures should also be installed to illuminate the front of a furnace, laundry equipment in a basement or garage, bathroom mirrors, and clothes closets. Fixtures in clothes closets must be located so that items can't be piled close to them or fall onto a hot bulb. This may require lowering a shelf, recessing a fixture, or using a fluorescent unit. Pendant fixtures are not allowed.

Switches. The switch for the main light fixture of a room should be located at the door to the room; at each door, if there is more than one. The switch must be on the latch side of a hinged door, so that the door does not interfere with the access to the plate when you enter the room. Do not locate switches in bathrooms where it is possible to reach them while using the shower or bathtub. Attic stairs must be illuminated by a light that is controlled by a switch at the foot of the stairs. Lights for basement stairs must have a switch at the

head of the stairs as well as an additional switch at any other entrance to the basement.

Receptacles. Receptacles, also called convenience outlets, must be located in every room no more than 12 feet apart. (The Code actually states that no point along the floor line of any wall is more than 6 feet from an outlet.) On a wall with more than one door opening, there should be at least one outlet unless the section of wall between the doorways is less than 2 feet wide.

Place receptacles for a kitchen counter no more than 4 feet apart. Standard practice is to install at least one outlet for each foot of counter.

Laundry rooms must have at least one receptacle positioned within 6 feet of any appliance.

Bathrooms should have at least one receptacle adjacent to the washbasin. All bathroom outlets must be protected by GFCI devices.

There must be at least one receptacle outdoors, as well as one in the garage and one in the basement. They must all be GFCI protected.

Appliances. Any 240-volt appliance or permanent 120-volt appliance should have its own receptacle or junction box.

Planning the Runs

When you have grouped the outlets and fixtures into circuits, walk around the room and mark the location of each box. Then plan how to run the cable in order to connect the boxes. You may decide to change circuit groupings because you see easier ways to connect the boxes and divide the load among the circuits.

Some local codes do not allow you to wire receptacles and light fixtures on the same circuit. Other codes do not allow wiring in exterior walls because it may interfere with insulation. Still other code jurisdictions require that all wiring be done with metal conduit instead of nonmetallic cable. Such restrictions will affect where you run the circuits, so check your local code during the planning stage.

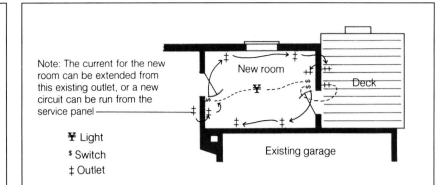

Note: The current for the new room can be extended from this existing outlet, or a new circuit can be run from the service panel

¥ Light
$ Switch
‡ Outlet

New room

Deck

Existing garage

A Typical Circuit

This wiring plan and the illustration show a general-purpose circuit of a room addition. The diagram shows three of the many symbols used in electrical plans. Notice that long arrows show the sequence of outlets from the source and that a dotted line connects each light fixture to its switch. A light fixture with two switches is marked S-3 to indicate a three-way switch.

As shown, nonmetallic cable is run through joists and studs and along the sides of studs. Holes are ¾ to 1 inch in diameter, drilled with a heavy-duty, ½-inch drill. A hole should be at least 1¼ inches from the edge of a framing member unless it is protected by a metal plate.

Stringing Cable

When running cable under a floor, try to staple it alongside the joists. Rather than crossing joists, drill holes through the center, preferably near the walls supporting the joists, rather than in the center of the span.

If there is any chance of a nail penetrating the cable, cover it with a nailing plate.

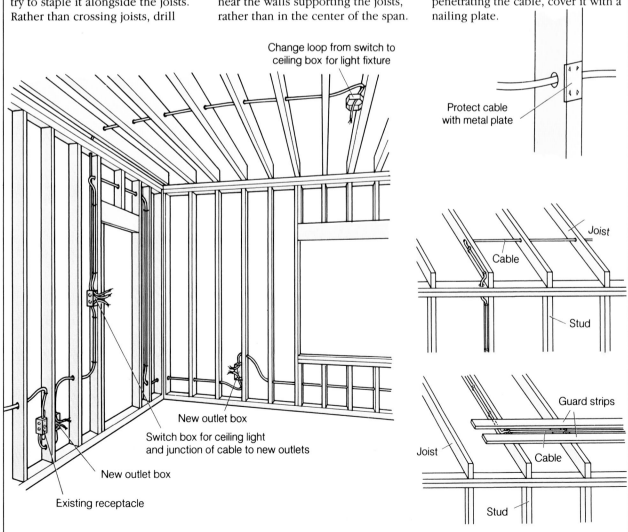

Change loop from switch to ceiling box for light fixture

Protect cable with metal plate

New outlet box

Switch box for ceiling light and junction of cable to new outlets

New outlet box

Existing receptacle

Joist

Cable

Stud

Guard strips

Joist

Cable

Stud

Boxes

Types of Boxes. Most codes allow either metal or plastic boxes. Electricians usually prefer one type over other. Metal boxes can be ganged together and are easier to fit wallboard around without leaving gaps. Plastic boxes are less expensive, a major consideration for large wiring projects but fairly incidental for small jobs. Both types are available with internal clamps and have various brackets and nail-on devices to make mounting easier.

Metal boxes must always be grounded to the system, which is a disadvantage in terms of inconvenience during wiring, but an advantage in providing one more guarantee of a well-grounded system. Some types of plastic boxes crack or break fairly easily during installation.

Installing Boxes. After you have planned the circuits, install a box for each fixture, switch, and receptacle. The type and size of box depend on the fixtures it will accommodate, the space it will fit into, and the number of wires it will house.

If you install boxes in open framing, extend the face of the box beyond the framing so that it will be no more than ¼ inch away from the finished wallboard surface or flush with any combustible surface.

Locating Boxes. The NEC does not specify box locations, but the following are typical for most areas:

- Switches: 48 inches from the floor.
- Outlets: 12 inches above the floor. Outlets above kitchen counters: 44 inches above the floor.
- Boxes for baseboard heaters: Usually 6 inches above floor; varies.
- Ceiling fixtures: Center of ceiling.
- Junction boxes: Wherever they will be accessible; they are not allowed to be concealed inside walls.

Types of Plastic Boxes

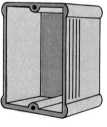

Standard Box

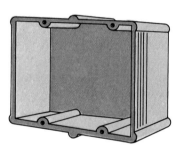

Gang Box

Types of Metal Boxes

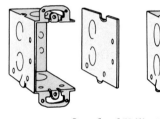

Standard Utility Box

Surface Box

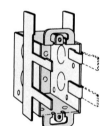

Plaster Box

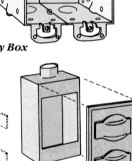

Outdoor Box

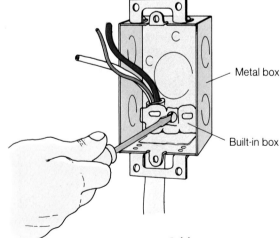

Metal box

Built-in box

Connecting Cable. Cables are connected to boxes with internal clamps or with connectors inserted through knockout holes. Plastic boxes do not require connectors if the cable is stapled within 8 inches of the box.

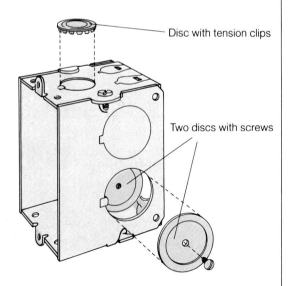

Disc with tension clips

Two discs with screws

Knockout Closures. If a knockout is removed from a metal box and the hole is not used, it must be closed with an approved metal cover.

Ceiling Boxes

Boxes for most ceiling fixtures are octagon shaped, and are usually located in the center of the room. They come with various mounting brackets so that you can position them precisely, depending on whether they fall next to a joist, under one, or in a cavity between two joists. Ceiling fans cannot be suspended from the ears of a ceiling box, whether metal or plastic. You must screw a base into a block of wood or use a bracket designed specifically for that purpose.

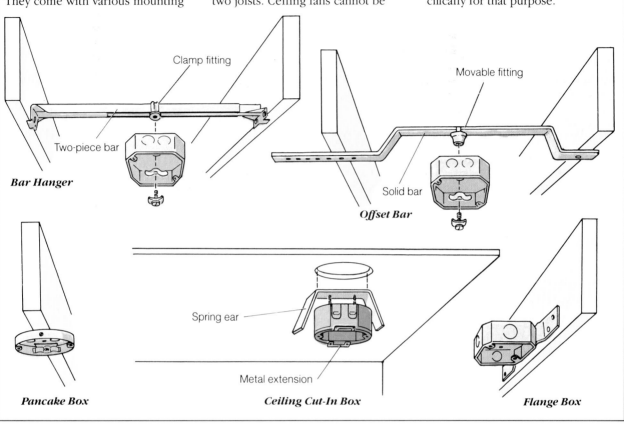

Bar Hanger
Clamp fitting
Two-piece bar

Offset Bar
Movable fitting
Solid bar

Pancake Box

Ceiling Cut-In Box
Spring ear
Metal extension

Flange Box

Choosing Boxes

The shape of the box you choose depends on what you will be using it for. Switch boxes, also called utility boxes or handy boxes, are the most common type, and are used for wall switches and receptacles. They can be ganged or bought in large sizes for multiple fixtures. Octagonal and round boxes are used for light fixtures. They are also used for junction boxes, as are square boxes. Specialty boxes are available for mounting on wall surfaces, in existing walls, or outdoors. Some fixtures, such as wall heaters and recessed lights, have their own electrical boxes built into the housing.

You can use the shapes and configurations that suit your needs, but the most critical attribute of a box is size. The NEC® is very strict about how many wires and fixtures can be stuffed into one. The accompanying box-fill table tells the size of box you will need for a particular situation. When using the table, include the following factors:

- Each hot or neutral wire (black, red, or white) counts as one conductor.
- All grounding wires together count as one conductor.
- Each receptacle or fixture counts as one conductor.
- All internal clamping devices and fixture studs count as one conductor.

As an exercise, choose the proper size for the switch box shown in the lower left-hand corner of the opposite page, assuming it will have one receptacle and the wire is No. 12. (The answer is 3 × 2 × 2½, for 5 conductors.)

Number of Conductors Permitted in a Box

Box Size	Maximum Number of Conductors			
	No. 14	No. 12	No. 10	No. 8
Round or Octagonal				
4 × 1¼	6	5	5	4
4 × 1½	7	6	6	5
4 × 2⅛	10	9	8	7
Square				
4 × 1¼	9	8	7	6
4 × 1½	10	9	8	7
4 × 2⅛	15	13	12	10
Switch Boxes				
3 × 2 × 1½	3	3	3	2
3 × 2 × 2	5	4	4	3
3 × 2 × 2¼	5	4	4	3
3 × 2 × 2½	6	5	5	4
3 × 2 × 2¾	7	6	5	4
3 × 2 × 3½	9	8	7	6
Junction Boxes				
4 × 2⅛ × 1½	5	4	4	3
4 × 2⅛ × 1⅞	6	5	5	4
4 × 2⅛ × 2⅛	7	6	5	4

Boxes in Wallboard Walls

1. Measure the box height from the floor. Draw an outline on the wall.
2. Cut through the wallboard by scoring it several times with a knife, or use a wallboard saw.
3. Run cable behind the wall. Pull it into a box. Fit box into the opening.
4. The type of box shown uses a separate bracket on each side to hold it against the wallboard. Other types include toggles or side flanges.

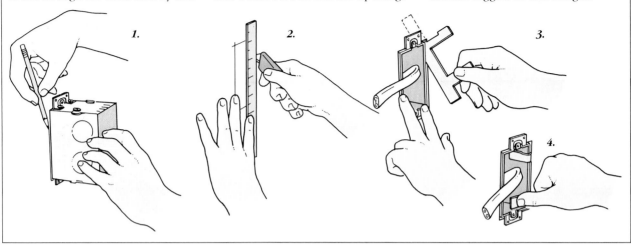

Boxes in Lath and Plaster Walls

1. Find a piece of lath by chiseling away some plaster.

    Tape the outline of the box around it, centering the box in the center of the lath. Cut through the lath and plaster with a keyhole saw, pushing in hard but pulling back very gently.
2. Move the ears of the box back by loosening and resetting the screws.

Chip away enough plaster for the ears to fit against the lath.
3. Pull the cable into the box and attach it to the wall by screwing the ears to the lath with wood screws.

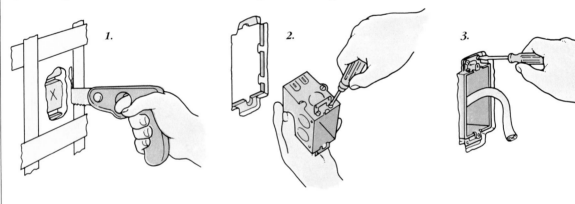

Boxes in Baseboards

1. Trace an outline of the box on the baseboard. Hold it horizontally if it will not fit as shown. Drill holes in the four corners and at the top and bottom; use them to start saw cuts.
2. Pull cable through the box and set the box in place. If the baseboard is thicker than $3/8$ inch, screw the ears of the box directly into the baseboard with small wood screws. Otherwise, use a toggle box.

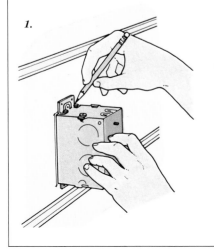
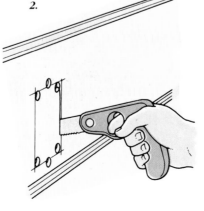
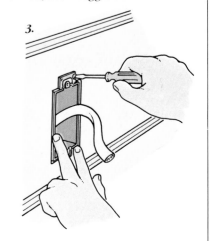

Ceiling Box From Above

1. Mark the location of the box by drilling a pilot hole up through the ceiling. Remove enough of the attic floor to enable you to install the box.

2. Trace an outline of the box onto the wallboard from above and drill holes in the corners.

3. From below, cut an opening for the box by sawing from hole to hole.

4. Install the box from above, using a bar hanger or piece of 2 by 4 blocking to suspend it between joists. Attach nailing cleats for replacing the attic floor boards.

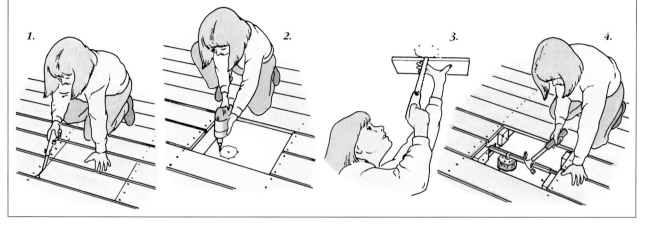

Box in Wallboard Ceiling

1. Saw out a square of wallboard where the box will go. Widen the hole enough to expose two joists.

2. Install the ceiling box by screwing each end of the hanger into a joist. Run the cable into the box. Cut a wallboard patch, with a hole for the box, to fit the opening. Nail the patch to the joists.

3. Tape the joints and texture the patch to match the ceiling.

Box in Plaster Ceiling

1. Chip out a channel the width of a lath between two joists.

Hold a piece of wood next to the outline of the ceiling box as you cut from marker hole to marker hole.

2. Cut the exposed lath on the outside of the two joists. Remove nails.

3. Once the box is installed, fill the channel with patching plaster, allow to dry, and smooth in a layer of spackling compound.

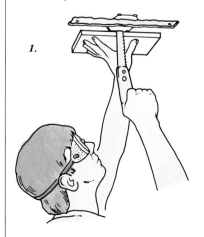

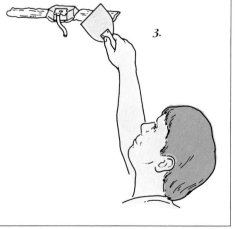

Running Cable

In new construction, you can run nonmetallic cable along the sides of exposed studs and joists or through holes drilled through their centers. If you are running cable through existing walls and ceilings, access is much more difficult, but not impossible. These two pages show techniques for connecting wall and ceiling boxes with cable, running it through the attic, under the floor, behind the baseboard, or between studs and joists.

Pulling cable behind walls is easier if you have a special wiring device called a fish tape. It is a coil of spring wire or stiff nylon rope which you can push deep into an opening or through a wall cavity to hook to the end of a cable and pull. It is a good idea to have a helper, but not more than one. With too many people it is hard to trace all the paths mentally and keep the wire connections sorted out.

Most of the cable you pull will be 2-wire-with-ground, either No. 14 or No. 12, so buy it by the coil. It is easier to buy all No. 12 to save the

bother of keeping both sizes on hand. You will also need 3-wire cable for multiwire circuits, 3-way switch runs, and 240-volt appliance circuits.

Always uncoil cable carefully from the roll so that it does not kink or twist. Such bends cause wire fatigue if they overheat, leading to possible short circuits caused by breakage.

When you have pulled all the cables into their boxes, do not connect any of them to fixtures or power until you test each one to check out which connections to make. Do this with a low-voltage continuity tester.

Through the Attic

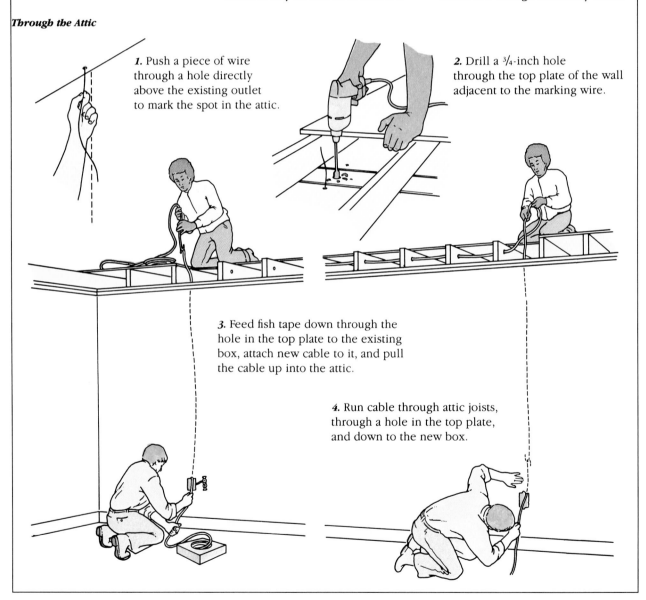

1. Push a piece of wire through a hole directly above the existing outlet to mark the spot in the attic.

2. Drill a ¾-inch hole through the top plate of the wall adjacent to the marking wire.

3. Feed fish tape down through the hole in the top plate to the existing box, attach new cable to it, and pull the cable up into the attic.

4. Run cable through attic joists, through a hole in the top plate, and down to the new box.

Behind Walls. This is a typical installation showing the necessary wiring for a new ceiling fixture and wall switch. In some places the cable is recessed in notches that have been cut into the studs or plates. If you do this, you must cover notches with metal plates at least $1/16$ inch thick to prevent nails from penetrating the wires. Avoid notching the bottoms of any joists, because it weakens them substantially.

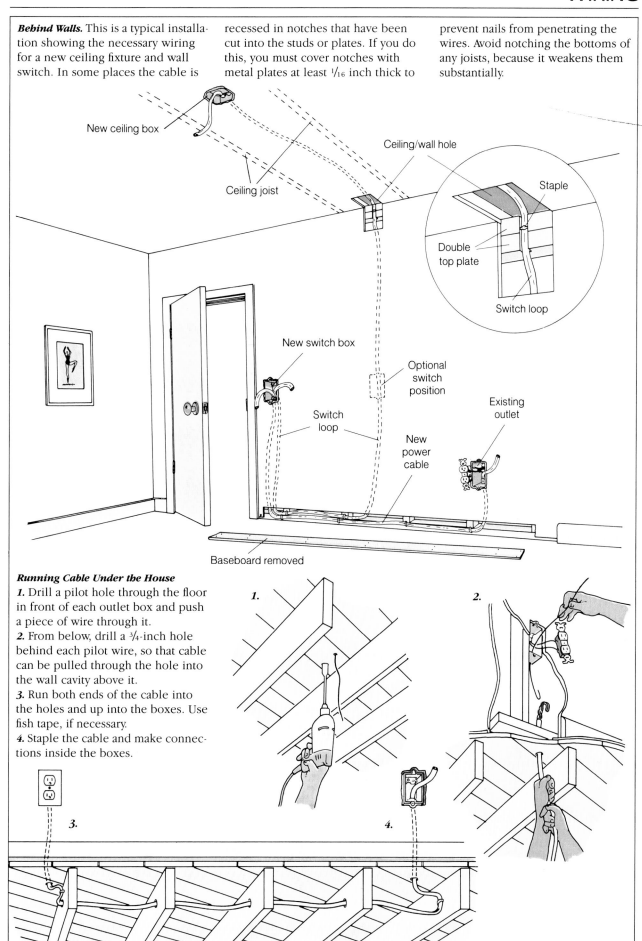

New ceiling box

Ceiling joist

Ceiling/wall hole

Staple

Double top plate

Switch loop

New switch box

Optional switch position

Existing outlet

Switch loop

New power cable

Baseboard removed

Running Cable Under the House

1. Drill a pilot hole through the floor in front of each outlet box and push a piece of wire through it.

2. From below, drill a $3/4$-inch hole behind each pilot wire, so that cable can be pulled through the hole into the wall cavity above it.

3. Run both ends of the cable into the holes and up into the boxes. Use fish tape, if necessary.

4. Staple the cable and make connections inside the boxes.

1.

2.

3.

4.

Wiring to an Existing Circuit

Most general-purpose circuits can handle an additional fixture. (Never tie into an individual appliance circuit.) You can connect the new wiring inside a junction box or at an existing fixture. Always turn off the power before working on a circuit.

The easiest connection is at a junction box. Connect all the white neutral wires together and all the black hot wires together. Connect the ground wires together and ground the box to them with a short pigtail of bare or green wire. The box must have a metal cover and be accessible.

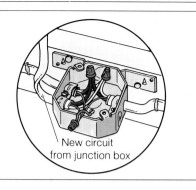

New circuit from junction box

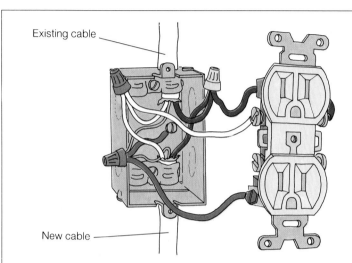

Existing cable

New cable

End-of-the-Run Receptacle

This is an easy place to tie into a circuit. However, first plug in a lamp to make sure the outlet is not controlled by a switch. If it is, do not add new wiring. If it is not, run the new cable into the box and connect neutral and hot wires to the receptacle, as shown. Connect the ground wire to the ground wire belonging to the old cable and both pigtails.

Middle-of-the-Run Receptacle

This box already has an incoming and an outgoing cable, in addition to a receptacle, so you will probably have to enlarge the box for an additional cable. Run the new cable into the box and connect it, as shown.

Note: The connections shown for middle-of-the-run and end-of-the-run receptacles are made by wiring

"through" the receptacle. Some codes require that hot wires and neutral wires from all the cables in the box be connected directly together, and that the receptacle be wired to them with short pigtails. Also, they sometimes require that ground wires be connected together with crimp-type collars instead of wire nuts, as shown in the illustrations.

Middle-of-the-Run Switch

If power from the source comes directly to the switch, the box will have two cables coming in and you can connect new wiring. If there is only one cable, it is a switch loop, which you should not tie into.

Before turning off the power, use a voltage tester to establish which of the black wires is the incoming hot source (be sure the switch is in the "off" position). Then shut off the power and disconnect that wire from the switch. Tie the black wire from the new cable and a short pigtail into it. Attach the pigtail to the switch. Connect neutral wires and grounds together, as shown.

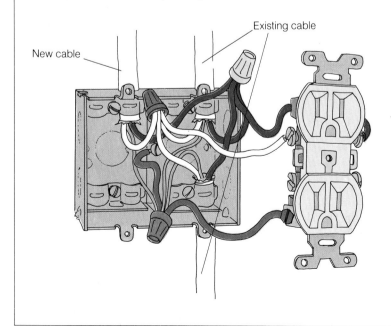

New cable

Existing cable

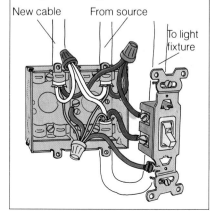

New cable   From source

To light fixture

Wiring a 240-Volt Receptacle

Ranges and dryers can be wired with a cord and receptacle for easy moving. The receptacle and plug must be mated and must match the rated amperage of the appliance, in this case 50 amps. The conductors must be sized as well (No. 6), and can be three-wire service-entrance cable. The neutral conductor, which carries only the current of the 120-volt lights, motor, or clock, can function as a grounding conductor if it is No. 10 wire or larger. Check local codes for other restrictions.

Each 240-volt appliance must be on its own circuit. This must originate in the service panel or a subpanel and be protected by a fuse or breaker. Locate appliances near the service panel or install a subpanel nearby to avoid long runs.

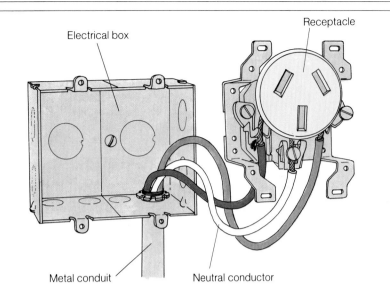

Electrical box

Receptacle

Metal conduit

Neutral conductor

Wiring a Water Heater

Appliances requiring 240 volts that do not have a cord set are wired directly to a junction box with flexible armored cable. A water heater only needs two-wire cable with ground because the heater has no 120-volt current requiring a separate neutral wire. The ground wire must be No. 10 or larger. It should be bonded to the junction box and wired through to the metal case of the water heater. Check local codes for other restrictions.

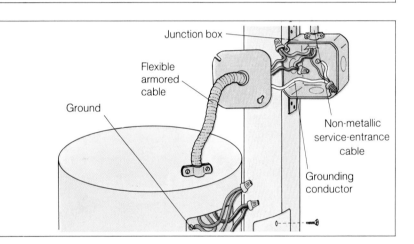

Junction box

Flexible armored cable

Ground

Non-metallic service-entrance cable

Grounding conductor

A Multiwire Circuit

Some codes allow two 120-volt circuits that are close to each other to be wired on the same three-wire cable, such as a dishwasher and garbage disposer or two small-appliance circuits serving the same kitchen counter. The black wire is the hot leg for one circuit, the red wire is the hot leg for the other, and the neutral wire serves both. Each hot leg has its own circuit breaker, and the handles must be connected to turn off both simultaneously.

Pictured below are receptacles along a kitchen counter alternately wired on different circuits, using the same three-wire cable. In some cases, local codes may require that the white neutral wires be connected together and joined to the receptacle with a short pigtail.

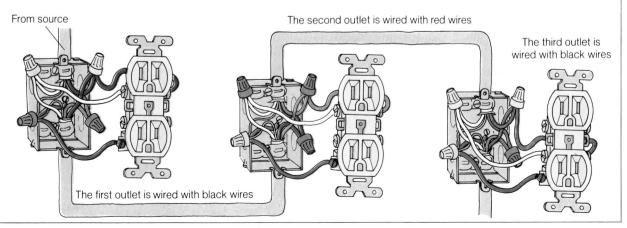

From source

The second outlet is wired with red wires

The third outlet is wired with black wires

The first outlet is wired with black wires

WOOD

Wood is beautiful, strong, lightweight, easy to work with, and, as if that were not enough, it even smells good. Wood is also natural, renewable, and readily available in an astonishing variety of species, grades, sizes, cuts, finishes, and products. This diversity can make shopping for lumber a bewildering experience, but if you become familiar with a few basic distinctions you will most likely find exactly what you need in one quick shopping trip.

One of the first considerations when choosing wood is the type of product you need, such as dimensioned lumber, milled products, or manufactured wood. When buying lumber, you need to specify dimension and length, as well as species and grade. The dimension of a board is the cross-sectional size, although the actual measurements may be less than the nominal size. Specifying rough or surfaced lumber also affects the dimension. Length, however, is more exact. The board will be at least as long as the nominal length, and sometimes it might be a couple of inches longer.

Recommended Cross-References
Most entries.

Most lumberyards store finish materials according to type, species, and length.

Moisture Content

When you buy lumber from a dealer you are usually concerned with size, length, strength, and appearance, but there are times when you should also be aware of the moisture content. Moisture content is expressed as a percentage that represents the additional weight of the wet lumber compared with the weight of the lumber when completely dry. Most framing lumber has a moisture content of 19 percent or less. Lumber for finish work should have a moisture content between 8 percent and 11 percent, a low moisture content that is achieved by kiln drying. A freshly cut tree, on the other hand, can have a moisture content between 100 percent and 200 percent, double or even triple the weight of the tree if it were completely dry.

Moisture content is an important factor in choosing lumber because wood will continue to lose moisture until it reaches equilibrium with the environment. If you live in a very dry climate, you need to choose lumber that has a very low moisture content. Otherwise, the wood will shrink as it dries, and the result will be cupping, bowing, and other types of warping. Even a small change in the amount of moisture will cause a board to bend or crack. If wood is concealed, this is not a serious problem. However, use kiln-dried lumber for trim, finish work, and critical structural members such as trimmer studs next to a door or window. Because wood shrinks across the grain rather than along the length, a large piece of lumber is prone to shrink much more than small-dimensioned material. This is especially true of headers over doors and windows. If headers are too green when installed, they can cause the wallboard nailed to them to split.

For most framing projects, use lumber with a 19 percent moisture content. Order the lumber several weeks in advance and stack it, placing scrap lumber between each row of boards. Weight the pile with heavy objects, like sacks of gravel or stones, to minimize warping.

Sawing Styles

Plain Sawed Lumber. Plain sawing is the fastest and least wasteful way to saw a log. Most construction-grade lumber is produced in this manner. Plain sawing produces flat-grain lumber with a pattern that resembles marble. The grain imparts strength, but the appearance of plain sawed lumber is not always suitable. In addition, plain sawed lumber is also prone to cupping and warping.

Quarter Sawed Lumber. Quarter sawed boards have vertical grain, which shows as parallel lines along the face of the board. Vertical grain is desirable for fine finish work and is durable when exposed to weather. More of a quarter sawed log ends as sawdust. As a result, lumber produced by this method, which is also known by the term rift cutting, tends to be rather expensive.

Veneer. Veneer is a continuous layer of wood that was peeled off a rotating log. It is used for making plywood and paneling, but thin veneers of fine woods are available for use in cabinetmaking. The grain pattern of a veneer resembles plain sawed lumber, but vertical grain veneers made from thin sheets of quarter sawed lumber are also available.

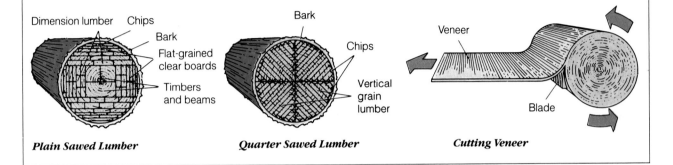

Plain Sawed Lumber

Quarter Sawed Lumber

Cutting Veneer

Grades of Lumber

Each species of lumber is subject to grading systems that evaluate many factors: strength, the number and size of knots, the amount of sapwood, the grain pattern, and surface appearance. Various associations throughout the country use different grading systems, so it is impossible to assume that the same term always means the same thing in regard to different species of lumber. Although there are many associations and many grading standards, the standards within one association are usually consistent. Not all lumber producers belong to an association, however, so obtain a copy of grading criteria from your lumber dealer and inspect the lumber yourself.

Your local building code probably specifies the grade of lumber you must use for framing and structural work. Failure to understand the grading terminology in a matter of code compliance could result in an expensive mistake. For instance, the term *construction* in one grading system refers to an inferior grade of lumber that codes would not accept. In other grading systems, however, construction-grade lumber is perfectly adequate.

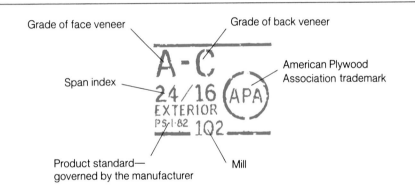

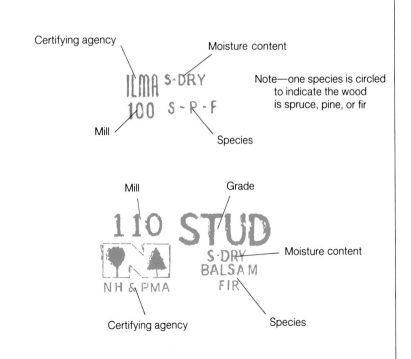

WOOD: continued

Selecting Lumber

Framing lumber is bound to have a few warped and blemished pieces. Make use of marginal lumber as blocking, or use curves to advantage to counteract the pull of gravity. Finish lumber, however, must be straight and free of splits or defects. Inspect any shipments before they are unloaded at your job site, and do not accept pieces that are totally unusable. Whenever possible pick up your own lumber at the yard, even if there is a slight charge.

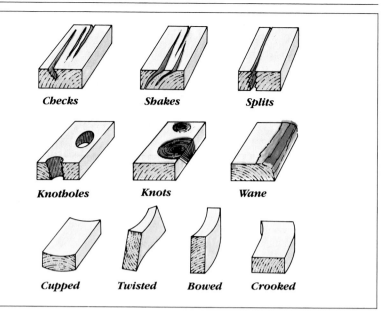

Checks   **Shakes**   **Splits**

Knotholes   **Knots**   **Wane**

Cupped   **Twisted**   **Bowed**   **Crooked**

Stacking Lumber

If you store lumber for any length of time before using it, stick it and stack it as shown. Set the stickers close enough so the boards do not sag. Add a few extra stickers every few layers to keep the stack stable. Pick a dry area and stack the pile off the ground. If you stack green lumber this way, it will be fully seasoned in about six months.

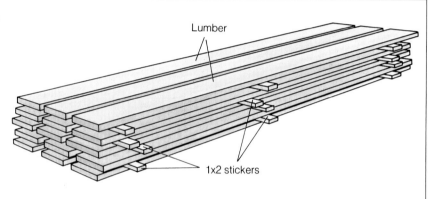

Lumber

1x2 stickers

Lumber Products

Technically, a board is less than 2 inches thick. The most common are 1-bys, which, in most cases, are actually ¾ inch thick. Some 1-by products may be ⅝ inch thick.

Lumber thicker than 2 inches is called dimension lumber. This includes the ubiquitous 2 by 4 as well as other 2-by and 4-by lumber. Anything larger than 5 by 5 is a timber.

Wood with contours and shaped edges is called a milled product and includes moldings, board sidings, and tongue-and-groove lumber.

Panelized wood is the final category of wood products. It includes plywood or one of the many forms of compressed board. Plywood consists of several layers, called veneers, cut from a log and glued to one another crosswise. Compressed boards, available in large panels or narrow boards, are manufactured from wood chips and particles compressed into a solid board by heat and pressure.

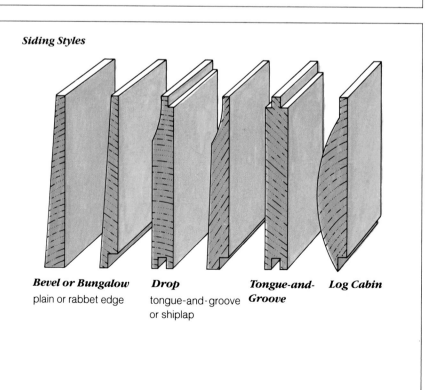

Siding Styles

Bevel or Bungalow
plain or rabbet edge

Drop
tongue-and-groove
or shiplap

Tongue-and-Groove

Log Cabin

490

Pressure-Treated Lumber

Most lumber is subject to decay and insect attack and is therefore unsuitable for outdoor or ground-contact use. However, it can be treated by a process of injecting preservatives under pressure, causing the preservatives to become locked permanently into the wood. Pressure-treated lumber is far superior to wood that has been merely sprayed or dipped in a chemical preservative. In many cases it will outlast naturally durable species like redwood, cedar, or cypress. Pressure-treated lumber is recommended when wood will be subjected to ground contact or buried; some codes actually demand that it is used.

The most common types of chemicals used for pressure-treating lumber are waterborne salts such as chromated copper arsenate (CCA) and ammoniacal copper arsenate (ACA). These preservatives are recommended where the wood will be close to plants; they can be used safely around the home except for surfaces that will be in direct contact with food or serving utensils. Other preservatives used are pentachlorothenol and creosote, but they are very toxic and the lumber cannot be painted or stained as easily as lumber treated with CCA or ACA. Penta applied with liquid petroleum gas (LPG) is an exception.

Pressure-treated lumber is slightly green or beige in color and does not darken if left to weather. When buying it, specify whether it is for ground contact (LP-22) or above-ground (LP-2) use. Sometimes it is incised or punctured on the surface to facilitate the penetration of chemicals. For projects where a smooth, unblemished appearance is critical, ask for pressure-treated lumber without incisement. It is also worth the extra cost to buy lumber that is kiln-dried after treatment (KDAT) to avoid extensive warping in exposed outdoor applications.

When you work with pressure-treated lumber, wear goggles and a dust mask when cutting it and gloves when handling it—especially if it is damp. Do not burn scraps; dispose of them in an approved landfill. Coat the ends of cut boards with an approved preservative.

Wood Finishes

Type Uses	Description
Oil Paint	Any of various opaque pigments suspended in linseed oil, or, more commonly, alkyd resin. Although flat finishes are available, oil-based paint is mostly used where a gloss finish is required. Clean applicators with turpentine or mineral spirits
Latex Paint	Synthetic rubber (latex) particles suspended in a water base. Less expensive than oil paint. Clean applicators with water
Varnish	Varnish is oil paint without the pigments. The type of resin used gives the varnish distinct properties. Polyurethane is recommended for most uses, it is clear and hard. Check labels on different varnishes for properties that meet your specific requirements. Clean applicators with mineral spirits
Shellac	Fast-drying clear finish. Use orange shellac over dark or stained wood; white shellac over light wood. Several coats produce a high-gloss finish, which can be dulled by rubbing with steel wool. Clean applicators with ammonia and water or alcohol
Stain	Oil-based stain is a suitable exterior finish and wood preservative for wood siding. Use water-based stain to darken and color interior wood. Apply to clean, unfinished wood

Plywood Veneer Grades

The following grades are listed in descending order of quality:

N. Smooth surface, natural finish veneer. Made of select grade wood. Free of open defects.

A. Smooth surface. Natural finish can be used if you are not too demanding.

B. Solid surface with circular repair plugs, shims, and tight knots. Some minor splits are permitted.

C Plugged. Splits cannot be more than $\frac{1}{8}$ inch. Some repair and broken grain permitted.

C. Tight knots up to $1\frac{1}{2}$ inch are allowed. Repairs, discoloration, limited splits, sanding defects, and stitching (piecing) are permissable if they do not impair the strength.

D. Knots and knotholes up to 3 inches wide are allowed. Splits and stitching are permitted.

Lumber Shrinkage

The following lumber sizes are those established by the American Lumber Standards Committee.

Nominal (inches)	Dry (inches)	Green (inches)
1	$\frac{3}{4}$	$\frac{25}{32}$
2	$1\frac{1}{2}$	$1\frac{9}{16}$
4	$3\frac{1}{2}$	$3\frac{9}{16}$
6	$5\frac{1}{2}$	$5\frac{5}{8}$
8	$7\frac{1}{4}$	$7\frac{1}{2}$
10	$9\frac{1}{4}$	$9\frac{1}{2}$

Nominal Lumber Sizes and Their Actual Equivalents

Nominal	Actual	Nominal	Actual
1 × 2	$\frac{3}{4} \times 1\frac{1}{2}$	2 × 2	$1\frac{1}{2} \times 1\frac{1}{2}$
1 × 3	$\frac{3}{4} \times 2\frac{1}{2}$	2 × 3	$1\frac{1}{2} \times 2\frac{1}{2}$
1 × 4	$\frac{3}{4} \times 3\frac{1}{2}$	2 × 4	$1\frac{1}{2} \times 3\frac{1}{2}$
1 × 6	$\frac{3}{4} \times 5\frac{1}{2}$	2 × 6	$1\frac{1}{2} \times 5\frac{1}{2}$
1 × 8	$\frac{3}{4} \times 7\frac{1}{4}$	2 × 8	$1\frac{1}{2} \times 7\frac{1}{4}$
1 × 10	$\frac{3}{4} \times 9\frac{1}{4}$	2 × 10	$1\frac{1}{2} \times 9\frac{1}{4}$
1 × 12	$\frac{3}{4} \times 11\frac{1}{4}$	2 × 12	$1\frac{1}{2} \times 11\frac{1}{4}$
		4 × 4	$3\frac{1}{2} \times 3\frac{1}{2}$

Manufactured Wood Products

Manufactured wood products include well-known materials, such as plywood, particleboard, and hardboard. Less widely known items include oriented strand board (OSB), laminated beams, and waferboard or flakeboard. All are becoming more common. Manufactured wood products are used for furniture, subflooring, sheathing, joists, underlayment, siding, shingles, and even framing. Strength, durability, and consistency of quality are often equal to or greater than the equivalent wood product.

Manufactured wood products are bonded with urea-formaldehyde or phenol-formaldehyde glues. These resins emit gases for a significant period of time. People who are sensitive to ureaformaldehyde (used in particleboard and some medium-density fiberboard) should choose a product made with phenol-formaldehyde, and test their reaction to it before building an addition or a new home. When buying particleboard or MDF, check for the mark "HUD 24 CFR PART 3280." This indicates that the product complies with federal standards on emissions of formaldehyde gas.

Sheet Products

Plywood. The plywood used in construction is made of laminated layers, each layer consisting of one or more veneer plies. It is widely used and comes in a range of grades, which vary according to strength and appearance.

Oriented Strand Board (OSB). OSB panels are made of compressed strandlike particles, arranged in layers at right angles to each other and bonded with phenol-formaldehyde. OSB is used for subflooring and for wall and roof sheathing. It is comparable to plywood in its ability to hold screws and nails.

Composite. This is made of veneer laminated to OSB with phenol-formaldehyde. It is available in framing timber sizes and standard 4 by 8 panels.

Waferboard. This is made of wood chips and flakes randomly compressed and bonded with phenol-formaldehyde. It can be used for paneling, as well as wall and roof sheathing. Its ability to hold nails and screws is fair, but is not as strong as OSB or plywood.

Particleboard. This is comprised of wood chips, sawdust, and other small particles bonded with urea-formaldehyde. It is used as underlayment for counter laminates and vinyl floors, the core of furniture and cabinet veneers, and the core of doors. It is very heavy. Its ability to hold nails and screws is poor; you must use specialized fasteners or attach it to solid wood.

Hardboard. This is made of wood fibers compressed and bonded with phenol-formaldehyde or linseed oil. It is used in furniture, drawers, siding, panels, pegboard, and doors. It comes tempered and untempered. The tempered variety is moisture resistant and is used for siding. Follow the manufacturer's instructions carefully to protect the warranty when installing hardboard siding.

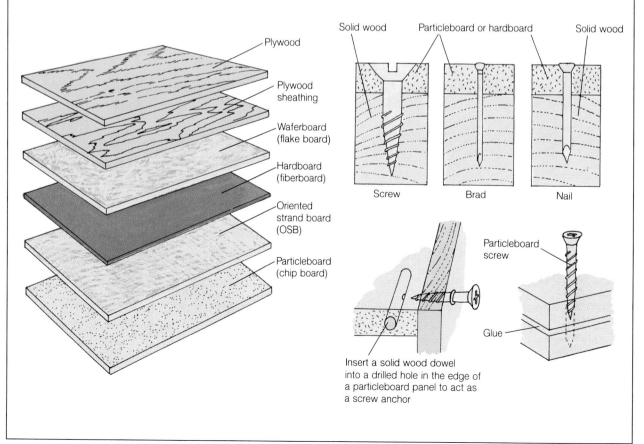

Fastening Particleboard or Hardboard

Manufactured Beams and Framing Lumber

Laminated Beams. You may be familiar with these large beams—called glulams—used to support roofs of supermarkets and churches. They consist of uniformly dimensioned lumber glued together in either a straight or curved form. The beams are stronger than sawn timbers of the same size, can be much longer—up to 60 feet or more—and do not shrink or warp easily. Even straight glulams have a slight curve built into them, so be sure to install them with the edge marked "top" facing upward. Connect glulams to other framing members with metal brackets and machine bolts, but be sure any saddle brackets you use are sized for glulams, which are narrower than sawn timbers of similar size. Notching or drilling through a glulam may weaken it significantly, so consult the manufacturer's specifications before you attempt to do so.

Laminated-Veneer Lumber. Referred to as LVL, this material is manufactured in layers of natural veneer, similar to plywood, and comes in standard lumber sizes. It is used most frequently for beams, headers, and other structural components. Unlike plywood, all the veneers in LVL are parallel, with the grain running in the same direction. It tends to be stronger, more stable, and available in longer lengths than most sawn lumber.

Parallel Strand Lumber. Similar to OSB, with most of the fibers and strands in the product oriented in the same direction, PSL comes in standard lumber sizes and is used for most framing applications. Its uniform appearance makes it suitable for exposed beams.

I Joists. These are a composite of plywood or OSB and natural lumber. The joists resemble I beams. They bear weight as though they were solid wood. As long as they are kept from twisting and are installed correctly, they result in flat, quiet floors that are very stable and strong. They also allow considerable flexibility in routing ducts and pipes through the webbings.

Plastic Lumber. This recently developed product uses recycled plastic and comes in standard lumber dimensions. It is not widely used or widely available. Standards are not uniform from one manufacturer to another, or even among batches from one manufacturer. It is not approved for structural use. It is used in areas subject to rot, such as dock decking, garden borders, and sign posts. It can be cut and worked like wood lumber.

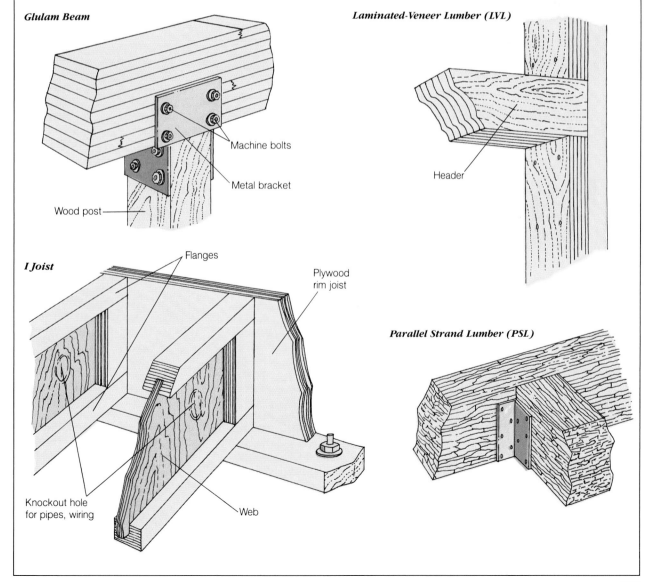

Glulam Beam

Machine bolts

Metal bracket

Wood post

Laminated-Veneer Lumber (LVL)

Header

I Joist

Flanges

Plywood rim joist

Knockout hole for pipes, wiring

Web

Parallel Strand Lumber (PSL)

WOOD-BURNING STOVES

Over the past few years Americans have demonstrated a renewed interest in burning wood for heat and the wood-burning stove has enjoyed a corresponding renaissance. A wood-burning stove—especially an airtight stove with a catalytic combustor or secondary combustion chamber—is the most efficient way to do it. A wood-burning stove distributes heat more efficiently than a fireplace and therefore heats more of the house for longer periods and with less fuel. A wood-burning stove actually costs less to install than a masonry fireplace and is safer and more durable than many prefabricated metal fireplaces.

If you already have a fireplace, it can be modified to allow installation of a modern wood-burning stove. Careful consideration should be made to the way the stove is installed. Though the existing chimney can be used, in most cases it was not properly designed for a wood-burning stove and should be relined.

Recommended Cross-References
Chimneys & Stovepipes, Fireplaces, Heating.

Clean-Burning Stoves
Airtight wood-burning stoves use fuel so efficiently that the cool exhaust gases cause two problems: creosote buildup in the chimney and air pollution in the atmosphere. New technologies minimize these problems. Stoves with secondary combustion chambers or catalytic combustors burn wood smoke a second time. The second burning captures more heat and burns particles that would otherwise cause creosote buildup or air pollution. If you are in the market for a new stove, consider buying a clean-burning stove. To increase the efficiency of an existing stove, install a catalytic device inside the stove or on the outlet. A retrofit is not as efficient as a stove designed to utilize a catalytic combustor, but it will boost efficiency significantly. In all cases, you should carefully monitor the functioning of the catalytic combustor and replace the catalytic element every 3 to 5 years.

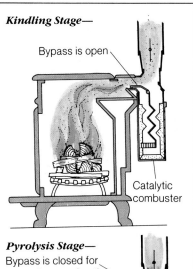

Kindling Stage—
Bypass is open
Catalytic combuster

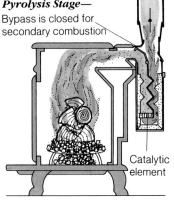

Pyrolysis Stage—
Bypass is closed for secondary combustion
Catalytic element

How a Wood-Burning Stove Works
To varying extents, all wood-burning stoves heat by conduction and radiation, but the most significant mode of heat distribution for warming a large space is convection. When wood burns in a stove, heat is conducted through the metal firebox and radiates from it toward objects in the room. The heated metal warms the surrounding air, causing it to rise and be replaced by cooler air near the floor. This moving air, called a convective current, circulates around the room. A fan can increase circulation and significantly increase efficiency. In addition, the best stoves have passages and ducts within them that enhance convection.

The efficiency of a wood-burning stove is also a function of how quickly the fuel burns. A large, hot fire burns fuel quickly, sending most of the heat up the chimney. A small, slow-burning fire provides constant heat over a longer period of time and loses smaller amounts to the chimney. Stoves that allow you to control the rate of burning by constricting air intake are called "airtight stoves." Actually, they are not completely airtight, but all the traditional leaks and gaps are sealed so all the airflow can be controlled. The more accurate term for this type of stove is "combustion-controlled."

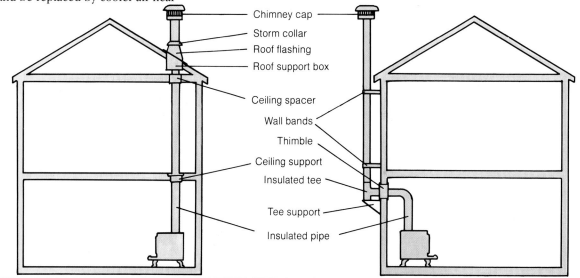

Chimney cap
Storm collar
Roof flashing
Roof support box
Ceiling spacer
Wall bands
Thimble
Ceiling support
Insulated tee
Tee support
Insulated pipe

Positioning a Wood Stove

Some rooms are more appropriate sites for a wood-burning stove than others. The ideal room is one that is central and has a low ceiling. In general, the more open and accessible the rooms are to stove heat, the better the convection throughout the entire house.

If you have a sprawling, ranch-style house, consider putting a stove at each end of the house. If you have a two-story house, put the stove downstairs, but not near the stairwell because all the heat will rise too quickly. Floor vents enable you to improve the circulation of heat upstairs. Do not put the stove in the basement unless you intend that the stove heat only this space; the radiant heat will be of no benefit to people upstairs.

If possible, keep the stove away from windows so that heat is not lost through the glass. If you place the stove by an existing fireplace, block the fireplace opening.

A further consideration is the need for an outside air intake near the primary air control of the stove. Combustion in the stove uses large amounts of air and because newer houses are built very tight the stove will have trouble functioning properly without its own source of oxygen. Most building codes now require that a vent be placed in the floor near the stove or behind it to allow outside air to be ducted directly to the stove.

In positioning the stove you should consider how you will route this air intake. In older houses the outside air intake is also a good idea because the stove will have a tendency to pull air from the room causing drafts around leaky windows and doors. This air will cool the interior of the house as it flows toward the stove. The outside air intake minimizes this effect.

Above all, safety must be considered in your choice of location. Although any room can be altered for a safe wood-burning stove installation, avoid rooms where combustion air may be limited, such as small, closed bedrooms. Also avoid rooms where small children play without close supervision.

Installation

Some stove dealers will install a new unit for you. If not, the salesperson can usually refer you to a local independent contractor. Installations take anywhere from a few hours to a couple of days. You can also install a stove yourself, as long as you comply with all local code requirements, safe installation practices, and manufacturer's instructions. Be sure the chimney is in sound condition, and be aware that not all chimneys are substantial enough to withstand the intense heat produced by a wood-burning stove. Hire a competent professional to inspect the chimney.

If you install the stove in front of an existing fireplace, connect the stovepipe to your chimney, either at the bottom or into a hole cut above the mantle. In the best installations using an existing chimney, a metal flue runs up the entire chimney. Specialized flues, usually stainless steel, are available for this purpose, and some are even flexible for curving around the throat of the chimney. Pack noncombustible insulating material around the flue after it is installed. Block up the remaining fireplace opening with a plate of metal or some other noncombustible material. Stoves that fit into the fireplace also require a flue and usually include all the hardware for blocking up the fireplace opening.

Whether installed in front of a fireplace or not, your installation must conform to local codes for distance to combustible materials and the nature of noncombustible barriers. Instructions included with the stove will give minimum clearances.

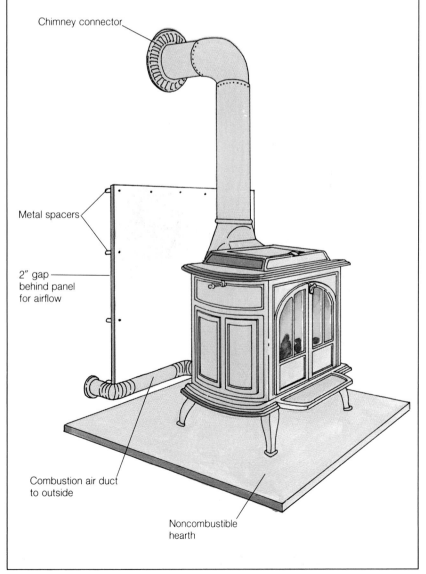

Chimney connector

Metal spacers

2" gap behind panel for airflow

Combustion air duct to outside

Noncombustible hearth

WOOD FLOORS

The warmth, beauty, and durability of wood make it one of the most popular flooring materials. Wood adds a feeling of quality and permanence to any room, and, in fact, it will last the lifetime of a house if properly installed. If well protected and cared for, wood will never even have to be refinished, but will only look better as it takes on the patina of age. Wood also has insulating properties and is comfortably resilient to walk on.

Wood is subject to moisture damage, either from spills or humidity. Take precautions when installing it around plumbing fixtures, over an enclosed crawl space, or below grade.

Although modern floor finishes are tough, a wood floor is still vulnerable to scratches and surface abrasion.

This might be a drawback in high-traffic areas or in beach locales, where sand is common.

Wood floors are made of either hardwood or softwood and, in some cases, the material comes prefinished. Most are hardwood: either red oak, white oak, teak, walnut, maple, pecan, or hickory. Softwoods, such as pine, Douglas fir, and redwood, can also be used as flooring materials, but they will scratch and pit more easily than the hardwoods.

Flooring is milled in three basic formats: strip, plank, and block. Strip flooring comes in widths of up to 3¼ inches. Strip flooring is usually ¾ inch thick with tongue-and-groove edges. Square-edged flooring, ⁵⁄₁₆ inch thick, is also widely used. Plank flooring is

wider than 3¼ inches, usually in random widths of up to 8 or 9 inches. It is ¾ inch thick and has tongue-and-groove edges. Sometimes the ends are held down with pegs or with screws that are countersunk and covered with plugs. Plugs are installed also for purely decorative purposes. Both strip and plank flooring are available with grooved edges. Wood flooring also comes in finger blocks that are arranged into parquet tiles.

Recommended Cross-References
Floors, Resilient Flooring, Sub-floors, Thresholds.

Widely spaced random-width planks give this floor a warm, rustic look. Specialized floor filler is used to fill the gaps between the boards.

Prefinished Wood Floors

Installing traditional wood floors requires a great deal of labor, followed by a messy sanding and finishing process. However, modern prefinished hardwood flooring can be installed by an average homeowner with excellent results. Be sure to check the durability of the finish and the installation requirements before you buy. Most prefinished hardwood flooring is too thin to be sanded more than once; and some can't be sanded at all.

Most prefinished wood floors are made of laminated material, which is more stable than solid wood and can be directly fastened to almost any subfloor, as long as it is level, dry, and tight. The floor can be glued to concrete, vinyl, or plywood.

There are two installation methods, one in which the floor is attached to the surface beneath it and the other in which the floor floats on a pad.

Attached Floor. Remove the baseboard to allow an expansion gap. Remove carpeting and repair any damage to the floor below.

Cut the door trim at the base so the new flooring will slip beneath it.

Move the flooring material into the room. Lay out test patterns to see how the flooring fits in doorways and irregular areas. Plan the layout. Make a paper template if necessary.

Cut pieces to length as needed. A backsaw or hand miter box will work, but a power miter saw is best. Cut pieces to width with a jigsaw or sharp handsaw. Protect the finished surface when you clamp pieces to be cut.

Mark the outline of cut pieces on the floor.

Apply adhesive with a notched trowel up to the guideline, following the manufacturer's instructions. Install the planks. Glue should not ooze up through the cracks; if it does, there is too much glue or you moved the plank too much.

Walk on the surface or use a roller to get a tight bond. Weight down any areas that don't adhere.

Continue to add flooring run by run. Spread only as much adhesive as you can easily cover in the time before it cures. Use a respirator and provide ventilation if the adhesive emits fumes.

Cut off the excess at the end of each run and use it to start the next run. Allow ⅜ inch for expansion and contraction at the walls.

When the flooring is laid, cover the gaps at the walls with baseboard.

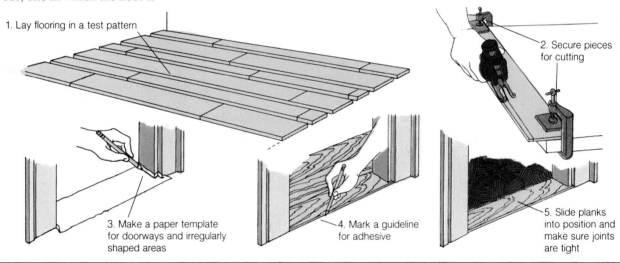

1. Lay flooring in a test pattern

2. Secure pieces for cutting

3. Make a paper template for doorways and irregularly shaped areas

4. Mark a guideline for adhesive

5. Slide planks into position and make sure joints are tight

Floating Floor

An easier installation technique uses a ⅛-inch foam pad under the floor and requires only a little carpenter's wood glue between the pieces. The tongue-and-groove fittings are very precise, so the pieces must be tapped together gently to ensure a tight fit.

Roll the pad into position and trim it as needed.

Lay the planks, leaving a ⅜-inch gap at the walls. Cut off any excess and use it to start the next run.

As you lay each plank, glue it to the one already laid next to it with a thin bead of carpenter's wood glue inside the bottom of the groove.

Tap the planks together, using a scrap piece to protect the edges.

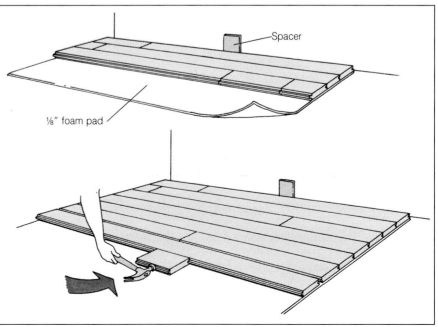

Spacer

⅛" foam pad

Preparing for Installation

As well as preparing the subsurface, you also need to prepare the door openings. To avoid complicated flooring cuts later on, saw off the bottoms of all door casings and door stops—but not door jambs. Saw them off just high enough for the flooring material to slide under snugly. Carefully pry off the baseboards and write an identifying mark on the back. If it makes it easier to work, remove the doors.

If installing wood flooring in a kitchen, realize that the new floor will effectively lower the countertop height by the thickness of the flooring material.

Wood flooring has a low moisture content and is subject to expansion and shrinkage from climatic conditions. Avoid deliveries during rain or snow, and make sure all concrete work, plaster work, and painting in the house are finished. Store the wood in the same room in which you plan to install it, or at least inside the house. The room should be dry and heated to 65° or 70° F. Stack the material log-cabin style or scatter it around the room, then let it acclimate for three to five days.

Planning the Layout

If you are installing strip flooring in only one room, simply start along one wall and work your way across the room. Laying boards with the tongue edge exposed makes it possible to blind-nail each board.

If installation extends to other rooms, or even a closet or hallway off of the room you are installing, you will have to plan the layout so that you can cover as much area as possible by working in one direction. At some point you will need to change direction. This may happen when you get too close to a wall to swing a hammer or when you run flooring into an alcove. To change direction, use a spline—a strip of wood that fits snugly into the groove. The spline converts a grooved edge into a tongued one.

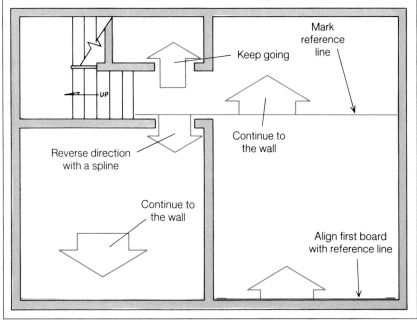

Establishing Guidelines

Strip flooring is generally laid perpendicular to the joists, with the blind-nailing centered over them. To guide the nailing, snap chalk lines over all the joists. You can determine their locations by looking for the nailing pattern of the subfloor. Mark the joist positions on the wall to help you snap chalk lines after laying building paper.

In some cases the flooring may

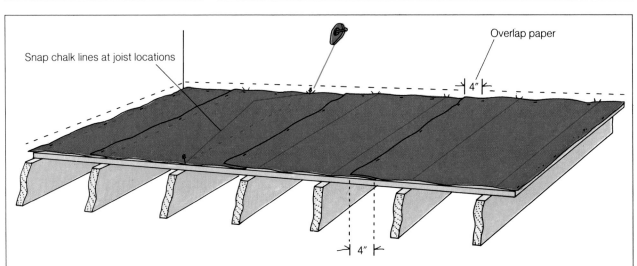

look better if it runs parallel to the joists. You can install it this way if the subfloor is at least ¾ inch thick and very sound. Then you just snap chalk lines on 16-inch centers.

Before snapping chalk lines, cover any floor that is not over heated space with 15-pound asphalt-saturated building paper laid perpendicular to the direction of the new flooring. Overlap edges 4 inches, and trim the paper around the wall so that it lies

flat. Staple or tack the building paper in place. Then snap chalk lines between the joist marks on the walls.

To establish a guideline along the starting wall, measure out ¾ inch at each end of the wall and drive a small nail into the floor. Stretch a string line tautly between these two nails. The ¾-inch space will allow the wood to expand without buckling the boards and the gap will be covered by the baseboard.

Installing the Starter Course

Align the first row of flooring with the string line. If the wall is not square with the rest of the room, which you can determine by measuring the diagonals of the room, you will have to adjust the starter line so that the flooring layout will be square. Follow the same layout techniques described for resilient tile to establish a centerline. Adjust the string line until it is parallel.

Lay the first board against the string line so that the left end is ½ inch from the side wall. (Floor installers refer to left and right with their backs to the starting wall.) Line up the groove edge along the string line. Beginning at the left end, carefully facenail the board with 8d finishing nails at every joist and halfway between them. Because facenailing can split the board quite easily, predrill for each nail.

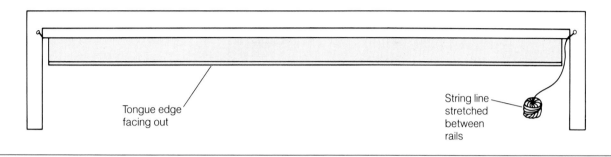

Tongue edge facing out

String line stretched between rails

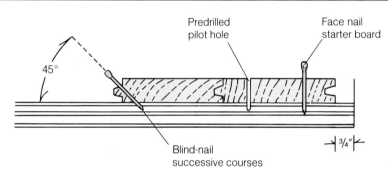

Predrilled pilot hole

Face nail starter board

45°

Blind-nail successive courses

¾"

2"

Nailing Tongue-and-Groove Flooring

Complete the starter course by facenailing additional boards. Cut the last board ½ inch short of the side wall, and use the cutoff piece to start the next course. Blind-nail the tongue edge of each board by hand. Drive in nails at a 45-degree angle, being careful not to ding the edge of the board. Set nail heads into tongue edges with a nailset.

Blind-nail the next two courses by hand, staggering the joints in a random pattern. Nail at each joist, at the midpoints between joists, and 2 inches from each board end. Every board should have at least two nails, no matter how short. Use a nailing machine for the rest of the floor.

Using a Nailing Machine. Stand so that your toes can hold down the board being nailed. When you hit the plunger with the mallet, it drives a nail into the tongue. Use a firm, easy swing, working from left to right.

Racking the Floor

To ensure a random joint pattern in the floor, loosely arrange six or seven courses of boards at a time, mixing long and short lengths. This process is called racking the floor. Be sure that all joints stagger at least 6 inches. Begin each course with the cutoff piece from the end of the previous course. Rack the boards loosely enough for you to have room to operate the nailing machine.

If you are installing flooring of various widths, such as 3-inch, 5-inch, and 8-inch plank flooring, separate the boards into piles of the same width before racking them. This will give you an idea of how many boards are available in each size so that you can maintain the same pattern without running out of a particular dimension.

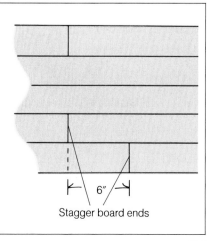

6"

Stagger board ends

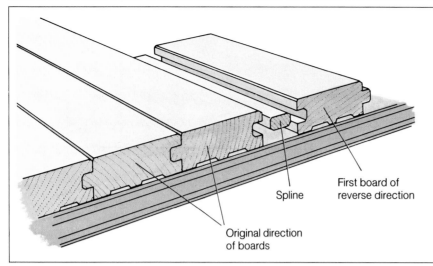

Spline

First board of reverse direction

Original direction of boards

Installing a Spline

If a hallway or closet is along the starting wall, or if there is a similar opening where one of the courses extends beyond the starting room, you will need to reverse the direction of the tongue edge. To do this, glue a spline or slip-tongue into the groove of the starter strip and proceed to install the reversed flooring courses. Lay the first board so that the groove interlocks with the spline. Tap it into place, using a scrap of wood to protect the tongue from being damaged by the hammer.

Nailing

Since not all wood floors are ¾-inch tongue-and-groove, they require different sizes of nails. Whenever possible, use nails designated for flooring. If you are repairing a squeaky floor, use spiral shank nails that resemble screws and hold better than plain nails. When facenailing, always set nails below the surface and fill the holes with wood putty.

Nail Schedule

This chart shows the nail sizes and spacing for various wood flooring materials. For planking wider than 4 inches, No. 9 or No. 12 screws are used for additional fastening.

Tongue-and-Groove Flooring Blind-Nailed

Flooring	Fastener	Spacing
½″ x 1½″	1½″ machine-driven fastener; 5d screw, cut steel, or wire casing nail.	10″ apart
⅜″ x 1½″	1¼″ machine-driven fastener; 4d bright wire casing nail.	8″ apart
¾″	2″ machine-driven fastener; 7d or 8d screw or cut nail.	10″–12″ apart
¾″ x 2¼″	2″ machine-driven fastener; 7d or 8d screw or cut nail.	10″–12″ apart
¾″ x 3¼″	2″ machine-driven fastener; 7d or 8d screw or cut nail.	10″–12″ apart
¾″ x 3″ to 8″ plank	2″ machine-driven fastener; 7d or 8d screw or cut nail.	7″–8″ apart into and between joists

(If subfloor is ½″ plywood, fasten into each joist, additional fastening between joists.)

Square-Edge Flooring Facenailed

⁵⁄₁₆″ x 1⅓″	1″ 15-gauge fully barbed flooring brad.	1 nail every 5″ on alternate sides of strip
⁵⁄₁₆″ x 1½″	1″ 15-gauge fully barbed flooring brad.	2 nails every 7″
⁵⁄₁₆″ x 2″	1″ 15-gauge fully barbed flooring brad.	2 nails every 7″

Source: National Oak Flooring Manufacturers Association.

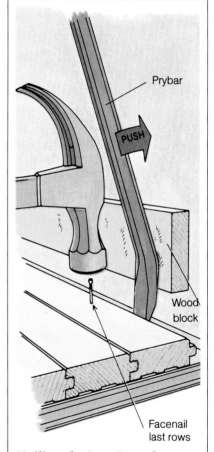

Prybar

PUSH

Wood block

Facenail last rows

Nailing the Last Board

When you reach the end wall, there will not be room for the nailing machine. Hand nail the last three courses. If you cannot fit a full-width board at the edge, rip a board to fit, cutting off the tongue edge.

To snug the last board into place, wedge a prybar between the board and the wall, protecting the wall with a wood block. When the board is in position, facenail it, predrilling a hole for each nail so that the board will not split.

Routed Strips

There are several ways to dress up a wood floor. If you have a router, you can inlay a strip of contrasting wood, such as walnut or hickory. You can also use matching wood on edge to give a different grain pattern. For emphasis, stain the strips darker or lighter than the floor.

Rout out grooves exactly the same width as the strip. Guide the router with a straightedge held to the floor with heavy weights or with 4d finishing nails. Then miter the corners of the strips, apply a strong adhesive, and set them in place.

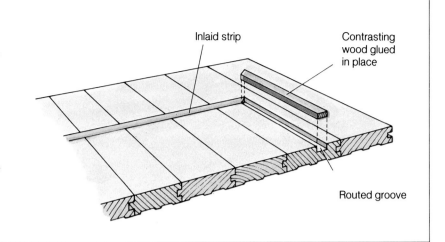

Inlaid strip

Contrasting wood glued in place

Routed groove

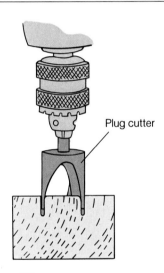

Plug cutter

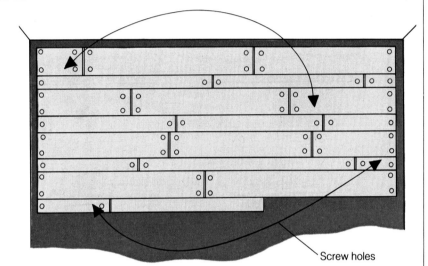

Screw holes

Floor Plugs

Plank floors with plugs at the ends of each board create a pleasing pattern. In some cases they conceal screws that are needed to hold down the extra-wide boards. In other cases they are merely decorative, simulating the pegged floors of bygone days. Many manufacturers offer plank flooring that includes easy-to-install wooden plugs.

Install plugged flooring the same way as regular tongue-and-groove floors, but first decide what plug pattern you want to establish. Since you must cut boards to fit each time you end a course, the boards along the right wall will have no plugs at one end. If you use the cut-off pieces to start new courses, they, too, will have no plugs at one end. However, if you start each row at the left wall with a new board, they will have plugs and you should plug all the

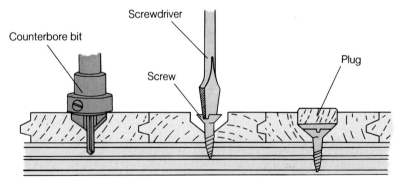

Counterbore bit

Screwdriver

Screw

Plug

boards on the right wall to match.

If you install your own plugs, use one at each end for 3½-inch boards, two for 6-inch boards, and three for 8-inch boards. If you are fastening the boards with screws, drill pilot holes, then counterbore them for the size plug you are using. Use No. 9 or No. 12 wood screws. Precut plugs are available at flooring suppliers,

which you should use if the flooring is prefinished. You can also make your own with a plug-cutting bit and electric drill. Glue the plug and tap it into the hole. If the flooring is prefinished, the plug should be flush with the top. Otherwise, you can chisel off the top of the plug and then smooth it flush at the same time as you sand the rest of the floor.

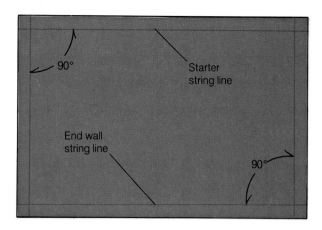

90°

Starter
string line

End wall
string line

90°

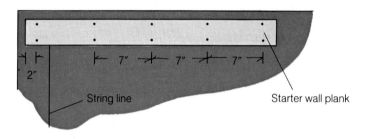

2"

7"   7"   7"

String line

Starter wall plank

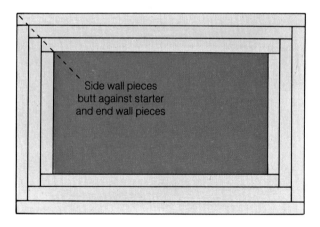

Side wall pieces
butt against starter
and end wall pieces

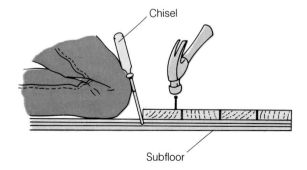

Chisel

Subfloor

Square-Edge Strip Flooring

Square-edge flooring is less costly than tongue-and-groove because it is less thick ($\frac{5}{16}$, $\frac{3}{8}$, and $\frac{1}{2}$ inch) and has less milling waste. However, all nail holes will be on the face and must be filled. It is usually 2 inches wide and often has beveled edges for V-groove joints.

Preparing the Floor. Lay down building paper, then establish a guideline along the starting wall as described for tongue-and-groove flooring, allowing a $\frac{1}{2}$-inch to $\frac{3}{4}$-inch gap along the wall. If you want a border, stretch string lines along the two side walls and back wall, squaring them to the starter line.

Laying the Starter Course. Begin the installation along the longest wall. Choose a long, straight strip of flooring and lay it inside the starter string line, leaving a $\frac{1}{2}$-inch to $\frac{3}{4}$-inch gap at the walls. Predrill nail holes about $\frac{1}{2}$ inch from each end of the board to prevent splitting. Facenail the board with two 1-inch flooring brads every 7 inches, predrilling if necessary. Complete the starter course.

Installing the Border. If you are including a border, install the course along the opposite wall next, followed by the two side walls, so that they fit tightly between the starting and ending wall courses.

To begin each side course, saw the end of the first board square. Align it along the string line so that the squared end fits snugly against the first course. Predrill holes and nail with two brads every 7 inches. Finish both side courses in the same way.

Complete the border by alternating the courses, log-cabin style. Use only enough nails to hold each board in place, but always nail in line with the 7-inch nailing pattern.

Nailing the Strips. Straighten bowed boards by using a chisel driven into the subfloor as a lever. Protect the board with a scrap of wood. Work your way down the board (on the 7-inch pattern), maintaining constant tension. If the tension slackens, the boards will split as you nail them.

When the border is complete, install the rest of the field in the same way, also nailing each board about $\frac{1}{2}$ to $\frac{3}{4}$ inch from both ends.

Finishing Wood Floors

Finishing a floor, whether new or old, involves sanding it smooth, applying sealer or stain, and covering it with a durable finish, usually polyurethane.

Cleaning. An older floor may not need refinishing if it is merely dulled by several layers of old wax and grime. To check, rub a small area with steel wool dipped in alcohol, removing all layers of wax. If damp-mopping the bare wood and applying paste wax bring satisfactory results, clean the entire floor.

Renting Sanding Equipment. Most rental agencies carry the specialized equipment required for sanding: a drum sander for the main part of the floor and a floor edger for corners and edges. Both machines are heavy-duty and require some strength to operate. Have the rental agent show you how; not all machines are alike. Pay attention to procedures for changing the sandpaper, lowering the drum, and emptying dust bags. You will need several grades of sandpaper in both sheets and disks. Take home plenty—you won't be charged for paper that you return unused.

Preparing for Sanding. Before sanding, make sure the flooring is at least ¼ inch thick by inspecting the board ends by a floor register or by removing an inconspicuous board. Then remove all furnishings, including curtains. Cover built-in units and doorways with plastic sheeting. Remove the baseboards, fill deep holes, and set any protruding nail heads. Make sure you have a dust mask and shoes with clean soles (not black rubber). You may also wish to wear ear protectors, since most sanders are noisy.

Using a Drum Sander. Make sure you know how to operate a drum sander—used improperly, it will scar the floor. Start with the coarsest grade of sandpaper for refinishing, with a medium grade for finishing a new floor. Always sand with the grain. Because the drum is constantly rotating, never let it engage the floor unless you are rolling the machine forward.

Start along the right side of the room, a few inches from the wall and behind an imaginary centerline. Sand toward the wall. Then pull the sander back over the imaginary centerline and, overlapping the previous pass by half the width of the drum, sand toward the wall again. When you have finished half of the room this way, turn around and sand on the other side of the imaginary centerline in the same manner. Sand any border separately—with the grain—after you finish the main area.

Sanding. Sand the entire floor once with the coarse paper. It will become rough and fuzzy, so the next step is to smooth the wood by sanding it with the medium grit. Replace the sandpaper when you do not see any results. The finer grit gets used up more quickly. When this second sanding is complete, fill any remaining open cracks or nail holes with a wood filler, using a broad putty knife. When the wood filler is completely dry, sand the entire floor with the fine-grit sandpaper.

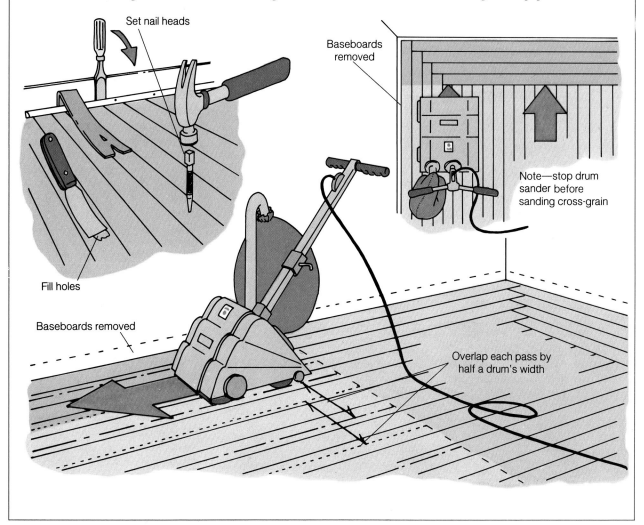

Set nail heads

Fill holes

Baseboards removed

Baseboards removed

Note—stop drum sander before sanding cross-grain

Overlap each pass by half a drum's width

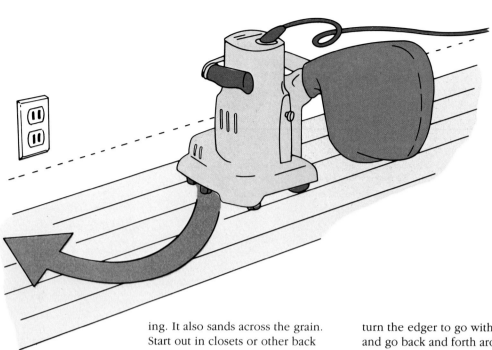

Sanding the Edges

The drum sander cannot reach every part of the floor, so you need an edger to sand along walls and in tight spaces such as closets. The edger is a rotary sander, and uses sandpaper disks. It is faster than the drum sander, and is more prone to goug-ing. It also sands across the grain. Start out in closets or other back spaces until you get the feel of it. Using a scallop motion of small semicircles rather than a straight back-and-forth motion helps to avoid gouging. As much as possible, avoid leaning the sander to the right or left, which forces the disk to gouge across the grain. In corners where the wood strips join at right angles, turn the edger to go with the grain, and go back and forth around that turn several times. Use the same grade of paper that you use for drum sanding, filling cracks and nail holes before applying the fine-grit sandpaper. Use a hand scraper to get into awkward corners and any other spots that are inaccessible to the sanding machines. Finish up those spots by hand sanding with fine paper.

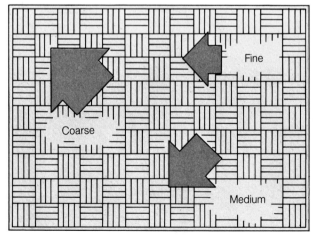

Sanding Parquet Floors

Using coarse paper, sand across the floor diagonally. Using medium grit, work across the floor on the other diagonal (thus forming an X). Finish with a fine grit, sanding parallel to the walls. Go over the floor with each grit twice, first walking with the drum sander and then pulling it back with you. Overlap each section half the width of the drum. Use the edger in the same way as for strip floors, but finish with the fine grit. A par-quet floor has many joints and cracks, so it is likely to need more filler than other kinds. Buy a 1-gallon can if your floor has excessive cracks and open seams and goop it on liber-ally before final sanding. The result will be a beautiful new floor.

Applying Sealer or Stain

Seal the floor the same day that you finish sanding to prevent it from absorbing moisture from the air. Sealers can be clear, tinted in wood hues, or even colored. Test them in a closet or on a scrap of wood.

No matter which type you use, excess sealer will not penetrate into the wood; unless it is removed it will leave dark splotches that obscure the wood. For best results, apply sealer with a sheepskin appli-cator, wiping away any residue after 10 or 15 minutes.

Buff the room with No. 2 fine steel wool after the sealer dries. Then vacuum and dust with a tack cloth. Apply the finish wax or plas-tic floor finish next, according to instructions. Use two coats, lightly buffing between them. Wait at least 24 hours after the second coat dries before moving furniture back in.

Even if your floor has a plastic floor finish, a coat of heavy wax will give added protection.

Damaged Boards

If a board in your floor has been damaged to the point where a good patching job is not feasible, you will have to cut it out and replace it. Before cutting, look over the piece to be removed. If there are nails, use a nail set to drive them as far through the board as possible.

1. Mark the edge of the damaged section of board with a square.
2. Drill holes along cross-cut line.
3. Slip out the damaged board.
4. Clean drilled edge with a chisel.
5. Cut a replacement board. Remove the bottom side of the groove, apply glue, and slip it into place.
6. Hammer down the replacement board, nail it, and finish it to match the rest of the floor.

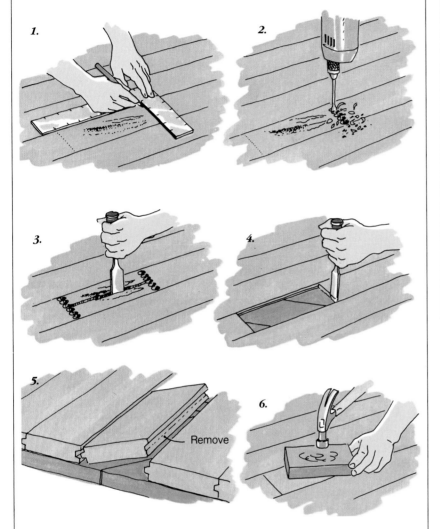

Remove

Split Boards

Repair immediately or the crack will enlarge and lengthen.

1. Drill pilot holes and drive nails at an angle beside the crack every few inches. Also drill and nail slightly beyond the end of the crack.

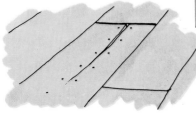

2. Countersink nails and fill nail holes and the crack with stained plastic wood or a matching putty.

Warped Boards

1. Remove wax and finish, then keep under damp rags for 48 hours.
2. Screw the warped board to the subfloor with countersunk screws. Tighten the screws a little each day until the board is level again.
3. Fill screw holes and refinish to match the original floor.

1.

2.

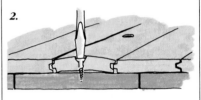

3.

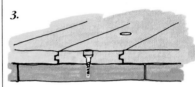

Adjacent Warped Boards

1. Remove wax and finish, then keep under damp rags for 48 hours.
2. Screw the boards to the subfloor with countersunk screws. Tighten screws a half turn or so each day.
3. When flat, refinish the floor.

1.

2.

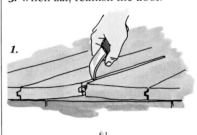

3.

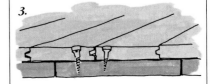

ZONING, CODES & PERMITS

Before you begin any improvement project, it is essential that you investigate local zoning laws, building codes, and the permit process.

To learn about the legal restrictions in your area, call or visit your local building department. If you want general information, the building department will probably refer you to whatever model codes it uses. Some departments distribute printed booklets that include additional requirements or exceptions; others have complete summaries that you can buy.

If you have a specific project in mind, take as many drawings or photos as possible to the building department to determine the feasibility of your plans. Most department personnel are unable to advise you on how to do something, but they can tell you if your plans comply with the code. Because laws vary from county to county, don't assume anything until you have inquired.

Recommended Cross-References
Most sections.

Zoning Ordinances

Zoning regulations usually affect only exterior construction, not interior remodeling. Zoning protects the quality of a neighborhood. In some areas, for example, codes allow only certain architectural styles. Ordinances also prevent the unsuitable use of property within a specific zone. If your neighborhood is zoned for single-family houses, for example, the code protects you from a business that wants to build a factory or fast-food restaurant right next door to you.

Zoning regulations also define setbacks. A setback is the distance a building must be from a property line. These distances vary from front to back and from side to side. For example, the front setback may be 25 to 30 feet; on the side, the setback may be only 5 to 10 feet. Know the precise location of your property lines. A fence or other boundary may not be an accurate indication of the actual property line.

There may be other special zoning requirements in your area; find out before you begin detailed planning. For example, your zone may limit building height. Be sure to investigate this possibility if the site slopes.

Zoning regulations can block your plans in a number of ways. For example, restrictions may require a larger setback on a second-story addition than on the existing first floor. Depending on the size of your lot, the regulation may mean that the only place you may build is the rear of the

house. You may be required to provide off-street, enclosed parking for your car; if so, you will have to scrap plans to convert your garage to living space. The building department may interpret an addition that provides living space for your parents as a conversion to a two-family dwelling. If your neighborhood is zoned only for single-family dwellings, the department may disallow your plans. The definition of second dwelling causes many problems. Some definitions would allow several families to live in the same house. Other definitions go so far as to categorize a home as two dwellings if it contains two ovens.

If you find that your plans conflict with the zoning regulations, consider applying for a variance, or exception, to the law. The permit appeals department will tell you how to apply for a variance hearing, if a hearing is necessary. Once you present your case, the decision is up to the local planning board.

In addition to zoning regulations, there may be other restrictions. For example, an easement gives someone else, such as a utility company or local municipality, the right to cross your property. The deed may contain a clause that limits or restricts use. If you own a condominium or belong to a homeowners' association, a set of conditions, covenants, and restrictions (CC&Rs) applies to your property. Eliminate problems by examining your deed and checking with the building department.

Building Codes

Local governments determine building codes in order to establish minimum standards of construction. They protect you and future owners of your property from safety hazards and faulty work. In addition, building codes can serve as valuable reference tools that cite technical information and proven construction methods.

Different codes are used in different regions. In the realm of basic construction, many local codes in states west of the Mississippi incorporate the Uniform Building Code. Local codes in southern states often include the Standard Building Code. The Basic Building Code is also often included in local codes.

Plumbing codes may include the Uniform Plumbing Code, the Standard Plumbing Code, or the Basic Plumbing Code. There are even more mechanical codes: the Uniform Mechanical Code, the Standard Mechanical Code, the Basic Mechanical Code, the Standard Gas Code, and the Code for the Installation of Heat-Producing Appliances. The only code in effect throughout the country is the National Electrical Code, which is actually a section of the National Fire Code. Finally, some states stipulate an energy code that specifies insulation, heating, cooling, and glazing requirements.

Your building department can tell you how to obtain a copy of the appropriate code. If you plan to do much building, buy a copy and study it. You may not need the complete code; a condensed version may be sufficient. If you have questions or disputes, however, refer to the complete code.

The building code influences your project by specifying:
• The type of materials you may use. Can you use plastic pipe for your water supply? What size wallboard do you need for the garage?
• Whether you may do the work yourself. Some codes require that a licensed professional handle electricity and plumbing.
• Structural requirements and installation techniques. For example, the code will tell you how large joists must be, or how posts must be attached to beams.

Building Permits

Improvement projects that change the structure, size, safety, or use of living space require a building permit. Projects that fall within the scope of normal maintenance, such as painting, wallpapering, roofing projects that leave the sheathing intact, or window and door replacement, do not require a permit.

To obtain a permit, you need to submit working drawings, a site or plot plan, a foundation plan, a floor plan, elevations, and sections or details of various components. If your project is small, a sketch and a brief description of your intentions will probably suffice. For larger projects, you may also have to submit engineering reports, soils reports, a certificate of worker's compensation insurance, and energy calculations.

Obtaining a permit takes anywhere from a few days to several weeks. A permit may require that work commence within a certain period, usually within 120 days. Some permits do not specify a completion date, but others do. A typical time limit is 9 months to a year. If your project is not finished by the completion date, you may need to obtain a new permit.

Besides compliance with the law, a permit confers several advantages. A permit validates any work done on your home that affects resale value. A permit decreases the possibility that an insurance company would cite your work as the cause of damage or fire from dubious origins. A permit also provides an incentive for doing work with a sense of pride and integrity. And, perhaps most important, the permit process necessitates thorough planning and estimating before you start a project—an effort that you will not regret.

Although building departments process most permits relating to home improvement, there are other departments that may issue separate permits or permit clearance. The planning commission will check for zoning compliance. The public health department usually regulates septic systems and wells. Public works departments check for easements and may require a survey. The fire department establishes regulations regarding smoke alarms and other life-protecting measures, although they are usually incorporated into local building requirements. Environmental review boards, flood control commissions, and architectural review boards may also have jurisdiction over your project.

Code Compliance

When you improve an older home, the codes usually apply only to new work. The building department generally does not expect you to bring your entire house up to modern standards—unless, of course, the building inspector finds something that is a definite hazard. Some existing conditions, such as plumbing, electrical wiring, and stairs, may be governed by modern codes, but most features of your home are governed only by the applicable code at the time of construction. If the improvement involves more than a specified percentage of property value, however, you will have to bring the entire structure up to code.

If you are doing extensive plumbing and wiring changes in an older home, it makes sense to modernize and bring your systems up to code even if it is not required. Spending a little more now may save a lot of grief later.

Inspections

Your permit will include a schedule of inspections. As a rule, the inspector will check an element of the job just before you cover it. The accompanying table lists the elements that will be of interest to an inspector.

Job element	The inspector will check
Foundation	Trench, forms, bare steel
Under the floor	Anchor bolts, floor framing, utility lines
Framing	Lumber grade, joints, shear transfer
Sheathing	Seams, nailing patterns
Rough plumbing	Pipe sizes, materials, pressure test
Electrical wiring	All elements
Roofing	Materials, flashing, fire rating
Energy efficiency	Insulation values, glass area
Interior walls	Wallboard nailing pattern
Flues and fireplace	Clearances, materials, leaks
Gas line	Fittings, pressure test
Final inspection	Electrical fixtures, plumbing fixtures, railings, furnace, smoke detectors

Even when a structure is built according to plans approved by the building department, the site inspector determines whether the construction meets code.

If the work does not meet the inspector's standards, you must correct the work and undergo another inspection.

Most inspectors are more than willing to answer questions about the code or about their inspection of your work, but they may not advise you on how to do something, nor will they tell you what needs to be done. They can only pass judgement on what has been done. If you are not sure if your work will meet code, have a professional builder who knows your building codes take a look first.

INDEX

INDEX

U.S./Metric Measure Conversion Chart

	Symbol	Formulas for Exact Measures: When you know:	Multiply by:	To find:	Rounded Measures for Quick Reference		
Mass (Weight)	oz	ounces	28.35	grams	1 oz		= 30 g
	lb	pounds	0.45	kilograms	4 oz		= 115 g
	g	grams	0.035	ounces	8 oz		= 225 g
	kg	kilograms	2.2	pounds	16 oz	= 1 lb	= 450 g
					32 oz	= 2 lb	= 900 g
					36 oz	= 2¼ lb	= 1000 g (1 kg)
Volume	tsp	teaspoons	5.0	milliliters	¼ tsp	= 1/24 oz	= 1 ml
	tbsp	tablespoons	15.0	milliliters	½ tsp	= 1/12 oz	= 2 ml
	fl oz	fluid ounces	29.57	milliliters	1 tsp	= ⅙ oz	= 5 ml
	c	cups	0.24	liters	1 tbsp	= ½ oz	= 15 ml
	pt	pints	0.47	liters	1 c	= 8 oz	= 250 ml
	qt	quarts	0.95	liters	2 c (1 pt)	= 16 oz	= 500 ml
	gal	gallons	3.785	liters	4 c (1 qt)	= 32 oz	= 1 liter
	ml	milliliters	0.034	fluid ounces	4 qt (1 gal)	= 128 oz	= 3¾ liter
Length	in.	inches	2.54	centimeters	⅜ in.	= 1 cm	
	ft	feet	30.48	centimeters	1 in.	= 2.5 cm	
	yd	yards	0.9144	meters	2 in.	= 5 cm	
	mi	miles	1.609	kilometers	2½ in.	= 6.5 cm	
	km	kilometers	0.621	miles	12 in. (1 ft)	= 30 cm	
	m	meters	1.094	yards	1 yd	= 90 cm	
	cm	centimeters	0.39	inches	100 ft	= 30 m	
					1 mi	= 1.6 km	
Temperature	° F	Fahrenheit	5/9 (after subtracting 32)	Celsius	32° F	= 0° C	
					68° F	= 20° C	
	° C	Celsius	9/5 (then add 32)	Fahrenheit	212° F	= 100° C	
Area	in.^{2}	square inches	6.452	square centimeters	1 in.^{2}	= 6.5 cm^2	
	ft^2	square feet	929.0	square centimeters	1 ft^2	= 930 cm^2	
	yd^2	square yards	8361.0	square centimeters	1 yd^2	= 8360 cm^2	
	a.	acres	0.4047	hectares	1 a.	= 4050 m^2	